PSYCHOLOGY
OF
MOTOR LEARNING

PSYCHOLOGY OF MOTOR LEARNING

Second Edition

Joseph B. Oxendine

Temple University

Prentice-Hall, Inc., Englewood Cliffs, New Jersey 07632

Library of Congress Cataloging in Publication Data

Oxendine, Joseph B.
    Psychology of motor learning.

    Bibliography: p.
    Includes index.
    1. Motor learning.   I. Title.
BF295.09 1984   152.3'34   83-13869
ISBN 0-13-736603-5

Editorial/production supervision and
    interior design: Helen Maertens
Cover design: Edsal Enterprises
Manufacturing buyer: Harry P. Baisley

Printed in the United States of America

10   9   8   7   6   5   4   3   2   1

ISBN 0-13-736603-5

Prentice-Hall International, Inc., *London*
Prentice-Hall of Australia Pty. Limited, *Sydney*
Editora Prentice-Hall do Brasil, Ltda., *Rio de Janeiro*
Prentice-Hall Canada Inc., *Toronto*
Prentice-Hall of India Private Limited, *New Delhi*
Prentice-Hall of Japan, Inc., *Tokyo*
Prentice-Hall of Southeast Asia Pte. Ltd., *Singapore*
Whitehall Books Limited, *Wellington, New Zealand*

To my son, James Thomas,
and daughter, Jean Marie,
from whom I continue to learn

Contents

Preface

PREFACE TO SECOND EDITION

When the first edition of *Psychology of Motor Learning* was published in 1968, the area of motor learning was a newly developing specialty within the field of physical education. In fact, no prior texts had been written which were devoted exclusively to this topic. Since that time a major surge of interest has engulfed the whole psychological domain of human movement. An enormous amount of attention in the form of research, conventions, conferences, and publications has been devoted to this general area. Recent texts have been published which deal with motor control, motor behavior, information processing, models of motor skill learning, sports psychology, perceptual-motor development, neurophysiology of skill learning, and instructional methodology related to motor skills. In addition, practically all college and university curricula in physical education, both at the undergraduate and graduate levels, have one or more courses devoted to motor skill learning. Many universities have graduate level program specialties in this area.

This second edition has been extensively revised and supplemented to reflect the almost geometric increase in the body of information regarding motor skill learning which has occurred during the past dozen years. Major portions of the book have been totally rewritten while other parts have been heavily revised. Chapter two on experimental methodology is entirely new. It grew out of the frequently expressed request of students for guidelines in conducting research in skill learning. Further, they sought help in selecting tasks appropriate for investigating particular problems. Consequently, this chapter has been included to provide specific assistance to young researchers. Chapter three has been expanded to include a discussion of current learning models in addition to the coverage of traditional learning theories. Greatly expanded attention to the topic of information feedback has been added to Chapter four, which previously was limited to reinforcement. In addition, a general updating of recent research and references has been included. More extensive use is made of photographs, charts, and other illustrations. At the same time, some obsolete references and content has been deleted. A point by point summary has been added to the end of each chapter which should aid the reader in synthesizing the chapter content.

This book is aimed at upper division undergraduate and graduate students with an interest in human movement and performance and is written principally for courses dealing with motor learning and skilled behavior. It is assumed that the majority of students will be in the area of physical education and related fields. However, in recent years, students from other areas of human behavior, particularly experimental, educational and developmental psychology are showing greater interest in skill acquisition and performance levels, and consequently should find this material helpful.

As with the first edition, the writing style is aimed at communicating easily and effectively with students who do not have extensive background in the scientific literature. At the same time, careful attention has been taken to ensure the integrity of the theoretical concepts and principles. I have attempted to present sound, verifiable information while avoiding the inclusion of excessive references. Extensive use of verbal illustrations are included to clarify and amplify theoretical concepts. These illustrations are selected from a variety of work, sports, leisure and developmental situations.

I am indebted to many persons who contributed immeasurably to this book; both in substance and process. The entire manuscript was read by Dr. Alan Applebee, Dr. Marcella Ridenour, Ms. Elizabeth Bair and Ms. Sharon Denny. Each of these persons contributed very helpful suggestions for improving the book, both from a technical and practical standpoint. Their keen insight as well as their knowledge of the field has resulted in a great many excellent ideas being incorporated in the text. In addition, Dr. Ridenour contributed the section on laboratory computers in Chapter two. Dr. Applebee provided extensive editing throughout the text.

Special thanks go to Sandra A. Weisberg who did most of the typing, including all of the final draft. Mrs. Dolores McNaughton provided valuable assistance in the difficult task of obtaining permissions, as well as coordinating some of the early typing. Mr. Robert Goodman did the photographs of most of the research equipment in Chapter two and the basketball backgrounds in Chapter thirteen.

Part I: General Learning Theory

1 The Nature of Motor Learning

INTRODUCTION

An investigation of the phenomenon of motor learning must begin with an analysis of learning in general. It is assumed that basic principles established as general learning theory underlie the acquisition of all types of skills and knowledge. In fact, those general learning principles and laws were established on the basis of research with a variety of tasks, including motor skills. Nevertheless, it has become clear that special techniques and more direct applications must be identified if maximum efficiency is to be reached in the teaching of motor activities.

It is now widely recognized that increased information on skill acquisition has far-reaching implications, affecting practices ranging from the nursery school to circus arobatics; from the little leaguer to the major leaguer. In the work world practically all occupations, including the laborer, the skilled tradesman, the clerical worker, the air traffic controller, and the surgeon, depend to some extent upon the efficiency with which motor skills are acquired and performed.

Therefore, the quest for a better understanding of human behavior is one of continuing fascination for psychologists, educators, and to some extent, the man on the street. Learning, one of the primary determinants of this behavior, has especially attracted the attention of those persons responsible for educational programs. Behavior in motor skills has gained widespread interest because of the easy observation of learning and performance phenomena and because of the strong general attraction to these activities.

The acquisiton of motor skills, while sharing many commonalities with learning in general, is more obvious in our daily lives. In most occupational skills, sports, routine daily activities, and in the developmental stages of young children, the results of skill learning are evident. In fact, motor skills are so common that there is a tendency to overlook their great diversity, and to forget that they do not arrive automatically but must be learned.

CHARACTERISTICS OF SKILLED BEHAVIOR

Soon after accepting my first university faculty position, I availed myself of the dental clinic that is operated by the university's dental school. As was the custom, a dental student in training was assigned the task of filling several cavities. For the

1

first time I became painfully aware of the fact that dentists are not born with the ability to look through a small mirror and make the proper (reversal) responses. Rather, these special skills must be acquired through practice. The dental trainee assigned to me, who later confessed that I was his first real patient, was nervous and uncertain. Although movements with the drill and the explorer were forceful, they were also shaky and often misdirected, frequently slipping off the tooth being repaired. I soon became thankful that he was drilling only my lower teeth, and not the uppers, which are in closer proximity to the brain. Finally, I was rescued by the faculty supervisor whose movements I found to be accurate, swift, and steady, reflecting not only superior motor skill but also much greater confidence.

As was evident with the dental faculty member, it is clear in most motor activities that the more highly skilled the individual, the less time and energy will be wasted. Skilled movement responses are smooth and seemingly effortless. For example, the skill of bricklaying looks deceptively easy when one observes the expert. However, this impression is quickly dispelled once the individual attempts to duplicate that performance. Similarly, highly skilled athletes make difficult plays "look easy." The best center fielder seems to glide under the ball in a fluid motion. The expert second baseman appears to make the double play effortlessly. A comparison of the Olympic ice skater or gymnast to novices in these activities reveals a clear and dramatic contrast.

In the entertainment and work world it is equally true that the more highly skilled person performs in a smoother, more relaxed manner; note the concert pianist or violinist, the skilled artisan, the plasterer, the typist, or the seamstress. Researchers have found that learners exhibit a higher degree of muscle tension during the earlier phases of learning. In mirror tracing, for example, new learners exert greater downward pressure and grip the stylus tighter than they do after achieving more skill in that activity.

We all regularly observe a multitude of motor activities in which the level of skill varies from somewhere below the aforementioned dental student to his faculty supervisor, from the novice skater to the Olympic-level performer. The higher level of skill leads to greater productivity and less hazards in work situations, greater success and recognition in the sports and entertainment fields, and increased satisfaction in all of these activities (both for the performer and for the recipient of those services). The same holds true for those routine daily activities that involve motor tasks.

Scope of motor skills

Careful observation of persons of all ages at home, school, or work reveals that the activities that depend upon movement skills are extremely prevalent and diverse. Too often it is assumed that competence in motor skills is important only in play or sports activities. Skills in the working world, or daily routine activities, are frequently overlooked. However, even casual observation reveals that most occupations make important use of motor skills.

Work skills.   Singleton (1978) presented an analysis of the motor skill components of thirteen occupations in Great Britain. Skills in these occupations range from the relatively basic functions of the farm worker and forester to the more complex motor behavior of the air traffic controller, the tea blender, and the architect as a designer. Further, he presents the Ministry of Labour's categories of occupations as skilled, semi-skilled, and unskilled, based upon the length and kind of training (see Table 1-1). According to Singleton, skilled occupations require extensive training, including an apprenticeship; semi-skilled occupations require some training; and unskilled occupations require no training at all.

TABLE 1-1.   Great Britain's Ministry of Labour Classification of Operatives

Group 5 Other skilled manual occupations	Group 6 Other semi-skilled manual occupations	Group 7 Labourers and unskilled occupations
Carpenters	Bottlers	Agricultural workers
Joiners	Printing machine assistants	Porters
Compositors	Plastic moulders	Dock labourers
Process engravers	Assemblers	Messengers
Steel erectors	Shepherds	Lift attendants
Bricklayers	Foresters	Kitchen hands
Plasterers	Paint sprayers	Caretakers
Glaziers	Warehousemen	Office cleaners
Tilers	Storekeepers	Window cleaners
Crane drivers	Packers	Laundry workers
Rubber moulders	Boiler firemen	
Photographers		

From Singleton, *The Analysis of Practical Skills,* University Park Press, 1978. By permission of publisher.

Although having some merit in very general terms, the Ministry of Labour's classification of trades is an oversimplification when viewed on the basis of motor skills criteria. For example, some of the motor skills in the "unskilled" area certainly require some learning before one can perform them safely and effectively. Having grown up on a tobacco farm in North Carolina, I can attest to the fact that agricultural work, even prior to today's mechanization, required substantial instruction and "practice" before one became proficient in milking a cow, plowing a straight furrow, putting up fences, training and caring for working animals, and harvesting tobacco and certain other crops when selectivity and speed are required. Similarly, to function effectively and safely, the forest worker must receive training in topping trees, using power saws, and handling heavy moving equipment. It is true, however, that once developed, the motor skill components of these occupations can be performed in a more or less automatic manner with little conscious attention to the task. At the same time, the more skilled trades require longer training periods, followed by regular, perhaps continuous, conscious control.

The U.S. Department of Labor has identified approximately 20,000 occupations in this country and categorized them according to the nature of the job or service performed. The categories, as presented in the 1977 *Dictionary of Occupational Titles* (4th ed.), are as follows:

1. Professional, technical, or managerial occupations
2. Clerical and sales occupations
3. Service occupations
4. Agricultural, fishing, forestry, and related occupations
5. Processing occupations
6. Machine trades occupations
7. Benchwork occupations
8. Structural work occupations
9. Miscellaneous occupations

A detailed analysis of these occupations, including a job-by-job review, reveals that motor skill performance is prominent in the majority of them, particularly in categories two through nine.

The Department of Labor further reviews the occupations to indicate the complexity of the worker's performance in relation to (1) data, (2) people, or (3) things. In relation to "things," job efficiency seems especially dependent upon motor coordinations and manipulative functions. Those functions requiring the use of equipment, machinery, and tools are described as: (1) setting up, (2) precision working, (3) operating-controlling, (4) driving-operating, (5) manipulating, (6) tending, (7) feeding-offbearing, and (8) handling (p. 1369).

Developmental skills.   The full range of human behavior motor skills (and perceptual-motor skills) may be divided into three broad categories according to the manner and purpose for which they are learned. First are the skills that are developed early in life and are primarily dependent upon maturation. These include activities such as crawling, walking, speaking, and general coordination of body movements. Although special teaching does not seem to speed this developmental process to any great extent, a favorable environment is essential for maximal development of these skills. The role of parents and teachers in regard to this early development is to provide the child with encouragement and opportunities for movement and exploration.

A second group of motor skills, high in perceptual component, involves those that are essential for the further development of educational objectives. The group includes communicative skills, such as handwriting, reading, and observation, which are used as tools for more advanced learning. The primary grade teacher is concerned with perceptual-motor learning particularly as it relates to the development of effective reading skills. For example, as the child learns to visually span two, three, or four words at a single glance, rather than one letter or word, reading efficiency improves. In clerical courses, students may develop typing and shorthand skills that may later aid in attaining other educational goals. Development of proficiency in these activities is also dependent upon certain other mental components, but perceptual-motor factors are strategic.

A third category of skills includes those that are taught for their own value, for benefits that are directly related to the activity. Generally, vocational and recreational skills are in this group. Teachers in different areas of specialization and at different levels of the educational program are responsible for the teaching of these skills. The physical education teacher is naturally responsible for developing sports and other recreational skills, as well as movement patterns essential for other specialized skill learning. The industrial arts teacher aids the student in developing skills in the use of a variety of manual and power equipment. These skills may later prove important for vocational or avocational pursuits. The science teacher demonstrates the proper techniques for using complex and fragile laboratory equipment. The home economics teacher promotes learning in the skills of sewing, cooking, and many other household tasks. In music class, students may develop skill in the use of a wide variety of instruments. The music teacher may also aid students in the development of voice control, projection, and enunciation. In the teaching of painting and drawing, it is clear that perceptual-motor factors come into use. All these activities provide an opportunity for motor learning that may continue for many years.

Even in advanced programs of study, the learning of motor skills is frequently important. Medical and dental students, as well as those in a great variety of technical fields, often find the development of manual skill important in their programs. Surgeons, engineers, and skilled artisans in many fields obviously need manual dexterity and skill in following instructions. These listings, though incomplete, provide ample evidence that motor skills are not restricted to the area of sports. Rather, teachers in a wide variety of subjects, from nursery school to the post baccalaureate levels and beyond, are involved in the teaching of motor skills.

THE STUDY OF LEARNING

The human infant begins life as a highly dependent, practically helpless being. Through maturation and learning, the child advances to a point that clearly distinguishes him or her from all other earthly inhabitants. The great capacity of humans for learning, along with a seemingly unlimited potential for motor development, sets them apart. Further, the more we learn about human capacities, the more we realize that we have hardly broken the surface in our understanding of human potential. The multitude and complexity of perceptual and motor capacities have intrigued authorities from several disciplines.

The term "learning" is used practically all the time by persons at all strata of society. Ironically, it is probably used with greater confidence by the person on the street than by the psychologist. The more naive individual assumes that "we learn what we are taught" and proceeds to teach children, apprentices, and others in the manner in which he or she was taught. Over the years parents, artisans, industrialists, farmers, and even teachers have functioned in this manner. Prior to the last century little concern was expressed about the complexity of the learning process.

During recent years it has become clear to teachers that in order to be most effective, they must *understand* the learning process more thoroughly. To simply remember how one was taught or even to have a wide range of approaches to teaching is not adequate. Unfortunately, some teachers appear limited to a "command style" methodology similar to that of the classic army drill sergeant. In this approach, a standardized technique is used to instruct the individual or the group. If, on occasion, this style does not result in success, the usual response is to increase the intensity within the learning climate, resulting in greater stress.

In contrast to the stereotyped command style of the drill sergeant, the teacher who understands the learning process and who understands the subject matter is able to *diagnose* a learning difficulty so that an appropriate alternative approach can be put to use. This alternative method is not selected at random but is specifically related to the learning difficulty. A thorough understanding of the learning process enables the teacher to detect clues that lead to a correct remedy. Consequently, this teacher is able to focus on the problem without going through an endless list of "trial and error" approaches.

Unfortunately, there is a frequently held assumption that "a good teacher can teach anything." The truth is that one who is not well acquainted with the specific subject matter is at a distinct disadvantage. Take the case of the volleyball player who has developed a service flaw that is so distracting as to reduce his previous successes by 50 percent. This player may not have the slightest idea where the problem lies. Only an instructur who is well acquainted with the intricacies of the volleyball service can break down the component parts and isolate the problem. Once identified, this teacher can provide the appropriate instructional cues and reinforcement to insure a rapid return to the original level and beyond. Consequently, the effective teacher is one who has a thorough understanding of the learning process *and* the material being taught.

Background of the study
of learning

During the latter part of the 19th century, experimental psychologists, and later educators, began seeking a clearer understanding of the learning process. Psychologists were interested in this topic because of its importance in determining behavior, while educators were interested in increasing the overall efficiency of the school program. Both groups have subsequently maintained a keen interest in learning, and their combined efforts have contributed importantly to the effectiveness of school programs.

The psychologist's quest for knowledge of learning is ultimately aimed at predicting and controlling behavior. By use of basic research techniques, he or she seeks to gather objective, verifiable, and detailed evidence regarding learning and behavior. This information is then organized into generalizations, principles, and laws that describe learning. (A more detailed discussion of these theoretical efforts is included in chapter three.)

when not so hungry. These all represent "changes in behavior," but they are not to be classified as learning inasmuch as they are not "persistent." That is, it is assumed that all will return to normal behavior after the temporary condition has passed.

Learning refers to those changes in behavior that result from "practice or experience." In addition to the temporary conditions suggested above, there are some persistent or even permanent changes in behavior that cannot be classified as learning. For example, as the individual grows older, there are changes in movement that are indeed persistent. This is perhaps most obvious in the changes caused by maturation, which occurs during the first few years of life. However, middle-aged and older persons also reflect changes in behavior that are more a part of the aging process than of learning. The onset of arthritis causes appreciable alterations in speed and range of joint motion in movement activities. The forty-year-old major league baseball pitcher behaves differently from the way he did as a twenty-five-year-old. One can note that the speed of his fast balls, and their frequency, has diminished. Because of reduced physical capacities, this "aging" pitcher is forced to rely more on "junk" pitches, better control, and an array of skills not necessary during earlier years. The change (reduced speed) in this pitcher's fast ball is not the result of practice or experience. Thus it does not represent learning. However, the multitude of subtle adjustments that he makes in his pitching style for continued success do represent learning. These changes in style were gained on the basis of experience, e.g., observation, trial and error, or coaching.

Those persons familiar with "masters" or "seniors" sports competitions in track or swimming are aware that performance standards are lowered progressively as performers reach the ages of forty, fifty, sixty, and beyond. These persistent changes in behavior do not represent learning since it was not practice or experience that caused the slower performance times. Persons approaching senility exhibit fairly dramatic changes in all types of motor behavior. Likewise, short retention skills for new information deteriorates.

In addition to age, serious illness or handicap often incapacitates the individual or limits activity so that behavior changes appreciably. The development of severe allergies, broken bones, or limb amputations usually restricts one's performance in a variety of motor skills either temporarily or permanently. Still, we would not call these changes learning. One does not usually *learn* to run with a limp, or to run less fast, or to begin wheezing during an asthma attack. While it is true that some learning may take place as one adapts effectively to diminished motor or mental capacities, the change in behavior takes place as a natural result of the causative factors.

The "change in behavior" aspect of the definition differentiates learning from such terms as improvement, advancement, progress, or other connotations of positive response. While it is the aim of teachers that learning lead to higher levels of performance, in motor skills, as with attitudes and verbal materials, learning may occasionally lead to a diminution in effectiveness or regression to a less desirable level. For example, those experienced in teaching motor activities often notice that deliberate or sometimes incidental changes in movement responses lead to a hindrance in performance. Occasionally this results from an effort to mimic someone admired, perhaps a sports hero or outstanding model whose style is copied. Teachers of junior high school students are often plagued with the tendency of students to develop fancy ways of performing traditional skills. Such behavior may become somewhat persistent, i.e., is learned; but it often does not represent an improvement in performance and frequently leads to failure.

At other times the individual may *inadvertently* pick up irregular movement habits that detract from performance. Most frequently the individual is not aware of these newly learned habits, e.g., a "hitch" in the baseball batting swing, looking up too early when swinging at the golf ball, taking the eye off the target in bowling, or raising the head too high out of the water on the butterfly stroke. Similar distracting responses develop in complex work skills. The responses, if ignored or undetected, often become well-learned habits and prove a major problem for teachers, coaches, and supervisors who must first identify the interfering habit, bring it to the attention of the learner, and then hopefully extinguish it.

Similarly, changes in attitudes, social habits, and verbal behavior clearly reflect learning, but that learning may not represent a positive change in behavior. Newly developed attitudes of racial or religious animosity, increased dependence on the use of mind-altering drugs, or a new receptivity to destructive religious cults all represent learning. However, few would argue that such change in behavior is beneficial.

Most authors define learning by describing behavior that can be rather objectively observed. A different approach has been taken by some who attempt to *explain* the learning process by discussing the physiological changes that are assumed to take place in the nervous system.

In the search for more precise answers to the phenomenon of learning, neurologists, physiologists, and biochemists have developed several models to put all of this into a framework. However, most of these constructs are still viewed as hypothetical. One of the earliest of such scientific theories was developed by Kappers (1917). He used the term *neurobiotaxis* to explain learning as the growth of dendrites* and axons** in the nervous system. This theory indicates that as one practices by participating in or observing an activity, electrical impulses pass through the nervous system and cause the development of "connections" at the synapses.† The greater the learning, the greater is this neural growth.

Kappers believed that in the first performance of any activity, impulses travel over previously unused paths of sensory and motor neurons. The learning and performance of the new activity is assumed to be difficult because of the resistance of undeveloped synapses to the transmission of impulses. The inability of these impulses to easily "jump the gap" results from the lack of neural development in the area of the synapse. As the individual repeats the activity, or as practice con-

---

dendrite: a branching nerve cell structure that transmits impulses toward the cell body.
    **axon:* a threadlike nerve cell structure that transmits impulses away from the cell body.
    †*synapse:* a juncture, or point of connection, between adjoining neurons.

tinues, the growth of dendrites and axons offers more connections, or "feelers," which help to transmit the impulse. This enables subsequent messages to travel over the nerve trunks more smoothly because of the greater neurological development in the synaptic area. According to Kappers, therefore, learning is the development of neutral connections that reduce resistance in the synapse.

Kappers' neurobiotaxis theory is not contradictory to the definition of learning suggested earlier. Rather it was an early attempt to explain the dynamics of the learning process physiologically. More recently, Sage (1971) has stated that ". . . changes in behavior called learning are in the last analysis a result of changes in the nervous system. . . . Learning may be viewed as a neural change which occurs as a result of experiences with stimuli in the environment." A great deal of research has been devoted to the question of determining precisely what neurological changes occur during the learning process. While discussing several anatomical, physiological, and biochemical theories on this topic, Sage concludes that ". . . we do not yet know the neural process by which they occur." Other psychologists, physiologists, and neurologists have expressed a variety of assumptions regarding structural changes or functional processes in the nervous system as a result of learning, none of which has been satisfactorily verified at this time.

Types of learning

Educators concerned with the teaching of principles in a variety of subject areas have often questioned whether learning is a basic or general process. That is, are there common characteristics that apply regardless of the material or skills being learned, or does the process differ depending on the material? For example, is learning to ride a bicycle essentially different from learning to skate? Aside from the obvious differences in type of response and muscle groups used, is the learning *process* similar, or is it different? Are the cognitive processes of a person who is learning dance steps the same as when that individual is learning to solve a complex mathematics problem? Can one assume that learning to dive is similar to learning to catch a ball? Is there something essentially different about verbal and motor learning? Answers to these questions have significance for teachers of all subjects.

Unfortunately, there is no consensus among authorities as to the precise nature of the learning process as it applies to different types of material or skills. However, it is widely agreed that all learning is dependent upon a complex system of information processing. The human organism is frequently compared to a computer that receives input, processes that information, and provides appropriate output, depending on the nature of the task. While "output" is the only phase that can be observed or measured, all recent explanations of the learning process acknowledge the input and processing phases. Students of learning agree that feedback is crucial for the effective learning of all types of skills, knowledge, or attitudes. Further, it is generally assumed that there is some mechanism for storing this material, probably on both a short-term and a long-term basis, along with a means of retrieving the information when needed.

Some authors categorize learning according to the nature of material, while others focus on the type of processing that is assumed to occur. Some believe that at the neurological level all learning is similar. Five patterns for categorizing learning are presented in Table 1-2. It can be noted that there is only limited similarity or consensus among these plans. However, a few types of learning, notably motor skill learning, problem solving, and the development of attitudes, do appear on several lists.

Motor skill learning differs most clearly from verbal learning in the output phase of the process. These differences may vary from a tumbling routine in gymnastics to an oral response to a problem in a math class. In addition, the input phase may also differ. For example, in verbal learning one may read a poem to be memorized or a math problem to be solved, while input for a motor skill may include observation of a volleyball spike or a cartwheel demonstration. On the other hand, the input phase of a motor skill may also be verbal, i.e., a written or oral explanation of the volleyball spike or cartwheel. Therefore, the distinctions between verbal and motor learning are not always clear. There is no certainty that the mechanism for processing, storage, and recall differ.

Hulse, et al. (1980) categorized all learning into two major groups that they believed to be basically different. Several others have agreed with this general notion. In the first type of learning, *classical conditioning* (sometimes referred to as Pavlovian conditioning), the learner responds to a particular stimulus. Classical conditioning was first demonstrated during the first decade of the 20th century with the well-known experiments of I. P. Pavlov, the Russian physiologist. He demonstrated that dogs could be trained to respond to a stimulus, such as a bell, with salivary secretion. In the experimental situation, the response is under the control of the investigator, who decides on an appropriate response and then trains the subject accordingly. The stimulus that is used also serves as the reinforcer. In classical conditioning, the learning organism plays a purely passive role so far as the delivery of the conditional or unconditional stimulus is concerned. Classical conditioning can be observed frequently today both in and out of schools.

In Hulse's second type of learning, *instrument-operant conditioning*, the learner must assume an active role in the process. Things are arranged so that the learner cannot obtain the reward, or cannot avoid punishment, unless he or she makes the proper response. However, after a correct response, the reward (reinforcement) is applied. A particular response or behavior is required for the reward, and responsibility for the response rests with the subject, i.e., one must do the trick before receiving the treat. As the name implies, the learner plays an "instrumental" role in producing rewards or avoiding punishment. Hulse's two types of learning seem equally applicable to the learning of motor and verbal skills.

Singleton (1977) categorized skills into *output-dominated, input-dominated,* and *cognitive* skills. This classification is based on what he considers the dominant functions of the process. Output-dominated skills are those in which physical activity is an obvious and consistent part, such as most sports activities, assembly line workers, and construction personnel. Input-dominated skills place primary

TABLE 1-2. Types of Learning as Suggested by Several Authors

Harris and Schwahn's process of behavioral change (1961)	Tolman's types of connections or relations (1949)	Kingsley and Garry's types of learning (1957)	Bloom's taxonomy of educational objectives (1956)	Gagné's learning outcomes (1977)
1. Skill learning—coordination of sensory and perceptual functioning in performance	1. Motor patterns—require simple conditioning	1. Perceptual motor learning	1. The psychomotor or motor domain	1. Motor skills—Executing a smoothly timed measurement response
2. Reasoning—a rational approach to problem solving	2. Cathexes—acquired relationship between drive and goal	2. Problem solving—learner must determine solution to a novel situation	2. The cognitive domain—development of intellectual abilities and skills	2. Cognitive strategies—Originating a solution to an unfamiliar problem
3. Attitudinal learning—involving the person's values	3. Equivalence beliefs—acquired relationship between drive and secondary or substitute goal	3. Conditioning—both instrumental and classical	3. The affective domain—dealing with interests, attitudes, appreciations, and adjustments	3. Intellectual skill—Demonstrating the relationship between symbols and things
4. Conceptual learning—generalizations concerning situations and signs	4. Field expectancies—learned signs or cues facilitate problem solving	4. Trial and error learning—refers to inefficiency of earlier behavior		4. Verbal information—Communicating ideas through language, oral or written
5. Group learning—interpersonal and social interaction are influential	5. Field-cognition modes (of a higher order than 4)—innate capacities contribute to readiness to learn in several ways	5. Discrimination learning—judgment between two or more stimuli is required		5. Attitudes—Tendencies that influence one's choice of action
6. Aesthetic creativity—application of original thought to aesthetic production	6. Drive discrimination—two modes of behavior are learned, depending upon the particular drive	6. Maze learning—learner must rely on memory of previous responses		
		7. Verbal learning		

13

importance on sensory input while the output is trivial. Input skills would include inspecting, monitoring, or serving as a "spotter." Singleton refers to cognitive skills as the "thinking" skills, placing most emphasis on information processing. These require reasoned judgments based on a body of information. The dance critic or the sports analyst would fit into this category.

CATEGORIES OF MOTOR SKILLS

Terminology relating to motor skills has expanded and come into greater prominence in recent years, during which time skill acquisition has been seriously investigated. Skills are often labeled or grouped on the basis of characteristics of acquisition and performance. The following discussion includes some of the more prominent categories represented in the literature today.

Motor skills
and verbal skills

Motor skills are those behaviors that are demonstrated through smooth, well controlled and coordinated muscular movement. Verbal skills are reflected in the communication of information through speech, writing, drawing pictures, "signing," or some other means. Use of the terms "motor" and "verbal" do not provide a clue as to the amount of *cognitive* or intellectual involvement required to perform the skill. It is clear, however, that in the case of motor skills the individual must be able to remember the sequence of timing of subskills in order to demonstrate a more complex movement response. In verbal skills, the individual must have gained some knowledge in order to communicate through speaking, writing, body language, or other forms. In addition to motor and verbal skills, Gagné (1977) identifies (1) intellectual skills, (2) cognitive strategies, and (3) attitudes. He refers to each of these as learned capacities that make up human performance. Although recognizing that the learning conditions and outcomes differ, he does not rank the various skills in any order with reference to difficulty, level of comprehension, or mental capacities required.

Some persons incorrectly create a dichotomy between motor and verbal skills with the assumption that mental functioning differs widely in the two kinds of skills. Such an assumption is not sustained when submitted to close scrutiny. It is true that some activities place primary emphasis on cognition with only secondary attention to motor output. Solving a riddle "in your head" is one such example. Other skills, such as learning to juggle, place the major emphasis on output. Still, mental and physical involvement are not mutually exclusive. The level of cognition depends upon the sophistication and complexity of the riddle or the juggling task. The riddle, for example, may vary from the simplest elementary school task to an Agatha Christie mystery. Likewise, the juggling task may vary from the use of only two objects to the most complicated of circus tricks. Consequently, the relevant mental involvement depends upon the complexity of the task and not whether it can be categorized as motor or verbal.

Some writers even object to the use of the motor and verbal distinction, arguing that all learning is both motor and verbal. It is true, of course, that in verbal learning (solving the riddle) certain physical components are brought into play. First, the senses are used so that the learner either sees or hears the problem as presented. Next, there is electrical or biochemical activity in the central nervous system that eventually results in the answer becoming evident. Finally, the learner must respond in some physical way to communicate the answer to the riddle. Still, such a response, be it oral, written, or even in pantomime, does not give evidence that a motor skill was learned. Rather, previously learned motor skills were used to demonstrate an answer that was arrived at mentally. Consequently, it does not seem useful to deny the distinction between motor and verbal skills, but it is important to point out that the difference is primarily one of output modality and not depth of mental comprehension.

Unlike riddles and juggling, a great many human activities cannot be so easily categorized into motor and verbal areas. Learning to play the piano or violin, typing or taking shorthand, painting or sculpting, or driving a car or flying an airplane all require both mental processing and motor output. Some skills are high in verbal involvement and low in motor responses while others are just the reverse. To force all human activities into these categories is clearly arbitrary.

The simpler, less complex tasks do not require continuous or even regular conscious control. They are more quickly relegated to an autonomous* or subconscious level. At the other extreme, there are highly complex tasks that require intensive, ongoing conscious control. Sometimes motor skills, such as walking, fall into the simpler, more habitual category, while verbal skills, such as solving riddles, fall into the latter category. On the other hand, many complex motor skills require more intensive cognitive control than do several verbal skills, i.e., compare the early stages of learning to fly a small airplane to the recitation of a well-learned poem.

It is reasonable to assume that motor skills are more frequently learned to the point at which they require little or no cognitive effort. Those skills requiring both verbal and motor involvement, e.g., typing, piano playing, or translating a language simultaneously, can be learned to the point at which they require little conscious control. Complex verbal skills with minimal motor involvement may afford less opportunity for being relegated to the level of subconscious responses. Still, even the highest level of verbal activity, when well learned and repeated often, can become practically automatic. For example, there is the old story of the university professor who once dreamed that he was lecturing to his class. In his dream he lectured on and on. Eventually he awakened and discovered that he was indeed lecturing to his class! Similarly, an analysis of political speeches leads one to assume that they are often repetitions of former speeches, learned to the extent that they can be delivered without conscious thought, much as the professional ice hockey

*See discussion of Fitt's phases of learning later in this chapter.

player can skate backwards without falling, while thinking about more important strategies of the game.

Therefore, motor skills and verbal skills are better understood in terms of their output than they are of an analysis of the intellectual or cognitive processes involved in the development of those skills.

Discrete, serial, and continuous skills

Motor skills are frequently categorized according to the temporal relationships of the stimuli and responses. Such groupings often serve as a comparative basis for research and other analysis. Terminology most frequently used for these temporally arranged tasks are *discrete* and *continuous*, with some intermediate tasks being identified as *serial*. Several researchers, including Fleishman and Parker (1962) and Naylor and Briggs (1961), have reported that continuous-type skills are retained more easily than are discrete ones.

Discrete motor skills are those that have a distinct beginning and end. The task is usually of short duration, sometimes involving a single action, such as a dart throw, a sit-up, or swatting a fly. These skills of short duration allow practically no opportunity for modification of response during the performance. However, some discrete tasks are somewhat more complex, perhaps having two or more component parts. They are still of short duration and have a clear beginning and end. These might include the golf shot, the volleyball spike, or opening a car door.

Serial tasks are similar to discrete tasks in that they also have a distinct beginning and end. However, serial tasks are more complex and involve a combination of responses performed in sequence that lead to a major culminating skill. They involve several discrete tasks joined together. For example, the bowling delivery involves several steps and an arm swing prior to the delivery of the ball. In this skill it is essential that all preliminary skills be performed accurately and in the proper sequence. The high jump, the springboard dive (including approach), and the gymnastics tumbling routine all involve several discrete tasks that must be joined together properly. In serial tasks, as with continuous skills, one has the opportunity to correct or adjust future responses on the basis of information received during the performance.

Continuous (or repetitive) skills are those that have no prescribed termination point. Walking, skating, swimming, juggling, or skiing are examples of continuous skills. In these activities, the same response is repeated over and over. One category of continuous skills contains those of a tracking nature, which require continuous observation and adjustment to a dynamic stimulus. In the laboratory the pursuit rotor task is an example of a tracking task. In more practical situations, driving an automobile or riding a bicycle in the correct lane, following a colored line through a hospital corridor, or sewing a seam while following a drawn pattern are other illustrations.

Closed and open skills

The technique of classifying skills according to their dependence upon environmental stimuli versus being "self-contained" was first developed by Poulton (1957) and later expanded by Knapp (1963) and Gentile (1972).

Closed skills are described as those in which environmental stimuli are stable, thus allowing for stereotyped responses on the part of the performer. During the performance of closed skills, the individual relies primarily upon proprioceptive control only and is therefore not forced to make temporal or spacial adjustments in movement pattern. Sports activities in this category include bowling, gymnastics, golf, the high jump, and the pitching delivery. In work situations, chopping wood, hammering a nail, and typing a manuscript are examples of closed skills.

In developing closed skills, the individual concentrates on developing an efficient movement pattern that can be performed in identical fashion at subsequent times. Hopefully the proper response will become habituated through practice. In bowling, a closed skill, all dimensions and conditions are standardized so that, once learned, the same delivery can be effectively used in all bowling lanes, particularly on the first delivery. However, a "spare" situation may require a somewhat different, though predictable, delivery on the second ball. In gymnastics, too, a movement routine can be habituated inasmuch as all equipment and floor dimensions are standardized and since the performer does not have to interact with any other person. So, too, with golf, since the ball is not moving and the distance to the green is predictable, the stroke can be "grooved." The high jumper, the baseball pitcher, and the diver can all perform with stereotyped movement patterns. The athlete who has learned the closed skill well is less likely to be affected by distracting psychological factors that may be presented, e.g., crowd noise for the free throw shooter, office noise for the manuscript typist, television cameras for the golfer, or the many distractions encountered by the London palace guards in the performance of their duties.

In *open* skills, stereotyped responses are not effective inasmuch as environmental factors that affect performance are unpredictable. Typically, the performer is required to make spatial or temporal adjustments in response to dynamics caused by people or things. Sports skills falling into the open category are tennis strokes (except the service), batting a pitched ball, riding a bucking horse, trapping a soccer ball, wrestling, fencing, and the martial arts. In none of these situations can the performer predict exactly when and where a response must be made. Obviously the tennis player cannot count on the ball arriving at a predetermined place or time. Consequently, one must practice a variety of responses in a wide range of circumstances. The same is true with the batter, the soccer player, and performers in combative activities.

In work situations, changes in environmental conditions are ever present in a wide range of circumstances. Common among these are driving a vehicle in traffic, translating a language simultaneously, directing traffic, taking dictation, or serving as a telephone operator. Persons in each of these situations must make intelligent use of input in order to respond adequately.

Not all skills are easily categorized as open or closed. Knapp (1963), in fact, suggested that skills should be placed on a continuum rather than in clearly open or closed categories. Certain complex tasks generally viewed as open contain subskills that are substantially closed. For example, driving an automobile is an open skill given the uncertainties of other vehicles, pedestrians, curving roads, and stop lights. Still, certain components of the overall performance, such as depressing the clutch, changing gears, accelerating, and braking are performed in a stereotyped fashion as "programmed" by the skilled driver. Similarly, the pass thrown by the quarterback in a game situation is clearly an open skill. However, once the situation is right, i.e., the receiver is open and there is an unobstructed lane in which to throw, he initiates the delivery. At this point the subskills, the planting of the foot, the cocking of the arm, the shifting of weight, the smooth delivery and follow-through, all seem to fall in place in a stereotyped (closed) fashion.

It appears that certain skills may start out in one category and shift to the other. Baseball batting, an open skill, may be used to illustrate. Several years ago I began teaching my son at a very young age to swing a baseball bat. The child learned to swing the small bat, at chest level, in a reasonable facsimile of a baseball stroke. I found that I could stimulate this stereotyped swing by simply yelling, "Swing!" Next I introduced a thrown ball (large, soft, fluff ball). By tossing the ball precisely at chest level while simultaneously yelling "swing," I found that he was able to strike the ball. In fact, he soon exhibited batting skill that was impressive to friends and neighbors. The swing was well "grooved." Only the toss was occasionally off target. Then gradually, as the child matured, he was able to see that it made a difference where he swung. Eventually he was able to make adjustments in the level and timing of the swing to strike an errant throw. At this point the skill became "open."

Gross motor skills
and fine motor skills

Motor activities may be arbitrarily categorized as gross or fine skills depending upon the magnitude of the movement. *Gross motor skills* are those that involve large muscle groups or move the body through space. Such sports skills as the high jump, a springboard dive, a jump shot, a football punt, or a tumbling routine are clear examples of gross motor skills. In fact, most major sports emphasize gross movements. In the work world, many unskilled and semi-skilled labor activities involve gross motor skills. Examples include the duties of the logger, the farmer, or the construction worker. Dynamic balancing activities and agility exercise are examples of gross motor activities frequently used in fitness testing or in research.

Fine motor skills are those involving small muscle groups or movement with a very limited range. Such activities usually emphasize timing and precision and frequently involve manipulative skills of the hands and fingers. In sports, this may include holding the football for the place kicker, putting in golf, squeezing the trigger in riflery, or more subtle components of larger movements, such as the follow-through in a basketball shot. The great majority of work-related motor skills in today's "skilled" trades and professions are fine. Examples include the operation of office machinery, the surgeon's skills, the dental technician, and even the operation of heavy machinery by levers and buttons. Similarly, most laboratory motor tasks used by experimental psychologists and physical educators fall into this group.

Clearly it is impossible to confidently place all motor skills into either the gross or the fine category. Rather, motor skills fall on a continuum ranging from those requiring the depression of a computer key to the high jump and beyond. It is of little value to place labels on all in-between skills. In research, however, it is helpful to identify the general magnitude of the movement so that assumptions can more confidently be made about the application of results.

Novel motor skills
and familiar skills

For research purposes it is important to distinguish between those skills that are novel to the learner and those that are familiar. Novel tasks, whether motor or verbal, are most frequently used by experimental psychologists and other researchers studying human learning and performance. Laboratory tasks such as the pursuit rotor, finger mazes, or mirror tracing fall into this category. These motor tasks have been used extensively by experimental psychologists in the study of learning. More recently developed tasks involve balancing, kinesthetic positioning, coordination movements, tracking skills, and a great variety of computer games, among others. These tasks offer distinct experimental control advantages over more familiar tasks. They can be compared with the *nonsense syllables* developed by Ebbinghaus and used extensively in memory studies during the late 19th century. The development of gross motor skills of a novel nature has greatly increased among researchers in physical education over the past two decades. (An extensive discussion of some of these tasks is presented in chapter two.)

Familiar motor skills are those with which the learner is at least partially acquainted. These are usually "meaningful" activities that have been performed or observed previously. Such motor skills frequently used in learning and performance studies include the basketball free throw, various swimming strokes, gymnastics skills, kicking a soccer ball for accuracy, archery, and tennis strokes. In many situations these tasks are modified to make them more "novel," and consequently, to increase their research value. This may be done by requiring the subject to use the nondominant hand or foot, changing the distance or speed, requiring a rebound or deflection, or by adding some other factor designed to reduce the effect of previous experience. Such measures, in effect, change familiar tasks into novel ones.

Perceptual skills, motor skills, and perceptual-motor skills

The terms *perceptual skills, motor skills,* and *perceptual-motor skills* are often used interchangeably. In a general sense, this is an acceptable way of referring to the whole category of skills that engage the senses, the neuromuscular system, or a combination of both. However, a more precise breakdown is necessary to understand the discussions of certain authors and to better comprehend some research reports.

Perceptual skills are activities one performs while responding to visual, auditory, tactile, kinesthetic, or other sensory cues. Some work situations that make use of perceptual skills include proofreading a manuscript, inspecting the quality of produce as it passes on a conveyer, and monitoring computer print-outs. In addition, the mechanic who listens to an automobile engine to diagnose a problem or the physician who listens to sounds through a stethoscope to determine cardio-respiratory problems relies on perceptual skills involving the auditory sense. On another occasion the doctor may palpate a body part to determine the normality of, or changes in, the patient's condition. In football, the "spotter," located in a position high above the field, observes the positioning and movements of players on both teams and makes strategy suggestions to the coach or quarterback who are not able to see these things. A somewhat similar role is served by "scouts" who, through trained eyes, observe future opponents and relay important information to the coach. The dance critic, the music critic, the choreographer, and the composer all rely heavily upon perceptual skills for success.

Motor skills are activities that place primary emphasis on movement efficiency. Such skills, however, are rarely, if ever, without a perceptual component. In some laboratory situations, special efforts are sometimes made to limit or eliminate sensory cues. Activities high in motor aspects and low in perception are sit-ups, running, swimming, and hopping. It is clear, however, that each of these skills makes use of the kinesthetic sense.

Singleton (1977) stated that perceptual skills are more complex than motor skills. He argues that whereas motor skills can be well-learned and shifted to the subconscious level during performance, perceptual skills are rarely, if ever, relegated to that level.

The term *perceptual-motor skills* recognizes both the sensory and motor components of human movement activities. Use of this terminology is prevalent among psychologists, particularly those working with developmental programs for young children. Still, the combination of perceptual and motor components is quite evident when one observes the sports or work tasks engaged in by adolescents or adults. For example, the baseball batter must make important use of visual perception in determining whether or not the pitch is to be in the strike zone, whether it is a straight ball or curving, and how fast it is traveling. Only after receiving and analyzing this information can the batter initiate the swing at the right time and place. The gymnast on the pommel horse must maintain a sense of balance and momentum in order to gauge responses effectively. In the automobile body shop, the worker gains perceptual input by looking at and feeling the fender while hammering and sanding the damaged area to a smooth finish.

THE LEARNING OF MOTOR SKILLS

Occasionally the assumption is made that little, if any, cognition is involved in the acquisition of motor skills. This is particularly true when skill learning is discussed in relation to other types of learning. For example, as illustrated in Table 1-2, Harris and Schwahn have separate listings for "skill learning" and "reasoning." Tolman referred to motor patterns as only requiring simple conditioning. Bloom's taxonomy lists separate "psychomotor" and "cognitive" domains, and Gagné's learning outcomes provide separate listings for "motor skills" and "cognitive strategies." A casual observation of such descriptions has led some persons to assume that motor learning is limited to simple physical stimulus-response associations, while other types of learning may involve symbol-manipulative processes. While it is true that such distinction seems apparent when one observes extreme examples of each type of learning, e.g., a very complex verbal or mental task versus a basic motor response, such a general dichotomy between verbal and motor learning is highly erroneous. In fact, it is impossible to categorize a great many skills because they involve both motor and cognitive components. Learning to type, play a musical instrument, drive an automobile, or perform a complex rhythmical maneuver obviously involves both mental and physical coordinations.

Motor skills require varying levels and degrees of cognitive involvement. The learning of most skills is a thoughtful, active process. For example, the fourth grade girl who is instructed to perform a cartwheel may observe another child, then attempt to put her own body through this sequence of movements. She then attempts to understand the relationship between her self-initiated movement responses and the overall results. After an initial try, she may receive advice from the instructor or her classmates and try again, varying her response on the basis of this verbal feedback as well as kinesthetic feedback from earlier trials. Use of this information in subsequent trials leads to effective learning. On the other hand, blind trial-and-error efforts are a poor way to learn a motor skill. Efforts that do not make use of feedback are not only frustrating but largely ineffective.

Certain motor activities are learned very slowly by some people because they are unable to understand the relationship between their motor responses and the results. A teacher may aid pupils by helping them to see this relationship. For verbal feedback to be effective, pupils must gain not merely an understanding of the verbiage, but an understanding related to the action. For example, an individual may understand the principle of inertia and still not be able to apply it while swinging a tennis racket or trapping and kicking a soccer ball. Action, feedback, evaluation, and repeated action are major factors in the successful performance of motor activities. Motor learning, therefore, is clearly a physical *and* a mental process.

Phases of motor skill learning

The most definitive and logical description of the phases or steps involved in motor skill learning was developed by Fitts (1964). This model has been commented on and expanded by several other authors. According to Fitts, there are three clearly defined phases in the acquisition of a motor skill from the beginning up to the level of mastery. These include: (1) the initial or *cognitive phase*, (2) the intermediate or *associative phase*, and (3) the final or *autonomous phase*. Robb (1972) has referred to these as the *plan formation, practice,* and *automatic execution* phases. Adams (1971) describes only two phases, using the term *verbal-motor* to parallel Fitts' first two phases and the term *motor* to approximate the autonomous stage. All authors agree that the phases are not separate and distinct, but that they gradually merge into each other. A review of the phases and processes illustrates just how skill learning occurs and how it can best be promoted.

Cognitive phase.   Fitts' first phase is characterized by efforts on the part of the learner to understand the task to be performed. The instructor aids in this process by providing the learner with all essential information about the task. Heavy emphasis is placed on perceptual mechanisms, with visual, auditory, and kinesthetic cues being highlighted. The early comprehension of the task is aided by explanations, demonstrations, films, charts, discussion, and initial trials. A slow, deliberate approach is needed so that the learner can observe cues and subtleties that might otherwise go unnoticed. Robb points out the need to intensify these cues when possible, such as using brightly colored tennis balls to increase visibility.

During the cognitive phase, the learner receives input from all sources and tries to internalize this information. For example, when a young girl learns to bounce (dribble) a basketball, she first observes another's performance, and, with encouragement, tries it herself. During initial tries, she receives visual input not only from watching a demonstration but also from observing the movement of the ball she is attempting to bounce. She receives kinesthetic cues by feeling the ball and by attempting to coordinate her movement response by striking the ball when it reaches the top of its bounce. She gradually realizes that hitting the ball prematurely or not forcefully enough results in inadequate impetus for the return bounce. Further, she learns through kinesthetic cues that a forceful downward "push" is preferable to a sharp strike for both power and control. Comments are provided by the teacher, coach, or parent, who not only encourages the activity but provides helpful information about the performance. Consequently, the visual kinesthetic, and auditory information is put to use by the learner in the initial stages of this relatively difficult coordination task.

During the cognitive phase, the learner begins to form an executive plan in which subroutines of the tasks are identified and organized for later use in the overall performance. Robb uses the term "plan formation" for this phase to emphasize the necessity of establishing a sequence, or ordering, of each of the routines that make up the overall performance. In other words, the learner must learn which responses follow which. Nothing is refined during this initial phase, and a precise form is not yet established. However, the learner does develop an understanding of what is to be done and establishes a plan for initiating each of the component parts in proper sequence. The cognitive phase is a relatively short period in the overall learning process.

Associative phase.   This phase, variously called the associative, fixation, or practice, is the period during which the individual approaches maximum efficiency in the task. The learner receives ongoing feedback, gradually eliminates errors, and makes fine adjustments. The temporal qualities of the task are refined during this phase. The learner establishes smooth coordination in the sequencing of the component parts of the task.

This practice-oriented phase lasts significantly longer than the cognitive phase, during which only gross adjustments in movement responses are made. The girl learning to dribble the basketball is now concerned not only with completing a series of successful bounces but with learning to dribble with fingertip control while moving at a rapid speed, changing directions, and without the benefit of visual cues, i.e., not looking at the ball. To reach this level of efficiency, the young player must engage in many hours of practice under favorable conditions. Most effective conditions involve proper attention to motivation, feedback, practice scheduling, whole and part organization, mental rehearsal, and other considerations. A wide variety of conditions, obstacles, and "game situations" will be presented, all of which are instrumental in developing versatility and confidence in dribbling. In addition to making use of augmented feedback, the learner develops the ability to detect her own errors and correct them.

Autonomous phase.   This final phase is one in which the task is performed easily, without stress, and with little, if any, conscious control. The skill eventually becomes habituated to the extent that the established executive program takes control of all aspects of the performance. All people have any number of skills that have been developed to this level. For example, all nonhandicapped adults are able to manipulate eating utensils and deliver food to the mouth on a fork without stabbing themselves in the cheek, thrusting it too deeply into the throat, or spilling the food prior to reaching the mouth. We seem to open the mouth just in the nick of time as the food approaches. This basic skill was not always so simple; note the two-year-old child who struggles to accomplish all the coordinations involved in this task with only moderate success. Or note the typical American in an Oriental restaurant who attempts to use chopsticks, a task "automatic" for the Oriental person who observes this custom.

The college or professional basketball player has learned the dribble to the point where it can be performed effectively without conscious control. Consequently, she can dribble full speed down court on a fast break, changing directions, even dribbling behind her back when necessary, while *thinking* about more important matters. She considers which opposing player is obstructing her path, her previous success against that person, perhaps even the tendency of the official to call a charging or blocking foul. On the basis of all this information, and in view of her awareness of the position of her teammates, she makes the decision to drive to the basket, pass off, or pull up suddenly for a jump shot. No longer does she think about the skill of dribbling. Rather, she thinks about strategy, the game situation, and which of several options is most suitable for this particular situation (see Figure 1-1).

Control of these well-learned routines is developed early in the learning process through the executive plan. Conscious attention is not required and may even interfere with effective performance of well-learned habits. Most of us can think of instances where we either get "tied up" or at least lose some smoothness when we decide to think our way through such a habit. If we decide to think about opening our mouths when the spoonful of soup is about to arrive, the whole process becomes mechanical and awkward. Years ago the story was told that New York Yankee catcher Yogi Berra, finding himself in a rare slump, was advised by manager Casey Stengel to start "thinking" more about batting. Yogi dutifully followed this advice his next time at bat, and after striking out returned to the bench in confusion to ask manager Stengel, "How can you *think* and bat at the same time?" Though the story made interesting copy for sports writers, Yogi knew best. You cannot bat effectively while thinking about swinging the bat. One can, however, think through the movement response (mentally rehearse) *prior* to the performance. At the time of performance, however, one should concentrate on the impor-

FIGURE 1-1.   Fundamental skills such as dribbling may become automatic, requiring no conscious thought on the part of the experienced player. (Photo courtesy of Temple University Department of Women's Intercollegiate Athletics.)

tant decision-making components, i.e., whether or not to swing at the pitch, and whether to hit to right, center, or left field. Once the swing is initiated, the mechanics of the performance function automatically.

Learning versus performance

Learning is invisible; it is never actually observed. Rather, it is evidenced only through performance. In essence, performance translates learning into behavior. Consequently, in order to determine whether learning has occurred, comparisons must be made in performance levels over a period of time. The most widely used mechanism for illustrating the occurrence of learning is the *learning curve*. More accurately, such a chart should be labeled a performance curve. However, because of the assumption that the changing levels of skill closely parallel performance scores, the term *learning curve* has traditionally been used. The validity of the learning curve as an indication of the actual status of learning is dependent upon getting an accurate measure of beginning level skill as well as a true measure of subsequent trials.

Representing actual data from three groups in an experiment, the learning curves in Figure 1-2 can be used to reflect typical patterns followed by individuals or groups who progress at different rates. Curve A represents a group of fast learners, Curve B a group of moderate learners, and Curve C a group of slow learners. The curves represent only the speed with which the learners developed proficiency at this particular task. All may arrive at the same level of performance,

FIGURE 1-2. Typical Learning Curve Representing Three Groups Progressing at Different Rates (From J. M. Harmon and J. B. Oxendine, Effect of different lengths of practice periods on the learning of a motor skill. *Research Quarterly*, March 1961, pp. 34-41. Copyright by the American Alliance for Health, Physical Education, Recreation and Dance, 1900 Association Drive, Reston, Va. 22091. Reprinted by permission.)

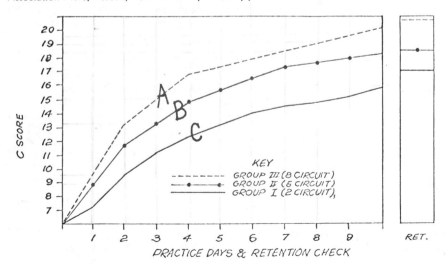

but not at the same time. The eventual level of proficiency is dependent not only on general aptitude, but on practice opportunities and motivation.

Typically, in plotting a learning curve, the units of time or practice trials are presented on the horizontal axis, or *abscissa*, while measures of learning or proficiency are plotted on the vertical axis, or *ordinate*. The rate of learning is reflected in the slope of the curve. The graphical representation, or learning curve, simply presents a picture of the relationship between practice and performance.

The measurement of performance as a means of determining level of skill at any time has many problems. Such problems exist in controlled laboratory studies, in sports skill performance, in job productivity, and in routine daily chores. Irregularities or inaccuracies in such measures may result from motivation variations, styles in performance, luck, or a multitude of personality variables. Performance variations from trial to trial usually vary more than does the actual skill level. Not only are chance factors involved, but sometimes scores are depressed deliberately. For example, students in classes sometimes learn to depress initial scores after they learn that an "improvement" score is a factor in course evaluation. In addition, years ago there seemed to be a tendency for teenage girls to downplay their strength and stamina in certain motor activities. Such a tendency has subsided appreciably. Still, the level of enthusiasm for both boys and girls in vigorous physical activities is often tempered to the extent that performance scores are lower than the actual motor capacity.

In competitive sports activities it is difficult to get a valid indication of one's level of ability on the basis of performance scores or records. This is particularly true in "open" skills where one is interacting with opposing team members or individuals. In high school wrestling, for example, one boy may wind up the season with a record of eight wins and four losses while another has a four and eight record. One cannot assume that the former is a more skilled wrestler without being certain that the level of competition was identical. In baseball, batting average is usually viewed as a fairly representative indication of one's batting proficiency, but this loses meaning if we do not know which league the person was in, what his slugging percentage was, how productive he was with runners on base, and how many successful sacrifice bunts he had, among other factors. Similar problems could be pointed out with a pitcher's earned run average, scoring average in basketball, or a team's won-loss record. Two comparably skilled skaters may wind up with vastly different scores on a routine because one performer presented a more difficult and daring routine that resulted in a fall, while the other skated a nearly perfect, but conservative program. Resulting scores may not reflect the comparable skill level accurately. However, performance scores in "closed" skills do more accurately reflect one's current level of skill. Archery, golf, riflery, and bowling scores are not so dramatically influenced by the skill level of the competition.

Singleton (1977) reports on the fallacy of using classical measures of performance to evaluate airplane pilots. In one study, pilot performances were compared on the basis of the closeness with which they adhered to the optimum approach line as they manuevered in for landing. Singleton reported that "highly experienced pilots when compared to inexperienced ones show greater deviation from this optimum because they make corrections less often." The more highly skilled pilot knows how far he can depart without danger. Less skilled pilots stick closer to the "letter perfect" pattern, which was not found to be strictly necessary. Similar findings are no doubt evidenced in many other job performances. In these jobs, as in sports, the very highly skilled person has the ability to be more casual, yet "get the job done." This individual is more interested in ultimate results than in absolute consistency. Since such problems often do not follow the prescribed performance, it is sometimes hard to measure skill level by using interim measures or checkpoints.

Motor learning refers to relatively permanent changes in performance levels. Consequently, those irregular fluctuations or measures reflected in learning curve are only rough indications of the individual's level of learning. Though such learning (performance) curves are clearly imperfect, they are the best indices available.

Generality and specificity in motor learning

It was traditionally assumed that the ability to learn and perform motor skills was a *general* factor, i.e., the person who could learn tennis strokes rapidly could also learn gymnastics or a complex manipulative skill equally well. Further, it was believed that those who could perform at a high level in basketball could exhibit similar proficiency in swimming and table tennis. In other words, some people were categorized as "natural athletes" and others "motor morons," with most falling somewhere in between.

In the area of verbal learning, a similar attitude of generality was espoused. This position held that a "bright" child could learn English grammar, spelling, mathematics, and science more quickly and easily than the less bright child.

As it turns out, neither of these widely held assumptions have stood up under close scrutiny in recent years. More than a half century ago, Thorndike and Hagen (1927) showed that there was little evidence to support a general factor of intellectual abilities, or the ability to learn a wide range of verbal materials similarly. This view was supported by Thurstone in his identification of seven "primary mental abilities." More recent studies have provided a rather convincing case that most human capacities are specific. Henry (1957), Fleishman (1964), Oxendine (1967), and others have shown that the performance of motor skills is essentially specific. In addition, ample studies are now available to show that the acquisition of motor skills is also task-specific, i.e., speed in the learning of one task is no indication that the person will be able to learn a different skill as quickly or as well.

There are conditions that give the impression of generality or carry-over from one task to another. Such is the case when the components underlying effective performance in two tasks are common. That is, the child who is a fast runner may perform well in sprint races in track and may also do well as a football runner. This is because the ability to run fast serves one well in each of the activities, as it would also for baseball and a variety of running games in the elementary school. However, for tasks that don't involve running, such as swimming, archery, pitching, or spiking a volleyball, such speed would provide no advantage. Similarly, the child with good reading ability (speed and comprehension) has an advantage in those school activities that place emphasis on reading, such as English, history, and geography, but would not have an advantage in music, algebra, or wood shop.

A second reason for the appearance of generality in the area of motor learning is the development of traits on the part of some students that help them excel. These include the habit of success, along with greater attention, motivation, and expectancy. Individuals with these characteristics are likely to be "good students" in all courses, whether or not they have any special abilities. (The topic of human motor abilities will be developed more fully in chapter twelve.)

THE LEARNING PROCESS

A brief overview of the learning process, in general, should serve as important background for the study of the special characteristics of motor learning. This discussion of the essential elements and the steps in the learning process will also be used to illustrate, to a limited extent, the application of basic learning principles to physical skills.

One of the clearest statements regarding the learning process was made by Woodruff (1948), who described six sequential steps in learning. This description is helpful in that it presents a step-by-step approach, which, according to Woodruff, occurs in all types of learning. Fitts' phases of skill learning, as presented earlier in the chapter, supplement Woodruff's statement.

According to Woodruff, the speed of learning depends upon (1) the capacity of the individual, (2) the degree of motivation, and (3) the nature of the task. First, more intelligent children, those with greater capacity, generally learn tasks more quickly than those who have less intelligence. Similarly, children who have greater motor ability develop proficiency in physical skills more quickly than those who have less coordination, strength, or general maturation. Second, when motivation is high, learning occurs more quickly than when interest is slight or nonexistent. Third, a task that is simple or of short duration is generally learned more quickly than one that is more complex. It is evident that the speed of learning is dependent upon a combination of these three factors. Woodruff's six steps, discussed below, appear to be characteristic of all forms of learning.

1. "Motivation within the learner makes him receptive to stimulation." Motivation refers to a condition of uneasiness within the individual that arouses or maintains activity. This is the most basic essential for learning and is a prerequisite for all other steps. All purposive behavior results from motivation. Motivation is not injected into the child by the teacher but develops within the individual and is the result of life experiences.

2. "A goal becomes related to motivation." When a general or undefinable state of motivation exists, the individual will seek some goal to satisfy that restlessness. As soon as the goal is selected, action toward that goal can begin. Depending upon the motivation, the goal selected might be of a physiological, social, or personal nature. In most school situations, social or personal goals are most prevalent. A teenager's desire to be able to dance, bowl, or ride a surfboard is usually of social origin and acts as a strong force in stimulating practice of these activities. The need for attaining a position on an athletic team in school can act as a powerful force for action. Aspirations to gain personal goals, such as the ability to read, swim, or drive a car are likewise strong incentives for action.

3. "Tension arises." When the goal is not immediately attainable because the individual cannot suddenly dance well, bowl, ride a surfboard, or drive a car, tensions arise. As in the case of all learning, a barrier exists. In these situations, the barrier is the inability of the individual to suddenly exhibit proficiency in the tasks. If the individual strongly desires the goal, considerable tension is developed. This tension can aid learning by enabling one to make a vigorous and sustained attack on the task. For example, social and personal needs can cause one to practice football, swimming, or dancing long and hard despite physical discomfort, fear, and embarrassment. It has been shown, however, that tension or anxiety that is too great can interfere with the efficient solution of a difficult task.

4. "The learner seeks an appropriate line of action to reach his goal." In every learning situation, there are usually several choices of action from which the individual may choose. The responses of the learner may vary from seemingly random or chance selection to those that are thought out and selected as logical or reasonable choices. For example, a novice bowler who is attempting to roll a hook might try different techniques, such as variations in starting position, speed of the approach, height of the backswing, release, and follow-through. However, another novice bowler might try to reason out the action that will cause the ball to hook and therefore try different ways of releasing the ball. In the first example, there is little cause-and-effect consideration. In the second situation, much of the trial-and-error explanation is from mental, rather than physical, activity.

As one's familiarity with a particular task increases, the degree of purely random activity decreases. For example, the novice golfer, after a poor shot, realizes that something went wrong with his swing, but he is not sure what it was. The more experienced golfer, however, quickly narrows down the problem to one or two alternatives. In either case, the golfer tries out the alternative that seems most appropriate. If that line of action is not correct and the shot is not improved, the learner starts over and tries other responses until success has been attained.

5. "The learner fixes the appropriate line of action." Determination of appropriate response usually comes from practice. Realization of the correct action and its repetition tend to fix that response to the particular goal. The first few successes might be rather accidental and, occasionally, no relationship may be seen between the behavior and the outcome. Sometimes the appropriate response is realized rather rapidly, after the first or second trial. On other occasions, the

correct action is suddenly realized after much practice, as when a performer, after long effort, suddenly gets the feel of how to perform a skip or a somersault in gymnastics. But realization of the appropriate action may be a slow process resulting from long practice. In most motor skills, learning takes place gradually by small degrees. Handwriting skill, dance performance, or swimming technique shows gradual improvement. The ultimate goal of excellent performance is not fully realized each time progress is made. Recognition of a small degree of success, however, results in some satisfaction, which leads to a reduction of tension. Tension is relieved in proportion to the progress one has made toward the ultimate goal.

(6.) "Inappropriate behaviors are stopped." When the learner realizes that certain activity is useless, that activity is terminated. In the early stages of learning most motor skills, much of the activity is wasted. An example is the running technique used by young children. Much of the action, especially the lateral movement, is not only useless but is actually a hindrance to running efficiency. However, when the junior high school boy or girl begins practicing with the track team, there is, hopefully, a reduction of movements that are not helpful in promoting speed. Efficiency in running, as well as in other skills, is closely related to the elimination of inappropriate behavior.

While placing strong emphasis on motivation, Woodruff's statement seems consistent with the majority of opinion on learning theory today. Each learning step is presented as distinct and recognizable by the keen observer. However, there seems to be no uniformity in the speed or ease with which different individuals progress through the different phases of the learning process. For example, an individual might progress through one step quickly, only to be slowed down by another one. The speed with which one learns the steps may vary from a relatively sudden occurrence to a very slow process.

In physical education, some time is devoted to the teaching of new skills, whereas in other situations, improvement in familiar skills is sought. There is often some question as to whether the same process is followed in both new learning and gradual improvement. Regarding both situations, Woodruff (1948) points out that

> They share in common these sequential steps: (1) motivation, (2) the setting up of a goal toward which action is directed, (3) the development of tension and readiness to act, (4) discovering a way of acting which brings progress, and (6) throwing aside or ignoring other ways which seem less promising. Whether the fifth sequential step (fixing the successful act) is present in behavior depends on whether one is trying to learn a line of behavior or is just trying to use one at the moment. . . . Nevertheless it is true that for both deliberate learning, and daily living and adjusting, the sequential steps are a sound basic formulation . . . (p. 59).[1]

---

[1] Used by permission of David McKay Co., Inc.

The necessary elements

At least four elements are necessary if learning is to take place: (1) a living motivated organism, (2) an incentive that leads to satisfaction of motives, (3) a barrier, or block, which prevents the organism from immediately gaining the incentive, and (4) effort or activity on the part of the organism to attain the incentive.

All *living organisms* can learn. It is true, of course, that some forms of life attain greater levels of discrimination than do others. In laboratory situations, lower forms of animals have shown behavioral changes that must be described as learning. These adjustments, or this learning, also take place in the organism's natural habitat. The different capacities and different types of learning among various species have long been of interest to the psychologist.

Incentives, which lead to the satisfaction of motives, are central to learning. Motivation, which is assumed to be an internal state of mind, arises from the organism's desire for certain incentives. Such incentives may take the form of food, a grade in school, or success in the performance of a specific task. The intensity of drives, wants, and needs determines the level of motivation. A comfortable or satisfied individual is not as receptive to learning as one who has a greater need for attaining a particular goal.

When the learner is *blocked* from immediately attaining the incentive that would satisfy a need, a learning situation exists. On the other hand, if the incentive or goal is obtained without any serious effort on the part of the organism, this is an indication that the learning has already occurred. An organism, if sufficiently stimulated, will make repeated attempts to attain the incentive. Most learning theorists agree that activity on the part of the individual is strategic for effective learning.

Initial *responses* may or may not prove successful. Goal-directed responses will often be inefficient and confused. Activity on the part of the organism may be overt, or it may primarily involve mental functioning. Occasionally, there may be chance successes. As the process continues, the more successful responses are selected and more often repeated, while the failures are gradually eliminated. The attainment of the incentive often involves the realization of a means-to-end connection on the part of the learner.

Regardless of the nature of the learning task, whether a child is learning to walk, a student is learning a scientific concept, or an adult is learning to drive a car, the essential elements are the same: a motivated individual, incentives that will lead to a satisfaction of the motive, an obstacle preventing the learner from easily attaining the incentive, and activity on the part of the individual.

SUMMARY

1. Because of its ease of observation and broad applicability, motor learning and performance have been of continuing interest to psychologists, educators, and the general public. Efficiency in much of our work, play, and routine daily activi-

ties is dependent upon well-learned motor skills. Some of these skills are developed as a normal part of maturation and activity during the early years of life. Other skills are developed largely to facilitate additional motor or verbal skills. Still others are learned for their own value, for benefits directly related to the skills.

2. For the past century, the topic of learning has been investigated in an experimental and theoretical manner. First, experimental psychologists, then educators, viewed learning as the strategic means of determining behavior, and further, the process by which the goals of education are transmitted.

3. Motor learning is a persistent change in movement behavior potentiality resulting from practice or experience. Learned movement behavior include newly acquired skills, improvement of previously established habits, adjustments necessitated by aging, handicap, or other limiting factors, and even distracting faults that are inadvertently acquired. Not all learning is taught, nor is all learning helpful in the performance of the skill.

4. It is uncertain whether the same principles of learning are followed for all materials and skills, i.e., whether or not the process involved in learning a verbal skill is similar to that for a motor skill. Nevertheless, it is widely agreed that all learning is dependent upon a complex system of information processing. The individual receives input, processes that information, and produces output, depending on the nature of the task.

5. Motor skill learning, along with other types, such as problem solving, attitudes, and verbal learning, is recognized by most authors as one of the prominent categories of learning.

6. Human skills are often categorized as either *motor* or *verbal.* Though a clear distinction is not always evident, motor skills are thought of as those that are demonstrated through smooth, well-coordinated muscular movement, while verbal skills reflect communication in some form. Most skills involve a combination of both motor and verbal components.

7. Depending on the temporal relationships of stimuli and responses, motor skills may be categorized as discrete, continuous, or serial. Discrete skills are those that have a distinct beginning and end, while continuous skills are repetitive, with no prescribed termination point. Serial skills have a beginning and an end, but they also involve a combination of discrete responses performed in sequence, leading to a culminating skill.

8. Motor skills may be categorized on a closed-open continuum according to their dependence upon environmental stimuli. Closed skills are those in which environmental conditions are stable, thus allowing for the development of stereotyped responses. Open skills require the performer to make temporal and spatial adjustments during performance in response to the dynamics caused by people or things.

9. Skills are often arbitrarily categorized as gross or fine, depending upon the magnitude of the movement required. Gross motor skills are those that involve large bodily movements, while fine skills require more limited responses. There is no

clear point of distinction between the two, but the terms are often used to categorize research tasks.

10. For research purposes, motor skills may be viewed as either novel or meaningful. Novel skills, those unfamiliar to the learner, are most frequently used for research purposes. Often these are performed in a laboratory with special apparatus. Meaningful skills are practical activities generally within the acquaintance of the learner or the general public.

11. Though often used interchangeably, the terms *motor skills, perceptual skills,* and *perceptual-motor skills* have different meanings. Motor skills are those tasks placing primary emphasis on movement efficiency. Perceptual skills are those tasks one performs while responding to sensory cues. The term perceptual-motor skill is used to give recognition to both sensory and motor components when they are predominantly used in the performance of a particular task.

12. Motor skill learning has been categorized into (1) the cognitive phase, the period during which the individual gains internal and external information about the task to be performed, (2) the associative phase, the period during which a great deal of practice is generated to master the skill, and (3) the autonomous phase, during which the task is performed with little or no conscious control. These phases are not distinct but gradually evolve from one to the next as greater proficiency is developed.

13. The learning curve is a widely used mechanism for charting performance at different points in the learning process. The decelerating growth curve is typical because rapid learning occurs early in the process in most activities. Actual learning rarely coincides with charted performances. Factors such as motivation, fatigue, or distractions can cause performance to fluctuate from one's true level of learning at any given time.

14. Both motor learning and motor performance are comprised of essentially specific rather than general factors, i.e., one's ability to excel in one motor activity is no assurance that he or she will be able to perform equally welll in a different skill.

15. The general learning process follows certain widely agreed upon steps, including (1) the emergence of motivation, (2) the identification of a goal to satisfy the general motivated state, (3) the development of tension when the goal is not immediately attainable, (4) activity, or responses, on the part of the learner, (5) the selection of the proper action to attain the goal, and (6) the elimination of extraneous or irrelevant activity.

SELECTED READINGS

AMERICAN ALLIANCE FOR HEALTH, PHYSICAL EDUCATION, RECREATION AND DANCE. *Motor Learning.* A. Rothstein, consultant, Basic Stuff Series I, 1981.

CRATTY, B. J. *Movement behavior and motor learning* (3rd ed.). Philadelphia: Lea and Febiger, 1973.

DROWATSKY, J. N. *Motor learning principles and practices* (2nd ed.). Minneapolis, Mn.: Burgess Publishing Co., 1981.

GAGNÉ, R. M. *The conditions of learning* (3rd ed.). New York: Holt, Rinehart and Winston, 1977.

HOUSTON, J. P. *Fundamentals of learning.* New York: Academic Press, 1976.

HULSE, S. H., EGETH, H. AND DEESE, J. *The psychology of learning* (5th ed.). New York: McGraw-Hill Book Co., 1980.

KERR, R. *Psychomotor learning.* Philadelphia: Saunders College Publishing, 1982.

LAWTHER, J. D. The learning and performance of physical skills (2nd ed.). Englewood Cliffs, N.J.: Prentice-Hall, Inc., 1977.

MAGILL, R. A. *Motor learning: concepts and applications.* Dubuque, Ia.: Wm. C Brown Co., 1980.

ROBB, M. D. *The dynamics of motor-skill acquisition.* Englewood Cliffs, N.J.: Prentice-Hall, Inc., 1972.

SCHMIDT, R. A. *Motor control and learning: a behavioral analysis.* Champaign, Ill.: Human Kinetics Publishers, 1982.

SINGLETON, W. T. *The analysis of practical skills.* Baltimore: University Park Press, 1978.

SINGER, R. N. *Motor learning and human performance* (3rd ed.). New York: Macmillan Publishing Co., 1980.

STALLINGS, L. M. *Motor learning: from theory to practice.* St. Louis: The C. V. Mosley Co., 1982.

TRAVERS, R. M. W. *Essentials of learning* (4th ed.). New York: Macmillan Publishing Co., 1977.

2 Experimental Methodology

ORIGINS OF EXPERIMENTAL METHODOLOGY

The phenomenon of learning cannot be fully appreciated without some acquaintance with the processes that have been used to create knowledge on this topic. Since it is primarily through experimentation that our current knowledge about learning has been established, this chapter will provide an orientation to the scientific methodology most frequently employed in skill learning and performance. This review is aimed at providing the reader with a greater understanding of the complexities of experimental research along with an increased ability to evaluate research results. It may also better prepare the student-researcher to conduct independent investigations in the area of skill learning. Rather than reviewing the full range of research methodology, this discussion will focus on those techniques and conditions that apply most closely to the learning of motor skills.

Scientific investigations of the learning process, including skill learning, began approximately a century ago. Empirical observations preceded the initiation of controlled experiments and have continued since that time. This process, *empiricism*, contributed importantly to our information about learning. However, without the support of systematic and controlled research, such observations are of limited value and, in fact, are often misleading. In contrast to empiricism, experimental research attempts to ferret out cause-and-effect relationships. Through use of the scientific method, particularly in the laboratory, maximum control can be attained.

In the earliest days of research into learning, prior to the beginning of the 20th century, motor skills were most often studied. Cratty (1973) reported that by 1903 sixteen experimental studies involving motor activity had been included in the psychological literature. Memorization of meaningful or nonsense verbal materials was also used, as were animal studies of considerable diversity. Because of the relative ease of observation and measurement, the use of motor skills in learning research has continued to be popular among experimental psychologists and physical educators.

Traditional approach
in the study of learning

The early work of psychologists was important in establishing some basic principles of learning as well as in refining the methodological aspects of research. Experimental psychologists interested primarily in the development of general theoretical positions were not completely satisfactory in meeting the needs of education. Their approach was viewed as not "practical" enough. Also, it has been found that research conclusions established under controlled laboratory conditions often break down when applied to the classroom, gymnasium, or elsewhere. In the latter situations, several different principles or laws that govern behavior may be operating, and when functioning at the same time, these may have opposing or canceling effects. Consequently, some of the original results of learning investigations had little practical value.

The direct application of laboratory-established guidelines to the teaching of practical motor skills is not only questionable but quite difficult. For example, how does one apply paired-associate memory results to the learning of typing, tying a necktie, or shooting a jump shot? Obviously, there is a question of how to apply much of the research, even if the teacher desires to make a direct application. Since research has often shown that short practice sessions generally have advantages over longer practices, just *how* short should these practices be for maximum efficiency? How many basketball free throws should a high school varsity player shoot each day? Should these free throws be distributed in any particular manner throughout the practice session? Is there a point of diminishing returns? Should practice schedules in tennis vary with different skill levels? Psychology does not offer specific answers to these questions. Rather its contribution has been in the establishment of broad principles. In order for these principles to be most useful in a practical way, further research must be done with regular physical education skills.

The exclusive use of fine laboratory tasks for establishing motor learning principles is inappropriate. Such an approach is somewhat artificial. On the other hand, "field" research (classroom or gymnasium) has problems, too, in that controls and measurements are often cumbersome. Consequently, the ultimate answer does not lie in the exclusive use of either laboratory or field studies. Rather, a well-coordinated combination of both is necessary. In this way replication of findings in each setting is possible.

Basic and applied research

Not all research can be expected to produce findings that have immediate and applicable usefulness for the teacher or coach. In fact, some research is conducted to develop new knowledge with little regard for practical application. Such investigation is referred to as *basic* research. In the purest sense, the basic researcher is concerned only with general research interests and has no regard for the usefulness of the findings. The attitude of Charlie Brown in the "Peanuts" cartoon (Figure 2-1) is illustrative of this concept.

On the other hand, there is research that is designed and conducted to find a solution to a particular problem. This is called *applied* research. However, studies in the area of learning and performance are not always neatly categorized into the basic or applied camps. For example, most researchers would not acknowledge that their work is remote from all practicality, though students and readers of the reports often do not readily see the applicability. Still, experimental psychologists,

FIGURE 2-1. Orientation of the Basic Researcher. © 1960 United Feature Syndicate, Inc.

leaning toward the basic research concept, have remained rather aloof from practical problems of education, striving instead for theoretical and far-reaching findings.

A reasonable extension of the basic-applied research continuum is frequently reported in physical education research literature. The use of feedback in learning may be used as an example. Toward the basic research end of the scale, college students may be engaged in a laboratory experiment using the pursuit rotor in which a whirring sound, buzzer, colored lights, or other stimuli might be activated to indicate when the stylus is "on target." Various groups may be given different types of feedback, including delayed feedback, or none at all, to determine its effect on the acquisition and retention of skill in this task. Toward the applied end of the feedback continuum learners may be taught to serve in tennis while making use of the videotape replay. Variations in delays, amount of videotape information, or supplementing videotape replay with coaching analysis may be applied to different experimental groups. In terms of applicability of findings to the teaching of tennis, the videotape project would be more useful than would the project using the pursuit rotor. On the other hand, the pursuit rotor project has the possibility not only for greater controls and diversity of conditions, but also broader application to other learning conditions. Using such a task under strict laboratory controls allows far more varied research designs and greater precision. It then becomes possible to determine not only if feedback makes a difference but what particular type, or arrangement, is most advantageous.

Basic research is very valuable in establishing fundamental information and, in fact, provides a theoretical framework for much of the applied research. The videotape tennis project is likely to produce information helpful in the teaching of tennis but will have little carry-over to the teaching of the breast stroke, driving a car, or sewing a curving seam. Nevertheless, such applied research has been the most popular approach used in the teaching profession. In recent years, it has become increasingly clear that both basic and applied research are necessary for our understanding of the learning process and as aids in the resolution of particular problems in the field of education.

Background of research
in motor skills

Systematic investigation of learning began late in the 19th century. These studies, however, were not usually conceived within a theoretical framework. Such was the case with the work of Hermann Ebbinghaus (1885), often called "the father of learning." Though his development of *nonsense syllables* is viewed as a milestone in scientific inquiry, his findings were not particularly helpful because he served as his own subject in memorizing lists of these materials. Application of his findings was therefore not appropriate for other persons or groups. An empirical or pragmatic approach was also taken by other researchers late in the 19th century. For example, Thorndike (1898) did extensive work with animal instrumental learning, and Bryon and Harter (1879) investigated the acquisition of telegraphic skill. Such studies collected a great deal of information about how skills are learned, but they were not designed within a particular theoretical framework.

The first half of the 20th century was characterized by the development of grand theories of learning. Researchers became primarily interested in the development of overall schemes to place learning knowledge within a specific theoretical framework. However, after 1950, there was some decline in this approach when it became clear that there were fallacies in many of the neat, clear-cut theories. They did not prove to be so all-encompassing and foolproof as originally assumed. More and more, new findings seemed to push all theories toward a common ground. In addition, there was the need for generating new information and solving new problems that did not fit into the classical framework of models. (A more thorough discussion of learning theories is included in chapter three.)

During recent years, both experimental psychologists and physical educators have investigated the learning and performance of simple motor skills. Such research has not usually been tied to broad theoretical models. Some persons have been motivated by the quest for basic knowledge while others are interested in improving performance in sports or other meaningful motor activities. Today the major emphasis in motor learning research is toward problem solving, i.e., seeking answers to specific behavioral questions, with less concern for a theoretical framework. Sound research information is viewed as important, regardless of the theory to which it may be affiliated. There may be some grouping of information, or constructs, on a smaller scale for greater usefulness in the educational setting. The emphasis is on applied research, is tightly controlled, and is aimed toward developing useful information for the classroom.

SOME EXPERIMENTAL CONSIDERATIONS
IN MOTOR LEARNING RESEARCH

The quality of any research is dependent upon the clarity of the problem, the adequacy of the design, the accuracy of the data collected, and the thoroughness of the analysis. Many factors have to be carefully controlled and analyzed to insure that findings will have value. Several of the factors particularly related to motor skill acquisition are included in this discussion.

Novel skills

Finding suitable material for research in skill learning has always posed a problem, as it has for verbal learning. It has long been recognized that novel, or unfamiliar, learning materials have many advantages over familiar ones. The first major effort to address this matter took place in 1885 when Ebbinghaus developed a list of *nonsense syllables* in his search for verbal material to use in comparing different methods of learning. These were conceived as a means of establishing uniformity in the difficulty and interest of the material to be learned. Nonsense syllables were constructed by placing a vowel between two consonants. Therefore, syllables such as B-U-H, V-O-F, and T-E-Z were selected because they were meaningless, or "nonsense." However, arrangements that did make sense, e.g., S-A-W or B-A-T, were not used. The practice of using these materials became widespread both in Europe and the United States. According to Bugelski (1977), ". . . thousands of experiments have been performed with nonsense syllables as the learning material" (p. 18).

More recent research with verbal material has made use of paired associated and serial lists. *Paired associates* utilizes combinations such as KAI-MES, where the first part is provided as a stimulus, and the subject is to respond with the second part. In this, the subject studies a list of associations during a short exposure to the paired lists. *Serial lists* require that the subject memorize a list of meaningless material. However, even with such lists, it is probable that absolute novelty is never achieved. Subjects are likely to have unequal levels of familiarity or appreciation for the items. Still they are viewed as *relatively* standard in their degree of meaningfulness.

In the area of motor skill learning, researchers have a similar need for selecting material that is somewhat "culture free," i.e., not within the experience or interests of certain subjects more than others. It is practically impossible to select a familiar motor task in which subjects have had equal exposure. Consequently, the most equitable technique has been to select an activity to which subjects have had *no* exposure. The purpose is to have all subjects start from a near zero level of proficiency. In this way the groups are not only equalized, but they are most likely to show significant improvement in the new activity. This may be contrasted with a familiar task in which subjects have approached their maximum performance level prior to the beginning of the experiment. In such a situation, little improvement would be shown in a short experiment.

Another distinct advantage for the use of novelty items in research is that these activities are not likely to be practiced between trials. When a more common activity is used, students, being naturally interested in performing well, often do "homework" on the experimental task. Admonitions to discourage such unauthorized practice are not always followed, especially when the task, or a similar one, is easily available to the subjects. Even laboratory tasks are not totally immune from these practice efforts. I recall an experiment in which seventh-grade boys practiced the pursuit rotor skill for ten days over a two-week period. Halfway through the experiment, one student reported with great confidence that he was going to do better on this particular day because he had spent an hour the previous evening "practicing." When questioned, he stated that he had taped a ten-cent piece to a 33 rpm record on his stereo set and had followed it around and around with a pencil. Since the speed was different and since the dime was going in the opposite direction of the pursuit rotor, I am not sure whether his nightly practice helped or hindered. It did, however, contaminate the data in his case.

Novel motor skills appear to have another advantage over most familiar activities in that they elicit greater interest on the part of subjects. There seems to be a ready willingness on the part of most people to respond to new challenges, particularly when there is no threat of punishment or embarrassment with failure. Further, subjects will not have developed any negative attitudes or "hang-ups," as is often the case with familiar skills. In an experiment involving seventh-grade boys from an inner city school in the use of several novel tasks, I was informed by the local teachers that school attendance for subjects was greatly improved during the course of the experiment. Students had been told that if they were absent on one day, they would have to be dropped from the experiment. After word got about the experiment spread, several parents complained to the principal because their children had not been included. Likewise, those students not selected by the sampling technique for inclusion showed great curiosity about the novel tasks.

It is not easy to find gross motor activities with which a large number of subjects in our society are unfamiliar. If not acquainted with the task itself, subjects often have familiarity with one or more other tasks that are reasonably similar. Still, ingenious researchers have developed or modified several tasks that meet the novelty criteria quite well. Some of these, involving both fine and gross movements, are discussed later in this chapter. These meaningless, sometimes bizarre, tasks usually have no value in and of themselves. They are not learned and used as vocational or leisure skills. Neither are they viewed as important prerequisites in the development of any subsequent activity. For example, there is no popular demand for persons skilled in the pursuit rotor, mirror tracing, maze performance, or a multitude of ingenious gross motor skill modifications. Consequently, such activities are not widespread in our society. However, the recent expansion of novelty tasks in amusement arcades and game rooms, as well as the development of electronic and television games, poses additional problems in the use of such novelty items in learning experiments. The great popularity of these games capitalizes on the seemingly inherent interest people display in learning new motor skills.

Novelty of motor items varies with different cultures. Just as developers of intelligence tests must be conscious of cultural and language patterns, so must those who select motor tasks. For example, because of the prevalence of soccer throughout Europe, children in those countries should excel in foot dexterity and ball kicking skills when compared with children in the United States. On the other hand, the popularity of baseball and basketball would likely give American children an advantage in throwing, catching, and ball bouncing skills. Similarly, regional peculiarities in this country are evident in major sport emphasis. Such factors must be taken into consideration in selecting a novelty task.

The setting: laboratory versus gymnasium

Physical education teachers and athletic coaches frequently express doubts about the value of laboratory research as a means of gaining useful information for teaching or coaching. Such laboratory research, as traditionally conducted, often seems remote. For example, it appears that most psychological research has been conducted with either college sophomores or white rats. Neither group is representative of anything else. It has been speculated that the behavior of the white rat is closer to that of the human infant than it is to that of the college sophomore. Yet neither is very similar to the second grader. In addition to belonging to a different species, animals cannot talk, which limits the information that can be obtained from them. University students, too, are not typical of the "normal" population.

Today's laboratory facilities in departments of physical education are primarily suited to fine motor skills, or at least to activities that limit one's movement. Physical dimensions do not generally allow large movement activities, such as those involving throwing, striking, kicking, or other skills that project objects or the body through space. Consequently, for most practical motor skills, a more "normal" setting is necessary. For example, the teaching and analysis of swimming strokes cannot be achieved effectively without a pool. Analysis of tennis skill demands a tennis court or at least enough space to strike the ball and receive it from some distance. Baseball batting, throwing or punting a football, striking a field hockey ball, or kicking a soccer ball all require more space and flexibility than is available in the typical research laboratory. Consequently, the gymnasium, pool, tennis courts, or field become the appropriate "laboratory" for this research.

Real game situations in athletics offer certain natural conditions for investigating the role of stress in performance as well as the effect of many other factors in such a natural setting. Still, there are many problems in obtaining permission to conduct such studies and in exercising the proper controls once permission is received. Coaches of athletic teams, often serious about the outcome of contests, are frequently reluctant to welcome researchers whom they believe to be distracting to players. Likewise, rules of various sports are so standardized that they do not permit the flexibility that may result in some interesting findings. For example, studying the effects of varying sizes, weights, textures, and colors of balls, striking implements, and flexible court and field dimensions under actual game conditions over a period of time would provide interesting data not possible under non-game conditions. However, such flexibility is not permitted within the rules of most sports.

One must conclude that neither the laboratory nor the gymnasium environment are fully adequate for generating and replicating research information about learning and performance. Rather, both bring strengths as well as limitations to this endeavor. Future research must continue to use both.

Experimental controls

Whether in the laboratory, gymnasium, classroom, or elsewhere, attention must be focused on all variables that could affect the experimental results. Controls must cover equipment, instructions, physical arrangements, and any other condition surrounding the data-gathering situation. A casual approach to these conditions lessens, or nullifies, the value of the project. Equipment must be checked and calibrated prior to data collection, and during the experiment, it must be closely observed. Equipment, whether sophisticated or simple, does not always function perfectly. All equipment can stop functioning without notice, or worse yet, it can *partially* stop functioning in subtle ways that are hard to detect. All researchers need to have at least elementary repair skills or have a technician constantly available while data are collected.

Physical arrangements within the research area must be held as constant as possible. Any particular room dimensions or physical layout is usually acceptable as long as there are no distracting conditions. However, the presence of other persons or the existence of irregular noises often do prove distracting. Consequently, every effort must be made to standardize all factors except specific experimental variables, including clear instructions that are precise and identical for all subjects. Too often inadequate attention is given to the clarity of verbal instructions provided for young children. To ensure clarity and consistency researchers frequently use tape-recorded instructions. On other occasions, they memorize the instructions and recite them precisely for all subjects to avoid variations.

Perhaps the best means of developing and refining proper experimental controls is in the conduct of *pilot studies*. These preliminary investigations are an absolute necessity for new researchers or for others who are working with new tasks or conditions. Pilot studies allow the researcher to gain familiarity with the experimental situation in order to reduce surprises or unanticipated difficulties when serious data collection begins. For example, persons who have not conducted research with seventh-grade boys simply cannot anticipate the kinds of reactions or the types of questions they are likely to encounter. Prior experience with animals or with university students will not adequately prepare one to work with a different age group. During pilot studies, instructions can be clarified and practice regimens refined to suit a particular group. Without such experience, researchers often find themselves providing unanticipated information or making impromptu responses that may affect the outcomes of the experiment.

Scoring performances in motor tasks

Scores in experimental motor tasks should accurately reflect the skill level or the capacity of the subject. Such scores may reveal speed, accuracy, precision, balance, strength, coordination, or a combination of one or more different components. For example, Snoddy (1935), believing that both speed and accuracy were important indications of skill in mirror tracing, devised a system whereby speed (in seconds) and accuracy (in errors) were reflected in each performance score. So, too, in many everyday skills the individual is often encouraged to devote attention to both speed and accuracy. Such activities as typing, "piecework" in industry, pitching a baseball, or automobile racing emphasize both speed and accuracy, each of which is measurable. In Snoddy's system of scoring, a "pacing" technique was used to discourage subjects from devoting undue attention to only one factor, a practice that would prove detrimental to the overall performance score.

Adequate score range.   In data collection efforts should be made to gather a range of scores that discriminates among differences in skill level at all points in the learning curve. Such differentiation is frequently difficult at extreme ends of the performance scale. Still, a good measure of human capacity is one in which the "floor" is adequately low and the "ceiling" is high enough. In a test of knowledge or of motor skills, no one should score a zero and no one should make a perfect score.* Scores for subjects that coincide with the absolute end of the scale are not likely to be accurate reflections of one's capacity or level of development.

Scales with a maximum capacity of 250 lbs are of little value for weighing persons heavier than that. When the scale registers 250 lbs, one cannot assume that the individual weighs *exactly* that amount. Therefore, scales with a capacity of 250 lbs would be inadequate for weighing a group of superheavyweight weightlifters because the "ceiling" is too low. Similarly, a manuometer registering up to 200 lbs is inadequate for measuring the grip strength of many strong athletes. In verbal material, test results of 100 percent, or a perfect score on a standardized test, may not fully reflect the ability of the individual in the area tested. Traditional skill tests in the areas of archery, badminton, volleyball, and tennis would be inadequate for

---

*There may be times both in the classroom and the gymnasium when it is appropriate to set a *criterion* level of performance, i.e., a standard that must be met by all. Such is the case when children are required to spell the complete list of words correctly, to learn the multiplication tables perfectly, to do forty sit-ups in two minutes, to run a mile in ten minutes, or to swim two lengths of the pool. While certifying that subjects do meet an assigned standard, such measures do not accurately measure one's full ability in those areas, nor does it discriminate among several students who have the same score.

measuring the skill level of Olympic athletes. These elite performers would be expected to make nearly perfect scores on those tests. Such tests, therefore, do not have an adequate ceiling.

In establishing motor learning tasks, it is frequently necessary to adjust the difficulty of the task to accommodate the level of maturity or the skill of the subjects. For example, a group of third-grade children performing on the pursuit rotor* may need the speed slowed to a level of 20 rpms to insure that they achieve some early success. Such a slow pace, however, may be inappropriate for college-age students because many of them would approach or actually reach a perfect score before too many trials had passed. The size of target areas, the complexity of tasks, speeds, and distances should be adjusted to insure that the level of difficulty is adequate.

Although experimental tasks need to be adjusted in order to challenge subjects throughout the experiment, they must be simple enough to detect even the slightest amount of skill. Target areas for kicking, throwing, or shooting must be of a size so as not to severely discourage subjects. A series of "zero" scores on a novel kicking skill does not provide an accurate indication of one's kicking skill. In fact, there may be several persons at somewhat different ability levels receiving these scores. In addition, such a series of trials discourages some subjects so that thereafter they are not likely to put forth effort with full concentration. All such tests should yield some quantitative measure of proficiency. For low-skilled persons, targets must be adequately large and speeds must be slow enough to detect even the slightest degree of skill.

Motor tasks should be so arranged that scores are spread over an adequate range. Unfortunately, some tasks are organized so that most scores fall within too few categories. Soccer kicks are sometimes scored on the basis of whether the ball landed in or out of the goal. Tennis serves may be scored simply as in or out of bounds, and basketball shots may be similarly scored as good or not good. Such crude measures do not reflect either subtle changes in skill level or small differences among subjects. In each of the tasks, greater precision should be brought into the scoring, perhaps by marking off the court or goal areas into several sections of differing point values. In the basketball shot, greater point value could be given for the near miss (one that hits the rim) than for the "air" ball (one that fails to contact either the rim or backboard). Such refinements in targets are likely to result in greater precision in measuring performance changes, and consequently, a greater "spread" of scores among subjects. Sensitive measures of speed activities are usually not a problem, assuming that adequate timers are used.

Selection of performance score.   In human performance measures it is not always clear just which performance score should be selected as being most representative of an individual's ability for a trial or a group of trials. Sometimes the average, or *mean*, of several trials is the best indication of the subject's ability.

---

* See discussion on the pursuit rotor presented later in the chapter.

This is usually true in accuracy measures, such as soccer kicks, tennis services, basketball shooting, or golf putting. When several trials are included, such averaging out accounts fairly for "lucky" shots resulting in a bull's-eye and even the misdirected shot that goes completely awry. The subject will still show improvement in the average score as the skill improves.

In other human performance activities, the *best* score is the most accurate indication of the individual's capacity. For example, if the object is to determine one's grip strength, the strongest or highest score of several trials is most representative. One cannot get "lucky" and squeeze more than he is capable of squeezing. Similarly, measures of running speed or high jumping ability should make use of the best score. One cannot run faster or jump higher than his or her current capacity. On the other hand, certain factors, such as fatigue, lack of motivation, or distractions may detract from performance. For speed, strength, and other maximal exertion activities, therefore, the best score of several trials is most representative of one's actual capacity.

In still other types of activities, the middle or *median* score may be more representative than either the average or best score. An example of this is reaction time testing, in which the subject is required to make a simple movement, such as depressing or releasing a button or telegraphic key. Typical response times for a given university-age subject might range from 130 to 180 milliseconds. However, as scores continue to be taken, an occasional 300 or 350 millisecond response will occur. This score is usually an indication that the subject had a lapse in concentration or began to daydream during the fore period. Such sluggish responses are more frequent when the fore period is more than four or five seconds. Therefore, even though the response time of 300 milliseconds is an accurate measure of the performance, it is not a good indication of the individual's reaction time capacity. On other trials in reaction time testing, an unusually quick score, perhaps 50 milliseconds, will appear. Such is not an indication of one's reaction capacity, but an indication that the subject "jumped the gun." That is, the response was commenced a short time prior to receiving the stimulus. Since neither of these extreme scores is a representative measure of true reaction capacity, both should be eliminated. The median score nullifies the impact of such extreme scores.

Treatment of human subjects

A general sense of fairness and reasonableness has always demanded that human subjects engaged in research projects not be abused in any physical, social, or psychological manner. The great majority of research over the years has adhered to such standards of concern and respect for the rights of research subjects. However, enough cases of physical and psychological abuse in the name of research have led to the development of certain safeguards against such practices.

In 1975 a code of federal regulations, *Protection of Human Subjects*, was formulated, demanding that specific experimental procedures be spelled out and approved when humans are used as subjects. Particular emphasis is placed upon informed consent. In 1973 the American Psychological Association published *Ethical Principles in the Conduct of Research with Human Participants*, which serves as a code of ethics for that organization. The ten major principles spelled out in the document place emphasis upon the following:

Informed consent of the subjects

The right of the subject to volunteer, decline, or withdraw from the experiment at any time

Discouraging the use of deception

Protection of subjects from mental or physical pain, discomfort, or danger

Most importantly, the integrity of the researcher in designing and carrying out the project.

These APA ethical principles were not universally applauded by all researchers, primarily because of the restrictions that the "deception" and "discomfort" guidelines place on research. Many argue that the use of deception is itself an important factor in much of the psychological and sociological research, and that without it a great many studies lose their value. They argue that subjects fully informed about the purpose of the study may respond in a biased manner. Further, without physical or mental stress, one of the primary tools for understanding human behavior is lost. Researchers in the field of physical education also have found that reasonably high levels of fatigue, sleep deprivation, psychological stress, or other "uncomfortable" conditions are valuable factors in understanding how humans functions under these conditions. Recent interpretations of both federal guidelines and APA principles indicate that a "reasonable" approach is acceptable, particularly with reference to deception and consent.

Federal regulations notwithstanding, it is important to state unequivocally that all studies with a potential impact on the long-term mental or physical well-being of human subjects should be done under the most closely controlled circumstances, with experienced and ethical researchers involved.

Beyond the legal requirements, or even the code of standards, there are frequent questions about the propriety of certain methods used in ongoing research. Such questions are sometimes raised with graduate students engaged in studies to determine effective teaching technique. In such studies several conditions are typically imposed on different groups, perhaps broken down by school class. These studies may provide different types of feedback to several groups, and perhaps a lack of feedback to some groups. Unfortunately, such experiments often involve groups in class situations where the total educational climate is seriously deprived of several important components. In some such projects, teacher-researchers not only remove feedback but practically all other teaching or coaching aids in order to test the effects of these factors. I recall one teacher of emotionally disturbed children who suddenly removed all the reinforcement to which the students had become accustomed in order to determine the effect of these practices. With vulnerable subjects, such dramatic change in daily routine could possibly prove harmful. Consequently, such research techniques should be taken only under the most carefully controlled conditions. Generally, researchers are discouraged from substituting any experimental condition for a practice ordinarily followed in the school setting when dealing with "special" groups. In fact, no condition should be imposed that is, by consensus, inferior to current practice.

Such stringent regulations are not usually imposed in animal research. This research has much greater latitude, extending even to the point of sacrificing the animal. Consequently, studies relating to feedback, motivation, sensory deprivation, and fatigue are practically unlimited. Researchers have found that parents of young children tend to object to the use of these extreme measures in the conduct of learning and performance research. University students are only slightly more cooperative. Consequently, some of the most ingenious research concepts for maximum motor performance are thwarted.

In animal research, guidelines have been established by societies for the prevention of cruelty to animals. Such guidelines are primarily concerned with insuring that the infliction of pain, starvation, and baiting be avoided. Still, animal research has fewer restrictions than does human research.

Quality in measurement data

The value of any research is obviously related to the quality of the data collected. Accuracy of measures taken is a basic concern for any experimental science. Those factors with obvious relevance for skill learning and performance are validity, reliability, and objectivity.

Validity.   This term refers to the extent to which the test actually measures what the researcher intends it to measure. Validity is the most crucial of all measurement criteria. Measurements may be meticulously taken and scores may be absolutely consistent, but if the test does not have validity, the scores are irrelevant. Measures of many motor components have advantages over certain verbal or other cognitive areas in that the factor being measured, e.g., strength, running speed, or throwing accuracy, can be easily observed and is often indisputable. On the other hand, measurements of intelligence, musical ability, or spatial perception are less clear. However, our current knowledge of certain motor components, such as balance, coordination, or rhythm, is also imprecise. Researchers investigating these components must go to great lengths to establish test validity.

In the area of skill learning, numerous tasks have been developed to study the learning process. Some of these, while having "face" validity (the appearance of validity), fall short when put to close scrutiny. Subjects frequently learn to outsmart the system or find ways to cheat that are not anticipated by the researcher. On other occasions, the task may be beyond the capacity of the individual to perform, due to inadequate maturation, strength, flexibility, or other limitations. Therefore, use of the handstand as a means of determining the effectiveness of several teaching techniques would be improper for use with three-year-old children or seventy-year-old men because the majority of those persons would not be able to perform the activity, although they may be able to conceptualize it.

The validity of some test results is distorted by the *Hawthorne effect.* This refers to the tendency of subjects to perform at a more effective level because of placement in a special program. The term comes from studies made by Roethisberger and Dickson (1939) at Western Electric's plant in Hawthorne, New Jersey, where female employees were studied under different work conditions. The subjects were assured that their employment was quite secure and that nothing would jeopardize their status. Further, they were told that they were partners in a scientific effort and that their cooperation was being sought as individuals, not as mere employees. The workers felt important and unique. Their morale and motivation were high. When the experimenters made changes in the working environment, the work productivity of the women began to rise. It soon became evident that the actual environmental changes had nothing to do with the productivity because the direction of the changes did not matter. If the work areas were better lighted, production rose; if the areas were darkened, production also rose. Changes in working hours, salary, and other conditions resulted in similar improvements. With every change, the women worked harder and more effectively than before. Simply knowing that something new was being tried (and that they were the center of attention) appeared to have a strong effect on their attitudes and motivation. Similar results have been noted in educational research. Teachers, in fact, use this concept of "special" treatment as a technique for motivating students to increased effort. However, validity is lessened when such a factor enters into the research setting.

Reliability.   Reliability refers to the consistency of performance and measurement, i.e., whether or not the response, or scores, can be replicated on repeated trials. Lack of consistency in performance may result from faulty measuring devices (counters, timers, or signals) that lack calibration. More often there are fluctuations in the physiological or psychological state of the subject, causing inconsistencies in performance. Fatigue, boredom, illness, or general arousal often contribute to inconsistent performance. In such cases the irregular scores do not accurately reflect the current skill level. On the other hand, systematic changes in scores are expected as one learns the task. Research involving even the most valid of tests or skills is rendered ineffective when performance is unreliable. Stringent controls and consistency in test administration is necessary to insure maximum reliability.

Objectivity.   Objectivity refers to the consistency of the experimental procedure or conditions. Conditions presented to the subjects on subsequent trials or to different subjects in the same experiment should be as nearly identical as possible. Objective conditions generally contribute to more reliable performance scores. Objectivity is exhibited when two experimenters are able to conduct a test or observe the same performance and come up with identical or very similar scores. This demands that instructions and measurements be identical. Generally, tasks involving timing performances, measuring distances, or recording numbers of repetitions are high in reliability. However, measures (or evaluation) of a synchronized swimming routine, a dance, or a gymnastics performance are likely to be less objective.

Where subjective judgment is involved, there is a greater problem with objectivity. In such cases, however, the more expert the judges, the more uniform is the judgment. For example, national-level gymnastics judges are more consistent in their evaluations than are inexperienced judges. Consistency in administering a skill test to a subject or in judging performance is dependent not only on a thorough understanding of the activity but also on freedom from a bias that might influence that rating. For example, it is frequently alleged that judges for Olympic sports are influenced by their national affiliation when scoring skating or gymnastics events. Even in this country there are frequent allegations of "hometown" decisions or calls by officials that favor the local constituency in major sporting events. Such occurences are examples of poor objectivity.

SELECTING TASKS
FOR MOTOR LEARNING RESEARCH

One of the most difficult jobs facing the investigator, especially the graduate student or beginning researcher, is that of selecting a suitable task for studying skill learning. This is especially true when one attempts to select a meaningful skill, particularly one involving gross motor movement. No one task is appropriate for all motor learning research projects. The nature of the skill selected must be related to the conditions or activities to which application is desired. Depending upon the topic to be investigated, or the general orientation of the research, there are a multitude of considerations. Consequently, the search for appropriate learning materials in both verbal and motor areas has gone on since Ebbinghaus developed his nonsense syllables nearly a century ago.

Over the years research has made use of a wide range of motor skills, along with a vast array of equipment. Early research involved laboratory skills almost exclusively, with emphasis upon those skills requiring fine motor movement. Such tasks have varied from the simplest of responses to the use of very complex electronic arrangements. The earliest tasks involved simple puzzles or responses that could be scored by observation. Early forms of mirror drawing or tracing fell into this category. Koerth (1922) made major advances by developing a pursuit rotor that was constructed to electrically record the time during which the stylus was held in contact with a target. This instrument (with variations) has been widely used for tracking tasks.

Elementary forms of mirror drawing or tracing were developed early in the 20th century and were subsequently used by numerous researchers investigating skill learning. These tasks have varied from simple pencil drawings (while looking into a mirror), allowing the experimenter to count the number of excursions outside a prescribed path, to the more complex apparatus in which scores are determined by electric counter and timer. Snoddy (1935) developed and refined a mirror tracing instrument called a *stabilimeter*, which he used for extensive research in practice scheduling. In like manner, mazes of various levels of complexity have been used.

During World War II and the years immediately following, more complex tasks and those involving large muscle movements of hands and feet were developed. The use of simulators for training airplane pilots during the war gave impetus to this development. Simulated equipment for other tasks, including space travel, has more recently come into use, both for training purposes and for research in skill learning. During the 1950s and 1960s Fleishman (1964) was instrumental in developing and using a vast array of fine and gross motor tasks, many of which required coordination of complex hand and foot movements.

During the past two decades, the development of learning and performance tasks has continued. Many of these have been related to familiar activities, such as throwing, kicking, balancing, gymnastics movements, dance, and juggling. Most tasks used in research have at least a degree of novelty. Although many are described in the professional literature, few have reached the level of acceptance (with convincing validity and reliability) necessary to become widely used.

Tasks used for research in skill learning and performance must be viewed as nothing more than tools, or a means to an end, in the investigation of learning phenomena. As such they must meet certain criteria in order to be of value in investigating particular problems. Many experiments, well-conceived and designed, have failed, or have been seriously weakened because the task selected was not suited for the experiment. Though no single task is adequate for investigating all questions in skill learning, it is noteworthy that A. B. Ammons and C. H. Ammons have used the pursuit rotor in literally hundreds of studies dealing with a variety of topics, including retention, feedback, and transfer. (Most of these studies have been published in *Perceptual and Motor Skills.* Others have been presented in the *Journal of Psychology* and the *Journal of Motor Behavior*.) Still, one could argue that this task would not be especially helpful for studying the learning characteristics of a gross motor skill of a ballistic nature, such as the shot put.

Criteria for selecting
skill-learning tasks

Criteria for task selection varies with the project. Considerations, such as the problem addressed, the subjects used, and the desired applicability of the findings, dictate the nature of the task to be used. For example, if the project is to have impact on training programs for nursery-school children, the experiment should involve young children and the task should be of short duration and within the performance capacity of children. An investigtion into the role of videotape feedback in skill learning should make use of a skill that demands clear overt responses so that distinctions in movement leading to success or failure may be easily recorded and observed on tape. Subtle movements may not be so easily observed on the monitor during replay. Consequently, prior to the selection of a motor task, the researcher should establish criteria that will provide a good chance of answering the basic question being addressed.

The following are some *general* criteria that should usually be met by motor skills selected for research in learning:

1. The task should be novel. It is important that all subjects begin the experiment with an equal level of proficiency, preferably near zero. This will tend to reduce the contaminating effect of prior experience. A novel task provides this advantage and also has the value of providing the subject with no opportunity for unauthorized practice.

2. The task should be one in which substantial improvement is likely within the experiment period. In order for learning to be studied, it must first occur. For this learning to be evident, the task must be within the capacity of the subject to learn and to perform. The greater the improvement within the experimental period, the greater the opportunity for detecting differences among experimental groups.

3. The task should involve an adequate degree of complexity. A sufficient "challenge" is necessary to sustain interest and to provide an adequate ceiling. On the other hand, researchers must guard against overwhelming immature or unskilled subjects with tasks that are too complex or difficult.

4. The task should exhibit high reliability of individual differences. Changes in scores should accurately reflect changes in skill level. Erratic scores reduce confidence that learning is being measured.

5. The task should provide an easy and objective means of measuring performance. Objectivity in data collection is essential for credibility in the study. This also provides an opportunity for the study to be replicated.

6. The task should be safe. There is an obvious need to protect the well-being of human subjects. In addition, the *appearance* of danger may add a distracting component to the environment.

7. The task must be practical and manageable. Tasks that require an inordinate amount of space or time, or equipment that is expensive, delicate, or not transportable, are impractical for many experiments.

CATEGORIES OF MOTOR LEARNING TASKS

There is no widely accepted classification system or taxonomy for motor skills. Consequently, different authors categorize motor activities in different ways, for example, according to open-closed skill factors, the availability of feedback, whether pacing is externally or self-controlled, processing demands placed on the learner, the hierarchical context of the movement pattern, or cognitive demands of the skills. Annett (1968), Farrell (1975), Fleishman (1967), Gentile et al. (1975), Miller (1967), and Singer (1981) are among those who have developed models or systems according to one or more of the above factors.

Over the next several pages is presented a rather arbitrary grouping of motor tasks that have been widely used in motor learning and performance studies. Since the purpose here is to aid the student-researcher in selecting an appropriate task according to several possible objectives, the grouping will be according to the nature of the response required of the subject. A much longer or shorter list of groupings could have been developed. The classification efforts of Dukelow (1977) and Annett (1968) will be reflected in this discussion. Included in the review are categories of tasks that have been widely used in learning studies, as well as some that are viewed as measures of motor capacities.

1. Positioning tasks

In positioning tasks, the subject moves an object of some type, often a lever, a predetermined distance, direction, or both. An attempt is made to duplicate an established position without benefit of vision or other specific sensory cues. The criterion is the accuracy of the "blind" response. Learning is reflected in increased accuracy, i.e., a reduction in the margin of error. During the learning process, the subject develops an improved kinesthetic awareness of a particular position.

Positioning tasks have been widely used in feedback studies. Thorndike's line drawing experiments (1931) were among the earliest positioning tasks used in controlled research. The *Research Quarterly of Exercise and Sport, Perceptual and Motor Skills,* and the *Journal of Motor Behavior* include numerous descriptions of tasks requiring the manipulation of levers, metal bars or knobs, and the sliding of objects along straight or circular tracks. Some positioning tasks require a timed measurement, i.e., reaching the prescribed positioning in a specified time. The scores may be recorded in distance error, time error, or both.

A type of response similar to positioning tasks are those involving *force reproduction.* In these activities, the subject is required to duplicate a force previously performed. Responses may be in the form of a ballistic movement or they may require continuous force application against some form of resistance. As in positioning tasks, errors are measured as variations from a standard measure of force.

2. Tracking tasks

Tracking tasks are frequently broken down into pursuit and compensatory categories. The difference between the pursuit and compensatory tracking tasks is the manner in which error information is presented on the subjects. In *pursuit tracking* a moving target is presented to the subject, who uses a stylus, control stick, or other indicator to keep in close proximity with the target. Holding a gun sight on a moving traget is an example of pursuit tracking. In the laboratory, the pursuit rotor is one of the most widely used of the pursuit tracking tasks. In fact, the pursuit rotor is probably the most frequently used instrument for the study of skill learning among humans. The traditional, or standard, pursuit rotor consists of a turntable or nonconducting material with a small target to be pursued by the subject with a stylus as the turntable revolves. When the stylus contacts the target disc, an electric circuit activates a timer to record the "time on target."

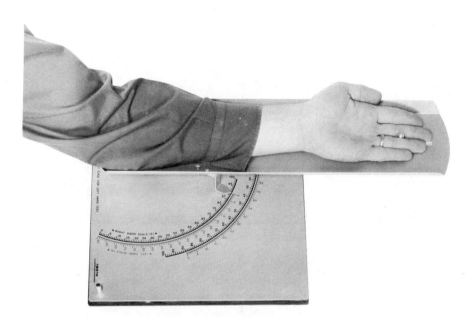

FIGURE 2-2. *Positioning Task* A blindfolded subject is asked to move the arm to a point previously assumed. The score is recorded in millimeters of error from a prescribed position. (This device, the *kinesthesiometer*, is manufactured by the Lafayette Instrument Co., Inc.)

Pursuit rotors may require direct contact between the stylus and target (as in Figure 2-3) or they may be of a photoelectric cell variety in which the clock is activated by a light beam on the target (as in Figure 2-4). Modification of this task allows tracking by foot response or while looking through a mirror.

In *compensatory tracking* the subject attempts to maintain a constant (speed, pressure, light) by making adjustments as necessitated by conditions. For example, responses required to maintain an automobile at a speed of 50 mph while going up and down hills illustrates compensatory tracking. A vivid example of compensatory tracking in sports is exhibited by the competitive ice skater during the performance of the compulsory "figure 8s." In this task, the skater attempts to skate exactly on a predetermined line drawn in the form of the figure eight. Error is measured

FIGURE 2-3. *Standard Pursuit Rotor* This instrument requires contact between the stylus and a 3/4″ diameter target to activate the timer. Speeds may vary frm 15 to 60 rpms. (Manufactured by the Marietta Instrument Co., Inc.)

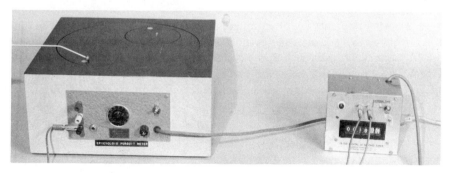

FIGURE 2-4. *Photoelectric Pursuit Rotor Apparatus* For this instrument, the standard rotary pursuit has been modified to incorporate a photoelectric circuit, which eliminates the need for any physical contact between target and pursuit wand. Sensitivity control permits use under varying lighting conditions. Speeds from 10 to 100 rpms in both clockwise and counterclockwise directions are possible. Patterns may be circular, triangular, or square. (Manufactured by the Lafayette Instrument Co., Inc.)

according to the distance between the performer's skate marks and the lines of the figure. Compensatory tracking behavior is also illustrated by the bicycle rider or the automobile driver who attempts to follow a marker on the road precisely. In work situations, the seamstress, the glass cutter, the highway line painter, and the carpenter using a skill saw exhibit compensatory tracking behavior.

In the laboratory, compensatory tasks may require that the subject keep the intensity of a light constant through lever, knob, or pedal adjustments. Such responses may also be designed to keep noise constant, or as near the zero level as possible.

Tracking responses are often tested, or taught, by use of simulators. The subject is required to manipulate one or more controls, which are often similar to those used in meaningful tasks, such as the cockpit of an airplane or an automobile (see Figure 2-5). In simulator tasks, subjects compensate by adjusting pedals, levers, a steering wheel, or rudder controls. The complexity of such tasks may vary greatly.

3. Mazes

In maze tasks, the object is to move along a predetermined path as quickly as possible without straying from that desired route. Frequently, time in seconds and

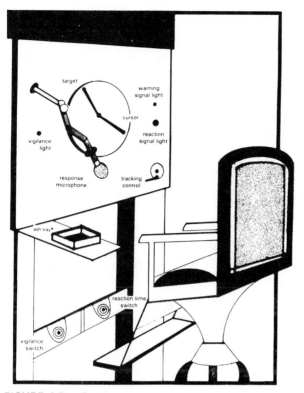

FIGURE 2-5. *Psychomotor Apparatus Used for Pursuit Tracking, Reaction, and Vigilance Response* In this task the subject sits with eyes approximately 48 cm from the complex psychomotor device. Located directly in front of the subject is a *pursuit tracking* display; the cursor and target needles have their origins at the center of the display. The target needle moves either clockwise or counter clockwise, via a 30 rpm reversible motor. At time on target is derived for the tracking task. Above the tracking knob, the signal lights located for a cued reaction time. To the left of the tracking display, a signal light with a green lens cover serves as the display for a vigilance task. (From J. D. Stone, et al., Annoyance response of nonsmokers to cigarette smokers. *Perceptual Motor Skills,* 1979, 49, 3, pp. 907-16. Reprinted by permission.)

accuracy in number of errors are used as the measures of proficiency. Errors may include going in the wrong direction (blind alleys) or in touching the edge of the path. Mazes come in many varieties, including pencil mazes, electronic or automatic tally mazes, walking mazes, and several types of mirror tracing tasks.

Learning experiments have made extensive use of pencil mazes (see Figure 2-6) and automatic tally mazes (see Figure 2-7). Blindfolds are usually employed in these mazes. In the pencil maze, the subject makes a line recording of his efforts to follow the desired path from beginning to end. With the automatic tally, a counter is used to record the number of excursions into blind alleys. In both cases a record is kept of the number of seconds required to complete the task.

Cratty (1964) developed a 40-yard-long walking maze in which blindfolded subjects learned to walk along the path using the volar surfaces of their hands (see Figure 2-8).

FIGURE 2-6. *Pencil Maze* This maze may be used for a variety of learning problems. Speed and accuracy can be studied with the aid of a stopwatch or clock timer. The subject is required to wear blindfold goggles when performing this task. (Manufactured by the Lafayette Instrument Co., Inc.)

A somewhat similar task, the hedge maze, has been in existence for hundreds of years in Europe and more recently in this country. A reproduction of the famous Hampton Court Maze has existed in Williamsburg, Virginia, since Colonial times. (See Figure 2-9.) This Palace Maze has been of general interest and a form of amusement to both children and adults. Small reproductions of this model have been used in conditioning studies with several types of animals. However, as far as can be determined, the hedge maze has not been used for controlled studies of human learning.

Mirror tracing and *mirror drawing* tasks are frequently placed in the category of mazes. Paths may be arranged in any pattern but are most often star-shaped. In mirror tracing, the subject is required to follow a prescribed route while viewing the pattern in a mirror. The mirror reverses the front-back relationship but leaves the left-right direction unchanged. Mirror tracing has been among the most widely used learning tasks in the field of experimental psychology. It has also been used rather extensively in physical education research. Many variations of the mirror tracing instrument have been developed, one of which is shown in Figure 2-10.

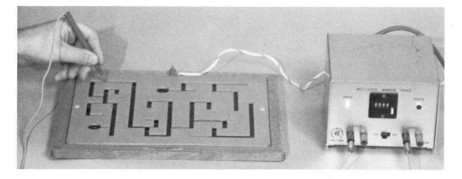

FIGURE 2-7. *Automatic Tally Maze* The automatic tally maze is connected to a single impulse center. This setup will tally the total number of wrong alleys entered. The number of trials to reach a perfect score may also be recorded. As in most such maze tasks, the subject wears goggles to prevent vision of the instrument. (Manufactured by the Lafayette Instrument Co., Inc.)

4. Movement time tasks

Reaction and movement time tasks have been used primarily as a means of measuring individual differences in speed. *Simple reaction time* (period from the stimulus to the beginning of the response) is not greatly influenced by practice. Consequently, it is not viewed as an appropriate task for the study of learning. Rather, it is simply an indication of one's response speed. However, if the complexity of the task increases (if choices must be made), the role of practice becomes important in speeding the responses. Greater complexity also means that the

FIGURE 2-8. *The Cratty Walking Maze* This maze was used by Cratty in several experiments employing blindfolded college subjects. (From B. J. Cratty, *Movement and Spatial Awareness in Blind Children and Youth.* Springfield, Ill.: Charles C Thomas, 1971. Reprinted by permission of the publisher.)

FIGURE 2-9. The Palace Maze in Williamsburg, Virginia (Reprinted by permission of the Colonial Williamsburg Foundation.)

FIGURE 2-10. Typical Mirror Tracing Instrument (Manufactured by the Lafayette Instrument Co., Inc.)

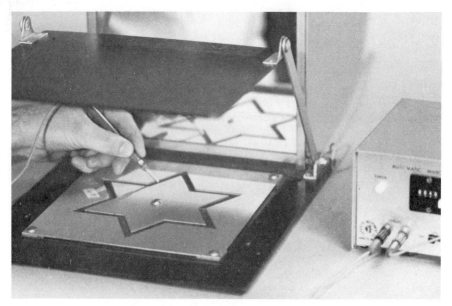

response time increases. Response for measuring simple reaction time include simple acts, such as lifting a finger from a button or depressing a telegraph key.

Choice reaction time (also called discriminative reaction time) requires the subject to select one of two or more responses after receiving one of several stimuli. Complex movement responses may require one to release a key, turn a crank one revolution, and strike another key, or some other movement combination. Though one can improve performance in such a complex task with practice, such an activity is still viewed more as a measure of movement capacity than of learning. Figure 2-11 illustrates equipment that can be used in the measurement of simple reaction time (by depressing the button on the left), or movement time (by the combined movement of releasing the button on the left and depressing the one on the right).

In addition to determining the ability of individuals to complete simple or complex responses, investigators have sought to determine *speed of repetitive movements.* Absolute speed in finger tapping, cranking a wheel in a rotary fashion, or making measured back and forth movements are examples of such repetitive movements. Figure 2-12 illustrates an apparatus used for simple tapping speed. Gross activities requiring such responses include running, swimming, bicycling, and skating.

The ability to make *rhythmical* responses, or responses at a uniform rate, is another timing factor of interest to researchers, and perhaps to musicians and those in several industrial fields where pacing is important. Investigators usually arrange tasks whereby the subject responds to a preset timer or metronome. Knob rotation,

FIGURE 2-11.   Simple Reaction Time and Movement Time Apparatus.

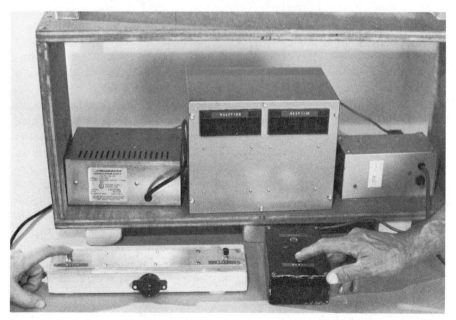

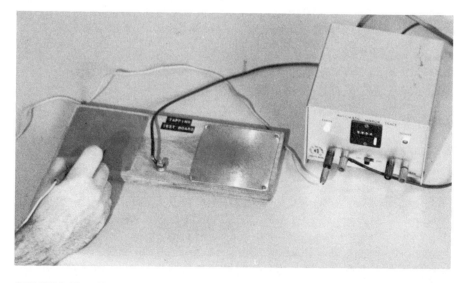

FIGURE 2-12. *Tapping Board* The task is to tap the metal plate with the stylus as rapidly as possible. A counter can be connected to record the number of responses within a given time period. An alternate task is to have subjects tap the metal plates at each end of the board alternately as rapidly as possible. (Manufactured by the Lafayette Instrument Co., Inc.)

hand cranking, tapping, and line drawing at a steady pace, or at a predetermined interresponse interval, have been employed. Error scores are expressed in variations from an established time pattern. This ability to make rhythmical responses is largely innate, and practice does not result in appreciably improved scores.

Another timing characteristic that has been investigated by several researchers is *coincidence anticipation.* This term refers to activities in which subjects observe a moving stimulus and attempt to time their responses to coincide with the arrival of the stimulus at a predetermined location. The idea is to intercept the target at a precise point. Error is recorded in time, distance, or both. The Bassin Coincidence Anticipation Timer, shown in Figure 2-13, has been widely used during recent years. The objective of the task is to "time" a response to coincide with the arrival of a moving light on the runway. The subject anticipates when the target lamp will be activated and responds by depressing the push button.

Other reaction or speed tests are those that require rapidity of *manipulation.* In such tasks, objects must be moved from one point to another with the criterion being either speed of movement or the time required to complete the task. The Minnesota Manual Dexterity Test (see Figure 2-14) is a popular example of such an activity. Others may be more complex, requiring the sorting of objects according to size, shape, color, or number. Such tasks have been used more as measures of hand and arm speed and dexterity than as measurements of learning.

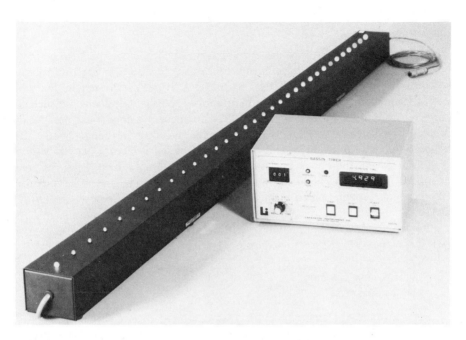

FIGURE 2-13. Bassin Coincidence Anticipation Timer (Manufactured by the Lafayette Instrument Co., Inc.)

FIGURE 2-14. *Minnesota Manual Dexterity Test* This widely used test of arm and hand speed requires that subjects transfer the 58 wooden cylinders from one part of the board to the appropriate holes in an adjacent panel. (Manufactured by the Lafayette Instrument Co., Inc.)

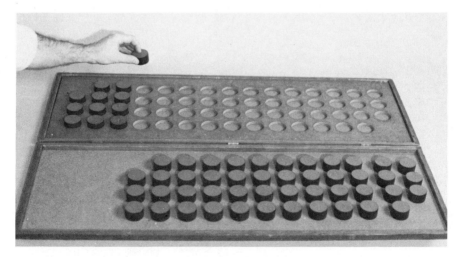

5. Balance tasks

Though individuals differ in their ability to balance, this component is sometimes used in skill learning experiments because performance in specific balance tasks can be improved with practice. Balancing activities usually require the subject to maintain an unstable position or to move his or her body while in such an unstable position for as long as possible. This is frequently done on some kind of apparatus. Balance tasks used in research have included the bongo board, the stabilometer, the ladder climb, and variations of the balance beam (usually within an inch or two of the floor). In classes students have engaged in one-leg stands, the tip-up (or frog stand), the hand stand or head stand, and others. Balance activities may be *static* (attempting to maintain one's balance in a stationary position) or they may be *dynamic* (attempting to maintain balance while moving). Figure 2-15 (static) and 2-16 (dynamic) present perhaps two of the most popular research tasks used for balance over the past two decades.

6. Throwing, catching, and juggling tasks

A multitude of learning tasks has been developed that require the subject to throw, roll, slide, or in some other manner *propel* objects at targets with a specific amount of force. Though the throwing of objects is not ordinarily viewed as novel, it may be made so by certain adjustments. For example, subjects may be required

FIGURE 2-15. *Stability Platform* This apparatus has arrangements for recording left and right imbalance as well as center balance. Also recorded are the test time and rest periods. (Manufactured by the Lafayette Instrument Co., Inc.)

FIGURE 2-16. *Modified Bachman Ladder* This has proven popular in research because it is unlike any popular sports skill; it requires all four limbs and does not necessitate extensive verbal preparation. At a signal, the subject begins to climb as high as possible without skipping rungs. Upon losing balance, he steps down to the floor and climbs once again. The score is the total number of rungs climbed within a given time period.

to throw at targets viewed through mirrors, to bounce objects off a wall to rebound into a target area, to attempt to bounce a basketball off the floor into the basket, or to throw a Frisbee for accuracy or distance with a specified type of delivery. Any time the customary practice of the throwing or catching tasks is adequately altered, it may be used as an appropriate learning task.

A variety of *juggling* and *cup tossing-catching* tasks has been used in studies of skill learning. Although several experimenters have used regular 3-object juggling in such studies, there are often problems with previous experience and control when juggling experiments extend for more than one session. As with other tasks, however, these can be modified in such a way as to reduce the likelihood of prior practice or unauthorized practice between sessions. For example, Corbin (1966) established a unique wand juggling routine that proved novel for the subjects in his experiment. A number of experimenters have used a cup tossing-catching task with success (see Figure 2-17). It should be noted that these tasks are generally more popular in Latin American countries, although they are becoming more so in the United States. Still, they offer a simple, interesting, and reasonable manual task for learning.

FIGURE 2-17. *Cup Tossing-Catching Task* Subject tries to catch ball in cup. Scores are recorded in the number of successful catches out of a given number of trials.

7. Striking

Striking tasks are extremely prevalent in instructional and sports activities. In fact, the striking of an object (usually a ball) with a body part or with an implement is one of the most popular of all sports skills. Some examples are the volleyball spike, soccer kick, tennis stroke, baseball hit, field hockey shot, and golf stroke. Consequently, researchers have made frequent use of such tasks. Usually the goal is to hit for accuracy, distance, or sustained repetitions.

Research projects usually demand that a degree of novelty be added to striking tasks. This may require that modified implements be used, that the nondominant hand or foot be used, that the object be rebounded off a wall or unusual surface, or that the object itself be novel. For example, Egstrom (1946) described a task in which subjects used a wooden paddle in the nonpreferred hand to strike a small rubber ball that had been projected into the air after rolling down a long tube. The subject was required to hit the ball into a target area on a wall 20 feet away. By striking the ball, the subject had to change its direction by 90 degrees in order to hit the target (see Figure 2-18).

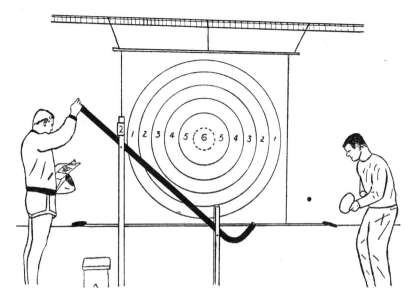

FIGURE 2-18. *Egstrom's Novel Ball Striking Task* Score values are represented on the target. (From Egstrom, Effects of an emphasis on conceptualizing techniques during early learning of a motor skill. *Research Quarterly*, 35, p. 474. Copyright by the American Alliance for Health, Physical Education, Recreation and Dance, 1900 Association Drive, Reston, Va. 22091. Reprinted by permission.)

8. Serial manipulation tasks

Serial manipulation refers to memory tasks in which the subject is required to initiate responses in a predetermined order. There are a great many serial manipulation tasks in which a combination of hand and foot manipulations are required (see Figure 2-19).

In recent years, several computerized toys have come onto the market that illustrate the serial manipulation concept. These are usually short-term memory exercises in which keys are depressed or other manipulations are made in a particular order. Pleasant tones may accompany correct responses whereas caustic buzzers are activated when an incorrect response is made.

LABORATORY COMPUTERS

One of the more dramatic developments in the area of motor skill research during recent years has been the creation and use of laboratory computers. Computers offer flexibility and versatility not possible with traditional types of laboratory equipment. As will be shown in the next few pages, results from laboratories using computers are beginning to appear in the research literature.

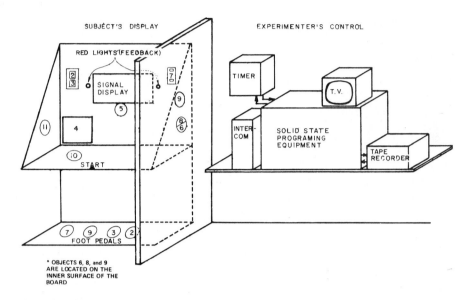

SUBJECT'S DISPLAY

EXPERIMENTER'S CONTROL

RED LIGHTS(FEEDBACK)

SIGNAL DISPLAY

TIMER

T.V.

INTER-COM

SOLID STATE PROGRAMING EQUIPMENT

TAPE RECORDER

START

FOOT PEDALS

* OBJECTS 6, 8, and 9
ARE LOCATED ON THE
INNER SURFACE OF THE
BOARD

FIGURE 2-19. *Serial Manipulation Apparatus: The Experimenter's Control Unit and the Subject's Display* The following are examples of task components and manipulations (numbers refer to numbers in the diagram). Hand Manipulations: 2—switch, high (2 alone, 3 alone, or either one in connection with foot pedals); 3—switch, low; 4—door, open 30 (knob can be turned either clockwise or counterclockwise); 5—punch bag (hit, press, or punch); 6—toggle switch, up position; 8—toggle switch, down position; 7—press switch, top buttton, bottom button, or both (any of these manipulations may be in connection with foot pedals); 9—press button, press in (can be connected to foot pedal); 10—pound button, press or pound; 11—rotary switch, turn in clockwise direction. Foot components 2, 3, 7—press-type switches (can be pressed alone or in connection with specific hand controls; 9—dimmer switch (pressed alone or in connection with a hand object). (From Singer, R. H. and Pease, D., A comparison of discovery learning and guided instructional strategies on motor skill learning, retention and transfer. *Research Quarterly,* 1976, 43, p. 790. Copyright by the American Alliance for Health, Physical Education, Recreation and Dance, 1900 Association Drive, Reston, VA 22091. Reprinted with permission.)

Laboratory computers currently have the capacity to duplicate, with greater sophistication, many of the tasks presented in the prior section of this chapter. For example, a pursuit rotor task can be programmed to be presented and performed on a monitor such as the one illustrated in Figure 2-20. In this task the subject uses a pencil-sized stylus to follow a light target that moves in a prescribed pattern and speed around the screen. As with the traditional apparatus, time on target can be recorded and tabulated by the computer.

As is clear with the great variety of home video games, an unlimited variety of tracking tasks are possible. In addition, other tasks, such as positioning, reaction time, and coincidence-anticipation time can be programmed with computers currently available. However, tasks that require the manipulation of objects, such as striking, throwing, catching, and juggling cannot be so easily programmed. Also,

FIGURE 2-20. A MINC laboratory computer (Manufactured by the Digital Equipment Co., Maynard, Mass.)

gross motor tasks that simulate sports skills are also difficult to program on the computer.

A laboratory computer can present the stimuli and record motor responses. Programs, called software, can be written to provide sufficient instructions for the subject at a terminal to complete the experiment with limited assistance from the experimenter. Software for the same computer will calculate and display the statistical analysis, provide optional performance feedback to the student, or both.

Most laboratory computers initially use BASIC statements, but for motor learning experiments, especially reaction time experiments, assembly-level statements are needed for precise timing of stimulus events and the recording of latencies. BASIC statements have a slow execution time with unacceptable and unpredictable time lags. A time-sharing computer, such as a remote terminal connected via telephone to a central computer with round-robin polling of terminals, also creates an unacceptable time delay. Therefore, single-user or real-time computers are required for motor learning experiments.

Printed instructions to the subject may be presented on a cathode-ray tube (CRT), which is similar to a television monitor, or a printer, which is similar to a typewriter. Oral instructions to the subject may be presented by a computer-controlled tape recorder, or voice synthesizer. To perform these tasks, the subject may be required to push a button; operate a multidirectional joy stick; draw a line, or touch points on a graphics table known as a digitizer. In addition, overall body movements reflecting potentiometer measured joint angles may be registered on an analog recorder. Interactive feedback to the subject from a computer is possible, although not required. Some laboratory computers have a capacity to display moving pictures as feedback, and others have the capacity to provide static color feedback on the cathode-ray tube (CRT). This color feedback is created from straight lines or little colored blocks.

Several examples of laboratory computer applications are found in recent motor learning literature. A reaction time experiment by Damon and Wickers (1977) used a CRT display for a one-dimensional tracking task and reaction time task using both single-task and dual-task condition. A linear movement task used a subject-held slider with a variable voltage output signal to communicate movement distance to a laboratory computer. For this task, a computer oscilloscope screen was used to provide a display of the line created to correspond with the subject's slider movement. Two conditions of feedback were investigated. For visual guidance conditions, a line appeared on the screen when the subject initiated the movement, and stopped when the slider stopped. For terminal feedback, the line appeared after the movement ended. This experiment, designed by Smith (1978), provides an excellent example of the use of the computer to provide visual feedback to the subject during a motor learning experiment.

An experimental set-up for recording reaction times and movement times in milliseconds is described by Glencross and Gould (1979). A laboratory computer was used to present all stimuli and signals and record all reaction and movement times. Summers used a laboratory computer for stimulus presentation, feedback, timing, and collection in an eight-part serial reaction time task. Klapp, et al. (1979) used CRT with a laboratory computer to present ready signals followed by either a simple or choice reaction situation on the CRT. The response was a verbal response to a voice key connected to the laboratory computer. After a voice response, the computer erased the CRT display and retained the blank CRT for a 3-second intertrial interval. The computer recorded all data for 50 trials and figured the initial data reduction.

A CRT display with a joy stick was used by Jagacinski, Hartzell, and Bishop (1978) to investigate Fitts' law as subjects are performing discrete movements using a joy stick that either controlled the position or the velocity of a movable light spot. For this experiment, the position and velocity of the target light spot were controlled by the computer, and the subject's success was sampled and stored every 5 milliseconds. The recording of linear displacement of a stylus in two dimensions (direction and extent) in the horizontal plane used a computer to code and store the position of a subject-controlled stylus. As the subject moved the stylus, the laboratory computer calculated the error scores (Christiana and Merriman, 1977).

Without question the laboratory computer will increase in use over the next several years. It will not only replace much of the traditional research apparatus and equipment, but it will also add speed and flexibility to the conduct and analysis of motor skills research.

SUMMARY

1. The phenomenon of learning is better understood if one is familiar with the experimental methodology used to establish principles, theories, and laws of learning. Consequently, this chapter provided an analysis of the most common techniques that have been used to develop our current knowledge of the learning process. Such information better prepares the student for evaluating the validity as well as the fallibility of our present assumptions about the learning process.

2. Scientific investigation of the learning process has been underway for approximately one hundred years. The initial milestone in this process was the work of Ebbinghaus in Germany during the late 19th century. Much of the experimental research, even from the earliest days, involved motor skills. Research with motor skills by experimental psychologists was conducted for the purpose of applying it to other types of learning.

3. Over the years, research has taken place both in the laboratory and in the classroom (or gymnasium). Laboratory research has proven especially popular with experimental psychologists because of the stringent controls possible in such a setting. On the other hand, the classroom has proven reasonably popular as a vehicle for research because of its practicality, and consequently, its application to the school setting.

4. Both basic and applied research have been widely pursued. In basic research, the aim is to create new knowledge about how people learn or behave with little regard to application. In applied research, the project is designed and conducted to find a solution to a particular problem.

5. Novel motor skills have been created, as have novel verbal materials, so that the learner will start from a near zero level of proficiency. This reduces the possibility of contamination from prior learning. Finding such culture-free tasks, however, has proven difficult over the years.

6. Stringent experimental controls regarding laboratory conditions, equipment, and administration are essential if results are to have any meaning. Equipment of increasing complexity during recent years requires increased sophistication to insure proper controls. Any laxity in equipment calibration, timing, instructions, and general climate lessen the quality of research.

7. Selecting the proper score in motor skill measurement is dependent upon many factors. On some occasions, the "best" score is most representative. At other times, the mean score is preferable, and at still other times, the median score should be used. Motor tasks should be conducted so that resultant scores accurately represent the individual's skill level. In addition, such tasks should have adequate range so as to accurately reflect the capacities of the very high and very low performers.

8. Professional societies, governmental agencies, and universities have taken steps to insure that human subjects will not be abused in the conduct of research. Standards and guidelines have been established to prevent physical abuse as well as

to reduce psychological and sociological hazards. Consequently, most universities and research institutes have established procedures for monitoring activities that involve human subjects.

9. The value of any research is dependent upon the quality of the measurement data collected. Most important of the criteria for data collection are validity, reliability, and objectivity. Stringent efforts must be made to establish the integrity of these measures prior to commencement of data collection.

10. The selection of an appropriate task for motor skill research is one of the more crucial aspects of any project. The search for acceptable tasks for various research problems has gone on for most of the 20th century. Usually such skills must be novel, have reliability, and be reasonably applicable to the kinds of learning to which results are intended to apply. During the first half of the 20th century, various forms of mirror tracing or drawing, pursuit rotary activity, and a multitude of mazes were used with success. Originating as crude tasks, recent instrumentation and design, as well as improved technical sophistication, have greatly improved these tasks as tools for research.

11. During and following World War II, more complex motor skills and those involving both hands and feet were developed. Many of these involved simulators of the type used by airplane pilots or space travelers. More recently, gross motor skills of a practical nature have been developed. Some of these are clearly novel, while others are major modifications of familiar sports tasks.

12. A list of criteria for the selection of tasks for motor skills research was presented and discussed. Though such criteria varies from one research project to another according to the particulars of the problem being pursued, the general criteria include the following factors: novelty; complexity appropriate to the ability range of the subjects; objective scoring; safety; and the ability of the investigator to manage the administration of the task.

13. Motor learning tasks appropriate for scientific investigation have been arbitrarily grouped and discussed in the following categories: positioning tasks; tracking tasks; mazes; balancing activities; throwing, catching, and juggling; striking; and serial manipulation tasks. Selection of the proper task is dependent upon the transfer application intended, the maturity and ability of subjects, and the resources of the investigator.

14. The use of computers in laboratory research has progressed rapidly in recent years. Computers are used to facilitate research through the use of programmed instructions, the presentation of the task, the measurement of the subject's response (scoring), and analysis of performance data. Much more extensive use of computers in skill learning research is likely within the next decade.

SELECTED READINGS

ANNETT, J. *Feedback and human behavior.* Baltimore, Md.: Penguin Books, 1969.
AMERICAN PSYCHOLOGICAL ASSOCIATION. *Ethical principles in the conduct of research with human participants.* Washington, D.C., 1973.

CARRON, A. V. *Laboratory experiments in motor learning.* Englewood Cliffs, N.J.: Prentice-Hall, Inc., 1971.

CRATTY, B. J. *Movement behavior and motor learning* (3rd ed.). Philadelphia: Lea and Febiger, 1973.

FLEISHMAN, E. A. *The structure and measurement of physical fitness.* Englewood Cliffs, N.J.: Prentice-Hall, Inc., 1964.

LOCKHART, A. S. AND JOHNSON, J. M. *Laboratory experiments in motor learning.* Dubuque, Ia.: Wm. C. Brown, 1970.

SCHMIDT, R. A. *Motor control and learning: a behavior emphasis.* Champaign, Ill.: Human Kinetics Publishers, Inc., 1982.

SINGER, R. N. and GERSON, R. F. Task classification and strategy utilization in motor skills. *Research Quarterly for Exercise and Sport,* Vol. 52, no. 1, 1981, pp. 100-116.

3 Learning Theories and Models

THEORIES AND MODELS

Scholars have traditionally sought to synthesize available knowledge about learning, translating it into widely applicable principles or generalizations. Learning theorists particularly have never been content to merely collect isolated information nor to solve narrow problems on an empirical basis. Rather, they have attempted to *explain* the learning process in general terms. Where no definitive guidelines existed, they conducted research to discover relationships between variables and to establish a theoretical framework that would enable them to predict behavior under widely varying conditions. Such generalizations have been expressed in terms such as theories or models.

The term *learning theory* has traditionally been used in reference to broad, sometimes grandiose, statements about learning. Learning *models*, on the other hand, are a more recent development and represent a functional approach to the study of behavior. The creation of models has accompanied the development of cybernetic and information theories during the past two decades. Theories and models both refer to statements or assumptions about how and why learning takes place. Though sometimes used interchangeably, a close analysis reveals some important differences. In the area of motor behavior, for example, models are often expressed in the form of a block drawing or schematics indicating a flow of action or the temporal sequence of events.

A *theory* represents a coherent group of general propositions or principles that explains a class of phenomena. Theories begin as speculations or guesses about how and why something occurs. Such unproven speculations or assumptions are referred to as *hypotheses*. Hypotheses gain some credibility because of their relationship to known facts. In scientific discussions, these hypotheses are stated in such a way as to offer a framework for investigation. After substantial research of several hypotheses relating to a common topic, greater confidence is established in concepts that were initially mere speculations. Thus, a theory evolves. To have credibility, a theory must be supported by substantial research.

Learning theories are attempts to explain what learning is and how it takes place. They summarize and synthesize the research findings and opinions of the theorist into concise interpretations of learning. In this process, some specific details may be lost because the theories are developed for application to a broad base of learning problems rather than for use as specific rules. Each theory reflects the point of view of the author, including terminology, research techniques, and those topics considered most important.

A *model*, as used in psychological terms, is a more limited statement (verbal or graphic) designed to illustrate a relationship of events or a system. A model is often very similar to a theory, but it is usually presented in such a way that it can be investigated more clearly than can a theory. The results of such investigation can yield specific information about the topic in question. Schmidt (1982) states that a model is analogous to a theory, that it enables us to visualize theories more effectively, and that it suggests predictions or solutions that are not so clearly seen or understood in the classical theory.

Models are effectively used for both research and teaching purposes. In mechanical engineering, for example, a model of a bridge enables students to test certain structural hypotheses. It also aids students in understanding relationships. A model of the heart and circulatory system or the muscular system aids one in planning research to test theories about how these systems work. Similarly, an electronic model of the brain may facilitate investigations of the physiological processes in the brain. In like manner, a well-defined learning model can aid in the investigation of specific learning phenomena.

As currently used in learning discussions, models are tentative explanations, often speculations, of how and why learning occurs. As such, they can be modified when additional information is made available. The model is less formal and is more flexible than the theory.

Models are often stated in practical terms, relating to real life situations. In contrast, theories are more remote and less practical. As such, models can aid in the "proving" of theories, inasmuch as they are easily translated into projects to be investigated. Classical theorists, however, do not always agree that the theories can be forced into the practical applications to which they are sometimes subjected.

In this chapter, a rather extensive review of the traditional theories of learning will be followed by a presentation of the more recent cybernetic theory and then several recently developed models of motor behavior. The discussion of traditional theories will highlight the prominent learning authorities, along with trends over the past century. The cybernetic theory, along with models, has been developed only during the past 25 years or so by psychologists and physical educators interested in the acquisition of skills. This, along with other theories and models will be discussed with reference to the learning of practical motor skills.

THEORIES OF LEARNING

Why learning theories?

There are several reasons why today's teacher should become acquainted with the major learning theories. First, one cannot really judge the merits of different teaching methods without understanding the primary assumptions upon which they are based. A thorough knowledge of learning theory enables the instructor to develop a systematic understanding of related principles so as to facilitate a more unified or developmental approach in teaching methodology. Where no such understanding exists, unrelated work patterns or unit assignments often prevail. It is not essential that the teacher develop a well-defined and explicit theory of learning, but such study enables one to avoid using a combination of contradictory techniques, a method that would not be advocated by any theoretical position. The teacher who is concerned with efficiency in teaching, the teacher who is more than a technician, will look beyond the method or task at hand and seek an understanding of the basic truths upon which the program is based.

Whether or not they realize or admit it, most teachers have their own theories about many aspects of learning. For example, the coach who stresses game situations in basketball practice reveals an attitude about the best way to prepare for competition. Some teachers introduce students to new skills early in the period and practice more familiar ones later on, based on the "theory" that the best time for learning is early in the practice period. Some years ago I worked with a basketball coach who, at the end of each practice, required players to shoot free throws and then run laps around the gymnasium. The player who scored the highest in shooting percentage did not have to run the laps. This coach certainly had a theory about the rule of motivation in performance. Even the parent who says, "Children learn to walk just as fast if you don't encourage them," illustrates a theory of learning.

Still, learning theories are not to be viewed as a panacea for teachers. In fact, they may provide only limited information of a specific nature as aids to the resolution of particular pedagogical questions. A rather cynical note was struck on this topic by psychologist Donald Snygg at the Kentucky Symposium in 1951. He stated: "The sad truth is that, after 50 years of careful and honest and occasionally brilliant research on the nature of learning, the only people who can be proved to have received any practical benefits from learning are the learning theorists themselves" (cited in Bugelski, 1970, p. 16). This extreme, even shocking, statement illustrates the inadvisability of taking a theory and precisely applying it to solve a particular problem. Still, learning theories do give a general orientation to pedagogical style. Also, they provide a framework for research projects designed to solve specific problems in education. It will be seen in the review of the works of the pioneers in the study of learning that there is much common agreement, and each has contributed to our understanding about how people learn. Each theoretical position presented has important implications for the learning of motor skills.

Categories of learning theories

Over the years there has been great diversity in the manner in which learning theories are grouped. For example, Kingsley (1946) and Hilgard (1948) organized the major learning theories into *association* and *field* theories. Hilgard (1956) later categorized most of the theories as *stimulus-response* (approximating the association group) and *cognitive* (approximating the field group). Hill (1963) described the two major theories as *connectionist* and *cognitive*, and Deese (1958) labeled them as *association* and *gestalt*. Perhaps the most encompassing terminology is provided by Bigge and Hunt (1962) who labeled the two main categories as *stimulus-response associationism* and *gestalt-field.*

For this discussion, the theories of Thorndike, Guthrie, Hull, and Skinner will be classified as stimulus-response, while the concepts of Tolman, Lewin, and the gestaltists will be referred to as cognitive. Of course, the distinction between these two groups is not always clear since there are points at which theories in different groups agree. There are also issues of controversy among the individual theories in each major category.

It is becoming increasingly difficult to break major learning theories into distinct categories. Some of the newer theories, and some interpretations of the older theories, do not fit into the traditional groupings. According to Deese (1958), the taking of sides on the major theoretical positions has declined. Even the development of elaborate theories has decreased. The differences within and between the major learning theories might be compared to the diversity in the Democratic and Republican parties in the United States. However, an effort will be made to show areas of distinction and identifying characteristics, or overriding concepts, of each of the two major groups.

STIMULUS-RESPONSE THEORIES

While stimulus-response and cognitive theories developed into major influences on education during the current century, each has roots in earlier centuries. In the United State the stimulus-response theories developed earlier than did the cognitive theories. Some impetus for the stimulus-response movement resulted from a desire among early American psychologists for theories more practical and objective than the relatively vague and subjective early German cognitive theories. The stimulus-response approach has been more "scientific." Stimulus-response proponents believe that behavior can be controlled by application of the *pleasure-pain principle.* Considerable attention is devoted to such matters as objective measurement, quantitative data, reflexes, and sequences of behavior.

The stimulus-response received a significant boost in the early part of the 20th century when Pavlov (1927) stated that "it is obvious that the different kinds of habits based on training. education and discipline of any sort are nothing but a long chain of conditioned reflexes." Earlier, Watson (1914) had stated that "it is possible to write a psychology . . . in terms of stimulus and response, in terms of a habit formation, habit integration and the like." Further, he urged a "scientific" approach to the study of learning, with the avoidance of gestaltist concepts such as will, imagery, mental states, and the like.

Watson (1930) is generally considered the founder of *behaviorism*, a philosophical position basic to the stimulus-response position. Behaviorism is perhaps most starkly illustrated by the following oft-quoted statement of Watson:

Give me a dozen healthy infants, well-formed, and my own special world to bring them up in and I'll guarantee to take anyone at random and train him

to become any type of specialist I might select—doctor, lawyer, artist, mer-
chant-chief and, yes, even beggerman and thief, regardless of his talents,
penchants, tendencies, abilities, vocations and race of his ancestors (p. 101).

This boast has neither been proven nor disproven. However, the basic concept, perhaps in more modest terms, would be supported by many psychologists in the
stimulus-response area today.

The term *stimulus-response (S-R)* is used to indicate that a particular stimulus
is connected or leads to a particular response. Stimuli that impinge upon the sense
organs are found throughout our environment Some of these stimuli cause automatic responses, such as the reaction of the pupils to varying intensities of light.
This behavior is unlearned. Other stimuli are connected to responses through learning, as when a typist sees the letter *t* and proceeds to hit the appropriate key, or a
baseball batter notices the thrown ball curve and makes the necessary adjustment in
his swing.

The association of a particular stimulus and response has long been
recognized by psychologists. English psychologists of the 18th and 19th centuries
established laws based on principles of association and used these laws to explain
memory, perception, and reasoning. When mental processes occur close together or
when the learner perceives several impressions at the same time, he tends to "link"
them. In the 18th century, Hume determined the qualities essential for association
to be resemblance and contiguity. Others gradually attached a cause-and-effect
relationship to things that usually followed each other. Psychologists later decided
that the association or connection was not an automatic link between ideas but the
result of thought on the part of the learner. Stimulus-response psychology arose
from this emphasis on the mental processes of the learner.

Stimulus-response theorists generally assume a direct cause-and-effect relationship with the learner seeing a connection between the stimulus and response.
They also emphasize the importance of reinforcement of this connection, or
stimulus-response *bond*. To the stimulus-response theorists, learning is the process
of building new bonds and organizing them into systems that develop into the
knowledge, behavior, and personality of the individual. When stimuli are connected
with responses that involve bodily movements, the connections are referred to as
motor bonds. Simple motor skills might involve very few bonds, while complex
skills might require many motor bonds.

The idea that learning consists of combining stimulus-response bonds, or
"parts," into "wholes" is emphasized. Determining how these connections are formed, and under what conditions, has led to the research upon which the stimulus-
response theory is based. The stimulus-response concept is therefore a molecular
theory in which the individual learns through *particular* responses or habits. General
understanding is not believed to take place to the extent assumed by the cognitive
theorists. Rather, understanding is restricted to habits appropriate to the particular
situation. Following is a brief discussion of the works of some authorities who have
been most influential in developing theories promoting the ideas of connectionism,
conditioning, part learning, or trial-and-error learning.

Thorndike's connectionism

Edward L. Thorndike (1874-1949) probably contributed more to our present understanding of learning than any other individual. He established the basis for early scientific approaches to educational problems. His suggestions were especially effective because they were specific and could be investigated by scientific means. His influence on American education has been monumental. Most early learning theorists used Thorndike's views as a reference point and then conducted experiments to test his views as well as to establish their own. Tolman (1938), in reflecting on the influence of Thorndike, stated:

> The psychology of animal learning—not to mention that of child learning—has been and still is primarily a matter of agreeing or disagreeing with Thorndike, or trying in minor ways to improve upon him. Gestalt psychologists, conditioned-reflex psychologists, sign-gestalt psychologists—all of us here in America seem to have taken Thorndike overtly or covertly, as a starting point (p. 11).[1]

Thorndike's learning theory is referred to as *connectionism* or sometimes as the *S-R bond theory* because of its emphasis upon the connection between the stimulus and response. He believed that learning requires the development of a bond between a stimulus and its appropriate response. Strongly influenced by the developing field of physiological psychology, Thorndike believed that the connections were products of biological changes in the nervous system. A major tenet in his theory is that learning takes place as a result of trial-and-error practice.

After conducting extensive research with cats in puzzle boxes, Thorndike established a number of principles for his trial-and-error learning. Among them are the following:

1. In the early phases of learning there is a great variety of activity and very little success.
2. The first successes are quite accidental and no connection is seen between response and desired result.
3. There is gradual elimination of wrong responses and useless activity.
4. The learner becomes aware of the connection between stimulus and response and gets the feel of the correct action.
5. Practice strengthens the correct response and the action becomes more efficient.

Thorndike's *laws of learning* have been used to a considerable extent as a guide for teaching techniques for half a century. The most widely known are his laws of readiness, exercise, and effect. The *law of readiness* states that learning will take place most effectively when the learner is prepared to respond. When an individual has reached a state of readiness, it is pleasurable to respond and unpleasant to be

---

[1] By permission of the American Psychological Association.

prevented from responding. Conversely, when an individual is not in a state of readiness, it is annoying to be forced to respond. Thorndike's readiness is a law of preparatory adjustment, primarily emphasizing psychological preparedness in interest and background knowledge. As an example of the need for background learning, one can imagine the difficulty that would be encountered by a person who takes an advanced course in statistics without having first taken the intermediate course. Today, the concept of readiness has been extended to include the interaction of maturation, prerequisite learning, and motivation. Thorndike, however, did not discuss maturation as a factor of readiness.

The *law of exercise* indicates that exercising or practicing a particular response under favorable conditions strengthens the connection between stimulus and response. Through repetition the bond is developed and strengthened; this is occasionally referred to as the *law of use*. Conversely, failure to exercise over a period weakens the connection, and this is sometimes called the *law of disuse*. Thorndike's early writings seemed to indicate that learning was almost automatic with practice, i.e., one learns in direct relation to the time spent in practice. Later Thorndike stressed that conditions must be appropriate for learning to occur. One of the essentials for an efficient learning situation is described as a satisfactory effect, or reinforcement.

The *law of effect* Thorndike considered of great importance, and this law became one of his most controversial. It refers primarily to the strengthening of an S-R connection if the experience is pleasurable. For example, if a basketball player finds that a certain maneuver fakes the opponent out of the way so as to gain an easy shot, this success is pleasurable and tends to strengthen the connection between the situation and the maneuver. Thorndike originally stated that when a response is accompanied by a painful or annoying experience, the bond is weakened. He later refuted this phase of the law by indicating that an unpleasant experience might indeed be well remembered.

Thorndike placed great emphasis on the use of motivational techniques to promote learning, and he encouraged the use of praise and rewards in support of his law of effect. He pointed out that rewards actually reinforce or strengthen the S-R bond. Although he emphasized motivation, he believed that above a certain critical minimum, additional motivation or greater rewards are not of value.

Thorndike believed that what is learned is a *specific* connection between the stimulus and response, and it is consistent with his view to assume that only such connections will be transferred. He stressed that only "identical elements" would be usable in a second situation. By identical elements he referred to substance (ability to handle spoken and written words, numbers, and symbols) and procedure (habits and attitudes regarding work). Thorndike's was a much narrower view of transfer than had existed prior to his time.

Guthrie's contiguity theory

Edwin R. Guthrie (1886-1959) developed the contiguity theory, which emphasizes the association between the stimulus and the response. He indicated that the mind tends to connect those things that come to it at approximately the same time. Guthrie believed that any response preceded or accompanied by a stimulus or a combination of stimuli will be repeated whenever the same stimulus or combination of stimuli is repeated.

Guthrie further believed that the connection between the stimulus and response is fully established in one trial. After this one-trial contiguous association, the strength of the association which has been established will not be altered by additional practice. This all-or-nothing theory (if a response to a stimulus is learned at all, it is learned to the maximum extent) is unique to Guthrie among the major learning theorists. According to this view, a specific response to a specific stimulus cannot be improved with practice.

One-trial learning would seem to eliminate the need for practice. However, Guthrie did advocate practice, and he emphasized drill. He believed that in every learning situation there are many connections made among the multiplicity of stimuli and responses. Skill learning results from repetition, therefore, because at each practice session additional associations can be made. Each learning situation presents a slightly different combination of stimuli. Correct responses (habits) need to be developed for each situation. Perfect performance results when the learner associates all appropriate responses with the right cues. According to Guthrie's theory, forgetting is not caused by disuse but by interference from subsequent learning. Drill helps the learner to make a greater number of correct responses, and more learned associations therefore result. Guthrie's explanation, though simple and plausible, is extremely hard to validate because of the difficulty in exactly duplicating a learning situation.

Guthrie was primarily concerned with things that could be seen or described. He was interested in the overt behavior that the individual exhibits in the learning process. He assumed a "black box" point of view regarding learning: We cannot really understand in a scientific way what takes place *in* the nervous system during the learning process. The role of the psychologist is, therefore, to match stimuli with their responses so that behavior can be predicted on this basis. Guthrie himself offered no clues regarding possible changes in the nervous system.

Guthrie disagreed with Thorndike's law of effect. He believed that motivation was not an important factor in the learning process, and he therefore did not emphasize praise or reward. Reward does not strengthen the stimulus-response connection directly, he stated. Rather, rewards are indirect aids effective in animal experiments because they remove the animal from the learning situation after a successful response. This removal prevents the animal from making incorrect responses that would interfere with learned habits.

Thorndike believed that the learner actually made a connection between the reward and response, whereas Guthrie discounted this suggestion of retroactive learning. He believed that rewards are important only as tools in promoting or discouraging learning *activity*. If it is desirable that a person continue practicing a skill in order to learn responses, then a reward may be effective in keeping him actively engaged in the learning process. Rewarding a person at the cessation of a practice period, however, would have no desirable learning effect, according to Guthrie.

Guthrie stressed the concept that people learn activities when they *do* them, not because they are rewarded after they do them. Similarly, they do not learn to perform an act by being punished for failure to do it. The validity of this point was impressed upon me in several child-rearing incidents in recent years. In one case, I made repeated efforts to develop within my son the habit of bringing trash cans from the street to the garage as he came home from school. On each trash collection day the boy got off the school bus at the corner of the street, walked past the empty trash cans at the entrance to the driveway, and came into the house. He did this despite being reminded and scolded by me on several occasions upon my arrival home from work. It soon became clear that this after-the-fact rebuke, despite its severity, had no effect. The boy continued to walk past the trash cans, oblivious of their existence. Finally I seized upon Guthrie's concept that one learns what he does, not what he get punished for not doing. Consequently, the next time I arrived home to find the trash cans in the driveway I did not scold him, nor did I simply ask him to retrieve them. Rather, I instructed him to walk all the way back to the bus stop, books in hand, and make the return trip, picking up trash cans en route. Two such "practice" sessions were adequate for developing in him the habit of returning all emptied trash cans from the street to the garage.

In like manner, the habit of covering his mouth while coughing was also developed. The young child, like all others, had no inherent tendency to protect others from his frequent coughs. Despite admonitions to "cover your mouth when you cough," he never seemed to think of this protective response until it was too late, nor could his parents "catch" him to provide a reminder prior to an eruption. A strategy was then devised. The child was instructed to cover his mouth and cough (a forced cough). The practice of covering his mouth while performing a "fake" cough was repeated a number of times over several days. This socially acceptable behavior became routine when the genuine cough occured.

Guthrie expected very little transfer of learning. He agreed generally with Thorndike about transfer of identical elements. His conditions for transfer were probably even more restrictive than those of Thorndike. Among the multiplicity of stimuli in a new learning situation, Guthrie believed that there would usually be enough differences to almost entirely negate the value of stimulus-response connections from old situations. To attain considerable skill in a new situation, therefore, a great deal of practice would have to take place.

Hull's reinforcement theory

Clark L. Hull (1884-1952) developed a theory that emphasized drive reduction as the prime essential in learning. According to Hull, an organism is usually in disequilibrium with its environment; the organism's *need* for something results in a *drive.* Needs are either primary (relating to physiological necessities) or secondary (relating to psychological wants). The drive causes energizing on the part of the learner. When the need is met the drive is reduced. The reduction of the drive is the reinforcement that causes the response to be learned. According to Hull's thesis, therefore, a stimulus causes a neural response that results in a drive. This drive evokes a response by the organism that ends in drive reduction. The drive reduction is the reinforcement that develops habits or learning.

Hull's theory of learning is an extremely well-developed system, although it does not have a highly integrated or centralized theme as is evident in the works of Thorndike or the gestaltists. Hull's definitions are in great detail so that each aspect can be investigated scientifically. He established the technique for reducing theory to well-defined components, and he developed a system of postulates that were designed to *explain* learning when most theories were generally descriptive.

Hull's system established a clear rationale for educational programs designed to meet pupil needs. Since children learn only to the extent that a need is reduced, according to Hull, educational programs should be based on pupil needs. School authorities who had held a philosophy of meeting the child's needs were given psychological justification for their programs.

In regard to transfer, Hull proposed that stimuli need not be exactly the same in order to evoke the same response. If the organization of stimuli is approximately the same, the individual will respond as if the stimuli are identical. An old response may be evoked because of the new stimulus' similarity in intensity or quality to the old stimulus. In this belief, Hull differed from Guthrie, who believed that slight differences in the combination of stimuli would create new situations in which old learnings would be less valuable.

According to Hull, mere contiguous repetition only promotes inhibition. In his system, reactive inhibition is described as the tendency to avoid repeating a response that has just been performed. In addition, the greater the amount of effort in the performance or the more often the performance, the greater is the reluctance to repeat the act. This inhibition subsides with the passage of time. Learning, there-fore, is not a function of a given amount of practice but depends instead upon reinforcement (drive reduction). To be effective, practice must be under conditions in which the learner has a physiological or psychological need. This concept is similar to Thorndike's law of effect but different from Guthrie's learn-what-you-do theory.

Skinner's operant conditioning

B. F. Skinner (b. 1904) developed a theory that emphasizes the reinforce-ment of the response as the critical factor in learning. This theory is referred to as operant conditioning. An operant, according to Skinner, is a set of acts, or responses. *Operant conditioning* is the learning process that makes a response more probable or frequent by reinforcing the desired act. Reinforcement, therefore, is contingent upon the correct response. While Thorndike believed that reinforcement strengthens the bond between stimulus and response, Skinner emphasizes that the reinforcement merely strengthens the response.

Skinner believes that the learner will tend to repeat in the future what he was doing at the time of reinforcement. By rewarding certain acts, the experimenter can get the learner to repeat those acts or to behave in a certain way. A great deal of research was done with pigeons and other animals in the "Skinner box." A particu-lar response was selected, and when the animal did it, a reward (food) was given. As a result, the animal performed the rewarded response more often, and frequently exaggerated or improved upon the reinforced operant.

Skinner believes that people's learning in daily life is somewhat more complicated but has the same basic nature as operant conditioning. He found very similar
properties in the learning processes observed in pigeons, rats, dogs, monkeys,
human children, and psychotic subjects. The species seemed to make little difference in the essentials of the learning process.

Skinner has been very scientific and has indicated that psychology can become almost perfect science. He disagrees with the old axiom that "A horse can be
led to water but cannot be made to drink." Rather, he insists that the science of
conditioning can be perfected to *assure* that the horse will drink. If the environment of animals or humans is controlled, behavior can be accurately predicted,
according to Skinner. Psychology should be able to determine what influences man
and the extent of this influence. It naturally follows that the probability of man's
responses can be predicted and his behavior controlled. Skinner's is a psychology
of naturalistic determinism opposed to the philosophy of personal freedom. This
determinism indicates that the behavior that results is the only behavior that could
have occurred. Skinner has indicated that as the science of psychology develops,
man will become more like a machine in that his behavior will be predictable.

Skinner's psychology is concerned entirely with measurable behavior. Like
Watson, he stresses that there is no place in scientific psychology for discussions
about one's "inner self." Discussions about the subconscious are, to him, make-
believe psychology and things of the past. Modern psychology has no need for
mystical discussions about internal motives, Skinner feels, when a study of the
environment could provide all the answers. Neither is the concept of "goal-
oriented" behavior acceptable to him. Rather, behavior is the result of conditioning. People do not perform acts because they are seeking results similar to those
of past responses. Skinner's theory differs from Thorndike's law of effect, which
requires a forward looking, incentive-seeking response. According to Skinner, it is
not essential that the individual see a connection between the operant and the
resulting reinforcement. Learning may take place, therefore, with or without the
individual's awareness of the consequence of his response.

Skinner views the teacher as the architect of behavior. Having first determined the desired behavior, the teacher skillfully uses reinforcers to condition the
learners in this behavior. A series of slight reinforcements is essential in effectively
controlling the environment. Because not enough reinforcers are available in ordinary classrooms, Skinner felt that the most effective control of learning requires
mechanical or automatic aids. This led him to develop "teaching machines" to
maximize and control reinforcement.

COGNITIVE THEORIES

Cognitive theories of learning are based on the assumption that the learner organizes
stimuli or perceptions into a pattern or whole, as opposed to the stimulus-response
concept, which assumes the reception of particular stimuli, both singly and in
groups. According to the cognitive theorists, stimuli from the environment are not

discrete and independent of each other. All things derive their character from their relationship to other things. Stimuli are observed against a background, or *field*. A customer, for example, in a clothing store may or may not like the music being piped in, or the lighting effects. These background factors influence his or her enthusiasm for the clothing being considered. The cognitive theories include ideas that stress the learner's awareness of the total field or combination of stimuli. Psychological reality is what the individual makes of all stimuli received. The individual, therefore, (1) relates stimuli to each other, (2) hypothesizes means-to-ends relationships, and (3) behaves in a goal-directed manner.

Another important characteristic of the cognitive theories of learning is their acceptance of the phenomenon of insight. It can often be observed in animals or humans that the learner suddenly "discovers" the solution to a problem. This "Ah, ha!" phenomenon is usually followed by rapid progress or much improved performance. It is generally assumed that insight results from conscious or subconscious consideration of the problem. Insight often appears to be much faster than the usually slow and awkward trial-and-error process. Very significant contributions to the study of insight were made by Köhler in his experiments with apes.

The cognitive concept has not been as scientifically exact as the stimulus-response theory because cognitive theorists recognize a greater number of intangibles that cannot be precisely measured by available evaluative tools. For example, cognitive theorists assume that behavior is a function of the total situation and a specific cause-and-effect relationship cannot always be shown. Motivation at any particular time cannot be attributed to a single stimulus, but is the result of a combination of internal and external forces. Even success and failure are recognized as strong motivators, with success being accepted as a significant reward. The teacher adhering to cognitive concepts will work with students to help them see the need for learning and for establishing goals.

Cognitive theorists stress the importance of signs, symbols, total stimuli, and structuring. The learner is a moving and changing energy system. The environment is also dynamic. The individual's process of interacting, adapting, modifying, and changing results in learning.

Cognitive psychology developed more recently in the United States than the stimulus-response theory. The basic tenets of cognitive learning theory originated with the gestalt psychologists in Germany during the 1920s and 1930s and continued with the work of Tolman and Lewin in the 1930s and 1940s. According to Hilgard (1960), learning experiments in the tradition of cognitive theory have sharply declined since the late 1940s. He believed that this decline results from the fact that (1) no major theorist came to champion this cause in the way that Hull developed the stimulus-response concept, and (2) the stimulus-response theory has been broadened to include many of the basic problems raised by early gestalt theorists.

The gestalt psychologists

The classical gestalt theory was more concerned with perceiving than with learning as such. However, since the learning process is so dependent upon how the learner discerns his environment, gestalt psychology developed into one of the major learning theories.

During the first two decades of the 20th century, three German psychologists, Max Wertheimer (1880-1943), Kurt Koffka (1886-1941), and Wolfgang Köhler (1887-1967), started conducting conditioning experiments that led to the development of gestalt psychology while stimulus-response and trial-and-error concepts were dominant in America. Wertheimer first presented the theory in Germany around 1912. A few years later, Köhler and Koffka were responsible for publicizing and establishing gestalt psychology in America.

To fully appreciate this theory and its application to learning, one must first understand the gestaltist concepts of *figure* and *ground*. The sensory field (visual, auditory, olfactory, etc.) is organized into a figure against a background. This can easily be observed when viewing a picture or any object against a background. One does not see the particular figure in isolation but observes the total visual field. Both the figure and the ground are important in presenting the total stimuli, or *gestalt*, to the learner. Wertheimer, generally regarded as the founding father of gestalt psychology, showed that when two optical stimuli are perceived by the human eye in quick succession, a simultaneous pattern is formed. This figure-ground concept applies to the other senses as well as to visual perception. A more thorough discussion of the figure-ground concept, with illustrations, is presented in chapter thirteen.

Recognition of and emphasis on *insight* has been another distinguishing characteristic of gestalt psychology. Köhler used this term to describe the sudden solution of a problem as the individual interacts with the environment. In his experiments with apes (described in *The Mentality of Apes*, 1925), he showed that the animals arrived at solutions without resorting to blind trial and error. In problem-solving situations, the apes were required to find an indirect way to obtain food. Such problems often involved placing boxes on each other to attain greater heights or connecting poles to extend their reach to secure the food.

It became obvious that the apes were "figuring out" the answers, and Köhler concluded that Thorndike's trial-and-error explanation of learning was inadequate. Similarly, it is clear in some classroom situations that the child reasons out answers to problems largely on the basis of related past experiences. The topic of insight had been largely ignored by American psychologists prior to Köhler's experiments. However, this concept later became a basic tenet upon which subsequent mental rehearsal studies were conducted in physical education.

Another important principle of gestalt psychology is that *the whole is greater than the sum of its parts*. The human mind not only connects the stimuli that come to it but transforms them into a pattern. According to the gestalt concept, the total pattern has properties of its own that are different from a mere accumulation of the individual stimuli. This idea differs from most stimulus-response theories (except Hull's), which assume that stimuli and responses are additive and that each stimulus or response is largely unitary and isolated.

Gestaltists believe that the organizing and reorganizing of stimuli by an individual in relation to the environment constitutes learning. They developed specific theories about the way in which the learner organizes the visual field.

Koffka (1933) was most instrumental in relating the gestalt theories to learning. He defined four laws of perception that seem to have implications for learning. His *law of proximity* indicates that the learner tends to group together things that are close in time or space. This concept is similar to Guthrie's view of association by contiguity. It seems logical to assume from this law that if the teacher organizes materials into groups, the children will perceive them in groups. If the learners see the material in proximity, it will be learned in proximity.

Koffka's *law of similarity* refers to the unintentional grouping of objects that are similar in shape, size, or color. This grouping of similar items applies also to the senses of hearing, touch, smell, and taste. Homogeneously grouped materials are more easily learned than materials grouped heterogeneously. More recent research has shown that material that falls into logical groups is learned more quickly and retained longer than isolated material.

Koffka's *law of closure* describes the tendency of the learner to complete any incomplete parts from the total field. The individual experiences a general uneasiness if a figure is incomplete or out of balance and is motivated to "complete" the pattern. Completion is satisfying to the individual and, according to Koffka, results in learning. For example, when three dots are presented, an individual may view them as a triangle, even though the dots themselves may be round. The *law of good continuation*, which is similar to the law of closure, states that the individual tends to continue the impressions that make a more pleasant whole. Very often, an individual is stimulated to complete an interrupted musical piece or visual pattern. Koffka believed that this continuation is a pleasant experience and results in the learning of the response. Both the laws of closure and good continuation are somewhat similar to Thorndike's law of effect.

Tolman's sign-gestalt theory

Edward C. Tolman (1886-1959) was instrumental in combining many of the gestalt concepts and developing them into an acceptable learning theory. Previous to his work, educators had not widely applied the gestalt ideas of perception to education. Because of his sensitivity to opposing points of view, Tolman did not develop a tight or exclusive theory like Hull's systematic behavior theory.

While stimulus-response theorists indicated that a series of individual movements (responses) were learned, Tolman believed that the individual perceived the nature of the situation. Learners get the general idea or learn the solution to the problem as well as the specific responses. The learner is goal-directed and is following "signs" or cues to attain an end. One does not routinely follow a definite movement pattern, but thoughtfully adjusts behavior in relation to current status in view of the goal. According to Tolman, learning is the formation of cognitions, i.e., the recognition of signs and cues in relation to goals. His *sign-gestalt concept* refers to the organization or patterning of the stimuli that act as guides or signs to the learner.

Tolman's theory is one of behavior. Despite his assumption of thought by the learner, he believed that the exact nature of the related mental processes could not be determined with great accuracy. He believed, however, that a human being does not automatically and passively respond to stimuli. Rather, the intelligence of the individual plays a part in his behavior and learning. The learner *thinks* when he organizes stimuli, gives them meaning, and responds with a purpose.

Tolman's theory is molar (large and generalized) rather than molecular (small and specific). Stimulus-response theorists broke behavior into small, discrete parts. Tolman emphasized the fact that behavior cannot be fully understood unless patterns or masses of behavior are observed. According to him, the pattern or whole is lost if the molecular approach is taken. Tolman, therefore, used the gestaltist's "whole is more than the sum of its parts" concept to describe behavior.

Tolman worked extensively with insight. He believed that in learning there is considerable implicit trial-and-error practice. The learner mentally tries out different ways of solving a problem before suddenly arriving at a solution. Like Köhler, he reported that insightful behavior is not restricted to man. Animals also show evidence of figuring things out. Mental practice was therefore proposed as an important ingredient in all types of learning.

According to Tolman's theory, rewards and punishments are important because they can be effective in regulating behavior by providing the learner with motivations to try harder or to continue an activity after he or she would have stopped. Motivation is not connected to learning in other ways, according to Tolman. He did not believe in any retroactive effect of rewards as reinforcers of past learning. Thorndike's law of effect was therefore not acceptable to Tolman, whose position on the role of motivation in learning is very similar to that of Guthrie.

Lewin's field theory

Kurt Lewin (1890-1947) developed a theory that emphasizes the complexity of stimuli acting on the learner. He was consistent with the gestalt theorists in his contention that the total pattern, or field, of events determines learning. He placed greater emphasis upon the role of motivation, however, than did the gestaltists. Lewin described the learner's "life space" as the external and the internal forces acting upon the individual. The internal stimuli are both physiological (resulting from hunger, thirst, heat, etc.) and psychological (including memories, dreams, and fears). External influences are received from other persons and from the multiplicity of stimuli that are encountered in the environment. Lewin compared this system of stimuli to a weather map, which includes many high and low pressure areas resulting in cold and warm fronts, rain, wind, and other atmospheric conditions. His theory has often been referred to as *topological psychology*. The interplay of external and internal forces determines the behavior of the individual. The differences in organizational complexity of individuals results in a different combination of forces for each, causing individual differences in learning and behavior.

In view of Lewin's topological explanation, one is able to better understand why the same statement made by a teacher to two children might motivate one while discouraging the other. The comment may challenge one student and humiliate another in an adjoining seat. The high school football coach may severely rebuke the whole team at half time and then wonder why some players "take it out on the other team" during the second half (the desired effect), while others resent the coach's action and sulk for a time thereafter. Lewin's revelations further explain why the same individual exhibits totally different responses to the same treatment on different occasions. In view of the dynamic internal and external life space of students, the sensitive teacher will attempt to treat all students fairly, while not treating them all alike.

Lewin described four types of learning, all of which deal with changes in cognitive structure. According to him, these changes might result from the cognitive field itself or from the motivations within the individual. Lewin believed that the change in cognitive structure (learning) might take place either suddenly or gradually as a result of repetition. Repetition might produce a change in the individual's knowledge of his environment or in his motivation. Not only might attractive goals occasionally become more attractive through repetition, but unattractive goals might also occasionally become attractive.

Lewin, more than anyone else, pointed to the distinction between incentives and goals and between reward and success. He emphasized that the individual's motivation or tension system involves more than reward. Motives are related to personal goals and not necessarily to a general incentive. Goals are established by the individual and are not the same as rewards that might be established by an external authority. A performer might, therefore, win first place or reach a recognized standard but not be very pleased because of not having reached a personal goal or level of aspiration. Conversely, a student might finish last in an activity but still receive considerable satisfaction as a result of attaining the goal being sought.

A related area of Lewin's work was that of social psychology, especially group dynamics. The major portion of his work in the rather new area of group dynamics came late in his life, and his basic tenets of group dynamics are consistent with the concepts of his field theory. Although group dynamics has not been firmly associated with Lewin's learning theory, both areas are based on similar assumptions.

REVIEW OF THE STIMULUS-RESPONSE
AND COGNITIVE LEARNING THEORIES

The differences in points of view expressed might well give the impression that the various theorists are in complete disagreement. In fact, some teachers feel that the philosophers and psychologists should theorize about the profound questions concerning learning and, "when they finally come up with solutions and agree among themselves, we'll put their recommendations to use in our programs." Neuman (1951) has suggested that, for the teaching of practical athletic skills, the psychologists' advice is worth about as much as a rabbit's foot. Although there is some logic to such lines of reasoning, the situation is not as chaotic as it may seem. An analysis of the theories reveals that there are a number of important principles that are characteristic of all of them.

Several attempts have been made to synthesize points of similarity among the major theories and to develop learning principles that are mutually acceptable to most scholars of learning. A number of difficulties are encountered when generalizing about the major theories. First, the theories were developed over a period of half a century and were largely independent of each other. Second, those who developed the theories used different experimental conditions for determining learning principles. These experimental conditions varied greatly in such matters as design, types of subjects, learning tasks, motivating techniques, and practice conditions. The learning periods ranged from a few minutes to many months, and evaluation of learning also differed. Third, the researchers themselves often had no chance to study opposing points of view. Nevertheless, several attempts have been made to establish basic points of agreement among the major theories.

Dashiell (1935) surveyed the major learning theories in the mid-1930s and attempted to develop a synthesis. On the basis of his study, he concluded that the following points were apparent in each of the theories: (1) the importance of motivation on the part of the subject, (2) the necessity of activity resulting from obstruction of motivated activity, (3) a multiplicity of responses to stimuli, (4) a gradual selection of appropriate responses and elimination of extraneous responses, (5) reinforcement of the appropriate responses, and (6) variations in improvement from gradual to sudden solutions.

McConnell (1942) also considered points of agreement among the learning theories. His conclusions were similar to Dashiell's but were structured somewhat differently. McConnell reported that each of the theorists emphasized the following points: (1) Stimuli and responses must be seen in relation to each other; (2) motivation is essential in that it initiates and gives direction to behavior that is organized to attain a goal; (3) the individual must recognize the appropriateness of his response and modify future responses in light of this awareness; and (4) future success in learning is dependent upon one's ability to discriminate between differences and generalize between similarities.

Perhaps the most extensive analysis of the major theories was conducted by Hilgard (1956) who, after reviewing the theories of learning, established fourteen statements upon which he believed most current theorists would agree. These statements are practical ideas that Hilgard developed for the benefit of the teacher:

1.   . . . Brighter people can learn things less bright ones cannot learn; in general, older children can learn more readily than younger ones; the decline of ability with age, in the adult years, depends upon what it is that is being learned.

2. A motivated learner acquires what he learns more readily than one who is not motivated. . . .

3. Motivation that is too intense (especially pain, fear, anxiety) may be accompanied by distracting emotional states, so that excessive motivation may be less effective than moderate motivation for learning some kinds of tasks, especially those involving difficult discriminations.

4. Learning under the control of reward is usually preferable to learning under the control of punishment. Correspondingly, learning motivated by success is preferable to learning motivated by failure. . . .

5. Learning under intrinsic motivation is preferable to learning under extrinsic motivation.

6. Tolerance for failure is best taught through providing a backlog of success that compensates for experienced failure.

7. Individuals need practice in setting realistic goals for themselves, goals neither so low as to elicit little effort nor so high as to foreordain to failure. . . .

8. The personal history of the individual, for example, his reaction to authority, may hamper or enhance his ability to learn from a given teacher.

9. Active participation by a learner is preferable to passive reception when learning, for example, from a lecture or a motion picture.

10. Meaningful materials and meaningful tasks are learned more readily than nonsense materials and more readily than tasks not understood by the learner.

11. There is no substitute for repetitive practice in the overlearning of skills (for instance, the performance of a concert pianist), or in the memorization of unrelated facts that have to be automatized.

12. Information about the nature of a good performance, knowledge of one's mistakes, and knowledge of successful results aid learning.

13. Transfer to new tasks will be better if, in learning, the learner can discover relationships alone and experience applying the principles within a variety of tasks during learning.

14. Spaced or distributed recalls are advantageous in fixing material that is to be long retained (pp. 486-487).[2]

Stallings (1982) has stated that the basic difference between the connectionist (stimulus-response) and the cognitive theories is one of emphasis. In the illustration below, she uses capital and lowercase letters to indicate the areas of emphasis in two categories. Where "s" represents the stimulus, "o" the organism, and "r"

CONNECTIONIST THEORIES   **COGNITIVE THEORIES**

S-o-R   s-O-r

the response, she illustrates that the connectionist theorists view the *stimuli*, or environment, as the most influential factor in explaining and controlling learning. On the other hand, cognitive theorists believe that the organism, i.e., the indi-

[2]E. R. Hilgard, THEORIES OF LEARNING, Second Edition. Copyright © 1948, 1956 by Appleton-Century-Crofts, Inc. Reprinted by permission of the publishers.

vidual's interpretation and use of external and internal stimuli, is most important. These two views are reflected in the different emphasis that the groups place on perception and cognition, motivation and practice. In recent years there has been minimal effort to synthesize these two major categories of learning theory.

THE CYBERNETIC THEORY

The *cybernetic theory*, although more recently developed than the traditional learning categories, is nevertheless one of the more widely discussed behavioral concepts in recent years. Interest in cybernetics has been particularly strong in the area of skill acquisition and performance, where applications seem especially relevant and fairly easy to investigate. Still, the cybernetic theory has not yet reached the level of recognition of the stimulus-response or cognitive theories. It does not involve the same kinds of analysis or follow the same format in analyzing the range of behavioral factors.

The cybernetic theory is based on the concept that information, or feedback, received *during* performance influences ongoing behavior in that particular task. In fact, several authors use the term *information theory* interchangeably with the cybernetic theory. In contrast to the stimulus-response and cognitive theories, the cybernetic theory places major emphasis on the importance of *inherent* feedback. It should be remembered, however, that Lewin (of the cognitive group) did point out that human behavior was strongly influenced by internal factors, both past occurrences and goals for future accomplishment. The cybernetic concept differs in that it focuses on simultaneous feedback, primarily kinesthetic, which provides clues as to how one is performing. The concurrent information then serves as a "steering" influence for ongoing responses.

The term *servo-mechanism*, which refers to a machine that is controlled by the consequences of its own behavior, is frequently used to describe the cybernetic theory. Falling into this category are guided missiles, rockets, thermostats, and a multitude of computer controlled, self-correcting instruments. For example, an airplane placed on automatic pilot will be brought back on course each time it drifts off by the servo-mechanism built for that purpose. The term is now used prominently in human behavior to refer to a complex self-correcting system in the performance of routine motor activities.

Human activities requiring self-correcting movement behavior are abundant in sports skills as well as in work situations. For example, in balancing tasks, corrective responses are made prior to one's conscious awareness of being out of balance. People performing on a bongo board, a balance beam, or the performer on a tightrope make rapid responses to feedback regarding their balance. So do persons on a kayak, canoe, or bicycle. People on horseback, particularly a rodeo performer on a bucking bronco must be sensitive to feedback in order to make proper positioning adjustments. The individual who trips on a rug or slips on the ice immediately responds to correct his posture, and subsequently realizes that he almost fell. On other occasions, when tripped or pushed beyond the point of righting themselves, one makes preparatory adjustments for landing safely. Depending on one's predicament, these responses may include putting out the hands to break a fall, assuming a posture for the forward roll, or sliding on the backside. Likewise, the skilled wrestler responds suddenly to changes in pressure applied by an opponent. All such preparatory responses are "automatic" and are made possible because the individual receives information that warns of the necessity for rapid action.

Recognition of the importance of feedback in learning predates the development of cybernetics as an important concept. In fact, Wiener (1961) cites an article on feedback by Clerk Maxwell in 1868. Thorndike's classic line drawing experiment (1931) was a study of feedback. However, specific attention to information *processing* on the part of human beings is a more recent development.

The cybernetic theory evolved over the past 30 years after receiving some attention related to the military efforts of World War II. Research on guided missiles and the use of human beings to control complex machinery provided the initial impetus for this movement. In addition, the development of the computer during recent years has also added substance to this concept, since the computer, like man, is a complex information processing system.

Following World War II, the cybernetic theory was developed and refined by several researchers. In a 1948 book on cybernetics, Wiener described the information processing basis of human behavior. Hebb's (1949) neurophysiological analysis of learning and retention added further support for the concept. Smith (1962), perhaps more than any other person, established cybernetics as a credible notion in the area of motor behavior. His extensive research and publications rejected the stimulus-response concept of the individual as largely a captive of surrounding stimuli. His work emphasized the dynamic nature of the individual's behavior within the environment, illustrating the importance of feedback in shaping motor behavior. In addition, Adams' (1971) closed loop theory and Fitts' (1964) three models of behavior (communication, control, and composite) provide important definition to the cybernetic theory. A number of British researchers, especially Welford (1969), have been equally active in studying cybernetics.

In the cybernetic theory, the human being is perceived as a computer who organizes behavior into a hierarchical order. The individual "programs" routine, well-learned functions and relegates them to a lower subconscious level. The central processing, or control, unit then activates those responses at the appropriate time. These behaviors do not enter into the individual's realm of consciousness. They reach the "autonomous" level, as described by Fitts. Consequently, the cerebral processes are freed from such routine activities for the purpose of receiving and storing new information as well as establishing new programs. The upper levels in this hierarchy establish the plan of action for a particular performance. As described in chapter one, the lower levels of the human central nervous system carry out the motor routines. Minor adjustments or corrections are made automatically.

MOTOR LEARNING MODELS

During recent years, a great deal of study has been devoted to the mechanism by which the individual makes use of feedback to affect behavior. These efforts have been particularly evident in the area of motor skill behavior. Consequently, "models" have been developed by several authors to illustrate just how the individual receives information and how this information is processed, stored, and subsequently used in the performance of a multitude of functions. The models focus on the process of motor behavior from beginning to end. Although all such models are speculations at this time, many have received substantial indirect verification.

There is presently no physiological evidence that any one of the models of behavior is entirely accurate. Their validity, therefore, is based on a black box* concept of human activity. Models of various authors differ because of the range of methodology used in these investigations or simply because of different interpretations of the same responses.

Figure 3-1 represents the simplest and most universally held assumptions about the processes involved in the learning and performance of motor skills. Essentially all models agree on the three components included here. This is a *closed loop* system because the feedback is automatically returned to the learner as a natural product of the output, or behavior. On the other hand, an *open loop* system model would reflect no such feedback. The majority of models presented in the literature do illustrate a feedback mechanism (closed loop) because of the assumption that in the normal process of learning and performing motor skills, feedback is usually provided, unless systematically curtailed. Despite the diversity of models, little difference is expressed in the input and output phases, although some report in greater detail as to the nature of those functions.

The primary difference in schematic models of skill acquisition models is the area of processing and sorting information. Figures 3-2 though 3-5, which are presented over the next several pages, reveal fairly complex systems that give greater definition to the area of processing, storage, and the use of feedback. However, they do not disagree basically with the simpler version presented in Figure 3-1, nor

FIGURE 3-1.   Simplified model of a closed loop system of motor behavior.

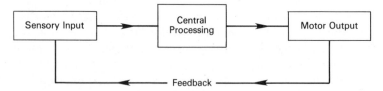

---

*In the black box approach to human behavior, a wide range of information (input) is presented and manipulated, while careful observation is made of the responses (output). Based on these observations (input and output relationships) inferences are drawn about the mechanisms *within* the black box (the central nervous system).

do they necessarily disagree with each other. Rather, they provide different interpretations of the processing mechanism.

One of the earliest models of skill learning was established by P. M. Fitts. In his model (Figure 3-2) the interacting components within the organism, the environment, and the "machine" are presented. The *internal* feedback mechanism (1-2-3-1) represents those simple processes that are relatively self-contained. Voice control in singing, combing one's hair, and brushing one's teeth are illustrative of this category of motor behavior. An *external* loop (1-2-3-4-1) engages the organism with the environment, which in turn influences subsequent behavior. For example, water in a pool, handball court dimensions, and gymnastic mats all represent environmental factors that give ongoing direction to one's performance. The *machine* loop (1-2-3-6-7-8-1) includes the organism with all interacting components. According to Fitts, this would include such items as the control mechanisms and gauges of an automobile. In sports or work situations, it would include equipment and apparatus that can be manipulated by the individual to interact with the environment in performing a task.

FIGURE 3-2.   Feedback loops involved in skilled motor performance. (From P. M. Fitts, "Factors in Complex Skill Training," *Training Research and Education,* ed. R. Glaser. University of Pittsburgh Press, 1962. John Wiley & Sons, N. Y., 1965. Used by persmission.)

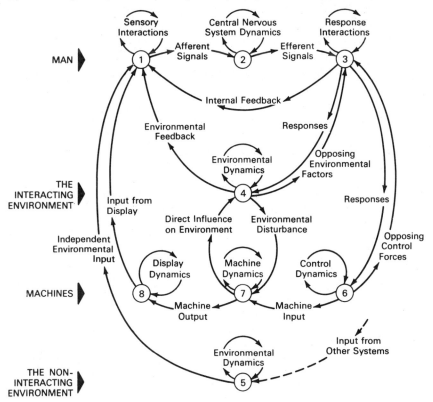

Stallings' model (see Figure 3-3) is reasonably similar to several schematic versions of skilled behavior that were developed during the 1970s. In addition to input, output, and feedback, this model is characterized by several other components. The *perceptual filter* enables the individual to screen the input on the basis of past experience. Although the sense organs are activated by a wide range of stimuli, we are conditioned to hear and see in certain ways. This "biased" observation is consistent with Levin's concept of "life space" and the gestalt figure-ground principle. When observed through the perceptual filter, our perception of stimuli is rarely limited to exactly that which is presented.

The *short-term store* accommodates the holding of information for a few seconds by the reverberation of impulses in neural nets. The short-term store is limited both in the length of time information can be held and in the amount that can be crowded in at one time. Information in the short-term store is lost within a few seconds unless put to use or rehearsed (a more thorough discussion of short-term memory is presented in chapter six).

The *limited concentration channel* represents the primary interpretive component of the model, including mechanisms for perceptual integration, translation of options, and planning for appropriate motor responses. This is the area concerned with cognitive processes related to performance. According to Stallings, the concentration channel is labeled *limited* to emphasize that the individual can concentrate on only one thing at a time. One who is asked to deal with two or more problems simultaneously is likely to become "overloaded" and consequently confused.

Memory refers to the mechanism by which the individual retains information or skills until time or circumstances call for initiating their use. In some models, this is referred to as *long-term store*. Knowledge or skills that have been experienced or practiced (therefore learned) are held in memory. As pointed out earlier, that which is held in memory influences both our perception (perceptual filter) and the choices or decisions for action (limited concentration channel) in turn.

FIGURE 3-3. Information Processing Model (From L. M. Stallings, *Motor Learning From Theory to Practice*. The C. V. Mosley Company, 1982. Used by permission.)

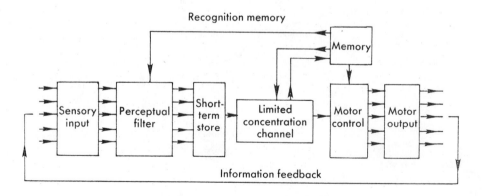

Once the sensory input has been processed and an action plan established, the _motor control_ mechanism is organized to command the muscles to perform the particular set of responses. This requires neuromuscular programming. Motor responses are often influenced by reflex mechanisms and conditioning. That is, after one has planned exactly what is to be done, previously established habits may make that performance difficult. In the Stallings model, motor control is influenced by closed loop, open loop, or goal directed mechanisms.

Welford's model (see Figure 3-4) reflects most of the same ingredients as that of Stallings', although it uses somewhat different terminology. Welford makes a clear distinction between categories of receptors as well as effectors, with the primary difference being whether or not the conscious control is involved in these processes. That is, some receptors, as well as some actions, are not within the general awareness of the individual. He also discusses at length the characteristics of short-term and long-term memory, and the distinction between them.

Gagné's model (see Figure 3-5) varies only slightly from those of Stallings and Welford. According to Gagné, learning begins with the intake of stimulation from the receptors and ends with the feedback that follows the learner's performance. To maximize skill acquisition, he encourages the instructor to provide a variety of external stimulation to precipitate several different processes of learning.

LEARNING THEORY TODAY

There are no longer serious attempts to develop elaborate, all-encompassing theories of learning. A few years ago, those interested in learning tended to choose sides and debate the major issues from opposing points of view. Although such arguments

FIGURE 3-4. Hypothetical Block Diagram of the Human Sensory-Motor System (From A. T. Welford, _Skilled Performance: Perceptual and Motor Skills._ Glenview, Ill.: Scott, Foresman, and Co., 1976. Used by permission.)

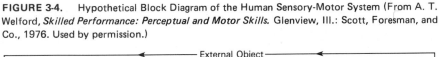
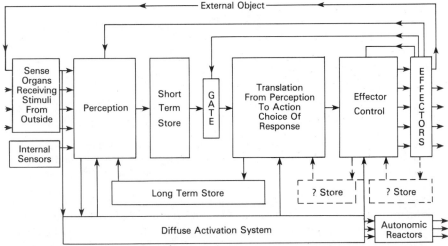

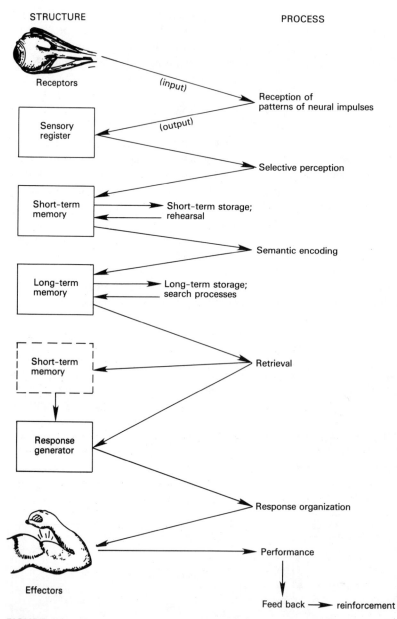

STRUCTURE   PROCESS

Receptors

(input)

Reception of
patterns of neural impulses

Sensory
register

(output)

Selective perception

Short-term
memory

Short-term storage;
rehearsal

Semantic encoding

Long-term
memory

Long-term storage;
search processes

Short-term
memory

Retrieval

Response
generator

Response organization

Effectors

Performance

Feed back ⟶ reinforcement

FIGURE 3-5. Processes of Learning and Memory as Inputs to and Outputs from Postulated Structures of the Information-Processing Model (From R. M. Gagné, *The Conditions of Learning,* 3rd ed., New York: Holt, Rinehart and Winston, 1977, p. 58. Used by permission.)

continue to exist, their prevalence in literature has declined. According to Deese (1958), there are several reasons for this change. For example, none of the current theories claims to answer all the questions about learning, so that there is no need to discuss the ultimate and exclusive correctness of one theory over another. In addition, detailed and specific answers are needed for learning problems, which are not solved by broad theoretical theses. Consequently, since no one position is able to answer all questions about learning, there is a need for a great many specialists, each of whom might contribute to the total field of knowledge.

In the area of motor behavior, the development of learning models has coincided with the decline of attention to the major theories. Interest in these models reflects a desire to explain the process of learning, as opposed to describing it from a behavioral position. Models are of both the closed loop and open loop type, the former assuming important uses of feedback as a part of one's behavior. While agreeing on the general nature of input, output, and feedback, there is substantial disagreement among researchers as to the nature of processing, storage, and use of feedback to influence ongoing or subsequent behavior. The move away from elaborate theoretical positions has also led to the popularization of the *functional* approach to learning. Functionalism is not particularly concerned with establishing broad theoretical interpretations, but emphasizes solving problems of interest to education. Functionalism assumes an eclectic position and has not been established as a major "theory" of learning.

Probably the majority of educational psychologists today would consider themselves functionalists. Their research has been conducted more frequently with human beings in a school setting than with rats or other animals in a laboratory. Functional theorists have been especially interested in investigating problems such as whole learning versus part learning, transfer of training, and reinforcement and practice distribution. As applied psychologists, they do not generalize far beyond the particular problem being investigated. In like manner, experimental psychology, which is directed toward the solution of specific problems., has become more popular within recent years. However, the problems investigated and the results obtained are not always clearly applicable to the classroom setting.

The functional approach has initiated research leading to the establishment of some principles of learning. Watson (1962) compiled a list of such established principles for the purpose of eliminating some of the confusion caused by the numerous learning theories. His list included fifty propositions "with which few knowledgeable psychologists of any school would disagree". These statements were established and organized into twelve areas important to education including learning process, maturation, individual differences, level of challenge, teaching method, discipline, and learning. In regard to these principles, Watson indicated that, "The educator who bases his program on these propositions . . . is entitled to feel that he is on solid psychological ground and not on shifting sands" (p. 4).

SUMMARY

1. Learning theories and models make statements about how and why learning takes place. Theories are more traditional and represent a broad and coherent group of general principles to explain learning. They are designed to synthesize all

available knowledge about learning. A model is a statement that illustrates (often graphically) the relationship of events leading to the acquisition of skills or knowledge. In addition, a model provides a framework that facilitates the testing of theories or hypotheses.

2. Familiarity with the major theoretical positions enables the teacher to bring consistency to the instructional program. Confusion and uncertainty in teaching techniques often result when instructors are unacquainted with the basic theoretical positions upon which those techniques are based.

3. Major learning theories address the issues of human capacities, the role of motivation, practice and insight in learning, and the processes of transfer and retention. Theorists differ on the degree of emphasis devoted to each of these topics.

4. Major learning theories are categorized into stimulus-response and cognitive areas. In addition, cybernetic and information theories have received wide recognition in recent years.

5. Though rooted in earlier centuries, the stimulus-response theories were developed and refined in the United States during the first half of the 20th century. The S-R theory is based on the concept that learning involves the development of connections or bonds between specific stimuli and responses. General behaviors are established by developing a great number of S-R connections through association, contiguity, reinforcement, or the pleasure-pain principle. Stimuli connected with bodily responses are referred to as motor bonds. Learning involves the development of new bonds and organizing them into systems, which in turn leads to knowledge, behavior, and a personality for the individual.

6. The major concepts included in Thorndike's correctionism, Guthrie's contiguity theory, Hull's reinforcement theory, and Skinner's operant conditioning are discussed within the stimulus-response category.

7. Cognitive learning theories are based on the assumption that the learner organizes stimuli or his perceptions into a pattern or whole and is not limited to specific S-R connections. Cognitive theorists do not believe that stimuli from the environment are discrete and independent from each other. Rather, all things derive their character from their relationship to other things. All stimuli are observed against a background, or field. The concept of insight is a major tenant of the cognitive theory.

8. The general concepts and specific contributions of the gestalt psychologists, Tolman's sign-gestalt theory, and Lewin's field theory are discussed, with emphasis on implications for motor learning.

9. Several efforts have been made to synthesize or to point out the common elements of the S-R and the cognitive theories. Such reports have usually concluded that all major theorists agree on the importance of motivation on the part of the learner, the necessity of activity and reinforcement, a gradual (or sudden) recognition of the appropriate responses, and recognized variations in improvement.

10. The cybernetic theory is a recently developed concept based on the idea that feedback received during performance influences ongoing behavior in a particular task. Concurring information serves as a steering influence for subsequent responses. Having its origins in the complex mechanism of World War II, the cybernetic theory has been additionally stimulated by recent advances in computer technology. Human beings are viewed as analogous to computers in terms of processing and using information. Further, people have the ability to "program" routine or well-learned skills and relegate them to a subconscious level.

11. Several motor learning models are illustrated and discussed. All such models include sensory input, central processing, and motor output. Closed loop models include a mechanism for feedback whereas open loop models have no such provision. The various models differ primarily in the area of central processing as well as in memory storage and processing.

12. In recent years the trend has been away from the development of major learning theories in the S-R or cognitive contexts. Rather, a functional or specific problem-solving approach is most often used today.

SELECTED READINGS

GAGNÉ, R. M. *The conditions of learning* (3rd ed.). New York: Holt, Rinehart and Winston, 1977.

GUTHRIE, E. R. *The psychology of learning* (rev. ed.). New York: Harper & Row, 1952.

HILGARD, E. R. *Theories of learning* (2nd ed.). New York: Appleton-Century-Crofts, 1956.

HILGARD, E. R., & BOWER, G. H. *Theories of learning* (2nd ed.). New York: Appleton-Century-Crofts, 1966.

HULL, C. L. *Principles of behavior.* New York: Appleton-Century-Crofts, 1943.

KÖHLER, W. *Gestalt psychology.* New York: Liveright, 1947.

LEWIN, K. *Principles of topological psychology.* trans. F. Heider & G. M. Heider. New York: McGraw-Hill, 1936.

MARTENIUK, R. G. *Information processing in motor skills.* New York: Holt, Rinehart and Winston, 1976.

SINGER, R. N. *Motor learning and human performance* (3rd ed.). New York: Macmillan Publishing Co., Inc. 1980.

SKINNER, B. F. The behavior of organisms: an experimental analysis. New York: Appleton-Century-Crofts, 1938.

STALLINGS, L. M. *Motor skills: development and learning.* Wm. Brown Co., 1973.

THORNDIKE, E. L. *Selected writings from a connectionist's psychology.* New York: Appleton-Century-Crofts, 1949.

TOLMAN, E. C. Theories of learning. In F. A. Moss (Ed.), *Comparative Psychology.* Englewood Cliffs, N. J.: Prentice-Hall, Inc., 1934.

WATSON, G. What psychology can we feel sure about? In W.C. Morse & G. M. Wingo (Eds.), *Readings in educational psychology,* pp. 3-7. Chicago: Scott, Foresman, 1962.

WELFORD, A. T. *Skilled performance: perceptual and motor skills.* Glenview, Ill.: Scott, Foresman and Co., 1976.

Part II: The Learning Process

4 Reinforcement and Feedback

INTRODUCTION

The process of learning has been perhaps the most intriguing of all phenomena related to education. A great deal of inquiry, therefore, has been devoted to the problem of determining the *nature* of the learning process. Only one who thoroughly understands this process can effectively promote learning in the variety of situations required.

The effective teacher must be able to diagnose learning problems in much the same manner as a physician or a skilled auto mechanic. Simply being able to perform a given task does not insure success in teaching it. Nor does mastering of a stereotyped teaching methodology that has been observed to be successful on former occasions. In order to meet the instructional needs of learners at different levels of maturity or at different stages in the learning process, or of those who are encountering diverse learning difficulties, it is essential that the instructor have a thorough understanding of how learning takes place.

Most authorities agree that the effective provision of information about performance, along with timely rewards, represents the vital key in the management of learning. From the time of Thorndike's law of effect to more recent reports on information theory, it is probable that no topic in the area of learning psychology has been of greater interest or more thoroughly investigated. Teachers who hope to be effective must become familiar with the concept of reinforcement and also skillful in providing information to learners about their progress.

Though having clearly different meanings, the terms *reinforcement* and *feedback* are so interrelated in present usage that it seems useful to deal with them in the same general discussion. Knowledge of results and reward are frequently used interchangeably with these terms and consequently will also be dealt with in this chapter.

Reinforcement refers to any condition that, if it follows a response, increases the probability that the same response will recur on subsequent occasions when similar stimuli are presented. Reinforcement comes in many forms, including such occurrences as the provision of food pellets to the laboratory animal after it depresses the appropriate lever, the awarding of a gold star to the second-grade child upon the completion of a reading exercise, or observation of the curving baseball by the young pitcher after having executed the newly taught finger-wrist snap during the delivery. In the last case, the particular finger-wrist response is reinforced by the observed curving of the baseball. Consequently, this behavior will most likely be remembered and repeated in subsequent situations when attempting to throw a curve ball. Similarly, the activity of the laboratory animal and the second-grade child are reinforced. That is, the food pellet and the gold star increase the likelihood of the same response on subsequent occasions when the same situation is presented.

Some reinforcement involves a "reward" of some type. The reward may vary from a tangible item, such as the pellet of food for an animal to the satisfying feeling upon the realization of success, as with the young baseball pitcher. Other reinforcement may be based upon information about the quality or quantity of particular behavior. For example, the baseball pitcher may find that a more vigorous snap at the release of the ball results in a more effective curve than does a more casual release. Such a discovery will reinforce the more forceful response when circumstances demand it. Since the control of information and the management of rewards are both such vital factors in learning effectiveness, and since both possibilities are available in the school setting, both will be discussed extensively in this chapter.

An understanding of the concepts of reinforcement and feedback along with some skill in effectively using them in a teaching situation is essential for teachers in all subject areas. Teachers of motor skills, however, can often make more direct and obvious application of reinforcement and feedback than can other teachers. This is because responses in motor skills are often more easily isolated and observed and, therefore, reinforced. Any lack of understanding of the concept of reinforcement, or lack of skill in its use, will seriously limit the effectiveness of those who seek to guide learning experiences. In this chapter, the strategic role of reinforcement in various types of learning experiences will be discussed with special attention devoted to its use in motor learning.

The meaning of terms

The terms *reinforcement, feedback, reward, knowledge of results,* and *knowledge of performance* are frequently used interchangeably. At times each of these terms appear to represent approximately the same occurrence or circumstance. At other times, they reflect widely different meanings.

With reference to factors that influence learning, *reinforcement* is the more traditional, and perhaps most inclusive, term in the area of learning psychology. As stated earlier, it refers to *any* condition that increases the probability of a given response occurring on subsequent occasions. Consequently, when any of the terms listed above (feedback, reward, etc.), enhances a particular response, it serves as a reinforcer. According to Travers (1977), feedback "falls into the category of events known as reinforcers, because it modifies the probability that a particular behavior will be repeated or inhibited on subsequent occasions" (p. 45). However, there are times when some of these factors may not be related to any specific behavior and are, therefore, not reinforcers.

Reinforcement may take many forms and may be described in many ways. The learner need not even be aware of its existence. It need not be a "reward" in the traditional sense, nor must it provide any information about the quality of a particular response. The story is told of the psychology professor whose students schemed to drive him out of the classroom through reinforcement. On the appointed day, as the professor paced back and forth across the room, all students, by prior agreement, commenced to reinforce those movements that took him closer to the door while providing negative behavior whenever he moved in the direction away from the door. That is, each time the professor took a step in the general direction of the door, all students gave the impression of great interest in the lecture, taking copious notes, leaning forward in their seats, appearing very studious, and "hanging on his every word." On the other hand, when he walked in the direction away from the door, students visibly lost interest, shifting their seats, looking around the room, yawning, looking at their watches, and exhibiting other distracting behavior. Further, the closer the professor approached the door, the more intense was the "scholarly" behavior, while the further he moved away from the door, the greater were the verbal and nonverbal distractors. Eventually the professor was found to be standing outside the room and leaning in to deliver his lecture. Without his knowledge, subtle student behaviors had effectively reinforced his actions leading to a particular goal.

Feedback refers to one's receipt of knowledge about a particular act or response. Bilodeau (1966) list "information," "reinforcing," and "psychological" as descriptive terms of feedback that have been used by one or more authors to define the different dimensions of this phenomenon. In this discussion, *information feedback* (IF) will be used to emphasize the informational nature of feedback. Bourne (1966) defines information feedback as a "signal occurring after or at the time of response, providing an indication of the correctness, accuracy, or adequacy of that response" (p. 299). As indicated by Travers, IF serves as a type of reinforcer. Reinforcement, however, is a broader term that includes circumstances in which no specific information is provided relative to the nature of the response. For example, the pellet of food for the laboratory animal would reinforce the pedal pushing behavior but may not provide any information about the quality of the response that will aid in subsequent modifications of the behavior. On the other hand, the pitcher who notices that a difference in the wrist snap results in a difference in the curve of the ball is receiving IF that results in a modification of that response.

Knowledge of results (usually referred to as KR in the research literature) has been used traditionally in much the same way as information feedback. Dukelow (1979) defines KR as "feedback which provides information about the degree of success in achieving the desired end product of a task performance." However, several authors, including Magill (1980), Schmidt (1975), and Bilodeau (1956), urge that KR be considered as that information about a response obtainable only from an *outside* source. This meaning has recently emerged to distinguish KR from the term *feedback*, often used in reference to *internal* information that the learner can sense himself. However, such a distinction has not yet gained universal acceptance. In this discussion, KR will be used to refer to all (externally provided as well as inherent) information about the performance. Dukelow has distinguished between KR and "knowledge of performance" (KP), with the former referring to an objective indication of one's success in achieving a desired goal and the latter referring to information about movement or form, i.e., temporal or spatial coordination of body parts.

In the management of learning, the term *reward* is probably even more obtuse than either of the related concepts referred to earlier. Although rewards occasionally do serve as reinforcers, this is not always so. For example, an athlete might be "rewarded" at the end of a practice period by praise from the coach, promotion to the first team, or favorable comments by teammates. Though stimulating, this type of reward would probably not strengthen any particular motor response. The performer probably does not know specifically which acts led to the reward. Therefore, no connection is made between motor response and reward. Rather, the player is likely to associate the reward to overall effort for the day and be motivated to duplicate that performance on subsequent practice days. For a longer period of time, perhaps for a full playing season, the performer may win prizes, all-star selections, or other forms of recognition. Although these recognitions are generally rewarding, they are of little value in strengthening particular stimulus-response relationships.

The use of punishment as a means of reinforcement is equally vague and, therefore, often ineffective. It is true that some types of punishment, or reward, if immediately and clearly connected to particular responses, do serve as reinforcement. But such a connection is frequently not the case. For example, the field goal kicker in football might be "punished" by jeers from spectators, criticism from the coach, or removal from the starting lineup. There is no assurance in these cases that the player forms a connection between punishment and the specific response that led to failure, perhaps the tendency to look up prior to the foot making contact with the ball. The lack of specificity in the usual administration of rewards and punishment makes them of little value in reinforcing learning.

Reinforcement does not always result in reward or punishment as the terms are generally used. While there may be a degree of satisfaction with the realization of success, and dissatisfaction with failure, these impressions are often too subtle to be viewed as rewards or punishment. Yet they do tend to reinforce related actions. An example of this might be seen when the novice soccer player learns to "give" with the body to more effectively trap the ball. Although there is some satisfaction in the successful performance of this act, the major result is not a reward in the traditional sense, but a reinforcement of the correct body action. In other situations, an act might lead to failure, which is a type of punishment. Nevertheless, the usual understanding of reward and punishment is not limited to the types of associations that reinforce learning.

Teachers use reinforcement techniques to change the response *probability* of a particular act. It may be desirable to increase the act's probability or, on occasion, to decrease the likelihood that the act will recur. All responses have a certain probability of occurring in a given set of circumstances. A particular eighth grader, for example, might be expected to serve a volleyball into the opposing court area 50 percent of the time, to make basketball free throws 30 percent of the time, or to throw a baseball into the target area 40 percent of the time. The teacher's aim is to increase the probability of success in each action to as near 100 percent as possible. This might be done by reinforcing the desired responses or even the intermediate improvements that might lead to the correct responses.

Repetition of the desired responses with related reinforcement tends to form a strong habit. Athletic coaches and physical education teachers are interested in students acquiring the correct responses so well that they are done automatically, without conscious thought.

Similarly, teachers of industrial arts or home economics and supervisors in numerous industrial jobs seek to teach motor skills in order to increase the probability of correct performance each time. Such a high level of probability is reached by repetition, or practice, which is reinforced by appropriate feedback or reward.

On occasion, the teacher wishes to *reduce* the probability that a particular response will occur. For example, an eighth grader might have a high probability of looking away from the volleyball before hitting it, of jumping off the wrong foot when shooting a basketball, or of looking at the ground just before throwing the baseball. A player might also have a high probability of arguing with the referee on all fouls called. The teacher's primary concern in such cases is to reduce the probability of these undesirable responses. Here too, the manipulation of reinforcers will be helpful. This might be accomplished by rewarding the more appropriate responses and removing all reinforcers from the undesirable behavior, or even "punishing" those behaviors.

REINFORCEMENT

Origin of the reinforcement concept

The term reinforcement was first used in connection with learning at the beginning of the 20th century. Reinforcement was closely associated with the idea of contiguity, i.e., any two ideas or concepts that were seen together in time or space would be connected. More recently, psychologists have concluded that contiguity alone does not insure a mental connection. Rather, the stimulus and the appropriate response must be related in some way to insure learning. Reinforcement is seen as the key to this connection.

Pavlov's stimulation substititon.   Ivan P. Pavlov's (1927) well-known conditioning experiments with dogs, conducted in the late 19th and early 20th centuries, led to the development of the earliest reinforcement theories, which were based on the concept of temporal contiguity. In Pavlov's experiments, a dog was placed in a soundproof room. Attachments were made to the animal's parotid salivary gland so the amount of salivation could be observed. It was noted that the sight, smell, and touch of food resulted in observable salivation. In the conditioning program, a tuning fork was sounded and food was then presented to the dog. Several sessions were held in which the sound of the tuning fork was always followed by the food. Later, the sound of the tuning fork alone resulted in salivation by the animal. The tuning fork had acquired the capacity for eliciting a salivary response because of its customary temporal contiguity to the food. Pavlov referred to the food as the unconditioned stimulus and the tuning fork as the conditioned stimulus.

Woodworth and Schlosberg (1963) interpreted Pavlov's first law as: "The occurrence of an unconditional reflex in temporal contiguity with a conditional reflex increases the strength of the latter" (p. 542). The second law is suggested as: "If a conditioned reflex is elicited without reinforcement by an unconditional reflex, the conditional reflex is weakened or inactivated" (p. 543). According to Pavlov's theory of reinforcement, conditioning is aided by reward (food), which tends to connect two stimuli. He assumed that without reinforcement, conditioning would not have taken place so effectively.

Thorndike's law of effect.   A concept similar to Pavlov's was E. L. Thorndike's law of effect. His theory was based primarily on the belief that the effect of the response was strategic for reinforcement. In *The Psychology of Learning*, published in 1913, Thorndike states:

> The Law of Effect is: When a modifiable connection between a situation and a response is made and is accompanied or followed by a satisfying state of affairs, that connection's strength is increased: when made and accompanied or followed by an annoying state of affairs, its strength is decreased. The strengthening effect of satisfyingness (or the weakening effect of annoyingness) upon a bond varies with the closeness of the connection between it and the bond. This closeness or intimacy of association of the satisfying (or annoying) state of affairs with the bond in question may be the result of nearness in time or of attentiveness to the situation, response and satisfying event in question (p. 4).[1]

His principle of reinforcement referred to any kind of reward or punishment that was instrumental in learning. This statement reflects the basic premise of reinforcement, although today the concept is not restricted to specific responses to isolated stimuli but is used more broadly.

Hull's drive reduction.   C. L. Hull stated that any stimulus-response sequence followed by a lessening of the strength of the drive will be reinforced. This is consistent with his reinforcement theory of learning, which indicated that learning takes place to the extent that a particular need is reduced. Such a need is

[1] E. L. Thorndike, *Educational psychology*, vol. 2. *The psychology of learning.* New York: Teachers College, 1913. Used by persmission.

connected to a particular drive, which may be either primary or secondary, biological or social. The value of the stimulus-response sequence as a reinforcer depends upon the strength of the relative drive. Hull emphasized that need-reducing reinforcement is advantageous to both learning and performance. In his later writing, he placed primary importance on reinforcement for improvement in performance. Thus, the attention-seeking child who disrupts the class and becomes its center of attention may be reducing a personal need for recognition. The reinforcement (need reduction) strengthens the tendency of the child to resort to similar behavior the next time this need occurs. An extension of this concept occurs on the athletic field, when social needs may enable young athletes to practice long and play hard in games even in conditions of boredom and fatigue.

Skinner's operant conditioning.   B. F. Skinner founded his theory of operant conditioning upon the concept of reinforcement. His work has contributed a great deal toward a broader understanding of reinforcement. A discussion of operant conditioning seems important to illustrate how much reinforcement may be used in controlling learning.

Skinner identified two types of behavior, *respondent* and *emitted.* His explanation of respondent behavior is much the same as the earlier theorists', i.e., particular behavior is the result of a particular stimulus. An eye blink resulting from a sharp noise, or a knee jerk are examples of Skinner's respondent behavior. Skinner differs from other theorists, however, in his discussion of emitted behavior. He describes emitted behaviors as those prompted by the individual that are not responses to any identifiable stimuli. Skinner, who suggested that most human actions are emitted, referred to these unsolicited behaviors as *operants.* He has seriously questioned much that was previously assumed to be responsive behavior in a cause-and-effect way. There is no reason, for example, why a speech causes applause at its end. Nor does a lecture cause note-taking by students. Certainly, a close play at second base does not cause the runner to slide. A zone defense in basketball does not cause the opposing team to use short, quick passes. According to Skinner, these behaviors are used because they have been rewarded in past situations.

Skinner stated that respondent behavior is not only very infrequent but is usually rather trivial. Since he feels that operant behavior is more frequent and more important, Skinner has devoted most of his attention to technique for shaping emitted behavior by rewarding (reinforcing) desired operants and punishing undesired behavior. The learner makes a connection between the response and the reinforcement to develop most skills, knowledges, and attitudes.

There is considerable evidence to show that whatever the individual is doing at the time of drive reduction will be reinforced, even if that behavior is incidental. Head scratching by a chimpanzee has been reinforced when it happened to be the animal's activity at feeding time. Most superstitions probably have developed in this way. Farming practices, such as planting corn "by the moon," are apparently based on accidental successes that earlier farmers had when using that method. The connection between moon position and successful farming has generally been lost because it was not consistently reinforced. For more superstitious individuals, however, even occasional reinforcement is sufficient to "prove" a connection.

Athletes tend to remember odd happenings or conditions that were present at success or failure. These "signs" are often trivial, such as the wearing of colored shoelaces, failure to shave, or having good luck charms. Nevertheless, reinforcement of these details leads to strong associations that stimulate great efforts to repeat "lucky" details and avoid "jinxed" ones.

Partial reinforcement or feedback

It would be unusual in everyday or school situations for reinforcement to be administered every time the correct response is given. Occasional or partial reinforcement is more often the rule. For example, the well-behaved first-grade child is not always noticed and commended by the teacher. A solid smash in baseball does not always result in a safe hit. Sometimes the opposing players catch the hardest hit line drives. The well-executed fake maneuver in sports does not always fool the opposition. So it is in other areas. The professional gambler does not win on every try. The hound does not catch the rabbit in every chase. The cat catches the mouse only sometimes.

Partial or occasional reinforcement may still be sufficient to keep the learner interested and working at the task. Humphreys (1936), for example, showed that reinforcement that was administered 50 percent of the time was practically as effective as reinforcement 100 percent of the time. Teachers should keep in mind, therefore, that reinforcement may be effective even if it is not given every time the response is emitted.

Retention is greatly affected by the regularity with which reinforcement has been administered during the learning period. Forgetting, or extinction, is much slower when the response has been only partially reinforced. Laboratory experiments show that animals that have followed a partial reinforcement schedule show greater perseverance in a particular response than animals that have been reinforced after every response. In fact, once a response has been learned, the more infrequent the reinforcement was during learning, the more difficult is the response's extinction. The performer who anticipates only occasional success will persist much longer than one who is used to absolute success. The gambler, for example, will continue his pursuits with greater expectations of success even after a series of responses has not been reinforced.

Habits that have been developed with partial reinforcement certainly seem more difficult to break than habits learned under full reinforcement conditions. The value of persistence, however, must be weighed against the value of speed of learning. Most authorities agree that learning takes place faster under conditions of very frequent reinforcement. For maximum learning *and* retention, the evidence seems to suggest a progressive decrease in the frequency of reinforcement, i.e., very frequent reinforcement in early stages of the learning process and less frequent reinforcement later.

Greater persistance resulting from partial reinforcement may apply to one's enthusaism for an activity as well as for learning. Perhaps this is why early maturing children who are star performers at the preteenage level appear more easily disillusioned when they get into more difficult competitions and occasionally experience failure. In comparison, children who are not in the habit of winning all the time seem less dependent upon the reward of winning.

Schedules of reinforcement.   Most typical schedules of partial reinforcement are based on the *number of responses* the learner must make or the *period of time* that must elapse between reinforcers. Travers (1977) has described four types of schedules for partial reinforcement using these two dimensions. The first is the *fixed-ratio* schedule, in which the individual is reinforced for an established amount of work. Fixed ratios operate as merit rewards based on what the subject has done. For example, a rat would receive a pellet of food for depressing a bar five times, and a child might receive a reinforcement after swimming each lap in the pool. "Piece work" in industry, where the individual receives payment for so many units of work, is another example of the fixed-ratio schedule. This schedule has been found valuable in keeping the individual interested in performing in a purposeful way. Because of its emphasis on maximum achievement, fixed ratios are widely applicable to the teaching of motor skills.

A *variable-ratio* schedule is one in which not all responses are reinforced and there exists uncertainty on the part of the learner as to when reinforcement will occur. For example, if it is determined that one-third of all responses are to be reinforced, then a random or unpredictable schedule must be established so that, on the average, one out of three responses is reinforced. Such a practice is commonplace in everyday work situations and in school settings. Skills or habits developed under these conditions are particularly resistive to forgetting.

The third form of partial reinforcement is the *fixed-interval* technique, in which the individual is reinforced according to a time schedule as long as work continues. Such a schedule is used in the laboratory when the animal is rewarded at regular intervals. The same system might be used for reinforcing the child who continues to swim or the worker who is receiving an hourly rate. Most industrial work uses the system of payment by the hour, week, or year. The technique is effective in keeping the individual active during the prescribed period, but it does not assure purposeful or enthusiastic participation. Because it does not emphasize maximum effort, the fixed-interval technique has not proven effective in sports activity or physical education.

Travers' fourth type of partial reinforcement is the *variable-interval* technique, which rewards the individual at irregular and unpredictable time intervals. This type of reinforcement is typical of many everyday situations. Variable-interval reinforcement has some weaknesses in promoting fast learning because the individual does not as quickly make the connection between the response and the reward. On the other hand, it has the advantage of developing behavior that is very resistive to extinction. One who realizes that reward could come at any time is more likely to persevere in that particular behavior. Variable-interval reinforcement comes naturally in many sports activities. This irregular schedule is also the type most often used by teachers in the administration of verbal reinforcement.

INFORMATION FEEDBACK

Information feedback (IF) is the provision of some signal to indicate the correctness, accuracy, or adequacy of a response or behavior. As such, IF is a widely used and very valuable type of reinforcement for learning and performance. It is a type of reinforcement that is based on information the individual can use to check or confirm the quality of performance. This information is valuable not only because of the data provided but because it often tends to motivate one to continue work on the task. Performance in any task is more meaningful when the learner is aware of progress.

Current thinking about IF has been greatly influenced by the development of the cybernetic or information theory over the past three decades. (This concept was discussed in chapter three.) Prior to the middle of the 20th century, most concerns about feedback were centered around the KR concept of externally provided information. Recently, information theory has focused attention on sensory information, particularly that which is provided by proprioceptors in muscles, joints, and tendons. The processing and translating of such information is particularly important in complex movement activities.

Authorities have long recognized that the learner improves more if *specific* information about the relationship of performance to goal is received. Students often seek this information even if they are not aware of any learning advantages. For example, they are not always satisfied with a simple letter grade, pass or fail rating, or even "better" or "poorer." They will often ask, "How far did I miss?" "*How* was the performance weak?" "In what way was it better?" "Which questions did I get right and which did I get wrong?" Even though these inquiries may be a source of annoyance to some teachers, they are often more than expressions of idle curiosity by the student. Answers to them can be instrumental in helping the student do better in future attempts.

People do not learn effectively, and perhaps not at all, without some sort of feedback. With no indication of how their performance compares with a desirable standard, they have no point of reference. Therefore, they would have no reason for altering their performance, or for that matter, continuing in the same manner. Without feedback they are essentially operating in the dark. This was, in fact, the technique used by Thorndike (1931) in his classic experiment to determine the effect of feedback on subsequent performances. In this experiment, students made 3,000 attempts to draw a four-inch line while blindfolded. During their practice, they were not told how closely their drawing approximated four inches. The 3,000 trials were organized into 12 sittings. It can be noted in Table 4-1 that although the performances varied, there was no general trend toward improvement. That is, the drawings in the later sittings were no better than those in the early sittings.

TABLE 4-1.   Distribution of the Responses of Each Sitting in Drawing Lines to Equal 4″ with Eyes Closed: Subject T.

Response	Frequencies in Sittings 1 to 12											
	1	2	3	4	5	6	7	8	9	10	11	12
3.7										1		
3.8									2			
3.9												
4.0			3						3			
4.1			4	1				1	3			2
4.2		4	8			1		3	6	1	2	1
4.3		3	9	1				4	5	3		4
4.4		13	12	6			3	4	12	2	4	3
4.5	3	18	18	14	2	7	3	15	14	8	7	11
4.6		20	23	23	3	7	8	13	14	8	14	11
4.7	6	20	14	22	11	14	16	25	13	9	14	21
4.8	6	22	15	18	14	27	17	16	18	15	19	26
4.9	13	17	24	24	22	28	18	21	16	10	18	30
5.0	25	20	16	24	26	21	29	25	14	24	19	20
5.1	27	10	16	12	25	32	14	15	14	22	31	22
5.2	24	11	8	12	24	21	23	25	16	18	28	16
5.3	30	8	2	11	21	13	17	8	18	18	16	12
5.4	17	4	2	8	10	10	7	8	12	12	7	7
5.5	12	1		4	13	8	7	3	10	13	4	3
5.6	7			2	4	7	4	1	4	5	2	2
5.7	3			1	4	2	5	2	6	4	3	1
5.8					1				1	2		
5.9	1				1					1	2	
6.0												
6.1									1			
6.2	1						1					
Total	175	171	174	183	181	198	172	192	200	175	190	192
Median	5.23	4.83	4.77	4.93	5.15	5.07	5.07	4.96	4.97	5.13	5.09	4.96
Q*	.16	.22	.23	.22	.19	.19	.21	.24	.33	.24	.21	.20

*Q is the half of the range required to include the middle 50 percent of the responses. From Thorndike, 1931, p. 9.

Kingsley (1957) conducted a similar experiment in which a group of students was asked to draw a four-inch line 400 times while the eyes were closed. This group (A_1 in Table 4-2) showed no improvement from the beginning to the end of the experiment, i.e., their percentage of error from four inches did not decrease. Following this experiment the same group (A_2) was asked to make four more attempts, and after each drawing, they opened their eyes and placed a four-inch strip of cardboard along the line they had just drawn. Table 4-2 reveals the dramatic improvement made by the group over the next four trials under these feedback conditions. (It should be noted that prior to the first trial no KR had been provided, so no percentage improvement was exhibited as compared with the first 400 trials). Another group (B) drew the lines under the same conditions as A_2, without having the benefit of the 400 trials without KR. Results were similar. A third group

TABLE 4-2.   Responses to a four-inch drawing task with the eyes closed,
under conditions of no KR, visual KR, and auditory KR.

Group . . . . A_1	A_2	B	C
Check. . . . . None	Visual	Visual	Auditory
Number of subjects. 7	7	14	15
Mean scores			
1st trial 16.1	21.4	21.6	22.0
5th trial. 15.9	2.9	6.2	6.7
10th trial. 11.4	2.7	4.4	4.1
15th trial. 13.0	4.7	3.1	5.3
20th trial. 17.3	2.2	2.0	3.7

From Kingsley, p. 257.

(C) performed four trials and were informed by the experimenter of the extent of their error. This group performed slightly more poorly than did the visual KR groups. Kingsley concluded that visual KR is slightly more advantageous than auditory KR in this task.

Without feeedback of any sort, it is unlikely that any learning will take place. A *change* in behavior can take place, but whether this change is in the desirable or undesirable direction is almost accidental. One can develop greater consistency in response but there is no assurance that the consistent response will be more accurate than initial responses. Such consistency may be in drawing a four-inch line, doing a plié in classical ballet, or swinging a golf club. The result may be a consistently *poor* response.

After a skill has been well developed, it may be retained without external feedback. In fact, the skilled or experienced performer is usually more sensitive to the reception of internal feedback than is the novice. Such an individual can more skillfully interpret subtle cues that give evidence of success. At this point the provision of feedback on a regular basis is no longer necessary.

Types of feedback

Information feedback may be provided in many forms. Consequently, it can be defined on the basis of the type of information received, the timing of that information, the senses receiving the information, the source of the information, and perhaps other factors. Dukelow (1979) has classified IF according to several of these performances (see Table 4-3).

Although authors differ to some extent on the terminology assigned to various forms of IF, the following terms are quite widely used in describing this phenomenon.

Intrinsic, or inherent, feedback is information that is provided as a natural result of performing the task. This information may be provided through any one of the senses or a combination of them. In some motor tasks a great deal of feedback is an inherent part of the performance. Archery, bowling, basketball, shooting, or serving a tennis ball are activities in which the effectiveness of the performance is

TABLE 4-3.   Classification of Information Feedback

Parameter	Classification Terms	
Type of Information	Knowledge of Results	Knowledge of Performance
Sense Modalities Receiving Information	Introspection	Exteroceptive
Time of Reception of Information	Concurrent	Terminal
Source of information	Inherent	Augmented

From Dukelow 1979, p. 19.

obvious to the individual, although the reason for that result may not be so clear. Dance, gymnastics, and diving are activities in which intrinsic feedback is far from adequate, especially in the early stages of learning the skill.

Intrinsic feedback may be further delineated as *reactive* (feedback that is produced by movement) and *operational* (information resulting from the effect of movement on the environment). Thus reactive feedback would include the kinesthetic sensations produced in bowling as the individual strides forward, takes the backswing, and delivers the ball. Operational feedback occurs as one observes the ball move down the lane and knock down a given number of pins.

Extrinsic, or augmented, feedback is that which is provided by an outside source. That source may be a teacher, coach, classmate, or a nonhuman mechanism, such as a videotape or a sound system (buzzer or bell) to indicate success or failure. The provision of augmented feedback is particularly important to those motor activities in which definitive information is not obvious to the performer, e.g., springboard diving or a cartwheel. Even in skills such as archery or bowling, augmented feedback is important to inform the learner of the *reasons* for success or failure. Augmented feedback may come in the form of verbal information, either oral or written, or it may be nonverbal, such as timers, distance indicators, buzzers, or via any of the other senses.

IF is often described according to the timing with which it is received by the learner. Consequently, *concurrent feedback* refers to information that is received simultaneously with the performance. *Terminal feedback* is provided at or following the conclusion of the performance. Concurrent feedback is most frequently provided by the kinesthetic sense. The experienced diver or the gymnast receives both kinesthetic and visual cues as to performance quality prior to receiving a rating from the judges. The "feel" of the tennis ball against the outside of the racquet or the baseball that is hit "on the handle" provides the performer with concurrent feedback of a poor stroke. In work situations, efficiency in tracking tasks such as driving, sewing, or using a skill saw is dependent upon the use of concurrent feedback. Many nontracking skills, such as welding, painting, and sanding are dependent upon both concurrent and terminal feedback. For example, the student driver receives concurrent information while operating the vehicle (observing the car's relationship to the center line and curves) and then also receives terminal feedback (perhaps in the form of a grade from the instructor) at the conclusion of the performance. In this situation, the learner would receive both verbal and nonverbal feedback.

Specificity of information feedback

To be most effective, feedback must be meaningful to the learner and specific in nature. In an early line drawing experiment (1932), Trowbridge and Cason showed that the value of feedback is clearly related to the precision of the information provided (see Figure 4-1). Groups given no KR or irrelevant KR (nonsense syllables) did not improve consistently. The group given qualitative feedback (right or wrong) did improve, but the group receiving more specific information (*how* short or *how* long) clearly performed best.

Salmoni (1980) had groups of third-grade students draw a 10 cm line, with one group receiving qualitative information (right or wrong) and two other groups receiving quantitative information (either the length of the line or the cms too long or too short). The groups receiving more specific quantitative information performed better than the group receiving qualitative KR.

There appears to be a limit on the amount of precision that one can process and use when learning motor skills. In a study involving junior high school boys, Bennett, Vincent, and Johnson (1979) showed a curvilinear relationship between the precision of IF and the amount of learning. Some degree of precision was helpful, but beyond a certain point there was no advantage in additional information. Subjects practiced 30-second trials on the pursuit rotor while receiving (1) no feedback (control group), (2) a two-point grading scale (pass-fail), (3) a five-point

FIGURE 4-1.   Performance Curves on a Line-Drawing Task for Groups with No KR, Irrelevant KR, Qualitative KR, or Quantitative KR (From Trowbridge and Cason, 1932.)

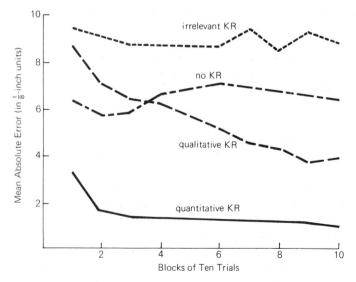

scale (ABCDF), and (4) a hundred-point scale (percentiles). Results of this study (shown in Figure 4-2) revealed that subjects receiving more precise information, the percentile and ABCDF groups, learned more than subjects receiving less information, the control and pass-fail groups. However, the former two groups did not differ significantly from each other, leading the authors to conclude that under these circumstances a five-point grading scale is as adequate as a hundred-point scale. They speculate also that the lack of acquaintance with the term *percentile* may have lessened its effectiveness with the 12- to 14-year-old boys. This study supports the use of a grading scale of ABCDF as opposed to a pass-fail system in the learning of motor skills.

In popular sports activities, the need for specificity is no less important. George Brett, American League batting champion in 1980, and teammate Hal McRae of the 1980 pennant winning Kansas City Royals praised batting coach Charlie Lau because of the clarity and precision of his feedback and instructions. In an article by sports writer Dick Young of the New York *Daily News* (October 30, 1980), McRae stated, "Most hitting instructors tell you to watch the ball and be aggressive, the way a doctor will tell you to take two aspirin and go to bed. Shoot, I heard that story when I was a kid. Old men talking across a checker board table talk like that. Use your hands they tell you. They don't tell you when to use your hands." In the same article Brett stated, "Charlie said he saw three things in my hitting that he could change and make me improve. . . . he moved me off the plate, closed up my stance, and told me to concentrate on hitting the ball from second base to the left field line." Both players went on to state that the thing that distinguished Lau from other coaches was the precision of his analysis.

If the information provided the learner is not clearly understood or if it is too general to be applied to a specific act, then it is of little value. Vague information or rewards that are not clearly connected to any particular behavior may be helpful for general motivation, but they are not very useful in promoting the learning of any specific skill or activity. This principle is important for both verbal and motor learning. In the classroom, it is not unusual for students to receive test papers or project reports from the teacher with no more than a letter or a numerical grade. Unfortunately, "correcting" papers today often means that the teacher applies a mark to the paper. With such limited knowledge of results, the student can only guess at the strengths and weaknesses of his work.

Even on objective examinations, the student may not find out which answers or solutions are correct, only that a certain number of the answers are incorrect. The teacher who uses tests as instructional as well as evaluative devices must provide performance information to the student. Ability to provide immediate, specific, and automatic feedback to the learner is the real strength of teaching machines and programmed instruction. Whether or not one uses these particular tools, the effective teacher will find some way to provide students with as much feedback as possible regarding their performances.

Perhaps teachers of motor skills have some advantage over teachers of verbal material in helping students receive specific knowledge of results. After all, the bat-

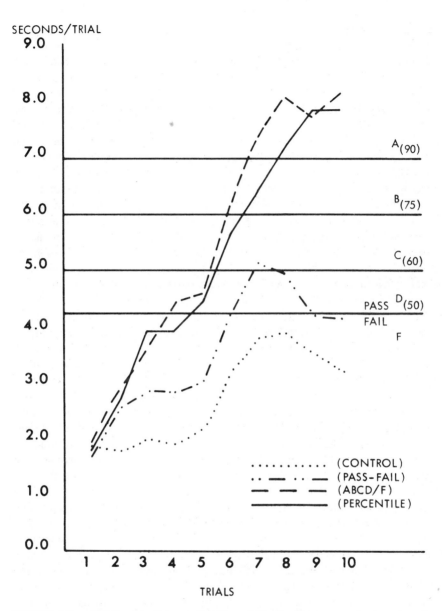

FIGURE 4-2. Relationship Between Precision of Grading Systems on the Learning of Fine Motor Skill (From Bennett, Vincent, and Johnson, *Research Quarterly,* 1979, 50, 4, pp. 715-22.)

ter in baseball either hits the ball or misses. The direction and force of the batted ball can also be observed. Some feedback is therefore obvious. However, there is much additional information that the physical education teacher or coach provides. In addition to giving *causal* information regarding success or failure in activities where the performer can readily see performance results, the teacher can provide an abundance of knowledge in activities in which the participant gets almost no feedback. For example, in the early stages of learning modern dance, diving, or swimming strokes, performers may have only a vague idea of the quality of their performances.

Feedback is automatic and easily observed in a great many motor skills. Archery, horseshoe pitching, typewriting, painting, bowling, and basketball shooting are some skills that provide early and definite feedback regarding success or failure. In other skills, however, *faults* that contribute to failure are not easily seen. Even when the end results can be observed, the performer often does not know exactly *why* the performance failed. An experienced teacher can be especially helpful in showing the learner the particular movement that contributed to the results. The performer is often unaware of the contributing response and, therefore, must find the solution by trial and error. Even professional athletes of the first magnitude sometimes get into "slumps" and are unable to determine what they are doing wrong. They have to depend upon coaches to identify their faults. In such cases, the coach provides some strategic knowledge of results, i.e., the actions of the performer that are contributing to success or failure. When students can readily observe the results of their efforts, the teacher may still increase the usefulness of this information as reinforcement in learning. Whereas students may receive specific results of performances in such activities as the broad jump, the 100-yard dash, or a push-up test, this does not insure that this information will be related to previous performances in the same activity.

Students usually do not take a scientific or analytical approach toward their abilities and progress. The teacher can be effective in getting them to keep records of their daily and weekly performances. In this way, knowledge regarding progress can be emphasized. Greater emphasis on self-evaluation will result in greater concern for learning and greater effort to improve. Too often, students go through practices or performances without considering whether or not they are operating at maximum efficiency. Record keeping and competition against personal standards usually results in greater motivation, more serious practice, and continued efforts to gain this type of detailed knowledge of results.

One word of caution must be made regarding the provision of augmented feedback. Too much information can confuse the learner. I can recall my early efforts to learn the game of golf as an adult after having played baseball for many years. One member of the foursome happened to be a golf instructor. After having watched me hit several drives, this individual availed himself of the opportunity to provide me with some much needed instruction. His comments went something like this: "You are standing too far away from the ball, so on the next drive, position yourself closer; you are hurrying the backswing, so try to bring the club back more slowly and in a straight line; you've been bending your forward arm, so try to keep it straight on the next shot; your head moved last time, disrupting your orientation to the ball; next time concentrate on shifting the weight to the front foot during the swing; get rid of your baseball swing and make more of an inside-out stroke;

and remember to keep your eye on the ball at all times." Being able to concentrate on only one thing at a time, I was caught in a "paralysis of analysis" predicament, unable to effectively use *any* of the information. Too much information confuses the learner. Therefore, teachers and coaches must remember to provide only as much information as the learner is able to comprehend and use at the time.

Temporal placement of information feedback

One of the most widely held assumptions over the years was that the effectiveness of feedback was directly related to the time at which it was received. That is, it was believed that feedback that was concurrent, or immediate, was most valuable, with progressively longer delays resulting in a gradual diminution of its effectiveness. After a substantial delay, feedback was assumed to be of no value because the learner would be unable to relate the feedback to a particular response.

Assumptions about the importance of speed in feedback were based in part on studies with animals that showed a relationship between speed of reinforcement and its effectiveness. Some evidence for this notion was provided by Shilling (1951), who reported an experiment in which rats waited from five to ten seconds after the response before a pellet of food was released. He observed that on the five-second delay schedule the rats became conditioned, and after the appropriate response remained at the food cup and made anticipatory movements for the food. Rats that had to wait ten seconds, however, generally moved away from the food cup and took part in unrelated activity. It appeared that the rats could remember up to five seconds and connect their response to the food. After a ten-second wait, however, they could not make the association. Spence (1956) observed that rats on a longer delayed reinforcement schedule might attain the same degree of learning, but that more trials would be needed.

In addition to the animal studies, general logic seemed to suggest that IF provided soon after performance would be more helpful than that which is long delayed. However, this assumption has not been substantiated by research over the past 20 years.

According to Bilodeau (1966), few variables have aroused as much dispute as the relationship between IF delay and learning. She argues that the theoretical basis for the IF delay is actually misapplied. After reviewing an extensive array of research, including her own, she concluded that delay *alone* is not important in reducing learning. However, a combination of temporal variables surrounding IF and repeated responses can make a difference in learning efficiency. These variables include (1) the period between the response and the IF, (2) the period between the IF and a subsequent response, and (3) the overall period between the two trials. Subsequent trials of the task involve the same variables. The variables are illustrated in Figure 4-2.

After surveying a great deal of research on this topic, Schmidt (1982) acknowledged that the predominance of studies suggests no negative effect related

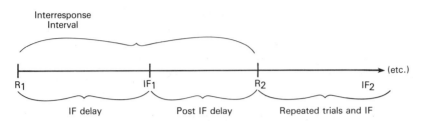

FIGURE 4-3. Temporal Relations in a Typical Skill Learning Situation.

to longer delay intervals. However, evidence is not unanimous. Further, Schmidt states that "... the conclusion drawn by J. Bilodeau (1966, 1969) and many others that KR delays have no effect on learning are not based on the proper evidence" (p. 543). He feels that faulty designs in most such studies, i.e., failure to use a transfer design, weaken the validity of those studies. The overall mix of available results is unconvincing in either direction.

Dukelow (1979) did an extensive review of the literature on temporal variables in motor skill learning and the timing of IF. He reported a great diversity of both evidence and opinion on the effects of delayed IF. He suggested that any effects of delay are influenced by (1) intervening activity, (2) the nature of the task, (3) the abilities of the learner, (4) the stage of learning, and (5) the type of feedback. He concluded that the optimal delay of IF is contingent upon each of those factors.

In recent years, some interest has been devoted to the effect of post-IF delay on skill acquisition. That is, after the IF has been provided the learner, what is the optimal delay prior to the next trial? Logic would suggest that the subsequent response be fairly soon so that the learner does not forget the information provided. There is some evidence that for simple motor skills such information can be retained for a long time, so that for even a day or more the value of the feedback will not be diminished. Responses initiated too soon after the feedback are largely ineffective because the learner may not have had adequate time to assimilate the information fully prior to commencing the next trial.

The effects of interpolated activities between trials, either before or after the IF, are not precisely known. However, it is probable that extraneous information or activity will reduce the clarity of the IF prior to the initiation of another trial. Such an assumption is consistent with studies showing that retention is interfered with by such interpolated activity.

One of the more confident statements that can be made about temporal arrangements is that if IF for a given performance is delayed until after a second trial, such information is practically useless. That is, when the learner is given information about the first trial following the second response, there is an inability to make the connection in a useful way. This factor would argue for fairly rapid IF, particularly in situations where the learner is making repeated responses to a given task.

The delay of IF in school learning varies widely. For example, after answering certain questions on a written examination, the student may have to wait days before learning whether answers were right or wrong. On the other hand, one who responds orally to a teacher's question in class receives almost immediate knowledge of whether the answer is correct or incorrect. In fact, the student often starts receiving feedback while still answering the question. It is not unusual for a student to start answering in one way and, depending upon the kind of feedback, to alter or even completely reverse the answer. Some examples of feedback that are likely to cause one to change such an answer are: the act of other students anxiously raising their hands while he or she is only halfway through answering; a surprised or amused expression on the face of the teacher at the beginning of the response; or a question such as, "Are you *sure* about that?" at the conclusion of an answer. Nonsupportive verbal and nonverbal responses cause the child to believe that he is on the wrong track. However, if the child receives an approving nod from the teacher, or if the hands of the other students start to come *down*, that student is already receiving IF as well as reinforcement for the answer. Much of the reinforcement from teacher to pupil and vice versa is extremely subtle.

Speeding IF in motor skills. There are times when the teacher wishes to provide IF to the learner very rapidly. This is especially true when the learner is making repeated responses or continuing to perform in that particular activity. In simple motor activities, delay of knowledge is usually short. Young children can immediately see results in handwriting, drawing, or cutting with scissors. When they are learning to whistle, they can almost immediately tell whether the lip formation and forced expiration are correct. The value of this feedback can be dramatically shown when children are prevented from seeing their work. When covering the writing hand or preventing the child from seeing his or her drawing, the work becomes distorted. Without knowledge of performance in these activities, improvement is much slower. The delay of automatic knowledge of results varies from one motor activity to another. In skeet shooting, the delay of IF is particularly short. The baseball pitcher must wait approximately one-half second to tell whether the pitch will curve in the appropriate manner or if it will go into the strike zone. In horseshoe pitching, there is a delay of a second or two. In the track and field events of javelin and discus throwing, the delay between response and IF is even greater.

It can be readily understood that a beginning bowler might forget the kinesthetic feel of a particular delivery by the time the ball strikes the pins. The thoughts, visual images, or distractions that enter one's mind between the release of the ball and the time it strikes the pins may serve to minimize the effectiveness of the IF. In discrete movement activities, even a slight delay may cause the person to lose an awareness of the intricacies of the movement. However, reinforcement may be aided by the early realization that the response will be successful. The basketball player who says, "I knew it was going in as soon as it left my hand," shows a degree of IF and reinforcement almost immediately. Teachers can often promote more immediate reinforcement by such techniques as spot bowling, which gives students feedback in about one-third the usual time. Although these interim reinforcements are not as definite as the final success, they may have special advantages because of the speed of the feedback. There are many activities that the teacher can select as checkpoints and encourage students to use.

Another way in which the teacher may provide earlier IF is by praising improvement or by pointing to errors in movement patterns *during* one's performance, regardless of whether the end result of the response is successful. The coach may praise the young batter who swings without the customary hitch even if the ball is missed. Similarly, the tennis player who is positioned in the proper manner and makes a smooth, level stroke should be reinforced regardless of the consequence of the stroke. The young basketball player who is learning the jump shot might receive an immediate "That's the idea" as soon as the ball leaves the hand. These efforts to shorten the delay in reinforcement are extremely valuable and should be more widely used by all teachers.

The amount of intermediate reinforcement that the teacher can give to each student is limited. The learning process will be enhanced if students learn to analyze their own performances and predict probable results on the basis of cues received during performance. Kinesthetic awareness of proper performance should be stressed so that the learner is able to detect correct and incorrect responses. Just as the player knows the basketball is going into the goal as soon as it is released, other performers, such as the place kicker in football, the golfer, the sprinter, the tennis server, or the horseshoe pitcher, might also be able to predict results.

Schmidt (1975) used the term *subjective reinforcement* to refer to self-generated error signals. In this process, the individual receives feedback through the eyes, ears, joints, and other senses. Schmidt and White (1972) report, however, that the individual is not able to generate such information in new skills. After one practices such motor activity for a period of time while receiving feedback from the instructor, the ability to detect errors is developed. Consequently, learners are better able to self-correct during the performance.

Evidence of self-analysis and its value in reinforcement are common in many sports activities. Even when the exact result may not be clear to the performer, subjective clues may provide an accurate general impression. Frequently, the comment made by the runner, the gymnast, or the competitive skier is, "I knew I did well but I didn't know I did *that* well." Millions of Americans watching the 1968 Olympic games on television saw long jumper Bob Beaman make his historic jump in Mexico City. Immediately after landing in the pit, Beaman leaped up with great joy and excitement. He knew he had made an excellent jump *prior* to being told that his jump of more than 29 feet had broken the world record by more than a foot. He had learned the interim cues so well that the end result was predictable within a narrow margin. Similar sensitivity can be developed by the gymnast, diver, discus thrower, or even the 400-meter or mile runner in the estimation of time.

Speed in IF or reinforcement appears to raise one's level of motivation for the given activity. In contrast, long delays tend to diminish enthusiasm. This was evident in "telegraphic" and "mailographic" athletic contests, which were prevalent some years ago. In these events, usually track and field, swimming, or some novelty events, each team performed at the home facility, recorded the results, and forwarded them to the opponent. There would then be a delay of hours or even days before the team found out whether they had won, lost, or tied. As a rule, the elation was not nearly so great as when the teams competed face to face and were immediately aware of the result. Consequently, despite obvious financial advantages, interest in such remote competition has not been sustained. One of the psychological advantages of face-to-face competition is the immediacy of results.

Augmenting feedback in motor skills

In many motor activities, individuals are not able to observe the effectiveness of their performance. Even when they do see the results, they often cannot detect the *reason* for the success or failure of their action. Consequently, the instructor has a responsibility to augment feedback in order to assist learners, particularly those who are encountering difficulty with their performance. Such feedback may simply provide verbal information about the performance. On the other hand, it may make use of novelty equipment, gadgets, or creative adjustments in the activity.

Individuals are often unaware that they are engaging in extraneous or irregular movement patterns, usually called splinter skills, which are detrimental to effective performance. The young basketball player who is being taught to shoot lay-ups with the left (nonpreferred) hand usually has a tendency to push off with the incorrect (left) foot. This often persists after having been informed of the correct mechanics of this new skill and even after going through the action in slow motion. I have heard many junior high school boys insist they pushed off the right foot when shooting the unfamiliar left-handed lay-up, when all observers agreed that the opposite was true. College students will make the same argument. In order to provide these learners with feedback about their behavior, that is, feedback they will believe, it must be done promptly. In fact, one must "catch them in the act" in order to be convincing. If the instructor stands at the point of lift-off and taps the student on the foot with a meter stick at the very moment it is lifted, then the feedback will be convincing.

Likewise, people learning to bowl often insist that they are not taking their eyes off the target (one-three pocket), and young pitchers believe that they have watched the catcher's mitt throughout the delivery when such is not the case. To convince these performers that their eyes wandered or their heads moved, I stood out in front of the performers and yelled "Ah ha" at the moment of the deviate behavior. Only when caught with their eyes off the target did they understand at what point this fault was occurring. Once this was accepted, they were receptive to changing their performance behavior. Such immediate feedback can be provided in other activities, e.g., to the girl who swings the field hockey club too high, the baseball batter who lift his head away from the ball at the beginning of the swing, or the bowler who fails to follow through adequately.

Young baseball batters frequently develop a "hitch" in their swing. This is a sudden lowering of the bat as if to wind up just prior to the swing. The hitch is clearly a distraction to an effective swing because it necessitates a change in direction at the last moment in order to contact the ball. Almost always, the batter is unaware of the hitch and questions the accuracy of the feedback. To be effective in extinguishing this distracting response, the instructor or coach must get alongside and perhaps tap the hands or forearms with a stick at the moment the bat is lowered. Beginning divers sometimes spread the legs while diving, yet insist that they were held tightly together throughout the dive. To enhance feedback on leg position, coaches often place a paddle board on some other item between the knees or ankles to see if it can be held there until the diver lands in the water. Of course, videotape is also a most effective method of providing feedback.

Some instructors or coaches ask performers to *exaggerate* the erroneous response to increase awareness of its existence. Deliberately overextending the baseball hitch or raising the field hockey stick may develop a keener understanding of such a movement on the part of the learner.

Some teachers or coaches make use of a variety of novelty items not only for general instruction purposes but to enhance feedback for the learner. Danny Litwhiler (1963), former major league baseball player and for many years the baseball coach at Michigan State University, developed a vast array of drills and novelty exercises, many of which provide feedback not easily communicated verbally. A chapter entitled "Gimmicks of the Game" includes more than two dozen such activities. One of the more interesting is a yo-yo pitching drill for teaching a young pitcher to throw a curve ball. Those who have attempted to teach this skill to young players recognize the difficulty of this task. One can observe the curve ball being thrown and, with instruction, can move his own hand and wrist slowly through the same general motion. Yet, like whistling, it is difficult to get the kinesthetic feel of the performance through such observation. As Litwhiler illustrates, it so happens that the effective delivery of a yo-yo requires almost the identical hand and wrist action of the curve ball. Therefore, he suggests the following routine:

Put the pitcher on the rubber, and have him assume the wind-up stance with the yo-yo in his hand. He takes his wind-up and follows through slowly with his delivery. As he comes through with his arm and hand, they follow the same path taken when throwing a ball. When the hand gets about at his head, he bends and shortens his arm. His palm is facing his face, and the yo-yo is held by the thumb, middle, and index fingers, so that it will roll off the side of the index finger, down toward his feet. This is an exaggerated way of spinning a ball for a curve. The yo-yo should go straight downward and spin at the end of the string. The pitcher should jerk it up and start all over again. After this action has been mastered, he should assume a set stance and go through the motion with his arm and hand. Soon, he should have a much better curve ball (p. 201).

Most persons have had experience in tossing a yo-yo. They know that when thrown incorrectly, in a twisted fashion, it will get stuck at the end of the string and will not return to the hand, thus providing rapid feedback that the delivery was not performed properly. If it returns rapidly and smoothly to the hand, this is evidence that it was thrown correctly. When the yo-yo routine is perfected in a simulated baseball delivery, the curve ball should then be more easily mastered.

Litwhiler and others have suggested the use of painted stripes on balls so that rotation can be observed more easily. Such stripes on a baseball give the pitcher clearer information as to the rotation of the ball. On a basketball such stripes (or the multicolored basketball formerly used in the American Basketball Association) vividly inform the performer whether the desired rotation is being achieved. The colors of the official soccer ball naturally privide this information.

The use of novelty ideas, or even gadgets, in the teaching of motor skills goes back beyond anyone's recollection and is probably as diverse as the number of teachers or coaches. Many of these ideas are designed specifically to provide feedback to the participant. The suggestions that follow are only a few of those with which I am familiar. (1) In *track* practice some coaches have required runners to hold eggs in each hand while running. This encourages the runner to relax the hands and arms while performing. There is some tendency for runners to develop tension without realizing it and they may even doubt the existence of that tension when informed by the coach. However, cracked eggs in one's hands provide vivid evidence that tension existed. (2) In *bowling* there is a tendency for beginners to bend the arm during the backswing as well as during the delivery of the ball. To aid the performer in correcting this, some teachers have taped a rod or other straight object to the upper and lower portions of the arm to prevent it from bending more than slightly. When one delivers the ball with such a contraption, any attempt to bend the arm will provide the perfomer with feedback of that action. (3) In *gymnastics* there are movements when it is desirable to keep the legs pressed tightly together. Therefore, requiring the performer to hold an object between the legs is one way of informing the learner if the legs spread (the object drops). Some coaches have used this technique for certain movements on the pommel horse. Similarly, diving coaches have used this with performers who begin with a standing start at the end of the board. (4) In *dance* some novices tend to slump forward rather than retain a more desirable upright posture. To aid performers in becoming aware of these slouching habits, some teachers have attached a straight edge that extends from the waist to the chin. Performing with this device for a time will clearly remind the individual of any slump in posture.

The list of examples for novelty ideas could be extended to all motor activities; it is limited only by the ingenuity of the instructor. Such techniques can be very helpful if used on a limited basis for the purposes indicated (feedback). One must guard against the performer beginning to lean on such gadgets as "props." In addition, other distractions can develop if the gadget is used continually. For example, if the yo-yo technique for the curve ball is used too long, this can adversely affect the follow-through in the baseball delivery. Consequently, one should effectively use such ideas for their dramatic and visible value in feedback but should remove them after a short time.

Teaching "form" in motor skills

There are occasions when it is desirable to actually withhold performance information from the learner. This may be true when the instructor is concentrating exclusively on developing the proper *form*, or body mechanics in the performance of certain activities. At such times all attention, including instruction and IF, should be focused on improving form and not on the performance results of the behavior.

The instructor who is interested in teaching the basketball free throw to beginners may wish the learner to observe and practice the bent knees, the lift of the body during delivery, the roll of the ball off the fingers, and the follow-through with forearm and wrist. In the early phase of learning, the development of these and other mechanical elements are the primary goals. Whether or not the shot is made is not important. Yet learners are influenced by the success or failure of the shot. In fact, such obvious feedback tends to nullify the effect of verbal comments about form. I recall demonstrating the free throw shot to junior high school boys, focusing all attention on form. While the students observed and listened dutifully, their comments were restricted to whether the shot was made or missed. They were clearly more impressed by performance than by words. Soon, I turned away from the basket and "shot" the ball to a selected student who was situated off to the side. Now the students could concentrate more fully on the form, without the distraction of success or failure. This technique subsequently was used not only to protect the ego of the instructor but to improve the learning climate as well. Furthermore, when organized to practice free throw shooting, students were also moved away from the free throw line and asked to "shoot" a perfect shot to a classmate. In this way complete attention could be focused on the learning of proper form.

In other activities, such as the shot put or discus, the instructor may wish to develop a new technique or to improve the one being practiced. Any appreciable change in one's habitual delivery will probably result in a reduction in immediate performance capacity. Emphasis on that decrement, or even the awareness of it, tends to counteract the effectiveness of the teaching technique. Therefore, it is advantageous to distract attention from the distance which the discus or shot is thrown. Distance markers should be removed and no indication of distance thrown should be reported. Rather, close attention should be given to movement form, or the delivery. All reinforcement should be directed to that end. Meanwhile, learners should be assured that when the new technique is perfected they will be able to equal or surpass their previous performance. When such level of efficiency has been established, it, too, can be used as a reinforcement for the new technique.

EXTINCTION

In physical education, as in other areas of the school curriculum, there is often a need for eliminating a particular response or some general behavior. This process, referred to as *extinction*, may be necessitated if the individual has developed a flaw in a response, if the skill or knowledge has been acquired incorrectly, or if improper social behavior is being exhibited. Extinction may be achieved by various techniques applied by the instructor. In the laboratory, many techniques for diminishing the strength of a response are used. This process is referred to as experimental extinction. For example, a rat that has learned to push a lever to get a pellet of food will respond in this manner each time it is hungry. If the experimenter wishes to eliminate the response, food is not given when the lever is pushed. The rat will continue to depress the lever for a time, then will gradually reduce and eventually eliminate this response. The connection between lever pushing and food getting will therefore be lost.

There is a tendency for the learner to continue responding for awhile after the reinforcement has been discontinued. This resistance to extinction depends on how well the response was learned originally. Behavior that has been learned thoroughly is most resistant to extinction. This has been demonstrated with animals in the laboratory and can easily be observed with children or adults in everyday life. Faults in motor performance that have been learned and practiced over a long period of time are the most difficult to eliminate. Physical education teachers and coaches have found, for example, that the baseball batter who is allowed to continue using a hitch in the swing or to step away from the plate has greater difficulty in learning the proper technique than does the person who is immediately corrected. Similarly, social behavior that is allowed to continue for a long period is most difficult to eliminate.

Eliminating improper social behavior

Children in school will forget an incorrect response and will eliminate improper behavior when it is no longer rewarded. For example, a child may have developed a tendency to clown in school after discovering that these antics got a laugh from classmates. After using this technique for awhile, however, the other children may no longer applaud. This behavior is, therefore, no longer reinforced. Eventually the association between the clowning technique and a pleasant response from classmates is lost. Another child may be motivated to argue with teachers because of status satisfaction received from a group of classmates. In a different class, however, the same child may find that arguing with the teacher is not popular with other class members. With no social reinforcement in this new situation, there would no longer be any encouragement to argue. If "baiting" the umpire proves popular with teammates, a player is likely to develop this habit. On subsequent occasions, when baiting loses its popularity, that action is reduced or eliminated.

Attention-getting behavior, both acceptable and unacceptable, is used because of the pleasant response that it brings to the person.

Coaches are often confronted with the young athlete who has a tendency to be a show-off. This behavior often detracts from the performer's concentration and that of his teammates in the game. Coaches, therefore, have attempted to eliminate such behavior by ignoring it, by punishing the show-off, or by rewarding alternative behavior. A universally effective method has not yet been determined. The effectiveness of any technique, however, will depend on its capacity for eliminating the reinforcement of the show-off's behavior. In this process, coaches and teachers should exercise care to avoid undue damage to the self-image of the child.

Eliminating movement faults

In physical education and sports, both social learning and skill learning may be eliminated by nonreinforcement. Participants often develop errors of movement or "faults" in sports activities. A direct attack on this fault by the teacher (punishment of the child) might be one way of reducing the incidence of the habit or eliminating it. Another technique would be to reward what the performer does correctly while ignoring the faults. If alternatives to the fault are reinforced while the fault itself is not, the alternatives will be learned because of their association with success or approval. For example, a common fault among young baseball players is overstriding when preparing to swing at a pitch. The coach might aid a player in correcting this fault by first pointing out the weakness of this technique and then complimenting the batter each time the stride is shortened. This emphasis on the correct way of doing things is a simple matter of "accentuating the positive."

The natural effect, or result, of a faulty response is often unpleasant in itself and will therefore prove instrumental in weakening the act. Such an unpleasant experience, or negative reinforcement, may be observed when the child who has been encouraged to tuck the head while doing a forward roll forgets to do it. Most often the head bangs into the mat or floor with some degree of pain, and this natural punishment will tend to speed the association between the tucked head position and a more comfortable forward roll. In horseback riding, incorrect coordination of one's body movement with the trotting horse will result in some physical discomfort for the rider. Similarly, the springboard diver who does not get the body in proper alignment will make a painful entry into the water. Improper body position while doing various stunts on the trampoline will become vividly apparent to the performer upon landing. The baseball player who hits the ball too near the handle of the bat will receive a somewhat painful sting. Occasions in motor activities in which improper performance is naturally punished with a painful or unpleasant experience tend to work to the advantage of the teacher who is attempting to promote a higher level of performance.

Inappropriate motor performance occasionally results in success. This is unfortunate for the teaching process since successful behavior becomes more resistant to extinction. For example, some beginning basketball players develop a tendency to take off on the wrong foot when attempting a lay-up shot. Naturally, the more this technique is practiced, the more correct it seems. Each success (making the goal) reinforcers this wrong foot takeoff. Efforts by the teacher to eliminate the fault are especially difficult becauwe early attempts in the correct manner may not result in success. Similarly, right-handed players who always shoot and dribble with the right hand, despite floor position or circumstance, do so because of greater immediate success with this hand. The coach who is interested in developing left-handed proficiency for the long-range development of the individual's playing ability therefore encounters considerable difficulty because of the greater reinforcement that the learner receives from his particular manner.

SUMMARY

1. Reinforcement refers to any condition that, if it follows a response, increases the probability that the same response will recur on subsequent occasions when similar stimuli are presented. Reinforcement may come in many forms, including reward, recognition, or knowledge of results. The concept of reinforcement as a factor in learning is found in the works of Pavlov, Thorndike, Hull, Skinner, and others.

2. Feedback, as one type of reinforcement, is the provision of knowledge about a particular action back to the individual. Information feedback (IF) refers to knowledge that gives the learner an indication of the correctness or accuracy of the response. It is clear that people do not learn effectively without such information. The term *knowledge of results* (KR) is often used interchangeably with *information feedback*. Several authors, however, restrict the use of KR to information that is obtainable only from an outside source.

3. Primary reinforcers are those that directly reduce a need of the individual. These needs may be physiological or psychological. A secondary reinforcer is one that carries importance because of its association with a primary reinforcer. Although the secondary reinforcer has no attractive quality in itself, it may serve to meet needs, especially psychological and sociological. Consequently, secondary reinforcers have traditionally been heavily used in the school setting.

4. It is impractical in most learning situations to provide reinforcement 100 percent of the time. However, when properly scheduled and applied, reinforcement for one-half or one-fourth of the time is practically as effective. Schedules of "partial" reinforcement have included (1) a fixed-ratio plan in which the learner is consistently and predictably reinforced for a specific amount of work or performance, (2) a variable-ratio plan in which reinforcement is provided at irregular response intervals, (3) a fixed-interval schedule in which the learner is reinforced according to a specified time schedule, and (4) a variable-interval schedule in which reinforcement is provided at irregular and unpredictable time intervals.

5. Information feedback has been categorized according to the type of information provided, the sense modality receiving the information, the timing of the feedback, and the source of the information. Consequently, IF may be described as *intrinsic, augmented, concurrent, terminal,* or *verbal,* along with a number of other descriptive terms.

6. To be most effective, IF must be specific in nature and meaningful to the learner. Vague generalizations may make the learner feel better and, consequently, put forth somewhat increased effort. However, it is not very helpful in one's attempt to make specific improvements in a skill or to eliminate a persistent response error.

7. Despite long held assumptions to the contrary, there is no convincing evidence available to show that the immediate provision of IF is more helpful than delayed IF in humans. This differs from the positive relationship that has been shown between speed of reinforcement and learning in animals. With humans, it appears that the effect of feedback delay is dependent upon the intervening activity, the nature of the task, and the type of feedback.

8. The intertrial interval is composed of IF delay, which is the period between the response and the provision of IF, and the post-IF delay, or the period from the provision of the IF until the next response is initiated. Although it is not entirely clear what the ideal post-IF delay period is, there is some evidence that responses should not be initiated too soon after feedback. The learner must have adequate time to assimilate the information prior to commencing the next trial.

9. Learners who are experienced in a particular activity are able to make use of inherent IF or cues generated during the performance. However, persons inexperienced in the task are not able to sense these subtle cues so easily, but must depend upon the augmented feedback or the obvious success criteria that are a part of the activity.

10. A primary function of the teacher is to provide feedback that is not otherwise apparent. The provision of such information in an obvious and immediate fashion is often necessary to convince the learner that it is accurate.

11. In motor activities in which form is important, initial concentration of feedback must be on movement response and not on the results (success or failure) of that response. Adjustments in body mechanics or response form can best be taught by providing precise IF on those motor responses and diverting attention away from the result of the activity. To assure full attention to those movement responses, instructors often find it helpful to screen out or prevent information regarding accuracy, times, or distances of the performance.

12. In complex motor activities, the teacher should provide feedback for gradual improvement or small progressive steps. Such tasks are never perfected suddenly but must depend upon continued improvement over an extended period. In these cases it is impractical to delay feedback until the skill is fully learned. On the other hand, a simple motor task may be mastered in a very few trials so that any augmented feedback may be delayed until it is fully learned.

13. The process of extinction, or the elimination of a particular response, is necessitated if the individual has developed a movement flaw or has acquired the skill or knowledge incorrectly. The most effective technique for extinguishing inappropriate responses, be they social, verbal, or motor, is to remove any reinforcement related to the improper response while providing reinforcement to alternative behavior. Another frequently used but less effective technique is to apply punishment to the inappropriate response.

SELECTED READINGS

BILODEAU, E. A., ed. *Acquisition of skill.* New York: Academic Press, 1966.

BIRNEY, R. C. and TEEVAN, R. C., eds. *Reinforcement: An enduring problem in psychology.* Princeton, N.J.: Van Nostrand, 1961.

HULSE, S. H., DEESE, J., and EGETH, H. *The psychology of learning* (5th ed.), New York: McGraw-Hill, 1980.

HULL, C. L. *Principles of behavior.* New York: Appleton-Century-Crofts, 1943.

KELLER, F. S. *Learning: reinforcement theory* (2nd ed.). New York: Random House, 1969.

PAVLOV, I. P. *Conditional reflexes.* Trans. E. V. Anrep. New York: Oxford, 1927.

SKINNER, B. F. Reinforcement today. *American Psychologist,* 1958, 13 (3), 94-99.

TRAVERS, R. M. W. *Essentials of learning* (4th ed.). New York: Macmillan Publishing Co., 1977.

5 Transfer of Skill

ASSUMPTIONS ABOUT TRANSFER

A great deal of what is taught in schools today is based on the premise that children will transfer what is learned to out-of-school situations. Learning in school would, in fact, be very ineffective if children learned only to solve the specific problems presented and were not able to apply this information to the solution of new and different problems. Consequently, all teachers agree that, to some extent, students generalize or apply the knowledge and principles learned in school to other situations. Few topics in education have proven more popular during this century than the matter of *transfer of training*. Perhaps no topic is more important.

Teachers in all phases of the school curriculum assume that children will transfer the skills that are learned in their particular subject area. For example, children are taught to write themes in English class not to help them write better themes in adult life but because of the belief that this experience will improve their general effectiveness in communication. Teachers of motor skills also assume transfer. In teaching swimming, land drills are often used not because of their value as a recreational or conditioning activity but because of the assumption that movement skills learned on land will be used when the individual gets into the water. In teaching soccer, the technique of dribbling around obstacles is often used with beginning players. It is rare, of course, that the exact obstacle pattern used will be appropriate in a soccer game. General skill in dribbling, however, will be helpful. Parents often encourage their children to take dancing lessons more for the expected skills of poise and graceful movement than for excellence in dancing per se. When one considers the learning experiences used by the successful coach and the physical education teacher, it becomes clear that transfer of training is just as appropriate for gross motor skills as for verbal learning or fine motor skills.

Expectation of transfer is not limited to communication, swimming, soccer, or other skills. It is also assumed that acquired social attitudes and emotional responses will carry over to other areas of a person's life. For example, certain democratic procedures, such as allowing team members to elect their captain, are often used more for citizenship-training values rather than to assure a wise selection. Kindergarten and first-grade teachers are interested in having young children develop positive attitudes toward initial school experiences in the hope that these attitudes will be transferred to other phases of the school program. In a particular subject, it is expected that attitudes developed in one phase will be reflected in other aspects of the course. An individual's negative attitude or anxiety concerning a particular teacher, coach, or opponent is expected to affect behavior in a completely different activity with which the same teacher, coach, or opponent is associated.

According to McGeoch and Irion (1952), "Transfer of training occurs whenever the existence of a previously established habit has an influence upon the acquisition, performance, or relearning of a second habit" (p. 299). Transfer may, therefore, be positive or negative. The English teacher hopes that the writing of themes will have a *favorable* effect upon the student's written and oral communication. The swimming teacher also strives for positive transfer. However, it has been found that previously learned habits in swimming sometimes interfere with the learning of new habits, especially if faults had been developed during one's early training. Similarly, golf instructors have found that baseball players often transfer undesirable movement patterns from the baseball swing that may interfere with their ability to learn to play golf.

After a certain age, perhaps the elementary school years, it is probable that we rarely learn anything that is entirely new. Whether motor skills, verbal material, attitudes, or whatever, all learning is influenced by previous learning that is somewhat related. Since it is practically impossible to factor out all such influences, most investigations in the area of transfer are to some extent contaminated. Researchers simply try to identify and, to the extent possible, control such factors.

The question of transfer of skill is, therefore, a complex one. Since the beginning of the 20th century a great deal of research has been devoted to questions such as: Does transfer occur at all? Are specific skills or general principles transferred? Can transfer be taught? How can transfer best be investigated?

Experimental designs in the study of transfer

During the past several decades, literally thousands of studies have been conducted on a wide range of topics. The type of task (verbal and motor) and the nature of the learning situation have varied in these investigations. Two basic types of experimental designs have been used. One type has been arranged to investigate the amount of *proactive transfer*, i.e., the effect that the learning of a task has on the learning or performance of a second task practiced at a later time. For example, proactive transfer would be exhibited if students performed better in diving after engaging in a unit on rebound tumbling (positive transfer), or if students did worse in baseball batting after playing softball for a period of time (negative transfer).

To investigate proactive transfer, the following experimental design has been used:

```
Experimental group. . . . .learn task A . . . . . . . . . . .test on task B
Control group. . . . . . . . .rest, or perform
                    some unrelated activity. . . . .test on task B
```

If the two groups perform equally well on task *B*, it can be concluded that there is no transfer from task *A* to task *B* (assuming that the two groups were equal on task *B* at the beginning). If the experimental group performs better on task *B* than does the control group, it can be said that there is positive transfer from task *A* to task *B*. Similarly, if the control group performs better on task *B*, this is evidence that negative transfer has taken place. In this general design, any number of experimental groups can be used. Different groups might vary the manner or degree to which task *A* is learned. One experimental group might even practice task *B* to determine how the transfer from *A* to *B* compares with a procedure in which all practice sessions are devoted to the learning of task *B*.

A second type of experimental design has been established to investigate *retroactive transfer*, i.e., the effect that practice on a particular task has on the retention of a previously learned task. Retroactive transfer might be illustrated if students with an established level of skill in tennis practice badminton for a series of lessons. If it is later determined that their proficiency in tennis had deteriorated as a result of the badminton practice, this deterioration would be an example of negative retroactive transfer, also referred to as retroactive inhibition.

For investigating retroactive transfer, the following design is generally used:

Experimental
      group . . . . . . .learn task *A* . . . .learn task *B* . . . . .test on task *A*
Control group. . . .learn task *A* . . . .rest, or perform
                        some unrelated
                        activity . . . . .test on task *A*

The important function of this design is to determine whether the learning of task *B* has any effect on the retention of task *A*. The critical comparison is made at the test on task *A*. Assuming that the two groups originally learned task *A* to the same degree of proficiency, they should perform equally well when this skill is tested, unless there has been some retroactive transfer. If the control group performs better at the test, this indicates that task *B* has a detrimental effect on the retention of the skill in *A*. On the other hand, if the experimental group is more proficient at the test for task *A*, it can be assumed that the learning of task *B* has a favorable effect on the retention of task *A*.

BACKGROUND STUDIES ON TRANSFER

Prior to the 20th century, the traditional concept of *formal discipline* was prevalent in educational practice. This all-encompassing theory of transfer was dominant for several centuries in Europe and the United States. Basic to the concept of formal discipline was the theory of faculty psychology, which postulated that the mind was composed of a set of faculties such as reason, will, attention, and judgment. Early educators believed that the study of certain subjects was especially valuable in developing the "faculties" for future use. The mind was assumed to be like a muscle, which becomes stronger, quicker, and more flexible with practice. Practice in reasoning, for example, would supposedly assist one in solving any kind of reasoning problem at some later date. Well-developed faculties were assumed to be helpful in all situations. Therefore, certain subjects were included in the school curriculum because of their "mental training" values.

In addition, the concept of formal discipline held that whatever was most difficult to learn was beneficial to the individual's development. In order to achieve maximum development, the *overload principle* was put to use. (In physical conditioning, the overload principle refers to the placing of unusual stress on the component to be developed.) The more difficult subjects in school were believed to be especially valuable in preparing one for subsequent hard work. The many failures in Latin and mathematics, for example, appeared to justify the belief that these subjects were hard and, therefore, most appropriate for training the mind.

The analogy between mental and muscular development seemed plausible and was, therefore, long accepted. It is true that effective use of a muscle can make it stronger, more flexible, and quicker in specific situations. However, studies have failed to produce any evidence that taxing the mind results in similar improvement. Consequently, modern educators and psychologists generally reject the doctrine of formal discipline.

Early experiments in transfer

Transfer was first objectively studied by William James and later by E. L. Thorndike. James (1890) tried to determine whether mental exercises were of any value in improving the mind. He and his students tested their memory abilities by learning Victor Hugo's poems. After an extensive training period of memorizing other authors' poems, they again tested their memory abilities on poems by Hugo. The difference in performance on the two tests was only slight. This led James to conclude that "one's native retentiveness is unchangeable. No amount of culture seems capable of modifying a man's *general* retentiveness" (pp. 663-664). He indicated that the best way to remember is to learn as much as possible about the material to be remembered. Many subsequent experiments were performed that indicated a lack of general transfer from one intellectual activity to another. Some later psychologists have concluded that James's views on transfer were too limited. However, his studies and writings opened a new era in the field of general faculty capacities and educational practice.

Early in the 20th century, a number of teachers became interested in "proving" the theory of formal discipline. The subject areas of Latin and mathematics were most often selected because of the prominent claims that they were especially important in developing one's faculties. These early research studies often shared a characteristic structural fallacy. For example, at the end of a high school program, students who had taken Latin courses would be given a test of mental achievement. This group's test results would be compared with those of students who had not taken Latin in high school. Usually it was shown that Latin students exhibited greater intellectual power, and it was assumed that study of Latin was primarily responsible for developing their greater reasoning ability. Weaknesses in this experimental design are obvious. A similarly structured study might be designed to compare the strength-building value of football and soccer. In such an experiment, the overall muscular strength of the football players (average weight, 180 pounds) would be compared to that of the soccer players (average weight, 150 pounds). Results would be easy to predict. Failure to select comparable groups at the beginning was a strategic weakness of the early transfer studies.

Thorndike and Woodworth (1901) investigated the allegation that the taking of "hard" courses such as Latin and Greek developed greater reasoning powers among students. Students selected from these courses and from alternative curricula were tested before and after taking the courses. The investigators found no important differences among curricula in the development of reasoning ability.

Later, when Latin was no longer advocated for mental discipline, a number of proponents claimed that Latin had special value in the development of English vocabulary or language knowledge in general. Several investigations were conducted to test this hypothesis. Hamblen (1925) reported that a Latin study group showed a gain in English vocabulary. The gain, however, was almost entirely in words of Latin origin. He suggested that perhaps a course in English would have been even more beneficial. Douglass and Kittleson (1935) and Pond (1938) reported no gains in English vocabulary following the study of Latin. Generally, it has been concluded from the Latin and mathematics studies that the difficulty of a school course, or other special intellectual activities, has no favorable effect on an unrelated subject or activity. (It should be noted that such studies did not address the possible effect of such course taking on the study regimen of students, i.e., it is conceivable that students taking such courses develop the habit of studying more seriously.)

Thorndike's theory of identical elements

The work of E. L. Thorndike, along with that of James, effectively refuted the theory of formal discipline. In addition, Thorndike was the first person to develop a prominent theory of transfer. When challenged with the supposition that superior intellectual powers resulted from studying a particular subject, Thorndike (1924) said:

> The chief reason why good thinkers seem superficially to have been made such by having taken certain school studies, is that good thinkers have taken such studies, becoming better by the inherent tendency of the good to gain more than the poor from any study. When the good thinkers studied Greek and Latin, these studies seemed to make good thinking. Now that the good thinkers study Physics and Trigonometry, these seem to make good thinkers. If the abler pupils should all study Physical Education and Dramatic Art, these subjects would seem to make good thinkers. These were, indeed, a large fraction of the program of studies for the best thinkers the world has produced, the Athenian Greeks (p. 98).[1]

[1] By permission of the American Psychological Association.

Thorndike concluded from his work that the best way to develop knowledge or skill in any subject area was to study that subject. Humphreys (1951) drew the following conclusion from the work of Thorndike and his associates:

> If you need accounting in your occupation, study accounting during your training and preferably the type of accounting you will need. If you want to read Cicero in Latin, by all means study Latin. If, however, you want to learn French, do not spend several years in the study of Latin, since you will be further ahead if you concentrate on French. If you want to learn to solve social problems, spend your time in the social sciences, not in the study of geometry (p. 213).[2]

Thorndike used newly developed intelligence tests to support his belief that there was no general transfer. Some of the tests involved novel problem-solving situations. He found that no high school subject was more effective than any other in aiding one to do better on intelligence tests. Generally, he advocated the direct teaching of any skill or knowledge to be learned.

Thorndike's famous theory of *identical elements* (1913) held that only specific skills, knowledges, or techniques are transferred. By identical elements, he meant "mental processes which have the same cell action in the brain as their physical correlate." He further explained that "It is, of course, often not possible to tell just what features of two mental abilities are thus identical" (p. 359). He believed, however, that approximate decisions could be accurate enough for practical use.

He indicated both "substance" and "procedure" were transferable when they were identical in the second situation. Under substance he included abilities to handle spoken and written numbers, words, and symbols. By procedure he meant habits of observation and study, attitudes of neglect or pleasure, and feelings of dissatisfaction and failure. His definition would seem to suggest a rather broad view of transfer. However, as a result of all his pronouncements on the subject, it has been assumed through the years that Thorndike held a rather limited view of the expected transfer of substance and procedure.

Thorndike's theory implied that transfer would occur to the extent that the same stimulus-response bonds were used in the second situation. Transfer would presumably take place if the stimuli were identical or if the responses to different stimuli were identical. Despite Thorndike's belief that approximate decisions regarding identical elements are of practical use, considerable difficulty and misunderstanding have resulted from the teacher's inability to know what is identical. In motor skills, for example, which movements or situations are similar enough to be considered "'identical'"? If the similarity were interpreted as strictly as Guthrie suggested, the possibility of any transfer at all would be remote.

In support of his transfer theory, Thorndike referred largely to studies of bilateral transfer conducted by himself and others. In these studies, it was found

---

[2] Lloyd G. Humphreys, "Transfer in Training in General Education," *Journal of General Education,* V, 213. By permission.

that similar movements or tasks *did* transfer to the opposite hand or foot. As a rule, Thorndike limited his predictions of transfer to the type measurable in these studies. It is difficult to relate his theory to transfer among different motor skills except to assume in a general way that transfer will take place to the extent that the skills are similar. For example, a person who had developed skill in tennis would have an advantage in squash only to the extent that the strokes are identical.

In view of Thorndike's explanation, one might expect enough identical elements to allow transference:

1. From rebound tumbling to diving, in which rotary and curvilinear motions as well as maximizing height could be used.
2. From the soccer kick to the soccer-type field goal kick in football.
3. From the overhand throw of a baseball to the overhead smash in tennis or in the tennis serve.
4. From the action of slinging a skipping stone across the water to the handball stroke.

Thorndike, with several other psychologists, effectively refuted the doctrine of formal discipline. He did not, however, offer a basis for an understanding of the full possibilities of transfer as now accepted.

Judd's theory of generalized principles

C. H. Judd differed sharply from Thorndike in regard to the nature and extent of transfer. Judd's theory of *generalized principles* emphasized that basic principles and laws, as well as specific skills, were transferred. He believed that the individual applied the general idea to a new situation.

Much of Judd's theory was supported by his classic study (1908) in which subjects threw darts at submerged targets. This motor skills study was designed to determine whether knowledge of a principle would aid an individual in a situation where the principle was applicable. In his experiment, two groups of fifth-grade and sixth-grade boys were required to throw darts at a small target that was placed under water. Prior to the testing program, one group was given a good theoretical explanation of the principle of refraction. The other group was not given this information. In the first few trials (with the target 12 inches under water), there was no appreciable difference in the performance of the two groups. Judd observed that even with the theoretical knowledge, a certain amount of practice was essential before the principle would be put into practice. Still, a difference between the groups eventually emerged in favor of those who had been taught the principle of refraction. The submerged target was next raised to 4 inches beneath the surface of the water. At this point, there was a sharp difference in the performance of the two groups. The group with the theoretical knowledge performed better. Judd believed that the superior performance resulted from their understanding of why the angle required at the 12-inch depth would not apply when the target was placed at a 4-inch depth.

Hendrickson and Schroeder (1941) conducted an experiment similar to Judd's dart-throwing study. Eighth-grade boys practiced the skill of air rifle shooting at targets submerged under water. The authors reported that (1) knowledge of the principle involved was valuable in facilitating transference; (2) this knowledge was an aid in the original performances in the first situation (contrary to Judd's findings); (3) thoroughness of theoretical understanding had an effect upon the degree of initial learning and transfer; and (4) insight, or sudden learning, was apparent.

Judd's theory was therefore more liberal than that of Thorndike. Judd's generalized theory suggests the transfer of basic principles as well as peripheral knowledges and skills. In Judd's theory a great deal more transfer would be expected than would be assumed in Thorndike's identical elements theory.

In view of the general concepts of Judd's theory, one would expect the following types of transfer to apply to sports skills:

1. From badminton to racquetball, not only would the forehand and backhand skills transfer but also the footwork, body positioning, and knowledge of rebounds and strategy.
2. Use of the concept of double teaming (2 on 1, 3 on 2, etc.) should be transferred among team sports such as basketball, soccer, field hockey, and lacrosse.
3. The follow-through technique should be transferred to throwing skills used in baseball, softball, football, and bowling, as well as to striking skills used in baseball, golf, tennis, or handball.

The theories of Thorndike and Judd have often been viewed as mutually exclusive, with one being correct and the other incorrect. Practice and research, however, have shown that transfer may take place either by identical elements or by general principles. As a result, recent educators have been concerned with establishing exact laws of transfer rather than proving one of the major theories right or wrong. This is consistent with the general trend in psychology to concentrate on functional principles rather than major theoretical positions.

TRANSFER IN MOTOR SKILLS

Transfer may be roughly classified as specific or nonspecific. *Specific transfer* occurs when the substance of the material or skill is transferred from one situation to another. Such transfer may be observed in racquet sports, bilateral use of the hands or feet, dance and gymnastics routines, or in the transfer of vocabulary from one language to another. *Nonspecific transfer* refers to the more subtle impact that one experience might have in a subsequent situation. Such transfer could include a general approach to problem solving, the carry-over of a strategy for handling a new task, learning how to learn, or the general warm-up effect that one activity may have on another. Both specific and nonspecific transfer may result in either a positive or a negative effect.

Transfer may take place either between tasks or within the same activity. In research reports this is referred to as either intertask or intratask transfer. *Intertask transfer* refers to the carry-over of skill or knowledge from one activity to a different one in which a similar response is required. It is often observed that catching, throwing, kicking, striking, or footwork skills are transferred to or used in different skills. *Intratask transfer* refers to the use of somewhat modified responses or different approaches within the same activity. Driving different types of motor vehicles, dribbling or shooting a basketball with the nonpreferred hand, switch-hitting the baseball, or doing reverse turns in skating, dance, or gymnastics would reflect intratask transfer. Research reports have focused on both intertask and intratask transfer.

General transfer among skills

The transfer theories of both Thorndike and Judd were to a great extent based on research involving motor skills. Support for Thorndike's identical elements theory came mostly from studies on contralateral transfer of simple skills. Judd's classical study made use of a motor skill in which a knowledge of the basic principle of activity was strategic to learning. Stylus mazes, tracking devices, electronic apparatus, mirror tracing, mirror writing, and numerous other skills have been used in subsequent studies on transfer. Ironically, findings from these studies have more generally been applied to verbal learning than to teaching of motor skills.

A limited amount of research has been devoted to the study of transfer among gross sports skills. One of the most extensive investigations of this type was conducted by Nelson (1957a). He studied the transfer of learning in a number of gross motor skills that had some similar elements and patterns. Specifically tested was the amount of transfer from (1) a badminton volley to a tennis volley (against a wall), (2) a volleyball tap for accuracy to a basketball tip for accuracy, and (3) a track starting stance to a football starting position. In these experiments, six groups of unskilled college men were used. Nelson found that initial learning of the tennis volley favorably affected the learning of the badminton volley; initial learning of the basketball skill favorably affected the learning of the volleyball skill; and initial learning of the track starting stance favorably affected the learning of the football stance.

Nelson also found that (1) when skills are taught separately, teaching for transfer helps more than when skills are taught alternately, and (2) teaching for transfer did not aid in the track starting skills. Some negative transfer was apparent when similar skills were interspersed. He concluded that skills involving similar elements should not be learned concurrently.

In another experiment, Nelson (1957b) investigated the effect of swimming on the learning of certain motor skills (volleyball tap for accuracy and running the high hurdles). In an investigation involving forty college men, he found that swimming had neither a favorable nor an unfavorable effect on the learning or performance of other skills. He reported that fatigue from swimming might have a detrimental effect on performance, but this was not a lasting interference. He detected no evidence of the negative transfer for swimming assumed by many during the past few decades.

Lindeburg and Hewitt (1965) conducted an experiment to determine whether practice with a basketball that was slightly larger and heavier than regulation size would aid or hinder one in performance with a regulation basketball. Experienced subjects were tested and retested with both the regulation and the experimental ball in the short shot, foul shooting, passing, and dribbling. The authors concluded that use of a basketball that was slightly larger and heavier than a regulation ball resulted in no differences in the shooting and dribbling tests. There was a slight negative effect on passing skills. In general, it can be assumed that use of a basketball that does not vary greatly from regulation size results in approximately the same development as would result if a regulation ball were being used. Teachers, therefore, who wish to use a larger than regulation size ball for young children need not be fearful of a great deal of interference. On some occasions these teachers may wish to use a ball, bat, or other equipment that is smaller than that used by older children or adults. Such miniature equipment may be less intimidating and more easily handled.

Contralateral transfer of skills

The ability of an individual to more easily learn a particular skill with one hand after it has been learned with the opposite hand is referred to as *contralateral transfer*. Other terms frequently used in reference to this phenomenon are *bilateral* or *cross-transfer*. In essence, contralateral transfer refers to the transference of any skill from one side of the body to the other side. However, this type of transfer may also be from the hand to the foot on either side of the body, and vice versa, or from one foot to the other. Studies as far back as the late 19th century have consistently shown evidence of contralateral transfer. Reviews of research that have shown the consistency of this phenomenon have been prepared by Bray (1928), Weig (1932), and Ammons (1958).

Bryant (1892) found that tapping ability was transferable between hands for children. At the same time, he determined that cross-fatigue (to the opposite limb) was independent of general bodily fatigue. Woodworth (1899) showed that the ability to draw straight lines was transferable between limbs. In skills involving speed and accuracy, Scripture (1899) discovered transfer between limbs of the body. Swift (1903) conducted a study of gross motor skills in which subjects were required to juggle two balls with one hand. He found that they could learn this skill more readily after it had been learned first with the opposite hand. Cook (1934) and Baker (1950) demonstrated cross-transfer with fine motor skills. Studies substantiating the existence of contralateral transfer have involved such fine motor skills as mazes, mirror tracing, operating adding machines, and handwriting.

A vivid example of contralateral transfer is described in an early experiment by Munn (1932). In this study, one hundred college students practiced a novel task that involved flipping a ball into a cup, the ball being attached to the cup by means of a string. Both the experimental group and the control group took 50 tries with the left hand. The experimental group then had 500 tries with the right hand, while the control group rested. But groups were then given 50 additional practices with the left hand. From the first 50 trials to the second 50 trials, the experimental group improved 61 percent, while the control group improved only 28 percent. Munn concluded that the advantage for the experimental group resulted from their right-handed practice.

The existence of contralateral transfer indicates that learning, when only one part of the body is overtly involved, is to some extent a general function. Certainly, this learning is not restricted to one particular limb or portion of the body. The reason for this transfer has not been entirely explained. However, neurological and muscular involvement may be comparable to the bilateral conditioning that reportedly takes place in muscles. For example, Hellebrant (1962) found that antagonistic muscle groups were developed along with protagonist muscular development. Earlier (1947) he had suggested that cross-transfer or cross-education are misnomers since the unpracticed limb is also exercised through isometric contraction. That is, it is probable that one who is asked to vigorously flex the right arm will at the same time (unknowingly) experience some tension in the left arm. Still, this appears to fit into the definition of transfer inasmuch as the original experience with the one hand provides some advantage during subsequent use of the contralateral limb.

Ammons (1958) has suggested that contralateral transfer is facilitated by visual cues, knowledge of appropriate body position, techniques in eye movements, relaxing effects as a result of the previous learning, and a general feeling of confidence. Johnson (1960) also suggested that improved performance on the second task may be due to increased confidence, acquaintance with the problem, and improved techniques of learning. The conditions Ammons and Johnson list are generally believed to facilitate transfer of all types, not just contralateral transfer. These conditions do not, however, suggest definite learning in the untrained body part.

The concept of contralateral transfer is no longer seriously challenged. It must be kept in mind, however, that the most efficient and direct way to learn a skill with the left hand is to practice with the left hand, not the right one. The wise coach would not teach a right-footed player to kick a football with the left foot for transfer value. Neither would the right-handed pitcher be taught to pitch left-handed. The most direct route in teaching these skills would be most effective.

In view of the advantages of direct teaching, of what value is contralateral transfer? While the punter in football and the pitcher in baseball would have little need to perform with their opposite limbs, many situations exist in sports and in everyday life in which contralateral skill is desirable. For example, the soccer player must develop kicking skill with each foot. Making effective use of transfer techniques may conserve practice time for the teacher. In addition, a more thorough analysis and understanding of the skill may result if the opposite side is used. Teachers who make use of the transfer concept will be able to promote more general or all-around skill development. By taking full advantage of contralateral training and transfer, teachers will avoid developing "one-handed" performers who can turn or break in only one direction.

The physical educator might make effective use of contralateral transfer in:

1. Teaching young basketball players to shoot and dribble well with either hand.
2. Teaching the wrestler to move effectively or to resist pressure from either side.
3. Teaching the dancer, the gymnast, or the diver to rotate the body to both the right and left.
4. Teaching the soccer player to dribble or kick with either foot.
5. Teaching the baseball player to switch hit.

Prerequisite learning

The development of skills and knowledge is a cumulative process. One viewpoint holds that all learning and performance in later childhood and adult life is the result of transfer from earlier learning. No doubt, there is a degree of validity in this theory. Teachers of motor skills, therefore, should start with more fundamental coordinations and progress toward more advanced activities. After developing basic skills, the child will, with appropriate maturity, be able to perform finer, more integrated tasks.

A serious mistake often occurs in motor development, as well as in verbal learning, when fundamental learning is prematurely passed over for the teaching of more refined skills. Not only does the learner have greater difficulty in learning the more advanced task, but certain movement fundamentals are omitted that limit other learning as well. It is possible to teach certain tasks to children before they have reached the optimum physiological or psychological level, but this practice results in an inefficient teacher-learning situation.

Learning and performance at each advanced level are best served if the instructor can assume certain prerequisite skills. The instructor in French II assumes that students have mastered certain concepts before beginning the course. The coach of a professional basketball team assumes that a candidate has all the basic moves. Similarly, a dancer applying for a role in a dance production is expected to have basic skills. It is essential, therefore, that teachers in the early grades concentrate on developing fundamental movement skills upon which a more sophisticated performance can be developed. The broader the base of early skills, the greater the possibility for developing proficiency in a wide variety of activities. Concentrating on the development of fundamental skills is often at variance with the sentiments of some overzealous athletic coaches who would have young performers specialize in a specific sport at a very early age. Although some success can be realized by specialization at a relatively early age, this practice tends to limit one's ability to develop proficiency in other physical skills.

Considerable attention in recent years has been devoted to the use of basic, or fundamental, movement activities as prerequisites for the learning of more specific skills. At the elementary school level, greater effort is being devoted to the use of such movement skills as running, walking, hopping, balancing, lifting, kicking, skipping, rolling, and climbing. These activities are taught so that other skills that require these movements can be learned more readily. The nature of the transfer from basic to more specific skills has not yet been fully explored. One of the greatest needs in physical education today is the establishment of a sound system of progression from the most fundamental skills to the most intricate movements for all activities included in the program. This task would require concentration of study in an area that has been woefully lacking in research.

GENERAL TRANSFER CHARACTERISTICS

Recent educational practice has sought to teach principles rather than all the specific facts that students may need in subsequent years. This practice was given a major boost by the work of Judd, among others, and was supported by the findings of Katona (1940), who had two groups of subjects learn the same set of numbers. One group was asked to look for a principle upon which the numbers were based. Lists such as the following were used: 912161923263033374044, etc. The group that was urged to search for a principle learned the lists much faster because they had less to learn, i.e., after the principle had been determined, the task became routine.

Emphasis upon a pinciples approach in teaching occasionally leads to criticisms that education is not "practical" enough. However, proponents of this teaching strategy point out that theory is the most practical technique. The rationale is that the individual who understands the concept or principle is able to use this knowledge in solving many problems. Consequently, greater useful knowledge can be gained from fewer concepts. On the other hand, the individual who understands specific facts without the underlying principles is limited to the application of only those facts. It is consistent with the principles approach to assume that the individual who has mastered basic movement or mechanical principles will be able to apply them to a wide variety of motor skills.

In accepting the generalized principles theory of transfer, there are dangers of assuming or expecting too much understanding and resulting application. First, it must be realized that theory which is not understood by the learner can hardly be expected to transfer. Unless there is understanding, there will be no application. In motor skills a basic or fundamental movement might be executed, perhaps accidentally, without any feel for the action or any appreciation for the general application of the movement. The wise teacher would, therefore, not assume that after one execution of a back somersault on the floor, a student would immediately be able to use this movement in a back dive off the springboard, a somersault on a trampoline, or at the end of a tumbling routine. The student must first get the kinesthetic feel of the movement and duplicate it *correctly* on the floor before being able to transfer the correct movement to another environment.

In addition, it should be pointed out that even when the principle or theory is understood, it will not necessarily be applied to a second situation. Correct theory is not always applied to appropriate situations. Burack and Moss (1956) conducted a study to determine if an understanding of the principle of centrifugal force would aid students in the solution of a problem. They found that not all students who understood the principle applied it to a new task that required use of the principle. They concluded that (1) relevant past experience is not always drawn upon and applied to a present problem, and (2) knowing the general principles and even receiving examples does not necessarily enable subjects to apply the principle.

Aside from the studies of Judd and Hendrickson and Schroeder, which have been discussed previously in this chapter, there is little evidence regarding the application of basic movement principles or physical laws in the learning of new motor skills. One study, designed to investigate the influence of knowledge of mechanical principles, was conducted by Colville (1957). This study did not reveal any particular advantages resulting from an understanding of the appropriate principles. Colville had women of college age learn principles relating to rebound angles, momentum, and acceleration. The subjects then learned (1) a ball-rolling skill that involved a rebound, (2) a catching skill (using tennis and badminton rackets), and (3) archery shooting from 20 to 40 yards. Colville found that instruction regarding the mechanical principles did not aid in the acquisition of tasks that were seemingly related to the principles taught. Nevertheless, she states:

> However, since it appears that some part of the learning period may be devoted to instruction concerning general principles without detriment to the motor learning of the students, it would seem desirable to include such instruction in order to provide this additional opportunity for acquiring some related knowledge about principles of mechanics and the application of forces (p. 326).

Transfer and application of principles are, therefore, not automatic. Teachers have found that students often fail to generalize or make connections. On other occasions, learners try to make application where the principle does not apply. There is a need for closing the gap between understanding principles and applying them to new problems. The teacher should therefore point out similarities of general movement patterns among different activities.

There is some evidence to suggest transfer advantages where only part of the components between tasks is similar. For example, Vincent (1968) showed transfer advantages in the motor components of skills where only the perceptual components were similar. Groups of college students practiced a balance task and a paper and pencil dot task for four weeks. Though substantially different from a jump board test and a second balance test (both of which were later used as the criterion tests) practice on the initial tasks did enable the experimental groups to perform better than did a control group. Vincent urged that tasks be analyzed according to both perception and motor components so that difficult tasks might be aided by allowing subjects to practice only the perceptual phase.

It seems probable that the teaching of general principles at the same time or in relation to a specific skill would have distinct advantages over such teaching in a neutral setting. The learner is likely to understand the concept in a more meaningful way. In turn, these principles would be transferred more easily.

Developing principles for transfer.   If an understanding of general principles or concepts is important in motor learning, a thorough knowledge of them is essential for maximum transfer. One should not equate the ability to state a principle with an understanding of its usefulness. Obviously, not all children understand the implications of poems they recite. The same holds true for verbal concepts, mathematical principles, or movement patterns. Of course, children with greater intelligence should understand principles and their applications more quickly than would less intelligent persons.

It is assumed that when students understand the principle of rebound, they will easily learn ball-playing skills in which this principle is important. Likewise, an understanding of the principle of inertia as reflected in follow-through is also expected to aid one in learning to perform certain sports skills. In order to promote rapid and thorough understanding of principles that are important for motor performance, it is often valuable to have students "prove" the concept in a practical way. For example, the principle of rebound angle and force can be effectively illustrated with a basketball rebound shot off the backboard or a bounce pass to a teammate. When shooting from the side of the basket, the beginning player has a tendency to bank the ball directly over the goal, thus causing it to miss the basket by coming down on the opposite side. In making a bounce pass, beginning players often erroneously bounce the ball halfway between themselves and their teammates, thus causing it to fall short of the target.

Novice catchers in baseball often misjudge pop fouls because they do not understand the principle that baseballs always curve in the direction in which the front of the ball is spinning (see Figure 5-1). Consequently, they stand directly under the pop-up only to find that at the last second it curves away from them, in the direction of the pitcher's mound. After the concept of the curve is learned, the

FIGURE 5-1.   Effect of Ball Rotation on Change of Direction.

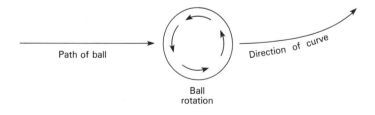

Path of ball

Direction of curve

Ball
rotation

catcher will anticipate this and compensate in the direction of the infield. Understanding the principle of the curve also helps outfielders anticipate that the ball hit near the foul line will always curve *away* from the fielder. Soccer players also learn to anticipate the curve of the ball on the basis of observed rotation.

The principles of inertia and momentum may also be illustrated in motor skills performance. For example, the inexperienced third baseman who must throw on the run and whose momentum is toward home plate will usually throw to the home plate side of the first baseman. The error in accuracy when one throws in a direction other than the direction of movement is reflected in many sports activities. The quarterback who is running parallel to the line of scrimmage tends to throw in front of the receiver who is running in the same direction. Conversely, he will most often throw behind the receiver who is running in the opposite direction. Similarly, people who have (mischievously) thrown objects out of a moving vehicle aiming to hit a roadside marker or tree have observed the same phenomenon, i.e., they miss the target on the side in which the vehicle is moving. A thorough understanding of the appropriate principles would make for more accurate passing in many sports situations. Although experienced performers eventually learn to apply most of the physical laws related to the activity, this takes a great deal of time and leads to needless inefficiency. Experienced teachers and coaches can reduce this waste of energy by devoting attention to the teaching of usable principles.

Selecting an effective technique for teaching a movement concept or principle is sometimes troublesome. Occasionally the use of an indirect method with alternative activities is helpful. For instance, if the pupil is having difficulty in learning one movement skill, another skill to which the same principle applies could be taught. With greater understanding of the basic principle, the student will more easily learn the desired skill. Teaching by transfer is often necessary when there is a lack of communication or if the student seems to have developed a psychological block to the first activity. Use of a familiar story, or parable, is often helpful in illustrating an important point.

A valuable aid in making use of general principles in motor activities is mental rehearsal. This practice may be encouraged either by verbal description or by visual imagery of the task to be performed. There is considerable evidence that mental practice aids learning and performance. It seems reasonable, therefore, to assume that general concepts of movement may be gained by mental rehearsal and may then be transferred to the appropriate skill.

The value of general principles in motor skills is obvious. Such principles as follow-through, opposition of arms and legs, conservation of energy, momentum, and even general strategy techniques have wide application in sports activities. Much rehearsal is needed, however, to determine the manner in which basic principles may best be taught and transferred among a wide variety of skills.

Learning how to learn

The story is told that science writer Isaac Asimov was once asked by his father where he learned all that he wrote. Isaac answered, "From you, Father." The father then pointed out, "But I don't even know those things." Whereupon Isaac replied, "Yes, but you taught me *how* to learn them."

The phenomenon of learning how to learn, sometimes referred to as learning sets, has been demonstrated on many occasions and with vastly different material. Learning how to learn is a type of nonspecific transfer, often giving the appearance of formal discipline. On occasion, there have been claims of a great deal of specific skill or knowledge transfer when such was not the case. The learner often learns how to approach a task in terms of technique in solving a problem. A second task is then learned more quickly than the first one, even if there is no similarity in specific material or theory. For example, some people seem to be able to solve puzzles or tricky problems easily. Their competence may come as a result of previous experience with problems that have a general similarity. It has been demonstrated that new lists of nonsense syllables can be learned better after lists of different nonsense syllables have been previously learned. Generally, if more lists have already been learned, the subject can more easily learn new lists. This technique of learning how to learn is often more important than any similarity of content.

Harlow (1949) showed that monkeys learn problem-solving techniques with practice. He later showed that children learn techniques that aid them in solving problems. As a result, he advocated that more attention be devoted to the development of techniques, and he stressed that a great deal of time and attention should be spent on the early trials of any task. After a good base or understanding of the techniques has been established, less time is needed for later related problems. Therefore, teachers of motor skills might be wise to spend extra time and effort in teaching the beginning or basic movements of a new skill.

Woodrow (1927) showed that skills in learning can be taught. He taught subjects how to memorize poetry, prose, and other materials. Subjects with practice showed greater improvement than those who had not been instructed. Woodrow's techniques for improving memory were similar to many in education today, i.e., recitation, analysis of meaning, and association.

Levinson and Reese (1967) found that children, college students, and aged persons developed general skills in problem solving as a result of working with problem-solving techniques. The more problems they solved, the better they were able to solve different problems. Postman and Schwartz (1964) reported that students benefited from a learning experience that followed an earlier one, even though the materials and procedures were different.

The existence of the learning how to learn phenomenon no doubt helped to propagate the doctrine of formal discipline. The two concepts, however, are distinctly different since formal discipline emphasized that the improvement of faculties would have application to all circumstances, while learning how to learn is assumed to apply only to situations where the method of attack is similar.

It is assumed by psychologists and educators that the phenomenon of learning how to learn occurs with all types of tasks. In motor skills, this concept is most often exhibited in the performance of novel tasks. In stunts, especially those involving reasoning or problem-solving abilities, persons with previous experience in similar tasks often perform at a higher level.

Developing psychological traits in sports

The development of certain psychological traits represents a type of learning that can have far-reaching effects. Such characteristics, for example, habits and attitudes that are developed in relation to one activity, have proven to be helpful in a wide range of other activities. As far back as the beginning of the century, Bagley (1905) reported that when neatness habits were taught to children as general principles, those habits were applied to all areas of the school program. General observation affirms that students who have established a habit of performing well in early school activities tend to sustain that habit in future school activities. These children, with their records and expectancy of success, exceed the performance of other children who have equal, and sometimes superior, ability. Success tends to beget success, and, unfortunately, failure tends to beget failure. Persons who have been taught, directly or indirectly, that they are not likely to do well often prove such a prophecy to be true. People who label themselves as "not being good in science" or being "poor at sports" often develop such attitudes on the basis of limited exposure to the area. Nevertheless, the negative effect carries over to the whole area of science or sports.

Athletic coaches have long believed that the habits of hard work and perseverance, once developed with reference to a particular sport, will carry over to all other athletic activities. Likewise, there is widespread belief that traits such as competitiveness, "toughness," and the willingness to tolerate pain or minor injury in sports, once learned, will become general habits of behavior, as will tendencies toward timidity, indecisiveness, and hypochondria.

Prior to around 1960 it was commonplace for football coaches to prohibit players to drink water during a two- or three-hour practice session, regardless of the heat and humidity. The general belief was that the consumption of water would make the players sluggish, and therefore less effective. Subsequently, ample evidence was produced to convince all reasonable coaches that the intake of some water did not hinder, rather it enhanced performance. In addition, the prohibition of water and the dehydration that sometimes resulted was shown to be the cause of a number of deaths. In view of this evidence, most coaches did away with rules prohibiting water at practice sessions. This was not universal, however. I recall hearing one coach go immediately from the argument that water would make players sluggish to the statement that withholding the water will "make them tougher." Though such a stance seems severe, especially for those who have had to endure such long, hot practices, there is a thread of truth in the coach's observation. The expectancy of avoiding all discomfort, or conversely, the willingness to tolerate moderate pains and inconvenience, are traits that can be developed. Coaches make a philosophical judgment concerning the merits of a "tough" guy (or girl) mentality as opposed to a more humanistic attitude on the part of the players. Having made such judgments, they then attempt to develop those traits they value most highly. Parents, too, make decisions as to the attitudes they wish their children to develop, and they work toward that end. Suffice it to say that a *proper balance* should be developed between such traits as intense competitiveness and total pacifism, hypochondria and unreasonable disregard for one's physical welfare, and timidity and "foolish" courage.

At another level, teachers find many opportunities to establish habits and attitudes that have clear transfer implications for times and places that are inappropriate. Unfortunately, physical education teachers and athletic coaches have long engaged in the practice of "punishing" misbehaving or underachieving students by requiring them to run laps, do numerous push-ups, or engage in other strenuous exercises. It is conceivable that the student actually enjoys running or doing push-ups under favorable conditions. However, when these same activities are used as punishment, the concept of punishment is transferred to running distances, doing push-ups, or whatever other activity is used. These activities therefore become things to be avoided. A similar negative approach is often used by other teachers who require students to write themes or perform other school chores, which then become related to punishment and ultimately avoidance.

Negative transfer

ERROR VS. IGNORANCE

It is almost as difficult to make a man unlearn his errors as his knowledge. Malinformation is more hopeless than noninformation: for error is always more busy than ignorance.

Ignorance is a blank sheet, on which we may write; but error is a scribbled one, from which we must first erase.

Ignorance is contented to stand still with her back to the truth; but error is more presumptuous, and proceeds in the wrong direction.

Ignorance has no light, but error follows a false one.

The consequence is that error, when she retraces her steps, has farther to go before she can arrive at truth than ignorance.

Caleb C. Colton

Negative transfer occurs when one task interferes with or inhibits the learning or performance of a second task, that is, inappropriate application based on an erroneous assumption about similarity between tasks or situations. Such misapplication may be a conscious or a subconscious act. In either case, such "error," as pointed out by Colton, can prove to be a significant distraction to the participant. Consequently, teachers in all subject areas are interested in preventing the development of such negative transfer. If such an error is allowed to persist, extinction becomes especially difficult. Therefore, while teachers are interested in promoting positive transfer, they are also concerned with reducing or eliminating negative transfer. Experimental designs for determining negative transfer (proactive and retroactive) were presented earlier on page 131 and 132.

C. L. Hull (1943) used the term *inhibition* in reference to the detrimental effect that the learning or performance of one task might have on a second activity, or the same activity at a later time. While inhibition and negative transfer are not synonymous, they are intimately related. Inhibition is a broader term referring to any reluctance on the part of the individual to perform the task immediately and correctly. One inhibiting factor is negative transfer. Hull describes the two types of inhibition as:

Proactive inhibition. This is interference that performance in one task might have on the learning or performance of a second task at a later time. That is, the second skill would be more difficult to learn because the individual had performed the first one.

Retroactive inhibition. This refers to interference that the performance of a task might have on the retention of one previously learned. Such inhibition results in the forgetting or weakening of performance of certain previously learned skills.

There is not overwhelming research evidence to prove the existence of negative transfer. In fact, Schmidt (1975) states that intertask motor transfer is never negative. Irion (1969) believes that such interference in motor skills is quite remote. However, Lewis, McAllister, and Adams (1951) did show significant negative transfer in the Mashburn three-dimensional continuous tracking task. In this task, subjects were taught to operate fast pedals in a right-left position and an aircraft-type control stick in both forward-backward and right-left positions. After having learned those responses, subjects were shifted to reversed responses for the interpolated task.

Irion reports that negative transfer is difficult to produce in research studies. However, most transfer studies have concentrated on the search for positive and not negative transfer, as did those studies conducted by Lewis, McAllister, and Adams. In addition, few studies have involved the open gross skills prevalent in today's sports activities.

Consequently, most of our opinions about negative transfers in motor skills are based on personal experience or observation of performers who participate in two or more activities similar in terms of motor response. The accomplished baseball player who takes up the game of golf often experiences considerable difficulty because of a tendency to swing the golf club like a baseball bat. This is an example of proactive inhibition. The well-learned tendency of the individual to swing across the body (outside-in) often retards the development of a proper golf swing (inside-out). Similarly, the interlocking or overlapping grip customarily used in golf is often more difficult for the person who has grown used to the baseball grip.

Though not unanimous, most baseball and golfing experts seem to agree with the interfering effects between baseball and golf. In an article in the *Philadelphia Inquirer* (May 3, 1981), sports writer Fred Byrod found support for this position in the opinions of golf professional Sam Snead and baseball slugger Mike Schmidt. Snead states, "If I was the manager of a baseball team, I wouldn't let my fellows play any golf until after the season. The swings are different." Schmidt states, "I think baseball can hurt a golfer. I would not want to see my golfer playing baseball . . . The baseball bat is much heavier than a golf club. When I go out after play-ing only baseball and no golf for a month, I can't slow it down [the golf swing]. It's like a feather. I top the ball. . . ." Though no formal evidence is available to prove or disprove these opinions, they clearly reflect the majority view of authorities in-volved with the two sports. It is probable that some retroactive inhibition is experi-enced when the novice tennis player is introduced to the game of badminton. It is likely that as one learns the fast wrist strokes of badminton, the proper tennis stroke (total arm swing) will be forgotten somewhat. In a retention test of the tennis stroke at a later time, the individual would probably have a tendency to use the badminton stroke with the tennis racquet. Most likely retention of the proper tennis stroke would be less than if badminton had never been played.

Switching from one-wall to four-wall handball might result in both positive and negative transfer. The person who is accomplished as a one-wall player will show positive transfer when the ball is played only off the front wall. However, when the ball bounces off the side or back walls the one-wall player will exhibit negative transfer. The initial movement response will be in the direction that the ball rebounds off the front wall. This response will tend to take him out of posi-tion for the second rebound off the side wall. The novice handball player will not be so likely to make this initial incorrect response.

Degree of initial learning

A factor that has proven to be important in determining the amount of trans-fer is the degree to which the initial task was learned. It has been demonstrated on numerous occasions that the transfer of verbal material is increased with additional practice of the first skill. Although this concept has not been fully investigated with motor skills, the same principle is assumed to exist. For example, an experienced driver can handle different types of automobiles with ease. However, a person who has not learned to drive the first car well will have great difficulty with different types of cars. Positive transfer can also be observed when an experienced musician learns a new instrument, or when a skilled typist learns to operate other office machines. Since much of what is taught in school is included for its transfer value, it is generally advocated that initial or basic tasks be overlearned for maximum transfer. The degree of desired mastery will often be more than the student thinks necessary.

Similarity and transfer

One of the most important factors in determining the amount of transfer is the degree of similarity between the tasks. This concept of similarity has been emphasized since Thorndike's work, which led to his identical elements theory. As has been pointed out earlier in this chapter, transfer can vary from highly positive (helpful) to neutral (no effect) to highly negative (interference). It is interesting to note that the relationship between degree of similarity and amount of positive transfer does not follow a straight line. Somewhat similar tasks may lead to interference, or negative transfer. Robinson (1927) illustrated this relationship (see Figure 5-2). The concept presented in this illustration is consistent with learning theory today.

Many years later Osgood developed a somewhat similar but more elaborate three-dimensional graph to summarize the transfer relationships involved in stimulus and response similarity. By use of a transfer surface (see Figure 5-3) positive and negative transfer are represented by vertical deviations above and below the horizontal plane. The long dimension of the plane represents response similarity, from completely opposite responses near the bottom, to unrelated responses in the middle, and identical responses at the top. The short dimension represents stimulus similarity between tasks, with the right portion denoting a neutral stimulus, and the left side an identical stimulus. According to this model, maximum transfer occurs when both stimuli and responses are the same. Negative transfer is greatest when stimuli are identical and responses are opposite. Where stimuli are correlated, transfer is always zero.

Another effort to generalize knowledge about transfer was made by Kingsley and Garry (1957). After surveying the available research, they developed a summary table to illustrate the amount of transfer that has been reported among several types of learning tasks (see Table 5-1). An analysis of their table reveals that the most similar tasks can be expected to benefit most from transfer.

FIGURE 5-2. *Effects of Task Similarity on Transfer* When tasks *A* and *B* are very similar or identical, transfer is high. When tasks *A* and *B* are only slightly similar, interference is great. When tasks *A* and *B* are very dissimilar, interference is slight. This is referred to as the Skaggs-Robinson Hypothesis. (From E. S. Robinson, "The 'Similarity' Factor in Retroaction," *American Journal of Psychology,* 39, 1927, pp. 297-312.)

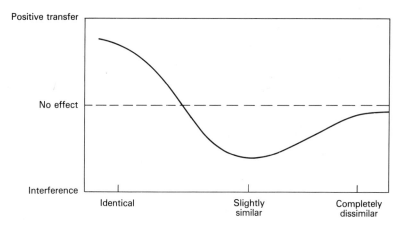

Similarity Between Task *A* and Task *B*

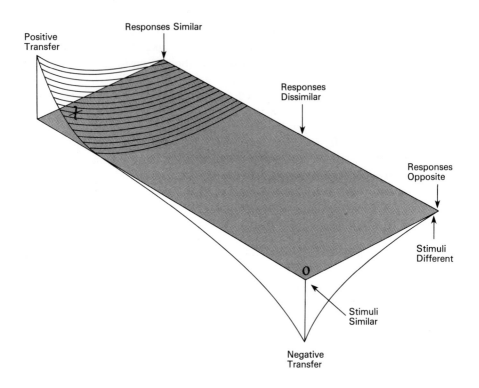

Positive
Transfer

Responses Similar

Responses
Dissimilar

Responses
Opposite

Stimuli
Different

O

Stimuli
Similar

Negative
Transfer

FIGURE 5-3. Osgood's hypothetical transfer diagram showing the relationship between response similarity and stimulus similarity of two tasks and the amount of transfer expected from one task to the other. (From Osgood, 1949.)

PRINCIPLES OF TRANSFER

On the basis of research evidence, opinion of learning theorists, and a consideration of the characteristics of motor learning, several transfer principles seem to emerge. Among those that are most widely accepted and that have implications for motor skills are the following:

1. The greater the similarity between two tasks, the greater will be the positive transfer. This principle has rarely been questioned, even by those with a very limited view of transfer, and it has been supported by research since the earliest studies on transfer. There is every reason to expect that this principle applies equally well to the learning of motor skills. Numerous examples of sufficient similarity among motor skills have been presented in this chapter. However, a great deal of research is needed in order to clearly determine similarity characteristics of both substance and technique in regular physical education skills.

TABLE 5-1   Amount of transfer resulting from different training experiences
in experiments on transfer of training

Amount of transfer reported	Training experience	Transferred to
Maximum transfer (over 50% gains)	Marking words	Other words
	Discrimination of shades of red	Discrimination of other colors
	Mazes	Other mazes
Considerable transfer (25%-50%)	Learning sets on object-equality discrimination	Similar problems
	Estimating areas of geometric figures	Similar mazes
	Memorizing techniques	Varied memory tasks
	Mental multiplication	Adding, dividing
	Biology, geometry	Biology and geometry tests
Moderate transfer (10%-25%)	Learning nonsense syllables	Learning prose, poetry
	Poetry	Prose
	Sound intensities	Brightness intensities
	Applying principles of refraction	Hitting underwater targets
Little to negative transfer (under 10%)	Poetry, prose	Dates, syllables
	Estimating line lengths	Similar task
	Cancellation of letters	Cancellation of nouns, verbs
	Card sorting	Reaction time typing
	Computation	Reasoning
	Latin	English vocabulary
	Latin	Spelling
	Biology and geometry	Other subjects

Source: Howard L. Kingsley and Ralph Garry, *The Nature and Conditions of Learning,* 2nd ed., © 1957. Reprinted by permission of Prentice-Hall, Inc., Englewood Cliffs, New Jersey.

2. Learning to make new responses to old stimuli results in negative transfer. This is evident when one attempts to break an old habit or to perform an established activity in a different way. The individual who learns to drive an automobile with a standard gear shift will experience some difficulty when attempting to drive one with an automatic shift. The stimuli are essentially the same, but different responses are required. The person will frequently stamp the floor with the left foot and reach for the gear shift with the right hand. Such behavior does not contribute to smooth driving performance. Similar difficulties result when the reverse learning procedure has been followed.

3. Learning to make old responses to new stimuli results in positive transfer. For example, a well-learned habit is easily applied to a new situation or a new

activity. The experienced automobile driver, though exhibiting negative transfer when new responses are required, shows almost immediate proficiency when driving different vehicles requiring essentially the same response. Different model cars, trucks, tractors, or other machinery may be driven quite easily if, for example, they all have a clutch and a standard shift. Likewise, body control skills that have been developed in gymnastics are easily put to use in other activities such as dancing, diving, or other new stimuli situations where the old responses apply.

4. Transfer among similar tasks is not automatic. Several studies have shown that established skills and principles are not always used in new situations. Often the learner does not recognize the similarity between the situations or is not stimulated to make use of available skills. The teacher's strategic roles are pointing to situations where established skills may be used and motivating students to use these skills.

5. An understanding of principles or procedures underlying the initial task will result in greater transfer to a different activity. This statement is supported by convincing evidence from verbal and fine motor skills research. Although little research on this topic has involved gross motor skills, it is reasonable to assume that an understanding of the principles of momentum, rebound, and Newton's laws of motion would prove helpful in the performance of many sports skills. Techniques of learning and performing have also been shown to transfer. The instructor should show the learner the general applicability of principles and procedures.

6. The amount of transfer varies according to the difficulty of the learning material and the capacity of the learner. Material that is so complex as to be confusing to the learner will not be transferred. Persons more intelligent in the particular activity make greater transfer than do persons of lesser intelligence. Learners with greater ability are able to make broader application on the basis of fewer basic principles. The instructor, however, can promote transfer among learners of lesser ability by clarifying common elements among learning tasks.

Teaching for transfer

All authorities agree that effective use of transfer principles can be a valuable aid in maximizing the learning energies of students. However, transfer must be planned for in order to be most effectively applied across the curriculum. Such transfer is not automatic, although some will take place without the intervention of the teacher. The amount that will take place is dependent upon the ability of the student and the degree of commonality between the two tasks or situations. Brighter students and those who are more highly skilled in the initial task are able to make more appropriate applications than are less talented or less skilled persons. Still, the amount of transfer for learners, regardless of ability level, can be enhanced by the instructor who plans for such transfer.

Several authors, including Davis and Lawther (1948), Nelson (1957a), and Drowatsky (1975) have listed guidelines for the promotion of transfer among motor skills. Many other persons have discussed teaching for transfer across the curriculum. Among the more generally proposed principles are the following:

1. Teach principles or generalizations that are broadly applicable. Such principles must be clearly communicated so as to be understood by the learner. For example, the employment of follow-through in motor skills is important for effective performance in many activities. However, the concept of follow-through is not automatically understood or appreciated by young performers. Years ago I was stressing the importance of follow-through in batting with a young baseball player when the young man asked, "What good is it to go through that routine after the ball's already gone? What good can it do then?" I explained that when one has no follow-through after striking the ball, or a very limited one, it means that the bat *started* to slow down before actual contact. For the first time the player seemed to understand that movement behavior after contact gave some clue as to what had occurred a split second prior to contact. Consequently, he was more receptive to instructions that he was to swing "through" the ball, and hopefully he was able to apply that principle to other striking or throwing skills.

2. Use a variety of illustrations or techniques to develop a thorough understanding of the principle. Verbalizing a concept such as the principle of follow-through does not insure that learners appreciate its importance and general applicability. The teacher or coach should not only explain, but should illustrate the effectiveness of a full follow-through as compared to an abbreviated one. Learners can then benefit by practicing both the full and the abbreviated follow-through, noting the differences in effectiveness.

3. For maximum transfer, the initial task should be well learned. There will be little transfer of the follow-through principles to nonbatting skills if it is not highly developed. The more thoroughly it is learned, the more easily it can be transferred to other follow-through types of movements. Verbalizing and illustrating the skill are important. However, it is even more important to have the learner practice the skill under guidance until it is properly and thoroughly learned. Transfer to a second skill will be most effective if the first one is developed as a strong habit.

4. Point out the similarity of the second task to the first one and the desirability of transfer. Once students have learned the principles of follow-through and have developed skill in its application in batting, they can easily transfer this skill to other tasks. Follow-through in the use of implements such as with the tennis stroke, hockey shot, volleyball spike, or the golf stroke are easily understood and applied. Follow-through in the soccer kick, football punt, baseball throw, bowling delivery, and basketball shot are also transferred once the similarity is pointed out and the first skill has been well learned.

Coaches have traditionally found that basic principles can be easily applied in a great variety of sports activities once they have been firmly understood and then applied in one situation. Among others these include: the double teaming principle, such as 2 on 1 or 3 on 2 in basketball, soccer, or field hockey, or "flooding a zone" as a football passing strategy; using slightly bent knees, spread feet, and weight on the balls of the feet for effective footwork as a defender in basketball, football defensive back, volleyball, wrestling, or boxing; putting "English" on the ball for use in tennis, slicing or hooking the golf ball, curving a baseball or bowling ball; or keeping a low center of gravity for effective tackling or blocking in football, wrestling, or other strength movements.

SUMMARY

1. Most instruction in school is based on the assumption that students will transfer what is learned to nonschool situations. Such assumptions apply to all subject areas, including tennis, wood shop, English grammar, swimming, and chemistry, among others. It is taken for granted that not only will specific skills be transferred, but also work habits, general principles, social attitudes, and emotional responses.

2. Transfer refers to the influence that an established habit has upon the learning, performance, or retention of a second habit. Such influence may be a help or a hindrance. Further, it may influence an activity or skill learned previously, or one learned subsequent to the transfer task.

3. Much observed transfer cannot be precisely related to a specific task. Rather, past learning often has a cumulative effect. In fact, after the adolescent years, it is probable that we rarely learn anything that is entirely new. Practically all learning, whether motor skills, attitudes, or verbal skills, is influenced by previous learning that is somewhat related.

4. Proactive transfer refers to the effect that the learning of a task has on the learning or performance of a second task acquired at a later time. Retroactive transfer refers to the effect that practice on a particular task has on the retention of a previously learned task. Research designs for investigating the existence of each of these are presented.

5. Prior to the 20th century, the concept of formal discipline had a major influence on education both in the United States and in Europe. Formal discipline assumed widespread transfer. This concept held that whatever was most difficult to learn was most beneficial for one's development. That is, the individual could train the mind on difficult subjects and this training would be useful in whatever study was undertaken at a later time. The inclusion of Greek, Latin, and other "hard" subjects were often justified on this basis. William James, Edward Thorndike, and several other psychologists refuted the validity of formal discipline early in the 20th century.

6. After criticizing the formal discipline concept, Thorndike developed a much more restricted theory of transfer known as *identical elements*. This held that only specific skills, knowledge, or techniques are transferred. The same stimulus-

response bonds are necessary in order for transfer to take place in the second situation. This "identical" requirement assumed very little transfer from one activity to another.

7. C. H. Judd, differing significantly from Thorndike's position, developed a theory of *generalized principles*. This concept asserts that basic principles and laws, as well as specific skills, are transferred. Thus, the general ideas or concepts are applied to the situation. Implications of Judd's theory, as well as Thorndike's, are presented as they relate to motor skills.

8. In addition to specific transfer in motor skills, such as contralateral transfer or transfer among racquet sports, nonspecific transfer may also occur. This refers to the more subtle impact that one experience might have on a subsequent situation. Approaches to problem solving, learning how to learn, strategy, and general warmup involve nonspecific transfer.

9. Information about transfer in motor skills has been based primarily on research with novel skills in the laboratory, or on speculation. A limited amount of research has been completed on meaningful gross motor activities. Still, available information lends credence to the belief that significant transfer is possible and that such transfer is widely applicable, i.e., not restricted to Thorndike's concept of identical elements but closer to the position proposed by Judd.

10. Contralateral or bilateral or cross-transfer is the transference of any skill from one side of the body to the other side. The terms are also used to denote transfer from hand to the foot on either side of the body, or vice versa. Extensive research into bilateral transfer was conducted by experimental psychologists early in the 20th century to confirm the existence of such transfer.

11. Many popular motor activities, such as basketball and soccer, require the use of both hands or both feet. In such activities, the effective use of transfer principles can conserve practice time for the teacher and the learner. Early attention to contralateral transfer can prevent the development of "one-handed" or "one-footed" players who have a distinct disadvantage when functioning with the opposite limb.

12. Prerequisite skills are necessary for effective learning and performance at advanced levels. The development of skills and knowledge is a cumulative process. Consequently, whether going from basic to intermediate swimming, French I to French II, or college basketball to the National Basketball Association, the coach or teacher should anticipate transfer of fundamental skills from the previous level of instruction.

13. In an effort to make the most economical use of time and effort, educators have emphasized the teaching of general principles. Such basic information is assumed to have broad usefulness in the educational setting in that the more basic principles will be applied to a wide range of applicable situations. However, when taken to the extreme, such an approach may be counterproductive because naive learners may not be able to make appropriate application.

14. The phenomenon of "learning how to learn" has been demonstrated with a great variety of skills and materials. This concept refers to the individual's learning to approach a task through the technique for solving a problem. After such a skill or strategy has been developed, subsequent tasks are then learned more quickly, even when there is no specific similarity with any previously learned material.

15. Psychological and sociological traits and habits developed in one situation tend to carry over to different activities. Work habits reflecting neatness, thoroughness, and perseverance seem to characterize one's approach to a wide range of activities. So do attitudes such as prejudice, tolerance, competitiveness, and hypochrondria.

16. Negative transfer refers to a situation in which one task interferes with or inhibits the learning or performance of a second task. This occurs when inappropriate application is made from one situation to another. Such misapplication may result from a conscious or subconscious effort to transfer. Negative transfer can prove to be a significant distraction in that it results in an erroneous performance. If such behavioral errors are allowed to persist, they can be difficult to correct.

17. Proactive inhibition is a term coined by Hull referring to the detrimental effect that the learning of one task has on the subsequent learning or performance of a second task. Retroactive inhibition occurs when performance in an activity interferes with the retention of previously learned material.

18. Transfer to a second task is enhanced by thorough learning of the first task. Both the specific components of similarity and the general concepts are more readily transferred when they are well learned.

19. Transfer between skills that are very similar is greater than transfer between dissimilar or slightly similar skills. On the other hand, slightly similar skills may result in interference, thus proving to be less helpful than activities that are totally dissimilar.

20. Both stimuli and responses affect transfer. Similar responses, despite the nature of the stimuli, lead to positive transfer while dissimilar responses, especially with similar stimuli, lead to negative transfer.

SELECTED READINGS

BERNARD, H. W. *Psychology of learning and teaching* (3rd ed.). New York: McGraw-Hill, 1972.

CRATTY, B. J. *Movement behavior and motor learning* (3rd ed.). Philadelphia: Lea & Febiger, 1972.

FISCHMAN, M. G., CHRISTINA, R. W., & VERCRYSSEN, M. J. Retention and transfer of motor skills: a review for the practitioner, *Quest,* 1982, 33 (2), 181-194.

GROSE, R. F., & BIRNEY, R. C., *Transfer of learning: an enduring problem in psychology*. Princeton, N.J.: Van Nostrand, 1963.

HULSE, S. H., DEESE, J., EGETH, H. *The psychology of learning* (5th ed.). New York: McGraw-Hill, 1980.

KINGSLEY, H. L., & GARRY, R., *The nature and condition of learning* (3rd ed.). Englewood Cliffs, N.J.: Prentice-Hall, 1970.

MCGEOCH, J. A., & IRION, A. L. *The psychology of human learning* (2nd ed.). New York: McKay, 1953.

STEPHENS, J. M. Transfer of learning. In *Encyclopedia of educational research* (Rev. ed.). New York: Macmillan, 1960.

TRAVERS, R. M. W. *Essentials of learning* (4th ed.). New York: Macmillan Publishing Co., 1977.

6 Retention and Forgetting

Passage of time seems to result in two types of alterations in learned material: quantitative changes (the amount retained) and qualitative changes (variations in the organization or character of the learned material). *Retention* refers to the persistence of knowledge or skills that have been learned. *Forgetting* is the failure to retain that which has been learned. Retention and forgetting are essentially opposites of the same phenomenon. For example, 100 percent retention is equal to zero forgetting and 20 percent retention equals 80 percent forgetting.

INTRODUCTION

The importance of effective retention is obvious when one realizes that learned skills that are not remembered when needed are of no value. The skilled teacher must not be ignorant about those practices that aid retention, nor those that interfere with the retention of learned material.

All learning experiences will be more valuable if the individual is able to remember them for a reasonably long time. Retention is essential if the person is to put to use what has been learned. If the information cannot be recalled on the appropriate occasion, the time spent in learning it has been largely wasted. In fact, there can be no improvement from trial to trial without some retention because the learning of advanced concepts or skills is contingent upon an understanding and retention of certain prerequisites.

It is axiomatic, therefore, that teachers should be concerned not only with learning, but with the retention of skills or materials that have been learned. Nevertheless, teachers in all subject fields have been traditionally concerned with immediate performance, often to the neglect of techniques that might improve long-term retention. There has existed a general assumption that if a high level of proficiency is exhibited in a particular task, this excellence will be retained. It has been shown, however, that the relationship between immediate proficiency and retention over a long period is not always high. A general concern for the fate of skills acquired has led to considerable investigation of retention and forgetting in recent years. Despite some success in establishing basic laws and general principles, much remains to be determined, especially in regard to the retention of gross motor skills.

Theories regarding retention have long existed in the minds of teachers and laymen. Some of these beliefs are based on research evidence or on empirical observation. Others are simply the result of traditional thinking. Teachers have long suspected that certain types of skills or knowledge are remembered longer than other types. It is also assumed that learning under certain conditions promotes retention. For example, it has been stated frequently that one never forgets how to swim or to ride a bicycle. On the other hand, the names of some state capitals, chemical formulae, or complex folk dance maneuvers are seemingly more quickly forgotten. Practicing a task after it has been well learned seems to aid one in remembering. Relearning an old skill, which apparently has been forgotten, seems to be easier than learning the skill for the first time. Similarly, a poem learned during childhood is seemingly learned more quickly by the individual twenty years later. What is the nature of retention? How can it best be promoted among the different types of skills? These are only two of the important considerations that relate to the retention of school learning. This chapter is devoted to a discussion of the most important aspects of retention.

The retention curve

A retention curve illustrates the amount of material or skill retained at various points in time following the cessation of practice. The retention of an unpracticed skill or unreviewed verbal learning follows a decelerating curve. The shape of this curve is almost as well known as that of the learning curve.

The retention curve was first outlined by Ebbinghaus in 1885. His curve of retention, which was based on memory of nonsense syllables, was one of his most notable contributions (see Figure 6-1). The relatively straight line plotted against

FIGURE 6-1.   Ebbinghaus' Curve of Retention for Lists of Nonsense Syllables.

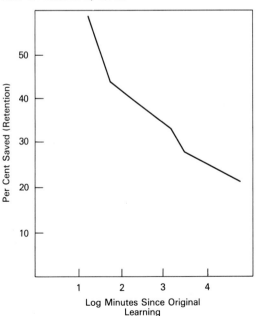

the logarithm of time indicates that most forgetting takes place soon after original learning. Studies since that time have also shown that retention follows a decelerating curve. Several researchers have plotted retention curves against the logarithm of time (as shown in Figure 6-1) so that the long and short intervals can be gotten into the graph without unduly crowding the short periods. Also, this technique has been used to show that retention declines approximately in proportion to the log of time. A typical retention curve without the logarithmic adjustment is shown in Figure 6-2. Retention of both verbal and motor skills has been shown to generally decline with time. However, special conditions of practice or of the skill itself, may result in reminiscence, a temporary rise in the retention curve.

It appears that forgetting is never complete. Thus, the true retention curve never reaches the base line. This is consistently shown when a sensitive measure of retention is used. Motor skills or verbal materials that are experienced only once are often recalled under certain conditions. Unusual or rare incidences of retention in everyday life seem to verify the belief that forgetting is never complete.

The descent of the retention curve is greatly affected by such factors as the type of material learned, its meaningfulness to the learner, the kind of practice schedule through which the material was learned, and the many experiences that come to the attention of the individual. Each of these factors will be discussed in some detail in this chapter.

SHORT-TERM MEMORY

Over the years almost all attention to the topic of memory has been focused on the retention of material or skills over relatively long periods. This has been consistent with the general definition of learning as a "relatively permanent" change in behavior. Consequently, teachers have been concerned with whether children could

FIGURE 6-2.   The Theoretical Retention Curve.

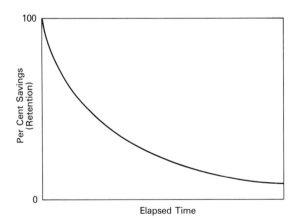

remember vocabulary words, chemical formulae, or other verbal material for days or even weeks after it was presented. Therefore, examinations are scheduled periodically to test retention of the material. So, too, the piano teacher, the driver education instructor, the gymnastics coach, and the carpentry foreman are all interested in whether their students can demonstrate skills taught during the previous session.

Recently, a more temporary phenomenon called short-term memory has attracted a great deal of attention among investigators. Identification of this concept, however, is not new. Even prior to the turn of the century William James (1890) distinguished between what he referred to as *primary retention* and *secondary retention*. He used the term *primary retention* to denote temporary or short-lived memory and *secondary retention* with reference to long-term memory. Others have used terms such as *short-term store* and *long-term store* (see Figures 3-3, 3-4, and 3-5 in chapter three). James was perhaps the first person to raise the question of a qualitative as well as a quantitative distinction between these two types of retention. Despite those early references to short-term retention, active research on this phenomenon did not commence until the late 1950s.

Hulse et al. (1980) classify memory of short duration into two categories: *sensory memory* and *short-term memory*. Sensory memory is described as the holding of a detailed representation of a stimulus for a fraction of a second, or on rare occasions, up to two seconds. A further breakdown of sensory memory is provided by Neisser (1967) who distinguishes between *iconic* and *echoic* memory. Iconic memory refers to the aftereffects of a visual stimulus that, according to him, may last up to one-half second. In support of this notion, Sperling (1960, 1963) conducted two important experiments to bring greater definition to iconic memory. He showed that subjects were able to hold a brief visual image (a series of letters) presented at 50 milliseconds, long enough to read out four or five of those letters. He found that larger exposures enabled subjects to reproduce a greater number of the letters presented. However, he reported that there was no increase in iconic memory when exposures lasted longer than 100 milliseconds.

Echoic memory results from auditory stimuli, and according to Massors (1970) lasts for approximately one-fourth second. Others (Crowder, 1969; and Daruein et al., 1972) present evidence that the sound of the human voice reading digits may be retained for at least two seconds. It should be noted that most experiments in the area of sensory memory have presented the visual or auditory stimuli for very brief exposures.

In contrast to sensory memory, Hulse reports that short-term memory without rehearsal may last for 20 to 30 seconds before fading away. In addition to the duration of this memory, a great deal of interest has been devoted to the amount of information that can be retained, a capacity often referred to as *span of apprehension*. Other terms sometimes used are *memory span*, the number of unrelated items, or *digit span*, the number of digits that can be remembered after a single presentation. In an article entitled "The Magical Number Seven, Plus or Minus Two," Miller (1956) proposed that immediate memory was limited to seven "chunks," plus or minus two. Just prior to the date of that article, Woodworth and

Schlosberg (1954) reported that the typical person can retain approximately the same number of digits, letters, or words. Still, there appears to be no proven way of quantifying all types of data into equal chunks. Organization of information is somewhat subjective and may well differ from person to person. The manner in which the material is organized will certainly make a difference in immediate retention.

The typical seven-digit telephone number (without area code) provides an example of a quantity of information that approaches the short-term capacity of most individuals. For example, as the telephone operator provides us with a number, that information enters the short-term memory system and we temporarily "know" the number. However, for most of us it will be quickly forgotten (sometimes before we are able to dial it) unless some special effort is made to remember it. Frequently we repeat the number, audibly or silently, several times while looking for a pencil and paper to write it down. If repeated enough times, or if associated with a meaningful sequence, it can be learned on a more permanent basis, and at this point it is transferred to the long-term memory system.

In an effort to increase the retention of telephone numbers, certain commercial firms arrange for "lettered numbers" to be used in advertising. Consequently, such numbers as "car loan" for an automobile financing company are easier to remember than 227-5626. What this does in effect is to reduce the number of "chunks" to two instead of seven. There is a greater likelihood that one who is presented with this information via a radio commercial, billboard, or newspaper advertisement is likely to recall the number if needed.

Forgetting in the short-term memory system is a decay process. The only way of preventing such decay, or forgetting, is through a rehearsal process. One can either keep repeating the telephone number, visualize it in one's mind, or use some other method to remember it. The same process is used in the retention of motor activities. When presented with a dance routine or any other movement activity that involves several components, the individual must quickly visualize that response or mentally rehearse to avoid forgetting it.

Actually, the fading of most information is desirable in that it prevents the long-term memory "store" from getting too cluttered with partially learned, useless information. A good deal of what we see or hear does not warrant being remembered. For example, at a baseball game in Philadelphia's Veteran Stadium in early June of 1981, I noticed that the scoreboard flashed the information that Pete Rose had 70 base hits for the year, giving him a lifetime total of 3,627, just three shy of Stan Musial's all-time National League record. This was noteworthy for the knowledgeable Phillies fan who had been informed by the local media of Pete Rose's record assault. Consequently, this information was considered, discussed with acquaintances, and transmitted to the long-term memory system. The typical Philadelphian was then able to recite this information without difficulty on the following day. More enthusiastic fans can recount the details of that scoreboard information for several weeks. However, at the same game, the scoreboard dutifully provided the same information about all other players. For example, it was shown that Houston Astros outfielder Jose Cruz was batting .277, with 62 hits in 224 times at bat. Further, he had hit nine homeruns and had batted in 33 runs. The typical fan looked at the scoreboard and noted nothing astounding about the data. Although it registered momentarily in the short-term memory mechanism, it was not viewed as noteworthy, i.e., Cruz was not the league leader, he was not closing in on an all-time record, nor was he the leading hitter on the Astros team. In this case, there is no reason to do anything more than note the information momentarily, then forget it. Most such information is viewed as trivial. Attempting to rehearse all this data for transmittal to the long-term store would clutter one's mind unmercifully.

Theories of forgetting

Researchers have long been intrigued by the question of just why people forget well-learned material. Consequently, a number of theories have emerged that seek to explain the phenomenon of forgetting. Perhaps the oldest and most popular one has been the *fading* theory, which is based on the law of disuse. (Several authors have referred to this as trace-decay.) According to the fading theory, skills that are not used regularly will gradually wither away. Forgetting is therefore assumed to be directly related to the passage of time. This theory has surface validity and is supported by the observation that as time goes by, most verbal material seems to become less vivid and motor skills appear to deteriorate.

In recent years, some doubt has been cast on the accuracy of the fading theory, at least as a total explanation of forgetting. The fact that people remember certain things longer than others raises a question about the traditional belief that time is the critical ingredient in forgetting. Clinical literature lists numerous cases of *hypermnesia*, i.e., unexpected incidences of recall during certain psychological states. In addition, most individuals experience occasions when they are surprised at their remembrance of a number, a name, or other information that they have not thought about for a long time. Also, a relatively high level of proficiency in certain motor skills is sometimes exhibited after a long no-practice period.

Doubt has also been cast on the fading theory by several studies in which sleeping and waking subjects were compared. These studies generally showed that during sleep, individuals remember more of what has been recently learned than during an equivalent waking period of normal activity. As a result, many current theorists believe that forgetting is not related to time, except that a longer period of time allows for more interruptive experiences. While seeming to have validity with reference to short-term memory, the fading theory and the principle of disuse appear inadequate as a complete explanation of forgetting.

A more recent theory considers forgetting the result of *interference*. According to this view, time as such is not a critical factor in retention. Rather, the most important consideration is that of interpolated experiences. This concept holds that nothing is really forgotten, but previously learned habits or skills are altered or obliterated by new experiences. Therefore, the only reason that a person forgets how to tie a particular knot, or balance on a bongo board, or shoot billiards skill-fully is that other activities have been learned tht interfere with the retention of these skills. This process of interference has been referred to as retroactive inhibi-tion, and it has been strongly supported by studies on the retention of sleeping and waking persons. Because the research evidence is so convincing, the basic idea of the interference theory is widely accepted by educators today. General acceptance of this concept, however, does not necessarily mean that interference is the only cause of forgetting.

Another theory of forgetting was developed by Sigmund Freud and expanded by later psychoanalysts. This clinical view holds that some forgetting is a result of *repression.* The individual subconsciously does not wish to remember a threatening event or activity. Forgetting is assumed to be a defense of the individual's person-ality. Usually the things most readily forgotten are unpleasant events or activities, especially those that evoke guilt feelings or shame. Forgetting is viewed as an active process of expelling ideas or skills from one's self, but this process of elimination is at the subconscious level and is not an act of which the individual is aware. The theory of repression is used to explain the occasional development of "mental blocks" regarding people's names, places, or events. Most individuals can recall inexplicable and embarrassing lapses of memory, and repression seems to be verified by many instances among both children and adults. The theory of repression does not seem adequate, however, to account for all forgetting, especially the deteriora-tion of skill.

One theory that has received limited attention explains forgetting as a *deterioration* of the neural connections that accompanied learning in the first place. This concept, referred to by Robb (1972) as the *memory trace theory,* is, in effect, similar to the fading theory discussed earlier. The deterioration theory is related to Kappers' theory of neural growth (discussed in chapter one), which explains learn-ing as the development of axons and dendrites around the synapse. The deteriora-tion theory is similar to the disuse theory because as a previously learned activity or skill is not practiced or used, the neural connections gradually degenerate. The deterioration concept includes the assumption that lack of activity causes atrophy in the unused nerve areas, just as lack of activity results in atrophy in muscular tissue. Sports skills, therefore, deteriorate during long periods in which they are not used. However, most theorists have been primarily interested in the behavioral aspects of learning and retention and therefore have given little attention to the neurological explanation of forgetting.

The complex phenomenon of retention will be discussed in terms of the many variables that appear to influence it. Most of the factors that affect retention seem to fall into the following categories: (1) techniques of measurement, (2) the nature and degree of original learning, and (3) interpolated experiences.

MEASUREMENT OF RETENTION

The retention of motor skills or verbal materials cannot be intelligently discussed without consideration of the conditions of measurement. Indications of the degree of retention vary greatly according to the manner in which retention is evaluated. One method of measurement might register a zero for retention, while another technique would show a fairly high degree of remembrance. The most popular techniques for determining degree of retention have been recall, recognition, and relearning. These methods vary greatly in sensitivity regardless of the type of learning being measured.

The *recall* technique is probably the most frequently used retention measure in schools. It is also the least sensitive method. In recall, the individual is asked to draw from memory without any cues the date of a particular event in history, the rules for a sports activity, or a poem that has been memorized. In short recall questions, the answers are usually entirely correct or entirely wrong, with no gradations. In other types of recall questions, such as reciting a poem, the individual can exhibit degrees of retention. As a rule, however, recall questions used in school do not measure the lower levels of retention, nor do they discriminate clearly between various degrees of competency.

The general technique of recall can be used quite successfully for determining retention in physical education skills. Such measures generally come in the form of retests. In movement skills, very low levels of retention are more accurately evaluated by the retest technique of recall than is possible with verbal material. The seventh-grade boy who is asked to demonstrate the recently practiced skill of shooting the left-handed lay-up shot can exhibit widely varying responses. He may perform very clumsily and even jump off the wrong foot; he may exhibit a technically correct but awkward response; or he may give a well-executed performance. Unlike the right or wrong answer on certain memory tests, some estimation of basketball skill can be made even if a successful goal is not accomplished. In other activities, students may be asked to demonstrate their retention in the cartwheel, archery, or rope skipping. In these activities, performers rarely get an absolute zero score for retention. In recall measures of verbal learning, however, the student often "draws a blank" or does not get the correct answer, even if a vague idea persists.

In some types of physical education skills, however, the weakness of the recall method is just as apparent as with verbal knowledge. Consider square dancing as an example. The individual might "completely forget" the correct moves for a particular dance when attempting to walk through the assignment while depending entirely on memory, i.e., without musical cues or other moving persons. On the other hand, if the person gets into a square in which the other people exhibit the right moves, their responses will very often evoke the correct moves on the part of the individual. The first situation, in which one attempts to recall moves strictly from memory, is an example of the straight recall measure and is likely to result in either a correct or an incorrect response. The second situation, in which the dancer uses the cues of the other dancers and the music, is a recognition situation. Recognition is a finer measure and is likely to evoke a more accurate indication of the individual's retention.

Test-makers and teachers have long been aware that questions of the *recognition* type will elicit greater reproduction of the correct responses than will simple recall questions. For example, people are sometimes heard to say, "I'll recognize the name as soon as you mention it." They are expressing confidence in their retention if it is tested in a particular way. The recognition technique of using cues is a more sensitive measure of retention. As stated previously, the square dancer is likely to fall right in line or quickly pick up previously learned skills if surrounded by skillful dancers. The movement of the others and the music serve as promptors. He recognizes the moves as parts of a particular pattern. Individuals often engage in group singing activities with reasonable effectiveness, even though they are only moderately familiar with the words to the song. In fact, if called upon to sing a solo, they may draw a virtual blank, recalling only a few of the words. However, in a group singing situation they may start a split second behind the others and thereafter receive enough cues to enable them to remember most of the lyrics as needed. Recitation of the pledge of allegiance and the singing of the national anthem are often guided in the same way, i.e., with cues from other participants.

While the novice bowler may become completely confused when attempting to recall the sequence of arm and leg movement in the approach, he may immediately recognize the correct approach in others who are demonstrating various techniques. Similarly, as soon as he happens to get off on the correct foot and starts the sequence, he can immediately recognize the familiar kinesthetic sensations and continue in the proper manner.

Written questions of the recognition type are familiar to all teachers. Multiple-choice questions are perhaps the most popular type of recognition measure. Consider the following example: Which of the following persons is credited with having developed the game of basketball? (1) Abner Doubleday, (2) James Naismith, (3) George Mikan, (4) Tyrus Cobb, (5) Frederick Jahn. Many people who would not clearly recall the name of the originator of basketball could look at the list and, through the process of elimination, along with very vague recollection, arrive at the name "Naismith." A person who may not be able to illustrate or describe the correct movement of a folk dance pattern may, when watching a group, realize whether the movement is done correctly or incorrectly. The individual who only vaguely remembers a particular movement response often is able to recognize whether or not his own movements are correct. This recognition appears to be based on cognitive and kinesthetic feedback as well as on the results of the movement. There is little question that the recognition retention measure is finer and more discriminating than the straight recall method. Although recognition is frequently observed in motor skills, it is not frequently used as a means of determining retention.

A measure of retention more sensitive than either recall or recognition is *relearning.* Occasionally, there is practically no evidence of retention when either the recall or recognition method is used. The student is sometimes not certain of any remembrance of the topic or skill. However, upon starting practice anew, the "feel" for the activity returns rapidly. At the very least the skill is learned in less time than it took to learn it originally. This economy or "saving" in relearning is usually evidence of the individual's having retained some skill from previous experience. Saving may be detected in cases of very low retention, such as when a person says, "I memorized that poem once, but now I don't even remember how it starts." It is also effective in cases of motor skills about which the person seems to remember nothing.

The sensitivity of the relearning technique was dramatically illustrated in an experiment by Burtt (1941) with his son who was less than two years of age. It was Burtt's practice to read traditional nursery rhymes to the child each day. For several weeks, however, he inserted three selections (twenty lines each) from Sophocles. These selections were read in the original Greek. Six years later, Burtt required the boy, who was then eight years of age, to memorize the same three passages of literature, and also three equivalent passages from the same volume. The boy required 435 readings to memorize the new passages but only 317 readings to learn those which had been read to him at the age of two. The earlier readings thus resulted in a 25 percent saving. Burtt's experiment has been offered as evidence of the persistence of earlier exposure. It is clear that only the relearning technique would have shown any evidence of retention in this case.

Almost invariably when an individual starts practicing or reviewing a previously learned skill, it is found that proficiency returns rather rapidly. The difference in the learning time between the first and the second experience is an expression of the degree of saving. Most persons can recall taking part in some apparently forgotten activity and having it "come back" rather quickly. The relearning technique is clearly the most sensitive detector of retention for both verbal and motor learning.

FACTORS AFFECTING RETENTION

An investigation of retention soon leads to the conclusion that the factors that influence learning also have an effect upon the manner in which that learning is retained. The type of task, degree of original learning, and conditions under which learning took place all make a difference when any sensitive test of retention is used.

Nature of the task

Several authors have suggested that not all learning tasks are remembered similarly. This assumption has been made especially when motor skills were compared with verbal material or when certain types of motor skills were compared with other types. In a recent report Fischman, Christina, and Vercruyssen (1982) state that "unlike verbal material, many motor skills, once learned, seem to be remarkably resistant to forgetting. Repetitive skills such as bicycling, swimming, and driving, once mastered, can be performed again even after lengthy periods without practice." However, statements about different degrees of retentiveness among different learning tasks are based more on empirical observation than on scientific investigation. The problem is especially difficult to solve by use of traditional research designs.

One problem encountered in attempting to compare the retentiveness of different tasks is the determination of equal levels of original learning. For example, if one learns to consistently shoot 70 percent of his free throws in basketball, how does this compare with the ability to bowl a score of 130? Obviously, it is difficult to say whether the level of skill is equivalent for the two tasks. When one considers more commonly used experimental tasks, the same difficulties are encountered. Does the ability to recite twenty lines of a twenty-five line poem represent as high a level of learning as the ability to name forty of the fifty state capitals? How do these verbal skills compare with the ability to shoot fifteen out of twenty-four arrows into an archery target at forty yards?

Just as difficult as determining equivalent levels of original learning among different skills is the matter of establishing comparable degrees of retention. Suppose, for example, that at the retention test the student had dropped from 70 to 35 percent in free-throw shooting. Is this comparable to a reduction in bowling score from 130 to 65? Similarly, if a learner is able to recite only ten of the originally learned twenty lines of poetry, is this equivalent to the retention of twenty of forty state capitals learned originally? Is *percentage* of retention an adequate means of comparing the retentiveness of different tasks? How can percentage of skating or swimming be measured? It is clear that these are not easy questions. Nevertheless, they are important in any attempt to determine and compare retentiveness among learning tasks.

The "chaining" of task responses in sequence aids in retention. The concept of chaining involves the connecting of a series of responses, each of which provide a stimulus for the next response. In this process what is actually learned is a series of stimulus-response connections. This notion was promoted by Skinner and several other S-R learning theorists.

Some tasks are more adaptable to chaining than others. Skills that involve a series of distinct responses are most likely to become connected in this manner. For example, playing a familiar tune on the piano from memory, reciting a poem, or performing a well-learned dance routine all fit into this category. In piano playing, striking and hearing one note stimulates one to respond with the next appropriate note, and so on until the tune is completed. On the other hand, when the wrong note is struck, the chain is broken because the correct stimulus is not provided. The performer must then begin all over in order to provide the proper stimulus for notes that follow. Beginning piano players and dancers find it hard to pick up a routine in the middle after an incorrect response has been made.

Relative retentiveness
of motor and verbal skills

It has long been suspected that certain types of material or skills are remembered better than others. Perhaps this is most frequently illustrated with the often stated assumption that motor skills are retained more easily than other types of skills or material. Despite the lack of convincing evidence, this view has been sustained by many authors over the years. Gagné and Fleishman (1959) reported that motor skills are retained longer than verbal material, while at the same time indicating that much of the observed difference results from the fact that regular motor skills are often learned more thoroughly. Nevertheless, they believe that even when original learning is equalized, motor skills are still retained longer than other types of learning. Further, they conclude after reviewing several research studies that, ". . . it appears that the kind of human activities most resistant to forgetting are motor skills of the type which are continuous rather than discrete (p. 173)". Skating, swimming, and bicycle riding are suggested as continuous activities. It might be assumed that discrete activities would include skills such as a soccer kick, basketball jump shot, or fungo hitting in baseball.

Leavitt and Schlosberg (1944) had subjects learn nonsense syllables and also develop skill in pursuit rotor performance. An attempt was made to equate the amount of learning by having subjects practice each task for ten thirty-second trials with a thirty-second rest between trials. When they tested for retention of these skills they found a higher percentage of original learning was retained in the motor skill (see Figure 6-3).

They suggested, however, that the greater retention of the motor skill could have resulted from better organization of that task. In a later study Van Dusen and Schlosberg (1949) made a particular effort to equate the organization of a verbal and a motor task. They reported no difference in retention at any point in time.

In one of the first studies on the retention of motor skills, Swift (1905) reported high levels of retention with juggling skills. He found considerable retention after periods of one and six years. He also reported a large saving in relearning the skill of typing after a two-year period. Swift's reports of high retention are not very helpful in comparing motor and verbal learning, however, because a comparable verbal skill was not learned and measured for retention. Also, practice in the interim was apparently not rigidly controlled.

Tsai (1924) reported a great degree of retention in the stylus maze habit. In this experiment, groups of subjects developed a high degree of proficiency in the skill. After periods of no practice from one to nine weeks, a very high level of skill was exhibited on retention tests. The skill retained varied from approximately 50 to 85 percent after nine weeks. Bell (1950) reported a retention of 71 percent in accuracy after a period of one year when the pursuit rotor was used. A very short period of practice was sufficient to bring the level of skill back to the original point. The original learning involved twenty trials. After one year, the original level of proficiency was reached after only eight trials. In other studies involving the skill

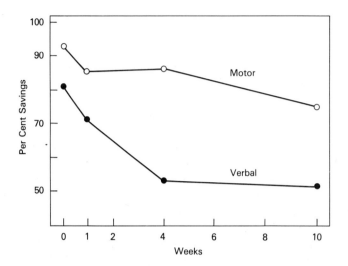

FIGURE 6-3. *Comparison of Retention of a Motor Task and a Verbal Sequence of 15 Nonsense Syllables* The mean savings at each interval was obtained by comparing the retention score of each individual with the score of his last learning trial. (From H. J. Leavitt and H. Schlosberg, "The Retention of Verbal and of Motor Skills." *Journal of Experimental Psychology,* 1944, 34, pp. 404-17. Used by permission.)

of typing, Towne (1922) and Rejall (1913) reported high percentages of retention when subjects refrained from practice for periods ranging from six months to four and one-half years.

Marx (1977) also supports the belief that motor skills are retained better than verbal skills, and further, that continuous skills are remembered better than discrete ones. He reports that "even after long periods of no practice we find that we are able to ice skate with all the grace and coordination that we had long ago." However, he adds that "the poem we learned in the third grade has little chance of recall."

Nevertheless, the claim for superior retention of motor skills is not universal. After noting the apparent difference between the retention of certain school learning and the motor skills of bicycle riding and swimming, Trow (1950) pointed out that such comparisons were unrealistic. He stated that:

> Bicycle-riding and swimming are relatively simple responses that have been many times repeated, while the items of knowledge are complex and numerous, and many of them have not been overlearned. A better comparison might be made between bicycle-riding or swimming and writing a capital letter A or giving the date for the discovery of America (pp. 605-606).[1]

[1] From *Educational Psychology* by W. C. Trow, used by permission of the publisher, Houghton Mifflin Company.

According to Trow, therefore, the important factors in retention are the complexity of the material and the amount of overlearning, not whether the task is verbal or motor.

It is important to point out, however, that evidence of long-term retention is not restricted to motor skills. Depending on the type of verbal material (especially its meaningfulness) and the manner in which retention is measured, great variation may be shown. Radosavijevich (1907) and McGeoch and Whitely (1926) report studies in which high degrees of savings were shown for both meaningful and nonsense syllables for four-month periods. Periods of prolonged retention of verbal material from five to forty-six years are reported by Worcester (1923), Ebbinghaus (1911), and Titchener (1923). Although experimental controls were not rigidly enforced in these studies, they do give some indication of the persistence of verbal learning.

Studies on the retention of school learning by young children indicate that school subjects are apparently retained in varying degrees, during the summer vacation, and in some subjects achievement even shows a gain. Further investigation reveals that subjects with less likelihood of being practiced during the summer months show the greatest loss. Conversely, subjects that are likely to be practiced, directly or indirectly, show the least reduction (or greatest gain). General proficiency in physical education, reading, and possibly social studies, remains highest during the summer months. While these observations have led some to conclude that physical education skills are retained longer, it is probable that the practice factor plays an important part in their retention.

Apparent differences.   Claims for an inherent advantage in the retention of motor skills have probably overstated any actual existence of such a tendency. The appearance of greater retention is caused by a number of factors other than whether the activity happens to involve motor movement. The tendency to overlearn the skill is probably more prevalent among motor skills than among other types of learning. The likelihood of learning the motor skill very thoroughly is enhanced by the fact that the individual sometimes enjoys the activity and participates beyond the point of having learned how to perform the task. The tendency to overlearn is often not as strong with verbal skills. For example, most persons who take a foreign language in school and who do not use the skills for several years thereafter seem to have "completely forgotten" the language when called upon to use it several years later. It is interesting to note, however, that those same persons can frequently "count to ten" in that language without difficulty. This is because counting to ten was perhpas the most overlearned phase of the language skill.

In common motor skills, the individual is likely to participate in the activity as a recreational experience long after the original learning has occurred. The activities of swimming, bicycle riding, and skating may be performed quite regularly during an individual's early years. The individual is often surprised to find that twenty years later he can still show some skill in these tasks. This motor ability is then compared with an inability to recite a poem or perform another verbal skill learned at approximately the same time as the motor skill. The individual may not consider that the verbal material was not regularly performed as a recreational activity.

Another reason why motor skills appear to be retained longer than verbal material is the usual manner of measuring the degree of retention. Very often a recall technique is used for the verbal material while the relearning method is used to test the retention of motor skills. For example, the person may be asked to recite a particular poem, to name the capital of a state, or to provide a chemical formula. This recall technique will usually result in an all-or-nothing response. For the motor skill, however, the person may be asked to demonstrate skill in dribbling a basketball, swimming, or bowling. Theoretically, if 50 percent retention existed for both the verbal and the motor tasks, this degree of proficiency would be exhibited in the motor skill, while a zero score might be obtained in the verbal material. After all, *almost* remembering a formula is of little value in a recall test.

Another point that is often ignored is that people *do* forget motor skills. In an experimental situation, Lersten (1969) had subjects learn a discrete task involving both a circular and a linear phase. He found that after a one-year interval, subjects showed a decrement of 79 percent on the circular phase and 29 percent on the linear phase of the task. Martin (1970) found that after four months, subjects showed a 50 percent retention loss on a discrete arm movement task. Numerous other research reports show a significant drop-off in performance level, even after a very high level of proficiency has been established.

In the area of sports and practical work skills, similar forgetting occurs, even when the individual has been away from the activity only for a short time. For example, the professional baseball batter who is apparently at the peak of his physical proficiency may go through a season with a batting average 40 points lower than his average of the previous few years. Often this loss of skill is not related to any physical disability but to the individual's inability to remember the fine points of his batting stroke when at his peak. All athletes, both professional and amateur, slump from time to time for no reason except an apparent loss of skill due to forgetting. The development of poor habits or movement errors may be a related factor. Performers in all sports activities forget how to perform for certain periods. This forgetting may be reflected in a small or large drop-off in performance.

More dramatic reductions in skill can be observed when the individual remains away from the activity for several years. As an example, while coaching a high school baseball team many years ago, I developed a high level of skill in hitting fly balls to outfielders with a fungo bat. Some fifteen years later, after not having practiced the skill during the interim, I took my ten-year-old son and several of his friends out to give them practice in catching fly balls. I assumed that the near pin-point fungo hitting accuracy of previous years would be retained. To my dismay, the skill was woefully lacking; successful hits were few and far between. Several practice sessions were required before coordination and timing could be regained to the point of reasonable success.

Meaningfulness of the task

Studies have consistently shown that *meaningful* material is remembered better than material that seems disorganized to the learner. The manner in which the material is structured, its relationship to the learner's previous experience, and the importance with which the individual views the material all help to determine the degree of retention. These details affect (1) the degree to which the material is learned in the first place, (2) the tendency of the person to think about it, or mentally practice, at a later time, and (3) the number of times that the person is reminded of the material in his everyday experiences. It also seems clear that the understanding or discovery of a principle that is basic to the material is an aid to retention. As mentioned in chapter five, Katons (1940) had two groups of subjects learn the same list of numbers. One group was encouraged to search for a principle upon which the numbers were arranged while the other group was simply asked to memorize the numbers. Katons reported that the "principle" group not only learned the list of numbers more quickly but also remembered them better. One must assume that numbers arranged in a logical sequence have greater meaningfulness for the learner. By comparison, simple rote memory is dull and not well remembered.

The teaching of the physical principles underlying motor performance usually adds meaningfulness to those tasks, thus enhancing their retention. For example, people who have been taught the principles of momentum and friction will develop and remember skills for driving in snow and ice, particularly on hills and in skids. Tennis players who understand the effect of "English" (spin) on rebound will respond more intelligently to a slicing stroke or a drop shot than players who do not understand that principle. Similarly, the individual who understands the principle of the curve ball will more clearly remember how to throw a curve and correct the slice or hook in golf. Consequently, the teaching of such principles or concepts is valuable for both learning and retention because it adds meaning to the activity.

Ebbinghaus' early experiments showed that meaningful material was retained better than nonsense syllables. Guilford (1952) similarly found that poetry was remembered much better than nonsense syllables. Naylor and Briggs (1961) reported that the organization of material was important in its retention. They found that verbal and motor tasks that were arranged in an arbitrary sequence were not remembered as well as the same material organized in a more meaningful manner. It was concluded that the motor-verbal factors were not as important in retention as the organization and difficulty of the material.

It has been reported on several occasions that the gist of a story is remembered longer than the minor or technical details. The basic ingredients are long retained, while names, dates, and numbers are quickly forgotten. Newman (1939) reported a study in which two groups of college women heard a story. In one group, the story was followed by eight hours of sleep. The other group followed the story by eight hours of normal daily activities. At the end of the period, both groups retained the general concepts of the story similarly. The working group, however, forgot a greater degree of the details of the story than did the sleeping group.

A similar study was designed to determine the verbal retention of elementary school children. In this project, one child was told a story and five minutes later was asked to tell the story to a second child. After five minutes, the second child was asked to tell the story to a third child. This procedure was followed until several children had listened, waited for five minutes, and told the story from memory. It was found that the basic ideas of the story were pretty well preserved while the details were obliterated. Names, places, and other specific information were forgotten and replaced by new information.

In like manner, fine movements or more detailed aspects of a motor skill are forgotten more quickly than the basic features of movement. Fundamentals that are taught early and stressed as the most important elements of a skill are more likely to be retained over a long period. When skills begin to deteriorate, the fine points that lead to the highest level of performance are the first to be lost. These skills are more recently learned and are perhaps not as meaningful as the more basic movement patterns learned earlier. Lawther (1966) reported that high levels of skill performance in piano playing, putting in golf, or other tasks where advanced performances may be exhibited, tend to drop down rapidly during periods of no practice. Robb (1972) reported that after a layoff, basic skills are retained, in-·cluding subroutines, but the temporal coordinations are not. Consequently, individuals may still be able to spike the volleyball, but usually the "timing is off." After a period of no practice, similar temporal difficulties can be noted in a complex gymnastics routine, a difficult springboard dive, rope skipping, or a complex dance movement.

Cook (1951) surveyed the research regarding retention and stated that learning involving problem-solving relationships and the operation of the highest mental processes are relatively permanent, and that unrelated facts and mere information are more temporal. Cook's contention seems to be supported by observation of high school or college students who appear to retain higher level abilities and techniques longer than they recall formulae, names, dates, and similar details.

The general orientation of the learner while receiving information or participating in an activity plays a major role in the retentiveness of that information or experience. For example, if one has a *need* to remember information while it is being received, it will be organized and dealt with in a meaningful manner. On the other hand, if one does not expect to be accountable for the material, it is more likely to "go in one ear and out the other." Much of the information heard on radio or television fits into this latter category. Students appear to recognize the importance of mental orientation with occasional comments such as, "I didn't know we were going to have to remember this" or "Will we be tested on this?"

Automobile passengers are frequently heard to say, "I didn't drive so I don't remember how to get there." One who expects to remember directions is more likely to make mental notes, watch for cues, and organize the information in a more meaningful way. Teachers who say, "You'll probably be tested on this" are using a not so subtle threat to encourage students to *plan* to remember what is being presented.

Several authors have reported that materials that are pleasant or acceptable to the learner will be remembered better than unacceptable or neutral materials. Edwards (1942) indicated, however, that more important than the pleasantness of the material was the frame of reference of the learner. The concepts or information most consistent with the beliefs of the individual will be remembered most vividly. On the whole, the experiences that most closely agree with one's point of view are also the most pleasant. Movement skills that *seem* appropriate to the desired action will be acquired and retained more readily than actions that do not appear to be closely connected with the results. This tendency to remember experiences that are pleasant or have greater meaning for the learner is just as applicable to motor skills as to other types or concepts.

Teachers of physical education may take advantage of the frame of reference by teaching certain rhythmical drills or dances while using familiar and popular pieces of music. The familiarity and pleasantness of the music may tend to evoke a positive reaction by the learner, and greater interest will aid both learning and retention. Perhaps just as important is the fact that on future occasions when the particular piece of music is heard, it will evoke mental rehearsal on the part of the individual. No doubt, the matter of mental practice is a factor that contributes to the increased retention of meaningful material. Conversely, it is unlikely that materials that are not meaningful to the individual will be reviewed during idle moments.

Degree of original learning

A factor that is most strategic in the retention of any type of learning is the degree to which the material or skill is learned in the first place. The amount or degree of original learning is usually reported either in terms of (1) number of practice trials or amount of time spent in practice, or (2) the degree of exhibited proficiency. The level of proficiency is often measured in terms of the speed, accuracy, distance, or number of successful repetitions in motor skills, or the number of successful responses in verbal material.

The term *overlearning* refers to the continued practice or study of a task after it has been learned. Overlearning is used to describe the amount of original learning of a particular task. When the child can recite a poem once without making an error, it is assumed that the poem has been learned. Theoretically, overlearning is not practiced for the purpose of improving performance on a skill, but rather to "set," or reinforce, the learning so that it will be remembered longer. The child who recited the poem without error will not improve performance with additional practice. The same is essentially true of the boy who continues to do headstands. Efforts to improve or refine a skill after success has been shown are not classified as overlearning. The diver who continues to practice a dive after it has been performed successfully is often attempting to polish or refine the execution of the task. Such efforts to make small changes and improvements are essentially new learning.

Overlearning is generally referred to in terms of the amount of extra practice that is taken. The amount of practice *after* the point of one perfect performance is compared with the amount of practice required to attain that level initially. A percentage of overlearning is computed from this comparison. For example, if the child required ten readings of the poem in order to recite it perfectly the first time, ten additional readings would represent 100 percent overlearning. For a girl who required six tries before being able to do a back somersault on the trampoline, three additional executions of the skill would be 50 percent overlearning. Most research studies report overlearning varying from 50 percent to 200 percent.

One of the early studies regarding the values of various degrees of overlearning was conducted by Krueger (1929). He had three groups of subjects learn one-syllable nouns, each group being given a different amount of practice. One group practiced only to the point of one successful repetition (thus no overlearning). Another group had 50 percent overlearning, and the third group practiced to the point of 100 percent overlearning. He found that 50 percent overlearning was very valuable in promoting retention, and 100 percent overlearning was only slightly more beneficial for retention (see Figure 6-4). The slight retention advantage of 100 percent over 50 percent overlearning did not seem to warrant the extra

FIGURE 6-4. Retention Following Different Amounts of Original Learning (Based on data from W. C. F. Krueger, "The Effect of Overlearning on Retention." *Journal of Experimental Psychology,* 1929, 12, pp. 71-78. From Gregory A. Kimble and Norman Garmezy, *Principles of General Psychology,* 2d ed. Copyright © 1963 The Ronald Press Company, New York. Used by permission.)

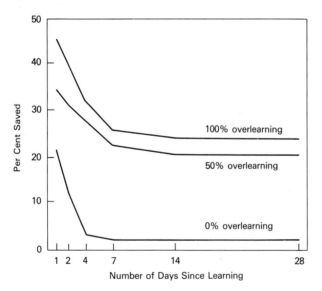

practice time. Krueger (1930) conducted a similar study with finger mazes and obtained approximately the same results. The tendency to get diminishing returns on retention for practice above 50 percent overlearning is consistent with several other studies of this topic. In addition, the following generalizations may be drawn from recent research literature regarding overlearning:

1. The value of overlearning increases as the time for forgetting increases.
2. To be fully effective, overlearning must be practiced as seriously as the initial task and with as much attention.
3. Less interference or negative transfer will result from material that is over-learned.
4. Positive transfer increases if material has been overlearned.

Hammerton (1963) had two groups of subjects learn a difficult tracking task to an established level of proficiency. One group then continued to practice to a higher criterion. After six months, the retention of both groups was tested by having each relearn the task to the level of the first criterion. Hamerton concluded that when a task is sufficiently difficult, overlearning does not prevent forgetting, but it does reduce the decrement with the passing of time. Garry (1963) stated that motor skills are overlearned more often than verbal skills and therefore give the appearance of having greater retention. In the area of verbal learning, one can readily see the effects of overlearning for retention. For example, we can refer to a poem learned in childhood or during the early years of school as a rough check. Many people who have not heard the poem in fifteen years would have no difficulty in completing the early portions of "Humpty Dumpty sat on the wall . . ." or "I think that I shall never see/A poem lovely as . . ." On the other hand, more recent (but less overlearned) knowledge might prove more difficult to retain. For example, the typical adult would have difficulty in giving the formula for hydrochloric acid or copper.

In motor learning, the practice of overlearning has long been advocated. Great stress has been placed on drills and practicing until one can perform blind-folded. Coaches have encouraged athletes to learn skills so well that they do not have to think about them. Conscious effort can therefore be devoted to higher level activities. The advantages of overlearning in sports are obvious. The soccer player who has to think about how to kick the ball will find that he is usually too late in getting the ball to the player who is open. The athlete has to perform most of his skills "instinctively." As used here, this term does not indicate that the player has inherited skills, but rather that the skills have been learned so well that they require no conscious thought.

Overlearning is usually a sound investment for teachers and students. Teachers must plan for overlearning. Too often there is a feeling that once you get the hang of it, you can stop practicing. The music teacher and the typing teacher use drills to enable the student to continue to practice skills that have just been learned, or at a level just reached. These drills tend to make the new (high) level of performance automatic. The individual will be less likely to regress to previous levels of performance at a later practice session.

The wise physical educator tries to insure that students hold onto any new skills they have learned during a particular session. Students practice their skills a few more times so that they will remember them the next day. The teacher or the coach, however, must be aware of the fatigue factor and not try to force new skills at the end of a long practice session. Too often, because of fatigue, players lapse into earlier stages of performance or learn and practice faults.

INTERPOLATED EXPERIENCES

Very soon after practice ceases, a decrement in the skill or knowledge can be noted. Even with the occurrence of reminiscence (an increase in skill following the cessation of practice), a drop-off in learning begins in a relatively short period of time. The reason for this inevitable reduction in skill has been of interest to psychologists and educators for a long time.

Among the theories of forgetting discussed earlier in this chapter, it was pointed out that the interference theory seems to be most widely accepted among authorities today. This theory holds that nothing learned is ever really forgotten. Rather, certain skills or knowledges are interfered with as other learnings occur and alter or eliminate the original skills. Whether or not one accepts this concept completely, the cross-effects of learning are widely accepted and can be well documented. An understanding of the effect of interpolated activities on retention is important for all teachers.

C. L. Hull developed the concept of *retroactive inhibition*, which refers to the interfering effects that certain experiences have on the retention of previously learned skills. This concept is essential to an understanding of retention. Teachers can most effectively manage school experiences only if they realize the role that certain interpolated activities have in the forgetting of previously learned skills.

In addition to cases of specific negative transfer, general interference is also evident in motor tasks. Not only may practice in football place kicking (with toe) interfere with the newly acquired soccer kick (with instep), but so may a variety of general movement activities. However, there is reason to believe that general and unrelated activities do not interfere as greatly as skills that are slightly related.

Several studies have been conducted in which it was shown that *general activity* tends to speed the forgetting of recently learned skills. Jenkins and Dallenbach (1924) compared the effects of sleep and regular, waking activity on the retention of nonsense syllables. The waking activity was unrelated to the tasks to be remembered. Two subjects took part in the study, and each was tested in the sleeping and waking conditions. Under both conditions, retention checks were made at one, two, four, and eight hours after original learning. The authors reported that a rapid drop-off in retention resulted under sleeping and waking conditions during the first two hours (though not as much for sleep). The sleeping subjects showed no further loss in retention from two to eight hours. However, the subjects following normal daily activities continued to show a decrement. A very high level of consistency is shown in the performance of the two subjects under each condition (see Figure 6-5). Van Ormer (1932) conducted similar studies and generally corroborated the conclusion that sleep tends to slow forgetting. The reason for the loss of remembrance during the first two hours of sleep and not afterward is not entirely clear. It has been suggested that this loss results because subjects do not go to sleep instantaneously after learning, and during the early stages do not sleep soundly. However, after the individual is fully asleep, there seems to be little interference until awakening.

The relationship between amount of activity and retention has also been illustrated among animals. Minami and Dallenbach (1946) showed that the retention of inactive cockroaches was dramatically higher than that of cockroaches that were moderately active. The skill that was learned and remembered was a simple avoidance habit.

Theories of retroactive inhibition

Retroactive inhibition occurs when the learning of material causes the forgetting of something previously learned. The existence of this phenomenon is widely accepted today. There are differences of opinion, however, regarding the reasons for this occurrence. The explanations most often given have resulted in

FIGURE 6-5.   Retention of Sequences of 10 Nonsense Syllables by Two Individuals After Varying Amounts of Sleep Immediately Following Learning (From J. G. Jenkins and K. M. Dallenbach, "Oblivescence during Sleep and Waking." *American Journal of Psychology,* 1924, 35, pp. 605-12. Used by permission.)

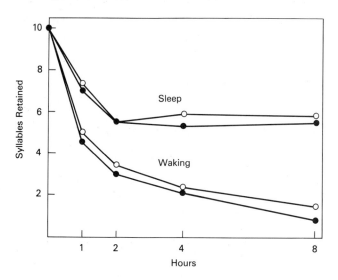

the development of two theories: the perseveration theory and the transfer, or competition, theory.

The perseveration theory.   This is a traditional concept of retroactive inhibition developed by Müller and Pilzecker (1900). According to this theory, there is a tendency for the learner to continue thinking about the task, or to perseverate, for a period after the cessation of overt practice. If a period of idleness follows practice, the individual engages in unconscious rehearsal that reinforces the learning that took place. However, if the individual takes part in another activity immediately after the work period, perseveration is interrupted and, as a result, the original activity is not learned as well, nor remembered. The exact nature or reason for the continuance of learning after practice has not been clearly established.

The perseveration theory seems rather plausible, especially when one considers the tendency of certain visual images to linger in the mind. Also, most people have, on occasion, experienced difficulty in eliminating certain musical tunes or even unrelated ideas from their minds. The tendency to experience lingering ideas is especially apparent following a particularly meaningful event. The result of that occurrence may be negative or positive. For example, most persons who have been involved in sports activities can recall anguishing over missed opportunities—the crucial tennis stroke in which the ball hit the top of the net and fell back, the free throw that hit the front rim, or the golf putt that stopped inches short of the cup. If the activity was viewed as important, we have an especially difficult time putting those errors out of our minds. We can still "see" those shots occurring, and at the same time make efforts to correct them, i.e., to hit the tennis ball a little higher or to make the necessary adjustments with the other skills. However, when these tasks are immediately followed by some other demanding activity, the opportunity to continue this related mental involvement is greatly curtailed. The perseverance theory, however, assumes that the continuance of learning results from *subconscious* rather than conscious activity. There has been no definite evidence of continued neural development because of perseveration, despite claims made by early physiologists in defense of the theory. In addition, if this theory were entirely adequate, the learned material should be rather free from interference once the perseveration is allowed to take place. But evidence indicates that a period of idleness following practice does not render one immune to interfering activities that may occur later. Though having some merit in terms of logic, the theory of perseveration is not generally accepted as a total explanation for retroactive inhibition.

The transfer or competition theory.   This theory assumes that forgetting caused by intervening activity is the result of transfer from one activity to the other or of interaction between the two activities. Many studies have shown that the degree of retention of one task is influenced by its similarity to the intervening task. This concept differs significantly from the perseveration theory, which holds that *any* activity following the original learning would interrupt the lingering mental processing and cause forgetting. According to the transfer theory, it appears that a person recalls the original and interpolated responses but is uncertain of which to use. The transfer theory is really one of *negative transfer* in which learning from one task intrudes upon the second task.

In consideration of the great variety and complexity of interpolated activity, one might wonder why we remember anything at all. Why is all learning not erased by more recent learning? There are several factors that seem to be crucial in preserving learning. Among these are the following: (1) Positive transfer is quite common among activities within the individual's experience; (2) many tasks are important and meaningful to the individual and, therefore, tend to be well remembered; and (3) much of what we learn is well learned or overlearned and, therefore, is likely to be long retained. The third factor is especially effective when the individual makes a conscious effort to retain the learned material or tasks.

Reminiscence

It is not an unusual occurrence in sports for an individual to return to an activity after a few weeks or months and exhibit a higher level of skill than when she last participated in it. This discovery is contrary to what one would expect from the retention curves. William James, however, indicated that something occurs within the individual even without practice. He postulated, for example, that people learn to skate in the summer and to swim in the winter. Do people really improve during periods of no practice? Under what conditions is the forgetting curve reversed?

The phenomenon of reminiscence is an interesting one and has long fascinated students of learning. Reminiscence refers to improvement during the period in which there is no practice. The term *reminiscence* was perhaps first specifically discussed by Ballard (1913). As inspector for the London county council school system, he visited a class to find that children were busy memorizing a poem. At the end of the period he asked them to write down as much of the poem as they could remember. He collected and scored the papers. Without having informed the children of his plans, he returned to the class the following day and immediately asked them to write down as much of the poem as they could remember. To his surprise, he found that they remembered more on the second day than at the end of the first day. He duplicated this experiment, with similar results, using other material, both meaningful and nonsense syllables. The retention curve showed a rise before the decline. He referred to this phenomenon as *reminiscence.*

This "improvement" during a period of no practice has been reported in various types of learning tasks and under widely differing circumstances. A typical experimental procedure is to allow practice on a particular skill, followed immediately by a test of proficiency; then a period of no practice, and a test of retention. As was indicated earlier, performance at the second test is occasionally at a higher level than at the test immediately following the practice period.

Several reasons have been offered to explain this phenomenon. The most common has been the assumption that some mental practice goes on in the individual at the subconscious level. This practice, or review, stands one in good stead at the time the retest is given. It has also been suggested that during rest periods the incorrect responses are more readily forgotten than the correct ones, possibly because the correct ones were reinforced.

Travers (1977) believes that reminiscence is not really a genuine phenomenon. He explains rather that the superior performance on the retention test results from the additional practice that the individual experienced during the earlier test period. A weakness in experimental design was therefore believed to be contributing to the erroneous assumptions. This idea was supported in a study by Ammons and Irion (1954) in which two groups were used. One group followed the traditional design of a test and a retest following the learning period. A second group omitted the initial test and therefore the practice that might occur from it. This second group did not exhibit the reminiscence phenomenon during the retention test. The authors concluded that the additional test was the source of additional learning, and that reminiscence did not, in fact, take place.

On a short-term basis in motor skills, it has often been shown that performance is higher after a period of no practice. This is possibly because of fatigue or inhibitions that may have developed during the period of intensive training. Much research is needed before definite conclusions can be drawn regarding the nature of reminiscence, or, indeed, whether reminiscence exists.

RETENTION OF MOTOR SKILLS

In comparison with verbal learning, many authors have reported a high degree of retention in motor skills. Several of these authors have been mentioned earlier in this chapter. Regardless of how the retention of motor skills compares with that of verbal learning, recent research seems to emphasize the fact that motor skills are retained at a higher level than is usually expected in verbal learning.

Purdy and Lockhart (1962) conducted an experiment to determine retention among five gross motor skills. College women learned novel skills including: (1) a nickel toss requiring timing and accuracy, (2) a ball toss involving hand-eye coordination, (3) a foot volley involving foot-eye coordination, (4) a lacrosse throw and catch requiring total body coordination and adjustments, and (5) balancing on a bongo board. Subjects were divided into three groups according to their ability to learn each of the skills. After a period of nine to fifteen months, thirty-six of the original seventy-five women were given a retention-relearning test on each of the skills. At this retention check, they practiced the skills for three days in the same manner as was followed from the original learning.

In analyzing the data Purdy and Lockhart found that:

1. A high degree of skill was retained after approximately one year of no practice. The total group retained 94 percent of its best performance on original

learning. Eighty-nine percent of the subjects displayed reminiscence on one or more skills.

2. Relearning to previously attained skill levels was rapid after approximately one year of no practice. After three days of practice the total group regained the level of proficiency acquired in the ten days of original learning.

3. The skill groups retained their relative positions in learning, retention, and relearning of gross motor skills. The high skill group had significantly better scores than the average and low skill groups; the average skill group had significantly better scores than the low skill group.

4. When proportion of skill retained and relearned was considered, differences among the classified skill groups were small. The average skill group retained 98 percent of its best performance on original learning, the high skill group 93 percent, and the low skill group 83 percent. The average skill group relearned in proportion more than the other two groups, attaining 122 percent of its best original learning performance on the second day of the retention-learning experiment and 121 percent on the third day. The high skill group attained 112 percent on the second day and 110 percent on the third day, while the low skill group relearned 102 and 99 percent respectively on the second and third days (p. 270).[2]

After observing the high degree of retention in these skills, the authors suggested that teachers probably spend too much time reviewing previously learned skills. Once a sound base of fundamentals has been established, performers should be able to go very quickly into more advanced skills. Long periods of review on more basic skills are generally a waste of time.

Ryan (1962) investigated the pattern of retention for two types of motor skills. He had eighty subjects develop skill in the pursuit rotor and the stabilimeter. The pursuit rotor involved rotary arm movement in which the subject attempted to keep a stylus in contact with a target revolving on a turntable. The stabilimeter was a total body balance task in which the subject attempted to maintain position with a minimum of movement while standing astride a bongo-board-type apparatus. After a standard amount of practice, subjects were divided into four groups to be retested after three, five, seven, or twenty-one days.

Ryan found that there was little loss in skill for periods up to twenty-one days. In fact, a gain in proficiency was shown on the pursuit rotor skill at all retention checkpoints. Retention on the stabilometer usually showed a slight decrement. It should be noted that shorter practice periods were followed for the pursuit rotor (thirty seconds) than for the stabilometer (one minute). Rest periods were a standard thirty seconds for both tasks. Since this constitutes a somewhat more distributed practice schedule for the pursuit rotor, Ryan suggested this as a possible

[2]B. J. Purdy and A. Lockhart, "Retention and Relearning of Gross Motor Skills After Long Periods of No Practice," *Research Quarterly,* **33,** Washington, D.C.: AAHPER, 1962, p. 270. By permission.

reason for the greater retention. He concluded, however, that the two different skills are not retained similarly.

Fleishman and Parker (1962) investigated the long-term retention of a complex tracking skill. The task was one that stimulated a pilot's actions in flying a radar intercept mission. The authors observed that retention of these skills over an extended period without practice is especially important. Seventeen practice sessions were held within a six-week period, each session including twenty-one 1-minute trials. Subgroups were then retained (as a test for retention) after periods ranging from one to twenty-four months. Some groups were retrained by use of a massed practice schedule (four continuous practice sessions), while other groups followed a distributed schedule (four practices scheduled one day apart). In analyzing the data, the authors found that (1) retention of this continuous perceptual-motor skill was very high, even for periods up to twenty-four months; (2) the small loss in retention was recovered in the first few minutes of practice; (3) no drop in the retention curve was shown between the first and fourteenth month; however, a decline was shown at twenty-four months; (4) the most important factor in retention seemed to be the level of original learning, not the conditions under which learning took place; and (5) retraining was more effective when practices were distributed rather than massed.

Ammons et al. (1956) conducted two experiments to determine the long-term retention of a complex type of compensatory pursuit skill and a second task involving sequential manipulation of controls. The task was learned by 538 male college subjects under twelve practice conditions, and they were given retention tests after periods ranging from one minute to two years. The authors found that loss in level of proficiency was not affected by degree of original learning. However, the groups with less original practice were poorer in proficiency at both the conclusion of practice and the retention test. Retraining to the earlier level of proficiency took longer for the groups having a longer no-practice period and for groups which had a higher original level of retention.

In two studies involving the skill of mirror tracing, I found practically no loss in skill for periods to four weeks. In one study (1959), junior high school boys practiced two days a week for five weeks. After a period of three weeks without practice, all groups showed improved performance at a retention test. The subgroup that had followed the schedule of short practices showed the greatest improvement. In another study by Oxendine (1965), college students practiced mirror tracing daily for ten consecutive school days. After a four-week period without practice, only a slight loss in retention was shown. In fact, all subgroups performed at a level that was equivalent to their ninth practice day.

SUMMARY

1. Retention refers to the persistence of knowledge or skills that have been learned. Forgetting is the failure to retain learned material.

2. Retention of an unpracticed skill or unreviewed material follows a decler-

ating curve. It is possible that learned material is never completely forgotten. Consequently, the forgetting never reaches the base line.

3. Short-term memory refers to the temporary storage of material that has been received by the sensory system and quickly transmitted to the short-term memory for a split second, or for several seconds. Much of this information is forgotten about as quickly as it was received. Other information, deemed by the individual to be important, is rehearsed in some fashion and then transmitted to the long-term storage area for retention.

4. Short-term retention may be broken down into sensory memory and short-term memory. Sensory memory refers to the very brief holding of sensory impressions, for perhaps up to two seconds. This phenomenon may be further broken down according to sense organ receiving the stimulus, e.g., iconic for visual stimuli and echonic for auditory stimuli. The more general term *short-term retention* may refer to retention for up to 20 seconds or so.

5. The typical individual can remember seven "chunks" of information, give or take two, without rehearsal. These units of information may be in letters, words, digits, or perhaps motor responses. The organization of these chunks and their meaningfulness will make a difference in the amount retained and the length of that retention.

6. Most attention by educators and researchers over the years has been devoted to long-term retention, i.e., remembering material over a relatively long period. Only material that is rehearsed and "learned" is held in the long-term storage system.

7. Reasons why people forget are not fully known. The factor generally believed to contribute most to forgetting is that of interference. Other theories receiving some support are the fading or trace-decay concept, repression, and deterioration.

8. Retention of material in school is most frequently measured by the techniques of recall, recognition, and relearning. Relearning has proven to be the most sensitive, revealing even the slightest retention of material in the form of a "savings" score. Recall, i.e., retention of material without the aid of cues or suggestions, is the least sensitive measure.

9. Amount of retention is affected by many factors, including the type of task or material, particularly its meaningfulness to the learner. Students have consistently shown that materials that seem disorganized are forgotten more quickly than meaningful materials arranged in some logical manner. The importance with which the individual views the material and its relationship to previous experience tend to aid original learning, and consequently, retention. These factors cause the individual to think about the material or the skill on subsequent occasions, thus promoting retention. Practice with the intention of remembering and with the awareness of possible distractions will aid retention.

10. Material that is better learned will be better retained. In the learning of motor skills or verbal materials, overlearning is a good strategy for aiding retention. In addition, learning material by following a schedule of distributed practices is

preferable to using a schedule of massed practices. Advantages are reflected not only in immediate performance but in retention as well.

11. There has been a longstanding assumption that motor skills are better retained than verbal skills. A thorough analysis of this topic reveals that there is little evidence to support this hypothesis. In addition, there is no evidence to support the popular belief that material learned more quickly is also forgotten more quickly.

12. The most widely held theory on forgetting is that of interference, which holds that new material or experiences alters or obliterates previously learned material. This concept, referred to as *retroactive inhibition*, has been supported by extensive research. Not only is similar material likely to interfere, but so can general routine or daily activities. Still, the more unique the learned activity, the less likely it is that interference will occur.

13. Reminiscence refers to gains made in learning during a period of no formal practice. Some evidence in support of this phenomenon has been demonstrated in both motor and verbal skills. Reminiscence is believed to be the result of conscious or subconscious mental rehearsal during periods between formal trials.

14. Research has consistently shown that motor skills are retained at a high level. In fact, well-learned skills show little deterioration over the first year. It is probable that most teachers spend too much time having students review previously learned skills. Of course the key is that skills must first be well learned.

15. Continuous or repetitive skills give the appearance of being retained longer than discrete skills. It is probable that continuous skills are simply overlearned to a greater extent and for this reason are better retained.

16. Good teaching involving appropriate motivating techniques, interesting learning tasks, and desirable practice conditions begets good learning. In turn, good learning begets good retention.

SELECTED READINGS

FISCHMAN, M. G., CHRISTINA, R. W., and VERCRUYSSEN, M. J. Retention and transfer of motor skills: a review for the practitioner. *Quest,* 1982, 33 (a), 184-94.

HULSE, S. H., EGETH, H., and DEESE, J. *The psychology of learning* (5th ed.). New York: McGraw-Hill Book Co., 1980.

KINGSLEY, H. L., & GARRY, R. *The nature and conditions of learning* (3rd ed.). Englewood Cliffs, N.J.: Prentice-Hall, 1970.

KRUEGER, W. C. F. The effect of overlearning on retention. *J. Exp. Psychol.,* 1929, 12, 71-78.

LEAVITT, H. J., & SCHLOSBERG, H. The retention of verbal and of motor skill. *J. Exp. Psychol.,* 1944, 34, 404-417.

MCGEOCH, J. A., & IRION, A. L. *The psychology of human learning.* New York: McKay, 1952.

PURDY, B. J., & LOCKHART, A. Retention and relearning of gross motor skills after long periods of no practice. *Res. Quart.,* 1962, 33, 265-272.

TRAVERS, R. M. W. *Essentials of learning* (4th ed.). New York: Macmillan, 1977.

Part III: The State of the Learner

7 Physical Readiness and Motor Performance

INTRODUCTION

Individuals vary greatly in their readiness for motor behavior at any given moment. This preparedness to perform differs not only among individuals, but also within the same person from time to time. No topic in education is more important than that of readiness to learn and to perform. The essential elements are first determining the state of readiness and then establishing a level of preparedness appropriate for the activity. Also included are the bases for task selection for persons at different age levels and the establishment of techniques for motivating students.

Physical educators have been concerned with the state of the learner in a different way from other teachers. In teaching motor skills to young students, the instructor must be cognizant of the physical as well as the mental maturity of learners. In addition, motor activities for children are selected not only with consideration for the ability of children to perform them, but also on the basis of their potential for promoting readiness for more advanced skills.

THE MEANING OF READINESS

At what age can a child be taught to tie shoelaces, thread a needle, or ride a bicycle? When can one learn to throw a curve ball, operate a lawnmower safely, or do a handstand? Can special exercises lower the age at which these skills can be learned? These are all questions about *readiness*. This topic is extremely important for the educator who is interested in the grade placement of activities. Teachers are also interested in determining what skills and experiences are necessary prerequisites for the learning of these activities.

Parents, too, seek to know the age at which children will be able to perform certain tasks. For example, when should a child start walking? Will special practice enable one to be an early walker? How old must a child be before toilet training will be effective? What factors are involved in bringing about readiness for a boy to learn to tie a necktie or a girl to set her hair? During recent years, teachers in all subject areas have developed a keen interest in the readiness of students to learn concepts and skills related to their particular subjects. The interest in readiness aims at matching instruction with pupil characteristics.

189

Individuals learn and perform best when they are "ready." This statement, though true, is only of moderate benefit to the teacher who is interested in specific information for program planning. Teachers and parents need to know what "readiness" means for each activity. They need to know how readiness can be determined, how it can be hastened, and what type of readiness can be expected at various age levels.

Readiness to learn refers to a condition of the individual that makes a particular task an appropriate one for mastering. Readiness for motor learning is dependent upon a combination of physical and mental maturation, prerequisite learning, the individual's motivation for the task, and any special feelings about the situation.

Readiness has important implications for the grade placement of activities in all areas of the school curriculum. Also, the particular sequence with which a set of tasks is presented should be arranged with careful attention to interdependence.

For efficiency's sake, the introduction of motor skills should be delayed until the learner is ready. However, care must be taken not to wait too long, i.e., past the period of optimal psychological and physical readiness. Such delay can prove as problemsome as introducing the tasks too early. For example, in the area of leisure skills the college student who has failed to develop competence in certain recreational areas is not inclined or encouraged to take part in these activities with peers. The same reluctance is evident among adults of all ages. People tend to be hesitant to expose their clumsiness or ineptness in front of acquaintances. In addition, most people are too busy with occupational and family responsibilities to develop the background skills necessary for effective performance in leisure activities. Therefore, readiness guidelines help us to wait just long enough before introducing learning activities.

The scope of readiness

The topic of readiness is much more complex than was suspected a few years ago. Traditionally, it was assumed that the development of motor skills depended solely on physical maturation, while verbal learning depended only on intellectual development. It has recently been pointed out, however, that the concept of readiness is not quite so simple. The interrelationship of physical, mental, and emotional factors in readiness has been emphasized by Zaichkowsky et al. (1980), Cronback (1951), Ausubel (1963), and Watson (1962). In discussing the factors that comprise the developmental process, Zaichkowsky et al. state that ". . . psychomotor, cognitive, and affective or social-psychological factors all interact during a life span. Physical activity can have a profound effect on the development of these three domains at every stage of a youngster's development" (p. vii). Cronback illustrates the complexity of the concept of readiness with the following statement:

> *All aspects of development interact.* A change in any facet of the child's readiness can alter his whole system of responses. When the normal sequence of development is interrupted in any way, effects are to be seen throughout the child's development.

Physiological maturing prepares one to profit from experience. Biological changes, especially in the nervous system, influence what one can learn. Pupils who differ in rate of maturing have different experiences and develop different personalities. . . .

Certain times in life are formative periods, which have a great effect on readiness for a particular activity. The period when a person first has a chance to engage in an activity is especially important. The formative period for physical skill is, roughly, from age 1 to 4. From the time he learns to creep through the "runabout age," the child is establishing a basic coordination pattern and developing confidence or timidity. The usual formative period for attitudes regarding one's intellectual abilities, reading, work with numbers, and school work in general is the first year or so of schooling. Success, failure, challenge, and conflict at that time precondition the reaction to all later schooling (pp. 89-90).

Ausubel (1963) states that the two principal factors in readiness are maturation (increments in capacity that take place in the absence of practice experience) and learning (specific practice on incidental experience). He indicates that a combination of the two is usually important, although for certain tasks only one might be strategic.

Numerous examples of the interrelationships of physiological and psychological phenomena can be pointed out. For example, a poor physical self-image can adversely influence all aspects of a young person's intellectual, social, and physical development. Physical exhaustion can greatly limit the extent of a student's intellectual pursuit. Similarly, a person who is limited in intellectual ability will have difficulty in learning a complex motor skill or in adapting to intricate teamwork and strategy. It is therefore unwise to assume that mental and physical maturation are separate and contribute to only one phase of the individual's development.

It is readily apparent that different levels of physiological maturity are essential for the learning of different motor skills. Usually children are ready for large and simple movement skills earlier than for fine and complex movements. It is therefore largely a waste of time to offer specific instruction in a fine skill before children have reached an appropriate level of maturity. It is also clear that certain activities cannot be taught before an appropriate level of psychological maturity has been established. For example, children cannot learn to swim well while they are afraid of water. Fifth-grade boys will have difficulty in learning to dance if they feel this activity is not appropriate for boys.

It is now generally accepted that interest is a strategic factor in affecting one's readiness to learn physical or verbal skills. Consider, for example, the reluctance of a group of eighth-grade boys to seriously practice dribbling a basketball properly. If this same group of boys had recently seen the high school star freeze the ball with his deft dribbling for the last sixty seconds in an important game they would be more ready to learn. Young children will be much more receptive to the learning of safety rules for descending stairs after a classmate has been injured on the stairs.

The adolescent girl will be ready to learn to set her hair if her girlfriends are also learning the skill or if she suspects a connection between hairdos and the interest of boys. These illustrations emphasize that readiness for the learning of a motor skill is not merely a matter of physical maturation.

Because of the interaction of physical, mental and emotional factors in determining one's readiness for learning, it is often impossible to pinpoint the reason for a child's inability to learn a particular task. The difficulty may result either from physiological immaturity or simply a lack of interest.

Despite the difficulty in discussing the various aspects of readiness separately, this chapter will be devoted primarily to the *physical* factors of readiness for motor learning and performance. Chapter seven will deal with factors related to psychological readiness.

Background of school readiness

The current interest in, and understanding of, readiness dates back to Thorndike's law of readiness (1913). This law referred primarily to emotional response to action or expected action. Today, the concept of readiness is broader than that proposed by Thorndike and is generally used in reference to learning or performance readiness. In the original law, the three circumstances for readiness are described as follows:

1. When a conduction unit is ready to conduct, conduction by it is satisfying, nothing being done to alter its action.
2. For a conduction unit ready to conduct, not to conduct is annoying and provokes whatever response nature provides in connection with that particular annoying lack.
3. When a conduction unit unready for conduction is forced to conduct, conduction by it is annoying (p. 128).

The rather vague term of "conduction unit" has been interpreted by Hilgard (1956) as "action tendency." In reference to this, he states, "When an action tendency is aroused through preparatory adjustments, sets, attitudes, and the like, fulfillment of the tendency in action is satisfying, non-fulfillment is annoying. Readiness thus means a preparation for action" (p. 18). Hilgard indicates that Thorndike did not develop, or even foresee, readiness for learning in the broad sense that it is understood today. He says ". . . it would be historically inaccurate to construe his law of readiness as an anticipation of maturational readiness" (p. 19).

In recent years, the topic of readiness has developed into one of the major topics of interest at the elementary school level. Reading readiness has received perhaps the greatest amount of attention. Readiness for drawing, printing, and writing has also come under considerable investigation. Relatively little attention, however, has been devoted to the necessary preparation for learning gross motor skills.

In regard to school learning, Bruner (1963) has stated that any subject can be taught effectively in some intellectually honest fashion to any child at any stage of development. Such a position seems to deny the need for educators to give special attention to readiness for particular activities. At the same time, his *spiral curriculum* is designed to enlarge upon the more basic concepts as the child develops greater ability and supporting concepts. Bruner's theory is disputed by Piaget (1966), who believes that the biological character of development limits learning or the understanding of concepts to a particular level of difficulty. Havighurst (1966), by stating that many concepts are beyond the capacity of first graders to comprehend, also disagrees with Bruner.

Components of physical readiness

For the purpose of this discussion, physical readiness for motor performances will include (1) maturation, (2) general motor development, and (3) prerequisite skills. These terms, with "growth and development," are often used almost interchangeably. Distinctions between them are not always clear because different authors indicate overlapping definitions. However, in this discussion, *maturation* is referred to as the early physiological development that increases the individual's motor capability to learn movement skills. This development may include changes in size, shape, and even skills not directly related to what is taught. Maturation refers to phylogenetic development, which is only slightly affected by environmental conditions. This process occurs early in life, most prominently in the first years but continues into the teens or early twenties. When viewed in the broadest sense, maturity continues throughout life.

General motor development refers to the improvement of one's motor abilities as a result of practice and experience. Such components as strength, coordination, speed, balance, and agility are fully developed only if certain exercise programs are employed. The same is true for such basic movement tasks as running, skipping, climbing, throwing, and kicking. A deprived or seriously limited environment retards the development of each of these basic tasks. General motor development, as viewed in this discussion, most closely relates to popular definitions of growth and development. Growth, however, simply refers to an increase in body size. This, of course, may result from a number of factors, including maturation, diet, and exercise.

Prerequisite learning refers to the development of particular skills that are, in turn, used in the learning or performance of more advanced patterns of movement. Prerequisite skills are relatively basic movements upon which more sophisticated skills are built. For example, ability to do a simple two-step is a prerequisite to learning the polka. Progression in teaching a particular activity is usually a matter of developing the necessary prerequisites in logical order. The significance of each component of physiological readiness for physical education will be presented in the following sections.

Phylogenetic development refers to those behavioral changes that occur rather automatically as the individual grows older and matures. This development is characteristic of the race and not a matter of individual or cultural origin. It dictates activities such as grasping, crawling, walking, and running.

Ontogenetic development includes those changes that result from learning. They do not occur automatically with maturation, but are acquired through such environmental experiences as driving a car, skating, catching, and all advanced mastering of recreational skills.

MATURATION

Maturation is defined by Eichorn and Jones (1958) as the emergence of any characteristics whose form and timing are chiefly controlled genetically. The development of these hereditary characteristics is primarily dependent upon neurological functioning and occurs during the early life of the individual. Maturation is only slightly affected by variations in nutrition, exercise, and other environmental conditions; it occurs essentially without effort by the individual. Although it does not produce learning, maturation makes learning possible. The rate of maturation does not follow a straight line. While chronological age is absolutely predictable, maturation is not. Heredity is primarily responsible for setting the pace at which children mature. This results in widely varying maturational levels for children of the same age, particularly during adolescence.

Motor skills are not developed until the child's neuromuscular system is sufficiently ready. When the required maturation level has been reached, the responses (grasping, walking, talking, etc.) will normally be made. However, the emergence of these skills does not occur suddenly and automatically with maturity. The child can be trained more easily and quickly after having reached a full state of physiological readiness for the specific activity. Therefore, the role of the teacher and the parent in promoting motor skill learning is to determine the time at which children are ready to learn skills and then to arrange the learning situation most effective for the development of the skills.

Research in maturation has generally been designed to determine at what age certain types of skills can be learned most effectively and if special training can speed the learning of certain skills. The studies have usually compared two groups of young children who take part in training at different chronological ages. This type of research has involved training in such diverse tasks are walking, talking, toilet training, climbing, throwing, and handling tools.

After studying different groups of children over two- and seven-year periods, Shirley (1933) and Bayley (1934) pointed out considerable consistency of behavior among them. Phylogenetic influences on early development seemed to be more influential than did environmental conditions. Children who had been compared by heredity seemed to develop the capacity to learn basic skills at about the same time. Several studies involving young twins have generally shown that the child who is untrained in the special task is able to catch up to the trained child with less practice at a later time. Even though some early advantage might be shown for the practicing group, these advantages are usually slight and are generally lost when the nonpracticing group begins work on the task at a more mature physiological level. Both Shirley and Bayley observed that serious illness or restriction of activity can slow maturation somewhat, but the social status of the parents seemed to make no difference in the maturation process.

Most rapid changes in maturation take place during the early years. The rate of maturation follows a descending curve until its completion in the early twenties. Bayley (1936) found that gross motor coordinations mature more rapidly than mental functions during the first two years of life. After this age, motor progress is comparatively slower. She reported a moderate correlation between measured mental and motor development during the first fifteen months. The relationship was lower thereafter. She found that performance in motor tests was less consistent than in mental tests. Cratty (1964) describes maturation in a broader context. He indicates that maturation continues throughout the life of the individual and views aging as the terminal phase of the process.

Developmental stages

During recent years, various authors have identified several stages of early human development. A great deal of agreement can be noted among the different authorities. Piaget (1954) describes two stages of intellectual development: (1) sensorimotor, which occurs during the first two years of life, and (2) conceptual, which occurs from two years until maturity. During the first two years, the coordination of simple motor actions seems dominant over the mental activity of the child. Piaget suggested that marked retardation in sensorimotor development at one year may be an indication of future conceptual retardation of the child. He differentiated the sensorimotor phase of development into six stages. The first month of life is referred to as the *reflexes* stage and is characterized by the prominence of simple reflexes. The second stage, which occurs during the second and third months, is referred to as *primary circular reactions*. During this period, the child engages in such repetitive motor actions as the opening and closing of fists or other simple movement of the hands. These actions are performed without any goal-directed purpose and without any result in which the child seems interested.

Piaget referred to the third stage of development as *secondary circular reactions*. The repetitive or rhythmical movements during this period (four to six months) seem to be performed because of the results they produce. For example, the child may kick repeatedly because of the pleasure resulting from this movement. This kicking action may cause a suspended toy to swing vigorously over the crib or make the carriage or stroller squeak or vibrate. Unlike the previous stage, the child seems to engage in these actions because of enjoyment in the change in environment that results. *Coordination of secondary reactions* occurs from the seventh to the tenth months. During this stage, the child performs a learned response in order to obtain a desired goal. Simple problem solving, such as pushing a pillow out of the way in order to obtain a toy hidden under it, may begin during this period. Piaget refers to the fifth stage as *tertiary circular movements*. This developmental phase occurs from the eleventh to the eighteenth months and marks the beginning of trial-and-error experimentation. The child uses different responses to obtain the same goals. He or she learns that movement and verbal actions can have considerable effect on surrounding events. The last of the six stages, *mental combinations*, takes place from the eighteenth month. During this period, the child learns to think through certain actions, considering possible consequences, before acting. This elementary foresight marks the beginning of conceptual thought. More advanced levels of conceptualization evolve during the remainder of childhood.

McGraw (1943) has identified four periods of neurological growth during the first two years of life, which are similar to those described by Piaget. The first period covers roughly the first four months and is characterized by reflexes and rhythmical movements of the newborn child. The second period ranges from the fourth to the eighth or ninth month. There is a reduction of activity in the pelvic girdle and lower extremities with an increase in voluntary movement in the upper spinal region. The third period ranges from eight to fourteen months and is evidenced by increased control of lower spinal region. Months fifteen through twenty-four are included in the fourth period, which is characterized by the rapid development of associated processes including communication.

Mussen, Conger, and Kagan (1974) suggest three major developmental trends during the child's early development. One of these is a *cephalocaudal* trend, which refers to the early development of the head and upper parts of the body. This tendency is evidenced by greater proficiency in head movements, visual skill, and eye-hand coordination during the early months, and the late development of walking and eye-foot coordination. Motor responses also develop in a *proximodistal* direction, from the central to the peripheral areas of the body. According to these authors, the trunk, shoulders, upper arms, and upper legs are controlled more quickly than are the forearms and hands, or the lower legs and feet.

The third trend described by Mussen et al. refers to a *mass-to-specific* muscular development, which indicates that children develop gross body movements and skills prior to the development of specific, or fine, skills. In addition, movements become more refined so that excess or wasted movements are gradually eliminated, and only necessary movements are used for more efficient performance.

Several studies have been conducted in recent years in an effort to determine the role of maturation in the learning of certain motor tasks, the age at which children can most effectively learn different skills, and whether special exercises or practice can speed maturation or physiological readiness.

Effect of special exercises

Several problems are faced by anyone contemplating the long-term effects of exercises or any other development programs involving young children. Perhaps foremost among these is the unwillingness of researchers to wait around for twenty or twenty-five years to publish the results of these long-term observations. Consequently, most of these developmental studies are concluded within months, with perhaps some follow-up in a year or two. Another approach is to use animals, which have a quicker maturation rate and shorter life span. Findings from these animal studies or short-term studies with human infants are often generalized for long-term human development. Such generalizations involve a great deal of speculation, and therefore, must be interpreted with caution.

A number of maturational studies (Gesell and Thompson, 1929; McGraw, 1935, 1943; Hilgard, 1932, 1933) have involved identical twins. These co-twin control studies have advantages because the two subjects have identical hereditary characteristics. In these experiments, one child begins practice on a particular task such as walking, stair climbing, or on finer skills such as cutting with scissors. The second child does not start practice at the same time, but usually begins a training program or is tested a few weeks or months later. The early practicing and late practicing twins are usually compared on (1) initial performance scores, (2) length of time required to reach a particular skill level, and (3) general proficiency at some later date.

Gesell and Thompson at the Yale University Child Development Center have conducted a number of studies with identical twins to determine the role of maturation in the learning of skills. In one study (1929), they had one child begin a daily program of stair-climbing sessions at the age of 46 weeks. After six weeks of this practice (at 52 weeks) the child was able to climb the staircase in 25.8 seconds. Practice was then discontinued for the first child, and one week later the other child began a similar training schedule. On the first practice day, the second twin climbed the stairs in 45 seconds. However, in just two weeks of training, this child was able to climb the stairs in 10.3 seconds. The two weeks of training at 53 to 55 weeks were therefore more effective for this task than were six weeks at the ages of 46 to 52 weeks. When practice was resumed for both groups at 56 weeks, the two children were practically identical in performance. McGraw (1943) reported similar results in a stair-climbing study.

Hilgard (1933) conducted an early study in which one twin (about five years of age) was given training in memory skills, tossing a ring over a peg, and walking a straight line on a narrow board. He found that the twin who was initially untrained caught up to the trained one in the performance of these skills and with fewer practices. He concluded that little was to be gained by early practice on complex skills. In another study, Hilgard (1932) trained children of two and three years in skills of climbing, buttoning, and cutting with scissors. In this study, the trained children showed superior skill immediately after the training session. After a very short practice period, however, the previously unpracticed group became as skillful as the trained children. He concluded that when children are sufficiently mature for an activity, a short practice period is as effective as a much longer period before the children have reached the appropriate state of physiological readiness.

Perhaps the most frequently quoted developmental study of twins was the Johnny and Jimmy project reported by McGraw (1935). McGraw worked with the twin boys from the time they were twenty days old until they were just over two years of age. Although these twins were not maternal, controls were such as to make this a milestone investigation. They spent eight hours a day, five days a week in the experimental situation. Johnny was selected as the "experimental" twin and was exposed to a highly stimulating environment, receiving short training sessions every two hours. Early experiences included stimulation of his reflexes, as well as encouragement to roll over, sit, and stand. Later, he was stimulated to climb stairs, inclined planes, and pedestals; to ride a tricycle, swim, skate, and manipulate objects; and to perform a variety of other tasks. In the meantime, Jimmy was given no specific training and, in fact, spent most of the time in his crib. However, from time to time, he, like Johnny, was tested for reflexes as well as for a variety of learned skills.

The age at which Johnny acquired certain complex motor skills was astounding, particularly for the mid-1930s. According to McGraw, he could swim 7 feet at the age of eight months and at fourteen months could swim 15 feet with his face in the water. Prior to the age of two, he could skate with the "broad rhythmical sway which was characteristic of the proficient skater" (p. 163). In comparative tests during and at the end of two years, McGraw reported that Johnny and Jimmy did not differ appreciably in reflexive responses, which, of course, are not influenced by learning. Neither did they differ in the onset of turning over, crawling, walking, and bicycle riding, where maturation appeared to be the primary determinant for performances. However, she did note that even in these activities Johnny showed more interest, less fear, and more confidence in performing the complex skills. Clearly, he excelled in the complex skills—skating, swimming, and diving—that had been taught. General coordination was enhanced and a more daring attitude was assumed. However, in novel skills he did not perform better at the end of the second year. Therefore, significant transfer was not observed in the particular tasks selected.

Another significant study in maturation was reported by Dennis and Dennis (1940). They conducted a study with the Hopi Indians to determine the effect of freedom of movement on the speed with which walking would be learned. While most of the mothers bound their children to cradle boards, which limited the movement of most parts of their body, the researchers persuaded some women to free their children at an early age to allow greater movement of their legs. If walking were a skill that could be learned earlier as a result of greater activity, it seemed that the less restricted children should learn to walk earlier. In this study, however, it was reported that the bound and unbound children learned to walk at about the same time. The authors concluded that learning to walk was dependent upon maturation and would not be learned earlier because of greater freedom of movement.

Despite the inability of special exercises to appreciably speed maturation or lead to the development of special skills, studies have shown some latent advantages for the exercising group. In one study, Gesell and Thompson (1929) reported that the twin who practiced stair climbing had greater agility, was more skillful, and was less fearful than the control twin after both had learned to climb stairs. McGraw (1946) reported similar findings in a study of motor development. Whereas initial tests indicated that a program of regular practice was of little value in the early stages of learning, a four-year follow-up study showed that the trained subject was more skillful and confident in the skills that he had practiced. Mirenvo (1935) found that twins who were specifically trained in jumping, throwing for accuracy, and bowling showed greater improvement than siblings who were not specifically trained. Rarick and McKee (1949) showed that children who had better play facilities performed better on tests of running, jumping, balance, agility, catching, and throwing. Nevertheless, these authors have not generally advocated special exercise programs for children during the first two or three years of life.

A noteworthy theory related to the developmental role of special exercise is that used by Doman (1960, 1964) and Delacato (1959, 1963) of the Institutes for the Development of Human Potential in Philadelphia. This theory is based on the assumption that many cognitive, motor, and perceptual problems are the result of poor neurological organization, and further, that most such problems can be remedied through an activity called "patterning." In essence, this is an effort to restructure the nerurological organization by retracting and redeveloping the crawling and creeping phases of development. The theory also places heavy emphasis upon the necessity for developing a hemispheric dominance. Though several successful case studies have been reported, the Doman-Delacato program has received criticism (Perkins, 1964; Oettlinger, 1964; Hudspeth, 1964) in the literature of both educator and medical specialists for its lack of scientific evidence to support the theoretical bases of its programs.

Restricted activity and maturation

Although special exercises do not seem to be especially valuable for the early development of skills, lack of activity may prove a hindrance to physical growth and skill development. Individuals who have had an arm or leg in a cast for a period of a few weeks will agree that atrophy takes place in a rather short period. Situations in which lesser degrees of inactivity are imposed will result in lesser amount of atrophy. A number of studies have been conducted in which the learner was deprived of normal activity. These deprivation studies have generally shown that unusual restriction of movement or experience will limit one's normal maturation.

Studies of controlled deprivation of children have not proven popular with parents. In fact, regulations that affect research techniques with human subjects now prohibit some of the studies conducted only a few years ago. However, a number of studies have been conducted with animals to show that those seriously deprived of movement over a long period will not develop in a normal manner. Also, if other types of learning experiences are restricted, the animal will experience limited development. In one significant study, Nissen (1951) reared a chimpanzee without restriction, except that it was unable to explore its environment with its hands and feet. These appendages were covered with cardboard tubes for two and one-half years. After the coverings were removed, the animal exhibited extremely retarded behavior and never developed normally thereafter.

Hebb (1958) reported an experiment in which a dog was reared in a situation where it did not have opportunities to learn normal self-protection techniques.

When the animal was later released into a more typical situation, it showed an inability to avoid bumping its head on a low pipe. It took this dog far longer than the normal dog to learn routine measures of self-protection.

Riesen (1947) reared baby chimpanzees in total darkness until the age of two. When exposed to light for the first time they were functionally blind and showed no visual discrimination. After several weeks, however, they began to make use of their eyes and eventually behaved like seeing creatures. Through this and other experiments, Riesen was able to show that animals must "learn to see." Thompson and Heron (1954) raised puppies in boxes so that for a year and a half they did not see anything but the sides and top of the box. When removed from this restricted environment, the dogs were totally naive about their environment. In addition to being less aggressive than other dogs, they were totally unfamiliar with pain and techniques for avoiding injury. Curiosity drove them to encounter fire, hot radiators, and sharp edges. The authors concluded that the dogs had to "learn to sense pain," eliminate hazardous behavior, and experience appropriate emotions.

In light of these findings, it seems fortunate that children have the urge for activity and change. Exploratory movement, even random activity, is apparently essential for normal development. The capacity of children for getting bored, therefore appears to be a desirable characteristic. Mednick (1964) reported a study in which university students were offered twenty dollars for every twenty-four-hour period they would spend in an especially unstimulating environment. The subjects were to lie on foam rubber beds with cardboard cuffs around their arms and with translucent goggles over their eyes. In addition they were to stay in a soundproof room. They could earn one hundred dollars for five days of this nonactivity. Few of the students, however, were able to continue this regimen for more than two or three days. The subjects reported that they experienced hallucinations and sometimes became panicky. In addition, they had difficulty sleeping or even thinking clearly. They performed poorly on intelligence tests that were given while they were in the room. Upon emerging from the restricted environment, many were confused, nauseated, disoriented, and fatigued for periods up to twenty-four hours.

Monkeys, rats, and other animals also show a need for activity and stimulus change. Researchers have shown that animals learn in some situations when the only reward is a change in scenery. Monkeys can be trained to push a particular panel that allows them to observe other monkeys, or even people, in a different room. On subsequent occasions, they open the panel to watch what is happening on the outside.

The need for change, both in movement and in what one observes, is strong enough to cause both humans and animals to bring about changes. However, special restrictions result in limited development or even deterioration. Normal activities and stimulation are necessary for normal maturation. Added stimulation appears to be helpful for growth.

Teeple (1978), while acknowledging the retardation in physical development that may result from childhood diseases, malnutrition, and extreme inactivity, reports that when these negative influences are removed, a "catch-up" growth phenomenon occurs. This is a metabolic rate increase that tends to bring the child to the level that would have been attained had those problems not been encountered. However, if the retarding influence lasts for too long, catch-up growth is not totally effective.

Hicks (1931) reported that young children benefited very little from practicing the complex task of hitting a moving target. He concluded that for young children the important need is for general environmental activity rather than specific skill practice. A study by Williams and Scott (1953) on motor development during infancy supports the need for activity during the period. Two groups of Black infants from sharply contrasting socioeconomic backgrounds were compared. The low economic group showed significantly greater development in motor skills than did the higher economic group. The authors believed that this difference was attributable to a permissive atmosphere and absence of cribs, playpens, high chairs, and similar restrictive equipment in the low socioeconomic homes.

Lawther (1978) encouraged the provision of a variety of programs, equipment, and arrangements for the overall motor development of children. He urged:

> Controlled outside-of-school play, tag, hopscotch, all types of pursuit games, ropes to jump, apparatus to climb and to swing on, mats for tumbling or wrestling, swimming and skating, dancing and team games, plus opportunities to use facilities under guidance, will foster children's development. They need encouragement and guidance from intelligent, interested, and able parents, from recreation and playground supervisors, and from teachers through unorganized and organized extracurricular programs. Community planners must arrange for space and equipment, especially with regard to the more complex skills—skating, swimming, badminton, tennis, team games. Gymnastics with apparatus seem to have more appeal at the younger ages than in the late teens, as does track, although supervision and guidance without pressure or forcing is needed. The appropriate activities will vary with the climate and with the sport skills employed by the adults of the community. Children like to imitate adults, and most youngsters will learn much informally by trial and error, and by playing with, observing, and imitating others, peers or adults (p. 33).

GENERAL MOTOR DEVELOPMENT

In addition to maturation, which usually takes place as a normal function of growing older, physical educators must also concern themselves with the development of motor capacities and the physical growth of the students. Physical fitness and general motor capacities are to a large extent dependent upon exercise or practice. These capacities are, in turn, important in establishing one's readiness to learn and perform more advanced skills.

The student cannot learn a routine on the parallel bars without first developing a degree of arm and shoulder strength. Agility and skill in footwork are essential for successful participation in handball. General body coordination and balance are needed for the learning of precise movements in a dance activity. Components such as strength, endurance, flexibility, and eye-hand coordination are strategic for participation in many motor activities. Different tasks are dependent upon, or emphasize, different capacities. Of course, various levels of performance require greater or lesser degrees of these capacities. A very important function of the teacher is to determine the most essential components and the levels necessary for each type of activity and to guide the students into these activities when they are ready. Another critical function, of course, is to promote readiness by developing the basic motor capacities.

The activity of an individual through the elementary school years will, to a great extent, determine readiness for a wide variety of activities or a few specific sports at the junior high school level. Activity tends to promote readiness for further activity. The best way of promoting readiness for learning and performance in motor activities is by encouraging general physical activity. This broad base of activity can be instrumental in the development of basic components essential for participation in a wide variety of activities.

Wickstrom (1977) presents an extensive review and analysis of the developmental components involved in walking, running, jumping, throwing, catching, skipping, and kicking. Through sequential illustrations and discussions, Wickstrom shows how these skills evolve from infancy to high levels of proficiency.

Numerous studies have shown that children of various ages who take part more regularly in physical activities score higher in motor capacity tests than do those who are less active. Rarick and McKee (1949) showed that superior performers in the third grade had a history of greater activity participation than did children with inferior performance. McCraw (1956) reported that junior high school boys who took part in varsity athletics scored higher than nonparticipants in tasks of running speed, the standing broad jump, and the softball throw. There are dangers, however, in generalizing from these studies about the value of these activities in motor development. It is not clearly established whether superior motor capacities were the cause or the result of greater participation in these activities. Most likely there is substance to both of these possibilities. There can be no doubt, however, that under well-controlled conditions, an increase in physical activity can result in improvement in most motor capacities. This improvement often represents an increase in readiness for various activities.

It is universally agreed today that muscular size and strength can be developed by physical activity. Numerous research reports describe the role of exercise in this process. Studies generally show that athletes exhibit greater development in all basic components of motor capacity than do nonathletes. McCraw (1956) reported that during a school semester athletes grew more in height and weight than did nonathletes. Kusinitz and Keeney (1958) found that favorable anthropometric changes took place in adolescent boys as a result of weight training. In these boys, waist girth declined while other measurements increased. Jokl (1964) compared men who were gymnasts with their twin brothers who did not take part regularly in any sports activity. The gymnasts had broader shoulders and were stronger and heavier than their brothers. The effect of exercise on muscular size and strength can usually be seen when one compares the most used and least used arms of professional baseball pitchers, bowlers, tennis players, or even carpenters.

Developing basic motor capacities and movement skills is a prime responsibility of physical educators, especially at the elementary school level. At the same time, it is difficult to develop basic skills among children who come to class with great variation in ability, without making the class especially repetitious and uninteresting for the advanced students. Unnecessary repetition has often been a valid criticism of many physical education programs. It seems possible, however, that practice on a particular trait might occur without repetition of the same activity. The needed skill can be incorporated into a new activity. For example, the skill of skipping may be used as part of a basic rhythm unit in the first grade. Perhaps not all of the students will develop a high level of proficiency at this time. In a later grade, a different activity such as "Skip to My Lou" might be used. This acitivity, which involves practice in skipping, may be new to the children. As a greater proportion of students learn to skip well, less time should be devoted to this activity. Other basic skills, such as throwing, catching, and kicking, can be brought into several activities in the same manner. The technique of changing the activity to improve the same skill will prove more valuable for students who develop early proficiency than will continuing practice of the same activity.

Motor development during childhood

Children today are maturing earlier and are taller and heavier than their parents were a generation ago. Much of this earlier development is assumed to result from improved dietary practices. The increase in physical size during recent years has been greater than differences in general motor ability or capacity. Despite outstanding athletic performances by a few teenagers, today's young people in general do not appear to be stronger, faster, or more flexible than the children of forty years ago. For tests in which comparable scores can be obtained, such as in strength and motor educability, today's children do not have the same superiority they do in physical size.

General statements about the readiness of an individual or group are of limited value. Readiness is always relative to the particular subject, topic, level of difficulty, and method used. Any age group in school represents different stages of development. Even a single individual may, for a time, waver back and forth in readiness for a particular task. However, norm tables regarding age-level characteristics provide some information regarding average or typical development.

According to Zaichkowsky et al. (1980), children progress through four phases of motor development. These begin with the reflexive and then *rudimentary movement abilities*, including sitting, crawling, creeping, standing, and walking. Next, during early childhood, *general fundamental skills* are developed. These are common to all children and are necessary for survival and functioning in our society. They include running, jumping, hopping, skipping, climbing, balancing, throwing, and catching. In late childhood, *specific movement skills* are developed. Here, fundamental movement skills are refined, and better form and accuracy are attained. The fundamental skills are further developed and used in sports or other motor activities. Then, at adolescence, *specialized skills* are developed. These include the advanced level sports (or work) skills that reach a high degree of specialization. To perform these well one needs strength, coordination, and well-developed fundamental (prerequisite) skills.

Seefeldt (1980) has developed a somewhat similar concept, which is illustrated in Figure 7-1. This model emphasizes the early development of reflex reactions and fundamental skills. These are precursors in the development of "transitional" motor skills and then specific sports skills and dances during late childhood and adulthood.

During the preschool years, there is a gradual improvement in the child's ability to run smoothly, to turn corners sharply, and to start and stop. These loco-

FIGURE 7-1. Sequential Progression in the Achievement of Motor Proficiency (From V. Seefeldt, "Guidelines for Pre-school Children." *Proceedings of the National Conference on Physical Fitness and Sports for All*, February 1-2, 1980, pp. 5-19. Used by permission of the author and publisher.)

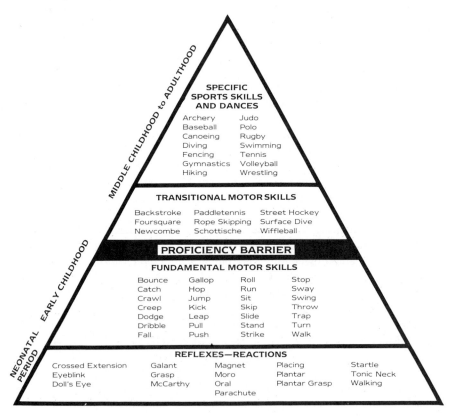

motor skills continue to develop into the primary grades. Gutteridge (1939) compared the motor development of children from three to seven years of age. Very rapid development was seen between ages four and seven in hopping, skipping, throwing, and galloping. At age seven, nearly all children were rated as proficient in each of the activities. Gross motor movement and coordination develop especially fast during this period.

Seils (1951) investigated the motor development of children in grades one, two, and three. Boys and girls were compared on a variety of motor ability tests according to grade level and age (broken into three-month groups). The children were tested in running, balance, agility, jumping, throwing, and striking. Generally, Seils found a gradual or consistent improvement in each of the components from grades one, two, and three. A few exceptions were found among girls, who often did not exhibit a significant improvement between grades one and two. However, grade three scores were always higher than those for grade two. When students were further grouped according to three-month age differentials, they generally showed a consistent improvement with each succeeding advancement in age. In addition to better performance at each level, it was found that students were taller and heavier. The increase in size was reasonably steady. While a moderate correlation was shown between performance and skeletal maturity, the relationship of physical size and age to performance was considerably lower.

There is no question that appropriate exercise is beneficial for physical development. According to Larson (1973), bones adapt to stress and benefit from exercise. Lack of stress, or inactivity, does not stimulate growth or development of bone tissue. Muscle tissues are more obviously related to exercise. Hypertrophy is one result of such activity while atrophy quickly results from lack of exercise. Body-building contests dramatically illustrate the effect of exaggerated weight training activity for both men and women.

Children become stronger as they grow older. Furthermore, the increase in strength is greater than the increase in body size. There appears to be a qualitative as well as quantitative change in muscle tissue. Rarick (1965) indicates that the muscle tissue actually becomes stronger or has the ability to mobilize more units. In addition, Asmussen and Heebell-Nielsen (1955) report that the effective use of strength becomes greater as the nervous system matures. This is exhibited in such activities as running and jumping.

Sex differences in growth rates

Individual differences in body size and in motor ability emerge most prominently during the adolescent years. This is especially apparent when one observes early maturers and late maturers. Boys and girls who mature early literally take off and leave the others. Early maturers, however, stop growing sooner and the late maturers close the gap to some extent but never completely.

Through the early school years, boys are slightly taller and heavier than girls. However, girls reach the maximum growth spurt approximately two years earlier than boys. As can be noted in Table 7-1 and in Figure 7-2, girls are taller and heavier at ages twelve and thirteen. Differences in time of maturation can cause considerable apprehension, especially for early maturing girls (who will appear unusually tall) and late maturing boys (who will be especially short). Table 7-1 includes average height and weight records for boys and girls from ages five to eighteen.

Figure 7-2, though using a different data source, reflects essentially the same trends. It can be observed that boys are slightly taller and heavier than girls up to age ten. For the next three years, girls take the lead over boys in both of these measures. The size differential in favor of girls reaches a peak at about age thirteen. After this, the growth spurt of the boys carries them past the girls in physical size.

A serious problem with height-weight norms is that they are outdated quite rapdily. Children (and adults) are becoming larger at all ages. On the basis of European and American data, Tanner (1970) reports that on the average, children increase each decade one to two cm between ages five and seven, and two to three cm between ages ten and fourteen.

In addition, children reach maximum height earlier now, usually around eighteen years of age. Another indication of earlier maturity is that the onset of menarche has accelerated by about four months each decade in Western European countries. The trend toward earlier maturation and larger adult size is related to better nutrition and advanced medical technology.

TABLE 7-1.   Height and Weight Records for Boys and Girls

Age (years)	AVERAGE BOY		AVERAGE GIRL	
	Height (inches)	Weight (pounds)	Height (inches)	Weight (pounds)
5	43.8	42.8	43.2	41.4
6	46.3	48.3	45.6	46.5
7	49.6	54.1	48.1	52.2
8	52.0	60.1	50.4	58.1
9	53.3	66.0	52.3	63.8
10	55.2	71.9	54.6	70.3
11	56.8	77.6	57.0	78.8
12	58.9	84.4	59.6	87.6
13	61.0	93.0	61.8	99.1
14	64.0	107.6	62.8	108.4
15	66.1	120.1	63.4	113.5
16	67.6	129.7	63.9	117.0
17	68.4	136.2	64.0	119.1
18	68.7	139.0	64.0	119.9

Source: Adapted from *Health Observation of School Children* by George M. Wheatley and Grace T. Hallock. Copyright 1951 McGraw-Hill Book Company. Used by permission of McGraw-Hill Book Company.

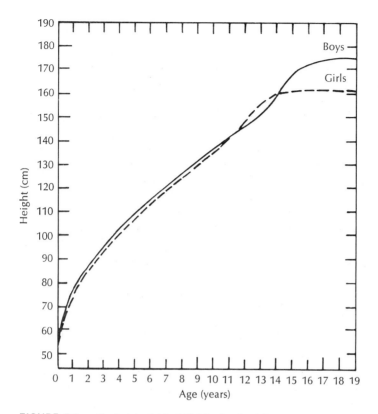

FIGURE 7-2. Typical Individual Height-Attained Curves for Boys and Girls (Supine Length to the Age of 2) (From J. Tanner, R. Whitehouse, and M. Takaishi, *Archives of Diseases in Childhood,* 1966, 41, pp. 454-71, 613-35.)

Sex differences in motor capacities

Few issues have evoked as much debate over the past decade as the comparison of males and females in regard to motor capacities. Several factors mitigate against a clear determination of the relative status of boys and girls or men and women in terms of physical ability. For example, there is little question that social and cultural considerations influence the performance of both groups in sports activities and in other physical capacity indicators. Frequently that influence is in opposite directions, i.e. encouraging males to become strong and aggressive in motor activities while promoting gentility and passivity for females. Social factors have also affected efforts to assess, interpret, and report the relative standing of the two sexes in such motor abilities. Performance data are not interpreted uniformly, nor are the implications of structural or physiological differences among males and females.

Measures of strength, speed, endurance, balance, coordination, or performance on particular sports skills reveal overlap between males and females, regardless of the age level. In other words, there are some girls in all school grades who can run faster and are stronger than some boys, and there are adult men who have greater flexibility and better fine motor coordination than do some adult women. Still, despite this overlap, motor performance test scores over the years have fallen into identifiable sex patterns, regardless of the reasons for such differences. These patterns are particularly evident when persons beyond the childhood years are tested.

In recent years, reports comparing the motor capacities of males and females have either presented performance scores on a variety of tests or they have analyzed physiological or anatomical characteristics that are presumed to predict differences in performances. First, some data showing performance comparisons will be presented. Table 7-2 contains some average physical performance scores for boys and girls from ages five to seventeen. These data are from a variety of sources. It can be noted that among young children boys proved superior to girls in gross motor activities. Boys seem to have a distinct advantage in throwing and strength items. The only measure in which girls perform as well as the boys is in the Brace Test of Motor Educability. It must be pointed out, however, that the types of items included here are those that our society emphasizes more for boys than for girls. Perhaps if skipping, balancing, or coordination activities had been included, girls would have performed as well or better. Differences in performance, therefore, apparently result from cultural as well as biological factors. In an early study, Bagley (1934) found little difference between boys and girls in motor ability. Garry (1963) reported that the motor ability of boys and girls is similar until adolescence.

Figures 7-3 and 7-4 reveal additional motor performance comparisons of school-age males and females. This information represents a variety in the types of measures taken. Further, Figure 7-3 presents comparative scores taken over approximately a seventeen-year period. These results show that while improvement has been made by both boys and girls during recent years, greater gains have been attained by girls. Corbin's chart (Figure 7-4) synthesizes the performance of boys and girls on a variety of fitness items as they vary over the school years. Table 7-3 includes summary information from many studies on male-female performance. These studies, conducted mostly during the 1950s and 1960s, showed that the superiority of boys or girls depends upon the particular traits being tested.

Early sexual maturation influences strength development and motor performance in preteenage and adolescent children. Gain in strength is greatest as boys and girls approach puberty, but this increase slows down afterward. Late maturers may follow early maturers in this change by as much as three years. The increase in strength during the pubescent period is greater for boys than for girls. During this period and thereafter, boys are superior in strength, jumping ability, speed, and power; while girls often excel in balance, hopping, flexibility, and coordinated movements.

TABLE 7-2. Some Motor Capacities of Children From Ages Five to Seventeen

Age (years)	Yards run (per second)	Standing broad jump (inches)	Jump and reach (inches)	Brace motor educability (score)	Distance throw (feet)	Hand grip strength (pounds) right	Hand grip strength (pounds) left	AAHPER sit-ups (number completed)	600-yard run walk[a] (minutes and seconds)
BOYS									
5	3.8	33.7	2.5	–	23.6	–	–	–	–
6	4.2	37.4	4.0	5.5	32.8	–	–	–	–
7	4.6	41.6	6.1	7.5	42.3	28	28	–	–
8	5.1	46.7	8.3	9.0	57.4	31	31	–	–
9	–	50.4	8.5	10.0	66.6	38	38	–	–
10	5.9	54.7	11.0	11.0	83.0	44	43	41	2:33
11	6.1	61.0	11.5	11.1	95.0	51	50	46	2:27
12	6.3	64.9	12.2	12.7	104.0	62	59	50	2:21
13	6.5	69.3	12.5	13.1	114.0	74	67	60	2:10
14	6.7	73.2	13.3	14.5	123.0	89	81	70	2:01
15	6.8	79.5	14.8	15.2	135.0	101	92	80	1:54
16	7.1	88.0	16.3	16.2	144.0	–	–	76	1:51
17	7.2	88.4	16.9	15.9	153.0	–	–	70	1:50

Continued on p. 210

TABLE 7-2. (continued)

Age (years)	Yards run (per second)	Standing broad jump (inches)	Jump and reach (inches)	Brace motor educability (score)	Distance throw (feet)	Hand grip strength (pounds) right	left	AAHPER sit-ups (number completed)	600-yard run walk[a] (minutes and seconds)
GIRLS									
5	3.6	31.6	2.2	—	14.5	—	—	—	—
6	4.1	36.2	3.5	5.5	17.8	—	—	—	—
7	4.4	40.0	5.7	7.5	25.4	23	22	—	—
8	4.6	45.9	7.7	9.0	30.0	28	27	—	—
9	—	51.3	8.7	10.0	38.7	31	31	—	—
10	5.8	—	10.5	10.5	47.0	37	36	31	2:48
11	6.0	52.0	11.0	11.1	54.0	42	42	30	2:49
12	6.1	—	11.2	11.8	61.0	53	51	32	2:49
13	6.3	62.1	11.0	11.8	70.0	60	56	31	2:52
14	6.2	62.7	11.8	11.9	74.5	66	61	30	2:46
15	6.1	63.2	12.2	11.5	75.7	64	59	26	2:46
16	6.0	63.0	12.0	11.8	74.0	—	—	26	2:49
17	5.9	—	—	—	—	—	—	27	2:51

[a]Low numbers represent better scores.

Source: Data from the Figure "Relative strength indices for boys and girls" by Anna Espenschade from *Science and Medicine of Exercise and Sports* edited by W. R. Johnson (Harper & Row, 1960); W. H. Peacock, *Achievement Scales in Physical Education for Boys and Girls* as adapted by H. M. Barrow and R. McGee in *A Practical Approach to Measurement in Physical Education*, Philadelphia: Lea & Febiger, 1964, and the American Association for Health, Physical Education, and Recreation, *AAHPER Youth Fitness Test Manual*, Washington, D.C.: the Association, 1965. By permission.

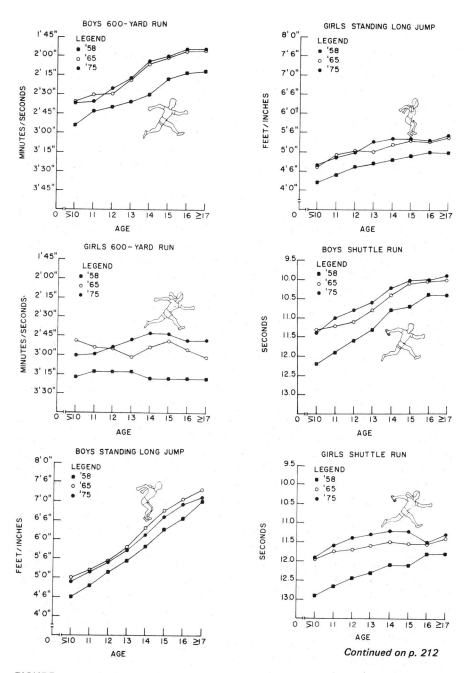

FIGURE 7-3. Comparative Mean Scores for AAHPER Youth Fitness Test, Coterminous, USA, 1975 (From P. Hunsicker and G. Reiff, "Youth Fitness Report: 1958-1965-1975." *Journal of Physical Education and Recreation,* January 1977, pp. 31-33. Copyright by the American Alliance for Health, Physical Education, Recreation and Dance, 1900 Association Drive, Reston, Va. 22091. Reprinted with permission.)

Continued on p. 212

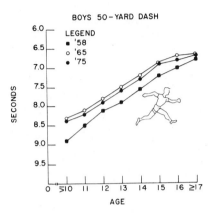

BOYS 50-YARD DASH

LEGEND
■ '58
○ '65
● '75

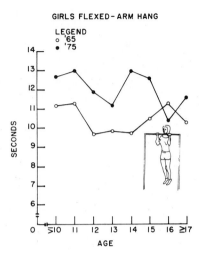

GIRLS FLEXED-ARM HANG

LEGEND
○ '65
● '75

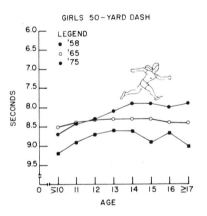

GIRLS 50-YARD DASH

LEGEND
● '58
○ '65
● '75

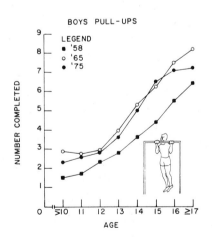

BOYS PULL-UPS

LEGEND
■ '58
○ '65
● '75

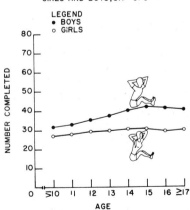

GIRLS AND BOYS, SIT-UPS

LEGEND
● BOYS
○ GIRLS

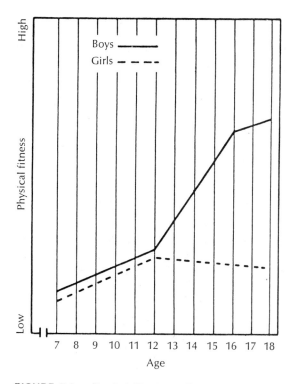

High

Boys ————
Girls – – – –

Physical fitness

Low

7 8 9 10 11 12 13 14 15 16 17 18

Age

FIGURE 7-4. Physical Fitness of Performance Differences Between Boys and Girls (From Corbin, 1973, p. 107.)

In general motor performance, girls usually show only slight improvement after the age of thirteen or fourteen. In fact, much of the data shows a decline for girls in some activities after this period. It is probable that this decline results more from cultural than from biological influences. There seems little doubt that girls *can* continue to improve motor performance for a time after age thirteen or fourteen. This has been shown by championship performances in many sports activities.

Zaichkowsky et al. (1980) suggests four reasons for the differences in motor performance between boys and girls: (1) body size, (2) anatomical structure, (3) physiological functioning, and (4) cultural factors. Prior to adolescence, *size* does not seem important, i.e., any difference in size is not as great as the difference in performance scores. In fact, in early adolescence girls are larger than boys, but in late adolescent years the reverse is true, and size does seem a logical factor.

During adolescence, but not earlier, *structure* appears to be a reasonable explanation for some differences. General structure of the pelvis area seemingly places girls at a disadvantage in running and jumping events. Also, after age eleven, boys have greater limb length and thus a mechanical advantage in some activities, such as throwing and striking with force.

TABLE 7-3.   Selected Studies Examining Sex Differences in Motor Performance

Motor Task	Age	Sex Superiority	Author
Agility	5-9	females	Keogh (1965)
Balance	7-9	females	Keogh (1965)
dynamic	7-11	females	Govatos (1966)
static	6-7	males	Cratty and Martin (1969)
Ball skills			
batting	6-12	males	Cratty (1970)
catching	6-12	none	Williams (1965)
kicking	8-10	males	Carpenter (1940)
	9-11	males	Latchaw (1954)
rolling	7-9	males	Witte (1962)
throwing (accuracy)	6-11	males	Keogh (1965)
(distance)	6-11	males	Keogh (1965)
	5-7	males	Jenkins (1930)
	5-17	males	Espenschade (1960)
	6-11	males	Crom and Pronko (1957)
	10-17	males	Hunsicker and Reiff (1966)
Fine Hand Movement	6-10	females	Connolly (1968)
Hopping	6-9	females	Keogh (1966)
Jumping			
Vertical	8-11	males	Johnson (1962)
	5-17	males	Espenschade (1960)
St. broad	6-11	males	Keogh (1965)
	5-17	males	Espenschade (1960)
Pursuit Rotor	5-8	none	Davol et al. (1955)
	8	males	Ammons et al. (1955)
Running Speed	6-11	males	Keogh (1965)
	5-7	males	Jenkins (1930)
	9-11	males	Latchaw (1954)
	5-17	males	Espenschade (1960)
Serial Motor	5-9	none	Zaichkowsky (1974)
Strength			
grip	11-17	males	Jones (1949)

From Cheffers and Evaul, 1978.

Rarick and Thompson (1956) showed that from an early age the male possesses more muscle tissue per unit of body weight, and that he is stronger per unit of muscle mass than is the female. Sex hormones play a prominent role in motor performance. In males, hormones favor strength development more than in females. Bayley (1951), however, showed that girls who ranked high in the masculinity physique were stronger per unit of body weight than were boys who had a feminine-type physique.

Sex and heredity play a major role in determining body type and composition. Research has shown that as early as age two girls have greater fat composition than do boys. Boys have heavier bones and greater muscular tissue. As children grow older, the differences in body composition become greater, reaching a peak during adolescence. Sheldon (1954) and several other authors indicate that body types are determined primarily by heredity and do not change a great deal from childhood.

During childhood, there is little difference in such *physiological* functioning as oxygen uptake or pulmonary ventilation. However, after about age twelve, Astrand (1976) reports some advantage for males in endurance activities. On the other hand, some recent reports attribute a physiological advantage to women in long endurance activities of moderate intensity.

Following a review of research on this topic, Herkowitz (1978) concluded that girls do not achieve the capacity for physical work as do boys at any age. She reported that females generally have smaller hearts, less blood volume, lower hemoglobin levels, less available oxygen, fewer red blood corpuscles, and less ability to absorb lactic acid.

Societal and *cultural factors* appear to best explain most differences during preadolescent years. Girls hop and skip more, engage in more balancing activities, and take part in more fine motor skills. As shown in Table 7-3, they perform better in tests of such activities. On the other hand, boys are more involved in gross motor skills and usually excel in those activities. Historically, girls have been discouraged from excelling in gross motor skills, but times are changing. For example, Wilmore (1974) has shown that female swimmers with intensive training have "closed the gap" on male swimmers. He shows that in the 400-meter swim, females today equal the times of men only 15 years earlier.

Children in endurance activities
and elite competition

It was traditionally assumed that vigorous or endurance activities were inappropriate for children and preteenage youth. Both medical authorities and educators believed that such activities were injurious to the health of children, and further, that children were incapable of these activities. Several persons in recent years have questioned both of these assumptions. Cureton (1964) and Astrand (1952) have reported research dealing with cardiovascular and respiratory functioning among children who are engaged in activity programs. In a study of the aerobic capacity of young children, Astrand reported that boys seven to eleven years of age and girls seven to nine years old reach practically the same oxygen intake as adults. In studies to determine endurance capacities of children, Cureton has used such measurements as oxygen intake, rate of oxygen debt, blood pressure, and electro-cardiograms to determine physiological responses to exercise. He has concluded that there is no evidence that a graduated progressive training program is injurious to the health of children.

Incidents are frequently reported in which young children perform outstanding feats of athletic strength or endurance. Children between the ages of five and ten years of age frequently run 10,000-meter races, and one boy of five ran a full marathon in 1978. Enough similar cases are observed to indicate that many children can perform activities of greater endurance than are usually recommended for regular school programs. Some physical educators who are convinced that children *can* engage in greater endurance events question the advisability of such activities. Cureton suggests, however, that programs limited in vigorous endurance activities (as are most school programs today) do not effect important changes in motor development. Rather, he recommends more endurance activities such as running, swimming, rowing, and cycling.

Nevertheless, medical authorities encourage caution in the selection of vigorous activities for health reasons. In view of the possibility that greater development may result from endurance programs, more research is needed on this topic. Continued acceptance of traditional beliefs (even of medicine) without evidence is unwise. Not to be ignored, of course, are the possible psychological implications of programs of strenuous activities. Longitudinal studies are necessary to determine the physiological and psychological implications.

Recent developments in "age group" competition has led to higher levels of competition for young people than were ever imagined just a few years ago. Young boys and girls are performing at a more advanced level and at an earlier age than ever before. This is particularly true in gymnastics and swimming. According to Fourther (1977), the average age of those attaining national and international championships has dropped approximately eight years since 1900. Still, they need the same years of training, i.e., the champion gymnast or swimmer of fifteen has been training since six or seven. It has been demonstrated, therefore, that young people can start training earlier and still learn efficiently. The advisability of this, however, is as much a philosophical as a developmental question.

DEVELOPMENTAL ACTIVITIES

In order to fully prepare children for the types of activities they will encounter in the school program, certain developmental experiences are necessary. A systematic program of such experiences will tend to raise the minimum level of readiness for all pupils. Such a program will also insure that physical competencies are attained as soon as the child is mature enough to gain them.

The idea of overall development (cognitive, affective, and motor) through movement and exploration is not new. Through the centuries, such educators as Rousseau, Socrates, Locke, Pestillozzi, Dewey, and more recently Piaget, have subscribed to this concept. Other recent advocates include Montessori, Getman, Radler, and Frostig, among others.

Ridenour (1978) describes two categories of programs designed to enhance the development of motor skills among infants. One of these, referred to as the *No Programming Plan* is advocated by Pikler (1968), a prominent pediatrician at the National Methodological Institute for Infant Care and Education in Budapest, Hungary. This plan is characterized by the lack of practice or stimulation for activity by any facilitator. The child is not held in position for any motor performance or assisted in any movement response. Neither is any special equipment used to stimulate activity or assist in the maintenance of postures not yet individually possible for the child. Toys and play equipment are made available, but the child must initiate use of them. Pikler does stress, however, that clothing, bedding, and other accessories shoud allow maximum freedom for the infant.

The second category, called the *Programming Plan* by Ridenour, is designed to stimulate activity in motor skills, using appropriate equipment to assist in the performance of those activities. Prominent among the advocates of this approach is Brnnie Prudden, whose publications (1964), lectures, and television programs are directed toward parents, nursery school leaders, and others responsible for children during the first several years of life. Prudden's approach emphasizes the stimulation of motor activity with minimal restriction to the child in the form of clothing, harness, or pens. However, she does encourage use of the infant walker and the baby bouncer because of their developmental value. In a similar approach, Levy (1973) describes an exercise program for children from birth to fifteen months of age that emphasizes four levels of activity according to age level within that period. He presents 55 exercises, some involving the manipulation of the limbs or trunk and others involving a great variety of colorful equipment and toys. Krottee (1971) also supports this "programming" approach with his development of an extensive curriculum of activities for children through the first year of life.

Though specific research evidence is not overwhelming, most American authorities in the area of child development favor some sort of programming plan as opposed to the no programming plan advocated by Pikler. At the same time it is conceivable that overprogramming or too rigid structuring could reduce the child's initiative and creativity.

As stated earlier, readiness for motor activities is dependent upon maturation, general physical development, and specific prerequisite learning. Little, if anything, can be done to speed maturation. With adequate nutrition and freedom from unusual restrictions of activity, maturation is relatively unaffected by parents and teachers. Special developmental activities are therefore not of importance for maturation. Prerequisite learning is related to proficiency in a particular activity. This concept has been discussed earlier in this chapter. In respect to the other essentials for readiness, several authors have recently suggested that *general* readiness for motor activities can be affected by the parent and the teacher.

Developmental or readiness training of very young children is primarily the responsibility of parents. Children who seriously lack basic readiness skills when they come to school may be regarded as retarded. However, the school will be able to speed the development of these skills if attention is devoted to them in the kindergarten or first grade. It would be even more helpful to establish a program of such developmental activities in prekindergarten programs such as Headstart and Get Set. When a child is retarded in the development of basic skills, this condition can be somewhat overcome by establishing a program of basic skills that is geared to the actual readiness level. Several motor development programs have been established especially for handicapped or retarded children. Among the most popular are those developed by Radler and Kephart (1960), Frostig (1964), Getman and Kane (1964), and Barsch (1968). An analysis of these programs, however, seems to indicate that many normal children would benefit from these activities during the early years. Montessori school programs (see Orum, 1965) place heavy emphasis on many of the same developmental activities.

Early developmental training should be aimed at establishing basic levels of proficiency in a wide variety of activities rather than excellence in a few. Exposure to a great many experiences is therefore essential. In regard to this, Radler and Kephart state:

> From a developmental point of view, the optimum condition is *not* high degrees of skill. *It is minimum ability in a wide number of motor activities.* . . . In any motor performance there is a minimum degree of ability which permits the child to perform the activity. This is the degree of ability which is important for his future development. . . . The law of diminishing returns sets in after the child has learned to perform the task adequately. *From the point of view of development, the acquisition of spectacular degrees of skill is not worth the effort required* (pp. 119-120).[2]

Developmental activities need not be uniform for all pupils. Individual differences demand that some flexibility and variety be built into the program. In any group, some children need to start at a more elementary level than do others. Equipment or apparatus of different size, shape, or complexity might be used. For example, some children can play with and control a relatively small playground ball, while others need a large one. Some children can bypass certain steps in the learning of stunts. Some can work with faster moving pieces of equipment, navigate greater distances or heights, or combine several stunts into one operation. Opportunities should be provided for children to develop basic motor abilities at their own rates.

Radler and Kephart indicate that motor skills are valuable in developing all-around school preparedness, not just readiness for physical education activities. They indicate that the kindergarten curriculum demands a level of readiness in the following areas of behavior: motor, symbolic, social, and numerical. Competencies in three of these areas may be enhanced by physical skills. These competencies assume a mastery of major and minor muscle movements, eye movements, eye-hand coordination, and a sense of laterality. In regard to motor behavior, the authors believe that the kindergarten child should be able to hop on one foot, skip, broad jump, high jump, and throw a ball accurately. In addition, the child should be able to build with blocks and to draw such simple forms as squares, circles, and crosses. Symbolic readiness may be exhibited by such physical tasks as drawing an object or a scene, or by reproducing forms or images with one's body. Social skills

---

[2] D. Radler and N. C. Kephart, *Success Through Play*, New York: Harper & Row, 1960. By permission.

of a physical nature are developed when the child learns to dress, tie shoelaces, or perform many of the social graces that require movement. Havighurst (1966) outlines the developmental tasks needed by young children as motor coordinations, learning to play in a group, oral language, moral consciousness, and concepts of the physical world. He points out the need for more complex skills as the child grows older.

During the early school years, many school functions are dependent upon motor development. For example, penmanship is a complex sensorimotor skill that may be aided by specific motor development. The five-year-old is able to begin associating visual and kinesthetic sensations so as to coordinate the muscular movements necessary for writing. During the early learning stages, handwriting should be large and free. Penmanship will improve as perception, memory for details, hand and finger dexterity, and strength are developed. These capacities can be developed through special physical exercise. Even the capacities of perception and memory of letter forms in penmanship, which are more removed from physical skills, can be developed by special activities.

SUMMARY

1. Readiness to learn refers to a condition of the individual that makes a particular task an appropriate one for mastering motor learning and performance. It is dependent upon a combination of physical and mental maturation, motor development, prerequisite learning, and the individual's motivation for the task.

2. Maturation refers to phylogenetic development, which increases the individual's ability to learn skills. This development, which occurs most dramatically during the early years of life, may include changes in size, shape, and even basic skills. Maturation is only slightly affected by environmental conditions.

3. General motor development refers to the improvement of one's motor abilities as a result of practice or experience. With proper exercise programs, components such as strength, speed, coordination, balance, and agility may be enhanced. In addition, certain basic movement skills, such as running, climbing, and jumping, are viewed as part of one's general motor development.

4. Prerequisite learning refers to the development of those skills that are, in turn, used in the learning or development of more advanced patterns of movement. Any sophisticated or advanced movement behavior is dependent upon the prior development of several prerequisite skills.

5. Several authors have described the maturational stages of children during the early years of life. Very early stages are marked by a predominance of reflexive and other sensory motor behaviors, whereas later stages place greater emphasis on cognitive processes. Other developmental characteristics during the very early years include trends in the cephalocaudal (head to foot), proximodistal (central to peripheral), and mass-to-specific directions.

6. Over the years many studies have been conducted to determine the effect of special exercises or environments upon early child development. Many such studies have involved identical twins. Most authors report that specal programs have a minimal long-term effect on maturational processes but may significantly affect long-term intellectual and motor capacities as well as social orientation.

7. Studies that have imposed severely restricted environments, mostly using animals as subjects, have shown that drastic restrictions do cripple the intellectual, motor, and social development of the subject. However, humans who have been subjected to a moderately or severely restricted environment do tend to show a "catch-up" growth phenomenon once that restriction has been removed.

8. General motor development during childhood and adolescence evolves through several stages. These include basic abilities such as crawling, creeping, and walking, followed by general fundamental skills such as running, jumping, skipping, throwing, and catching. During late childhood, more specific skills are developed along with continued development and refinement of fundamental skills. During adolescence, more specialized skills are developed, including the use of refined skills in sports or game situations.

9. During the early childhood years, there is little difference between boys and girls in body size, though boys are slightly taller and heavier. However, since girls reach their maximum growth spurt approximately two years earlier than boys, they are actually taller and heavier for a short period during the twelfth and thirteenth years. At around age fourteen, boys begin their maximum growth spurt and surpass girls in height and weight. In America and in Western Europe, children are maturing earlier and becoming larger as adults. This is apparently the result of better nutrition, less serious illness, and other environmental conditions.

10. Despite some overlap between males and females, most studies reveal that males excel in measures of strength, speed, power, and gross motor activities. Females excel in balance, flexibility, and some coordination tasks. While there are some indications of physiological and anthropometrical bases for these differences, most authors agree that a major factor in such measured differences are socially and culturally based.

11. Young people are reaching national and international championship level competition at much earlier ages than they did several decades ago. It is not unusual for world class competitors in swimming or gymnastics to be in their early teens. In order for this to be accomplished, however, a long training session is still essential. Consequently, such individuals must begin training seriously in their sport by the age of seven or eight. It is now acknowledged that children of a very early age can take part in long endurance activities. This is contrary to the widespread belief of two decades ago that a young child's heart could be damaged by some vigorous and long endurance activities. However, the advisability of young children engaging in such endurance activities or restricting their programs to one sport at such an early age is a philosophical question of considerable importance.

12. In the placement of learning activities at an appropriate age and grade level, teachers must determine both the mental abilities and motor capacities of children at various grades and also the status of prerequisite skills required for more advanced learning. Without such planned sequencing, programs are introduced that are either too difficult for the learners or that involve undue repetition.

13. Developmental programs for children, though long a part of the educational process, have received increasing attention during recent years. Some authorities advocate that no particular stimulation or activities be provided for young persons. The basic assumption is that when opportunities are available to the child without restriction, special stimulation or additional efforts are not needed. Another strategy is to provide a program to stimulate appropriate activity in motor skills. The assumption here is that children develop more rapidly and avoid possible weaknesses when special well-rounded programs are insured. Several developmental programs with a particular orientation toward handicapped students are presented.

14. Several techniques have been used in an effort to determine developmental readiness for various activities. These include age, size, grade level, skeletal age, classification systems based on motor skills, secondary sex characteristics, or some combination of such techniques. These have proven somewhat helpful in grouping children for activities on a reasonably equitable basis.

SELECTED READINGS

AMERICAN ASSOCIATION FOR HEALTH, PHYSICAL EDUCATION, RECREATION AND DANCE. *Motor development* (K. Haywood, consultant). Reston, Va., 1981.

CORBIN, C. B. *A textbook of motor development.* Dubuque, Ia.: Wm. C Brown, 1973.

FROSTIG, M., & HORNE, D. *The Frostig program for the development of visual perception.* Chicago: Follett, 1964.

GETMAN, G. N., & KANE, E. R. *The physiology of readiness.* Minneapolis: PASS, Inc., 1964.

MCGRAW, M. B. *Neuromuscular maturation of the human infant.* New York: Columbia, 1943.

MUSSEN, P., CONGER, J., & KAGAN, J. *Child development and personality* (4th ed.). New York: Harper & Row, 1974.

PIAGET, J., *The origins of intelligence in children.* New York: International Universities Press, Inc., 1952.

RADLER, D., & KEPHART, N. C. *Success through play.* New York: Harper & Row, 1960.

RIDENOUR, M. V. *Motor development: Issues and applications.* Princeton, N.J.: Princeton Book Co., 1978.

WICKSTROM, R. *Fundamental motor patterns.* Philadelphia: Lea and Febiger, 1977.

8 Motivation and Arousal

INTRODUCTION

Physical and mental maturity are only two of the factors contributing to one's readiness for learning and performing motor skills. Overall motivation is no less important. In fact, probably no type of human activity is as vividly affected by emotional arousal and general motivation as is performance in motor skills. An investigation of the various levels of arousal and their effects upon the learning and performance of different types of skills is explored in this chapter. Also addressed are some popular techniques for promoting the desired motivational state for different types of motor activities.

DIMENSIONS OF AROUSAL

One of the most universally accepted concepts regarding learning is that the individual must be interested in a particular task before effective learning can occur. It is therefore best if the child in school is somewhat aroused or excited about a specific task or learning situation. This principle of motivation has been widely agreed upon through the years from the early learning theorists to today's classroom teachers. A "motivated" condition is essential not only for *learning*, but also for effective *performance* in motor skills. For this reason, educators in general, and physical educators and coaches in particular, devote considerable effort toward motivating students.

While generating widespread interest over the past few years, the topic of psychological readiness for motor performance has proven to be a most complex issue. Several different terms, though not identical in meaning, are used by various authors in reference to this general topic. Among the more common of these are motivation, arousal, anxiety, and alertness.

Motivation, as used in this discussion, refers to the process whereby needs are created within the individual, forcing him to seek particular goals to satisfy those needs. Motivation refers to one's *internal* state, which may be initiated from within the person, as in the case of a biological need, or from the outside, as in the case of a social need. If the need is a basic or urgent one, a state of intense emotional arousal may develop. Generally the motivated person is more active than one who is not motivated. This activity is directed toward particular goals that, when attained, satisfy the individual and lead to diminished activity. In the school setting, the goals most often sought are social or psychological values such as achievement, recognition, or belonging. It is by making effective use of these motives that the teacher is able to stimulate students to outstanding accomplishments.

Arousal refers to one's level of alertness. The individual's state of alertness at any time may be placed on a continuum from very high to very low activation, ranging over the scale from "blind rage," highly excited, alert, relaxed, drowsy, sleep, coma, to (ultimately) death. Different levels of arousal parallel different physiological activity, which is controlled by the autonomic nervous system. The aroused state may be viewed as positive, i.e., elation, joy, love, and the "thrill of victory." On the other hand, the arousal state may be a negative one, such as in anger, fear, embarrassment, rage, jealousy, and the like. Arousal is accompanied by certain physiological responses regardless of the stimulus that evokes the condition or the name given to the psychological state.

During the past several years the term *anxiety* has come into widespread use as a description of one's psychological condition that impacts on the readiness of that person for some particular activity. Anxiety has traditionally been referred to as one's tendency toward a generalized feeling of stress or apprehension. Spielberger (1970) has divided this concept into two areas, i.e., *state anxiety* and *trait anxiety*. State anxiety refers to a temporary condition describing one's response at a given time to a particular situation. Trait anxiety, on the other hand, refers to the general orientation of the individual toward stress. As such, trait anxiety may be viewed as a stable personality characteristic, e.g., the "nervous" individual, whereas state anxiety is a short-lived arousal condition, e.g., the "psyched" athlete. Clearly, the particular anxiety level will make a major difference in the performance of motor skills, as it will with other human activities.

An aroused or highly motivated state most obviously affects the individual in three ways. First, such a condition results in *physiological changes* that take place within the person. These changes usually involve an increase in heart rate and blood pressure, a flushed face, and other processes that are more difficult to observe, except by scientific measurement. Second, within the individual there are *conscious sensations* that accompany excitement. These sensations are attributable to physiological changes and are not usually noticed by other persons. Third, an aroused emotional state is usually reflected in *more activated behavior* on the part of the individual, who will often exhibit gross and strong movements and may become awkward and clumsy. This activated behavior can be easily observed and measured. Physical educators have been particularly interested in physiological changes and in resulting motor behavior.

People in everyday life and in the sports world are often impressed with the physical performance of persons who are highly motivated or emotionally aroused. The following case was described in a newspaper a few years ago. A man, after having jacked up his station wagon to change a tire in his driveway, was called into his house. Moments later, one of his children, who had been observing the proceedings, ran into the house to tell his father and mother that the car had fallen off the jack and on another child. Both parents ran outside, and the quick-thinking father immediately began resetting the jack in order to lift the car off the child. The mother, seeking more immediate results, took hold of the car and manually lifted it so that the child could crawl out from under! So great was the strain that, in the process, a bone was broken in her back. Certainly this feat was outside the expected performance possibilities for the woman, who was described as average in size. Other incidents of unusual physical acts under emotional stimulation are within the experience of most individuals.

Physical responses resulting from stimulation are strange and varied. Motivation or stress may result in *positive* effects, such as increases in (1) speed of movement: the running speed of a frightened child or sprinter under pressure of intense competition; (2) strength: the angry man is stronger than the contented one; the woman who was able to lift a car because she was emotionally aroused; and (3) endurance: the athlete will endure or persevere longer without showing fatigue if the competition is especially exciting. Likewise, a reasonably high level of motivation in the classroom may aid one in focusing attention on the task at hand. It will lift one out of a sense of lethargy, ensuring alertness.

At other times, *detrimental* effects may result from a high state of emotional excitement. Quite often there is a reduction of bodily coordination. For example, a very excited young pitcher might lose control in a close game, a basketball player will miss a higher percentage of easy shots, or a child who has recently learned to tie shoelaces might be all thumbs when pressured by the teacher to hurry. Mental performances also are sometimes adversely affected by emotional excitement. Consider the case of the child (or adult) who forgets a well-learned speech when standing up before a group. Some adults indicate that their minds occasionally go blank under pressure. In the classroom such stress may be focused on the child's fear of the teacher, fear of receiving poor grades, or some other type of punishment. Such reactions tend to have a negative effect not only on that learning situation but on one's attitude about the total school experience.

FOUNDATIONS OF MOTIVATION

The basis for motivation has traditionally been explained with reference to the concept of *homeostasis*. Homeostasis refers to the tendency of the body to take compensatory action for the purpose of maintaining a physiological balance at all times. Physiological adaptations are regularly required. For example, the human body contains mechanisms for maintaining its temperature at approximately 98.6° F. People occasionally work for short periods of time in temperatures ranging from below 0°F to above 170°F. Even under such extreme conditions, a variation in body temperature by as much as six degrees would not be expected. The ability of the body to maintain an even temperature balance is one of the clearest examples of homeostasis.

Homeostasis is also revealed in the tendency of the body to maintain a reasonably constant supply of blood sugar, despite wide variations in intake of sugar. Similarly, the acidity-alkalinity balance in the blood is held reasonably constant regardless of variations in intake. To maintain healthy conditions for life, similar internal adjustments must be made regarding the water content of the blood and lymph, the oxygen content of the blood, and the numerous minerals in the body. In the event of a failure in homeostasis, the individual is forced to seek a body balance by other means. The seeking of substances to meet bodily needs, therefore, becomes the basis for motivated activity.

Richter (1942) conducted extensive research with animals to illustrate how a disturbed homeostatic state results in overt behavior on the part of the organism. In his studies, various ductless glands were removed from rats in order to upset the normal homeostatic ability of the body. The rats responded by taking compensatory action such as selecting unusual but appropriate food to obtain certain minerals, or building larger and warmer nests to make up for unusual heat loss. He concluded that "... in human beings and animals the effort to maintain a constant internal environment or homeostasis constitutes one of the most universal and powerful of all behavior or drives" (p. 64).

There can be little doubt that there is merit to the homeostatic theory of basic drives. However, this concept, when restricted to biological conditions, is not broad enough to include the total range of human motivation. People are not merely biological beings. Personal and social conditions play a major role in influencing behavior. In fact, even lower animals give evidence of reacting to social influences. It has become very clear that psychological or sociological needs may act as stimulus for action, just as do physiological deficiencies.

Types of motivation

Motivation may be categorized according to the stimulus or the condition that serves as the source for the aroused interest. One such source could be an incentive related to participation in the activity. Additionally, the task itself may serve as the stimulus, and on still other occasions the need for achievement may transcend both the incentive and the task. In a broad sense, the use of incentives can be viewed as external motivation, while task and achievement motivation would be categorized as internal.

Incentive motivation occurs when reward or reinforcement is used to change the direction of motivated behavior. When children receive reinforcement for appropriate behavior in relation to the teacher or classmates, they are then motivated to behave similarly on subsequent occasions. The anticipation of such teacher or peer approval provides the incentive. At other times, a specific incentive in the form of grades, recognition, or prizes may be used as incentive.

Task motivation refers to the interest or pleasure created by participation in the activity itself. Sometimes such motivation occurs with the mere anticipation of an event or activity, while at other times it results from such participation itself. This type of intrinsic motivation is most helpful in the school setting in that it capitalizes on curiosity and exploration. In view of the reciprocal relationship between learning and motivation, Ausubel (1968) insists,

> It is unnecessary to postpone learning activities until appropriate interests and motivations have been developed. Frequently, the best way of teaching an unmotivated student is to ignore his motivational state for the time being, and to concentrate on teaching him as effectively as possible. Some degree of learning will ensue in any case, despite the lack of motivation; and from the initial satisfaction he will, hopefully develop the motivation to learn more (pp. 365-366).

Although practical experience does not support Ausubel's views in all cases, there appear to be times when there is little choice but to follow the procedure suggested. All experienced teachers will agree that despite their most ingenious motivation techniques there are times when some students seem totally disinterested in the task at hand. To delay the teaching process until all students are clearly motivated would be a greater disruption than would moving forward without a 100 percent level of interest. Besides, it can be demonstrated that learning can take place without motivation or interest in the topic. For example, those persons within earshot of a radio or watching television are frequently bombarded by commercials with monotonous regularity. Despite a total lack of interest in the product, the individual often finds that he has learned something about the product, perhaps even memorizing the jingle. Ingenious commercial writers find ways to "capture" the attention of a disinterested audience.

Achievement motivation refers to the tendency to strive to achieve or excel in whatever challenge is presented. For example, some persons develop a need to "master" any task that is presented. This concept, also referred to as achievement need, was first developed by Murray (1938). He suggested that most children, if sufficiently bored, will be aroused by almost any new activity or challenge. The lack of challenge in other activities becomes a factor in the new activity, i.e., practically any new task will result in some increased motivation.

Many authors suggest that once achievement motivation is developed as a habit, it can provide motivation for a wide range of activities, including school learning. For example, Kifer (1975) suggests that continued school success over several years leads to a positive self-concept and an attitude for achievement, which then becomes a basic characteristic of the individual's personality. Careful observation of students at all levels of education reveals that those who exhibit motivation to achieve high standards usually establish records higher than their abilities would imply.

Murray reported that achievement motivation emanates either from (1) the hope for success, or (2) the fear of failure. The hope for success is somewhat related to the concept of "level of aspiration," which is discussed later in this chapter. The fear of failure can clearly be shown to be a motivating, though perhaps distracting, factor in many areas of human endeavor. Observation of children at play, young people in school or sports activities, or adults at work gives evidence of motivation to avoid failure. The fear is of the *consequence* of failure, which may be internally or externally imposed.

An example of the fear of failure leading to achievement motivation was illustrated in a report found on the sports pages a few years back. The incident involved the quarterback of the football team at a university in the southeastern part of the United States, an institution famous for its football teams, and perhaps even more famous for its coach. During the course of an important game, the quarterback committed the unpardonable sin of throwing a soft pass into the flat, where it was easily intercepted by an opposing defensive back who immediately began running for a touchdown. The quarterback, realizing his error, and, further, remembering the wrath of his coach following such mistakes, began chasing the ball carrier with an extraordinary burst of speed caught him before he reached the end zone. When asked by sports writers after the game how he was able to overtake a player who had a reputation for being a much faster runner, the quarterback replied, "You see, he was running for a touchdown, but I was running for my *life*." Fear of failure from an internal source may be just as strong, but it is rarely so clearly articulated.

The AAHPERD publication *Psycho-Social Aspects of Physical Education* (1981) reports, "The need to achieve is a relatively stable disposition to strive for success. An individual with a high need to achieve has a positive approach tendency toward achievement-oriented situations and a positive success tendency" (p. 20). The same publication also identifies (1) the fear of failure, (2) the need to fail, and (3) the fear of success as tendencies that influence certain individuals in their performance.

Needs and drives

Needs and drives form the basis of human motivation. Both are often related to the concept of homeostasis. A need generally refers to a deprived state or a lack of an essential element. This deprivation may exist in physical, psychological, or social necessities. A physical need would be illustrated by a body depleted of its food supply. The physiological need for food eventually results in an awareness of this need and a desire to overcome the deprivation. The desire to obtain food is referred to as a drive. The physiological need, therefore, results in a psychological drive.

Needs are sometimes categorized as primary and secondary. This classification, however, can be misleading since the so-called secondary drives are, on occasion, stronger than the primary drives.

Cole and Bruce (1959) classify human needs into *physiological* and *psychological* groups. Earlier, Murray (1938) used the terms *viscerogenic* and *psychogenic* to mean much the same thing. Such categories, though more descriptive than "primary" and "secondary," can still lead to confusion because of the difficulty in always clearly distinguishing between the physical and the psychological or sociological influences.

Physiological needs and drives

Cole and Bruce suggest the following as the most important of the physiological needs that may result in drives:

Food and Drink.   The body survives on chemical ingredients supplied by food and water. Obviously, food and drink are important, and their unavailability results in powerful drives.

Rest.   The fatigued tissues of the body are repaired during rest periods. When man is sufficiently tired, he will rest in spite of external efforts to stimulate him to action.

Sexual gratification.   When a state of excitement exists, sexual gratification becomes one of the strongest human drives. Unlike the other needs listed here, sexual gratification is not life-threatening when not satisfied. Still, the need is clear, and is physiologically (hormonally) as well as psychologically based.

Self-protection.   All human beings have a need for protection from physical harm or destruction. Safety and a feeling of security are among the strongest needs.

Elimination.   Regular elimination of waste products from the body is a strong physiological need for all persons.

Most recent authors substantially agree with the Cole and Bruce list of physiological needs. In addition, the drive for *activity* has been discussed by Leuba (1961), Bertner (1962), and more recent authors. Observation of caged rats on an exercise wheel shows that they engage in a great deal of movement activity with no reward except for the activity itself. Humans, especially children and young people, also exhibit a high level of activity. The strength of this drive becomes particularly evident when animals or persons are restricted or deprived of movement activity.

The need for *oxygen* is certainly among the most basic and universal for all life. A lack of oxygen leads to immediate and desperate overt activity on the part of humans and animals. Perhaps no need is more obvious, and no other deprivation leads to a more violent response. Certain other physiological needs, such as *drug* dependency, may be acquired for a period of time.

Psychological needs and drives

Maslow (1943) presents the following as the most important needs in the psychological and sociological areas:

Belongingness and love.   All normal human beings need affection, warmth, acceptance, and a place in a group. After the physiological needs have been satisfied, love needs emerge as perhaps the strongest drive.

Self-esteem.   Individuals have a strong need for self-respect, self-confidence, and a feeling of adequacy. This need is satisfied to a great extent when one receives the recognition, attention, and appreciation of others.

Self-actualization.   Individuals in our society need opportunities to realize their full potential. When this has been achieved, the individual experiences a fulfillment that is conducive to a healthy adjustment.

Bortner (1962) presented a rather similar list of social drives that he considered the most common and most demanding. They included the following:

1.   The drive for security
2.   The drive for mastery
3.   The drive for recognition
4.   The drive for belonging

Bortner pointed out that it is essential that these drives be satisfied in order for the child to develop a healthy, integrated personality. These needs and drives provide the teacher with a sound basis for motivating students.

Thomas (1923), Symonds (1934), Carroll (1940), and Leuba (1961) discuss psychological needs and drives that are similar to those mentioned by Maslow and Bortner. Primary differences are in terminology and length of the lists. The longer lists contain greater specificity and refinement of the general concepts mentioned by Maslow and Bortner.

How needs become drives

A drive is a tendency to behave in a manner to fulfill a need. Needs give rise to drives, and drives give rise to behavior. Physiological needs result in psychological drives. For illustrative purposes, Cole and Bruce (1959) describe the following sequential stages in the hunger cycle to show how drives, or motivated activity, may result:

Physical deficit. The stomach is empty and the blood's supply of food is depleted.

Body tensions. The physical deficit of food may be accompanied by contractions of the stomach, tensions in the muscles, and general irritability.

Psychological awareness of these changes. With the conscious awareness of hunger, there is a craving for food.

Seeking food and eating. Motivated action eventually results in the individual's securing food.

Full stomach. The need is eliminated, and there is a relaxation of physical tensions.

With the conscious awareness of hunger, the need for food becomes a motive for action. Obviously, this motive can be very strong, driving human beings to determined actions. Other physiological needs can be broken down and analyzed as the source of emotional arousal in much the same way. The psychological and sociological needs, though more complex to break down, might also be logically analyzed in this manner.

The relative strength of different drives

As suggested by Maslow, not all needs and drives are equally strong. Some seem to underlie or act as prerequisites for others. For example, certain needs do not manifest themselves until hunger and thirst have been satisfied. Persons who have been deprived of food and water for long periods report that intellectual, sexual, or social matters fade in importance during these periods. This effect of starvation is illustrated in a study reported by Cole and Bruce (1959) of a World War II experiment in which conscientious objectors volunteered for fasting studies designed to gain information helpful in the rehabilitation of starving people. Despite the initial enthusiasm of the volunteers, as time passed, their thoughts centered more and more on food. As their preoccupation with food reached an obsessive height, some subjects secretly secured food for consumption and others experienced severe psychological repercussions from their conflicting drives. Travers (1963) pointed out that Buddha is pictured with a fat belly because of the belief that the mind can be fully devoted to serious matters only when physical needs have been met.

A number of personal and environmental factors affect the strength of the various drives. This adds to the difficulty of organizing needs by strength or importance. However, Maslow (1943) listed the following broad categories of needs in rank order, from strongest to weakest:

1. Physiological needs
2. Safety needs
3. Love and belonging needs
4. Esteem needs, including achievement and recognition
5. Self-actualization needs
6. Desires to know and understand

Although Maslow's ranking may meet with general approval, certain of the personal and social needs at the end of the list occasionally become stronger than the physiological and safety needs. Extreme examples of the domination of personal and social needs are seen in the individual who becomes a martyr, goes on a hunger strike, or commits suicide, and by a parent's sacrifices for a son or daughter. Therefore, classification of needs into primary and secondary groups, or into lists of strengths and weaknesses, must be viewed with some reservation.

Management of needs and drives

Positive reinforcers in school usually involve the provision of incentives to energize behavior on the part of the child. An alternative to this is the *frustrative nonreward*. Scull (1973) has shown that animals, when denied an anticipated reward on one trial, will exhibit increased energy on the subsequent trial. Ryan and Watson (1968) report similar results with young children, though when they are frustrated too frequently, this technique loses its effect as a motivator. Such positive results from nonreward occur when the response is not perceived by the subject as a failure. A response viewed as a genuine failure by the subject (one's inadequacy causing the nonreward) results in a reduction of motivation and a lowering of energy output. Though the technique of frustrative nonreward has not been fully researched, Travers (1977) speculates that occasional withholding of praise or other reward might be more important than consistent praise for everything the child does. Perhaps the use of one of the schedules of partial reinforcement (as discussed in chapter four) would prove helpful in this motivation technique.

Teachers should organize and conduct their programs so that each child has an opportunity to meet needs. Whether the need is basic or derived, teachers will be more effective if they work in accordance with, rather than contrary to, needs. In today's typical school setting, the children's physiological needs have been cared for quite well. On occasion, slight difficulties may arise regarding uncomfortable classroom temperature, furniture, lighting, or the like. In physical education, however, the total range of physiological, psychological, and sociological needs can be encountered in a manner that is unique in the school situation.

Quite a wide range of physiological needs and drives becomes evident in physical education classes and in varsity athletes. The individual is often encouraged to withstand some degree of pain, fatigue, and fear of impending danger. A strong tendency to surrender to these needs may be countered by other needs, such as achievement, recognition, and belonging. For example, the undersized high school football player may experience mixed feelings when faced with the necessity of hurling his body into the path of a hard-charging fullback. The need for self-preservation encourages him to avoid contact while the need for accomplishment demands that he stop his opponent at all costs. The personal need to excel in front of one's peers may on other occasions cause the young person to practice long and hard for perfection or to continue an all-out effort in a wrestling match long after fatique has appeared. The physical educator and the coach are, therefore, in a unique position to manipulate personal and social needs for developmental purposes.

Along with the process of maturing, and with education, comes the ability to control drives or to delay gratification. For the infant, this capacity does not exist at all. However, the individual is gradually able to be reasonably satisfied with a promise of "Not now, but later." The capacity to delay gratification satisfactorily may never be fully attained; thus adults vary in their ability to discipline their desires for satisfaction. Psychopaths are especially weak in the ability to delay the satisfaction of a drive. One major concern of educators is to develop appropriate drive control and restraint in children.

According to Travers (1977), all advanced cultures use a system of delayed rewards. In fact, he observes that our entire promotion system is based on delayed rewards in order to be equally effective. Further, he reports that those individuals responding well to delayed rewards are more mature, intelligent, and socially responsible, and have high ego control. They also respond better to social reinforcement than to material reward. In contrast, those persons responding best to immediate rewards tend to be more impulsive, have lower social competence, and more frequently come from disadvantaged classes. They also tend to seek predominantly material rewards. The development of responsible, mature behavior is a duty of the school at all levels. Progress in this task can best be made when the teacher is familiar with the psychological and physiological needs of the children.

EMOTIONAL AROUSAL

Physiological responses

During periods of excitement, certain physiological changes occur that are measurable with modern scientific equipment. The particular responses depend upon the nature and the extent of the emotional arousal. As stated earlier, these emotional states may range from a high of "blind rage" to a low of deep coma, with the more activated states producing an accelerated response and the quiescent states resulting in subdued responses.

W. B. Cannon (1929), probably the most influential pioneer in the study of emotional reactions, described physiological responses with his book *Bodily Changes in Pain, Hunger, Fear and Rage.* Other authors use a variety of different terms to describe conditions of arousal or excitement. These include anger, hate, sorrow, embarrassment, joy, or simply the state of being "psyched up." The longer such a list becomes, the more the words begin to overlap in meaning. However, even when the conditions or states are easily understood and clearly distinguishable, the physiological responses are not so. All arousal states have a great deal of overlap in symptoms, though there may be special characteristics of each depending upon the stimulus that created the response.

Cannon worked extensively with both humans and animals to identify physiological responses with various types of situations. He pointed out that strong emotions prepare the organism for vigorous activity during emergencies. To illustrate the types of physiological changes that take place during periods of stress, he cited the following situation:

If a cat is quietly eating and digesting its meal and is suddenly confronted by a barking dog, the following changes take place within the cat:

1. Digestive movements of the stomach stop.
2. Blood pressure rises.
3. Heart rate speeds up.
4. Adrenalin is secreted into the blood system.
5. The cat arches its back and is ready to fight.

Cannon pointed out that when adrenalin is secreted into the blood system, it (a) increases the blood pressure, (b) builds up the supply of sugar in the blood, (c) causes the blood to clot more easily, and (d) makes the cat less sensitive to pain. Most of the responses observed in the cat can also be measured in humans. For example, it is a rather common occurrence for athletes to discover after a game that they have a fairly severe bruise or cut, an injury that they do not remember having received. During a relaxed state, a similar injury would be noticeably painful.

Physiological changes in response to emotional excitement are controlled by the *autonomic nervous system*, which regulates the secretions of the endocrine glands and controls the smooth muscles of the body. The autonomic nervous system is made up of the sympathetic and parasympathetic systems, each of which influences the same bodily organs but generally with opposite effects. The sympathetic system acts as an emergency system, being most active during excited states, and serves to mobilize the body for violent action. The parasympathetic system functions primarily during normal or quiescent states and takes care of regular metabolic functions. For example, the sympathetic system stimulates the adrenal gland and thus increases the heart rate. The parasympathetic system is instrumental in slowing down both of these processes.

The physiological responses that are initiated by the autonomic nervous system during excitement are many and varied. The full range of reactions is not yet known. However, some of the bodily responses that have been described by various authors are as follows:

Galvanic skin response. During periods of excitement, there is a detectable increase in electrical impulses on the skin. This response, which is intimately related to sweat secretion, is one of the most widely used indices of one's level of activation. The galvanic skin response (GSR), also referred to as skin conductance and skin resistance, may be measured in microamperes by use of an ammeter or galvanometer. One important advantage in using the galvanic skin response as a measure of excitement is the immediacy of the measure. Whereas certain other types of physiological analysis (gas, blood, urine) usually require a relatively long time, skin responses to sudden stimulation can be detected in a few seconds. These measures may be taken by attaching electrodes to the palms or, in some cases, by placing the fingers on the poles of an ammeter. Harmon and Johnson (1952) and Fort (1959) have used the GSR in studies of athletic performances.

Heart rate. During periods of excitement, the heart rate speeds up and becomes more intense. The rapid, pounding heart is one of the most obvious signs of excitement. Even routine mental activity stimulates the heart to a faster rate than exists during sleep or other quiet periods. Testers who have sought to use the pulse rate as an indication of physical fitness have found that one's emotional state at any given time is often more important in determining heart rate than is physical condition.

Blood pressure and volume. Blood pressure is almost always higher during periods of excitement. Startling occurrences cause dramatic increases in blood pressure and circulation. In certain emotional states (extreme depression or shock), blood pressure may be lowered. Also, there is sometimes a displacement or movement of the blood supply, for example, into the tissue near the skin of the face when blushing or of the neck when angry, and away from the surface of the face when one is frightened.

Blood composition. During periods of emotional excitement, the endocrine glands secrete certain hormones into the blood to aid the body in its responses. Perhaps the most important of these hormones is adrenalin, which aids the body in performing many physical feats. Variations in hormone secretions can best be measured by a blood test or urinalysis. In addition to hormones, extra red blood cells may also be released into the blood to aid the body in obtaining more oxygen. The extent of this hormonal secretion may be determined by a blood test.

Muscle tension and tremor. This is one of the most obvious and common reactions to a stressful situation. The individual is unable to relax because of conflicting internal desires. This tension leads to an inability to control fine muscular movements as efficiently as when one is relaxed. Considerable evidence (Duffy, 1957; Malmo, 1959; Woodworth and Schlosberg, 1963), has been collected to show that the tension level of various muscles reflects the motivation level and, generally, the level of activity or arousal.

Eason and White (1960) have shown that tension level of the head, neck, shoulder, and arm muscles reflects the amount of effort exerted during performance of physical tasks. Evidence shows that muscular tension, measured electromyographically, will reveal how well an individual performs a task in relation to the amount of effort exerted, i.e., how *efficient* the performance is. This technique has possibilities for showing whether fluctuations in performance are due to motivation or a change in skill.

Respiration. During certain types of excitement, respiration may become faster and shallower, so that there is sometimes a gasping effect. Deep breathing is difficult during excitement. On the other hand, when the individual's level of excitement is less than normal or if bored, one may show signs of lack of air, such as yawning or sighing.

Pupillary response. During emotional excitement, the iris contracts and, as a result, the pupils of the eye dilate. This seems to happen especially during pain, anger, or extreme tension. During quiet states there is a tendency for the opposite reaction to occur.

Pilomotor response. During certain types of emotional situations, goose pimples may appear on the skin. This may happen when an individual hears a screeching sound, or even when affected by a profound emotional experience. The same circumstance will often cause the hair to stand on end and give a person a "creepy" feeling.

Encephalography. During stressful situations, there are changes in the nature of brain waves. The development of accurate and simplified techniques for measuring brain waves may hold the key to the determination of emotional states in the future.

Salivary secretion. Research indicates that there is a reduction of salivary secretion during most periods of emotional excitement. Many athletes experience dry mouths before important contests. This phenomenon apparently led to the establishment of at least two "lie detection" practices, the basis of which was probably not known by the participants.*

Among other physiological changes within the body during excitement are a slight rise in oral or skin temperature, a change in gastrointestinal activity, and an increase in the frequency of blinking. However, information regarding the exact nature of these changes is not refined enough to be of special importance to most physical educators.

Several of the physiological responses included in this discussion serve to affect performance, while others are merely symptomatic or descriptive. For example, increased heart rate and the greater intake of air actually provide more food and oxygen to the muscles as needed. In addition, increased adrenalin in the system breaks glycogen into glucose within the muscles for quick energy. On the other hand, responses such as the pilomotor reaction or blushing have a much more remote impact on subsequent performance.

Conscious awareness

People often become aware of certain changes in internal functioning when excited. Emotional arousal is therefore a physiological and a conscious experience. *The James-Lange theory* of emotional reaction, which resulted in considerable debate soon after it was introduced, was based on the concept of the individual's awareness of physiological responses. Their theory was the reverse of traditional ideas about the sequence of emotional response. It had generally been assumed that (1) one observes an impending dangerous situation, (2) interprets the hazards and becomes frightened, and (3) reacts in a manner to reduce the danger to self and possibly others.

During the 1890s, William James, of Harvard University, and George Lange, in Denmark, independently disputed traditional beliefs about the sequence of emotional responses. According to their theory, humans react rather instinctively to

---

*One such occurrence was the medieval practice of "ordeal by morsel," whereby an accused person was required to eat a chunk of dry bread. If the suspect choked on the bread, this was evidence of guilt. Theoretically, the guilty person would be more anxious about getting caught, which would lead to a reduction in salivation that would make it difficult to swallow dry food. An innocent individual, having confidence in the integrity of this practice, would feel no such fear. It is conceivable that this practice led to the uncomplimentary label of "choking" in sports.

Certain African tribes engaged in a different technique for determining guilt, although it was based on the same physiological phenomenon. In this practice all suspects were lined up and asked to stick out their tongues. The ruling elder then approached each person and momentarily placed a preheated sword upon the tongue. The innocent persons, having a moist tongue, would feel little, if any, pain. The guilty person, suffering a cessation of salivation, would experience severe pain and consequently would be forced to cry out. Modern lie detection tests involve a great number of physiological responses and are (perhaps) more reliable. However, in any such system, the "pathological liar" tends to thwart detection.

dangerous situations, and conscious awareness of danger comes *later*. This theory holds that we become afraid after we run from danger, and we become sad after starting to cry. The physiological response that accompanies one's general reaction was seen as a strategic factor in promoting emotional arousal. The theory is based on the concept that humans have the capacity for acting appropriately in hazardous situations without foresight. Nature then takes care of the necessary bodily functions to prepare us for fight or flight. After one has acted appropriately, an awareness of bodily changes occurs. For example, after narrowly escaping a major accident on the highway, people often say, "After I pulled the car over to the side of the road, I noticed that I was really shaking."

Despite the interest and debate caused by this theory soon after it was introduced, it has never gained general acceptance among psychologists. It does, however, emphasize the awareness of physiological phenomena associated with emotional excitement.

What physiological changes are people aware of during excitement? The symptoms vary according to the situation and the individual. Just before an important contest, athletes usually exhibit tense behavior and often report feelings ranging from mild excitement to nausea and intense fear. In a locker room prior to a particularly important football game, many players are irritable and most show some signs of edginess. The tone is often quieter than usual, and there is a lack of frivolity or horseplay. Such a climate usually continues until the game begins. Of course, such symptoms are not limited to football. A few years ago the Philadelphia 76er's basketball team had a popular player who frequently ran off the floor and into the locker room during the playing of the national anthem. This behavior of seeming disrespect for the anthem evoked some critical comment from fans and sports writers until word got around that this highly excitable player simply had to make still another trip to the urinal.

Other circumstances in life may, of course, evoke similar responses. One of the most important studies of the conscious symptoms of a stressful situation was conducted by Shaffer (1947) with flying men during World War II. In his study, the subjects were asked to indicate the unusual physiological symptoms of which they were aware during a combat flight mission over enemy territory. The results are included in Table 8-1.

It is not necessary to involve persons in a life-threatening situation (as in the Shaffer study) or even in a physically combative sports encounter in order to bring out strong physiological responses. Leedy (1977) had ranked chess players engage in a chess tournament while being monitored for heart rate, blood pressure, respiratory rate, and galvanic skin response. She found that these highly competent players exhibited dramatic arousal symptoms during game competition, particularly at crucial points in the match. For example, the heart rate of these chess players increased from 25 to 120 percent above the resting rate. At times, blood pressure increased from 20 to 60 percent, and respiration more than doubled, reaching 40 breaths per minute for some subjects. It becomes clear, therefore, that even quiet, practically motionless activities can lead to high arousal if the activity is viewed as important by the participants.

TABLE 8-1.   Signs of Fear During Aerial Combat

"During combat missions did you feel":	"Often"	Percent reporting "Often" or "sometimes"
A pounding heart and rapid pulse	30	86
Feeling that your muscles are very tense	30	83
Being easily irritated, angry, or "sore"	22	80
Dryness of the throat or mouth	30	80
"Nervous perspiration" or "cold sweat"	26	79
"Butterflies" in the stomach	23	76
Feeling of unreality, that this couldn't be happening to you	20	69
Having to urinate (pass water) very frequently	25	65
Trembling	11	64
Feeling confused or "rattled"	3	53
Feeling weak or faint	4	41
Right after a mission, not being able to remember details of what happened	5	39
Feeling sick to the stomach	5	38
Not being able to concentrate	3	35
Wetting or soiling your pants	1	5

Source: L. F. Shaffer, "Fear and Courage in Aerial Combat," *Journal of Consulting Psychology,* 1947, **11**, 137-143. By permission. Based on reports of 1985 flying officers and 2519 enlisted fliers of World War II.

EFFECT OF AROUSAL ON MOTOR PERFORMANCE AND LEARNING

Emotion has long been recognized as an important factor in one's learning and performance of motor skills. Logic, empirical evidence, and research support this concept. The exact nature or extent of its effect, however, has not been determined. This seems to depend heavily upon the nature of the emotion-producing situation. The emotional condition may be one of tension, anxiety, stress, or general excitement regarding a pending situation. Just as the meanings of the terms that are used to describe emotional arousal both differ and overlap in some ways, so does the effect of these different conditions on performance. Therefore, in order for one to clearly discuss the role of these conditions on performance, particular stimuli and responses must be described.

It is clear that emotional excitement has a profound effect on an individual's *performance* in a wide variety of activities, both motor and verbal. For example, there is little question that the level of excitement influences the ability of an individual to lift a heavy load, to throw a baseball for distance or for accuracy, to make a convincing speech, to perform well on a written examination, or to play a piano skillfully. The emotional state is likewise influential in one's ability to *learn* skills of various types. In some situations, high states of emotional excitement seem to help, and in other cases, great excitement seems to prove a detriment. Effects on both performance and learning will be discussed in some detail.

Specific questions are raised by the assumption that one's emotional state affects performance in motor skills. For example, just how much motivation is needed for maximum performance? Is a condition of emotional excitement equally beneficial for the performance of different types of skills? What are the best techniques for motivating students in different activities? These questions have been investigated by psychologists during the past few years. Some research has been conducted under laboratory conditions, while other investigations have been carried out in regular classroom or athletic situations.

In relating arousal to performance, three theories are worth noting: the *Yerkes-Dodson law*, the *inverted-U hypothesis*, and the *drive theory*. The *Yerkes-Dodson* law, described by Eysenck (1963), was developed in the early part of the 20th century by Robert M. Yerkes and John D. Dodson of Harvard University. According to this law, complex tasks are performed better when one's drive is low, while simple tasks are performed best when drive is high. Therefore, a drive that is either too great or too low for a particular task may result in impaired performance. It is assumed that "drive" as used here is roughly equivalent to motivation or arousal. There is some evidence to support this widely accepted generalization and, in addition, several plausible explanations as to its validity. Nevertheless, the Yerkes-Dodson law fails to answer many questions for the teacher or athletic coach interested in gaining more specific guidelines for the conduct of activities. For example, which tasks are "complex" and which are "simple," and, what is "high drive" or "low drive"? Given such latitude, the researcher or the practitioner can explain any results on the basis of the task being either complex or simple or the level of drive being either high or low, whichever supports the results obtained. Such reflective explanations, however, are of little value in predicting performance. Though offering a rough guide as an explanation of arousal and performance, the Yerkes-Dodson law does not provide the specificity needed for today's teachers and coaches.

The *inverted-U hypothesis* described by Hotkinson (1940) has also gained a high degree of recognition. This hypothesis states that as one's arousal level moves from drowsiness to alertness, performance improves, but movement from alertness to high excitement leads to a deterioration in performance. Thus the mid-range (general alertness) is proposed as ideal for performance, with a gradual diminution in effectiveness as one's arousal moves in either direction. (See Figure 8-1.) Although it is valuable as a general guide, the inverted-U concept has a major limitation in that it generalizes that performance in *all* activities is best when the individual is in a state of moderate alertness. General observation, logic, and some research evidence suggest that ideal arousal levels differs for the individual required to carry a heavy person out of a burning building, the brain surgeon involved in a microscopic operation, the presidential candidate engaged in a televised debate, and a defensive football tackle in a goal line stand.

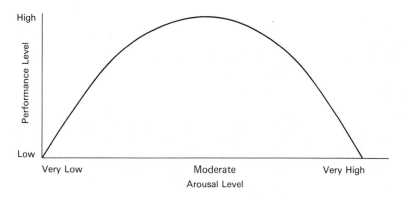

FIGURE 8-1.   The Inverted-U Relationship Between Arousal and Performance.

The drive theory was developed by Hull (1943) and later modified by Spence and Spence (1966). Originally this theory suggested a linear relationship between drive and performance, i.e., as drive increased, performance increased proportionally. As revised, the theory indicates that increased drive raises the probability that the *dominant* response will be made. Therefore, habitual responses, whether correct or incorrect, are more likely when one is aroused. In newly learned skills, increased drive or stress may cause one to revert to older (incorrect) habits because those are more dominant. However, when the newly learned skills become habitual, their performance will be enhanced by increased drive. Although the logic of this theory is attractive, supportive evidence is sparce. In fact, it is practically impossible to test this concept with motor skills because of our inability to precisely determine the habit strengths of the several skills that may be interacting.

Precise conclusions based on convincing data are not yet available. In one of the most thorough reviews on the arousal-performance issue, Landers (1980) encourages that in order to bring adequate definition to this topic, a multidimensional approach is necessary. He encourages situationally specific measures as well as a multimethod approach to combat the many "little studies" that have been prevalent in recent years.

Generalizations*

On the basis of research reports, the opinion of the authorities as reported in the scientific literature, and empirical observation, the following generalizations are offered on the arousal-performance topic:

1. A very high level of arousal is desirable for optimal performance in gross motor activities involving strength, endurance, and speed.

*Portions of the next five pages are from J. B. Oxendine, "Emotional Arousal and Motor Performance," *Quest*, 1970, **13**, 23-32.

2.   A very high level of arousal interferes with performances involving complex skills, fine muscle movements, coordination, steadiness, and general concentration.

3.   A slightly above average level of arousal is preferable to a normal or subnormal arousal state for all motor tasks.

Strength, endurance, and speed

As an illustration of the relationship between arousal and *strength*, an incident was cited early in this chapter in which a woman lifted a station wagon that had fallen on her child. Similar incidents of unusual feats of strength are reported with some regularity in the daily press. Such situations run the gamut from "superhuman" actions by men during war to little old ladies carrying refrigerators down stairs and out of a burning house. In fact, most of us have observed emergency situations where unexpected physical strength was exhibited.

D. L. Johnson (1965) reported that subjects with induced motivational techniques made significant gains in strength, whereas a nonmotivated group did not. One technique, which simulated the competitive aspects of an athletic contest, increased strength scores to a greater degree than other motivational techniques. Johnson further reported that subjects with below average strength and subjects with above average strength made proportional improvements under conditions of motivation. Gerdes (1958) found that motivated subjects increased performance in pull-ups and push-ups.

On the basis of research and observation, there is every reason to believe that the highest arousal state will result in the most extraordinary strength performances. Therefore, the gymnast performing an "iron cross," the weightlifter pressing a heavy weight, or the student doing a leg lift with a dynamometer would each do best if greatly aroused.

As an example of the relationship between arousal and *endurance* I am reminded of the following personal incident that occurred several years ago. I was nearing the completion of a three-mile run that ended with a long uphill climb through a wooded area, and the customary painful level of fatigue had become very evident. Suddenly, out of the brush sprang two large Weimaraner dogs, noticeably unhappy, and, in fact, exhibiting a high level of unwarranted hostility. After about 15 seconds of stressful uncertainty, I was rescued by the owner. As I resumed jogging, I realized that not only had my pace increased, but there was a total absence of any sensation of fatigue. I could not attribute the sudden burst of energy to the 15-second "rest."

Cannon (1929) cites the case of John Colter who, along with a companion, was seized by a group of Indians in Montana in 1808:

> Colter was stripped naked; his companion, who resisted, was killed and hacked in pieces. The Chief then made signs to Colter to go away across the prairie. When he had gone a short distance he saw the younger men casting aside everything but their weapons and making ready for a chase. Now he knew their object. He was to run a race, of which the prize was to be his own

life and scalp. Off he started with the speed of the wind. The war whoop immediately arose; and looking back, he saw a large company of young warriors, with spears, in rapid pursuit. He ran with all the speed that nature, excited to the utmost, could give; fear and hope lent a supernatural vigor to his limbs, and the rapidity of his flight astonished himself. After nearly three miles his strength began to wane. He stopped and looked back. Only one of his pursuers was near. The Indian rushed towards him, attempting to cast his spear and fell headlong. Colter seized the spear, killed his enemy and again set out, with renewed strength, feeling, as he said to me, as if he had not run a mile (p. 226).

Fatigue results in an increase in the threshold of a muscle and, thus, motor responses become slower. During fatigue, muscle thresholds increase from 100 percent to 200 percent and occasionally much higher in situations involving extreme amounts of work. Muscles usually return to their normal condition in 15 minutes to two hours of rest. Cannon (1929) reported research in which fatigued animals were injected with adrenalin immediately after the cessation of long work periods. He reported that animals with threshold increases of 150 percent had this decrement cut in half within five minutes as a result of the adrenalin. Rested animals did not increase their muscle response time with the injection of adrenalin. He concluded, therefore, that the injection of adrenalin had a counteraction on the effects of fatigue.

While it is unlikely that spear carrying Indians, Weimaraners, or injections of adrenalin will be used as a regular means of increasing endurance in sports participants, it does seem clear that situations eliciting strong emotional arousal will result in significant endurance gains.

Incidents that seem to show a positive relationship between fright, anger, or other forms of arousal and *speed* are within the experiences of most persons. Unfortunately, accurate measures of speed are not usually recorded in these situations. While feats of strength are often verifiable, it is rare that anyone is available to clock frightened people over a measured course. Nevertheless, the belief remains that a child being chased by either a bully or a ghost will run faster than when told by a teacher, "Run as fast as you can." In experimental situations, a relationship between movement speed and motivation has been shown by several researchers. For example, Gerdes (1958) had subjects perform tasks involving speed, strength, accuracy, and certain sports skills under several motivation conditions. The speed tasks were the sixty-yard dash and a zigzag run; strength items were pull-ups and push-ups; accuracy items included a volleyball wall volley and basketball passing test; and skill tasks were the baseball throw and basketball wall volley test. Gerdes used such motivating techniques as competition between individuals and groups, encouragement on an individual basis and in class situations, scale scores, and individual testing in a class situation. He reported that each of the motivational techniques proved beneficial for performance in most of the activities, but that encouragement and the use of test scores were especially helpful. Henry (1961) showed that motivation resulting from electric shock can be effective in speeding simple reaction time. In addition, the resulting speedup was transferable from a simple to a more complicated movement. Miller (1960) and Strong (1963) showed a similar relationship between speed and arousal. Consequently, there is ample reason to assume that sprinters will run faster and swimmers will swim faster when aroused.

Complex and fine movement responses

Numerous situations can be cited from sports in which highly motivated or aroused individuals performed less well on *complex tasks*. The typical young baseball pitcher who becomes highly excited in a tense game situation is less likely to throw strikes than in practice or under less stressful game conditions. Similarly, erratic or subpar performance in a high pressure situation may be expected from the basketball player shooting a free throw, a gymnast in a balancing routine, or a diver attempting a complex springboard dive. Frequent interference in activities requiring complex and controlled movements appear to support the Yerkes-Dodson law.

Matarazzo and Matarazzo (1956) reported that performance on a more complex maze problem is adversely affected by anxiety. A simple maze task, however, was enhanced by a moderate level of anxiety. Taylor and Spence (1952) reported that a high level of anxiety is a detriment to performance in a complex verbal choice-point problem. Wechsler and Hartogs (1945), after research with a mirror drawing task, concluded that fine motor coordinations and discriminations were adversely affected by anxiety.

The effect of a psychic stressor on the depth perception, steadiness, blood pressure, and simple eye-hand coordination of freshmen college women was investigated by Hennis and Ulrich (1958). They found that there was an elevation in blood pressure when the stressor was used. There were also changes in depth perception, steadiness, and coordination, but these changes were not consistent in direction.

The interference effects of high emotional arousal appear to be more detrimental with tense or highly anxious persons than with those less anxious. Carron (1965) reported that a shock stressor (electric shock from a constant current electronic simulator) had a detrimental effect on highly anxious male college students in a *balancing* task, whereas low anxiety subjects were unaffected. Late in the learning period, however, the detrimental effect of the stressor on highly anxious subjects was lessened. In reviewing several research studies in this area, Carron concluded that in tasks of low difficulty, highly anxious subjects were found to be superior to low anxiety subjects. However, in *tasks of high difficulty*, low anxiety subjects proved superior. Stress seemed to be particularly detrimental when persons were largely unacquainted with a particular activity. Experience in the activity tended to reduce the adverse effects of stress. Bergstrom (1967) reported that experienced airplane pilots performed less well on a *complex motor task* during stressful conditions. The stressful situation consisted of distracting flashing lights and the performance of a secondary task along with the main task. Bergstrom reported that the human pilot can perform extremely difficult and complex tasks in a calm laboratory situation or a simulated cockpit. When the system is airborne, however, the pilot's performance seriously deteriorates as a result of the stress. Pinneo (1961) reported that as tension increased, so did the errors in a complex tracking task.

In a study of *steadiness*, Eysenck and Gillen (1965) reported that high drive subjects performed at an inferior level to low drive subjects in a hand steadiness test. Basomity et al. (1955) found a decrement in performance in hand steadiness following the administrations of adrenalin, and Hauty (1954) reported an increase in fine tremor after the administration of a stimulant drug. Several authors report that muscle tension and tremor is a normal characteristic of increased tension. Such tension may easily result in the inability of the pass receiver in football to catch the ball. The same may be true for the basketball player attempting to catch the ball or retrieve a rebound, or the field hockey player unable to exercise the typical "give" with the stick when receiving the ball.

Several studies have been conducted in which induced noises and other distracting conditions were used to determine their effect on motor performance taking place at the same time. Grimaldi (1958) conducted one such study in which a coordination task was performed under quiet and noisy conditions of various frequency ranges and intensities. There were more errors and less precision when noise was evident. Further, response times were slower and the number of errors was greater when noise levels and frequencies were highest. Grimaldi concluded that intermittent noise has a reducing effect on an individual's ability to perform quick and precise movements.

According to Hussman (1969), functioning *intelligence* goes down as emotional arousal goes up. Of course, effective intelligence is an important factor in athletic contests, not to mention I.Q. tests and the performance of general routine tasks. However, rising emotion and declining intellectual functioning is probably not a straight line relationship. That is, there is no evidence to indicate that an emotional state slightly above normal is less effective than a "normal" or even below average level. Nevertheless, there is little question about the distracting effects of extreme levels of emotion on any type of performance involving reasoning powers. Such interference may be particularly harmful when the performer is involved in an activity requiring quick thinking or fast decision making. Extreme examples of this interference occur when the individual "freezes" or "goes blank."

Individual differences in arousal response

The level of proficiency.   Individuals having different levels of proficiency often react differently to a stressful or motivating condition. In two verbal tests, Gates (1924) found that proficient students performed less well in front of a large audience. Rasch (1955) reported that the most outstanding aviation cadets were more seriously hindered by the realization of failure than were cadets who were not as proficient. Similarly, in a verbal test, Sullivan (1927) found that an intellectually superior group was more adversely affected by failure than was an inferior group.

Not all evidence, however, supports the concept that stress has a more detrimental effect on superior performers. L. A. Miller (1960) reported that track performers who were rated as poor performers by their coaches showed relatively little emotional stress prior to track meets, good performers exhibited a greater degree of emotional stress and also greater consistency of performance. In a simple maze test with young children, Abel (1936) found that the performance of more intelligent subjects was enhanced when a group situation was introduced.

The personality of the individual.   In addition to the individual's level of skill and the type of task, personality plays an important part in determining one's performance in a stressful situation. Highly anxious individuals are more disturbed by stressful conditions and have greater difficulty in novel situations than do less anxious persons. Parsons, Phillips, and Lane (1954) found that stress was detrimental to steadiness. Baker (1961) found that stress inhibited the performance of high anxiety subjects and aided the performance of low anxiety subjects. Breen (1959) showed that there is motor incoordination even among normal subjects under stress. Also, neurotic patients were found to have less general coordination and manual dexterity.

Some people seem more resistive to distraction than do others. Some athletes are more consistent or steady performers while others tend to be "hot" one day and "cold" the next. It can be observed by those who follow major league baseball games that some players are more susceptible than others to slumps and hot streaks. In like manner, there is great variation in the consistency of track and field performers. Characteristically, all people's performances fluctuate from time to time. This variability is evident among both outstanding and poor performers and among anxious and nonanxious individuals. Physiological causes cannot always be found when the individual performs at an unusually high or low level. Personality traits seem more influential in determining one's response to different emotional situations. Although there is little dispute about the influence of personality, very little conclusive evidence has been gathered in this difficult area of investigation.

The realization of failure seems to have a detrimental effect on subsequent performance in motor skills. Rasch (1955) investigated this phenomenon with aviation cadets during World War II. After the cadets had taken the final flying test to qualify for their wings, instructors informed each student that he had failed (but accurate scores were kept). After this "failure," students were given subsequent flying tests to determine if their performances would be affected by knowledge of failure. Rasch found (1) subsequent performances were significantly poorer than original test performances; (2) performance was adversely affected for four days after the failure; and (3) flyers who were rated highest in previous performances were more adversely affected than were poorer flyers.

Sullivan (1927) observed a similar phenomenon when he reported that an intellectually superior group of students was hindered more by a realization of failure than was an inferior group. Possibly, this was because the more intelligent group was not as used to failure. Memorization of nonsense syllables was used in Sullivan's study. McClelland and Apicella (1947) found that failure produced less efficient subsequent performance in a card-sorting task. Willingham (1958) also showed a decrease in motor performance following failure.

L. A. Miller (1960) evaluated the emotional stress of varsity high school track performers immediately before all meets for the months of March and April. The degree of stress was determined by taking pulse and respiratory rates and measuring palm perspiration. The students also completed a checklist to give an indication of their confidence. A significant relationship was found between emotional stress and consistency of competitive performance. Poor competitors (as rated by coaches) showed less emotional stress than did good performers.

Performance in sports activities

Research dealing with the role of emotional arousal in ordinary sports activities is sparse. Some studies have attempted to determine the level of arousal associated with participants in different sports without specifically relating that arousal to subsequent performance. Other studies, designed to relate arousal to performance level, consider the team as a whole in making generalizations about a particular sport. One of the few studies in this specific area was conducted by Harmon and Johnson (1952) who found that a major college football team played its best game when aroused to the highest level of the season. On the other hand, the team performed poorest when the arousal level was at the lowest state. However, to generalize that a football player performs best when he is most highly motivated is a rather crude generalization. The game of football is so varied and complex that optimum emotional arousal for the different skills may vary from near the norm line to extremely high levels. For example, the offensive guard or tackle required to block the individual straight across the line will probably exhibit speed and power most effectively if he is aroused to the highest possible degree. On the other hand, the open field runner is required to exhibit agility, balance, and judgment in direction as well as good running speed. Since he must remain "in control" a moderate level of arousal may be most helpful. Finally, the quarterback, when throwing a pass, and the field goal kicker would probably perform best at a low level of arousal so that they relax and focus their attention on the task at hand, thus making the accurate and rather delicate responses necessary for success. For the performance of individual tasks in football, therefore, it appears that different levels of arousal would be ideal for players at different positions.

Without adequate research relating emotional arousal to specific sports skills, suggestions as to the most appropriate level for different sports activities are speculative. Nevertheless, Table 8-2 includes a summary of suggestions regarding the optimal arousal level for the typical participant in a variety of sports activities. These are based on some reflections on the research and opinions that relate to the components necessary for performance in the activities listed.

In Table 8-2, the #5 level refers to extremely high levels of excitement approaching "blind rage" while the #1 level suggests a condition only slightly more intense than a normal relaxed state. Skills are placed on the scale at a point seeming

TABLE 8-2.   Optimum Arousal Level for Some Typical Sports Skills

Level of Arousal	Sports Skills
#5 (extremely excited)	football blocking and tackling performance on the Rogers' PFI test running 200 meters to 400 meters sit up, push up, or bent arm hang test bench press
#4	running long jump running very short and long races shot putt swimming races wrestling and judo
#3	basketball skills boxing high jumping most gymnastic skills soccer skills
#2	baseball pitching and batting springboard dives fencing football quarterback tennis
#1 (slight arousal)	archery and bowling basketball free throw field goal kicking golf putting and short irons skating figure 8's
0 (normal state)	

Modified from J. B. Oxendine, "Emotional Arousal and Motor Performance," *Quest* XIII, 1970, 23-32. By permission of Human Kinetics Publishers.

to reflect the needed ingredients for excellent performance. That is, those activities high on speed, strength, or endurance needs but low on complexity, fine muscle control, and judgment are placed nearer to #5. Those activities placing high priority on fine muscle control and coordinated movements but low on strength and speed are placed nearer to #1. Of course, many skills require a combination of these several factors and, thus, fall somewhere in between #1 and #5. For example, the boxer, though needing the strength, speed, and endurance afforded by high emotion, must devote attention to analyzing his opponent's moves and figuring out a way of maximizing his own strengths while exploiting his opponent's weaknesses. In addition, he must protect himself. Consequently, the boxer who becomes unduly angry or "loses his head" is an easier target for the more composed boxer. Similarly, the sprinter in a short race is likely to lose some efficiency at the start of the race and during the first few steps if a state of extreme tension exists at the starting blocks. However, in a slightly longer race, i.e., 200 meters, the negative effects of extreme tension would be minimized while the benefits (speed and endurance) would be maximized. For even longer races, such as a mile or greater, there is a tendency for the highly aroused runner to throw caution to the winds, fail to pace himself properly, and tire badly near the end of the race.

For an activity such as golf putting, an extreme level of arousal is often devastating. The golfer is likely to putt the ball much too strongly because of a high level of general muscular tension or, on the other hand, much too easily, for fear of overputting. The same holds true for other skills emphasizing accuracy and precision. I have never known a basketball coach to say to a young player who has just missed an important free throw, "You did not try hard enough." Rather, most problems arise when an individual tries *too* hard.

The direct influence of an emotionally stimulating situation is more obvious in motor performance than in motor learning. Nevertheless, it has been consistently pointed out that the most important condition for learning is motivation on the part of the learner. This widely accepted principle is important both for motor skills and for verbal concepts, but the exact role of different types and intensities of motivation in the learning of different skills is not entirely clear.

Several factors seem to affect the role of tension or excitement in the learning of motor skills. Most investigators have reported that simple motor tasks are learned more effectively under tension, while the learning of complex tasks is adversely affected by tension. Also, Wechsler and Hartogs (1945) reported that high levels of anxiety hinder the learning and performance of tasks involving fine motor coordination. A third factor is the induced tension's characteristics and relation to the task. Tension from both physical effort and emotional stress has been used in studies. Physical tension, which is nearer the performing body part, appears to be most influential.

The existence of tension seems to have varying effects on mental tasks of different degrees of complexity. A moderate amount of tension seems to aid simple mental tasks. Bills (1927), for instance, found that subjects who were squeezing hand dynamometers in both hands were better able to learn nonsense syllables, memorize and add columns of digits, and recite scrambled letters. Zartman and Cason (1934), however, reported that continuous tension (a foot applied to a resisting pedal) did not aid subjects in solving a complex arithmetic problem. Freeman (1938) found uneven effects when he attempted to affix an optimal tension load to different types of mental and motor tasks. He concluded that the more complex tasks would be inhibited by tension.

A number of studies have shown that during the early stages of learning tension is high, but that it subsides as greater skill is developed in the task. Stroud (1931), in a maze problem, found that less downward pressure was exhibited by subjects as they developed skill. Greater tension was shown when subjects encountered the more difficult portions of the maze. He also found that physical tension could be induced by suggestion. When subjects were told that they had to produce three perfect trials, greater downward pressure on the stylus was evidenced.

Daniel (1939) and Ghisselli (1936) obtained results in general agreement with those of Stroud. Both found a reduction in tension as learning increased. Daniel reported that high tension was associated with greater speed while lower tension resulted in fewer errors. Stauffacher (1937) found that good learners were hindered by increased tension while poor learners were aided by tension. He theorized that prior to induced tension the poor learners were operating at below maximum level.

Farber and Spence (1953) reported that nonanxious subjects developed proficiency in a stylus-maze task more quickly than did anxious subjects. After arriving at similar findings, Ausubel, Schiff, and Goldman (1953) concluded that anxious individuals were not able to improvise or adjust to changes in a learning situation. Matarazzo and Matarazzo (1956) reported that subjects learn a simple maze task more easily when a moderate level of anxiety exists rather than a very high or very low level of anxiety. Very anxious or overly tense individuals apparently do less well in most learning situations and perform even more poorly in situations that require progressive discrimination.

In a situation in which airmen were attempting to learn a complex manipulative skill, Fleishman (1958) used verbal encouragement to increase the motivation level. The experimenter made comments that indicated that future assignments would depend upon how well one performed. These comments were made prior to and during the performance. Fleishman reported that performance scores improved significantly when this motivational technique was used. Many other authors have reported that the motivational level attained through written or oral praise is beneficial for the learning of both motor and verbal skills.

TECHNIQUES IN MOTIVATION

The idea that excitement or tension level has an effect on performance is no longer seriously questioned. For some types of motor performance or learning, a very high level of motivation may be sought by the teacher. Such a situation exists when maximum performance on a pull-up test is sought, or if the coach in football wants his linemen to play at their peak. In another situation, the coach may want the player to develop a relatively low level of motivation. This condition may prove best for the quarterback in football, the novice diver or gymnast in an important meet, or the child who is taking a balance test in a physical education class. In other situations, the teacher or coach would like to develop a motivation level between these two extremes.

In addition to *determining* the most advantageous level of arousal for each type of activity and for children of different personality types, teachers need to give more serious study to the matter of effectively *changing* the tension levels of children. In many situations, students in class or athletes on the field need to be motivated or brought to a higher level of excitability. On other occasions, they need to be "demotivated" or calmed down for most effective performance.

In regular school classes, motivating techniques are needed very frequently.

The arbitrary bell schedule often runs counter to the interests of the child. For example, the student may be interested in a particular problem in history when the bell rings. Then he must immediately be ready for math; another bell and his interest must be in a soccer lead-up game, then in some project in wood shop. Obviously, students may have great difficulty in changing their psychological readiness with the class schedule at school. Sound motivational techniques are therefore needed to quickly capture the student's attention in each class situation.

Numerous motivating techniques have been tried, both in experimental and practical settings. An analysis of the effectiveness of some of these may aid the teacher in determining the most appropriate method to use in several different situations.

Different states of emotional excitability seem to have varying effects in different learning and performance situations. Some factors that seem important are (1) the nature of the emotion-inducing stimulant, (2) the type of skill involved, (3) the level of proficiency of the participant, and (4) the personality of the participant. Each must be considered if one is to fully understand the effect of motivation. With each of these conditions, several alternatives are possible. For example, the emotion-inducing stimulant may be a challenge, threat, reward, ridicule, praise, or environmental distraction. The type of skill may vary from simple to complex, from fine to a gross movement, or a meaningful to a novel laboratory task. Similarly, studies have shown that the level of skill of the performer is influential in the degree of excitement that may result from a particular set of circumstances. One's personality also plays a major role in the response. For example, empirical evidence indicates that some individuals become unduly rattled under stress while others "rise" to the occasion. It becomes clear that a blanket generalization cannot be made for all circumstances.

Experimental techniques

A number of projects have been conducted in which several motivating techniques were studied at once. In one study, Strong (1963) had sixth-grade boys and girls take physical fitness tests following six different methods of motivation. He reported that best performances took place when subjects were organized as members of a competing team and then were individually able to choose their desired level of performance. Another effective method was encouraging the children to try to set a record. Individual competition against either (1) a classmate of near equal ability, (2) a classmate of different ability, or (3) all classmates was not as effective. Generally he found that motivated children performed better than unmotivated children. He also reported that these techniques of motivation were more effective with boys than with girls.

Gerdes (1958) compared the techniques of (1) verbal encouragement, (2) team competition, (3) use of previous scores, and (4) retesting on four types of physical tasks that involved speed, strength, accuracy, and sports skills. He pointed out that the motivating techniques did not demand any specially constructed apparatus and therefore were usable in a regular class situation. Gerdes generally concluded that all the techniques resulted in improved performances (especially in strength), but that no method was singularly most effective. He observed that the validity of fitness testing is dependent upon the motivation used.

M. M. Martin (1961) tested the effect of four motivational techniques on performance in a jump and reach test. Individuals performed either with the group or alone, and some were told their results while others were not. She found that the informed groups did better than the uninformed groups. Also, performing in the presence of classmates resulted in better achievement than performance alone. J. Nelson (1962) used ten different techniques to get college men to exercise to exhaustion on the elbow-flexion ergograph. The motivating situations varied from verbal encouragement to several competitive situations in which subjects were told that they were being compared with Russian students or that their performances were being used to set standards for the selection of astronauts. Most of the special techniques resulted in improved performance, with none of the methods proving particularly outstanding.

Occasionally, the practice of *hypnotism* has been used by some researchers in an effort to stimulate the individual to greater effort or to determine one's true capacity in such components as strength, endurance, speed, and general muscular control. It has been found that hypnotism can be effectively used to delay fatigue, to enable one to withstand pain, and to control various psychological inhibitions. It has also been reported that hypnotic suggestion can reduce the effective strength of the individual. However, there are inconsistencies among studies in regard to the value of hypnosis for *increasing* strength. Some researchers have found that inhibitions regarding performing without a warm-up can be effectively controlled by hypnotism. For several reasons, however, hypnosis is not recommended as an appropriate technique to motivate public school children.

Traditional techniques

The techniques most often used to promote greater interest in learning and performance are *reward* and *punishment*. The advisability of selecting either reward or punishment for learning cannot be easily generalized because the choice depends upon the circumstances. The personality of the learner is one important consideration. Some individuals respond well to both reward and punishment while others respond better to one method. Quite frequently, punishment results in a detrimental effect on subsequent learning and performance. All experienced teachers have observed children who sulk for long periods after being punished. Other factors that influence the effect of these techniques are the age and sex of the individuals and the manner in which reward or punishment is administered.

Rewards may be classified as (1) material, (2) symbolic, or (3) psychological. Material rewards are those items that have value in and of themselves, and this value is often monetary. Athletic prizes, such as blazers, watches, jewelry, sports equipment, or radios, would fall into this category. The professional golfer or tennis player receives prize money according to the order of finish, and consequently is encouraged to play well in order to receive more money.

Symbolic rewards are those external signs or symbols that indicate success or approval. Athletic letters, inexpensive trophies, reinforcing praise, school grades, gold stars, or selection to an all-star team all represent symbolic rewards. Such awards, although having little or no monetary value, can have great motivating power if presented in the most advantageous context. Some prominent coaches have found that handing out jelly beans or M & M candies has important impact when they symbolically represent approval of the coach. Years ago, gold stars were frequently given out by primary-grade teachers as a means of rewarding children for school work or good behavior. It was interesting to note that the world champion Pittsburgh Pirate baseball players during the 1979 season and in the World Series aggressively sought gold stars for placement on their caps because they were given out by popular team captain Willie Stargell for outstanding performance on the playing field. The appeal of these gold stars was certainly not limited to their inherent value.

Psychological rewards represent "internal" motivation and are viewed as the highest order or most noble of all types of motivation. These represent items such as one's personal desire to improve, enjoyment in participation and a desire to achieve, or mastery of a task for its own sake. Internal motivation is deemed by educators to be the most essential goal, although external rewards are frequently used as an interim measure to promote outstanding performance.

The most important advantages of rewards seem to be that they tend to create a pleasurable association with the desired act; they engender enthusiasm; and they enhance the learner's ego. Numerous studies with both verbal and motor skills reveal advantages of praise. There are some disadvantages, however, especially if too frequent use is made of praise. The most important disadvantage is the individual's tendency to develop a dependence upon extrinsic rather than intrinsic motivation and, therefore, develop false values (interest in the reward rather than the activity itself). Another disadvantage of external rewards in physical education and intramural activities is that the same few children seem to excel most of the time. It appears that the winners of external rewards are usually the children who need them least for subsequent enthusiasm.

Traditionally in schools, reproof or some form of punishment has been used about as frequently as praise and reward. The most important advantage of punishment seems to be that it *is effective* with some children. In motor skills, punishment is sometimes associated as a natural result of an activity. As such, the punishment can aid in the elimination of certain undesirable responses. Apparently a degree of discipline is needed by all children, but there are more agreed upon disadvantages of punishment than advantages. For example, when used often, punishment loses its effect. There are situations in which punishment may reinforce the undesired act by creating fear in the mind of the learner. Very often rapport between the teacher and student is lost. Punishment is often humiliating for some students and reinforces a feeling of inadequacy. This is damaging to the self-concept of the individual. On the other hand, some students, especially extroverts, are stimulated more by reproof than by praise. In the use of punishment, however, one drawback is the inability to establish an equal punishment for all students. It is often clear that what is real punishment for one child is only a minor challenge for others.

A popular technique that has been used to stimulate individuals to greater effort has been the *pep talk* immediately before the beginning of athletic contests. The nature of these pregame talks has varied from a tense, stirring, oratorical appeal to the emotions of the participants, to a quiet, logical, and instructional talk. The former type, popularized by Knute Rockne and several other football coaches, has perhaps been the most popular technique for team games in schools and colleges. Recordings of such speeches or events are used for pregame motivation in a similar manner. Films with emotional overtones occasionally have been used before athletic contests and even during wartime to evoke a certain arousal on the part of participants. There can be little doubt that the pep talk and other precontest techniques have often been effective in motivating young people to exert greater effort.

The use of *music* as a motivating device has recently become popular. However, very little reasearch has been done to determine the effect of music on one's attitude toward or performance in subsequent activity. The practice of using music in the locker room to generally excite the players for the upcoming contest is common. Each year at basketball tournament time there are reports of coaches who use music prior to games and during half-time intermissions. It is logical to assume that certain types of music, with a stirring, rhythmic beat and with progressively increasing volume and tempo may result in a measurable increase in excitability on the part of young people.

On other occasions, music is used *during* the performance of an activity for the purpose of stimulating the individual to greater effort. Band music for marching has traditionally been used by armies because of the psychological stimulation as well as for regulating the pace at which the troops walk. "Exercise" records are frequently used in schools as well as in adult aerobic classes. In addition to the verbal instruction, music is designed to motivate students to vigorous activity. In the use of such music to accompany exercise, care should be taken to select music that is appropriate for a given age level. I have observed junior high school girls exercising to the accompaniment or rock and roll music and elementary school children exercising to the "William Tell Overture" and the "Sabre Dance." These selections seemed to promote maximum effort as well as blending with the interest level of the children. The effectiveness of aerobic dance is strongly related to the music selected. Thus, physical educators and coaches, in addition to dance teachers, have begun to use music for the stimulation of positive attitudes as well as for rhythm.

Competition has been one of the most frequently used techniques for motivating young people to perform with greater enthusiasm. Physical educators and coaches have consistently found that individuals seem to try harder if they are competing against another individual or team. The technique of competition has therefore been used as one of the primary means of promoting maximum effort by performers. As early as 1897, Triplett found that the mere presence of other persons caused changes in an individual's performance. Sometimes the performance improved, while on other occasions a decline resulted. He observed that the inconsistency in direction of change seemed to be caused by the personality of the individual.

W. R. Johnson (1949) studied the effect of competition in causing a buildup of anxiety among a group of team sport (football) members and a group of individual sport (wrestling) members. Heart rate, blood pressure, and blood sugar were used as the measures of anxiety. He reported that the wrestlers became more excited immediately before the contest than did football players. The individual challenge seemed to present a greater competitive threat to the participants than did the group challenge. In another study of college football players, Johnson (1950) reported a close relationship between the performers' level of excitement regarding an upcoming game and their performance in the game. Games that were preceded by the highest level of excitement also had the highest level of performance. In the game of football, Johnson theorized that the higher the level of arousal, the better would be the performance.

Research projects dealing with the role of motivation in physical activity have used several forms of competition. Competition is not only effective, but it is easy to create in almost any school situation. Students may compete against other teams or against other individuals. Team competition may be on the varsity level, the intramural level, or within a particular class. Individual competition may be strictly individual in nature, as in a challenge tournament, or it may involve individuals as team members, as in a gymnastic or track meet. In working with sixth-grade children, Strong (1963) reports that competition was more effective in motivating boys than girls. In his study, he showed that boys were more responsive to a competitive situation than were girls. Today, one must suspect that the attitude of girls toward competition has changed, at least to some extent.

In athletics, competition is often used by coaches to stimulate individuals or teams to greater effect. Frequently, coaches will search for an ingredient to heighten the feeling of competition. Coaches of favored teams are careful to avoid making any comment that could be viewed as derogatory, lest the coach of the opposing team use it to incite the underdog team to extraordinary effort. Favored teams or individuals tend to "let sleeping dogs lie."

Several years ago, a wrestling coach of my acquaintance used the competition factor as a strategy for increasing the arousal level of one of his wrestlers. The wrestler was outstanding in natural ability and technique. Late in the season he was still undefeated as his team approached a match against a team that had a wrestler in the same weight class who was also undefeated. The coach observed that his outstanding wrestler's one weakness was his inclination to be complacent and easygoing, rarely exhibiting adequate ferocity, or the "killer instinct." For this important match the coach devised a plan to arouse the young man to a higher level: He wrote him a letter and signed the name of the upcoming opponent. The letter contained most uncomplimentary statements about the wrestler, including derogatory comments about his courage, his institution, and even his heritage. Furthermore, the letter promised that the local wrestler would not only be beaten but humiliated in the upcoming match. As it turned out, the coach's devious strategy produced the desired effect—the wrestler was clearly angry with his opponent at match time. His ferocity and determination, according to general consensus, were greater than in any other match during his career. Consequently, he was a clear winner over an equally competent opponent. The effectiveness of this bit of coaching strategy could not be disputed. However, the ethics of this technique, and its long-term effects on coach-player relationships are another matter. When word got around that the coach was the author of the letter, I was never certain that the players would trust him again. Still, the incident illustrates the point that exaggerated competition can arouse one to more aggressive physical performance.

Competition is often presented in a much more subtle manner than is observed in major sporting events. Still, wherever present, it can have a motivating effect. As an example, my wife recently handed me a pickle jar to open while I was sitting at the dinner table. She had been unable to open it and, after giving it a try, neither could I. As I was ready to return it to her, my fifteen-year-old son eagerly said, "Let me try it, Dad." Suddenly I realized that this was no longer a casual matter, and there were implications beyond the pickle jar. Sensing this challenge, I was aroused to put forth a greater effort, determined either to open the jar or to be absolutely sure that my son could not open it. With renewed energy I was able to open it, thus keeping my threatened ego intact—at least for the moment.

In addition to competing against other persons, one might compete against personal records or against various class or school records. Such competitive situations are especially appropriate and easy to establish in physical fitness tests, circuit training or obstacle courses, track and field events, and sports skills tests. A useful and effective method that is employed by many teachers is reminding children of their previous performance on a particular task and encouraging them to surpass that score in subsequent trials. Such competition is particularly dependent upon the student's receiving *knowledge of results* from all participations. This proves to be a meaningful challenge for most students. Outstanding performers can be encouraged to try to break the class or school record. The total class, as a unit, might compete against established school records. Secondary school boys are often motivated to work harder if a situation is established in which they are competing against Marine Corps scores or scores of children from another country. Competition is most effective when each child has a reasonable chance to win. If one child is either completely outclassed or is an easy winner in a contest, motivation will be weakened rather than enhanced.

General motivation or enthusiasm for a class activity may be prompted if the instructor *teaches for success* on the part of the student. There is wisdom in the cliché: "Nothing succeeds like success." It is obvious that students develop greater interest in an activity if their early attempts meet with some degree of achievement. On the other hand, if their first few trials result in total failure, students' interest will rapidly diminish. Therefore, class methods should be varied so that even those with a very low level of skill can, to some extent, reach the objectives of the activity. Modifications can be made in certain drills in order to attain this success. Consider the situation in which the instructor attempts to teach the fast break to a group of novice basketball players. If the drill is organized so that three offensive players are coming down court to be met by three defensive players, it is practically certain that the offensive team will meet with failure. In the early stages of learning basketball, defensive skills are more advanced than are offensive skills. Therefore, to increase the probability of a successful fast break, the teacher could start with three offensive players against one defensive player. Later, he might use two defensive players, but restrict their movement to about one step. The same general technique might be employed in soccer, since the lack of dribbling and passing skills makes it practically impossible to score goals unless certain restrictions are placed on the defensive team. Some technique for assuring a degree of success will certainly add to the interest and general motivation of students.

Reducing arousal level

Sometimes it is desirable for the teacher or coach to *demotivate* or calm down individuals. Demotivation may be necessary both for efficiency of performance and for safety reasons. First, it has been pointed out that a high level of excitement or stress is likely to hinder one's performance in some tasks, especially those involving precision or complexity of fine motor movement. For most efficient performance in such tasks, therefore, efforts should be made to reduce the tension of performers in certain situations. Second, there may be dangers if certain individuals with heart ailments, epilepsy, or other handicaps get too excited and overexert themselves in vigorous activity. When such individuals show evidence of too great tension, efforts should be made to relieve the tension or to remove them from the situation. Sometimes young people under the stimulation of emotional excitement attempt dangerous activities for which they are not yet ready. In advanced diving, tumbling, or gymnastics, hazardous stunts are often attempted as a result of undue motivation, as is reckless play in such sports as football or soccer.

Ironically, some of the general techniques used to motivate performers are also effective in reducing motivation or tension. For example, talking with an individual or a group in a calm and relaxed manner might have just the opposite effect of a pep talk. Likewise, music that is soft and flowing, rather than loud marching music, might have a calming effect. Hypnotism, progressive relaxation, and deep breathing exercises have also been used to soothe persons who are in a state of high tension.

Stress management, the control of harmful anxiety, has taken many forms in recent years. These include progressive relaxation, autogenic training, yoga, zen, meditation, and imagery. These techniques involve self-regulation or control as opposed to drugs or the use of environmental stimuli to reduce tension.

Recently *biofeedback* has become popular as a means of stress management. This term refers to the process of feeding back to the individual biological or physiological information by visual or auditory means. Such information, provided by some sensing device, can aid the individual in regulating physiological responses. As it is, most people have little awareness of their internal physiology in any specific way. However, when provided with such information, one can often make alterations in these responses.

According to Zaichowsky (1979) biofeedback affects at least the following modalities: (1) heart rate, (2) blood pressure, (3) muscle tension, (4) peripheral skin temperature, (5) brain waves, and (6) skin potential response. These techniques have been developed and used primarily with patient dysfunction, where problems result from stress or tension.

The use of biofeedback as a technique in reducing arousal level or stress among athletes in a practical setting is mostly speculative. Zaichowsky reviewed his own work and the research literature regarding the use of biofeedback in the laboratory setting and in restricted athletic situations. The data are too sparse and narrowly directed to be helpful in a practical sense at this time. Still, as a tool for developing self-regulation, biofeedback certainly has great potential for enhancing motor performance, particularly in areas where arousal level needs to be lowered.

LEVEL OF ASPIRATION AND GOAL SETTING

A concept that is intimately related to motivation and performance is the topic of level of aspiration. It has long been suspected that a relationship exists between one's goals and achievement. However, the idea of expectations and their influence on performance was first investigated by Lewin before he left Germany. Frank (1935) reported that the term *level of aspiration*, in reference to expectation, was originated by Hoppe. Other authors have reported that Dembo (1931) first coined the phrase. Both Hoppe and Dembo were students of Lewin.

A generally accepted definition of level of aspiration is given by Frank as: "The level of future performance in a familiar task which an individual, knowing his level of past performance in that task, explicitly undertakes to reach" (p. 119). In the general use of this term, primary thought has been devoted to what one *expects* to achieve as opposed to what one would *like* to achieve. In support of this distinction, several researchers, Martire (1956), Clarke and Greene (1963), and Wylie (1961) found no relationship between the level of aspiration and the achievement need of the individual. Other authors, however, have suggested that one's general level of motivation probably has bearing on the achievement one expects. Most authorities agree that *once the level of aspiration is set, it can serve as a strong motivator for the individual to reach it.*

Measurement of level of aspiration poses a problem. Merely asking the subject what he expects to attain in a particular performance does not always provide an accurate score one really expects to achieve. Lewin (1944) suggests that there are three levels for each task: (1) what the person *says* that he expects to attain, (2) what he *really* expects, and (3) what he would *like* to attain. Weiss (1961) had subjects respond to several aspiration questions. On the basis of these, he was able to identify two major categories: the judgmental or expectational dimension, and the motivational or aspirational dimension. Current research seems to indicate that a high or low level of aspiration is not a general personality characteristic that is the same for all tasks. Instead, level of aspiration is specific to a particular task.

A participant who attains or surpasses an established level of aspiration for a particular task is considered to have succeeded. On the other hand, inability to reach the predicted level would constitute a failure. The participant's future levels of aspiration are affected substantially be previous performances. However, some individuals seem to consistently set levels that are not attained. Others establish levels that are close to their actual performances, while a third group sets levels that are far too low. Children who regularly set unreasonably high levels of aspiration apparently feel a need to put themselves in a high category or promote the feeling that they have tried very hard. Those who select too low levels seemingly need to play it safe and assure themselves of success. It is also possible that they do not wish to try very hard. In general, one's level of aspiration for a task tends to vary up or down with prior successes or failures. However, subsequent aspiration levels are influenced more by successes than by failures.

Price (1960) had college women take part in a wide variety of motor skills to determine if there was a relationship between level of aspiration and performance. Significant correlations were found between aspiration and achievement. The reason for this relationship was not suggested. Strong (1963) found that one of the most effective ways to motivate children to perform was allowing them to choose their own desired level of performance.

Worell (1959) found that college students who set a reasonable level of aspiration concerning their academic work had greater contact with reality and were generally successful in grade achievement. Students with levels of aspiration far above their previous records were generally unsuccessful or poor students. Walter (1951), in a study of children from the fourth to twelfth grades, found that boys had a higher level of aspiration than girls.

Sears (1940) investigated the level of aspiration of a group of children in grades four, five, and six who had long histories of chronic failure in reading and arithmetic. These children were compared with another group that had histories of consistent success in these subjects. She found that the children with successful backgrounds set their aspirations at a reasonable or realistic level while the failure group set their aspirations with little regard to their previous achievements. Sears inferred that many of the failure group completely ignored reality and were living out of contact with their ability. Apparently these children continuously set higher aspiration levels in an imaginary world, where the mere gesture of setting high goals was accepted as achievement instead of real success.

The establishment of aspiration levels seems to be affected by the social setting. Children seem to express aspiration levels that conform to some extent with the group mean. According to Hilgard, Sait, and Margaret (1940), "One with a good score does not wish to brag, and so asserts that it was a matter of good luck and next time the score will be lower. Similarly, one with a low score does not wish to admit that he is a deviate, attributes the low score to bad luck, and expresses an optimistic estimate" (pp. 419-420).

A very important role of the teacher is helping the student to establish realistic goals. In this way, success and failure can be regulated to some extent. Without guidance, some students select tasks or levels of proficiency inappropriate for their ability. Such indiscriminate goal setting often leads to frustration or, in some cases, habits of selecting tasks that are not challenging. On the basis of previous performances, students' feelings about their abilities, and other factors, the teacher should suggest appropriate aspiration levels (goals). Individual guidance is especially necessary in physical education activities were performance standards vary so widely. In the same class, one boy may well be encouraged to high jump 5 feet and to run a mile in six minutes, while another boy should reasonably be expected to jump only 4 feet and to run a mile in seven and one-half minutes.

For many years, teachers have found that the simple practice of *goal setting* can serve as an important determinant of behavior. Some recent evidence has supported that general notion. Barnett and Stanicek (1979) reported that in archery the practice of goal setting led to higher performance levels than when no performance goals were established. Their results with university students in beginning archery classes support the concept that performance goals serve as potent variables affecting behavior.

Nelson (1978) tested the effect of norms and goals on endurance testing with college men. Three groups, which were given some sort of expected standard, performed better than did a group receiving no such guidelines. A group receiving very high fictional norms performed highest, but their performance was more varied than that of a group receiving realistic norms and another group given a set goal. Nelson concluded that endurance is highly influenced by established goals.

A goal that has been stated or becomes known by others provides an especially strong incentive for the individual. As an example, several years ago, before the beginning of the great popularity of jogging, I recall starting the practice of running around the perimeter of a school in my neighborhood. It so happened that ten times around the school grounds was a near maximum workout and one that I most frequently followed. One day some neighborhood children asked me how many laps I could run, and I replied "ten." From time to time on subsequent days, I noticed the children observing. On one particular day, while running, I felt listless and could not generate the energy or enthusiasm necessary to complete the full ten laps. Consequently, on lap five I made a decision to stop after six laps. While rounding the last turn on lap six one of the children yelled out, "Only four more to go, Mr. Oxendine!" Public knowledge of my "goal" had an immediate effect on my need to meet that standard. Obviously, the only option at that point was to endure the misery and complete the ten laps.

In other situations, people strive to achieve scores that "look" good. Consequently, maximum scores on endurance tests most frequently cluster on round numbers such as 25, 30, 50, etc. For example, if a high school girl is asked to do as many sit-ups as possible, she may get to 38 or 39 and find that she is very tired, but being close to 40, she will force herself to do 40 and then stop. A person will strain very hard to reach a round number such as 50 but will have no strong motivation to go to 51 or 52. Therefore, round numbers often serve as goals in pull-ups, bent arm hangs, breath holding, distance runs, and other physical activities.

SUMMARY

1. Motivation refers to an energized state that directs the organism toward some goal. Such a condition is viewed as crucial for effective learning and performance. Motivation is an internal state that may be initiated by stimuli within the individual or from the surrounding environment.

2. Arousal refers to the general level of alertness on the part of the individual. This term is used in reference to physiological phenomena that place the individual on a continuum from very high excitement to a very subdued or passive state.

3. Anxiety has been used to indicate one's general feeling of stress or apprehension. In today's literature, *state anxiety* refers to a temporary condition of stress, while *trait anxiety* refers to the chronic orientation of the individual toward stress.

4. Activated or aroused states are reflected in (1) physiological changes within the individual, (2) conscious sensations accompanying this excitement, and (3) more activated behavior. Such a state of arousal, depending upon its intensity, may positively influence behavior or may prove detrimental.

5. Motivation may be categorized according to the stimulus or condition that serves as the source of one's arousal. For example, incentive motivation occurs when the reward or prize serves as the primary stimulus for one's activation. Task motivation occurs when the activity itself proves pleasurable and is sought as an end in itself. Achievement motivation refers to the tendency on the part of some persons to strive for mastery or a high level of accomplishment in any task undertaken.

6. Needs and drives serve as the basis for human motivation. Human needs are often categorized into physiological and psychological groups. Unfulfilled needs gives rise to drives. A discussion of the various categories of needs and drives is presented.

7. Effective motivation in school depends upon the skillful management of needs and drives. Effective teachers learn to use incentives to energize behavior on the part of students. As students mature, more inherent motivational techniques can be applied. Further, students learn to delay gratification in order to attain more long-term goals.

8. Emotional arousal results in a complex but predictable series of physiological responses. Depending upon the intensity of the stimulus and the individual's

personality dynamics, this arousal may send a person into a "blind rage" state. On the other hand, a lack of stimulation may result in regression to a quiescent state of lethargy or boredom. A discussion of the physiological concomitants to arousal is presented.

9. Arousal may result from a genuine, life-threatening crisis. On the other hand, a more modest level of excitement or arousal may accompany challenges (or threats) in one's occupational domain, athletic contests, major written examinations in school, or any number of interpersonal encounters. The athletic coach is able to observe and elicit both physiological and psychological behaviors in a way not possible in other school settings.

10. The Yerkes-Dodson Law, the inverted-U hypothesis, and the drive theory are presented as explanations of the effect of arousal on performance. Each of these is sound in terms of a general framework for the potential positive and negative influences that stress may have on behavior. However, all are broad generalizations and lack the specificity needed by the practical teacher or coach.

11. Whereas a very high level of arousal is desirable for optimal performance in gross motor activities involving strength, endurance, and speed, such a condition would interfere with performance in complex skills, fine muscle movements, coordination, steadiness, and general concentration.

12. Implications of the wide range in arousal levels and their effect on performance in motor activities are presented along with suggested optimal levels for several popular sports activities.

13. Motor learning seems best under conditions of mild arousal. Research indicates that conditions of high stress distract the individual when learning a new skill. On the other hand, a condition in which one is not motivated at all leads to mediocre levels of output and effectiveness.

14. Determining the optimal level of arousal is only one of the ingredients needed for effective motivation. The other is to develop effective techniques for raising the level of motivation, or in some cases, lowering that level. Several techniques for intensifying arousal in the school setting are presented. In addition, some techniques for lowering the energy level, or relaxing, are suggested. Included in this discussion are such techniques as use of rewards, competition, verbal communication, music, and biofeedback.

15. Use of goal setting and level of aspiration are widely recognized as appropriate in the school situation. A discussion of these concepts and their implementation is presented.

SELECTED READINGS

CANNON, W. B. *Bodily changes in pain, hunger, fear and rage* (2d ed.). New York: Appleton-Century-Crofts, 1929.

COLE, L. E. and BRUCE, W. F. *Educational psychology.* New York: Harcourt, Brace & World, 1959.

LANDERS, D. M. The arousal-performance relationship revisited. *Research Quarterly for Exercise and Sport,* 1980, **51,** 177-90.

LANDERS, D. M. Arousal, attention, and skilled performance: further considerations. *Quest,* 1982, **33** (2), 271-83.

OGLESLY, C. *Psycho-social aspects of physical education,* basic stuff series I. Reston, Va.: American Alliance for Health, Physical Education, Recreation and Dance, 1981.

SELYE, H. *The stress of life.* New York: McGraw-Hill Book Co., 1956.

SUINN, R. M., ed. *Psychology in sports: methods and applications.* Minneapolis, Minn.: Burgess Publishing Co., 1980.

WOODWORTH, R. S. and SCHLOSBERG, H. *Experimental psychology* (rev. ed.). New York: Holt, Rinehart, and Winston, 1963.

YOUNG, P. T. *Motivation and emotion.* New York: John Wiley and Sons, 1961.

Part IV: Conditions for Learning

9 Practice and Rest Distribution

SCHEDULING WORK PERIODS

The conditions under which a task is presented to an individual are strategic in the learning process. Instructor-controlled practice variables affect both the rate and the thoroughness with which the task is learned. The distribution of practice periods as well as the length and internal makeup of each work session are important factors that the instructor can control. Work schedules should be arranged based on available knowledge concerning attention span, fatigue, inhibition, and general interest.

Efficiency in teaching and learning is to a great extent dependent upon the intelligent scheduling of work periods. For this reason, the arrangement of schedules has always been an important concern of teachers and school administrators. It is acknowledged by authorities that individuals do not learn simply because they "study" or "practice." Thorndike emphasized that "exercise" must take place under favorable conditions in order for effective learning to take place. In addition, our current understanding of the attention span of children and recently developed knowledge about the learning process indicate that some traditional methods in work scheduling are inadequate. Still, in today's schools the assumption often persists that learning is simply a matter of time spent in practice or in study—in other words, the more you practice, the more you learn.

Physical education teachers and athletic coaches have many practical questions about daily, weekly, and yearly schedules of work periods. For example, how long should daily practices be for a high school football team? How can the many skills of field hockey be broken down into short units of practice within a work session for most effective results? In baseball batting practice, is it best to take one round of twelve swings or two rounds of six swings? Should one begin the season with short practices and gradually lengthen them, or with long practices that are later shortened? Should a coach have the team skip days of practice late in the season? Unfortunately, teachers are often guided by nothing more valid than tradition when planning work periods or unit schedules. Athletic coaches seem particularly guilty of arbitrarily scheduling practice sessions with little uniformity in length and structure and with almost no scientific evidence upon which to base their judgments.

Much research has been organized and administered to determine the relative effectiveness of massed and spaced practices. *Massed*, or concentrated, schedules are those having little or no rest (or alternate activity) between the beginning and the completion of practice on the activity. *Spaced*, or distributed, schedules are those in which work periods are spread out or separated by either rest or some activity that is different from the one being practiced.

Research designs

The degree of massing or spacing of work periods is generally expressed in terms relative to alternative schedules. In most experiments, two or more groups are involved, each of which follows a different concentration of practices. A rather typical research design was conducted by Snoddy (1938). His experimental design (illustrated in Figure 9-1) was arranged to determine the relative effectiveness of three practice schedules in the development of skill in mirror tracing. While looking through a mirror, subjects traced a star-shaped path. Performance score on this task was determined by the length of time required to complete the circuit (number of seconds) and accuracy (number of errors).

All groups completed twenty trials in Snoddy's experiment. One group practiced on a massed schedule in which no rest was allowed between trials. A second group followed a relatively massed schedule in which a one-minute rest was allowed between each of the 20 trials. The third group practiced on a distributed schedule in which a 24-hour period elapsed between each of the trials. All groups, therefore, had the same amount of practice. Each group was tested at the end of the experimental period to determine which schedule was most effective for the learning of the skill. Snoddy found that the group having the 24-hour period between trials performed significantly better than did either of the other two groups. Further, the group having a one-minute rest between trials performed better than the group following the massed practice schedule.

Many variations in research designs have been used to solve particular learning problems. Practice schedules most often used are those in which (1) no rest is allowed between practices; (2) a standard rest period is used following each trial; (3) progressively increasing rest periods are administered; and (4) progressively decreasing rests are given. Of course, any number of variations in the relative degree of massing or in the length of practice periods may be arranged. For most studies, the total amount of practice has been held constant for all groups. A second major

FIGURE 9-1.   Snoddy's Design for Three Experimental Groups Following Different Practice Schedules.

Groups	Trials	Test (order of finish)
A	(continuous practice—no rest between trials)	3
B	(one-minute rest between trials)	2
C	(24 hours between trials)	1

variable in practice studies is introduced if different amounts of practice time are assigned to the different groups. This is often done to determine if variations in distribution can offset advantages of a greater amount of practice.

PRACTICE EFFECTS
IN DIFFERENT ENVIRONMENTS

The important problem in scheduling is the determination of the optimum *amount* of practice and the most ideal *spacing* of practice periods for maximum learning. Solutions to this problem vary with different types of skills and at different points in the learning process.

Intervals between work sessions are usually helpful. However, intervals that are too long are probably just as problemsome as intervals that are too short. In cases of long intervals between work sessions, a "warm-up" period is often needed to bring the performer up to the original level of functioning. Welford (1976) points out that brief pauses between work sessions are often as helpful as long periods. Such short periods have some advantage in that the learner does not have to warm up or become reacquainted with the task.

Many questions still exist regarding the most efficient means of scheduling practices for different types of learning. Following is a discussion of some research, theories, generalizations, and implications regarding the topic of practice scheduling. The research is discussed according to the tasks learned, i.e., verbal materials, laboratory motor skills, and meaningful motor skills.

Verbal materials

The first experimental work dealing with practice schedules and learning was reported by Ebbinghaus (1885). He served as his own subject for extensive research with meaningful poetry as well as nonsense syllables, and he concluded that a given unit of material could be learned in less practice time and retained longer when rest periods are taken between study sessions. This first significant effort to deal with temporal relationships served as a beginning for experimental work in all aspects of learning. Ebbinghaus' work with practice schedules stimulated others to test his findings.

Lyon (1931) had subjects memorize meaningful materials on two practice schedules. One group learned a short section each day while a second group practiced continually until they had learned all the material. The short-section-per-day group retained the material much longer. On the basis of his study, Lyon suggested that: (1) progressively increasing rest periods should be used, and (2) the optimum learning schedule varies with different individuals and different tasks. Hahn and Thorndike (1914) used elementary school children in an arithmetic experiment that lasted for 90 minutes of practice. Most effective work periods varied from 10 to 22½ minutes depending on the grade level. In working with meaningful material, Jost (1897) found that two readings every day for twelve days was far more effective than eight readings a day for three days. English, Welborn, and Killian (1934) showed that fewer readings were required to learn poetry and prose when the readings were distributed.

Pyle (1919) compared results from practice periods of 15, 30, 45, and 60 minutes as subjects took part in a card-distributing experiment. For economy in learning, he found that the 30-minute work period was most effective. He suggested that the 15-minute period was too short for this type of learning, while the 45-minute periods were too long. For the longer periods, very little gain was made after 30 minutes. He presumed this decline in efficiency was due to fatigue.

The suggestion that fatigue interferes with learning has frequently been made. Pyle's study, however, seemed to indicate that practices that are too short are not desirable, and that, possibly, it takes some time for the person to warm up to the activity. Reed (1924) also varied the length of the practice period from 10 minutes to 60 minutes. He found that addition of two-place numbers was learned more quickly in 20-minute periods than in shorter or longer practice periods. Perkins (1941) used different sized blocks of nonsense syllables and varying time intervals. She reported that the length of the work period was much more important than the length of the interval. After conducting extensive research with rote learning, Hovland (1940) concluded that distributed practices are most effective because less interference is developed with such practices. In a study of meaningful physics material in a classroom setting, Leith, Biran, and Opollot (1970) reported a distinct disadvantage when using spaced practices rather than massed practices.

After an extensive literature review, Travers (1977) concluded, "Information distributed over time is more efficiently learned than information learned in a concentrated session. Even an interval between trials as short as a minute may facilitate learning" (p. 297). He insists that the advantage of distributed practices holds true in the classroom as well as in the laboratory.

A few researchers have reported some disadvantages in distributed practices under certain circumstances. After experimenting with subjects in learning finger mazes, Cook and Hilgard (1949) concluded that easy skills could best be learned with massed trials, whereas difficult tasks could best be learned with spaced practices. Rubin-Rabson (1940) found no difference in the effectiveness of massed and distributed practices when subjects were memorizing piano music. Eaton (1937) reported that the nature of the interpolated activity between work periods was strategic in determining the value of the interim periods. After working with various types of verbal material, he concluded that the greater the amount of concentration demanded by the interpolated activity, the greater would be the interference with the regular learning material. Franklin and Brozek (1947) suggested that the most advantageous schedule depends upon the individual, the difficulty of the task, and the stage of learning.

Laboratory motor skills

A great deal of research regarding practice distribution has involved novel motor tasks. Experimental psychologists have conducted studies with these skills to establish principles for learning in general. A more complete rationale for the use of these activities was presented in chapter two. Snoddy developed a mirror-tracing instrument and used it in several early studies of practice and rest. In one study (1935), he had five groups of university students learn the motor skill, each on a different practice schedule. On the basis of his findings, he suggested that there are two processes in mental growth, and, further, that these processes are directly opposed to each other. These two opposed growth processes were called primary and secondary. Primary growth takes place early and is stable. It is the foundation for secondary growth. Secondary growth comes later and is less stable. The stability of secondary growth is greatly dependent upon the adequacy of primary growth. Snoddy further stated that early growth is enhanced by distributed practices while later growth occurs best when practices are massed. Rest intervals tend to have opposite effects on primary and secondary learning. Snoddy's theory, therefore, advocates spaced practices in the early stages of learning and massed practices later. Lorge (1930) had college students learn mirror tracing as well as verbal tasks involving nonsense syllables, code work, and mirror reading. He found that for each type of task, a 24-hour interval between practice trials was more effective than was a continuous schedule or one with a one-minute rest interval.

In a study of young women training to be teaching nuns, Massey (1957) had subjects learn mirror tracing according to three different practice schedules. The variables of diet, rest, and daily routine were controlled to a great extent. Practice schedules used were (1) daily (Monday through Friday), (2) three times per week, and (3) an *adapted additive* pattern, which starts with massed practices and continues with progressively longer rest periods. Each practice period was held constant for all groups. All groups practiced (on their respective schedules) for a five-week period. It was shown that groups with greater massed practices at the beginning exhibited greater initial learning. In later practices, the Monday through Friday group reached a higher level of performance. The higher level of performance for this group, however, was not in proportion to their greater number of practices. The more distributed practices were far more efficient in terms of time spent in practice.

In a 1965 study, I had college students practice mirror tracing on three different schedules. The length of each succeeding practice period increased progressively for one group. Another group practiced on a schedule in which each succeeding practice became shorter. The third group used constant units of practice throughout the learning period. During the experimental period, all groups completed the same amount of practice. At the end of the learning period, the group using constant units of practice performed best, followed in order by the increasing practice group and the decreasing practice group. A retention test administered four weeks after the final practice revealed that the groups remained in the same relative positions.

In a study by Harmon and Oxendine (1961), three groups of junior high school boys had different *amounts* of practice while developing mirror-tracing skill. Each group practiced two times a week for five weeks. Only the length of the practice period varied. One group had 2 trials on each practice day, while a second group had 5 trials and a third 8 trials. At the conclusion of the experimental period, therefore, one group had completed 20 trials, another group 50 trials, and the third group 80 trials. The authors reported that during the early stages of the experiment, the groups using relatively long practices showed advantages over the groups using shorter practices; i.e., the 8-trial group performed best, followed by the 5-trial group and the 2-trial group respectively. After the early stages of learning, however, the groups seemed to learn equally fast despite the differences in amount of practice.

Humphrey (1936) reported that during the early periods of learning, greater increments took place between practice periods than between trials within the same practice. He found, also, that after a substantial degree of skill had been developed, greater improvement took place during the work period. I reported this same phenomenon in both 1961 and 1965. In the 1965 study involving mirror tracing, I stated, "During the early stages of the experiment, greatest gains took place between the last practice of one day and the first circuit of the following day . . . whereas the average increment per circuit within the first practice day is 58 percent, the between-days increment is 68 percent. During the second day, the per circuit increase is 8 percent, compared with a 14 percent increment following the second day of practice. The per circuit increment on the third day is 2 percent, compared to 7 percent following the third day. Late in the learning period an opposite reaction seemed to take place" (p. 313). This appears to support Snoddy's recommendation of early spaced practices followed by later massed practices.

Kimble has conducted extensive research with the pursuit rotor to determine optimum spacing of practices. In one study (1949), he reported that learning took place during the first five minutes of practice. After that, all gains occurred during the rest period, and all decrements occurred during practice. Duncan (1951) had college women develop skill with the pursuit rotor. He used two groups in an experiment that lasted 20 minutes for each subject. Each group worked five minutes, had a ten-minute rest, then worked five more minutes. During the five-minute work period, one group practiced continually while the other group worked ten seconds and rested 20 second. The latter group, therefore, had only one-third as much practice as the former group. The group that took the 20-second rest, however, still was superior to the continuous practice group in the prerest and postrest sessions.

Meaningful motor activities
and sports skills

Several researchers have used meaningful motor tasks in the search for information regarding the most desirable distribution of practice. The advantage of research with meaningful tasks is that results are more clearly applicable to other gross motor skills offered in the school program. There are certain disadvantages, however, in exercising experimental control. In one study, Harmon and Miller

(1950) had four groups of inexperienced college women practice the skill of billiards. One group practiced daily, another group one time a week, the third group three times a week, and the fourth group used an additive pattern (rest periods getting progressively longer). New set shots were added at each practice while one shot was held constant throughout. The additive pattern proved more efficient than either of the other plans. Harmon and Miller concluded that relative massing was desirable during the early stages of learning, but later practices should be more distributed. Lawrence (1949) did a retention check on the same subjects one year later. Based on the 60 percent of original subjects who took part in his study, Lawrence found that after a 12-month period, the additive-pattern group retained a significantly higher level of skill than the other groups.

A novel basketball skill was used in an experiment reported by Singer (1965). In this task, college men were required to stand behind the free-throw line and attempt to bounce the ball off the floor and into the basket. Three groups had a total of 80 practice shots plus 20 shots on the test. One group practiced the 80 shots consecutively; a second group had a five-minute rest following each 20 shots; and a third group had a 24-hour rest between each of the 20-shot practices. Singer reported that the most distributed practice group (24 hours between 20-shot practices) did best on a test that was administered at the conclusion of practice. However, this group performed poorest in a retention test that was administered one month later.

Selected fundamental basketball skills were used in a study by Wagner (1962) to determine the effect of three different lengths of practice periods on learning. The skills were field goal shooting, speed dribbling, free-throw accuracy shooting, and wall volleying. He reported that the longer-practicing group exhibited early proficiency at a higher level than the shorter-practicing groups. After the initial practices, however, the shorter-practicing groups appeared to learn just as much. More consistent performances were evident among the longer-practicing groups.

Breeding (1958) conducted a study to determine whether women's archery classes held on Monday, Wednesday, and Friday for 40 minutes would improve the archery achievement of beginners to a greater or lesser extent than would classes conducted on Tuesday and Thursday for 60 minutes. The participants were 70 freshmen and sophomore women. The final test to measure archery achievement was three rounds shot from a distance of 40 yards. The difference between the mean improvement of the two groups was not statistically significant. It was concluded that one method of spacing the archery practices, as set up within the limits of the study, was as effective as the other method in teaching beginners.

In an early study, Lashley (1915) experimented with archery target shooting. During the early learning period, he found no distinction in performance whether practices were massed or distributed. During the second half of the experiment, however, better results were obtained when practice periods were spaced. Lashley's results were somewhat different from those of Young (1954), who had students practice archery and badminton on two-day-a-week and four-day-a-week schedules. The four-day-a-week schedule proved more effective for learning archery while the two-day-a-week schedule was more effective for badminton. It should be noted, however, that even a four-day-a-week schedule is relatively spaced.

In other studies, Murphy (1916) found practices on three days a week to be more effective than practices on five days a week when learning to throw the javelin; Webster (1940) reported that shorter, more frequent practice periods were most effective in learning bowling; Pyle (1915) found distributed practice far superior to massed practice when learning the skill of typewriting; and Knapp and Dixon (1950) reported similar results in favor of distributed practices in working with the skill of juggling.

ISSUES REGARDING WORK
AND REST DISTRIBUTION

The learning-performance question

On the basis of extensive research from the late 19th century through the 1950s, it has been widely reported that spaced practices offer distinct advantages over massed practices in the learning of skills. However, in recent years, several researchers and authors (Stelmach, 1969; Whitley, 1970; Schmidt, 1975; Singer, 1980; and Magill, 1981) have suggested that such advantages are temporary. That is, the differential effects of spaced practices are limited to immediate *performance* and do not affect *learning* in the long run. Observation is made that most research has reported immediate practice effects and has not included any long-term training results. In addition, Epstein (1949) and Adams (1952) showed that long-term effects were more similar than were the immediate practice scores. Nevertheless, their follow-up scores still showed the distributed practice groups to be somewhat better than the massed practice groups. The "closing of the gap" between the two types of practice groups led some authors to conclude that once the fatigue or boredom has passed, the scores should be equivalent for the different groups.

A study by Godwin and Schmidt (1971) can be used to illustrate the concept that practice under fatigued conditions has a more differential effect upon immediate performance than on more permanent learning. Figure 9-2 illustrates the results of their study in which the performance of a group of fatigued college women is compared with that of a nonfatigued group. A "sigma" task, requiring subjects to rotate a lever for speed and accuracy, was employed. As can be observed in Figure 9-2, the nonfatigued group (NF) performed substantially better than the fatigued group (F) during day one (the first 20 trials). However, three days later (trials 21 through 30), when neither group was fatigued, the differences between the groups were not as great. The authors pointed out that fatigue was a greater performance variable than a learning variable. Several other studies have yielded similar results, i.e., the differences between fatigued and/or massed practice groups are reduced after a rest period. Some argue that massed and distributed practice have *no* differential learning effects. For example, Stelmach has concluded,

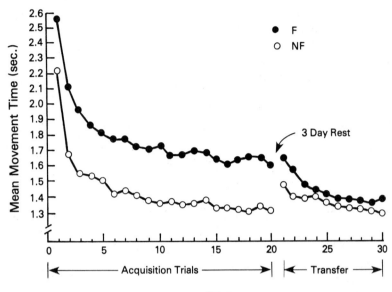

FIGURE 9-2. Mean Movement Times for Groups F (fatigued) and NF (non-fatigued) Over Two Days of Practice (From M. A. Godwin and R. M. Schmidt, "Muscular Fatigue and Learning a Discrete Motor Skill," *Research Quarterly,* 42, 1971, p. 379. American Alliance for Health, Physical Education, Recreation and Dance, Reston, Va. Used by permission.)

". . . the learning of a motor task is a function of the number of trials and is independent of conditions of practice distribution."

Perusal of the recent research clearly indicates that massed practices tend to depress performance levels more severely than learning. That is, during the latter stages of a massed practice, the performance of the individual appears to be poorer than the actual state of comprehension or the true learning of the task. However, I am persuaded that there remains a distinct *learning* advantage to the proper type of distributed practice. The study reported by Kimble and Shatel (1952) is offered as one of the most convincing cases (see Figure 9-3). In this study, two groups of college students practiced the pursuit rotor for fifteen 50-second trials each day for ten days. Consequently, a substantial amount of learning was acquired. The distributed practice group had 65-70 seconds between each trial while the massed group had 5-10 seconds. As can be noted, through the first three days the groups performed similarly on the first few trials but differed substantially in later trials. Beginning with day four, the initial trials are also clearly different, although not so great as the *performance* differences in later trials. Further, the differences become greater as the groups proceed toward day ten in the experiment. If only performance differences (and not learning) were observed, the beginning scores for each day would be nearly equal.

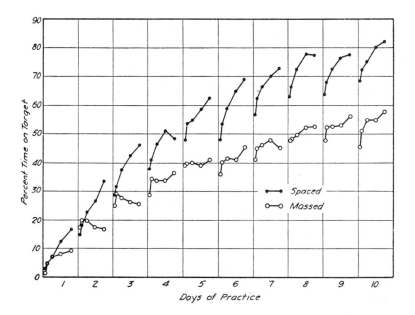

FIGURE 9-3. *Massed and Spaced Practice on a Pursuit Rotor Task* Curves are smoothed within each day except for the first, second, and last trials of each day, which are shown as recorded. (From Kimble and Shatel, 1952.)

In the Kimble and Shatel study, it is significant that a great deal of learning took place over the ten-day period. Consequently, there was ample opportunity for a difference between the groups to emerge. A more recent study by Austin (1975) took place over a six-week period and involved elementary school girls in a throwing task. The distributed practice group had ten trials on each school day as compared with 50 trials on one day per week for the massed practice group and no trials for a control group. Austin found a clear advantage for the distributed practice group, reporting that this group "... evidenced a continuous linear trend during the six-week experiment session while the massed and control groups had no such learning trend" (p. 27). Many other studies, including several of those used to support the argument claiming no difference in learning scores, were completed in one session.

In sports or other meaningful motor skills, one might suspect that the amount of learning is more closely related to performance level than it is in the case of certain laboratory skills. For example, in the practice of the pursuit rotor, one may be performing at the 50 percent time-on-target level while at the same time gaining a level of understanding that will aid in subsequent performance at a higher standard. Essentially, the individual is performing the *same* skill, whether at the 30 percent, 50 percent, or 70 percent level of efficiency. On the other hand, for the typical sports skill, one is required to make *different* motor responses as improvement or learning occurs. In learning a springboard dive or a cartwheel, it can be

271

noticed that performance in the latter stages is progressively more advanced than performance during the early stages. Therefore, performing poorly or at a lower level does not prepare one for performing the responses required at a more advanced level, at least not as well as does actually performing at that higher level. Continuous performance at an elementary level does not prepare an individual to make the subtle progressions essential for performing at a more advanced level of that task. Consequently, in the practical setting, those practice factors that contribute to a depression in performance are also likely to inhibit learning.

Limitations of distributed practices

Short work sessions do not seem to be most advantageous in all situations. Woodworth and Schlosberg (1963) suggest that the advisability of spacing versus massing depends upon (1) the type of skill, and (2) the length of the interval between practices. They present evidence to support the contention that *short lessons* or tasks are best learned in one long practice rather than in several shorter ones. Less forgetting appears to take place if the task can be completed in a short period of time.

Woodworth and Schlosberg also pointed out that widely spaced practices are detrimental to the learning of tasks that demand much exploration to discover the correct response. It is often observed that a brief review or warm-up is valuable in enabling one to get into the swing of the activity. This seeems especially important if the activity is very complex. Numerous research reports show a rapid warm-up effect (improvement) during the first two or three trials of a particular session. (As an example, see Figure 9-2.)

It is possible that massing can aid in the *variability of attack* on a rather unfamiliar problem. If one is taking several trials of a task, there is a tendency to avoid the immediate repetition of an erroneous response. On the other hand, if practices are widely spaced, one is likely to return to a logical but incorrect choice. This is especially true if a fault has been developed in some movement. Table 9-1 presents a summary statement regarding situations that call for either short, frequent trials or longer, less frequent trials.

Generalizations

1. In most circumstances distributed practices are more efficient for performance and learning than are massed practices.

2. Relatively short practices (in time or number of repetitions) promote more efficient learning than do longer practices.

3. Progressively decreasing the concentration of practice periods during the learning period seems advantageous.

4. Proficiency gained over a long period is retained better than proficiency developed within a short period.

5. A high level of motivation enables one to benefit from longer and more concentrated practices than would be possible with a lesser degree of motivation.

TABLE 9-1.   Factors that may influence your choice of massed or distributed
practice organizations.

	Shorter and More Frequent	Longer and Less Frequent
If the task:	is simple, repetitive, boring	is complex
	demands intense concentration	has many elements
		requires warm-up
	is fatiguing	is a new one for the performer
	demands close attention to detail	
If the learner:	is young or immature (unable to sustain activity)	is older or more mature
	has a short attention span	is able to concentrate for long periods of time
	has poor concentration skills	has good ability to focus attention
	fatigues easily	tires quickly

From *Motor Learning*: Basic Stuff Series I, A. Rothstein, Scholar, 1981, p. 40.
American Alliance for Health, Physical Education, Recreation and Dance, Reston,
Va. By permission.

6. Individuals or groups who are more competent in a particular activity can effectively practice that activity for longer periods than can persons or groups who are less competent. Similarly, older children are able to practice longer than younger ones.

7. Short, simple tasks are best learned under conditions of distributed, short practices while longer and more complex material is best learned in relatively longer sessions.

8. In physical education or sports activities, the number of repetitions or trials (shots, throws, dives, etc.) should be considered as the unit of practice rather than the time spent at the work session.

9. Some group or team activities can be practiced for longer periods than individual tasks because of the fewer trials that the person may have, i.e., one often has a rest period between turns in a group activity.

PRACTICE DISTRIBUTION
IN THE SCHOOL PROGRAM

How can the principles of practice distribution be put to use most effectively in the regular school curriculum? Unfortunately, educators have devoted very little attention to the exploration of implications of the research. Nevertheless, the problem of applying distribution principles derived from the research seems to have implications for (1) the daily conduct of classes, (2) unit planning, and (3) year-to-year schedules. Athletic practices and season schedules should also make use of these principles. Rest intervals may therefore refer to minutes, weeks, months, or years.

All teachers must function within the structure of the school day and the school calendar, but even these schedules may be altered to obtain a more effective plan. For example, some school systems now operate on regular six-week to eight-week sessions, followed by a one-week vacation, rather than on the traditional schedule in which vacations are associated only with national holidays. In addition, the length of school days may vary, just as the number and length of recesses or the length of the lunch period may be altered within the school day. These schedules are based largely on what administrators believe to be the most effective learning regimen for their children.

Nevertheless, for the teacher in the classroom, planning must fall within the time allowed for that class. Therefore "ideal" schedules based on very unusual conditions cannot be used. The 24-hour day, the 7-day week, and the 12-month year are not under the auspices of the teacher. Furthermore, in many cases, physical education classes do not meet every day, but follow schedules such as Tuesdays and Thursdays or Mondays, Wednesdays, and Fridays. Athletic teams, however, usually meet for practice on every school day. Within the school's schedule restrictions, there are still ways in which practices may be arranged effectively. Some of these possibilities will be discussed briefly.

Scheduling during the class period

According to Hull's theory of inhibition, students can be expected to develop inhibitions after performing a given task several times. This means that they will become relatively ineffective (temporarily) in learning that particular task. Students may, however, practice different skills with full effectiveness. Inhibition is, therefore, distinguishable from fatigue, which would render the individual incapable of fruitfully practicing anything. Complete rest is not necessary when inhibition occurs, but a frequent change in the task being practiced is useful. According to Belzer and Peters (1972), inhibition may actually subside more rapidly during a different motor activity than during idleness. All major physical education and sports activities have several subtasks that can be practiced to allow variety without changing to a completely different activity.

Welford (1976) suggests that very brief pauses between practice sessions can be as effective as longer ones. This is based on the idea that the perseveration that follows each trial and provides the advantage for distributed practice really lasts only for a short time, and, therefore, would take place during a brief rest period. He speculates that when subjects are able to function at their own pace, they often perform as well with continuous practice because they take short breaks for a few seconds between trials. Consequently, long rest periods during the practice session are probably not essential.

During a unit of basketball, the instructor may attempt to teach dribbling, lay-up shots (with the right and left hand), jump shots, free throws, rebounding, passing (different types), faking, guarding, fast breaking, and many other fundamentals of individual and team play. Some teachers might take a full period to try to do a thorough job in teaching one or two of these skills. Consequently, a rather long practice (especially in number of repetitions) for one or two skills results. On the other hand, the teacher who makes effective use of short, distributed practices would have the students move more rapidly through a greater number of the skills during the class period. This might mean that each player gets only three trials at a particular pivoting maneuver during the early part of the class. However, the teacher might well take the class through more than one "round" of the skills during a single period. It is probably better that the student practice two rounds of five left-handed lay-ups, rather than one round of ten trials of the same shot. The technique of going through the circuit of skills more than once, or covering a greater number of skills during a class period, seems to be an effective use of short and distributed practices.

The practice session in athletics

The distributed techniques described for class periods can be used equally well by athletic coaches in any sport. The football coach who uses team A and team B to run alternate plays against the red shirt team is making more effective use of distributed practice than the coach who has team A work for ten minutes and team B for ten minutes.

In baseball, one skill that needs regular practice for improvement, or even to prevent deterioration, is batting. It is not unusual for a practice session to be arranged so that each player has a total of 15 swings at batting practice pitches. The coach could have each player come up and take the whole of the batting practice at one time. However, this does not appear to make the most effective use of the distribution principle. It is likely that the player who takes 15 swings consecutively will not gain as much from the eleventh to fifteenth swing as from the first to fifth swing. Only part of the reduction in efficiency results from fatigue. Therefore, it seems desirable to break up each player's total swings into two rounds of eight and seven swings, or three rounds of five. A coach may also develop a progressively decreasing work schedule, with batting rounds of seven, five, and three swings. Such decreasing schedules are often used by professional teams just before a game. Sometimes each of the starting players participates in several one-swing rounds just before the end of the batting session. These techniques seem much more effective for the improvement of skill than the system of taking all the swings at one time.

Even in individual sports that require no waiting, distribution in skill practice can still be realized. For example, after all the skills have been introduced in golf, a person may practice the different strokes by using a different club after every five strokes. Or, at the driving range, a participant may "play" holes of different distances by first driving, estimating the distance remaining to the imaginary green, and then selecting a club and attempting to hit the ball the proper distance. Holes of various distances would require the selection of different clubs for the second shot on each hole.

Most athletic teams probably practice too long. It is often obvious to the outside observer that late in the practice period the players are not performing any better than they did a half hour earlier. Fatigue often occurs and learning diminishes. In addition to the cessation of learning, players often lose some enthusiasm for the activity when practices are too long and grueling. It is understandable that motivation would be lessened when improvement no longer seems possible. A decline in performance is even more frustrating. Teachers and coaches need to keep in mind that enthusiasm for the activity is vital to both learning and performance. Additional *physical conditioning* is frequently needed even after learning has substantially slowed. A different activity, often more suitable for conditioning, can be selected. The alternate activity, which can be a fun game or drill, tends to eliminate the negative impressions that often become associated with the original sport when longer and more frustrating practices are used.

During a practice session, substantial gains in learning and performance may occur. On the other hand, as fatigue and/or inhibition develops, improvement may slow down or stop completely while practice continues. Even after improvement ceases, one may believe that there is no harm in continuing to practice because some degree of learning might take place. Also, performers may need the additional conditioning that could result from such practice, or perhaps the experience of participation while fatigued—a frequent experience during competition.

While striving to maximize learning and conditioning and exposing athletes to the experience of performing while fatigued, the alert coach must be aware of liabilities that develop when practices persist for long periods. One of these is the development of an erroneous movement response that, if allowed to continue, will become habitual and remain a relatively permanent part of the individual's behavior. A second liability is the greater risk of accident or injury when players become tired. Such fatigue hazards are obvious when one is performing intricate gymnastic routines on apparatus. Diminished strength or speed can result in falls and injuries. In many different types of activities, e.g., pitching a baseball, running the hurdles in track, springboard diving, or playing football, basketball, or field hockey, tired athletes get hurt more frequently. A third liability is the probable diminution of enthusiasm on the part of the performers. Even those persons who persist in the activity and give the appearance of continued interest usually experience a reduced level of enthusiasm.

Unit and season scheduling

The technique of spacing or distributing units of learning material can be applied to large segments of material that require weeks or months for completion, as well as to smaller units that are completed within one session. Such larger segments include units of verbal material that are taught in the classroom, specific activity units in physical education, or a playing season in a varsity sport.

In physical education, when classes meet only two or three days a week, segments of material are quite naturally presented in a rather distributed manner. The classes are generally separated by at least one day. In most classroom courses, however, lessons are more concentrated, meeting five consecutive days a week. The five-day-a-week schedule is also followed in most varsity sports. Depending on the activity, however, varsity practices are interspersed with one or two games a week.

Providing distribution during the day by frequently changing the task being practiced makes it necessary to introduce the same tasks on several occasions in order to develop adequate skill. For example, in the discussion of daily basketball practice, it was mentioned that several fundamental skills should be included each day. During the first few days of practice, it seems desirable to spend a *relatively* long period on each skill as it is introduced. On following days, after some degree of success has been attained, a shorter period will be devoted to the specific skill. Other new skills should be introduced on successive days and handled in a similar manner, with relatively long practices immediately after the skill is introduced. In this manner, several activities are included within each class period with the possibility of devoting different amounts of time to each. Group activity, whether in a lead-up drill or the total game, can also be conducted in this manner. One way of achieving distribution is to include game play (with other activities) only for a short period during the class time. Another way is to devote the total class time to the game but to introduce sufficient rest periods for the purpose of instruction, whether in fundamentals or in team strategy.

Many athletic coaches have used techniques that seem to be suggested by the research presented earlier in this chapter. One technique is using longer practices in the beginning of the season and gradually shortening work periods as the season progresses. Football coaches often hold two practices a day during the first two or three weeks of the season and then cut down to one practice a day.

The term *staleness* was used by coaches for several decades to refer to athletes who were no longer performing at their customary level of effectiveness, presumably as a result of a long series of practices or games. Other terms often used with similar connotations are *overtrained, flat,* and *burned out.* Such a condition appears to parallel Hull's description of reactive inhibition. Staleness in athletes is distinctly different from fatigue. Further, it is not simply a reduction in motivation. For example, late in a basketball season a high school basketball team may have a high level of fitness and indeed would score at the top of the scale on a conditioning test. In addition, their level of interest may be very high as they approach important tournament games. Yet the team may still show signs of burn out, performing far below the level of efficiency exhibited earlier in the season. Such a condition is also noted in individual golfers, tennis players, gymnasts, baseball players, and others. As with short-term inhibition (within a single session), the most reasonable cure for the seasonal lull or "slump" is to get away from the activity for a period of time. It is not unusual for one to come back to the activity after such a lay-off and immediately go on a "hot streak." Efforts by well-trained athletes to overcome their poor performance by working harder or training longer usually exacerbate the problem.

Consequently, wise coaches will be alert to signs of reactive inhibition during the season and will take steps to counter such depressed performance. The elimination of practices, use of short sessions, or engaging in alternative activities, such as novelty games, or other techniques to "break the routine" are frequently effective. In view of the high level of conditioning and the small degree of learning involved in many late-season practices, these procedures should probably be used more often.

SUMMARY

1. Efficiency in learning and performing motor skills is, to a considerable extent, dependent upon wise scheduling of work periods. Motivation, warm-up, attention span, fatigue, and "burn out" all play a role in determining the optimal practice arrangements for learners at varying levels of development and for materials of differing complexity.

2. Practice schedules may be organized as massed or distributed work sessions. Massed practices are those with little or no rest or alternative activity between the beginning and the completion of practice. Distributed practices are those in which work periods are separated by either rest or some activity different from the one being practiced. The task of the teacher is to determine the optimal amount of practice and the ideal spacing of practice periods for maximum learning. It is conceivable that optimal arrangements will vary with the type of task and one's stage in the learning process.

3. A majority of research with verbal materials has concluded that information distributed over time is more effectively learned than information presented in a concentrated manner. Even short intervals between trials of a minute or so still facilitate learning. There are, however, some exceptions to this, particularly if the total task is very simple or if it may be learned within one session from start to finish.

4. Studies with motor skills, both novel and meaningful, also conclude that short sessions with some rest periods interspersed are advantageous over longer sessions or massed practices. The advantage of such practices is particularly evident in immediate performance scores but also evident in long-term learning.

5. Distributed practices appear to have a differential effect on learning and performance. Immediate performance is seriously depressed when an exaggerated schedule of massed practice is followed. However, the long-term effect of such practice on learning is not so dramatically shown. Nevertheless, the learning scores are negatively affected. This detrimental effect is particularly important in motor skills where the individual's depressed performance does not enable him to function

at the most advanced levels of the activity. Not being able to perform at increasingly sophisticated levels obviously inhibits one's ability to learn those advanced responses.

6. There is no agreed upon explanation as to why distributed practices are advantageous for performing and learning. The most widely accepted theory is that of reactive inhibition developed by C. L. Hull. Other authors suggest a range of reasons varying from fatigue to maturation.

7. Short and distributed work sessions are not universally advantageous. For example, very short lessons on a small body of material and simple tasks may be best learned in longer sessions. In addition, practices that are too short limit exploration or the variety of approaches sometimes necessary to discover the correct approach to problems. Likewise, a warm-up period is usually essential before the learner can begin to function at a maximum level of efficiency.

8. In the school setting, the principles of schedule arrangements should be taken into account when arranging (1) daily classes or practice sessions in athletics, (2) unit or seasonal schedules, and (3) yearly schedules. Suggestions for such practical applications are presented in the text.

SELECTED READINGS

KIMBLE, G. A., and SHATEL, R. B. The relationship between two kinds of inhibition and the amount of practice. *J. Exp. Psychol.,* 1952, **44**, 355-59.

KNAPP, C. and DIXON, R. Learning to juggle: a study to determine the effect of two different distributions of practice in learning efficiency. *Res. Quart.,* 1950, **21**, 331-36.

MASSEY, M. D. The significance of interpolated time intervals on motor learning. *Res. Quart.,* 1959, **30**, 187-201.

SCHMIDT, R. A. *Motor skills.* New York: Harper and Row, 1975.

SNODDY, G. S. *Evidence for two opposed processes in mental growth.* Lancaster, Pa.: Science Press, 1935.

STELMACH, G. E. Efficiency of motor learning as a function of intertrial rest. *Res. Quart.,* 1969, **40**, 198-202.

TRAVERS, R. M. W. *Essentials of learning* (4th ed.). New York: Macmillan Publishing Co., Inc. 1977.

WOODWORTH, R. S. and SCHLOSBERG, H. *Experimental psychology* (Rev. ed.) New York: Holt, Rinehart and Winston, 1963.

10 Mental Practice

THE MEANING OF MENTAL PRACTICE

Conceptualization and its relation to motor learning is receiving increasing attention from teachers and researchers. Covert rehearsal accompanying the overt practice of a particular skill is a condition that takes advantage of the intelligence of human beings for faster learning, and perhaps better comprehension, of skills. Although the teacher cannot have absolute control over this process, he or she can often stimulate the student's attention to appropriate cognition and create a climate that is likely to maximize learning.

Teachers of physical education and coaches of athletic activities have traditionally viewed practice in terms of the overt or physical performance of the task to be learned. The amount of practice and subsequent learning has generally been assumed to be a function of the period of time the individual participates or the number of repetitions that are completed. This emphasis on active practice or performance has been consistent with John Dewey's philosophy of "learning by doing". At the same time, relatively little attention has been devoted to the mental, or imaginary, practice that may precede, accompany, or follow the performance. Some recent evidence, however, suggests that physical proficiency might be considerably enhanced by mental rehearsal, by observing others perform, or by just thinking about the task.

The term *mental practice* is used to signify the introspective or covert rehearsal that takes place within the individual. Other terms that have occasionally been used in reference to this process are *conceptualization, ideational functioning, introspection,* and *imaginary practice.* Actually, references to mental practice and physical practice are somewhat misleading since they seem to indicate that the individual functions at a purely physical or mental level. The truth is that in the physical performance of a task there is usually some degree of related mental activity, while in mental practice certain neural and muscular responses are evoked. In light of this, the concept of mental practice may perhaps be understood better if it is thought of as sedentary practice.

The emphasis upon overt performance, with a neglect of the associated mental processes, does not take full advantage of man's intellectual abilities. The physical practice technique seems to have been patterned after conditioning experiments with animals. In these experiments, amount of practice was generally based on the number of repetitions or the length of time spent in practice. Although such a trial-and-error approach usually results in learning, it is a rather slow and unpredictable process. Too often, learners seem to go through the motions rather mechanically, without much thought or kinesthetic awareness of the essential movement responses.

Despite the traditional emphasis on overt practice, few teachers would doubt that the learner occasionally thinks through the performance *between* the physical work periods. In fact, these mental activities have occasionally been encouraged by teachers. It is not known at this time just how much of the practice is "physical" and how much is "mental." Neither is it known how much learning results from going through the motions and how much is from related mental activity. It appears that if the mental and physical practices were effectively combined, the tasks might be learned more rapidly and perhaps with greater understanding.

It is now recognized that mental practice or imagery can be used effectively at the highest levels of athletic competition. In an article by Joel Greenberg in *The New York Times* (September 8, 1981), Thomas Tutko, a psychologist at San Jose State University, stated that imagery will be "the single most important factor in the sports world" during the 1980s. He reports that in his "sports psyching" program, athletes "relive" their best performances over and over again until they can revert to top form almost automatically. He relates this to a computer model in which persons "program" themselves to perform in a certain manner.

The general concept of learning without performing was advanced by Professor Harold Hill in Meredith Wilson's popular play, *The Music Man*. When forced to explain his plan for teaching band music to boys and girls of River City, he stated, "I have a revolutionary new method called the Think System where you don't bother with notes . . . it's really very simple—as simple as whistling. No one has to show you how to use your lips in whistling. You only have to think a tune and have it come out clearly." It must be acknowledged, however, that the quality of music created by those band members was not a clear endorsement in favor of mental rehearsal.

The role of conceptualization in motor skills has not been widely investigated by general psychologists. Apparently, this is because the concept of applying mental rehearsal to the performance of motor tasks is not characteristic of the type of learning in which they are most interested, i.e., verbal learning. In addition, it is not possible to actually observe and measure the process (mental practice) as it is taking place. Rather, the process must be *inferred* from subsequent behavior.

Why mental practice?

There are several reasons why teachers of physical education should give serious attention to the systematic use of mental practice in addition to traditional overt performance. Perhaps the most important reason is that the learner may develop proficiency in the skill more quickly, more thoroughly, and possibly with greater retention. Research reports have suggested each of these possibilities.

The intelligence of people should be recognized and brought into use when a task is being taught. Too often it has been assumed that motor learning is a rather automatic process. It is reasonable to expect that human beings do some thinking when they go through the motions of a particular activity. Nevertheless, more specific information regarding types of related mental activity can increase the effectiveness of the intellectualizing process.

Another important reason attention should be devoted to mental practice is that more efficient use might be made of the crowded facilities and limited equipment in many schools today. Large classes make this problem especially important. If the nature of between-trial learning were more clearly understood, more effective use could be made of these periods. When a facility or a piece of equipment is unavailable, or when one is waiting for a turn, the time might be used to promote learning. Some research has shown that a systematic program of mental practice in conjunction with physical rehearsal might result in as much learning as spending the full time in physical practice. Alternating groups of students between physical and mental rehearsal, therefore, might allow more students to take advantage of the facility or equipment for physical practice. Systematic use of both physical and mental practice should prove valuable not only in crowded conditions, but even in nearly ideal class conditions.

It is possible that individual differences in mental and motor abilities might be more adequately met when techniques of mental rehearsal are skillfully used. It has been shown that mental rehearsal is an effective practice for individuals of widely differing intelligence levels. In two separate studies, Start (1960, 1962) found that children of low to average intelligence could make effective use of mental practice. It is essential, however, that the individual *understand* the skill to be rehearsed. Some variation in technique might therefore be necessary with pupils of very low intelligence.

Getting students into the habit of thinking about or analyzing skills in an intellectual, kinesthetic, and mechanical way is a desirable result of the use of mental practice. Most people are not used to rehearsing in this manner. Perhaps greater personal discipline is needed to enable the student to make effective use of the time between performances. For each new skill learned, the individual is likely to gain a greater understanding, which should result in increased retention of the task.

It should be emphasized that mental practice is not proposed as a substitute for, or at the exclusion of, physical performance. Physical practice offers numerous advantages that cannot be matched by conceptualization. In addition to helping one learn the skill, overt practice also tends to promote fitness, comradeship among participants, satisfaction from movement, and enjoyment as a result of participating with and against others. Mental practice cannot achieve these goals very effectively. Nevertheless, the full possibilities of conceptualization must be thoroughly explored because of its learning advantages.

DEVELOPMENTS IN THE STUDY
OF MENTAL PRACTICE

Mental rehearsal has long been practiced to a limited extent in the learning and performance of motor skills. Undoubtedly, athletes have always gone over in their minds ways in which they might improve their performances in a particular activity. Despite such long-term and widespread use, mental practice has not been thoroughly investigated or discussed. This is somewhat surprising in view of the fact that learning in general has become the subject of extensive research and theorizing. One reason for the lack of attention to this topic has been the obvious difficulty of isolating, observing, and controlling the mental activity related to a particular skill. While it is quite easy to control and measure the number of seconds or minutes a person spends actively practicing a skill, or even the number of trials, the related mental processes cannot be easily detected. The degree of concentration or the intensity of mental activity also cannot be accurately measured.

Another reason why mental practice has not been widely investigated has been the popularity of the concept that stresses that learning is reflected in observable *behavior*. Guthrie and Skinner especially emphasized the need for demonstrable behavior in learning. They were not particularly interested in explaining the functioning of the nervous system. Therefore, learning has generally been viewed as the resulting observable and measureable behavior. Such an outlook has not stimulated interest in the informal mental activity related to the task. Study of this mental activity, however, might result in an understanding of the task that would be important in areas other than the specific measurement of learning. The importance of related understanding has generally been minimized.

Gestalt contributions

The concept of mental rehearsal first came into sharp focus with the work of Köhler during the second and third decades of the 20th century. He devoted considerable attention to the matter of *insight* in relation to gestalt psychology. In his experiments with apes, it became apparent that the animals were figuring out answers to problems without always resorting to overt trial and error. Tolman, another learning theorist, indicated that learning often results from *implicit trial-and-error* practice. He believed mental rehearsal to be an important element in all types of learning.

It became a basic assumption of the gestalt psychologists that mental activity, or thinking, is important in the learning of any skill. The concept of insight is essentially the belief that the learner actually figures out the answers to problems. Tolman believed that the individual uses intelligence in problem solving and does not mechanically and automatically make connections. Problem solving is assumed to be a factor in both verbal and motor learning. The emphasis that gestaltists placed on the learner's intelligence and thought would indicate their assumption of mental practice.

Experimental Designs

Studies of mental practice have generally been organized into the following type of experimental design: First, two or more groups are established to learn a new or relatively new skill. One group is then assigned a physical (overt) practice schedule that is followed for a designated period of time. A second group engages in covert practice by *imagining* themselves performing the task, or perhaps reading a detailed description of the correct execution of the daily activity. A third group serves as a control, engaging in neither overt nor covert practice. Additional groups may be assigned a combination of physical and mental practice. The allocated practice time or number of trials is usually the same for all experimental groups.

Table 10-1 presents the daily practice regimen for four experimental groups employed in a study involving accuracy of soccer kicks that I undertook in 1969. One group took part in overt practice only while the other groups followed different combinations of mental and overt trials. This schedule was followed for nine consecutive school days, and a posttest was administered on the day following the last practice. Other experiments have typically extended from one day to four weeks. At the end of the experimental period, groups are tested to determine which type of practice schedule resulted in the greatest amount of learning.

EXPERIMENTAL STUDIES IN MENTAL PRACTICES

Experimental studies relating mental activity to physical performance date back to at least 1890. Wilson (1961) reviewed several of the early studies that make at least peripheral reference to mental or imaginary rehearsal. Most of the earliest studies, however, did not clearly isolate and attempt to control mental rehearsal as opposed

Table 10-1.   Daily Practice Schedules for Groups in the Soccer Kick Experiment

Groups	Daily Units of Practice	Posttest
S-1	12 overt trials (kicks)	
S-2	3 mental and 9 overt trials sequence = M-0-0-0 (repeat 3 times)*	
S-3	6 mental and 6 overt trials sequence = M-0 (repeat 6 times)	
S-4	9 mental and 3 overt trials sequence = M-M-M-0 (repeat 3 times)	

*M refers to a mental trial or an imaginary kick while *0* refers to an overt trial or an actual kick. The order in which the trials were taken is shown.

From J. B. Oxendine, Effect of mental and physical practice on the learning of three motor skills. *Research Quarterly,* 1969, **40**, 763-775. Copyright by the American Alliance for Health, Physical Education, Recreation and Dance, 1900 Association Drive, Reston, VA. 22091. Reprinted with permission.

to overt activity. During the 1930s, Jacobson (1932, 1934) showed in several electrophysiological studies that when subjects imagined their performance of a particular motor response, they reacted by subconsciously flexing muscles that were used in the overt performance of the task. In addition to the slight response in the muscle groups used in physical performance, action was also noted in such areas as the eyelids, tongue, and lips. Jacobson also showed that subjects who were skilled in relaxation techniques were unable to visualize movement activities when in a state of relaxation. As a result of his research with progressive relaxation, he concluded that complete relaxation of the body can take place only when the mind is free from activity.

In a somewhat similar study, Shaw (1938) found that weightlifters exhibited muscular action when they imagined themselves lifting weights. He further reported that greater vividness in imagination, or thoughts of lifting heavier weights, resulted in proportionally greater muscular action.

Recent studies relating to mental practice may be grouped into two categories: (1) those involving novel or unusual tasks, and (2) those in which common skills are used. The novel tasks may be laboratory skills or others that are new to the subjects. The common motor tasks are ones that are relatively familiar to the subjects.

Perhaps the first "mental practice" study was conducted by Sackett (1935). In his experiment, four groups of college women learned a finger-maze skill. One group engaged in overt practice of the task, while three groups took part in various amounts of mental rehearsal. One of the mental rehearsal groups was asked to think through the task once at each practice session. A second group was asked to think through the task three times, and a third group had five such practices. A control group was asked not to think about the activity at all. Sackett reported that the physical practice group learned more than any of the mental practice groups. It was found, however, that the symbolic practice did aid subsequent performances and also promoted retention. Sackett reported that the greater the prescribed mental rehearsal, the greater the learning. However, he concluded that a small amount of mental practice was relatively more beneficial than a large amount.

Perry (1939) reported that some types of tasks were better learned by mental practice than by physical performance. The relative effectiveness of mental and physical practice seemed to vary according to the type of skill. Rubin-Rabson (1941) reported that mental review reduced the amount of keyboard practice needed in the learning of musical scales. In his experiment, mental review proved especially effective in promoting retention. However, he reported that prolonged periods of mental practice before one had actually taken part in the activity were not of great value. After students had gained some experience in the physical performance of the activity, mental rehearsal was much more effective.

Studies involving novel motor tasks.   In W. E. Twinning's (1949) study, 36 college men practiced a ring-tossing task emphasizing accuracy. The subjects, divided into three groups, were tested by throwing 210 rings on the first and twenty-second days. In addition, one group practiced by throwing 70 rings on each day in between the test days. For the same period, a second group was asked mentally to throw the rings for 15 minutes daily, but to refrain from any simulated movements. A third group did not have any type of practice between the test days. Twinning found that the no practice group showed no significant improvement when tested on the final test day. The group with the daily ring-tossing practice showed the greatest improvement. The mental practice group showed significant improvement at the final test but not as much as the regular physical practice group. He concluded that both physical and mental practice aid in learning the ring toss.

A novel paddleball task involving six groups of college men was used in a study by Egstrom (1964). Subjects practiced for ten days, with each group following a different combination of manual drill and conceptualization. He found that the groups that showed the greatest improvement were those following a regular physical practice schedule for the full period and those regularly alternating between mental and physical practice. He also reported that a group that followed a mental practice schedule for the first half of the experiment and then changed to physical practice showed improvement in both phases of the experiment. However, a solid program of conceptualization during the last part of the experiment did not prove beneficial after the first part had been spent in manual practice. He suggested that a technique of alternating between physical and mental practice in regular physical education activities would result in effective learning and would also reduce the pressure in terms of facilities and equipment in today's school programs. He concluded:

> There appear to be some advantages in the use of a method which alternates manual and conceptualizing practice during the learning of a gross motor skill . . . Perhaps the inclusion of a period of manual practice between periods of conceptualizing practice provided reinforcement through additional knowledge of results and heightened sensory impressions which resulted in more meaningful perceptions and subsequent improved performances.
>
> . . . There appeared to be cause for considerable skepticism about the value of conceptualizing practice which was not accompanied by frequent experiences with manual practice (pp. 479-481).[1]

Corbin (1965) had 120 college men practice a novel juggling task that required them to toss and catch a wand by use of two other wands that were held in each hand. The wand being manipulated was not touched by the subjects during the performance. Three groups of subjects practiced for 21 days under conditions of overt practice (30 tries), mental practice (30 imaginary trials), and physical-mental practice (15 overt and 15 imaginary). A fourth group was used as a control. Corbin

---

[1]G. H. Egstrom, "Effects of an Emphasis on Conceptualizing Techniques During Early Learning of a Motor Skill," *Research Quarterly,* **35,** Washington, D.C.: AAHPER, 1964, pp. 479-481. By permission.

found that the schedule of overt practice proved most effective. In addition, the data offered some support for a schedule that combined mental and physical practice. It was reported in this study that the skill level of the subjects was not a factor in determining the most effective technique of practice; i.e., less skillful subjects benefited from mental and physical practice in a manner similar to those who were more proficient. Therefore, he made the recommendation that ". . . the best method of teaching should be found and used regardless of the skill level of the S [subject]" (p. 102).

In Corbin's study, mental practice did not appear to be of value when used as an exclusive practice technique. He suggested that prior experience was needed before mental practice would prove valuable. This conclusion is supported by Trussel (1958), who reported that mental rehearsal was ineffective except in combination with physical practice. Her study involved a ball-juggling task that was new to all her subjects.

I employed the pursuit rotor in a study (1969) that had four groups of seventh-grade boys practice according to different mental and physical schedules. In a design similar to the one illustrated in Table 10-1, one group engaged in overt trials only. A second group had 75 percent overt trials, along with 25 percent covert (mental) trials, i.e., watching the revolving dot on the pursuit rotor while remaining stationary. A third group had 50 percent overt and 50 percent covert trials, while the fourth group had 25 percent overt and 75 percent covert trials. During the two-week training period, which involved ten sessions, all groups improved significantly, with the first three groups showing the greatest gains. That is, the group having only 25 percent overt trials fell behind the others on both the test and retention checks. All other groups improved similarly, leading me to conclude that up to 50 percent of assigned practice time could be devoted to covert practice without detracting from learning effectiveness.

The pursuit rotor was also used by Rawlings et al. (1972) in an experiment involving female subjects. They reported nearly equal learning effects of overt and covert trials in this study, which involved practice over a ten-day period. One group actually performed the task on each of the ten days, while another group mentally rehearsed the task without the apparatus being in view. The control group engaged in neither type of practice. As can be seen in Figure 10-1, the physical and mental practice groups performed similarly after ten days of practice according to their particular schedule, while the control group showed only minimal improvement.

Studies involving popular sports skills.   Several studies have involved meaningful motor tasks, i.e., activities familiar to the subjects. In these studies there are experimental control disadvantages, such as varying degrees of familiarity with the task or the possibility of unauthorized practice during the experimental period. However, the ease of applying such findings to the regular school situation involving gross motor skills is obvious. Perhaps the earliest study of this type was conducted by Vandell, Davis, and Clugston (1943). These researchers had boys from junior high school, senior high school, and college practice the skills of basketball free-throw shooting and dart throwing. Three groups that were equated in motor and

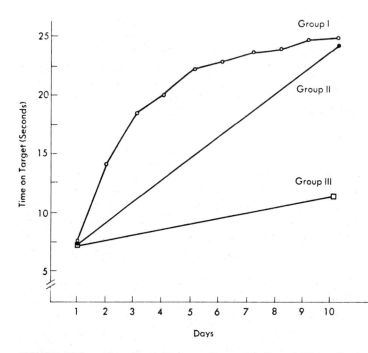

FIGURE 10-1. Mean Total Time on Target for Days 1-10 for Group 1 (physical practice), Group 2 (mental rehearsal), and Group 3 (control) (From E. Rawlings, I. L. Rawlings, S. S. Chem, and M. D. Yilk, 1972.)

mental ability learned the basketball skill. Another three groups, similarly equated, practiced dart throwing.

All subjects were given proficiency tests in free-throw shooting or dart throwing on the first and the twentieth days. However, from the second through the nineteenth days: (1) one group engaged in overt practice each day; (2) another group had 15 minutes of mentally throwing the basketball or darts; and (3) a third group did not take part in either physical or mental practice. At the test given on the twentieth day, the physical and the mental practice groups showed significant improvement over the first day's test scores. The amount of improvement was almost identical for these groups. The no-practice group showed no improvement. Results from the basketball and dart-throwing skills were very similar. The authors concluded that, under the conditions of the experiment, mental practice was practically as effective as physical practice for improvement in performance.

Clark (1960) also used the basketball free throw in a mental rehearsal study. High school boys practiced the one-hand foul shot. Groups were equated into mental and physical practice groups on the basis of intelligence, arm strength, and basketball-playing experience. On the first day, both groups were given instructions followed by 25 practice shots and then 25 shots for score. For each of the next fourteen school days, the physical practice group practiced 5 warm-up shots and 25 shots for score. For the same period, the mental practice group was instructed to imagine shooting five warm-up shots and 25 shots for score. The daily mental practice of this group was preceded by their reading through a work sheet that described the correct execution of the shot. The work sheet was used to enable the boys to focus their attention on the task and to concentrate more effectively.

After the fourteen days of practice, Clark administered a retest to both groups. He found that both the physical practice and the mental practice groups showed highly significant gains in shooting ability. The physical practice group showed only a slight advantage over the mental practice group. This advantage was evident primarily with those who were lowest in skill. All mental practice subjects reported a gain in the ability to visualize, or imagine, shooting techniques. Clark also reported that arm strength seemed to make a difference in shooting performance.

Wilson (1961) investigated the relative effects of mental practice and physical practice in the learning of tennis drives. Her subjects, 75 college women who had recently completed a course in tennis, were divided into a physical practice group, a mental practice group, and a control group. The physical practice group hit tennis balls in the gymnasium daily. The mental practice group engaged in daily imaginary practice in the classroom. This group received coaching cues that were slightly different from day to day. Wilson found that both experimental groups made significant improvement during the practice sessions, while the control group did not improve. The physical practice and the mental practice groups showed approximately the same amount of improvement. In addition, it was reported that highly skilled performers maintained their superiority in each of the groups. Phipps and Morehouse (1969), who studied gymnastics and jumping skills, and Wills (1965), who studied football passing for accuracy, found that mental practice groups excelled over groups not engaging in formal mental rehearsal.

Start (1960) had a group of 35 boys mentally practice the underhand basketball free throw. Although the boys were familiar with basketball in general, they had not previously practiced the particular task. In addition, the investigator reported that unscheduled practice would be impossible during the period of the experiment. After an initial test to determine the general shooting ability among the boys, nine daily mental practice sessions of five minutes each were given. At the end of the experimental period, a final free-throw test was given. The group showed significant improvement at the final test. According to Start, the effect of the initial test and intelligence were effectively controlled. He believed, therefore, that confidence could be placed in the fact that the improvement resulted from the mental practice.

Effect of intelligence and imagery ability on mental practice.   Given the fact that mental practice requires imaginary rehearsal or "thinking," several authors have raised the question of whether one's intelligence, age, imagery ability, or other factors matter in the ability to gain significantly from such practice. Consequently, these factors have been addressed in several studies. In Start's study, reported earlier, subjects were divided into two groups to determine if general intelligence was a factor in the amount of gain that resulted from mental practice. He found that the high intelligence group (I.Q. from 106 to 117) did not gain more in mental rehearsal than did the lower intelligence group (I.Q. from 83 to 105). The ability to improve motor skill through mental rehearsal, therefore, did not seem to be related to intelligence.

In a study involving three separate groups learning the pursuit rotor, a soccer kick for accuracy, and a modified basketball jump shot, I also (1969) found that intelligence scores were not related to one's ability to gain from mental practice. The groups involved seventh-grade boys from three separate Philadelphia public schools. Clark (1960) found that within the normal range of the subjects in his study, intelligence was not a factor in the ability to benefit from mental practice. Similarly findings were reported by Jones (1963).

Several researchers, including Clark (1960), Corbin (1967), Sarborg (1968), and Whitehall (1964) speculated that imagery ability might influence the capacity to gain from mental practice. However, in a study of this concept, Smith (1974) found that college subjects with average visual imagery ability gained more from mental practice than did either the low visual imagers or high visual imagers. Imagery ability was established on the basis of a composite score of both objective and introspective tests. The learning task was a modified Bachman ladder climb. She also reported that long-term retention in the ladder climb is not dependent upon visual imagery ability.

In a review of research on other factors, Smith reported that neither (1) intelligence, (2) sex, (3) age, (4) motor ability, (5) kinesthesis, nor (6) initial skill level were related to the ability to benefit from mental practice.

TECHNIQUES TO PROMOTE
MENTAL PRACTICE

In view of the proven benefits to be derived from the use of mental practice, how can this process be promoted most effectively? How can the track coach get a high jumper to understand the execution of the skill so as to properly conceptualize the task? For effective use of mental practice, it is essential that the learner understand the task and develop skill in conceptualizing its performance.

If mental practice is to be used at all, it is important that a proper technique be used. When a poor method is used, it is likely to be ineffective, and time will be wasted. More important, if an incorrect movement, or a fault, is practiced mentally, this undesired response will be learned. Some thought should therefore be given to *how* mental practice should be used. A starting point in such an investigation is for teachers to consider some of the techniques that have been used by researchers in the past few years.

No one has yet been able to control or measure the exact amount and type of mental activity. As a result, the nature of mental practice is to some extent open to question. Some investigators have gotten subjects' reactions and impressions of mental functioning during periods of practice. Questionnaires or other techniques have been used in an effort to determine how long the subjects could concentrate, what types of suggestions seemed to evoke the most valuable responses, impressions regarding the understanding of the task, and other observations. Such surveys, whether by questionnaire or interview, are limited to the subjective opinions of the learner. Most effective techniques must therefore be determined by analyzing the *results* of different methods used to promote such practice.

Despite the inability to determine scientifically the techniques that stimulate most effective mental activity, a discussion of the different types of programs that have been used should offer some guidance. Two types of mental rehearsal techniques will be discussed: (1) those reported in experimental studies, and (2) the practical techniques that have been observed in informal use.

Experimental techniques

An investigation of the techniques used in experimental studies should provide some useful information on the range of methods that have been used. The effectiveness of the various techniques offers some guidance to the teacher who wishes to promote the use of conceptualization.

In Clark's study (1960), primary emphasis was placed on getting the student to understand the skill before beginning mental practice. Clark believed that comprehension was essential for the skill to be practiced properly. In his basketball free-throw experiment, he set up the following instructional program for those who were to engage in mental practice. First, the student read a printed description of the proper technique. Next, he stepped up to the free-throw line and, as the instructor demonstrated and gave oral instructions, slowly went through the motions of the shot (without the ball). At different sequential positions, the subject was stopped momentarily in an effort to get him to remember all phases of the skill. Clark encouraged the subject to see himself and the instructor in the different bodily positions, and to *feel* the movement with his eyes open and then closed. Next, the subject took 25 shots at the conclusion of which any necessary changes were pointed out. The students later reported that they gained greater confidence through this method of mental practice. They also expressed the belief that this technique enabled them to visualize the skills more effectively and to instantly recognize an incorrect response.

Start's (1960) mental practice sessions involved both instructor-led exercises and individual practices. In the first case, the instructor described in detail the proper technique for shooting a free throw. At the same time he asked the boys to picture themselves performing the skill. Next, they were asked to mentally perform the free throw without an oral description. This was followed by another short instructor-led practice. Students remained seated for the entire session. At subsequent sessions, the instructor would concentrate on certain specific aspects of the performance. In some practices, the students were asked to picture themselves from the time they left the bench in the gymnasium, through the execution of the free throw, and until their return to the bench.

In Wilson's study (1961), which included the learning of tennis strokes, all subjects came to the mental practice session together, and all left at the same time. During the practice period, they were given coaching cues that varied from day to day. They were asked to review the cues on their own and then mentally practice 14 forehand and 14 backhand drives (the same number that the physical practice group was taking). An interesting feature of the study was that the subjects were asked to feel the body going through the stroke, not to picture it, because when a stroke is actually performed, one does not see it. Further, when a poor hit was made, students were asked to analyze it and try to correct it. Eyes could be kept either open or closed during this rehearsal.

In Harby's study (1952), motion pictures were used in an effort to stimulate the desired mental activity. Harby believed that this technique would have the same effect as a demonstration, and that it would extend the period of time that the student could effectively engage in mental practice. In his study, however, the films did not prove particularly valuable in helping subjects to learn the underhand free throw. W. E. Twinning (1949) asked subjects of college age to mentally throw rings for 15 minutes. He reported that they had great difficulty in mentally practicing for this length of time. The college-aged subjects said that they were able to effectively concentrate on this type of activity for only about five minutes. The remainder of the time was usually devoted to trying to figure out new ways of performing the skill or to random mental activity.

After teaching seventh-grade subjects to kick a soccer ball in a novel setting on the first experimental day, I (1969) then instructed them in specific techniques for mental rehearsal. I recited for students the following memorized message:

> Now that you know how to do this skill, I'm going to have you take part in a special kind of practice. Part of the time you will kick the ball just as you did yesterday. Then, at other times, you must *imagine* kicking the ball in exactly the same way. During the imaginary kicks you will go up to the starting place behind the ball and concentrate on making a perfect kick. When you do this, however, you will not be allowed to move.
>
> Your first kick today will be an imaginary kick. When you do this I want you to stand at your starting point behind the ball, pick out the spot on the ball that you should kick, then imagine that you slowly lean forward and take the step with the right foot. The left foot then swings forward and the toe hits the ball right at the spot that you are watching. Kick the ball straight and hard enough so that it will bounce back near the center of the target area. Try to actually *feel* yourself doing this without moving your body. Do you get the idea?
>
> Okay, step up to the starting spot and go through this imaginary practice. As soon as you have finished it, let me know.

On each of the subsequent six practice days the following reminder was given to each of the mental practice groups:

> Today's practice schedule will be exactly like yesterday's. Your first trial will be an imaginary kick. Remember that you are to concentrate as hard as you

can on doing everything right when you kick the ball. *Feel* yourself going through the movements smoothly and kicking the ball in exactly the right spot. When you are ready, step up to the starting spot and take the imaginary kick. Let me know when you have finished this.

Reaction to mental
practice instructions

It is probable that some teachers or coaches hesitate to use formal procedures for mental practice because of the unusual nature of such a process in a practical setting. It is possible that many students would think it strange. With this in mind, I observed students' behavior during mental practice rehearsal, and recorded their responses to questions at the conclusion of the experiment (1969). Common behavioral elements were evidenced whether the students were engaged in the pursuit rotor, the modified soccer kick, or the modified basketball jump shot.

It seemed obvious that formalized mental practice was a new experience for most of the subjects. This was suggested by the quizzical reactions to the initial verbal suggestions, as well as comments made at the conclusion of the experiment. Nevertheless, there was a ready willingness on the part of all subjects to cooperate in this type of experience.

The overt behavior of the students during mental practice could be categorized into three general areas: (1) visual responses, (2) postures assumed, and (3) movements of the body. Perhaps the most diversified behavior was visual response. Many subjects closed their eyes during the mental practice sessions, with some tightly clenching their eyelids as if to increase concentration. Several held one hand over their eyes. The majority of subjects stared in the direction of the apparatus or task to be performed. Some moved their eyes as if simulating a performance, i.e., around and around for the pursuit-rotor performance or following the flight of the ball in an imaginary jump shot or soccer kick. Still others stared at a blank wall or vaguely into the distance.

The posture of most subjects during mental practice indicated a general state of readiness for action. This was particularly true of the soccer kick and jump shot where most leaned forward or leaned on one foot as if ready to jump and shoot or kick the ball. Most students let their arms hang down to their sides, but some grasped their hands behind their backs or put them in their pockets. During mental practices, the entire body was usually tense.

Even though subjects were told that they were not allowed to move during the mental practices, some did engage in seemingly spontaneous movements. These included swaying back and forth, swinging the arms slightly, flinching, or rolling the head around as if watching the pursuit rotor. No gross movements, or anything resembling the overt trial, was permitted. In the jump shot and soccer kick, the length of time consumed for a mental practice was usually the same as that for an overt trial. Three or four subjects, however, required exceptionally long periods for the mental practice.

The personal reaction of each subject to the mental practice was solicited after the last session. Almost all expressed the belief that these practices helped them learn the skill. Some said that it was fun, "like a game." Others reported that it helped a great deal, especially in the beginning, that the task was easier after mental practice, and that they thought about it at times other than at the regular practice session. A few subjects reflected a somewhat negative reaction, such as "They're OK but I liked the 'real' practices better." Almost all negative comments came from subjects who had a predominance of mental practices (75 percent mental and 25 percent overt) during each session. On the basis of observing student behavior during the experiment, as well as talking with them later, I am convinced that the use of a formal system of mental rehearsal is a useful and acceptable technique. The students were more than willing to cooperate consciously in the process. In fact, school attendance for these seventh-grade boys during the two-week experiment was far better than usual. While it was not representative of all ages or grade levels, the response of these seventh-grade boys appears to be fairly typical of the school-age population in general. Therefore, it lends some credence to the belief that the use of systematic mental rehearsal is a viable exercise.

Practical uses
of mental practice

Away from the research laboratories, teachers and coaches often do not take advantage of opportunities to promote mental practice among students. Consequently, skills and habits are often not developed in the use of these rehearsal techniques. Nevertheless, mental practice has been observed, and to a modest extent, advocated by teachers and coaches for many years. Yet, the only aid or prompting for this mental activity has been comments such as "Take your time" or "Don't rush." These comments have been assumed to be valuable aids only in getting the performer to relax. More specific guidance is needed to enable the individual to use mental rehearsal for most effective learning and performance. Since most students do not know *how* to mentally rehearse effectively, coaching in the use of techniques should prove valuable.

It can be observed in many activities that performers do not appear to make deliberate efforts to improve through mental practice. For example, the golfer who fails in the first attempt to blast out of the sand trap often rushes into the second or third shot without thoroughly analyzing the first. If the individual would seek to determine the cause of the initial failure and then mentally rehearse a perfect performance, the second attempt would often be more successful. When this procedure is not followed, however, a particular fault is often repeated several times. The tendency to rush through performances and repeat mistakes can often be observed among bowlers, young baseball pitchers, high jumpers, and many other performers. The use of mental rehearsal, or review, following the performance may provide feed-back that would not otherwise be perceived by the learner.

There are several ways in which the individual might practice mentally for improvement in movement proficiency as well as in game performance. This conceptualization may come in the form of (1) review that immediately precedes, follows, or coincides with the performance; (2) formal or informal rehearsal that takes place between work periods; and (3) decision making that relates to the strategy or other conceptual phases of the activity. The latter may occur *during* the practice or game or *between* these events.

Review techniques.   The learner may be encouraged to mentally review the total performance and attempt to sense kinesthetic and other cues associated with the act. Such a rehearsal should be used to enable the individual to exactly duplicate the perfect performance that has just been imagined. This brief preperformance review is often used by individuals in such diverse activities as gymnastics, bowling, diving, the high jump, and the pole vault. Although such a rehearsal may be used in most motor activities, it seems most easily applied in individual activities of short duration. During this short rehearsal, the performer focuses attention on the task at hand and thinks through the entire routine. This is done so that during the actual performance that follows, the sequence of movements will be most vivid in his mind. Frequently, it can be noticed that the individual who is upset following a failure will proceed with the performance without such a rehearsal.

On some occasions, the learner may attempt to analyze a previous performance and concentrate on avoiding a particular fault or error that has been committed. For example, the diver may realize that in the previous dive he opened out of his tucked position too soon or that his knees were not drawn into the body tightly enough. During the ensuing mental rehearsal period, this individual can review the total performance and make a special effort to avoid duplicating specifical erroneous responses. The high jumper might realize that the trailing leg was held at the wrong angle. In like manner, the basketball player who has missed the first of two free throws can concentrate on making the necessary adjustment on the second one. Not all review must be based on the need to make adjustments, however. Quite often the learner may attempt to duplicate a previous perfect performance.

One famous golf professional *replays* each poorly hit shot; i.e., he takes a second swing at an imaginary ball from the same position. He apparently analyzes the first shot, determines the error, and attempts to correct it or "play it the way it should have been played." This seems to be an effective way of preventing the remembrance of an incorrect swing. The technique used by this golfer is an effort to reorient himself to the proper swing to insure that it will be remembered. Perhaps a similar procedure after a perfect performance would also be desirable as a means of reinforcing the correct response. The technique of mental rehearsal and simulated movement used by this golfer seems to be an excellent procedure that teachers should advocate. Another professional golfer, Billy Casper (1970), encouraged golfers to "picture" the shot prior to addressing the ball. According to him, "You should assess every shot, even the putt, from behind the ball even before you assume your stance... Pause a moment to imagine just how you would like the ball to fly ... once this is all decided you'll be ready for good swing execution."

Some individuals verbally remind themselves to perform correctly *during* the performance of the activity. For example, the golfer may tell herself to take a slow backswing, to keep her eyes on the ball, or to keep her head down during the backswing. The skier sometimes tells himself to shift his weight or to execute other bodily maneuvers while descending the hill. Bowlers sometimes remind themselves of the correct technique during their approach. Other performers, such as the baseball pitcher, the discus thrower, or the free-throw shooter, orally remind themselves to focus their attention on the most important aspects of the performance. Such methods are actually the result of the instructors' frequent and forceful emphasis of particular points and the performers' belief that they will forget these points unless they remind themselves. Of course, it is not essential that one talk to oneself while performing. However, this practice is indicative of accompanying mental activity, which is advantageous to learning and performance.

Teachers can aid the performance of their students by encouraging them to slow down, relax, and review the skill before beginning. This technique should be encouraged in athletic coaching and with students in a regular class. Instructors can be very helpful by developing habits of preperformance rehearsal among learners.

Between-practice mental rehearsal.   Conceptualization between daily practice periods has rarely been emphasized by teachers when they have attempted to develop motor skills among students. However, there is research evidence to support the belief that a planned program of mental rehearsal might effectively supplement physical practice. Occasionally an individual who has experienced little success in rebound tumbling or in shooting a jump shot will return to the activity at a later time and exhibit skill that was seemingly impossible at an earlier practice. The learner often says, "I think I've figured out how to do it," or "I know what I've been doing wrong." The phenomenon of reminiscence (improvement between practice periods) may result from this type of informal practice. Perseveration, or the persistence of imagery after the cessation of practice, is frequently offered as the reason for this improvement. Mental deliberation may be a conscious or a subconscious act. Nevertheless, a planned program, and one in which some specific guidance is offered, seems more likely to result in useful conceptualization than will an informal or unstructured program.

Research seems to suggest homework assignments in which students would conceptualize the tasks that are being overtly practiced in school. In addition to techniques such as mentally performing the task a given number of times or reading a detailed description, the learner may gain a clearer concept of the correct performance by observing outstanding participants in action or by watching a demonstration film. Simulated practice may also be advocated in which the learner stands before a mirror and executes the movement response, whether it is swinging a baseball bat or stepping through a dance routine. When a student develops kinesthetic awareness of the action by watching the skill in a mirror, or possibly by watching an instant film replay, improvement often becomes apparent during the next practice session.

Situational decison making.   The type of mental activity most frequently stressed by athletic coaches has to do with game strategy or rapid decison making during a contest. It is assumed that more intelligent behavior will result if the performer engages in concentrated rehearsal of the various eventualities that might occur in the game. This type of conceptualization might take place during the contest, by replaying the game after its completion, or by planning ahead for the next contest. It is not uncommon for a baseball coach to tell a player, "Assume that every ball will be hit to you and plan ahead so that you'll know what to do with it." This planning ahead is probably the reason some players seem to make "instinctive" responses in certain game situations. Performers who repeatedly make such correct decisions are assumed to have good athletic "sense." It is likely that such individuals simply plan ahead for various possibilities.

Teachers and coaches should devote greater attention to the matter of getting students to make valuable use of the time available during a team activity. There are many ways in which an individual can spend idle moments. For example, between pitches the shortstop in baseball might (1) mentally prepare for any situation that might occur on the next pitch, (2) think about unrelated activities, or (3) simply rest. Coaches should encourage all performers to plan what they will do if certain situations arise during the next play. Assuming that there is a runner on first base, what will the shortstop do if a ground ball is hit hard to his left or slowly straight at him? After considering all the possibilities, he will be able to react more intelligently than if he has been idling away his time. Coaches who encourage this type of mental rehearsal or situational planning will find that their players make fewer mental errors.

The athlete will surprise an opponent more often after having planned for several options. This planning should be based on previous actions and the opponent's responses, as well as the strengths and weaknesses of both. With such planning, the receiver in football might figure out ways in which to run a pass pattern that will be unexpected by the opponent. The pitcher in baseball, the wrestler, the fencer, and the quarterback should think through the available possibilities rather than routinely doing what seems to come naturally. Without considerable reasoning, the individual will usually do the natural and the obvious thing. Teachers should emphasize the habit of thinking ahead. Spot checks and drills can be conducted for this purpose.

Mental rehearsal, or review, should be used at the beginning of a class or practice period more often than it is currently used. Mental review of recently learned skills can save time by reducing the usual amount of routine physical practice. In addition to general class orientation, each particular task should be mentally rehearsed prior to the beginning of performance. After this technique has been developed into a habit, time need not be taken from general class activity for such individual conceptualization. The teacher can be very effective in promoting both general class and individual mental rehearsal sessions.

In mental practice, as in other aspects of learning, a high level of motivation is essential for optimal benefits. There is a strong tendency for individuals to think often about things in which they are interested and to ignore things in which they are uninterested. It is therefore advantageous for teachers to keep interest in the task to be learned at a high level. In addition, they have a responsibility for teaching learners how to conceptualize effectively and to develop the learner's understanding of the importance of mental practice. Because of the relative newness of this topic, many questions regarding mental rehearsal remain unanswered. Research will continue in this area in coming years. Meanwhile, teachers should take advantage of the intelligence of their students by having them use their heads while learning motor skills.

SUMMARY

1. Mental practice refers to introspective or imaginary rehearsal. To mentally practice a motor skill, the individual "thinks through" the task without actually going through the motions.

2. Mental practice has been employed to some extent by athletes from the beginning of sports competition. However, formal analysis of the concept began with the study of insight by gestalt psychologists in the early part of the 20th century. The first studies of mental practice as an isolated factor in motor performance were conducted in the 1930s.

3. Studies have consistently shown that groups engaged in some formal system of mental practice benefit from it almost as much as from overt practice in the learning of motor skills. Learners often report that mental practice aids them in understanding the skill.

4. To be most effective, mental practice should be used in combination with overt practice and not in place of it. There is no evidence to suggest that exclusive use of mental practice proves superior to exclusive use of physical practice.

5. Several studies have reported that the rank beginner does not profit as much from mental practice as does the individual who has some skill in the particular task. Consequently, some experience or acquaintance with a particular motor task is necessary before mental practice can be fully effective. Apparently this is because the inexperienced person is unable to focus concentration on the appropriate movement responses.

6. Mental practice results in below-threshold muscular responses, which usually accompany the overt performance of a particular motor task. These responses, however, are so slight as to be negligible for physical conditioning purposes.

7. Some evidence suggests that mental rehearsal that is rigidly directed by the instructor may prove less effective than rehearsal sessions in which the learner is allowed greater freedom of imagery. After a certain amount of guidance, students apparently need some freedom in organizing their own patterns of conceptualization.

8. Mental practice can be effectively used with students of widely varying age, intelligence, motor ability, and imagery levels. Consequently, within the range

of abilities found in the typical school or college setting, all students should profit from mental practice.

9. Instructions for formal mental practice must be carefully developed with respect to the age and educational level of the learners. Terminology and directions that are difficult for learners to comprehend detract from their concentration on the task. Learners should focus on the kinesthetic sensation of the performance, and not on interpreting the directions of the instructor.

10. Mental practice may be used in several ways with motor skills, including a preview of the task immediately prior to performance, rehearsal between practice sessions, in planning strategy for upcoming performances, and in preparation for various eventualities that could occur in athletic situations.

SELECTED READINGS

CLARK, L. V. The effect of mental practice on the development of a certain motor skill. *Res. Quart.,* 1960, **31,** 560-69.

EGSTROM, G. H. Effects of an emphasis on conceptualizing techniques during early learning of a gross motor skill. *Res Quart.,* 1964, **35,** 472-81.

JACOBSON, E. Electrical measurement of neuromuscular states during mental activities. II. imagination and recollection of various muscular acts. *Amer. J. Physiol.,* 1934, **94,** 22-34.

NIDEFFER, R. M. *The ethics and practice of applied sport psychology.* Ann Arbor, Mich.: Mouvement Publications, 1981.

OXENDINE, J. B. Effect of mental and physical practice on the learning of three motor skills. *Res. Quart.,* 1969, **40,** 755-63.

RICHARDSON, A. Mental practice: a review and discussion, part I. *Res. Quart.,* 1967, **38,** 95-107.

SINGER, R. N. *Motor learning and human performance* (3rd ed.). New York: Macmillan Publishing Co., 1980.

START, K. B. Kinesthesis and mental practice. *Res. Quart.,* 1964, **35,** 316-20.

VANDELL, R. A., DAVIS, R. A., and CLUGSTON, H. A. The function of mental practice and the acquisition of motor skills. *J. Gen. Psychol.,* 1943, **29,** 243-50.

WEINBERG, R. S., The relationship between mental preparation strategies and motor performance: A review and critique. *Quest,* 1982, **33**(2), 195-213.

11 Programming Units for Instruction

INTRODUCTION

Another condition for learning over which the instructor has primary control is the organization of the task or material into units that are most appropriate for acquisition. Learning tasks may be broken into small or large segments and may be related to the whole activity, or each task may be a separate unit in and of itself. The preparation of "programs" for motor activity learning and behavior can promote individual practice as well as self-reliance in motor behavior.

To achieve maximum efficiency in the teaching situation, consideration must be given to the manner in which bodies of material are presented to the learner. An analysis of this topic requires both a study of the way in which the learning units are organized, or programmed, and the size and form of the units. In this chapter the organization of learning material into a context of self-teachable units will be viewed with reference to the development of *programmed* instruction. The selection of units of this material will be discussed in terms of *whole* and *part* concepts.

PROGRAMMED INSTRUCTION IN PHYSICAL EDUCATION

Programmed instruction is essentially a method of organizing material into progressive steps so that it can be easily acquired by the learner. It is simply an attempt to present the material in a logical manner, from the start of practice until the achievement of a designated goal. A program is generally arranged so that the learner can make progress without the constant aid of an instructor. This autoinstruction has generally taken the form of teaching machines or programmed textbooks. The principles upon which programmed instruction is founded were established many years ago. B. F. Skinner credits S. L. Pressey with introducing teaching machines during the 1930s, but in reality it was Skinner who initiated the modern movement in teaching machines and programmed instruction during the 1950s. During the following decade or so, programmed instruction developed to the point that most subject areas from the primary grades to the college level made some use of its techniques.

Pros and cons of programming

There are numerous advantages as well as problems related to the use of programmed instruction in the classroom. The most notable advantage is the flexibility of accommodating individual differences by enabling students to learn independently and at their own rate. Fast learners are not held back by slower children who, in turn, are not overwhelmed by the pace established by other class members. There are even programs for nonreaders, which require the use of buttons or levers. When instruction is programmed, teachers are freed from routine tasks to deal with particular students or problems that need special attention. Since programs require regular intelligible *responses* from the learner, constant attention to the task at hand is assured. In other words, students cannot daydream as easily during the session as they might during teacher-led instruction. Inasmuch as programs are arranged to reward each correct response, a high level of motivation can be developed, at least with many students. In addition, programs do not scold or punish students as many teachers do. It has also been pointed out that well-developed programs, when used in a supplementary manner, tend to compensate for teacher inadequacies.

Despite the obvious advantages of programmed instruction, there are several significant problems related to its use. Some of these have, in fact, prevented the advancement of the programming movement to the level that was anticipated during the early 1960s. One of the more serious complaints concerning programs is that while they are good for promoting minute step-by-step learning, they are usually ineffective in developing broad concepts and students' attitudes or values. Also, several authors have expressed the concern that programmed learning does not require serious thought or creativity on the part of the learner. They maintain that the program developer does all the thinking while the learner merely becomes conditioned to respond in a particular way. Another serious criticism leveled at many programs is that they are developed on the basis of the "least common denominator." That is, in order to accommodate the slowest students in class, the program is started at a very low point and progresses in such small steps that the more able students are slowed down and become bored by such a slow, meticulous process. Theoretically, individual teachers can develop their own programs to meet particular class needs, and teachers in several areas have done this. It has been found, however, that the development of a good program requires a great deal of time and extensive testing. Most teachers do not have the time or the ability to develop useful programs.

Among the other problems associated with programmed instruction is that extensive use of this technique tends to make the school climate impersonal. In certain programs, students can easily look ahead for the answers and "cheat." That is especially apparent when the instructor is removed from the teaching situation and depends too greatly upon the program. However, most of these problems can be minimized when the program is kept in proper perspective and is only one technique used by the teacher.

Consequently, programmed instruction has not proven to be a panacea for instruction, nor is it likely to be in the next few years. The hopes and expectations of many psychologists and educators in the 1960s have not yet been realized. Still, programmed instruction is finding its place in new and different ways. For example, the advancement in computer technology during the past decade has provided an important new dimension to programming. Literally thousands of instructional programs have been written and are available for use with the computer. The potential of computer programming in all subject areas, including movement activity, is unlimited.

Problems in programming physical education

Programming in motor activities has not been extensively developed during recent years. Motor skills are simply more difficult to program than are verbal skills. While most courses have been primarily concerned with the acquisition of verbal concepts, physical education has placed major emphasis on the development of physical skills with secondary emphasis on related knowledge. Of course, the verbal skills associated with physical education, as well as with health and safety education, are as convenient for programming as are other primarily verbal courses. Krause and Barham's (1975) programmed text on biomechanics, Leyshon's (1974) text on anatomy, a series of health and safety programmed texts by the Behavioral Research Laboratories (1966), and Penman's (1964) text on college physical education give evidence of this.

While the knowledge areas of physical education are easily adaptable to programming, efforts to program movement tasks have not been very successful. Effective programming is dependent upon the individual's reception of immediate and accurate feedback regarding appropriate and inappropriate responses. This type of information is difficult to arrange for all the graduated steps in learning skills. This difficulty in providing feedback is probably why general concepts are also not effectively taught by programmed techniques. In complex tasks especially, conscious awareness of body position is not very vivid for the person who is performing a skill for the first time. Some simple motor tasks, however, offer more definite knowledge of results.

An example of a program that involves some motor activity is the set of instructions that one attempts to follow in assembling a piece of equipment or machinery that has been purchased. Detailed instructions for each step, along with checkpoints and illustrations, are usually provided. When parts lock into place or line up so that bolts fit properly or resemble the sequence of illustrations, the individual knows that the verbal instructions have been followed accurately. When mistakes are made in these assembly tasks, the person can revert to an earlier step to check his progress. Unfortunately, the progression steps in such programs are often too great for the unskilled individual.

Despite certain inherent problems, the programming of physical skills has been accomplished, or appears to be feasible, in each of the following situations:

(1) the learning of new motor skills and the improvement of old ones, (2) the notation, or writing, of dance movements and sequences, (3) the development of regular conditioning programs, and (4) the arrangement of remedial activities.

WHOLE AND PART PRESENTATION

For several decades serious attention has been devoted to the study of techniques by which materials may be organized for presentation to the learner. Much of this investigation has centered on the topic of whole versus part learning. Answers have been sought to such questions as the following: Is it more economical to memorize a poem by studying it as a whole or part by part? Can a folk dance be learned more easily if it is presented as a total unit or if it is broken into parts? In teaching the game of soccer to a group for the first time, should skills in dribbling, passing, and kicking for goal be developed first, or should one begin with a game situation?

The term *whole learning* has been used in reference to situations in which the total block of material is seen or studied at once. An example of this in verbal learning is the study of a poem as a unit (reading it from start to finish) until it can be recited in its entirety. In *part learning*, initial attention is devoted to only a portion of the material. In memorizing a poem by this method, a line, a sentence, or verse is studied until it is thoroughly learned before the next segment is studied. After all the parts have been learned, the individual connects them so that the total poem can be recited. In addition to these very different techniques, several variations or combinations of the two methods are used, for example, whole-part and progressive-part techniques. In such plans, whole and part techniques are used alternately in an effort to take advantage of the special values of each.

In motor activities, part learning refers to the plan in which practice is devoted to a particular phase of the task until it is learned quite well before other parts of the overall task are introduced. For example, if one were to learn the tennis serve by the part method, he or she would first practice tossing the ball into the air until this could be done properly. This would be followed by practice on shifting the body weight, then various aspects of the swing. When all the separate parts of the service had been learned, the serve as a unitary response would then be practiced. On the other hand, if the whole learning approach were used with this task, the learner would be made aware of the total act of serving by demonstration, explanation, film, or some other method. The total act of serving would then be practiced from the beginning.

In team games, such as basketball or soccer, the part method emphasizes the early development of proficiency in the separate fundamentals, such as dribbling, passing, and shooting. When the whole method is used, early attention is devoted to acquainting the learner with the total activity or at least with combinations of several parts. It is important to note that the whole method does not simply throw groups of children into an activity without instruction and guidance. Rather, the whole method organizes the material so that the learners are able to view the total activity from the beginning.

The concept of part learning has been most closely related to stimulus-response theories of learning. Within this framework, students have been encouraged to learn one thing at a time and to learn it well. Educational methods have been based traditionally on proceeding from the simple to the complex. Although the part principle has considerable merit, its extreme use has been challenged by cognitive psychologists. These theorists insist that learning is not additive in nature, i.e., knowledge about any given activity or task is not simply knowledge of the sum of the individual parts.

Interpretations of gestalt psychology from its earliest days have led to the belief that learners should become acquainted with the broadest possible view at the earliest moment. Recent gestaltists have urged that unitary wholes be developed first and that parts or skills be refined later. According to this view, stress should be placed on the learner's perception of the interrelationships of the parts of the material to be learned. Current evidence, however, does not suggest that one method should be used exclusively. Rather, each method seems to have merit in different situations.

Whole learning and part learning are relative terms. In the practical setting, it is rare that any teacher adheres to an absolutely whole method, i.e., involving the total activity or game from beginning to end, or conversely, teaching only discrete units entirely. Rather, several of the component parts are joined together into a unitary whole that still does not encompass the total activity. For example, a "three on two" drive in field hockey involves more than a single part, but it is obviously less than the full game. Therefore, while one's approach at a particular time may be *relatively* more whole or more part, it is rarely an absolute adherence to either method.

Factors influencing
the method to be used

There are several factors that determine whether the whole or part method should be used. Under certain conditions, the whole approach may prove most effective, while in other situations the part method seems best. On occasion, they may be equally effective. Some learners, especially those who are highly motivated, seem to learn well in all situations.

One of the most important factors in determining the most effective method is the *learner* himself. More mature learners, those with a longer attention span, are able to comprehend larger units of material than can less mature individuals. Likewise, more intelligent learners can understand larger wholes or relationships among more complex parts. Such individuals are more likely to become bored with continuous repetition of small segments of the task. At the same time, slow learners and those with short attention spans are likely to become bewildered and frustrated with the complexity of some large blocks of material. In their case, smaller units would be advisable. Of course, some activities or bodies of material are so large or so complex that they must be broken down for even the most advanced learners.

The nature of the *material* or task to be learned is also influential in determining the appropriate technique. Most important considerations are the difficulty and length of the material, and whether or not there is a relationship among the parts that gives meaning to the whole. In some situations, there is no particular advantage in attempting to learn all the parts at once. Certain movement skills in sports activities are not very closely related to other aspects of the sport. For example, batting in baseball does not form any logical whole with fielding a ground ball. Therefore, regularly practicing these skills in close proximity does not seem particularly beneficial. On the other hand, movements that follow each other in a logical sequence probably have a relationship to each other. The whole method is therefore advocated for the learning of such sequential activities.

The *instructor* is also important in determining the best method to be used in particular situations. Some teachers seem to be more skillful with one technique or the other. Either method, to be very effective, must be mastered by the instructor. Other considerations in determining the best method to use are (1) the manner in which *practice periods* are distributed, (2) the particular *variation* of the part or whole method used, and (3) the method to be used for *measuring* the amount of material that is learned.

An AAHPERD (1981) publication has presented a synthesis of the literature on this topic. As can be noted in Table 11-1, highly interconnected and simple activities are best acquired through the whole method while independent, discrete, and complex tasks are best learned through the part method. On the other hand, more mature and more highly skilled individuals are able to make faster gains with the whole method.

According to Murray (1979), the advisability of either the whole or part technique is dependent upon the individual learner's "cognitive style." She used a

TABLE 11-1. Factors that influence choice of whole or part practice.

Practice should/can emphasize:		
	Wholes	Parts
If the task:	Has highly dependent (integrated) parts.	Has highly independent parts.
	Is simple.	Is made up of individual skills.
	Is not meaningful in parts.	Is very complex.
	Is made up of simultaneously performed parts.	If limited work on parts or different segments is necessary.
If the learner:	Is able to remember long sequences.	Has a limited memory span.
	Has a long attention span.	Is not able to concentrate for a long period of time.
	Is highly skilled.	Is having difficulty with a particular part.
		Cannot succeed with the whole method.

From *Motor Learning* (Basic Stuff Series I), 1981, p. 38. Copyright by the American Alliance for Health, Physical Education, Recreation and Dance, 1900 Association Drive, Reston, VA. 22091. Reprinted with permission.

modified cognitive map and the lateral eye movement phenomenon to identify learning characteristics. Groups of students organized into holistic or sequential information processors were taught to juggle three tennis balls by either the whole or part method. She found that "holistic" learners acquired the skill best using the whole method while "sequential" learners did better using the part method. Opposing assignments resulted in substantially inferior learning. Murray's results are reported as consistent with those of Lopez (1977) and Hartnett (1974).

Research involving whole and part presentation

Studies that have been organized to determine the relative merits of whole and part teaching techniques have generally been designed in the following manner: (1) one group is designated to practice the total task, or some major part thereof, from the beginning; (2) a second group practices a particular part of the overall task and does not go on to the next part until the first part is well learned; and (3) a third group is sometimes included to practice some combination of the whole and part techniques. At the conclusion of the training period, the groups are compared to determine which technique proved more effective.

Most of the early research in whole and part learning dealt with the memorization of verbal material or the learning of various novel types of physical tasks. In recent years, however, a significant number of studies have involved more common motor activities. Knapp and Dixon (1952) compared the whole method with the part method for developing skill in juggling. Paired groups of college students were used. The group following the whole method learned juggling more rapidly. Cross (1937) used whole methods, minor games, and whole-part methods in teaching basketball to ninth-grade boys. He found advantages for each method, depending on the complexity of the skills to be learned. The simpler skills were learned best by the whole method, while the more complex ones were acquired more quickly with the whole-part method. McGuigan and MacCaslin (1955) found that army trainees learned rifle marksmanship better by means of the whole method. The whole method was superior to the part method for both slow and sustained firing.

Theunissen (1955) compared the whole method to the part method in teaching golf. After ten weeks of instruction according to these methods, the paired groups played eighteen holes of golf. Instruction was continued for six more weeks after which another round of golf was played. The group on the part method proved superior in the first test, but those following the whole method did best on the second test. The whole method also proved best for indoor golf instruction. O'Donnell (1956) showed that college women learned tennis better by the whole method than by either the part or progressive-part methods. It was noted that in final playing ability (as measured by the Dyer test), the whole-method group was significantly better. In specific tests of forehand, backhand, and serving ability, however, the whole-method group was not significantly better. Thomas (1923) found that junior high school boys developed skill in ordinary sports activities when they were placed in a competitive situation faster than when attention was concentrated on the movement patterns of the activities. This seems to support the whole activity concept rather than specific skill practice. Lambert (1951) found that interference resulted when a two-handed manipulatory skill was taught separately with each hand.

Although the bulk of experimental evidence shows some advantage for the whole method, the results have not been unanimous. Niemeyer (1958) taught 336 students to swim, to play volleyball, and to play badminton by whole and part methods. He found that persons who were taught by the whole method learned to swim sooner, faster, farther, and with better form than those who were taught by the part method. In learning to swim by the whole method, arm and leg action, as well as breathing, were developed simultaneously while in the part method these skills were introduced separately. In volleyball, greater improvement was shown by the group that followed the part method, i.e., individual skills (serving, setting up, spiking) were developed before being put together in a game. In badminton, neither method proved superior. On the basis of his study, Niemeyer suggested that (1) the part method is best for the learning of team sports; (2) the whole method is best for individual activities; and (3) dual sports are learned equally well by either method. Although this may be an oversimplification, it does appear to be somewhat consistent with the conclusions presented in Table 11-1. That is, it is probable that team sports such as basketball or field hockey are made up of independent skills and are very complex. At the same time, individual sports such as archery and skating are made up of highly dependent parts that are not meaningful when separated. Still, it would seem unjusitified to assume that all team and individual sports fit into these categories and should consequently be taught by the part or whole method as suggested by Niemeyer. A better strategy would be to analyze each activity in view of the factors presented in Table 11-1.

Naylor and Briggs (1961) investigated the effects of task complexity and organization on the efficiency of whole and part methods. They reported that when tasks were unorganized, part practice was most efficient. However, under conditions of higher organization, the whole method proved most efficient.

In a study of a gymnastic stunt on the horizontal bar, Shay (1934) found that a progressive-part method resulted in greater speed of learning than did the whole method. Peckstein (1917), Reed (1924), and McGeoch (1931) have also reported good results with the progressive-part method for the learning of various types of verbal material. In this technique, the individual first learns one part of the task, then a second part and, at this point, practices both parts together. This procedure is followed until all parts are learned and practiced as a total unit.

ORGANIZING MATERIALS FOR TEACHING

It is important to point out that teachers need not adhere completely to the whole method or to the part method. A good teaching program might well combine both of these concepts to a greater or lesser degree. Recent research seems to indicate, however, that the whole method should be used to a greater extent than it has been in the past. The size of the whole should be given serious study by those who are planning teaching units. The amount of material that can be comprehended will depend largely upon the intelligence of the learners. Research seems to indicate that less intelligent learners should be given smaller wholes than brighter pupils. Some may learn a whole dance routine, while others would need it broken into several "wholes."

In discussing the whole and part concepts in the teaching of tennis, Ragsdale (1950) states:

> It is probably well to begin with a concept of the game as a whole and some preliminary trial in it as a whole. Very soon, however, special practice on part-activities must be begun. As each part is moderately learned, it should be applied in further trial of the game as a whole. This alternation of part and whole practice carries all parts along approximately together and keeps them constantly adapted to the requirements of the total activity. This procedure also assures that no important part is underlearned, that practice is constantly motivated by reference to the whole game, that transition between part-activities is learned as the parts are learned, and that meaning and relationship are preserved and developed at all stages of skill (p. 85).[3]

Whole learning

In whole learning, the separate parts and the integration of these parts into a meaningful unit is established at once. When the part-learning technique is used, extra effort is needed to connect the parts together after they have been learned. A situation in which the individual has learned the parts but not the whole can sometimes be noted in classes where sports skills are tested. I have had students who scored high on tests of individual sports skills, but in subsequent class tournaments in the activity did not rank at the same relatively high position. This is consistent with the gestalt concept, "the whole is more than the sum of the parts." Clearly the game of basketball is more than the sum of its separate skills. Some players are excellent shooters in basketball, but when harassed by opposing players they cannot make routine shots. Dance teachers likewise report that some students are skillful in the various techniques or positions of a particular dance but are mediocre in overall dance performance.

The introduction of a new activity by the whole method is much more complex than just starting with a game. Putting children in an unfamiliar team game would, in fact, not often result in any clear understanding of the total game. The concept of the whole method implies that the learner gains an *understanding* of the whole and the relationship of the parts to the whole. An experienced teacher of soccer knows that to put children immediately into a game without some preparation would result in mass chaos. Little understanding of the real game would take place. For many activities, therefore, alternative measures must be taken. The

[3] By permission of the National Society for the Study of Education.

teacher might discuss the basic purposes and rules of the game along with chalk-board illustrations of positions and movements. Additional activities might include the showing of a film in which soccer is played as a game or taking students to see a soccer game. These techniques would all give the student a general acquaintance with the game and an idea of the necessary skills. The student might then be taken onto the field and walked through some game situations. At this time, emphasis would be placed on position responsibilities and team strategy. Later, the students might move to activities such as full speed games, practicing skills, and lead-up games. This whole-part approach is, therefore, very different from merely rolling out the ball.

In a discussion of the gestalt approach in the teaching of tumbling, Dahlern (1960) encouraged the grouping of tumbling activities into families of similar stunts. According to him, the student should not view each stunt as an isolated entity but should be made to see that rolls, cartwheels, and turns are all activities involving rotation of the body. This big family of activities can be further broken into subfamilies depending upon the type of movement involved. Stands and balances can be grouped because of similar general principles. Using combined tumbling stunts also gives the student a larger perspective of total body movement. Dahlern emphasizes that individual stunts are easier to understand and learn if one sees them as part of a larger whole.

Teaching wholes in sports skills.   From a practical standpoint, a division of the whole may be necessitated when the total material is too long or complex. Just as a poem or play may be broken into stanzas or acts, a complex motor activity may be broken into several wholes. Any individual who is familiar with sports can think of situations where several skills together make a logical sequence. For example, consider the receiver in football who is practicing pass catching. The customary procedure is to have the player take his set position, start on the snap of the ball, run to a given spot, fake, accelerate movement, catch the ball, cradle it in the arms, and sprint for about ten more yards. This sequence involves a number of parts that obviously go together. Practicing the parts separately would not enable the player to run the pass pattern smoothly. Learning to fake well is not of much value unless the individual can move quickly away from the unsteady defender. Learning to catch the ball well and quickly moving into a full gait (with ball properly cradled in arms) involves more than being able to catch the ball and being a fast runner. The total pass pattern, therefore, is a logical whole. There are times when one needs to isolate the separate parts of a whole for specific attention and practice. However, one must guard against devoting too much attention to the separate skills, lest they become disjointed from related skills.

There are many other sports situations in which sequential skills should be practiced together. The baseball player practicing the drag bunt should follow each bunt by taking a few quick steps toward first base. Knowing how to bunt the ball and being able to run fast will not necessarily make one a good drag bunter. The two skills must be put together for the fast getaway that is needed in a game. In like manner, the most effective infield practice for the shortstop involves fielding the ground ball *and* throwing to first or to second base. This makes for a more effective play than does fielding grounders at one time and throwing to the base at another time.

Conversely, one can think of other situations in sports where it is meaningless to try to tie things together into a whole. Sometimes this is done rather artificially with little apparent advantage. The football coach, for example, might have the receivers break from the huddle, go to the line of scrimmage, wait for the signal, and start the play pattern. When the players get set to wait for the signal, the first "whole" has been terminated. The next meaningful sequence starts with the signal. The pass receiver who practices extensive broken-field running after the catch seemingly has no whole-method advantage over the one who stops after a few steps. Broken-field running can be practiced in isolation from pass catching. In trying to determine the advantage of whole or part techniques, therefore, one must determine whether any "connecting" advantage is gained by putting them together.

Novice wrestlers often learn one move at a time, and then unfortunately continue to use moves in isolation. The sit-out, turn-in, switch, wrist roll, and takedown might be learned quite well as separate skills. However, unless the instructor devotes some time to aiding the wrestler in putting these skills into a rapid and smooth sequence, they may be of little value in a wrestling match. Practices should be conducted so that several series of moves can be put together for greater effectiveness. Also, boxers who have a good repertoire of punches will be much more effective if "combinations" are developed. The dancer who learns a particular movement or position without understanding how to get to the next position or movement smoothly will exhibit a disjointed style. In a wide range of activities, from fencing and wrestling to all varieties of dance, greater fluidity and effectiveness are promoted by encouraging learners to practice several skills in sequence.

In addition to possible learning advantages, the whole-game approach, or a modification, might offer motivational advantages. It is obvious that learning to dribble in soccer will interest the learner little unless some relationship can be seen between dribbling skill and success in the total game. Learning to trap the ball without understanding the use of trapping in the game is next to useless. Young children, especially, are interested in early gratification of their efforts. This gratification is most often supplied in an activity that has variety and climax in itself. Modified or lead-up games offer excellent variations from the total game situation. Lead-up games serve as "small wholes" that allow the learner to join several parts without becoming overwhelmed by the total activity, which may be too complex at a given moment in the learning process.

Part and whole-part learning

There are definite limitations in the use of the whole concept in teaching that make strict adherence to this technique inadvisable in several situations. Sometimes the learner cannot effectively comprehend large units of material or the complexity of an activity. In such situations, the learning material can be organized in parts adjusted to the capacity of the individual. Sometimes motivation can best be promoted by the part method because of the more immediate improvement that the learner is often able to observe. For example, students who are exposed only to the whole method for the learning of a complex dance may leave an early learning session with the idea that they really do not know any part of the dance. Such an experience usually leads to a lack of interest on the part of the learner. On the other hand, if some attention is devoted to a particular part of the dance, that phase may be mastered with the result being greater satisfaction.

Part learning is also essential on occasion to enable the learner to improve particular responses. When the whole technique is used exclusively, improper responses, or faults, are likely to be practiced repeatedly. If not isolated for special attention in the early stages, these faults will be well learned and thus more difficult to eliminate at a later time. Coaches who have been especially interested in correct form and technique have traditionally devoted a great deal of attention to the practice of parts.

Combination techniques in which learners are exposed to both whole and part learning, perhaps on an alternating basis, have been used with considerable success. Variations of this method have been described as whole-part, part-whole-part, and progressive-part. The whole-part method has been used in situations in which the students are first introduced to, and begin work on, the total activity and later revert to practice on particular parts. It is assumed that when learners understand the place of the separate skills in the overall activity, practice of the skills will be more meaningful. The whole-part approach is used quite often in teaching beginning swimming. The individual must be taught the overall act of swimming before refinement of arm strokes, kick, breathing, and other parts can effectively take place.

The part-whole-part technique, as generally used, is similar to the whole-part technique except that alternation back and forth occurs more regularly. In using the part-whole-part, teachers or coaches have learners practice the fundamental skills, participate in the overall activity, and then return to practice of the skills. This technique often has advantages over the exclusive practice of specific skills in terms of meaningfulness and motivation. Similarly, the part-whole-part technique is often better than exclusive game play because more specific attention can be directed toward the improvement of weak skills.

The progressive-part method refers to the gradual accumulation and combination of the separate parts of the activity. If this technique were used in basketball, the students would first learn passing and then a second skill, such as dribbling. The two skills would then be combined in an activity requiring the use of both. Now a third skill (such as shooting a lay-up) would be practiced separately. Then the skills would be combined in an activity, such as a weave, which results in a lay-up shot. Similarly, the remaining skills would be learned, one at a time, and connected to previously learned skills.

A traditional and effective way of combining several parts into a whole has been the use of *lead-up* games in sports. In these activities, several fundamental skills are combined to form an interesting game. There are several advantages in the use of lead-up games. Such activities are usually more interesting to the participant than practice of the separate skills. With the enthusiasm engendered in this competitive situation, it is reasonable to expect that greater learning of skills will result. In addition, several of the skills are related or tied together in these activities, much as they are in the regular game. Students are able to see the importance of the separate skills with regard to success in the total activity. Numerous examples of developmental lead-up games are presented in a recent book by Blake and Volpe (1964).

Selecting the best technique

Whether or not the whole or part method should be used with a particular activity depends on many factors. Numerous studies have shown that material that is meaningful is learned more readily than material that is not meaningful. It has been suggested that practicing the total or complex task is preferable when a reasonable degree of success is possible. If the total concept is within the grasp of the learner, the part method, which requires learning the parts *and* putting them together, probably wastes some time. However, if meaning in the overall activity is not apparent, a key part or a simplified whole is desirable. Neither the whole nor the part method is invariably better than the other. The desirable method depends upon the complexity, length, organization, age, intelligence, and motivation of the learner.

The whole method seems best when the amount of learning does not exceed what the learner can comprehend. This method is also better when learners are older, brighter, more highly motivated, and have a background in the task. The whole technique is also favored in late stages of the learning process and when practices are distributed. When the opposite conditions exist, part methods seem best. A combination of the two methods is sometimes most successful. It seems desirable, therefore, that all teachers be able to make effective use of each technique and a combination of the two. An essential of good teaching seems to be flexibility, which is also important in the use of whole and part organization of learning tasks.

SUMMARY

1. Programmed instruction involves the organization of learning materials into self-teachable units for easy learning. Progressive steps are based on a logical presentation of the material from beginning to the achievement of a designated goal. Popular techniques have made use of programmed textbooks, teaching machines, and most recently, computers.

2. Programmed instruction has the advantage of allowing learners to make progress without the constant aid of the instructor. Students learn at their own rate without being held back by slower learners or being rushed along by faster learners.

Consequently, teachers are better able to devote attention to students who have special needs.

3. Although programmed instruction has not proven to be a panacea for schools as had been believed by some researchers in the early 1960s, there are several distinct advantages of this technique, particularly if it is only one of the approaches used and if it is appropriately applied.

4. Programmed instruction has certain problems, including its concentration on minute steps in learning that largely ignore major concepts. In addition, these programs are criticized (1) because of their alleged weakness in developing attitudes and values on the part of the student, (2) their tendency to make the school climate impersonal, and (3) their weakness in developing creativity on the part of students.

5. Programmed instruction with verbal material, including that related to health and physical education, has proven less problemsome than the programming of motor skills. Automated feedback regarding graduated steps in the development of motor skills has not been very successful. A discussion is presented of the programming of new motor skills, dance notation, conditioning programs, and remedial physical activities.

6. Whole and part learning refers to the manner in which the total body of material is presented to the learner. Whole learning refers to situations in which the total block of material is seen or studied at once. In part learning, only a portion of the material is presented. Most motor activities can be taught by either of these techniques.

7. The advisability of following either the whole or the part method is dependent upon the orientation of the learner, the style of the instructor, and the nature of the material. More mature learners are able to comprehend larger units of material than are less mature learners. Instructors differ in their preference and skill in using the whole or the part method.

8. Learning material that involves a strong relationship among its parts (thus giving meaning to the whole), should be presented by the whole-technique strategy when possible. On the other hand, materials that are disjointed or lengthy and difficult may best be taught by breaking them into parts.

9. Complete adherence to a whole or a part method is generally not advisable. Motor activities should be analyzed according to the connectedness of various components when planning a teaching strategy. A combination of whole and part methods is often best, including alternating from one to the other.

SELECTED READINGS

AMERICAN ALLIANCE FOR HEALTH, PHYSICAL EDUCATION, RECREATION AND DANCE. Motor learning (Basic Stuff Series I) A. Rothstein, et al. (consultant), 1981.

CRATTY, B. J. *Movement behavior and motor learning* (3rd ed.). Philadelphia: Lea & Febiger, 1973.

DETERLINE, W. A. *An introduction to programmed instruction.* Englewood Cliffs, N. J.: Prentice-Hall, Inc., 1962.

KRAUSE, J. V. and BARHAM, J. N. *The mechanical foundations of human motion: A programmed text.* St. Louis: The C. V. Mosby Co., 1975.

MARGULIES, S. and EIGEN, L. D., eds. *Applied programmed instruction.* New York: Wiley, 1962.

MORGAN, R. E. and ADAMSON, G. T. *Circuit training.* London: G. Bell, 1957.

MURRAY, M. J., Matching preferred cognitive mode with teaching methodology in learning a novel motor skill. *Res. Quart.,* **50,** 1979, 80-87.

PENMAN, K. A. *Physical education for college students.* St. Louis: Mosby, 1964.

ROYAL CANADIAN AIR FORCE. *VBX Plan for physical fitness.* Ottawa: Roger Duhamel, F.R.S.C., Queen's Printer and Controller of Stationery, 1962.

WOODWORTH, R. S. and SCHLOSBERG, H. *Experimental psychology* (rev. ed.). New York: Holt, Rinehart and Winston, 1963.

Part V: Individual Differences in Learning and Performance

12 Dimensions of Human Differences

INTRODUCTION

When children report to school at the beginning of the year, differences in appearance and behavior are immediately apparent to the teacher. Many other differences, perhaps the most important ones, are not as easily observed. Teachers concerned with motor skills now realize that cognitive factors, personality characteristics, and unobservable motor capacities are equally as important as physical structure and those motor capacity factors that can be easily observed. Individual differences (both obvious and subtle) are influential in the child's learning and performance in all areas of the school curriculum. Of course, certain types of differences are more strategic in some subject areas than in others. To be fully effective, the teacher must understand (1) the nature of the differences among children, and (2) the effect of these differences on the learning and performance of the child in various activities.

In the area of motor skills, children seem to vary a great deal in their capacity to benefit from practice and in their ability to excel in skills. While it is obvious that different children succeed in different physical activities, some seem to excel in a great number of skills. Physical educators have long been interested in determining the particular factors that contribute to differences in motor capacities. Also of interest is the question of whether they can be further developed through practice.

GENERAL RANGE OF HUMAN DIFFERENCES

When one observes a group of young children playing a run-and-tag game, skipping, or bouncing a ball, it is apparent that some of them are more skillful than others. When a new activity is introduced, a few of the children will almost immediately get the idea and exhibit a reasonably high level of proficiency. Other children will work hard at the activity with little success. Still others will have no interest in the game and will pay little attention to instructions. In performance of motor activities, therefore, it soon becomes clear that physical, mental, and personality factors are important. Individuals differ in each of these areas in ways that are important to the learning and performance of motor skills.

Despite the problems that may be presented to the teacher, individual differences prove a distinct asset in our culture. Vocational and avocational pursuits in our society require great diversity of motor and verbal skills. Great variety in interests and backgrounds also proves valuable. Even in sports, different types of strength are required for the many athletic activities (and positions in each) available in the modern school program. Then too, differences among individuals, and the resulting variety in attitudes and activities, add interest and strength to both small and large groups.

Nevertheless, in the school setting, the teacher is faced with an important problem when attempting to meet the needs of the different class members. Success depends upon an understanding of the important differences among pupils and the teacher's resourcefulness in responding to these differences. Even the neophyte teacher can usually pick out gross differences among children but may at the same time have little skill in making program adjustments to meet these differences. However, the effectiveness of the teacher in dealing with pupils' differences will determine how well students reach the direct and related objectives of the programs.

The problem of differences cannot be solved completely by homogeneous grouping, which reduces only the range of the trait that is used as a basis for grouping. Other physical, mental, and social traits may vary widely for such a grouped class. For example, if some test of motor ability were used as a means for grouping in physical education, special sports skills as well as interests in the activities might still cover the total range of the school population. Therefore, the practice of ability grouping, despite certain pedagogical advantages, does not lessen the need for the teacher's attention to differences within the class.

Within the most highly skilled as well as the most poorly skilled groups, differences become readily apparent. Among high school varsity basketball players, for example, some shoot the ball more accurately, pass with greater speed and accuracy, and generally perform better than their teammates. Some boys and girls seem to be "natural" players in certain activities, while others, with great effort and perseverance, manage to perform only adequately. Even on professional athletic teams, some players consistently perform at a high level and become the stars in the league, while others barely make the squad. When observing baseball players, one can see that certain outfielders get the jump on the ball and run a true course to the point where the ball is to be fielded. Others, sometimes with greater running speed, get off to a slower start and often misjudge the flight of the ball.

Teachers have often wondered why some children are much better than others in the performance of certain skills. One might hypothesize that the more proficient children have had more experience. Even with a new activity, however, some children learn more rapidly and perform at a higher level than do others. It seems that some people have a greater innate capacity for learning and performing in certain skills. Upon close observation, it can be detected that the better performers are not always the biggest children or the smallest. Physical size and body build do not always give a reliable clue as to the reason for differences in abilities to learn and perform motor skills. Physical educators have shown some concern in recent years for determining the physiological and psychological components that contribute to differences in motor skills. In addition, they have been interested in establishing whether or not these traits are inherited, to what extent they can be developed, and how they can be measured most effectively.

The Declaration of Independence states that "all men are created equal." It is obvious, however, that this equality is a legal rather than a biological concept. It was clear even before the document was written that not all men were the same height, weight, or had the same shoe size. Experimenters today, with more sophisticated measuring instruments, have discovered countless traits in which human beings differ. Probably the most widely used instruments in American schools during the past decades have been those designed to determine the students' intelligence or special mental abilities. Today, physical educators, as well as specialists in other subject areas, are becoming more interested in determining the basic traits that enable an individual to attain outstanding success in a particular specialty.

Garry (1963) has categorized individual differences into the following areas, each of which might affect school performance to a greater or lesser degree:

1. Physical differences include age, height, weight, sex, vision, hearing, motor ability, and handicaps.
2. Social differences include socioeconomic status, religious and ethnic background, family relationships, and peer group relationships.
3. Personality differences include character traits, motivational needs, interests, attitudes, and affective reactions.
4. Capacity differences refer to general intelligence and a wide variety of special aptitudes.
5. Achievement differences refer to previous accomplishments in in-school and out-of-school activities.

Within any class there are variations among students in each of these components. Teachers in different subject areas are, of course, interested in the traits that are most influential in their particular field. Physical differences, therefore, are of greatest importance to the physical educator. However, the influence of physical and other differences overlaps in several areas. Certainly social and personality components help to determine the child's interest and work habits in certain motor activities. On the other hand, it is obvious that physical components such as vision, hearing, and general state of health can affect the child's achievement in reading. Similarly, general intelligence is a component that seems to influence the individual's performance in a wide range of activities.

Whatever the trait selected, human differences will be distributed in a predictable pattern around an average score. In such a distribution, greater numbers will cluster around the average, with decreasing frequency the farther one varies in either direction. Figure 12-1 presents a bell-shaped, or "normal distribution," curve representing general intelligence scores in the broad population. A similar type of

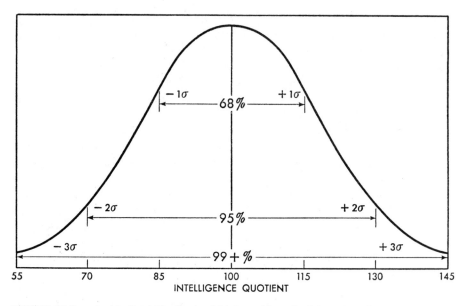

FIGURE 12-1. *An Idealized Distribution of I.Q.s to Show the Percentage of Cases Falling Within Various σ-Ranges.* A small fraction of 1 percent of the population have I.Q.s over 145 and below 55. (From Kimble, 1956.)

distribution could be illustrated for any other trait, be it the ability of fourth-grade girls to throw a tennis ball for distance, the family income of students in the eleventh grade, the visual acuity of 50-year-old men, or the reaction time of first-year dental students. However, absolute symmetry does not always occur in such measures. Skewed or lopsided curves may be caused by many factors. For example, visual acuity scores of any group as determined by the Snellen eye test would show a skewing in the direction of poor vision simply because there is much greater range in that direction. From a "normal" score of 20-20, one might range in the superior direction to 20-10 or slightly better. However, in the inferor or defective direction, scores might range as high as 20-200 or beyond. Still, all group scores tend to concentrate around the mean, usually in a fairly symmetrical manner.

Motor abilities

In Garry's list of physical differences, motor ability has received the greatest attention from physical educators. Unfortunately, an acceptable taxonomy of motor abilities has not yet been developed. In fact, there is no unanimity as to the meaning of the term "general motor ability." However, in recent years the term has been used to describe one's proficiency in a wide variety of rather basic skills and general fitness activities. Clarke (1959), Fleishman (1964), and several other authors have outlined and described the components of motor ability. Clarke's list includes elements that have traditionally been assumed to be important in the performance of *gross motor skills*. This list, which has attained considerable recognition among physical educators, includes the following:

Muscular strength. The maximum force that can be exerted in a single muscular exertion.

Muscular endurance. The ability to continue muscular exertions of a submaximal magnitude.

Cardiovascular endurance. The ability to continue moderate contractions of large muscle groups for a relatively long period of time and requiring adjustments in the cardiorespiratory system.

Speed. The rapidity with which successive movements of the same kind can be made.

Agility. Speed in changing body position or direction.

Balance. Ease in maintaining or controlling body position.

Muscular power. The release of maximal muscular force in the shortest period of time.

Eye-hand coordination. The ability to make precise movements of the hands when vision is used.

Eye-foot coordination. The ability to make precise movements of the feet when vision is used.

Fleishman (1964) identified the following list of *psychomotor ability components* that he believed to be somewhat independent of physical proficiency or fitness factors. These motor abilities were established after extensive factor analysis studies:

Control precision. Fine movement dexterity with the hands or feet.

Multilimb coordination. Simultaneous control of the movements of a number of limbs.

Response orientation. The ability to make rapid and correct movements to different stimuli.

Reaction time. The speed with which the individual is able to respond to a stimulus.

Speed of arm movement. The rapidity with which the person can make a gross discrete movement where accuracy is not required.

Rate control. The ability to make anticipatory adjustments to objects that change speed and direction.

Manual dexterity. Speed of skilled arm-hand movements of relatively large objects.

Finger dexterity. The ability to manipulate small objects that primarily involves use of the fingers.

Arm-hand steadiness. The ability to make finely controlled positioning movements.

Wrist-finger speed. The ability to make rapid movements of the wrist and fingers, such as in tapping.

Aiming. The ability to make rapid controlled movements requiring the touching of targets placed in an irregular order.

In another report, Fleishman, Thomas, and Munroe (1961), analyzed several gross motor abilities, particularly those related to speed, flexibility, balance, and coordination. The following six "primary factors" were identified among these gross motor abilities: (1) speed of change of direction, (2) gross body equilibrium, (3) balance with visual cues, (4) dynamic flexibility, (5) extent flexibility, and (6) speed-of-limb movement.

Cratty (1973) has illustrated the great number of motor ability traits as identified by Fleishman and his colleagues (see Figure 12-2). These traits are organized into large muscle and small muscle groups. The one popular trait not specifically mentioned is that of coordination. However, an analysis of the smaller muscle traits reveals that several of them involve what is popularly referred to as eye-hand coordination.

The "natural athlete"

Research over the past 30 years has refuted the widespread belief that motor ability is a general trait. Rather, it has been determined that people have aptitudes specific to a particular task, not a "general" motor ability. Consequently, general motor ability tests, which were popular in earlier years, have proven to have little validity in determining one's overall capacity or potential in motor skills. As was suggested in chapter one of this book, the concept of the "natural" or "all-around" athlete is a misnomer because it implies that certain individuals are outstanding, or potentially so, in all athletic activities. Research over the past three decades by F. M. Henry, E. A. Fleishman, and others has demonstrated that such is not the case. However, it often appears that one observes natural or all-around ability when watching a group of children or young people in motor activities. This results from the fact that a particular child may be talented in several specific abilities that are especially useful for effective performance in the activities being observed.

Figure 12-3 presents a theoretical picture of the concept of how motor abilities may vary among individuals. Those abilities that are independent of each other will reflect no overlap. High potential for muscular strength is not an indication that arm-hand steadiness will be above average, and one who has low potential in speed of limb movement may actually excel in balance. This lack of overlap holds true to the extent that the factors are *independent* of each other. It must be pointed out that an agreed upon listing of motor abilities that is complete and does not contain overlap among the different factors has not yet been developed. As a rule, the longer the list of such abilities, the more likely there will be overlap, i.e., positive interrelationships. For example, if muscle power were added to the list in Figure 12-3, one could expect some positive correlation with muscular strength, though these factors can be defined as separate entities. A similar relationship might be shown between running speed and agility.

The concept of the natural or all-around athlete is commonplace in the literature as well as in the minds of the general public. This term implies that certain individuals have an innate capacity for excelling in all motor activities, that he or she has outstanding *general* motor ability. Although there is no evidence to support

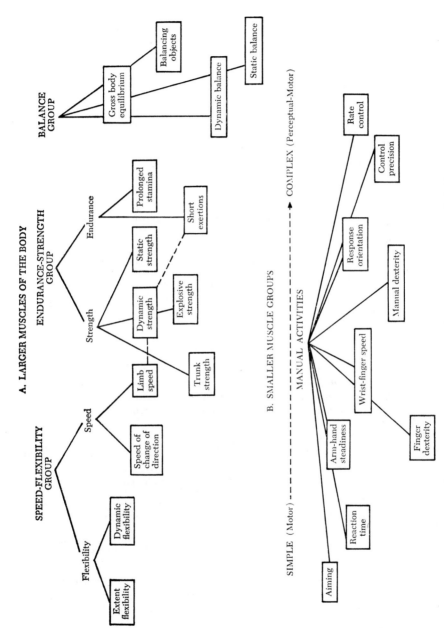

FIGURE 12-2. Motor Ability Traits Identified by Fleishman and Illustrated by Cratty (1973).

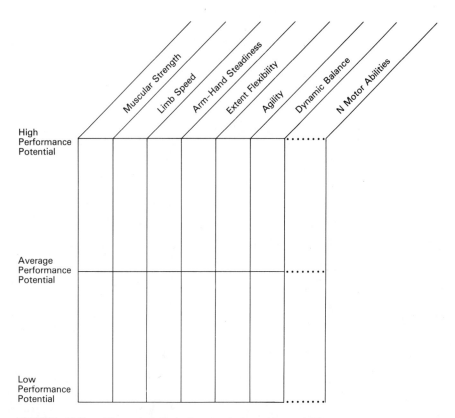

FIGURE 12-3. *Theoretical Basis for the Independence of Motor Abilities* The list of specific components in this chart is only illustrative and is far from complete. Each individual has N number of independent motor components. A high potential in one trait provides no clue as to how that individual will measure up in a second independent trait.

the generality of motor abilities, certain children and adults *appear* to excel in most of the motor activities presented to them. For example, television "superstar" competitions identify athletes who excel in several different sports events. In addition, outstanding decathlon performers exhibit a high level of skill in several different track and field events. It can be noted, however, that among competitors, different performers excel in the different events. That is, the competitors do not fall into the same rank order for all ten events.

There are probably both physical and psychological reasons for this. In the physical realm, the individual may have high potential in the particular traits that underlie effective performance in certain activities. For example, the child who has high performance potential in speed and agility will do well in a host of elementary school activities, such as run-and-tag games, dodge ball, and races. In addition, several major sports activities, such as soccer, field hockey, basketball, football, and track, would be enhanced by these traits. However, high potential in speed and agility is no indication that the same individual will have above average potential in the arm-hand steadiness and precision that aids one in riflery, archery, penmanship, or drawing. Similarly, the child high in speed and agility potential might experience difficulty with the balance beam or walking on the hands (activities strongly dependent upon dynamic balance) or in the ball throw (dependent upon muscular power and coordination).

It must also be pointed out that having high potential in speed and agility is no indication that one will be *low* in other abilities. Clearly, some individuals exhibit high potential in a greater number of all the components than do others. That is, all persons are not equal on the aggregate of motor activities. Those persons who exhibit high potential in the traits that underlie the most popular athletic activities are commonly referred to as natural athletes. However, the argument against the concept of a general trait is that one's potential in an untested motor activity cannot be predicted on the basis of other unrelated skills.

A second factor that contributes to the appearance of a gifted all-around athlete is general psychological orientation. On the basis of previous experience, some persons develop the habit, and the expectation, of success. This psychological orientation plays an important role in actually contributing to such results. In addition, there is a carry-over, or transfer, of certain strategies and methods from one activity to another. These help the individual with modest motor ability in a given area to perform at an above average level.

The argument for the "motor moron" is also erroneous. The fact that one is *below* average in eye-hand coordination provides no assurance that the same individual will be below average in muscular strength or running speed. Evaluative judgments can be made only in areas that have been specifically investigated. It is true, however, that many young people and adults describe themselves as "poor at sports" or having "two left feet." Such an attitude tends to be self-defeating.

In addition to the general motor abilities and psychological orientation just discussed, there are other distinctions among individuals that may cause variations in their achievement in physical activities. The most important of these differences seem to occur in (1) general intelligence, (2) kinesthesis, (3) visual abilities, (4) reaction and movement time, (5) lateral dominance, and (6) anthropometry. These components are somewhat related to both learning and performance in a wide range of motor skills. Because of this relationship and because of the differences among individuals, each will be discussed separately.

INTELLECTUAL DIFFERENCES

The role of general intelligence in motor learning and performance has intrigued the physical educator for many years. Many questions relating to this topic have been investigated and are still being explored. For example, is an intelligent person likely to learn a rather simple motor task, such as shuffleboard, more quickly than a person with less intelligence? Does the same rule apply for a more complex skill, such as an intricate rhythmical drill? Does the learning of a motor skill require the use of one's intellect? Does general intelligence include motor aptitude, or is there a special kind of motor intelligence?

An investigation of these questions first requires an analysis of the topic of general intelligence. Is intelligence inherited, is it developed, or is it a combination of both? Several years ago this was a popular question for debate, research, and general discussion. The nature-nurture controversy has never been completely resolved because of the difficulty of isolating and controlling all the important variables. However, extreme "hereditarians" and "environmentalists" are decreasing in number. Most psychologists today agree that both heredity and environment interact to influence the development of one's intelligence.

What is intelligence?

According to Wrightsman and Sanford (1975), intelligence is the most highly valued psychological attribute in our society. They also conclude that it is the most thoroughly measured and studied of all enduring human traits. Yet there is a lack of consensus as to precisely what it is, and what the factors are that contribute to its development.

Intelligence has been pragmatically defined as that which intelligence tests measure, or the ability to do well on an intelligence test. Although these explanations apparently contain a degree of truth, they do little to clarify the issue. It is extremely difficult to get a consensus among authorities on a clear definition of intelligence. In view of this, Spearman (1923) stated that ". . . this word in its present day usage *does not possess any definite meaning . . .* neither its utterers nor its hearers appear to have behind it any clear idea whatever" (p. 20).

Hebb (1959) has suggested that intelligence has two meanings. A theoretical one, referred to as Intelligence A, is an innate potential to develop and to grow into a given capacity to function appropriately. Secondly, a behavioral definition, referred to as Intelligence B, refers to the demonstrated level of performance or comprehension at a specific time. Intelligence B is that which is observed in various test situations. Generally we can only speculate about Intelligence A, and not even intelligence tests claim to measure it. Elsewhere, intelligence has been described as (1) the ability to adjust to a new situation, (2) the ability to do abstract thinking, (3) that which distinguishes man from lower animals, (4) the ability to think rapidly, (5) the ability to solve problems, and (6) one's manner of behaving in the face of a variety of problems. A synthesis of the many definitions would include most of these qualities.

Wechsler (1944) offers the following definition, which has attained a reasonable degree of acceptance: "Intelligence is the aggregate or global capacity of the individual to act purposefully, to think rationally and to deal effectively with his environment" (p. 3). He points out that intelligence is made up of differential elements or abilities and their *combination*. According to Wechsler, therefore, intelligence is more than the sum of one's special abilities.

Ideas about intelligence have changed considerably during the past century. A great deal of generality has traditionally been assumed to exist among the various abilities of the individual. Stern (1914) advocated this concept of intelligence in his general factor theory, which implied that the person who has outstanding intelligence or ability in one activity or trait will also have outstanding intelligence in all other areas of human ability. All specific abilities (referred to as s) accrue from the general factor (referred to as G). A person is, therefore, equally intelligent in all areas. According to Stern's theory, the more intelligent person learns mathematics, mechanics, music, or spelling better than the person of lesser ability. Uneven abilities or skills are assumed to result from one's environment or one's greater interest and experience in some areas.

The concept of intelligence as a general factor was supported conditionally by Spearman (1927). He described two integers: a general factor g common to all tasks, and a specific factor s peculiar to a particular task. No two people have identical combinations of g or s. The specific factors or abilities were listed as verbal, numerical, mechanical, attention, imagination, and mental speed. Unlike Stern's theory of a large G with perfect intercorrelations among special abilities, Spearman described a small g with the suggestion of a *tendency* toward a correlation among abilities. The individual who was above average in numerical ability was assumed to have above-average ability in mechanics, mental speed, and all other capacities.

Thorndike and Hagen (1927) described intelligence as an accumulation of specific abilities *(S)*. According to this theory, an individual's general intelligence was derived by adding all the S factors, i.e., $S_1 + S_2 + \ldots S_n$. They discussed intelligences rather than intelligence and indicated that there is a special intelligence for each task. They assumed no g factor, and the S abilities were viewed as unrelated. The fact that a person is intelligent in one area is no indication that he or she will be above average in another field. For example, the skilled mechanic may exhibit a very low level of skill when thrust into a group leadership role. The politician may experience similar failure when presented with a mechanical problem. On the other hand, there is no assurance that the relationship will be a negative one.

In a view similar to that of Thorndike and Hagen, Thurstone (1938) believed general intelligence to be made up of seven "primary mental abilities." His theory is similar to the one proposed by Thorndike. Thurstone, however, assumed some correlation to exist among certain of the abilities. The primary abilities were listed as (1) numbers, (2) word fluency, (3) verbal meaning, (4) memory, (5) reasoning, or ability to solve problems, (6) space, and (7) perceptual speed. The last two abilities listed seem especially important in the learning and performance of motor skills. Although the question of intelligence is not yet settled, the most popular ideas on this topic do not appear to differ greatly from Thurstone's theory.

Though most intelligence tests today involve a variety of factors, there is still heavy emphasis on verbal ability, with secondary attention to mathematical skills. One is expected to read words, or listen to them, and behave appropriately. One may also be required to respond to visual arrangements or mechanics. Persons who do well on one intelligence test may not do so well on others, depending upon what the test emphasizes. Some tests, especially for young children, concentrate on performance items, such as perceptual-motor responses or form board tasks.

The relationship of intelligence to physical proficiency

It has often been assumed that intelligence is important in enabling one to learn motor skills. Aptitude in motor activities may be one of the many "intelligences," or special abilities, every person has. The ability of some persons to more quickly determine the relationship between a particular physical response and desired result may be considered an example of motor intelligence. Anyone who observes a group of elementary school children can see that some can more easily coordinate all parts of their bodies for certain types of activities. Those with greater aptitude in motor coordination can more quickly learn to perform in activities that depend heavily upon that aptitude. Is general intelligence also a factor in this motor aptitude?

Several authors have suggested a relationship between intelligence and the ability to improve with practice in motor skills. Among them, R. A. Davis (1935) claims a relationship between intelligence and the learning of *complex* skills but no relationship with easy tasks. He states that:

> Skills of the simple types require a limited amount of mental coordination and direction and therefore bear little relation to intelligence. The simpler skills are primarily dependent upon reflexes and instincts where intelligence and training are not essential. In the complex skills intellectual control and training are necessary. Complex skills, therefore, become an index to intelligence (pp. 138-39).[1]

Vince (1953) also emphasizes the relationship between intellectual and motor activity in the following statement:

> At the same time it has been shown that this intellectual activity cannot be considered in separation from the motor activity: in that the subject's idea of the pattern is to some extent determined by it, and in that the development of the intellectual activity may depend very largely on the character of the motor response . . . (p. 85).

Several studies dealing with the topic of intelligence and motor performance have been conducted in recent years. However, the variability in design and conduct of research has often confused the issue. For example, some studies have related *physical fitness* to academic achievement. Such studies are based on the assumption that good health and fitness enable people to more nearly reach their potential capabilities in various intellectual activities. Typical of such studies was a recent analysis of the dropouts from U.S. military academies. A disproportionate percen-

[1] From *Psychology of Learning* by R. A. Davis. Copyright 1935 by McGraw-Hill Book Company. Used by permission of McGraw-Hill Book Company.

tage of the failures was especially low on physical fitness components. Also, Nason (1965) recently stated that, "children with high motor proficiency make higher grades in reading and writing than children with poor coordination" (p. 36). Though lending support to the relationship between fitness and school achievement, these statements do not provide a strong clue to the role of intelligence in the ability to learn a new skill.

On other occasions, efforts have been made to analyze the effect of athletic *participation* on academic achievement. In such studies, the school grades of athletes and nonathletes have been compared. Comparisons have also been made among participants during the sports season and during the off-season. Participants in a single sport have been compared with participants in several sports, and varsity players with intramural players. Such studies have generally led to the conclusion that those who participate in athletic activities represent the full range of ability and achievement levels found in the school. But these studies have added little to an understanding of intelligence and motor learning ability.

It seems reasonable to assume that intelligence would have little to do with one's ability to *perform* a simple muscular response involving power, speed, or endurance. For example, items such as pull-ups, a softball throw for distance, and a running speed test appear not to be affected by intelligence. However, when several types of movements are combined into a rather complex activity involving coordination, reaction to different stimuli, and use of general strategy, a relationship seems more plausible.

Another question frequently raised is whether high intelligence (as determined by performance on a general intelligence test) aids one in the *learning* of new skills. Still others have dealt with the relationship between intelligence and speed of improvement in relatively familiar skills. A positive relationship was reported in some studies, while no significant relationship was shown in other studies. Consequently, different questions related to the intelligence-motor ability issue have resulted in different answers, many of which have confused the observer.

Research favoring a positive relationship

Harmon and Oxendine (1961) investigated the relationship between the intelligence of junior high school boys and their ability to develop skill in mirror tracing. Scores on the Pintner Intermediate Test (Form *A*) were obtained for 135 boys. These scores were then correlated with the subjects' initial performance in mirror tracing as well as performance at various points throughout a five-week learning period. The authors reported low positive correlations between general intelligence scores and mirror-tracing performance. There was a tendency for subjects with higher intelligence to exhibit better initial proficiency and to perform better at all phases of the learning process than subjects with lower intelligence scores. The correlations were too low, however, to have a predictive value.

Kulcinski (1945) had fifth-grade and sixth-grade boys and girls learn eleven easy and eleven hard stunt exercises. He reported a definite relationship between various degrees of intelligence and the learning of the exercises. Children in the high

I.Q. group exhibited slightly superior motor performance in the new skills than did children in the normal intelligence group. Further, the normal group exhibited superiority over the subnormal group. Ellis (1938) investigated the learning ability and performance of groups of normal and retarded children. He found that normal children learned more quickly, had better overall performance, and had better retention than retarded children. There was also less inhibitory potential among normal children.

In an early study, Burt and Moore (1912) reported a correlation coefficient of .60 between general intelligence scores and mirror-tracing scores. Elementary school children in England were used as subjects. Others who have studied the relationship between general intelligence and mirror tracing were Schott (1923), Calfee (1913), and Snoddy (1926). All reported low positive correlations. Subjects in these experiments ranged in age from elementary school to college age.

Garfiel (1923) compared intelligence scores with general motor ability. Although he found a low positive correlation, he concluded that motor ability represents a group of abilities different from mental ability. Thompson (1952) found only a slight relationship between motor ability and general intelligence. Ray (1940) compared mental and physical abilities with scholastic achievement among high school boys. He reported that physical ability was a more reliable predictor of academic standing than one's intelligence quotient. Brace (1946) tested the ability of feebleminded girls to learn gross motor skills. The mean I.Q. of the girls was 53. He found a slight relationship between intelligence and the ability to learn sports skills.

Fitzhugh and Fitzhugh (1965) reported a significant relationship between certain small motor movements and general intelligence in a group of brain-damaged patients. Children were organized into intelligence levels from below 60 to above 90. Each group was given tests in finger-tapping speed, tactile finger recognition, and fingertip number writing. They reported that intelligence, within the range of the group, was positively related to each of the skills.

In recent years, several reports have shown that on both fine and gross motor skills the performance of *mentally retarded children* is well below that of intellectually normal children. Further, the more severe the mental retardation, the greater the performance deficit. In one of the more significant studies of this topic, Dobbins et al. (1981) compared the motor performance of 71 intellectually normal and 71 educable mentally retarded boys. Subjects were tested on 12 motor performance and seven anthropometric measures. Although superiority in performance was shown for the intellectually normal boys, the authors stated that when adjustments were made for differences in body size, performance gaps between groups were eliminated on approximately half of the items. While agreeing that intelligence plays a part in motor performance, Dobbins et al. point out that the retarded children have (1) an anthropometric disadvantage (much greater subcutaneous fat and less height), (2) less opportunity to be physically active, and (3) less motivation to be physically active. The authors suggest that these factors tend to exaggerate the motor performance differences between intellectually normal and retarded persons.

Studies not showing a relationship

Not all research has shown a relationship between general intelligence and motor learning. Clinton (1930) gave intelligence tests to a group of elementary, high school, and college students. Each of the subjects then took a five-minute mirror-drawing test. The score on the test was simply the amount that could be traced during this initial period. Mirror-tracing performances of pupils with the highest and lowest intelligence were then compared. There was no significant difference between these scores. This led Clinton to conclude that "There is no positive relation between mirror-drawing ability and general intelligence" (p. 228).

In three separate experiments I (1969) found that intelligence scores did not correlate consistently with the motor performance scores of seventh-grade boys. The motor tasks were the pursuit rotor, a soccer kick, and a modified basketball free throw. Intelligence scores from a test administered one year earlier were obtained from the school records. For one experiment, the mean I.Q. score for groups was 114. The other two experiments had group means of 109 and 95. For each of the experiments, the I.Q. scores were compared with the initial scores, test day scores, retention scores, and the overall amount of improvement. Despite a few scattered correlations that proved to be significant, there was no consistency in these relationships either in terms of significance or direction. I concluded that even with groups ranging from 95 to 114, intelligence test scores were not indicative of performance in either of the tasks.

Start (1962) tested 180 grammar school boys in Australia to determine if there was any relationship between game performance, intelligence, and "streaming" (selection for a tract, or particular course of study, in secondary school). Game performance, which was used as an indication of motor ability, was determined by whether or not the boy was selected for either rugby union or association football. Streaming was based upon the boy's performance on the annual scholastic examinations. The intelligence scores used were those obtained in the Secondary School Selection Examination, which was taken prior to the boy's entering grammar school. Start reported an insignificant correlation between game performance and intelligence quotient. The difference in game performance between the group with I.Q.s from 121-141 and boys in the 106-120 range was insignificant.

In addition, Start found no significant difference in the proportion of school players in each stream. This would indicate a lack of relationship between school achievement and sports performance. He also reported a low positive correlation (.19) between intelligence quotient and performance on the annual scholastic examinations. Although this was reported as significant at the 1 percent level of confidence, it is admittedly low. A high score on an intelligence test, therefore, did not give strong assurance of success in grammar school.

Start indicated that the selection of the sample may have been an important factor in showing no relationship between intelligence and athletic performance. The measured intelligence quotients of the subjects ranged from 106 to 141. He suggested the need for determining whether similar results would be found if a lower intelligence group were used. One should therefore conclude from this study that *for boys in the 106 to 141 intelligence range* there is no relationship between general intelligence and motor skill as measured by selection on a rugby or football team.

Ryan (1962a) tested the speed with which 80 male college students learned a novel balancing skill. He then correlated each subject's score with academic capacity, academic achievement, athletic ability, and relative achievement (academic achievement related to ability). The only significant correlation was between motor learning and relative achievement. He suggested that the *motive to succeed* was a more general characteristic than either intelligence or motor ability.

Westerdarp (1923) showed a negative correlation between mental ability and the physical traits of agility and coordination. Hertzberg (1929) compared motor ability tests with the intelligence scores of kindergarten children. He found no relationship at this age level. DiGiovanna (1937) found no relationship between general intelligence scores and (1) athletic ability or (2) motor ability of college men. G. B. Johnson (1942) showed that there was no relationship between the performance of college freshmen on the Thurstone Psychological Examination and the Johnson Physical Skills Test.

Intelligence and motor learning

Evidence concerning the relationship of general intelligence to motor learning is not consistent and therefore not entirely conclusive. Several studies report a low positive correlation, while others show no significant relationship. Almost no studies report a negative correlation between intelligence and the ability to learn skills. It seems reasonable to assume that, within the I.Q. ranges in most regular school situations, there is no more than a slight relationship between intelligence and the ability to learn the types of tasks reported in the literature. It should also be noted that correlations between general intelligence scores and school grades are also low, usually between .40 and .60. However, when feebleminded or very low I.Q. subjects are used, a more substantial positive relationship is found between intelligence and motor-learning ability. This suggests the existence of a point below which intelligence becomes important in learning. According to Lawther (1977), when I.Q. scores go below the normal range, they become significantly related (negatively) to motor learning ability. Furthermore, the lower the I.Q., the more profound the relationship. However, he states that when measured intelligence is normal or above, there is no relationship.

From the available evidence, it must be assumed that motor intelligence and general intelligence (as measured by tests today) are *different* factors. Does this mean that the ability to learn skills is not related to intelligence or that this learning is not an intellectual process? This question has not been answered in the research. Immediately open to question is the validity of current I.Q. tests for determining overall general intelligence.

One might well question which of the following is the more accurate indication of general intelligence: (1) the ability to remember the definition of a word and to analyze the sequence of a series of numbers, or (2) the ability to learn to drive an automobile and to coordinate one's body in a skilled gymnastics movement. Word definitions and number analysis are rather arbitrarily described as intelligence measures, while the last two items are not. Therefore, if intelligence is defined as "the ability to do well on an intelligence test," then this factor is no more than slightly related to the learning of most skills. If, on the other hand, intelligence is the "capacity of the individual to act purposefully" (Wechsler) or to adapt to new situations, perhaps motor-learning proficiency is as accurate an indication of intelligence as is the learning of a mathematical skill.

According to Rarick (1980), "The question would in fact seem to be not so much are cognitive functions required in the skillful execution of motor skills, but rather what kinds of cognitive functions are needed for such tasks . . . clearly the learning of a motor skill requires concentrated mental effort" (pp. 188-189). Rarick concedes, however, that we do not yet know precisely how the cognitive processes function in skill learning or how they differ from those functions considered primarily "intellectual."

It can be concluded that the ability to learn motor skills, i.e., to relate specific body responses to results and to use coaching suggestions and cues, is *different* from the ability to solve certain mathematical problems or to do some types of verbal reasoning. Which of these is most closely related to general "intelligence" is still an unanswered question.

SUMMARY

1. Individual differences in physical size, motor ability, intelligence, and social traits that permeate society in general are reflected in the school setting. Consequently, the teacher must develop an understanding of these differences and their implications for performance. The development of techniques for teaching children who differ in a variety of abilities must also be addressed.

2. General intelligence and motor abilities, along with all other human capacities, are distributed in a predictable fashion around an average.

3. Performance in gross motor activities is most heavily influenced by height, weight, age, and a host of specific motor abilities.

4. Motor ability is no longer assumed to be a general trait. Rather, lists of very specific motor abilities have been identified by several authors. Still, there is no universally agreed upon taxonomy of such abilities.

5. Persons with outstanding special abilities that happen to be strategic in the performance of certain categories of sports activities are often referred to as "natural" or "all-around" athletes. Usually these individuals excel in speed and strength traits that are prominent in several popular sports. However, one cannot assume that the same individuals will exhibit above average skill in motor activities that do not depend upon these particular traits.

6. Some individuals are aided in the performance of a wide range of human activities by certain psychological traits. These include a positive self-image, the

expectancy to excel, encouragement of parents, perseverance, and the habit of success.

7. Intelligence is one of the most highly valued psychological traits. Even though it has been extensively studied and discussed, it is still not well understood. General intelligence has proven to be easier to describe than to measure. Definitions generally include the ability to think creatively and to solve new problems. Yet, intelligence tests are still heavily dependent upon one's verbal ability and do not effectively measure problem solving. In fact, those persons excelling in word fluency, which is a special trait, tend to excel in intelligence tests.

8. Earlier theories of intelligence stressed the generality of mental abilities, i.e., a "bright"child could learn all subject matter better than a less bright child. However, it has been shown during the past several decades that there is little overlap among the identified mental abilities. For example, the fact one can excel in reading comprehension is no assurance of high abilities in mathematics, mechanics, swimming, or music.

9. Measured intelligence is only minimally related to the ability to learn new motor skills or to perform at a high level in any motor activity. Therefore, the ability to learn and to perform a motor skill is different from the ability to do well on an intelligence test.

10. Among mentally retarded persons, intelligence does relate positively to motor learning and performance. Severely retarded persons are especially limited in motor performance.

SELECTED READINGS

ANASTASI, A. *Psychological testing* (2nd ed.). New York: Macmillan, 1961.

BRACE, D. K. *Measuring motor ability.* New York: Barnes, 1927.

BUROS, O. K., Ed. *The sixth mental measurement yearbook.* Highland Park, N. J.: Gryphon Press, 1965.

CLARKE, H. H. *Application of measurement to health and physical education* (4th ed.). Englewood Cliffs, N. J.: Prentice-Hall, 1967.

FLEISHMAN, E. A. The perception of body position in the absence of visual cues. *J. Exp. Psychol.,* 1953, **46**, 261-70.

FLEISHMAN, E. A. *The structure and measurement of physical fitness.* Englewood Cliffs, N. J.: Prentice-Hall, Inc., 1964.

GARRY, R. *Psychology of learning.* Washington: Cen. Appl. Res. Educ., 1963.

GUILFORD, J. B. A system of psychomotor abilities. *Amer. J. Psychol.,* 1958, **71**, 164-74.

GUILFORD, J. P. *The nature of human intelligence.* New York: McGraw-Hill, 1967.

HENRY, F. M. Specificity vs. generality in learning motor skills. *Annual Proceedings.* College Physical Education Association, 1958, **61**, 126-28.

JENKINS, J. J. and PETERSON, D. G. *Studies in individual differences: the search for intelligence.* New York: Appleton-Century-Crofts, 1961.

RARICK, G. L. Cognitive-motor relationships in the graving years. *Research Quarterly Exercise and Sport,* 1980, **51**, 174-92.

THURSTONE, L. L. Primitive mental abilities. *Univer. of Chicago Psychometr. Monogr.,* 1938, 1.

13 Visual and Kinesthetic Perception

PERCEPTUAL DIFFERENCES

The senses offer the means by which humans learn from the environment. The sense organs, therefore, contribute greatly to the manner in which people respond. The senses that seem most strategic for motor learning and performance are those that relate to perception, from both external and internal stimuli. Vision and kinesthesis are particularly strategic. Even though other senses may prove important in certain physical performance situations, general applicability is not as extensive. This chapter will therefore be devoted entirely to perception resulting from visual and kinesthetic cues. As with general intelligence, individuals differ in their capacities of kinesthesis and vision. In fact, abilities in these traits are distributed over a normal curve.

The relationship of vision and kinesthesis to the acqustion and performance of skills becomes clear upon close investigation. For example, vision is clearly a capacity that is both distributed over a wide range among different individuals and is strategic in motor performance. There are several types of visual abilities, each of which falls into a distribution curve much the same as general intelligence scores. This is contrary to the often held concept that one's vision is either 20-20 or poor. The important role of vision in overall school performance makes an investigation important for all teachers. Physical education teachers, especially, should be familiar with (1) the different types of visual abilities, (2) the range of these abilities among different persons, (3) how each can be measured, and (4) their role in motor learning and performance.

The kinesthetic sense, one's awareness of body position and movement, is of vital importance in most motor activities. The crucial nature of this sense is evident whether one is (1) moving the total body through space, as in the springboard dive or a high jump, (2) controlling limb position and movement, as in hammering a nail or drawing a straight line, or (3) maintaining balance, as in doing a handstand or walking on a balance beam. Despite longstanding interest on the part of many, efforts to establish the dimensions and measure this "sixth" sense have proven difficult.

VISUAL PERCEPTION

There are many kinds of school achievement in which visual perception plays a vital role. Teachers in several subject areas have only recently begun to gain a full realization of the important effect that the various visual capacities may have. One school activity that is very strongly influenced is motor-skill acquisition and performance. Recent research is beginning to answer some longstanding questions regarding the relationship of vision to athletic performance. For example, must one have exceptional vision to be an outstanding athlete? In what particular activities is good vision most beneficial? What are the key components of visual perception, and can they be developed or improved? In what activities can the visually handicapped person participate most effectively? Can visual tests be used as a screening device to determine one's potential for performing at a high level in certain activities?

In areas other than physical education, individual differences in vision also result in variations in performance. It seems likely that the person who learns to read with great speed has special visual abilities that may be measurable. Such abilities may be special inherited capacities or acquired skills. For efficiency and safety in driver education or industrial arts, it is important that the individual's visual abilities be appraised. In addition, the student's ability in painting or other artistic work may be influenced by special perceptual abilities. Teachers in the arts, as well as those in physical education, have a particular interest in visual differences.

The gestalt psychologists expressed great interest in visual perception and emphasized its intricate involvement with learning. The manner in which one observes the environment is considered strategic to learning. Despite their attention to perception, the gestaltists placed little emphasis on individual differences in vision and the role of these differences in learning. Neither did they identify or discuss the different types of visual abilities.

Unfortunately, thorough and scientific investigations of vision and its relationship to the learning and performance of motor skills have not been undertaken on a large scale. Perhaps this lack of attention has resulted from an assumption that differences in vision within the normal range are not important in performance. Although it has been accepted that a weakness in vision proves a handicap in activities in which seeing is important, little attention has been devoted to the possibility that outstanding vision might prove to be an asset. Some of the special visual abilities that have been identified in relation to motor performance will be discussed briefly.

Depth perception

Depth perception refers to the ability to distinguish the distance of objects or to make judgments about relative distances. This capacity, also called distance perception, adds the third dimension to height and width. Binocular vision (simultaneous vision with both eyes) is the primary basis for depth perception. The two eyes focus on an object from slightly different angles. These overlapping fields of view help provide depth in one's perception. Conversely, monocular vision (seeing with one eye) tends to flatten things in the distance. Of course, closer objects require the two eyes to converge at a greater angle than do more distant ones. This more advantageous angle facilitates keener distance discrimination for nearby objects.

In an attempt to illustrate this concept, Bannister and Blackburn (1931) reported that rugby players had greater distances between their eyes than non-players. The authors assumed that the players' greater interpupillary distance provided them with outstanding depth perception, which contributed to their playing ability. However, there is no indication that subjects were controlled for body or head size. Of course, it is probable that rugby players are larger than nonplayers, and naturally have larger heads with greater interpupillary distance. Due to the rugged nature of rugby, it is likely that large men would have been drawn to this activity more often than smaller men. A relationship between interpupillary distance and depth perception has not been substantiated by more recent research.

In addition to binocular vision, the individual is aided in making judgments about the distance of objects by certain learned visual aids. These cues include the distinctiveness of the object, brightness, texture, relative size, overlapping shadows, perspective, and in some cases, relative motion. Once learned, these secondary factors prove helpful in judging distance. Objects of a known size that are closer, beside, or farther away help the individual in estimating a second object's size and distance. For example, when driving, the distance of an oncoming automobile can be guessed fairly accurately by observing its relationship to the highway and other objects in the visual field. At night, judgments are often based on the observed distance between and the intensity of headlights. However, these guides may prove inadequate for passing, since a smaller automobile with a shorter distance between the headlights would appear farther away.

In motor activities, there are many opportunities for making judgments about the distance of people or objects. For example, the passer in football needs to determine with considerable accuracy the distance of receivers and opponents. To be sure, this judgment is aided somewhat by timing and kinesthetic perception established through practice. Still, visual perception is a vital factor in locating the receiver. Similarly, the receiver must be able at all times to make an accurate judgment about the distance of the thrown ball. The golfer on the fairway must make an accurate estimate of the distance to the pin in order to determine which club to select and how hard to swing. The high jumper, pole vaulter, or broad jumper in track needs to make an accurate estimation of the distance to the take-off point, or he will be required to make a last-second adjustment in stride. A misjudged fly ball in baseball results from a poor estimation of the distance and speed of the ball. The batter with poor depth perception would appear to be most susceptible to a change-up pitch. In most motor activities, and especially in ball games, the ability to distinguish distances is strategic to efficient performance.

Depth perception is generally assumed to be an inherited physiological trait that cannot be improved appreciably by practice. However, the ability to identify and accurately judge distances in terms of absolute measures apparently can be improved to some extent. For example, some persons who have a keen sense of depth seem to have little awareness of a distance of 100 feet or a quarter mile. I recently asked a nationally ranked collegiate bowler what the length of a bowling lane was. This young woman, currently averaging around 190 pins per game, considered the question for a moment then answered, "around 30 feet." The actual distance is 63 feet. Surely her depth perception is not that faulty. In fact, she would probably notice the difference if a lane were two feet short of "regulation." The problem is faulty estimation of distances, not depth perception.

In a study of the practice effects of judging distances, Gibson and Bergman (1954) conducted an experiment in which individuals observed targets at distances ranging from 39 to 435 yards. During a pretest period, the subjects made 18 different judgments and were told the correct distance after each. They had five practice trials of 18 judgments each and a posttest. The percentage of error decreased considerably during the pretest trials but changed very little during the remaining practice and posttrials. Therefore, a short training period for judging distances seems helpful.

The golfer who can accurately judge the distance-to-pin to be 120 yards and not 135 yards can make a more intelligent club selection. Professional golfers, not wishing to depend upon this casual judgment, frequently "walk off" distances during practice rounds. Military service personnel, especially those in artillery divisions, use training techniques to prepare for shooting in combat.

Olsen (1956), using the Howard-Dolman apparatus[1], found that male college varsity athletes had better depth perception than did male students who participated in the intramural program. The intramural group in turn had significantly better depth perception than did a group of male students who had never participated in athletic activities on formal teams. Olsen assumed that depth perception was a necessary component for outstanding performance in the varsity team sports used in his study. He concluded that college athletes were able to perform at a higher level because of their greater inherent depth perception and that the trait was not being developed as a result of participation.

Montebello (1953) found a keener depth perception among baseball players than among nonplayers. However, there was no significant correlation between depth cues and batting averages among the players. Graybiel, Jokl, and Trapp (1955) reported that differences in depth perception were found between Olympic performers and nonperformers. He also found differences among performers in different sports activities. D. M. Miller (1960) showed depth perception to be one of the important distinctions between outstanding performers and low-skilled performers in a variety of sports activities.

In a study by Dickson (1953), however, no relationship was found between depth perception and basketball shooting ability. He administered five tests of depth perception to three groups of college men. The groups were skilled, semi-skilled, and unskilled players. He found that the five measures of depth perception used did not identify those who performed well in the shooting tests. In a similar

---

[1] The apparatus was devised by Howard in 1919 to serve as a screening test for determining those aviation cadets who might not have keen depth perception. The test requires the subject to line up two black rods from a distance of 20 feet. The rods are mounted on parallel tracts and are maneuvered by tugging on the 20-foot-long cords.

study, Shick (1971) found a relationship between foul shooting and depth perception among female college students. However, in studies involving popular sports, other factors, such as prior training effects and motivation, may be expected to outweigh the influence of components that are not especially prominent.

Peripheral vision

Peripheral vision is often called "field of vision" and has been traditionally referred to as the ability of an individual to see to the side while looking straight ahead. In addition, some recent researchers have investigated "vertical" peripheral vision, which refers to the range of up-down vision while looking straight ahead. According to Sage (1971), "field of vision refers to the entire extent of the environment which can be seen without a change in the fixation of the eye" (p. 148). An individual who has very limited peripheral vision is said to have "tunnel vision." Peripheral vision is determined by the placement of rods and cones in the eyes. While looking straight ahead, most individuals are able to see about a 90° angle to each side, or a total field of vision of 180°. Among a group of normal individuals differences in peripheral vision range from approximately 155° to 205°. From a central point, Olsen (1956) reported that most people see farther to the right than to the left. Peripheral vision cannot be appreciably improved by practice. One might, however, become more alert and possibly make greater use of his innate field of vision.

Peripheral vision has been measured with several types of apparatus. In using most apparatus, the head and eyes are held stationary while the subject is required to respond to stimuli that are presented on each side. In Olsen's (1956) experiment, the McClure perimeter was used. With this apparatus, the subject presses his face against a darkened periscope-type viewer that has movable arms on each side. As the arms swing farther to each side, the subject monitors a signal in the front center while responding to miniature lights that flash in either or both arms. Some driver education programs have used a cruder method in which the subject's face is pressed against the apparatus while pegs are moved farther to each side until the subject indicates they are out of visual range.

Williams and Thirer (1975) compared college-age male and female athletes with nonathletes on vertical and horizontal peripheral vision. The authors speculated that vertical vision, or the range of view from top to bottom, might be as important in athletic performances as peripheral vision on a horizontal plane. The authors reported that athletes exhibited a greater field of vision than did nonathletes. There were no sex differences among athletes and nonathletes except that female athletes exhibited greater high vertical range of vision.

In his study to determine the relationship between certain physical capacities and proficiency in sports, Olsen (1956) found that varsity athletes in college had greater peripheral vision than did those who did not take part in varsity sports. Also, intramural participants had greater peripheral vision than did college men who had no history of organized athletic competition. Olsen surmised that greater innate peripheral vision aids one to perform at a higher level than persons with more limited vision. McCain (1950) reported slight visual differences between high school athletes and nonathletes. Stroup (1957) found that basketball players had above average peripheral vision.

Graybiel et al. (1955) reviewed some research relative to peripheral vision that was conducted at the 1952 Olympic Games. A test project was set up in which athletes performed in various activities under conditions of normal vision, limited peripheral vision, central vision, and no vision (blindfolded). In javelin throwing, movements became clumsy, and the distances of the throws were significantly shorter when peripheral vision was excluded. The javelin also could no longer be thrown in a direction at right angles to the base line. The throwers with imposed limited peripheral vision reported that they were unable to see the tip of the javelin at the moment of maximal thrust of the arm, and this fact was believed to be responsible for the disorganization of the normal performance patterns. Throwing performances were poorest when vision was totally eliminated.

Discus performances were very poor when peripheral vision was excluded and best with unimpeded vision. Total elimination of vision proved at times to be less of a handicap than did interference with peripheral vision. Similar results were found with hammer throwers. In a 400-meter track race, no appreciable decline in efficiency was found with the elimination of peripheral vision.

With slalom skiers, the elimination of peripheral vision resulted in marked deterioration in performance. The athletes found it difficult to follow the course, and their judgments of distance were extremely poor. Figure skaters experienced a serious loss of symmetry, precision, and timing of movements when peripheral vision was excluded; on elimination of central vision, less difficulty was encountered than resulted from the exclusion of peripheral sight. Gymnasts experienced similar problems.

Although the research of Graybiel et al. clearly illustrates the problems caused by an immediate deprivation of one's peripheral vision, one cannot be certain what the long-term effects are. Perhaps if the performers had been given time to adjust to this state, improvement in performance may have occurred. The importance of peripheral vision in sports activities is clear when one considers the many situations in which this lateral vision is essential. The middle person on a fast break in basketball needs to be able to see to each side without turning the head. The defensive football player with limited peripheral vision is likely to be hit from the "blind" side most often. In soccer, field hockey, and all other team sports, it is advantageous for the individual to be able to observe both teammates and opponents over a wide range. However, it seems that for certain other activities, such as track, tennis, golf, or bowling, the ability to see well to the side is not particularly important.

Individuals who have an especially limited visual field, either to the right or left, may be wisely placed in certain positions on the team so that their weakness will not play a major part in their performance. For example, the soccer forward with a weakness in vision to the right side may be positioned at right wing because in this position most of the action would be to the left side. Such a practice, however, is dependent upon accurate measurement of peripheral vision.

In activities other than sports, good lateral vision is often important for performance and for safety. The automobile driver who is entering an intersection or who is driving in the center lane of heavy traffic will have a safety advantage if he can see at wide angles to each side. It is also to the pedestrian's advantage to be able to see cars approaching from either side. In many work situations with moving machinery or vehicles, one's safety is enhanced by good vision to both sides.

Speed of vision

The speed with which individuals are able to observe objects may be discussed in terms of two types of capacities: (1) span of apprehension, and (2) pursuit movements. Span of apprehension refers to the individual's ability to observe several objects in a short period of time and retain a knowledge of what has been seen. This component may be measured by use of a tachistoscope, which flashes several numbers, words, or images onto a screen for a short period of time. The subject then identifies what has been presented. Pursuit speed is the ability of the individual to visually follow an object or image that is moving at particular velocities. This component is often measured by use of high speed eye movement cameras. As with other visual traits, people differ in speed of vision.

In Olsen's (1956) study, span of apprehension was measured by means of a tachistoscope that flashed black dots onto a white screen for one fifth of a second. The number of dots varied from four to 13. After each exposure, subjects were asked to write down the number of dots that appeared. If 12 dots were flashed, the individual did not have time to count to 12 by the one-two-three technique. Rather, he had to try to get an impression within one fifth of a second and retain the image long enough to count during the brief period after the flash had passed. Subjects differed greatly in the ability to see and distinguish objects quickly. Olsen reported that almost all persons could accurately distinguish four or five dots within one fifth of a second, but very few could consistently count 12 or 13 accurately.

How is span of apprehension important in motor activities? Very often the player in a team game situation will look up and see the total field within his view. A quick analysis of the position of his opponents and teammates in relation to a goal can be of great importance. A momentary delay in seeing the set-up, if it results in a delay in decision and action, can allow compensatory actions on the part of opponents. The person with a limited span of apprehension will often move just a little too late. The halfback in football who breaks through the line of scrimmage must size up the situation and make a quick decision. There are many other situations in sports where a multiplicity of visual stimuli must be observed and analyzed in a minimum of time. Olsen reported a relationship between scores on his test and proficiency in team sports among college men. Perhaps this same speed of vision in spanning is what enables some children to span a greater number of words and therefore read faster than other children.

Morris and Kreighbaum (1977) compared three groups of female college athletes on dynamic visual acuity. This term is used to refer to one's ability to perceive an object when there is relative movement between the observer and the object. It is the ability to process ball flight information quickly even though the exposure may be of short duration. According to Cratty (1973), dynamic visual acuity plays a more important role in activities such as ball playing or driving than does visual acuity of a more static nature. In the Morris and Kreighbaum study, dynamic acuity was determined by use of a slide projector with a zoom lens. A rotating mirror projected the moving target on a screen extending 180° around the subject. Varsity volleyball players were compared with basketball players. In addition, high percentage shooters in basketball were compared with low percentage shooters (based on shooting percentages during the season). The authors reported that there were no differences in mean dynamic visual acuity scores among the groups. However, the high percentage basketball shooters were less variable in this ability. The authors took note of the fact that the test situation involved a stationary subject and a moving target, whereas in basketball just the opposite is true, i.e., there is a moving subject and a stationary target.

When one observes a moving object, the retinal image becomes blurred unless the eyes keep pace with the object. If the eye follows the moving object in a smooth sweep, vision of the object remains vivid. When this occurs, stationary objects within the field of vision become blurred. Individuals develop some skill in tracking objects as a result of learning what kind of movement to expect and by practicing. New visual activities involving movement, especially when the movement is caused by an external force, result in difficulties in focusing. After all, as the fixed object starts to move, the image is displaced from the center of vision. The individual must then make corrective movements in order to catch up to the target. The pursuit movement may be too fast or too slow until experience with the particular task has been gained. Individuals, however, differ in their ability to develop skill in tracking objects moving very fast. Some persons are able to develop a smooth pursuit movement while others must rely upon jerky (jump-pause, jump-pause) action. Hubbard and Seng (1954) and Mott (1954) have reported a relationship between pursuit speed and proficiency in motor skills.

Figure-ground perception

The term *figure-ground* refers to a particular manner in which humans perceive the environment. In normal vision, the individual organizes the perceptual field into two parts, one dominant and unified and the other more diffuse. The dominant object, usually serving as a focus, is referred to as the "figure," while the surrounding field or background is the "ground." The concept of figure-ground was developed and investigated by the gestalt psychologists, particularly Rubin (1958) and Wertheimer (1958), during the early part of the 20th century.

In classifying the differences between figure and ground, Rubin (1921) pointed out that: 1) the figure has form, while the ground is relatively formless; 2) the ground appears to extend continuously behind the figure and is not interrupted by the figure; 3) the figure has the appearance of a "thing" while the ground appears more like unorganized "material"; 4) the figure suggests more meaning and is better remembered than is the ground. Most of these concepts have been upheld by more recent investigations.

According to Herkowitz (1971), the ability to differentiate figure from ground is related to development, sex, and personality. She reported that the most rapid progress toward figure orientation occurs between eight and thirteen years of age.

Several persons have questioned the relationship between the figure-ground trait and perceptual motor performance. Krieger (1962), using an embedded figures test, showed a positive relationship between figure-ground perception and spatial adjustments in tennis. Torres (1966) showed a relationship between ball catching skill and performance on an embedded figures test. Gallahue (1968) showed a similar relationship between the gross motor patterns of kindergarten children and their figure-ground patterns.

Several recent studies have not illustrated a clear relationship between measures of figure-ground perception and motor performances. In two studies, Ridenour (1979, 1981) reported no relationship between visual background patterns of subjects and 1) their ability to predict the directions in which an object is moving, or 2) coincidence-anticipation performance. However, in another study (1980), she showed that vertical and vertical-horizontal patterns of the background behind a moving object did influence the prediction of an object's directionality by girls.

In a practical sense, the figure-ground phenomenon has been a matter of interest to athletic coaches and teachers. Tennis teachers concerned with maximum visibility of the ball pay careful attention to the background, often using backdrops to screen out a distracting ground. Also, colored balls are often used to sharpen the contrast with the background. In baseball, batters are extremely sensitive to the background visual stimuli surrounding the pitcher. The pitched ball that approaches the batter from out of a maze of white shirts in the centerfield bleachers or lights from a parking lot is difficult to "pick up." A more ideal arrangement for the batter is the centerfield view of Wrigley Field in Chicago, which contains a view of thick green trees and ivy. In this situation, the figure (the white baseball) presents a clear visual contrast to the ground (the green ivy). Outfielders frequently experience difficulty in visually following a batted ball because it is coming out of a background of spectators behind home plate.

Basketball coaches are very cognizant of the figure-ground dynamics of the basketball goal. This is true despite the fact that players are never encouraged to shoot at the net, nor are they told to notice the shape of the backboard or the lines on the board. In fact, they are usually encouraged only to shoot just over the front of the rim or to the back rim. Yet the effect of the "ground" factors are so widely recognized that basketball rules require that all conditions be standardized, even to the point of requiring that the rim be painted orange. Fan-shaped backboards are not "regulation" in most leagues, and therefore are not allowed in competition. Neither are blue nets or polka dot backboards, despite the aesthetic advantages these might offer over the colorless glass boards.

Figure 13-1 illustrates the impact that the "ground" can make on the "figure." In all four illustrations the figure (the basketball rim) is identical, i.e., exactly 18 inches in diameter and ten feet from the floor. However, the "ground" (visual stimuli surrounding the rim) differs appreciably. Experienced basketball players recognize that these conditions make a big difference in their shooting effectiveness. Experienced players would probably have greater shooting success in the (a) setting since the field, or background, surrounding the rim is more familiar

FIGURE 13-1.   *Figure-Ground Relationship Confronting the Basketball Player* In each picture, the *figure* (the rim) is identical. However, the ground is varied greatly by (1) the shape of the backboard (square or fan-shaped), (2) the texture of the board (glass versus wood or plastic), (3) the painted rectangle on the backboard, (4) the existence of the net, (5) the visibility of support structures, or (6) the lack of a backboard.

(a)

(b)

(c)

(d)

and provides additional cues as to the location of the rim. Less success would be attained in the (b) or (c) setting because of the disturbing nature of a rim without a net or a fan-shaped backboard. Greatest difficulty would be experienced in situation (d), the goal sitting atop a standard, where the player has no background against which to focus. The problem exists even when the player is not attempting to "bank" the ball off the backboard.

Figure 13-2 reveals additional visual stimuli encountered by basketball players. Spectators in the background and their movement may prove distracting. Of course, crowd noise provides nonvisual background that may either interfere with or encourage players.

General acuity

General visual acuity is a form of brightness discrimination that contributes to one's ability to see his way around, to read, or to take part in routine daily activities. This type of vision may be adequately measured by the Snellen eye chart, which contains rows of printed letters or symbols of decreasing size. The importance of visual acuity in most motor activities is clear. Just as a person on the street

FIGURE 13-2.   Visual Field Observed by Basketball Players in a Game.

needs to see people in order to keep from walking into them, the player on the athletic field needs to see the opponents clearly so as to avoid or intercept them and to see teammates so as to work with them.

Visual acuity among different individuals seems to be spread over a range that approximates a normal distribution with the typical person having 20-20 vision. This means that the individual with such vision can see at a distance of 20 feet what the average person can see at 20 feet. Almost all people fall within the 20-10 to 20-40 visual range. The child with 20-10 vision has excellent visual acuity in that he can see at 20 feet things that the average child can see only at 10 feet. Such outstanding visual acuity would appear to give the child an advantage in activities requiring keen vision at some distance. On the other hand, the child with 20-40 vision can only see at 20 feet what the average child can see at a distance of 40 feet. This inferior vision would prove a disadvantage in most activities requiring good vision.

When visual acuity has been weak enough to handicap an athlete's performance, glasses or contact lenses have been used with satisfactory results to improve the visual acuity of the performer. Performers in all sports activities are using glasses or lenses more than ever before. Traditionally, players have hestitated to wear glasses because of the fear of serious injury or the possible stigma attached to wearing them. It is not unusual today to find several players on a major league baseball team wearing either regular glasses or contact lenses. Obviously, if eye glasses can aid in overcoming visual acuity handicaps, they should be worn.

Other visual characteristics

Several other visual abilities seem to have a limited relationship to general motor performance. These include eye dominance, color vision, night blindness, and glare recovery. *Eye dominance* refers to the fact that one eye is stronger in acuity or is preferred for certain sightings over the other eye. It has generally been suggested that the right eye is dominant in most children. Special training does not appear to affect eye dominance. An optometrist, Teig, in a New York News Service report (*Philadelphia Inquirer*, February 12, 1981) described the testing of 250 major league baseball players on a number of visual capacities. Most prominent among his findings was his report of cross-dominance among more than half the players. By contrast only 20 percent of the general public displays such cross-dominance. Teig described as cross-dominance a situation in which a right-handed batter had left-eye dominance, or a left-handed batter had right-eye dominance. As it turns out, such a situation places the dominant eye closest to the pitcher, with a better view of the oncoming ball. However, not all persons would agree with Teig's definition of cross-dominance. Not all "left-handed" batters are left-handed in unilateral tasks, nor are all "right-handed" batters right-handed. Consequently, Teig classified some players as having cross-dominance even though they had hand and eye dominance on the same side.

Several additional visual traits appear to have more remote connections to motor skills performance. One of these is *color vision*, which is the ability to make discriminations on the basis of wave length as well as intensity of light. Color "blindness" proves a handicap in sports activities where subtle color and shade differences exist between team uniforms. This forces the performer to make distinctions on the basis of cues other than color, an adjustment which may slow response time.

Night blindness refers to the unusual difficulty some persons experience in becoming acclimated to relative darkness. Normally the eye is capable of adapting to great ranges in light intensities. However, a diminution in sensitivity to light may occur in some persons, particularly where there are vitamin A deficiencies. This condition is not usually noticed in well-lighted situations, but can prove a distinct handicap when driving at night or performing other skills under darkened conditions. Light adaptation refers to the ability of an individual to recover to normal vision after going from bright light to relative darkness, or vice versa. All persons experience some difficulty in recovery when going from a darkened room into bright light, such as from a movie theater into the afternoon sunlight. Similar difficulties are realized when going from a bright environment into a darkened one. Automobile drivers notice this when rapidly entering a tunnel on a sunny day or at night when attempting to recover from the glare after passing an automobile with "bright" lights.

Apparently the individual's *total* visual capacity is more important than particularly strong vision in any one of the components discussed. The gestalt, or combination of visual abilities, seemingly offsets a weakness that may exist in one area. This strength from the combined visual abilities appears to be present in certain outstanding athletes who are especially poor in one or more of the individual vision traits.

While most ball games and many other activities make great use of vision, many motor activities do not place such a high premium on visual perception. Vision is apparently of minor importance in swimming and in some types of dancing. Some outstanding swimmers and dancers have very poor vision. Some dances, however, do emphasize space perception and require the individual to coordinate movements with those of a partner.

KINESTHESIS

Kinesthesis has often been referred to as the muscle sense or the motor sense. In addition, it has popularly been called the sixth sense because it was the first recognized addition to the traditionally acknowledged five senses. Although physiologists demonstrated the existence of the kinesthetic sense approximately a century ago, it is still relatively unknown to persons outside scientific fields. Until very recently, a surprisingly small amount of study had been developed relative to kinesthesis even in the scientific area. This neglect probably results from a number of factors, including problems and differences of opinion in defining kinesthesis, difficulties in measuring it, and problems related to isolating and studying kinesthesis without the interference of other senses.

Guyton (1974) describes the "somesthetic system" as including (1) exteroceptive sensation, (2) proprioceptive sensation, and (3) visceral sensation. *Exteroceptive* sensations generally emanate from the skin and include temperature variations, pressure, touch, and pain. *Proprioceptive* sensations include tension of tendons and muscles, changes in joint angles, and deep pressure responses to weight. (This term is used in much the same way as the kinesthetic sense is used by other authors.) *Visceral* sensations usually come in the form of discomfort or malfunction of the internal organs. Clearly there is overlap in these sensory systems, particularly in the areas of pain, heat, and pressure. It is also clear that each of the systems may have some impact on motor performance. However, since the proprioceptive system is most directly related to movement responses, analysis will be devoted to that area, with only superficial attention to the exteroceptive and visceral systems.

The terms kinesthesis and proprioception are sometimes used interchangeably, and have essentially the same meanings in professional literature. However, the kinesthetic sense, emphasizing skeletal movement, is the more popular term with psychologists and educators; consequently it will be used most frequently in this discussion. Proprioception is frequently used by physiologists to refer to receptivity from all bodily systems. In a more limited way, this term comes from proprioceptors, which are the sense receptors located in the muscles, tendons, and ligaments.

According to Dickinson (1974), the term *proprioception* was invented by Sherrington (1906) in a paper just after the turn of the century. Other scientists made frequent references to different aspects of this phenomenon. However, the first substantial effort to define and analyze proprioception was made by Boring (1942) in his book *Sensation and Perception in the History of Psychology.* More recently, Dickinson's book (1974), *Proprioceptive Control of Human Movement,* has contributed importantly to our knowledge of this topic.

The kinesthetic sense is generally considered to be the "feel" or awareness of body position and body movement. However, more thorough and specific definitions offered by authorities may help to clarify and outline the scope of this capacity.

Scott (1955) defined kinesthesis as ". . . the sense which enables us to determine the position of segments of the body, their rate, extent, and direction of movement, the position of the entire body, and the characteristics of total body motion" (p. 325). According to Magruder (1963) kinesthesis is (1) the ability to recognize muscular contractions of a known amount, (2) the ability to balance, (3) the ability to assume and identify body position, and (4) the ability to orient the body in space. Phillips and Summers (1954) referred to kinesthetic perception as "the conscious awareness of the individual of the position of the parts of the body during voluntary movement" (p. 456). Dickinson defines proprioception and kinesthesis similarly, as "the appreciation of movement and position of the body and parts of the body based on information from other than visual, auditory, or superficial cutaneous sources" (p. 10).

After looking at these and other definitions, it can be noted that there is considerable agreement regarding the general meaning of kinesthesis. Four factors seem to be quite common in the many statements: (1) positioning of body segments, (2) precision of movement, (3) balance, and (4) space orientation. These concepts offer a basis for developing tests to measure kinesthesis. When tests have been developed, however, a great deal of specificity has been noted in kinesthesis, thwarting efforts to develop a single, all-encompassing test for this trait. This in turn has required more specific listings of what abilities are to be measured.

Basis for kinesthesis

Most sense organs depend upon stimulation from outside the body. For example, the eyes, nose, ears, skin, and taste receptors receive external impulse. The kinesthetic sense, however, is dependent upon internal stimulation. Nerve endings, called spindles or proprioceptors, are located in the muscles, tendons, and ligaments, and apparently aid in the coordinated movement of the body. Labyrinthine receptors located in the inner ear are strategic for body balance. Both coordination and balance are important elements of kinesthesis.

Authorities do not entirely agree regarding the physiological basis for the kinesthetic sense. Traditionally, it has been assumed that the proprioceptors in the muscles are stimulated by contraction or stretching of the muscle cells. Tendon and ligament proprioceptors are stimulated by the stretching or movement that results from muscular contractions. The constant flow of stimuli from these receptors enables the individual to sense the position of the body part without the benefit of vision. In addition, he is able to make smooth coordinated movements and antigravity adjustments without even being conscious of sensations from receptors.

This explanation of kinesthesis is supported by Cooper and Glassow (1963) who identify the sense receptors as muscle spindles, Golgi tendon organs, and Pacini corpuscles. They state that each of these is stimulated by changes in tension, and nerve impulses initiated in them are conducted to the cerebral cortex where they serve as the basis for kinesthetic sensation and perception. The 1965 edition of *Neuro-Functional Anatomy* lists four types of proprioceptors as endings; the first three are related to the sense of position and movement, while free nerve endings (and Pacini corpuscles) are sensitive to deep pressure.

There is some difference of opinion, however, regarding the exact source of kinesthetic information. Rose and Mountcastle (1959) express doubt that stretch receptors in muscles provide information regarding movement or position. They state that "... it appears that classical proprioceptors may not contribute at all to the arousal of 'proprioceptive' sensations" (p. 388). Gardner (1963) also expresses the belief that muscle spindles do not play an important role in kinesthetic reception. Rather, she states the Ruffini endings and Pacini corpuscles are primarily responsible for kinesthesis. Thus, the precise source for the reception and transmission of kinesthetic information during movement has not been determined to the satisfaction of all those who have worked in this area.

Equilibrium, or balance, is very closely related to the overall kinesthetic sense. Just as the individual is aware of general position changes, he is also aware of head movement and position. Labyrinthine receptors located in the inner ear are activated by changes in head position or movements of the head in connection with movements of the body as a whole. The ability to assume good posture or to maintain an upright position when external force is exerted against the body is evidence of the usefulness of these receptors. Since effective motor performance is dependent not only upon coordinated body movement but upon balance control of the body, the equilibrium receptors are assumed to be part of the mechanism for kinesthesis.

Measurement of kinesthesis

Research in the area of kinesthesis has generally fallen into two categories: (1) studies dealing with the selection of tests and the measurement of kinesthesis, and (2) studies dealing with the relationship between kinesthesis and motor performance or learning. Even research in the second category has been forced to deal with the matter of measurement. The concept of kinesthesis is relatively easy to define, but it is very difficult to measure effectively. As a result, there is more consistency among the definitions than among the tests that have been developed. Although many evaluative tools have been used for measuring kinesthesis, most do not possess established validity.

Authorities who are most familiar with this topic have concluded that *the kinesthetic sense is not a general capacity.* Rather, it is composed of specific elements. For example, Scott (1955) suggested the following specific abilities as those which determine the kinesthetic sense: (1) muscular contractions of a known amount, (2) balance ability, (3) ability to assume and identify body positions, (4) precise use of the hands, and (5) orientation of the body in space. Others have developed different lists of specific abilities. Therefore, in order to measure kinesthesis, a number of different capacities must be measured. This requires not one, but several tests. In attempting to measure the many elements involved in kinesthesis, various researchers have administered batteries of tests involving 15 to 25 items. Very low correlations have usually been shown among the different tests. This lack of relationship has substantiated the belief that no single ability or single test is sufficient to cover the total kinesthetic sense.

Analysis of the different measures of kinesthesis reveals that most test batteries are designed to measure the following capacities: (1) dynamic and static arm functioning, (2) thigh and leg functioning, (3) balance, and (4) vertical and horizontal arm movements. It is assumed that visual or tactile senses should not be used in these measures. No single test is adequate for measuring all these kinesthetic traits.

In addition to difficulties in identifying the measurable components, a second major problem encountered in testing for kinesthesis is similar to the difficulty in measuring other traits ranging from intelligence to motor ability. It is virtually impossible to select test items that are equally novel for all subjects. Research has shown that performance on most tests used in the measurement of kinesthesis can be improved with practice. Therefore, a basic question arises regarding the results of kinesthetic testing: Did the individual perform well because of a high degree of sensory capacity, or did the outstanding performance result from previous experience in the test activity or an activity similar to it? Although there is little research on the subject, one is led to suspect that, like intelligence, kinesthetic performance is affected by both heredity and environment.

Typical tests of kinesthesis require the subject to perform the following types of activities:

1. Duplicate or assume a given space, position, or angle with the arms and legs.
2. Exhibit accuracy in arm movements on a horizontal and on a vertical plane.
3. Exert a given amount of force against some measurable resistance.
4. Jump a given distance or height.
5. Walk a certain pathway in a particular manner.
6. Throw an object for accuracy in direction or distance.
7. Touch or point at a particular target.

Phillips and Summers (1954) described one technique for measuring body alignment or position. In their study, subjects were blindfolded and asked to assume a certain standing position. A floodlight was placed in front of the subject, which caused his shadow to be cast on a board that was marked off in degrees. The subject's score was determined by the number of degrees of variation from the desired position. A similar technique is used when the individual stands against a board that is marked off in degrees at fingertip distance from the body. Here the subject assumes different arm positions, and measurements are taken in variations from the desired position.

In summary, efforts to develop a test of kinesthesis have resulted in the conclusion that there are several specific elements that require a *battery* of tests for adequate measurement. Although several of these elements have been identified by different researchers, no agreement exists regarding the best means for measuring each of them. Since kinesthesis is assumed to be dependent upon the proprioceptors and labyrinthine receptors, it is generally concluded that tests for kinesthesis should not make use of one's vision. Finally, several of the tests used for kinesthesis have shown a high level of reliability, but validity has not yet been established.

Relationship of kinesthesis
to motor performance

Proprioceptive feedback is related to practically all physical performance. However, not all of this feedback enters the conscious awareness of the participant. Dickinson (1974) has speculated that ". . . if proprioceptive feedback is relevant to skilled movement, the greater the proprioceptive sensitivity, the higher the level of skill with other aspects constant" (p. 65). This proposition has formed the basis for much of the research in kinesthesis during recent years.

Several researchers have reported a high positive relationship between performance on kinesthetic tests and general tests of motor ability. In addition, it has been shown that outstanding athletes score higher on kinesthetic tests than do nonathletes. Conclusions from such studies, however, are limited by the unproven validity of the test.

Phillips and Summers (1954) reported a relationship between motor-learning ability in bowling and kinesthesis. They classified 115 college women as fast and slow learners on the basis of improvement in bowling scores shown in 24 class periods. Then a kinesthetic test involving positional measures was administered to all subjects. The authors reported that kinesthesis was more highly related to early learning than to the later learning stages of bowling. In this study, the authors also reported a difference in kinesthetic perception between the preferred and nonpreferred arm. It was suggested that habitual use of the arm might result in this perceptual difference. In another study involving bowling, Greenlee (1958) found a relationship between dynamic balance and bowling, but not between other measures of kinesthesis and strength and bowling. Also, no relationship was shown between static balance and bowling.

Clapper (1957) administered tests of kinesthesis to high school girls who were grouped into low, medium, and high socioeconomic levels. The tests involved target pointing, arm raising, finger spreading, and ball balancing. She reported a low correlation between motor-learning ability and the accumulative scores of the test battery. When test items were analyzed individually, insignificant findings were reported. She also reported that performance in the test items used in the study could be improved somewhat with practice. Wiebe (1954) reported that varsity athletes performed at a higher level than did nonathletes on 21 tests of kinesthetic ability. Taylor (1952) found that boys who were successful in making the varsity basketball team scored higher on a kinesthetic test than did unsuccessful candidates. Gross and Thompson (1957) reported that individuals who have better dynamic balance can swim faster and have better overall swimming ability than do individuals with poorer balance. The Bass test of dynamic balance was used to establish one's balance score.

Young (1945) investigated the relationship between kinesthesis and selected movements used in gymnastics and sports. A group of 37 college women took movement tests involving arm and leg movements, throwing, kicking, hitting, grip, and balance. Although some question was expressed regarding the validity of the kinesthetic test items used, the author concluded that there is a positive relationship between kinesthesis and some typical movements used in gymnastics and sports. In another experiment involving college women, Roloff (1953) administered the Scott motor ability test and eight tests for kinesthesis to 200 students in physical education classes that reflected different levels of ability. A positive relationship was shown between these two test batteries. Roloff concluded that there was merit in the kinesthetic tests used, and further, she developed a regression equation for a battery of the test items involving arm raising, weight shifting, arm circling, and the stick balance.

Norrie (1952) had instructors divide students in physical education classes into good and poor groups according to physical ability. A battery of kinesthetic tests was then admininstered to each group, and it was found that a positive relationship existed between performance in these tests and motor ability as evaluated by the instructors. Witte (1962), however, reported no relationship between positional measures of kinesthesis and the ball-rolling ability of boys and girls in the first and second grades. Also, there were no differences between boys and girls in these measures of kinesthesis.

Development of kinesthesis

The possibility of improving the kinesthetic sense has been of considerable interest to physical educators. However, the probability of improving a basic sensory capacity through practice seems remote. There is no convincing evidence that kinesthesis can in fact be improved. What *can* be improved is a particular position or movement response. Generally, the more one practices a certain response, the more skillful he or she will become in that movement or similar movements. For example, Widdop (1963) showed that ballet training improved the ability of college students in limb positioning and limb position awareness. There is little doubt that such an activity might enable one to perform better on certain types of kinesthetic tests. Nevertheless, it appears that the Widdop study, as well as several similar ones, shows only that certain types of movements and positions can be learned.

Despite the assumption that no basic capacity of kinesthesis can be developed through a program of exercises, there appear to be distinct advantages for participating in a wide range of motor activities. Greater body control, balance, and movement skill should result from this widespread activity. The more movement responses and positions the individual practices, the more likely he or she will develop some skill for movement behavior that will be required in the future. Therefore, the person who takes part in a variety of dance, gymnastic, and sports skills will probably be able to exhibit a higher score on any future measure of kinesthesis that involves bodily movement. This argues for the early exposure of children to a wide range of movement activities. Resultant general development of movement skills gives the appearance of kinesthetic development. Actually, it only represents the development of skills that will be duplicated or transferred to similar skills in the future.

Use of kinesthesis in teaching

Persons with a keen kinesthetic sense apparently remember correct motor movements easily because of vivid position sensations received from the proprioceptors. For example, when learning to type, such an individual develops an early awareness of what it feels like to touch each of the keys. Once this sensation has been established, the person can thereafter depress the correct key with the proper finger without looking. The finger will not often come down between keys or strike two keys at once. The same kinesthetic knowledge may be put to use by the piano player or by the automobile driver who is able to step on the brake pedal or the accelerator without looking.

In sports activities, the ease and skill with which the individual is able to initially assume certain positions or execute particular movements is evidence of the level of kinesthesis. The individual with a high level of kinesthesis will therefore be easily able to repeat the proper starting position for track or football or the baseball batting stance once it has been done correctly the first time. In addition, this person will be able to duplicate or execute a movement more consistently. The ability to regularly execute a cartwheel, fancy dive, or a baseball swing properly is evidence of good kinesthesis. In order to perform in this manner, the individual must clearly sense the movement involved.

To perform effectively and consistently in motor skills, the learner must be guided by his own sensory clues. On the spot instruction by the teacher can be helpful, but in the final analysis the performer must know if he is performing correctly. He must develop a feel for the correct way to swing, to throw, or to jump. In most situations, instruction is necessary in order to effect the initial performance in gymnastics, dance, or some other activity. Following this, the person must remember the sensations of the movement in order to duplicate it at a subsequent time.

The instructor can be helpful in enhancing the performer's kinesthetic awareness of the movement necessary for a particular response. In addition to the natural and obvious sensations the learner receives without guidance, the teacher should aid the performer in conceptualizing the movements for more conscious awareness of the sensations. This greater receptivity to the sensations from proprioceptors should aid the learner in reviewing the performance and mentally rehearsing for future performances.

Some aids are occasionally used by the teacher to promote proper mechanics in movement and student awareness of these responses. The traditional body mechanics technique of having students balance a book on the head while walking up and down stairs, sitting and standing, or walking around the room is one method. Techniques in sports include the use of weighted golf clubs, baseball bat, or tennis racket (with press) to help the learner develop a proper follow-through. Such a weighted bat or club will *force* the individual to follow through and perhaps experience this response for the first time. Once the correct movement is being performed, the instructor can be very helpful in alerting the performer to its sensations.

SUMMARY

1. The senses that are most vital to the learning and performance of motor skills are vision, which receives external stimuli, and kinesthesis, which relates to internal stimuli.

2. Vision is important for overall school performance. A great majority of all learning material in the school is presented visually. Consequently, in the typical classroom, normal visual acuity is viewed as adequate for effective learning. However, in motor skills, some special visual abilities play an important role in determining whether one will perform in an outstanding, average, or inferior manner.

3. Depth perception refers to the ability to distinguish the distance of objects or to make judgments about relative distances. Although binocular vision is the primary basis for depth perception, individuals learn to use a variety of cues to make intelligent estimates of distance.

4. Many situations in sports are presented in which the performer must make accurate judgments about the relative distance of objects or persons. Several studies have shown that athletes perform better than nonathletes on tests of depth perception.

5. Peripheral vision is the ability to see to the side or up and down while looking straight ahead. This sometimes is referred to as field of vision. Most persons can see about 90 degrees to each side, for a total field of about 180 degrees. Peripheral vision is determined by the placement of rods and cones in the eyes.

6. Several studies have shown a relationship between peripheral vision and effectiveness in sports participation. In addition, driving effectiveness and safety, as well as efficiency in certain occupations, are dependent upon adequate peripheral vision. Unusual restriction in one's peripheral vision is sometimes referred to as "tunnel vision."

7. Speed of vision includes both the ability to see and identify objects or images quickly (span of apprehension) and the ability to follow moving objects (visual pursuit). Research has shown a relationship between each of these capacities and motor performance.

8. Several other visual capacities, such as eye dominance, color vision, night blindness, light adaptation, as well as general acuity, have also been identified. These characteristics have been identified and investigated as general visual phenomena and not often with relationship to motor skills. Some would seem to have obvious application to special aspects of motor performance.

9. Kinesthesis, often referred to as the muscle sense, provides individuals with information on body position or body movement. This information is provided by proprioceptors located in muscles, tendons, and ligaments. Information regarding body balance, also viewed as a part of kinesthesis, is provided by the labyrinthine receptors located in the inner ear.

10. Efforts to establish a single test for "the general kinesthetic sense" have proven futile. Rather, it has been determined that the kinesthetic sense is not a general capacity, but a series of specific capacities. Consequently, tests that measure different aspects of the kinesthetic sense show little relationship to each other.

11. No convincing information has been reported to show that the kinesthetic sense can be improved. On the other hand, what can be improved are specific movement skills that may aid one in the performance of several related activities.

However, apparently no kinesthetic sense to aid unrelated activities can be established.

SELECTED READINGS

BORING, E. G. *Sensation and perception in the history of experimental psychology*. New York: Appleton-Century-Crofts, 1942.
DICKINSON, J. *Proprioceptive control of human movement*. Princeton, N.J.: Princeton Book Co., 1976.
GRAYBIEL, A., JOKL, E., and TRAPP, C. Russian studies of vision in relation to physical activity and sports. *Res. Quart.,* 1955, **26**, 480-85.
HOCHBERG, J. *Perception*. Englewood Cliffs, N. J.: Prentice-Hall, 1964.
MUELLER, C. G. *Sensory psychology*. Englewood Cliffs, N.J.: Prentice-Hall, 1965.
OLSEN, E. A. Relationship between psychological capacities and success in college athletics. *Res. Quart.,* 1956, **27**, 79-89.
PHILLIPS, M. and SUMMERS, D. Relation of kinesthetic perception of motor learning, *Res. Quart.,* 1954, **25**, 456-69.
SCOTT, G. M. Measurement of kinesthesis. *Res. Quart.,* 1955, **26**, 324-41.
WILLIAMS, J. M. and Thirer, J. Vertical and horizontal peripheral vision in male and female athletes and nonathletes. *Res. Quar.,* 1975, **46**, 200-205.
WOODWORTH, R. S. and SCHLOSBERG, H. *Experimental psychology* (rev. ed.). New York: Holt, Rinehart and Winston, 1963.

14 Structural and Dominance Differences

INTRODUCTION

One of the most obvious differences that one observes in a group of boys and girls is the variety of sizes and shapes. These differences are considerable from the time the children first enter school. Once the children start to participate in physical activities, whether they are writing, throwing, kicking, or swinging clubs, handedness and footedness also become apparent. For any age level, somatic or anthropometrical differences are normally distributed over a wide scale. Such an even distribution does not exist in dominance since most children favor right-sidedness. However, among children who exhibit a right or left dominance, there appear to be strengths or degrees of this dominance.

Differences in both structure and lateral dominance characteristics are related to learning and performance in motor skills in two important ways. First, these differences have an effect on how successfully, as well as the manner in which, the individual performs in various activities. In most school activities, size differences have limited importance for performance, but this does not hold true in physical skills. Generally, the big child with a good physique will excel over the child who is small or has a frail body structure. Although body structure alone cannot be used as a means for determining performance potential, it is one important factor. Differences in handedness or footedness affect the manner, and possibly the level, of performance. Adjustments on the part of the teacher and the child must be made in the case of left-handed children.

The second way in which structural and dominance differences are related to motor activity is influential in the development of these characteristics. Children who engage in vigorous activity from an early age will have a somewhat different structural development from children who are more restricted or limited in their activity. Similarly, the nature of one's early activity plays a role in the development of handedness or footedness. Physical educators have an excellent opportunity to observe, and possibly affect, both of these characteristics.

ANTHROPOMETRY

The term *anthropometry* refers to the investigation of variations in body structures. These somatic factors have been of particular interest to physical educators because of the effect of body structure on performance, and the effect of physical activity on body structure. Certain other persons, including psychologists and medical doctors, have also shown an interest in this area because of the possible relationship between body type and personality, physical health, and mental health.

It is a truism in any sport that "A good big athlete can beat a good little athlete." The same principle holds true for children in physical activities. In addition to physical maturity, the larger, well-developed children will have distinct performance advantages in general motor performance. Among older children and adults, specific performance advantages for particular types of body dimensions are not so clearly understood. Some authorities, though, have described particular physiques as best suited for various sports activities. They encourage greater investigation of this topic so that children and youths may be guided in the selection of activities in which they will be most successful. Although somewhat scientifically valid, as well as reasonable, some would argue that such an approach will ultimately lead to the manipulation of the lives of young people, i.e., the society determining the sports patterns of citizens.

Today there are two general methods used to describe the physique of the individual. First, there is the classification of the total body into one of several categories. Traditionally, such descriptions as heavy, medium, and slender were used for classification. This is a somewhat subjective procedure, although the techniques are now reasonably well standardized. Second, the body may be described in relation to specific body proportions. For example, the length of the forearm, upper arm, lower legs, the trunk, or the total body may be measured and compared with the width of the hips and shoulders, the width and depth of the chest, the girth of the neck, upper arm, or waist. Such measurements and comparisons may be used as means for describing body structure. Each of these measurements and many more may be studied in relation to some other factor such as performance in some physical activity.

Historical background

It has long been recognized that no two human beings are exactly alike in physical characteristics. Man's interest in body variations and in ways of classifying them dates back more than 2000 years, at least to the Athenian Greeks. Perhaps the persons most influential in pioneering the area of anthropometry in relation to physical education during modern times have been Edward Hitchcock, in the latter half of the 19th century; Ernest Kretschmer, in the 1920s; and William Sheldon, in the 1940s.

Hitchcock (1893) at Amherst College began the first systematic work in anthropometric measurement in the United States. Measurements were taken on each student soon after he entered Amherst and again near the end of each school year. These measurements included ". . . eight items of age, weight, height, chest girth, arm girth, forearm girth, lung capacity and pulse. . . ." (p. 5). Each student was shown how he compared with others in these measurements, and how his own dimensions had changed since previous measurement periods.

Kretschmer (1925) divided body types into the following classifications: (1) *asthenic*: characterized by a lack of thickness and width in all parts of the body and generally a low level of strength; (2) *athletic*: a vigorous body build with strong skeletal and muscular developments, and (3) *pyknic*: compact development of the body cavities and a great deal of fat distribution around the trunk. After working with mental patients for several years Kretschmer concluded that physique was related to temperament.

Since around 1950, a widely used system for describing body types is the plan developed by Sheldon (1954). This system, which is similar to that of Kretschmer, uses the following terminology for describing three body types: (1) endomorphy: relative predominance of soft, round tissue throughout the body with short, heavy arms and legs, and a large midsection; (2) mesomorphy: relative predominance of muscle, bone, and connective tissue throughout body; a heavy, rectangular body outline; and (3) ectomorphy: relative predominance of linearity and fragility; a frail, thin body.

Body type and general motor performance

R. N. Walker (1952) reported that important relationships exist between the motor behavior and body types of two-, three-, and four-year-old children. Using Sheldon's terminology, he described mesomorphic children as having good gross coordination and being energetic. Thin ectomorphs, however, exhibited poor gross coordination with a lesser degree of energy and drive for active participation. Cunningham (1927) found that among nursery school children, body build was more important in the performance of gross motor tasks than was instruction or verbal ability. In a study of first-grade boys and girls, Bauer (1956) reported that boys of medium build tended to be stronger than boys of linear or lateral physique. For girls of this age, however, physique did not seem to be related to measures of strength.

Several studies have reported that athletes who participate in long duration events, such as distance running or cross-country skiing, have lower percentages of body fat than athletes who do not participate in activities requiring such endurance. In a somatotypic analysis of athletes at the 1968 Olympic Games in Mexico City, deGaray, Levine, and Carter (1974) found that male divers, cyclists, sprinters, boxers, rowers, and field event participants were very high in the mesomorphic component with slightly higher measures in ectomorphy than endomorphy. On the other hand, marathon runners were very low in endomorphy and slightly above the midrange in both mesomorphy and ectomorphy. In most comparable activities, women athletes exhibited slightly higher endomorphic and lower mesomorphic measures than did men. Sinning, et al. (1977) did an analysis of men and women who were members of the U. S. Nordic Ski Team while in training for the 1976 Olympics. Both men and women skiers compared favorably with the leanest athletes in any sport. A distinctive body somatotype was identified in the ecto-mesomorphic area for men and endomesomorphic for women. These somatotypes were confined to a small area of the somatochart, suggesting a select body type for the sport of Nordic skiing.

Body composition and body build of high-quality female ballet and modern dancers were compared with each other and to college-age nonathlete females by Dolgener et al. (1980). The percent of body fat among the two groups of dancers was practically identical, although modern dancers had greater hip girth and thigh skinfold measurements. The authors pointed out that the number of years of dancing was almost twice as long for ballet dancers as for modern dancers. Non-dancers were heavier and had larger girth than the combined groups, except for calf girth, which was not any different. The nondancers also had more body fat and were less dense than the dancers. However, when these data were compared to information on nine female distance runners from an earlier study (Brown and Wilmore, 1971), the runners were found to have less fat and to be taller, lighter, and more dense than the dancers. Dolgener et al. concluded that dancers are different from nondancers in body build. They did not speculate on whether the differences were the result of, or a contributing factor in, dance performance.

The relationship of body size to physical performance was investigated by Bookwalter (1952). He compared the Wetzel Grid ratings of 1,977 elementary school boys with performance on the Indiana Physical Fitness Test. Bookwalter reported that (1) boys of average size and thin physique perform better than boys of average size who have a medium physique; (2) very obese boys were the poorest performers of any group studied; (3) maximum size and shape do not produce maximum physical performance; (4) very large boys who are thin perform equally well with those who are average weight; and (5) large and fat boys vary more in physical performance than do normal or thin boys.

Cozens (1929) administered several tests of athletic performance to college men who were grouped according to weight. The tests included measures for strength, speed, jumping, throwing, kicking, diving, and agility. The author found distinct relationships between stature and athletic performance. Specifically, he reported that (1) both tall men and those of medium height were superior to short men; (2) heavier men were superior to slender ones; and (3) men of medium weight were superior to those who were slender.

College women athletes were compared to nonathletes in body strength, anthropometic measurements, and somatotype by Morris (1960). Comparisons were also made among athletes who competed in different sports. Significant anatomical differences between performers in particular sports were found in limb lengths, hip widths, and the ratio of shoulders to hips. The athletic group was more mesomorphic and less ectomorphic than the unselected women. While the athletes were generally rated as mesomorphic endomorphs, divers, gymnasts, and track women were particularly high in mesomorphy, and participants in hockey, basketball, swimming, softball, and golf were relatively high in endomorphy. Morris reported that total strength was not as important in athletic performance as was the ratio between strength and weight. Perbix (1954) found that women physical education majors in college exhibit high mesomorphic traits. She also reported a significant relationship between mesomorphy and knee push-ups but no relationship between body type and flexibility.

Hawthorne (1952) investigated the relationship between the somatotype ratings of college men and their performance on selected motor ability tests. The tests included strength, speed, jumping, throwing, and coordination items. The ectomorphic-mesomorphic group did best on these tests, while the mesomorphic-ectomorphic group did poorest. In general motor ability, those high in ectomorphy were best while the mesomorphs were highest in strength items. Sills and Everett (1953) related performance in physical fitness items to the somatotype of the participants. The authors reported that the mesomorphs did best, with the ectomorphs and endomorphs following in that order. Willgoose and Rogers (1949) reported that strength increases with mesomorphy, and that the fitness level of extreme mesomorphs is very high.

Physical size, with age, serves as the basis for two widely used methods of grouping children for physical activity. The McCloy *classification index*, long used as a means for class grouping and equating teams for athletic competition, includes the components of height, weight, and age. A different index is used for the elementary school, the high school, and the college levels. In the elementary school, only age and weight are used, thus indicating that height is not a major determinant for performance at this age level. The index for the college level includes only height and weight, but the high school index includes all three characteristics. The *Neilson and Cozens classification index* is very similar to that of McCloy except that it is limited to the elementary and high school levels. Both of these indices emphasize the role of height and weight in athletic performance. Sills (1950) suggests that children be grouped, and therefore graded, in physical education according to their body type.

Racial differences

It has been observed that at certain periods there are disproportionate percentages of persons from particular racial groups in certain sports. For example, during the past half century, boxing has had, at different times, an abundance of Americans whose heritage was Irish, Italian, Black, and Latin American. During recent years, Black athletes have practically dominated short-distance running events in this country. They have also excelled in baseball and basketball, but not in swimming, golf, or tennis. At least some authors (Metheny, 1939; Steggerda and Petty, 1940; and Tanner, 1964) attribute some of the performance differences to anthropometric characteristics. It used to be commonplace to attribute performance differences by certain racial groups to inherent physical differences. Recent research has provided little support for this notion. Participation and success seem more related to cultural factors.

According to Brown (1973), the Black athlete has become the major force in modern American sport. He stated that this is particularly true in boxing, baseball, football, and basketball. To illustrate this, he pointed out that in the 23-year period between 1949 and 1972 Black athletes accomplished the following in baseball: ten National League batting titles, 14 home-run titles, and 15 M.V.P. awards, with somewhat less impressive statistics in the American League. In basketball there were ten Black N.B.A. scoring leaders, 15 rebound leaders, and ten assist leaders. In professional football there were 16 N.F.L. leading rushers, eight A.F.L. leading rushers, four N.F.L. leading receivers, and five A.F.L. leading receivers. Certainly there has not been a diminution in the achievements of Black athletes in these sports since 1972. Statistics of their performance in boxing hardly need to be cited, and the same is true in track and field. While discussing at length some of the social ramifications of this matter, Brown draws no conclusion as to the *reasons* for the excellence of Black athletes in these areas.

In an effort to control the effect of culture on performance differences, Dinucci and Shows (1977) compared six- to eight-year-old Black and White girls in measures of endurance, speed, muscular power, balance, and flexibility. They found no differences in any of these measures. However, they reported that the White girls excelled in grip strength and a shuttle run, while the Black girls performed better in agility. No clear superiority was established for either group in the 28 motor test items.

Lee (1980) compared the motor performance ability of White and Black children selected from low socioeconomic neighborhoods in a small Louisiana community. The children were further categorized according to the authoritarian style of the mother. Lee reported that Black children, regardless of parental style, were superior to White children in both running and jumping. In addition, children of nonauthoritarian mothers excelled when compared to children of authoritarian mothers. She does not conclude that the differences are racially based. Rather, she suggests additional research to include peer influence, sibling attitudes, parental attitudes, different measures of parental control, and the use of different types of motor skills.

In an early study, Metheny (1939) reported numerous differences in anthropometric measurements between Black and White students at the college level. She theorized that these differences offered the Black students advantages in athletic activities. She pointed out especially that the structure of the lower leg and ankle may offer some advantage in jumping events. However, no effort was made in her study to determine if there was a relationship between the observed structure and performance level. Despite the fact that Metheny's study has been quoted often since its publication, very little effort has been made to duplicate its findings. Neither has research demonstrated the relationship between the anthropometric characteristics described and outstanding athletic performance. In a comparison of Black and White college women, however, Steggerda and Petty (1940) reported that all linear measurements of appendages were greater for the Black group. The arm span of the Black women was reported as 105 percent of the standing height, whereas for the White group the relationship was 99 percent.

Tanner (1964) described Black athletes at the Olympic games as having longer arms and legs than White athletes competing in the same event. Also, Black athletes had more muscle in the arms and thighs, but more slender calves and hips. In a performance study, Hutinger (1959) found that Black children in the elementary school ran faster in a 35-yard dash than did White children at the same grade level. He suggested that the difference may have been due to a faster reflex time, although this was not tested in Hutinger's study. Age, size, and environmental differences were not controlled or suggested as factors in the speed differences. Herzstein (1961) found that at the college level, Black men had higher scores on the Sargent vertical jump test than did white men.

In addition, certain *nationalities* have seemed to dominate in some sports to a greater extent than would be anticipated by population numbers or any other visible reason. For example, during the 1970s and early 1980s, Little League baseball teams from the small country of Taiwan clearly dominated the annual World Series. In world competition, men's field hockey teams from Pakistan have practically ruled that sport, as have table tennis players from China, ice hockey players from Canada, and gymnasts (and ballet dancers) from the U.S.S.R. During the 1950s, Australia seemed to have a corner on the market in swimming and tennis.

Such incidence of near national dominance seems to have waned somewhat over the past decade. Possibly the growing popularity of the Olympic Games and sports in general has contributed to wider visibility and participation in a greater number of sports in all countries. Still, one wonders about the disproportionate prevalence and excellence of national and ethnic groups in particular sports and their obvious absence from others. Among the reasons offered has been the suggestion of anthropometric advantages of certain racial groups for some activities. Some related physiological differences have also been offered as a reason.

Aside from a few obvious situations, such as the height and weight disadvantage that Oriental performers might have in basketball or American football, are there physical differences among racial groups that are important in athletic performance? Unfortunately, there has been much more speculation than research on this question. Wyndham, Strydom, Morrison, Peter, Williams, Bredell, and Joffe (1963) found that there was no difference among various ethnic groups in oxygen intake when the physical condition of the subjects was similar. This tends to refute earlier assumptions that Black athletes were incapable of performing well in distance or endurance events because of limitations in lung physiology.

A word of caution must be offered regarding the tendency to categorize all athletes according to particular body dimensions. It has consistently been found that persons with widely differing somatotypes excel in each sport. Also, many who have an ideal body type for some activities yet fail to win over others who are apparently less well-endowed. One must conclude, therefore, that there are many factors that go into making an outstanding performer. Body structure is only one of these components.

It is a major understatement to say that there is a lack of convincing evidence regarding the matter of ethnicity or nationality and sports performance. Research into this topic, with adequate sociocultural controls, has simply not taken place in recent years. As has been found in intelligence testing, such controls are practically impossible to manage. In addition, the possibility of studying adequate numbers of "pure" Blacks, American Indians, or Chinese in this country is becoming increasingly remote. Related research and general speculation suggest that social and cultural factors are far more influential than are racial determinants.

LATERAL DOMINANCE

Lateral dominance refers to the habitual use, in unilateral motor tasks, of one hand, foot, or eye in preference to the opposite member. In bilateral tasks, dominance is exhibited by the member that performs the more complex maneuvers or provides the greatest power. Other terms used in reference to the concept of lateral dominance are *laterality, preference, sidedness, dominance,* and in a more limited context, *handedness.*

In addition to common motor tasks, people exhibit sidedness in smiling, chewing, winking, sleeping positions, handling eating utensils, and many small manual skills. Lateral dominance and body asymmetry, with resulting habits, are characteristic to some extent of lower animals. The most easily observed aspect of lateral dominance in humans is handedness. This trait also affects more movements and habits than the other dominance characteristics. As a result, most of the attention in the area of dominance centers on handedness.

Handedness has been a phenomenon of considerable social interest for centuries and in all cultures. Since the beginning of recorded history, man has been concerned with the occurrence and significance of left-handedness. Sinister moral and mental implications have been associated with this trait. Recent scientific interest has also been devoted to this topic and particularly to questions such as: Is handedness inherited, or is it developed as result of environmental conditions? Can handedness be changed without resulting in stuttering or other emotional problems? Are there particular advantages or disadvantages in performing motor skills either right-handed or left-handed? Is it advisable to change handedness, and if so, how can this be done most effectively?

Several terms have been developed to describe the conditions that exist in lateral dominance. The predominant use of the right hand for unilateral skills is referred to as *dextrality.* When the left hand is used for such tasks this is called *sinistrality. Ambidexterity* refers to a condition in which the two hands exhibit approximately equal skill and are used to perform similar tasks. Perfect ambidexterity, however, is rarely found. Hildreth (1950) has inferred that most ambidextrous people are naturally left-handed but have acquired a great deal of skill with the right hand.

Homolaterality refers to the situation in which the hand, eye, and foot on the same side are dominant. *Contralaterality* is used to denote mixed dominance in which the individual has some dominance characteristic on each side, such as being right-handed and left-eyed. The term *ambisinistrality* has been used recently in reference to a condition in which neither hand has been developed to an adequate level of efficiency and, therefore, no dominance is present. This is contrasted with ambidexterity in which a relatively high level of skill has been developed in both hands.

The incidence of dominance

Percentages of lateral dominance of one type or another seem to vary with the particular culture. In the United States, it is estimated that approximately 5 percent of the population is left-handed. However, the range in research reports often varies from about 3 to 12 percent. It has been reported that in Russia and in China the percentage of left-handers is far less than in the United States. Anthropologists indicate that in some cultures, past and present, the proportion of left-handers to right-handers more closely approached a 50-50 ratio. According to Hildreth (1949a), incidence of left-handedness has run as high as 33 percent in prehistoric times.

It has been theorized by one psychologist that about 25 percent of the population is naturally right-handed, 25 percent is naturally left-handed, and 50 percent has no innate dominance. According to this theory, all those who are naturally right-handed remain so; all those with no dominance become right-handed; and most of the naturally left-handed persons develop a right-handed dominance.

Right-handedness has apparently prevailed in all cultures as far as man can trace. Tools, relics, and drawings, however, indicate that left-handedness was more prevalent among primitive men than among people today. The strong shift to right-handedness probably originated in religious ceremonies and was reinforced by the design of military weapons and methods. Superstitions that associated left-handedness with evil spirits resulted in great pressure for the development of right-handedness in all children. Dextrality then became a social code and a cultural law. Prejudice and superstition regarding sinistrality still exists in some cultures.

Incidence of lateral dominance seems to be related to the age and sex of the individual as well as to the culture in which one lives. Left-handedness is more common among boys and men than among girls and women. In a study of 13,438 elementary school children, Blair (1945) reported that 6.4 percent of the children used the left hand for writing. Of this sinistral subgroup, 62 percent were boys and 38 percent were girls. Brain (1945) found that left-handedness was twice as common among males as females. Apparently boys are less concerned with conformity in laterality, or possibly they participate in more activities in which the left hand is developed. In addition to dominance preference, boys exhibit less strength difference between the hands than do girls. In one study, it was shown that among boys the strength difference between the right and left hand was 6 to 7 percent, while among girls the difference was 10 to 12 percent.

Children exhibit a greater degree of ambidexterity than do older persons. For example, more five-year-old children will show a right-handed dominance than will three-year-olds. In fact, during the first few years of life, there is a fluctuation in hand preference. The tendency toward right-handedness increases during the first few years of school. Thereafter, any significant change in handedness is rare. College students appear to have the lower incidence of left-handedness than do any younger group.

Simply reporting the number of people who are right-handed or left-handed does not present a complete picture of hand dominance. There appear to be *levels* or *degrees* of handedness that vary among people and among tasks. Rife (1951) has indicated that 5 to 8 percent of the population are totally left-handed while 30 percent are inclined to be left-handed in certain activities. The particular method used to identify or measure handedness makes a difference in the percentage reported. Some persons write with one hand but throw a ball with the other one. Some may swing a tennis racket with the right hand but swing a baseball bat from the left-handed side of the plate. In addition, some people have approximately equal strength in each hand while others have a great difference between the two. For these reasons, labeling a person as "right-handed" or "left-handed" or simply reporting the percentage of people who fall into each category does not completely illustrate the status of handedness.

Dominance of the feet and eyes does not follow the extremely one-sided pattern prevalent in handedness. That is, a much higher percentage of people are left-footed or ambidextrous with the feet than are left-handed. This may be due to the fact that since foot dominance is less obvious, less pressure is exerted upon people to make dominant use of one foot. The situation often results in a condition of contralaterality. It is estimated that from 65 to 85 percent of all right-handed people are also right-eyed, but probably a smaller percentage have foot dominance on the same side as hand dominance. In a study by L. M. Jenkins (1930), for example, it was reported that at age five, 3.3 percent of the subjects exhibited both left-hand and left-foot dominance, whereas 7.7 percent were left-handed and right-footed.

People are able to make a pretty accurate judgment of their hand dominance, but an accurate identification of foot dominance is more difficult. Even the selection of hand dominance can be troublesome, however, as reported by Fox (1963), who found that a sizable percentage of people preferred the use of the right hand even though tests indicated that the left hand was stronger and more skilled. Most people assume that the right foot will be greatly dominant, but left-handed people will select the left foot. In many activities, the individual performs in a manner that seems most natural without being aware of which leg is being used in a dominant manner. Personal judgments about eye dominance or leg dominance are often inaccurate. Visual tests, however, can easily be established for acuity, peripheral vision, or other capacities.

Measurement of lateral dominance

A series of tests must be administered before a clear determination can be made of the type or degree of handedness. Fuzak (1961) indicated that lateral dominance can be expressed only in terms of the traits measured. To be most accurate, therefore, one must indicate the skill or activity in which the person exhibits a preference. Since people exhibit different hand preferences for different activities, no single test can be adequate for measuring dominance. Children especially alternate hand preferences as they move from one task to another. Although eye and foot preference are not easily observed, they, too, vacillate during the early years of life.

One technique that has been used in some studies is to solicit information from the subject by means of a *questionnaire* or *interview*. Rather than seeking the subject's general estimation of his dominance, it is more accurate to ask specific questions about habitual performance of certain routine tasks. For example, which hand is used in cutting with scissors, writing, throwing a ball, or using a tennis racket? Also, in what manner is a baseball bat swung, wood chopped, or leaves raked? Which foot is used to kick a football, as a takeoff for a high jump or broad jump; and which leg is used for the hurdle step in diving? Such questions can give a fairly accurate picture of the individual's preferred or habitual use of hands and legs.

A second technique for determining functional handedness, footedness, or eyedness, is to have the individual actually *perform* tasks as the investigator observes. Such a procedure is often used with preschool children as they draw a picture, throw a ball, use a hammer, cut a form with scissors, screw nuts on a bolt, sight objects, or jump over an obstacle. This will provide information regarding functional dominance in cases where it cannot be given by the individual verbally.

Dominance may also be tested by administering a *series of tests* and comparing the strengths and weaknesses of different body parts in each. Tests of speed, strength, fine and gross dexterity, and skill level may be administered to both hands or both feet. Comparisons between the right and left can be made to determine not only the dominant member, but the amount of difference in each type of movement. Provins (1956) tested each hand of subjects for speed of tapping and for sensitivity to applied pressure against a steel bar. The same measures were administered to the big toe on each foot. In addition, an aiming test (dart throwing) was taken with each hand. Significant differences were found in tapping speed in favor of the preferred hand and in accuracy for the preferred hand. No differences were noted for the sensitivity test.

A comparison of the capacities of each hand and foot offers the most helpful means of classifying handedness and footedness. Manuometer tests can be administered to determine the strength of each hand. The ball throw for distance and for accuracy provide a valuable comparison of the power and skill associated with each. Different dexterity and skill tests may be used for other types of comparison. Tests for leg strength, kicking for distance and accuracy, and jumping distance off each foot provide similar comparisons. Only when such a battery of tests is used can a thorough analysis be made of the individual's dominance.

In practice, children may be categorized according to their *degree* of handedness, i.e., some children may be viewed as extremely right- or left-handed, while others are more nearly ambidextrous. Such a classification may be based on the percentage of tasks one performs with a given hand, or the relative strength or proficiency advantage one hand exhibits over the other. Theoretically, the ambidextrous person is one who performs tasks equally well with either, i.e., a 50-50 balance. Others may have a 60-40 right-left balance, or, in extreme cases, a 90-10 balance.

Characteristics of left-handed persons

It has often been asserted that stuttering or other speech defects are associated with left-handedness and with children to whom attempts have been made to change handedness. Durost (1934) reported that sinistrality is linked with reading difficulties, stuttering and stammering, and a lack of physical coordination. He expressed the view that these difficulties resulted from both neural confusion and environmental pressures. It has also been reported that confusion resulting in opposite hand movements such as typing the letter *d* instead of *k*, or *i* instead of *e* is more prevalent among left-handed persons.

Several researchers have reported a disproportionate number of mentally retarded and defective persons to be left-handed. In one study of institutions for the feebleminded and psychopaths, K. L. Martin (1952) found from 16 to 30 percent of the patients to be left-handed. Other studies have also reported three or four times as many left-handers in such institutions as are found in the general population.

Those who have reported a connection between left-handedness and school failure or other difficulties have not usually suggested a cause-and-effect relationship. Rather, it has generally been theorized that the frustrations and pressures encountered by the left-hander in a right-handed culture have been considerable. Lack of success, lack of appropriate facilities or equipment, and efforts to subdue the preferred hand in favor of the unpreferred hand may result in *some* children developing emotional or motor development problems. Apparently, these problems do not adversely affect all, or even the majority, of left-handed children.

Traditionally, the left-handed person has been forced to modify or adjust to many situations in and out of school. For example, the right-handed teacher explains or demonstrates the proper technique for throwing, batting, jumping, or kicking for the right-handed student. About the only consideration given to left-handed persons is that they are instructed to "do just the opposite." That person is required to interpret or adapt this technique to the opposite side for his own purposes. Further, left-handed persons are required to use right-handed desks, tools, baseball gloves, bowling balls, and, in some cases, omit an activity entirely. Over the years, in certain cultures, there has been considerable contempt for left-handers. The Latin word for left, sinister, does not help the image of this trait. Neither does "he's out in left field," "two left feet," or "a left-handed compliment." In short, the left-hander is a member of a minority group. Some persons respond healthily to such stimulation; others do not.

Some attention has been devoted to the need for developing a dominant side. It has been reported that individuals with no clear dominance and with little motor skill exhibit more severe problems than persons with either a right or left dominance. Doman (1960) and Delacato (1963) reported that when a clear dominance is established in retarded children, significant motor and intellectual development results.

Despite such claims, there has been no convincing evidence that cross-dominance leads to any difficulties in intellectual development, speech patterns, or motor development. In fact, there is some opposing evidence. Tyler (1971) reported on a study that showed that hand preference and cross-dominance did not interfere with one's ability to learn new motor skills. As was reported earlier, Teig (1981) found that more than 50 percent of all major league baseball batters had a cross hand-eye dominance. This is compared to about 20 percent of the general population who have such cross-dominance.

Changing handedness

There are special problems that a left-handed person growing up in our society will naturally encounter. Some of these were alluded to in the previous section. For this reason, it has often been considered fortunate if a child naturally grew up to be right-handed. Furthermore, some parents and teachers have thought it desirable to change any children who seemed to be developing left-handedness. In some quarters, this desire to reverse handedness assumed a degree of urgency. Most often these attempts centered around the task of handwriting during the early school years.

Efforts to switch the handedness of children resulted in several problems (real and imaginary) in speech and general school progress. A fear of changing handedness therefore developed. Recent research, however, has cast serious doubt on the assumption that attempts to change handedness will necessarily result in emotional or other problems. In fact, most authorities today do not feel that this procedure causes stuttering or is emotionally upsetting. However, particular attention should be devoted to the manner in which the change is attempted. One of the most extensive studies dealing with the reversal of writing handedness was conducted by Blau (1946) in Elizabeth, New Jersey. In this study, an effort was made to reverse 250 left-handed students during the first years of school. Within a four-year period all but 66 of the children were regularly writing with the right hand. No cases of defective speech or emotional problems were reported. It may be assumed that since 66 children were *not* reversed, undue pressure was not exerted upon them. While some children are quite susceptible to reversal training, others are very resistive. Blau's study points out that training to a degree sufficient for reversing most children may be conducted without emotional problems.

When attempting to change handedness among children, patience and understanding are needed to avoid emotional repercussions. It is also best that the reversal be attempted early, preferably before the ages of seven or eight, although some children can be changed years later. When developing the nonpreferred hand, simple gross movements should be initiated. After some skill has been developed, finer and more complex tasks can be introduced. For example, in developing handwriting skill, large figures written on the chalkboard may serve as an appropriate preliminary activity for paper and pencil writing.

It is important that parents and educators keep in mind that children do not *have* to become right-handers. Before attempting to reverse left-handers, some thought should be devoted to whether or not it is worth the effort. Accommodations are more readily available today, and the culture is more tolerant of left-handers than ever before. In some situations, including certain sports activities, they appear to have an advantage. As a result of these developments, researchers indicate that the number of left-handed persons in this country is growing.

Lateral dominance
and motor performance

In athletics it has often been suspected that left-handed performers had a slight advantage over right-handers when competing in a face-to-face situation. This was based on the assumption that the left-handed person is more used to such a confrontation than is the right-hander. For example, in combative activities, such as boxing, wrestling, fencing, and judo, the strengths and typical moves of the right-handed participant may be quite familiar to his left-handed opponent, whereas the reverse is not true. In football, the quarterback who rolls out to his left and throws with the left hand may cause some adjustment problems for the charging defensive lineman. In softball, the left-handed pitcher may have a slight advantage because the delivery is not as common. However, in sports not requiring interacting competition, such as swimming, track and field, bowling, and gymnastics, handedness would seem to make little difference.

Research relating lateral dominance to motor proficiency has been slight. Several related studies, however, are reported in the literature. Sinclair and Smith (1957) investigated the relationship of hand, eye, and foot dominance to proficiency in swimming the crawl and side strokes. Subjects were freshmen and sophomore college women. The investigators reported that swimmers who breathe to the right side while doing the crawl stroke generally swim the side stroke on the left side. Similarly, those who breathed to the left side in the crawl stroke did the side stroke on the right side. Dominance of the hand, eye, or foot was not established as important for side selection in swimming or breathing. Rather, the authors concluded that teaching methods and social customs were more important factors in determining sidedness in swimming.

Fox (1957) administered a response test to determine hand dominance of women students in a bowling class. Twenty subjects were selected who exhibited a left-handed dominance, but who preferred bowling with the right hand. In the experiment, 16 of these subjects were taught to bowl with the preferred hand, while four were taught to bowl left-handed. The two groups of students were equated in general motor ability. After equal sessions of practice, the right-handed bowlers performed better. In this particular study, therefore, the *preferred* hand proved more effective in bowling than did the *dominant* hand (as determined by Fox). Though the sample was very limited, the author theorized that total body coordination and previous experience were perhaps as important in performance as was hand and arm dominance. It was suggested that hand preference rather than hand dominance be used as the basis for arm choice in bowling.

In another study, Fox (1963) investigated the dominance indices of girls with high and low motor ability. No difference was found between these ability groups in dominance indices. Mixed dominance was prevalent among both groups. From this study, she concluded that lateral dominance was not related to motor performance.

Way (1958) administered tests in archery, bowling, badminton, and tennis to 410 college women to determine the relationship between these activities and certain measures of lateral dominance. Hand, eye, and foot dominance were established for each of the subjects. Certain laterality measures seemed particularly important in activities stressing accuracy of direction toward a fixed target, such as archery and bowling. The author concluded that women with mixed dominance are superior in motor ability to those with homolateral preferences.

It should be clear that left-handedness does not inhibit outstanding sports performance. Uhrbrock (1970) reported that of the 144 most prominent athletes, a higher percentage was either left-handed or had mixed dominance than a group of students whose interest in athletics was nominal. Babe Ruth, Sandy Koufax, Reggie Jackson, and Steve Carlton are but a few names from baseball, but they provide ample evidence that left-handers can attain a high level of success in this sport. In other fields, Harry S. Truman, Gerald Ford, Marilyn Monroe, Dorothy Hamill, Caesar, Charlemagne, Michaelangelo, and da Vinci also reached high levels of success in a variety of fields despite left-handedness.

Teaching ambidexterity

In many athletic activities, it is desirable for the instructor, to teach ambidexterity in the performance of the particular task because of the need for the performer to be able to use both hands or both feet skillfully. For example, in basketball the good player must be able to dribble or to shoot lay-up shots with both the right and left hand. When one does not have this ability with each hand, the defensive team has a decided advantage by concentrating its attention against only one side. In soccer, the player who can kick with only one foot has limited effectiveness. In football, the ability to block or tackle on either side is advantageous. Many other examples can be brought to mind in which ambidextrous skill is essential for effective participation. In some activities, however, bilateral dexterity is not of particular value. In handwriting, playing tennis, pitching baseball, or shooting archery there is little advantage to having a high level of skill with the nondominant hand.

When developing skill in the nondominant or less skillful hand, it is desirable to emphasize large and simple movements in the beginning. After some skill has been developed in basic or fundamental elements, practice can begin with finer and more complex movements. This technique has been used where handwriting has been developed in the nonpreferred hand for the reversal of handedness. Large, smoothly curved figures have usually been presented in the early sessions. The development of skill in the nondominant hand is therefore similar to the recommended practices for original learning.

When introducing soccer to a group for the first time, should skill in dribbling and passing be developed first with one foot or should practice take place with both feet concurrently? The advisability of simultaneous versus separate practices has not been clearly determined for gross motor skills. The possibilities for positive bilateral transfer as well as negative transfer (interference) must be considered in each situation. The majority of evidence suggests, however, that practice with both hands or both feet should proceed simultaneously. Lambert (1951) conducted a study in which male college students learned a novel two-handed psychomotor task. In this experiment, some subjects practiced the skill first with the dominant hand, while others practiced initially with the nondominant hand. The author concluded that for learning the two-handed task, it made little difference which hand was trained first. When subjects switched from the use of a single hand to the use of two hands, poorer performance resulted. Lambert recommended, therefore, that attention be devoted to training both hands concurrently.

SUMMARY

1. In motor activities, physical size and structure have a more profound effect than in other areas of school achievement. In motor skills, the big child with a good physique generally excels over the small, frail child. Further, children who engage regularly in vigorous activity grow and develop more athletic physiques than those who lead a sedentary life.

2. Anthropometry is the study of variations in body structure or general physique. This field also encompasses investigation of the relative proportion of body parts to each other and their effect on motor performance. Because of the obvious interrelationship between body structure and motor performance, physical educators have a particular interest in this topic.

3. The study of physique and body dimensions dates back at least to the ancient Greeks. However, this field has received greater attention and definition with the work of Hitchcock during the second half of the 19th century, Kretschmer in the 1920s, and Sheldon in the 1940s and '50s.

4. Studies over the past three decades have developed a rough profile of body types and sizes for athletes who excel in a wide range of activities, including long distance running, weightlifting, cycling, boxing, and ballet.

5. All categories of athletes are relatively high in Sheldon's classification of mesomorphy. The relative strength of endomorphy and ectomorphy vary with the particular type of athletic ability. For example, it would be very unusual to find an individual high in endomorphy playing forward in the N B.A. or one high in ectomorphy playing defensive tackle in the N.F.L.

6. There are some general physical characteristics that relate athletes to different sports, as well as to particular positions in those sports. However, there is enough overlap and mix so that it is impossible to restrict individuals to those sports and positions. There are many exceptions that defy the general descriptors.

7. Racial and nationality groupings appear to emerge in certain sports areas. However, the lack of well-controlled research and the evidence of exceptions tend to discourage broad generalizations about any physical advantage or disadvantage of any racial or nationality group for a particular activity.

8. Lateral dominance refers to the habitual use in unilateral motor tasks of one hand, foot, or eye in preference to the other. Terminology related to the area of dominance is presented.

9. The incidence of left-handedness varies widely among cultures. In the United States, the number of left-handers is reported to be between 5 and 10 percent. In more restrictive societies, the percentage of left-handedness is reported to be much less. Foot and eye dominance are closer to a 50-50 split.

10. The measurement of handedness is complex because of the varying degrees or strengths of handedness among individuals. Whereas some persons use the same hand for practically all unilateral tasks, others spread the skills more evenly between the two hands, e.g., writing with the right hand but playing tennis with the left hand, or using scissors with the left hand and handling a spoon with the right hand. Some persons even alternate hands from time to time while performing the same task. Consequently, thorough tests of handedness must involve a range of motor tasks.

11. The establishment of handedness does not have precise timing. Rather, preference for one hand or the other vacillates back and forth with most children for the first three or four years of life.

12. It has been widely believed by some that changing handedness will lead to speech, reading, or other educational achievement problems. However, adequate studies have shown that such change can take place with many children without psychological or educational problems.

13. Despite the claims of some therapists, there is no convincing evidence that cross-dominance leads to any educational or motor performance problems.

14. There are numerous difficulties and adjustments encountered by the left-handed person growing up in a "right-handed society." In motor skills, such difficulties can be minimized by the thoughtful teacher. Adjustments or position assignments in motor sports activities enable left-handed persons to participate with minimal difficulty. In fact, there are often distinct advantages for left-handed athletes because of the unusual nature of their movement response as viewed by a right-hander.

15. There are numerous motor skill situations in which it is helpful for the athlete to be able to perform with either hand or foot. In such activities it is helpful to teach ambidexterity from the beginning of one's participation in that activity.

SELECTED READINGS

BLAU, A. The master hand. *Amer. Orthopsychiatr. Ass. Res. Monogr.*, 1946, no. 5.

BROWN, R. C. The black gladiator—the major force in modern American sport. *Proceedings of the NCPEAM,* 1973, 43-50.

CURETON, T. K. *Physical fitness of champion athletes.* Urbana, Ill.: University of Illinois Press, 1951.

DELACATO, C. H. *The treatment and prevention of reading problems.* Springfield, Ill.: Charles C Thomas, 1959.

DINUCCI, J. M. and SHOWS, D. A. Comparisons of the motor performance of black and caucasian girls ages 6-8, *Res. Quart.,* 1977, **48,** 680-84.

GARRITY, H. M. Relationship of somatotype of college women to physical fitness performance. *Res. Quart.,* 1966, **37,** 340-52.

GESELL, A. and AMES, L. B. The development of handedness. *J. Genet. Psychol.,* 1947, **70,** 155-75.

LEE, A. M., Child-rearing practices and motor performance of black and white children. *Res. Quart. for Exercise and Sport,* 1980, **51,** 494-500.

METHENY, E. Studies of the Johnson test of motor educability. *Res. Quart.,* 1939, **9,** 105-14.

SHELDON, W. H. *Atlas of men.* New York: Harper & Row, 1954.

TANNER, J. M. *The physique of the Olympic athlete.* London: G. Allen, 1964.

UHRBROCK, R. S. Laterality of champion athletes. *Journal of Motor Behavior,* 1970, **2,** 285-90.

15 Reaction and Movement Speed

REACTION TIME VERSUS MOVEMENT TIME

An important behavioral characteristic in which individuals differ greatly is speed of reaction. This component seems strategic in distinguishing between outstanding, average, and poor performers in many motor skills. Athletic coaches have traditionally assumed that persons with the fastest reaction times become the better athletes. For this reason, coaches have shown considerable interest in reaction speed and in determining which performers can move most rapidly. Experimental psychologists have also exhibited a great deal of interest because reaction speed is one of the important response variables among people and because it is conveniently available for rather objective measurement.

Several meanings are often attached to the term *reaction time*. Some people use it in reference to such traits as the ability to get quick starts, i.e., to take the first few steps most rapidly, or to have quick movements. Others have a more limited concept of the term. For measurement of reaction time, physical educators and psychologists have usually restricted the subject's response to small finger movements. Occasionally, large motor responses have also been used. To clarify the issue, reaction time and movement time will be discussed as components of speed of reaction.

Reaction time is the period from the stimulus to the beginning of the overt response. It is not what the term might seem to imply, i.e., the time occupied by the execution of the response. Rather, reaction time is the time required to get the overt response *started*, or the stimulus-to-response interval. Following the stimulus, there is a period before movement commences. The response simply cannot come out of the organism as soon as the stimulus goes in. There is a latent period while the impulse is transmitted from the sense organ to the central nervous system and then back to the muscles. The muscles must then contract to begin movement. Although all of these actions take some time, the most time is probably taken in the motor areas of the brain. This is especially true if any decision making is required. According to Woodworth and Schlosberg (1963), reaction time ". . . includes sense-organ time, brain time, nerve time, and muscle time" (p. 8). In experimental situations the measurement of reaction time has involved some simple responses, such as releasing or depressing a button or telegraph key. Since even these small responses require some movement through a distance, they are not "pure" measures of reaction time. Still, such responses have been the customary way of measuring reaction time, and as such, are viewed as reasonably accurate.

During the past two decades or so, analysis has been devoted to a further breakdown of the components of reaction time. These components were recognized by Woodworth and Schlosberg's reference to "muscle time" in addition to nerve time and sense-organ time. The necessity of muscle time is evident in traditional measures of reaction time, which requires that some response occurs before it can be measured. In most experimental situations the subject is required to perform a simple act, with the time being recorded. A departure from this approach has been the recent development of the concept of *fractionated reaction time*, a term used to distinguish between the point when there is action potential registered in the muscles and the point at which a criterion response has been completed.

Investigators verify that there is a period of muscle activation prior to movement. The activation is experimentally detected by surface electrodes placed over the relevant muscle groups. According to Schmidt (1982), after the muscle is activated, no movement occurs for 40 to 60 milliseconds. He refers to the interval from the stimulus to the first EMG responses as the *premotor* reaction time. The period from this response to the criterion movement, e.g., depressing the key, is the *motor* reaction time. The premotor phase seems to represent processing, interpretation, and decision time, while the motor stage represents muscular functioning.

In addition to reaction time, movement time has been of special interest to athletic coaches and physical educators. Experimental psychologists, on the contrary, have not investigated or discussed this component widely. *Movement time* refers to the period from the beginning of the overt response to the completion of a specified movement. In the measurement of movement time, a rather large movement is usually employed. The total movement response, therefore, encompasses both reaction and movement times; reaction time being the stimulus-response interval, and movement time being the period required for the response itself. The term "reaction time" has occasionally been used erroneously to include both of these concepts, even when the movement phase was quite long. Figure 15-1 illustrates the components of overall response time.

FIGURE 15-1. Components of Response Time.

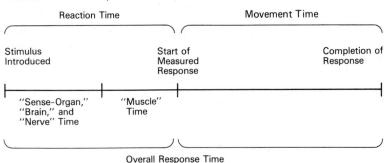

Quickness and speed of movement have always been popular topics with athletic coaches because of their interest in how rapidly an individual can perform an act that is important in some motor activity. These coaches have been interested in determining which players can perform certain acts most rapidly. For example, in a face-off situation in hockey, can the person move fast enough to gain control of the puck? The same question would apply in a drop-ball situation in soccer. In other situations, does the player have quick hands so that he can catch a fast moving ball or one that suddenly appears from a short distance? The individual with fast movement time exhibits this capacity in numerous sports situations. Speed of movement is therefore quite different from the speed of the neural impulses in reaction time testing.

It has traditionally been assumed that there is a rather high relationship between reaction time and movement time. That is, the individual with a fast reaction time was believed to be able to move more quickly or to run faster than a person with a slower reaction time. This particular question has been investigated quite thoroughly during the past few years. As a result of this research, considerable doubt has been cast on the traditional assumption. According to Guilford (1958) and Henry (1952), the natures of reaction time and movement time are quite different.

Guilford (1958) classified *impulsion* (the rate of starting movements from a stationary position) and muscular strength as general factors that are primarily dependent upon heredity. *Speed* (the rate of movement after it is initiated), static precision, dynamic precision, coordination, and flexibility are listed as traits that seem to be dependent upon experience. According to Guilford, therefore, simple reaction time (impulsion) is inherited, while the movement phase of reaction time (speed) is developed. This would suggest little, if any, relationship between the components of reaction and movement time.

Henry (1961b) stated ". . . muscular force causes the speed of a limb movement, whereas reaction latency reflects the time required for a premovement operation of a central nervous system program-switching mechanism" (p. 65). Movement time, on the other hand, is caused by muscular force. On the basis of these concepts and his research, he suggests a zero correlation between the two traits. This is contrary to the longstanding beliefs of some coaches and physical educators.

Hodgkins (1962) found that reaction time and movement time were unrelated for subjects ranging in age from six to eighty-four. In several studies, Henry (1952, 1960a, 1960b, 1960c) found no relationship between reaction time and speed of movement. Slater-Hammel (1952) and L. E. Smith (1961) have also reported insignificant correlations between these two components. However, Kerr (1966), Pierson and Rasch (1959), and Hipple (1954) have reported statistically significant correlations between measurements of reaction time and movement time. They theorize that reaction time is an aid to one's movement speed. It appears, however, that the majority of research generally shows no relationship

Another question that has been investigated during recent years is the *generality of reaction time*, i.e., do people who have fast reaction with the right hand also have fast reaction with the left hand, the feet, or other parts of the body? Evidence regarding this topic is rather inconsistent. Seashore and Seashore (1941) reported a high correlation among the reaction time of hands, feet, and even biting movements. In their study, the speed of the hands did not differ greatly from each other, nor did the speed of the feet. These correlations demonstrated a high degree of individual consistency. However, they did show that foot movement was slower than hand movement. Rangazas (1957) also reported hand movement to be faster than foot movement. After an extensive study with children between the ages of seven and thirteen, McArthur (1957) differed with Seashore and Seashore's assumption of generality in bodily movement speed. He found no relationship among the movement speed of various parts of the body or among different types of movement. McArthur concluded that: "No satisfactory conclusions regarding the general response patterns of subjects can be drawn from a series of testings based on one neuromuscular response such as the tapping of a finger, the flexion of a hand or the extension of a foot" (p. 128).

SIMPLE AND CHOICE REACTION TIME

In the literature and in discussions of speed of reaction, a distinction is made between simple reaction time and choice reaction time. In *simple reaction time* testing, the individual is asked to make a simple response, such as depressing or releasing an electric key or switch when a light goes on. Under these conditions, one type of stimulus is given, and one response is solicited. When the stimulus of light is used in such an experiment, reaction time will generally be in the vicinity of .15 to .25 seconds, depending on the magnitude of the response required. If a buzzer or another sound stimulus is used, the time may be slightly less. These times are relatively fast because there are no alternatives for the subject to consider. One knows in advance what stimulus to expect and what response to make. This has been referred to by Massaro (1975) and others as Type A reaction time.

In *choice reaction time*, there are alternatives for the subject to consider. Other terms used in reference to this type of response are *discriminative* or *disjunctive* reaction. In one situation, Type B, a red light may require the depression of key 1, while a green light requires the depression of key 2. In such an experiment of choice reaction, the stimuli are alternated in an irregular order. The subject, therefore, must observe the stimulus and make a choice of which response is appropriate. Needless to say, the time for choice reaction is slower than that for simple reaction. A third type of reaction time, Type C, requires the individual to make a single response to a particular option among two or more choices, e.g., if the green light goes on, he depresses the key, but if the red light flashes, he makes no response. Response time in this situation would be somewhere between simple and choice reaction time (with multiple options) as discussed earlier. These options are presented in Figure 15-2.

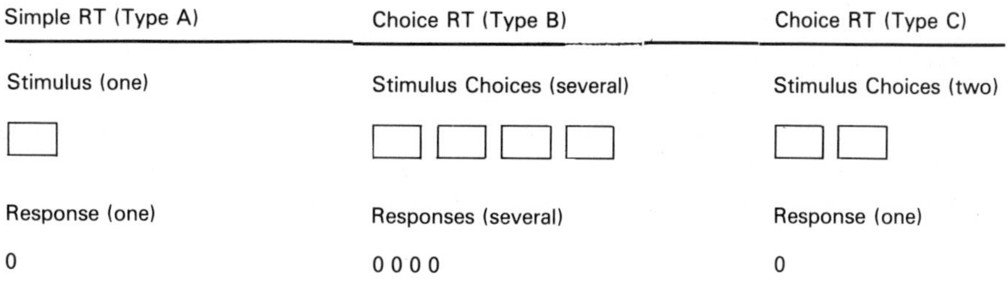

Simple RT (Type A)	Choice RT (Type B)	Choice RT (Type C)
Stimulus (one)	Stimulus Choices (several)	Stimulus Choices (two)
☐	☐ ☐ ☐ ☐	☐ ☐
Response (one)	Responses (several)	Response (one)
0	0 0 0 0	0

FIGURE 15-2. *Designs for Testing Simple and Choice Reaction Time* In simple reaction time testing, the subject receives only one stimulus and makes one response. In choice reaction time, Type B, any one of four stimuli may be presented, to which the subject selects one appropriate response. In choice reaction time, Type C, one of two possible stimuli is presented to which the subject must make a "go no-go" decision before responding.

Choice reaction time requires four distinct processes. First, there is the reception of the signal by the sense organ and the conveyance of that information via the afferent nerves to the brain. Second, the signal must be identified. The third process involves the making of a choice to correspond with the identification of the signal. The fourth step is the initiation of the appropriate response. The first and fourth processes occur relatively quickly, as in simple reaction time. The majority of time in choice reaction is taken up in processes two and three, the identification of the signal and making the appropriate choice. Choice reaction might include only two options or as many as ten. It has been found that the greater the number of choices, the slower is the reaction, i.e., a longer period of time is required for interpretation and decision making.

Researchers are interested in both simple and choice reaction time. In sports, there are many occasions when the player must decide on the most appropriate response. For example, the volleyball player who receives a service near the back line must make a decision whether the ball will be "in" or "out" before initiating a return. The softball batter must make a decision whether or not the ball will be a strike before starting to swing. The defensive halfback must decide whether there is a chance for an interception on a pass, or whether to stay back and play the receiver. On other occasions, a simple movement response is called for. The defensive lineman in football, for example, looks for a single stimulus (movement of the ball by the center) as a key to making a single, predetermined response (charging into the gap between two players).

In nonathletic situations, similar reactions must be made. Most often, reactions in the adult world require a choice. The automobile driver, upon entering an emergency situation, must decide the most appropriate response. It may be to slam on the brakes, speed up, blow the horn, or steer the car to the right or left. In such a situation, it is of little value for the response to be fast if it is the wrong response. Certain workday situations require that the worker "grade" products before they are processed. This necessitates observation of several options and corresponding responses. In other occupations, however, simple reactions are often the rule. In routine machine work, especially, the worker expects one type of stimulus and is prepared to make one type of response. In such a situation involving rapid response, a fast, simple reaction time is most advantageous.

There is no doubt that there are *individual differences* in reaction time. All researchers report differences among individuals, whether the testing is on simple reaction, choice reaction, or movement time. Within individuals, however, there are a number of factors that contribute to speed of reaction.

FACTORS AFFECTING REACTION TIME

The reaction time of an individual depends upon several variables. These variables may be classified as (1) external: principally dealing with the stimulus; or (2) internal: having to do with the state of the individual. Several of these conditions can be controlled by the experimenter. A thorough knowledge of them is therefore essential if the tester is to get optimum reaction speeds, or if he is to get accurate measures that can be compared. In addition, some knowledge of the influential conditions is essential if the reader is to make valid judgments about particular research reports. The most important variables affecting reaction time will be discussed briefly. The first two of these, of course, are external, having to do with the stimuli used, while the remainder deal with the individual's condition.

Stimulation of the sense organs

In pioneer work on reaction time at Columbia University, Cattell (1947) found that which sense organ is stimulated makes a difference in the speed of reaction. He established the following order of senses for speed from fastest to slowest: hearing, seeing, pain, taste, smell, and touch. Table 15-1 from Brebner and Welford (1980) includes information from several other researchers over a 50-year period that generally confirms the results of Cattell.

Rangazas (1957) also showed that reaction to sound was faster than reaction to vision. However, it has been shown that touch may elicit as fast a response as sound, especially when the more sensitive spots, and those closest to the brain are used. In testing, the senses of sight, hearing, and touch are relatively easy to isolate and stimulate separately. However, the senses of taste and smell, as well as the temperature receptors, are extremely difficult to stimulate suddenly without affecting the touch receptors. Mowbray (1960) found that choice reaction is improved when more than one sense is stimulated simultaneously. From various studies, it seems evident that the individual who reacts quickly to one stimulus also reacts quickly to others.

Intensity of the stimulus

Cattell reported that the intensity or strength of the stimulus makes a difference in the speed of reaction. Research by Rangazas substantiated this conclusion. A very loud noise is likely to result in a faster response than noise at a lower inten-

TABLE 15-1.   Some values of the simple reaction time for different sensory modalities

Study	Stimulus	Reaction time (msec)	Comments
From Woodworth and Schlosberg (1954)	Light	180	
From Woodworth and Schlosberg (1954)	Sound	140	
Robinson (1934)	Touch	155	
Kiesᵣw (1903)	Salt on tip of tongue	308	One subject
Kiesow (1903)	Sugar on tip of tongue	446	One subject
Baxter and Travis (1938)	Rotation of the person	520	
Baxter and Travis (1938)	Change in the direction of rotation of the person	720	
Wright	Intense radiant heat	330	An approximation

From Brebner and Welford, 1980.

sity. The sharp sound of a starter's gun in track should therefore elicit a quicker response than would the oral command, "Go." When color is used as a stimulus, a brilliant or vivid color will result in a faster reaction than the softer shades. The general physical setting of visual stimuli also affects one's response. Similar findings regarding the effect of more intense stimuli seem to prevail for the other senses. Woodworth and Schlosberg (1963), after reviewing the research, suggest that each increase in intensity of stimulus results in a faster reaction time. The decrements become smaller and smaller with each subsequent increase in stimulus. The correlation between reaction time and intensity is a curving rather than a straight line. It seems, therefore, that above a certain point, additional increases in intensity of stimulus would not prove beneficial.

Height of readiness

Researchers have long been interested in the period of greatest attention, or the time at which the subject is likely to exhibit the fastest reaction. This is an important factor in the speed of reaction. Investigators have consistently found that the peak of attention does not last indefinitely. If the foreperiod is too short, the subject will not have time to get sufficiently ready; but if it is too long, the readiness will gradually fade away. Cattell (1947) suggested the period between two and four seconds following the stimulus as the moment for maximum response. Other recent researchers have generally established the period of highest concentration as from one to three seconds following the stimulus.

General muscular tension is natural during the foreperiod. This tension is especially evident in the muscle to be used in the expected response. R. C. Davis (1940) attached electrodes to the skin over the muscles to study muscular tension during expectant periods. He concluded that muscular tension begins about .20 to .40 seconds after the "ready" signal and tends to increase until the moment of reaction. He also found that the reaction was quickened with greater tension.

Knowledge about the moment of greatest readiness has significance for physical education teachers and athletic coaches. Starters in a sprint race in track are interested in the length of delay between "set" and the gun. If the length of the foreperiod is regular, tension will be greatest at the point of expected stimulus, and the reaction quicker. Starting signals in football, from the time the team is down in position until the snap of the ball, should be arranged to fall within the period of maximum concentration. Of course, efforts may also be made to avoid the opposing team's maximum readiness period. Either a long count or a quick snap of the ball may prove effective. The pitcher in baseball, after coming to a "set" position with a runner on base, often tries to avoid a regular one-second delay, either by waiting a shorter or a longer period. This break in routine is done for two reasons: (1) to avoid the period of highest attention for either the batter or the runner, and (2) to prevent the runner from anticipating time of delivery so as to get a "jump" on the pitcher. A long (three-second) delay will usually cause the batter to begin wondering when the pitcher will deliver the ball and whether or not to step out of the batter's box. Obviously, such thoughts tend to interfere with one's concentration on the pitched ball.

Practice as a factor

The effect of practice on the speed of reaction has been investigated by a number of individuals. These investigations have been aimed at determining whether reaction time, as usually measured, is inherited or developed. Simple reaction time is so routine that one would expect a person to reach maximum speed after a very few trials, i.e., once the idea is clearly established. However, Woodworth and Schlosberg (1963) report that the average person continues to improve for several days or for several hundred trials, though the change after the first 50 or 100 trials is slight. About 10 percent improvement is shown after the first day of practice. Blank (1934) showed very small diminishing values for practice after the first day. McArthur (1957) administered five trials of a reaction time test to boys and girls. He found the fourth and fifth trials were faster than the first. For the five trials, there seemed to be gradual improvement. Hodgkins (1962), however, reported that reaction time was not significantly improved from the first through the tenth trial. Tweit, Gallnick, and Hearn (1963) found that total body movement time can be improved. This was "movement time" as previously defined, and they concluded that athletes may develop this type of reaction.

Age

During the developmental years, reaction time improves rapidly. As the peak period is approached during the late teens and early twenties, there is a leveling off in speed of reaction. After the adult level has been reached, there is very little change up to the age of sixty. The lengthening of reaction time begins to occur rapidly when the individual approaches feebleness. Miles (1929) showed that maximum speed of reaction was reached at about twenty-five, and practically no change was evident up to age sixty. Hodgkins (1962) reported that peak reaction time was reached at age nineteen and noted a greater drop-off than Miles by age sixty. (See Figure 15-3.) In her study, movement speed and reaction time developed and deteriorated in almost identical patterns, even though there was no correlation shown between these two factors. It should be noted that her "movement time" was limited to an arm swing of approximately 2 feet. One could speculate that if a gross, total body movement had been required, a more rapid drop-off may have occurred with increased age.

Sex

Hodgkins (1962) and Rangazas (1957) showed that males are faster than females in both reaction and movement time. Also, peak performance is maintained longer by males in movement time. Females, however, retained a relatively high level longer in reaction time. McArthur (1957) found boys to be faster than girls in movement time, and boys were also less variable. Fulton and Hubbard (1975) reported that from age nine through seventeen, both males and females developed faster during the earlier years, but males continued to improve during the later

FIGURE 15-3.   A Comparison of Males and Females in Speed of Reaction (From J. Hodgkin, Reaction time and speed of movement in males and females of various ages. *Research Quarterly,* 1963, p. 338. Copyright by the American Alliance for Health, Physical Education, Recreation and Dance, 1900 Association Drive, Reston, Va. 22091. Reprinted by permission.)

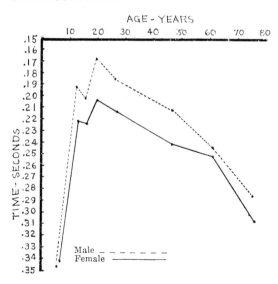

years as the speed of females leveled off. Movement times also improved with age, with males being consistently faster.

Drugs and alcohol

The effect of drugs on one's reaction time has long been a matter of interest to researchers. Cattell (1947) found that alcohol slows reaction time to the extent that it is evident in the blood system. The detrimental effect of alcohol and several drugs on reaction time has been shown by a number of other investigators. Straub (1938) reported that reaction time is lengthened by 10 percent when the alcoholic content in the blood reaches .35 and by 24 percent when the 1.4 level of alcohol in the blood is reached. This problem has been especially important in traffic safety research. Most medicines, taken in normal doses, do not have an appreciable influence on reaction time. When large doses are absorbed, most drugs slow one's reaction and speed of movement. However, certain drugs have recently been found to improve reaction time slightly. Nevertheless, use of these drugs for the purpose of improving speed has been strongly discouraged. Since the possibility of harmful or habit-forming effects is a possibility, such drugs have no place in school athletic programs.

Accuracy and movement response

Research has generally shown that movement time is slowed when accuracy of response is required. Furthermore, the more precise the movement, the slower the response. Goggin and Christina (1979) found that movement time was slower under both simple and choice reaction conditions when subjects had to make contact with a smaller target. When subjects moved a stylus to contact a larger target, movement responses were faster. The authors concluded that the increase in time for movement to the smaller target was due to the increase in time needed for programming the response.

When maximum speed of hand movement is to be measured, it should not require a response of great precision. For example, for one to turn a knob or even to depress a button at the conclusion of a movement will usually require that the response be slowed prior to completion so that the accuracy component will be completed. Ideally such a response would require only that the hand be moved through a plane where a photoelectric cell would break a circuit to stop a timer. In a practical setting, the defensive football lineman charges more quickly across the line in his initial steps if he is anticipating a pass. In such a case he can charge toward the quarterback without fear of having to stop, change direction, and tackle a ball carrier. Because of this habit, a "draw" play (fake pass and run) is often effective. Similarly, the baton exchange in a relay race requires a slowing down of movements on the part of both runners to increase precision and insure a successful exchange.

REACTION TIME AND ATHLETIC PERFORMANCE

Westerlund and Tuttle (1931) reported a high relationship between reaction time and running speed in the 75-yard dash. Several subsequent studies, however, have failed to show a relationship between reaction time and running speed or similar activities. On the other hand, correlations have been reported quite frequently between general athletic performance and various measures of speed of movement. Most studies designed to determine the relationship between reaction time and performance have compared individuals of different ability or experience in athletics.

Keller (1940) reported a relationship between movement time and athletic ability among male subjects. He found that athletes performed better in "quickness of movement" activities than did nonathletes at both the high school and college levels. He also found that team sport athletes (baseball, football, track) were quicker than individual sport athletes (wrestlers, gymnasts, swimmers). Olsen (1956) found that varsity athletes in college exhibited faster reaction times than did intramural participants who, in turn, showed greater speed than nonathletes. In another study of male athletes, Wilkinson (1958) reported that athletes had a faster reaction time than nonathletes. Further, he found that wrestlers and baseball players exhibited greater speed than did several other groups of athletes. In a study by Cureton (1951), champion athletes in different sports activities were shown to have different reaction speeds. Pierson (1959) reported significant differences between male fencers and nonfencers in movement speed.

SUMMARY

1. Reaction time is the time period from the stimulus to the beginning of the response. This latency period from stimulus to response is composed of sense organ time, nerve time, central nervous system time, and muscle action time.

2. Movement time is the period from the beginning of the overt response to the completion of a specified movement. Obviously, a large, complex movement will take more time than a small, simple response.

3. Simple reaction time occurs when the subject is asked to make a simple response to a single, predictable stimulus. Choice reaction time occurs when one or more stimuli are presented to which the individual must make a choice and then respond in one of several ways. Obviously, choice reaction time requires a longer period than simple reaction time. Further, the greater the number of choices, the greater the time required for a response.

4. Reaction time and movement time are unrelated, i.e., persons with quick reaction time are not likely to have a faster movement time than persons with a slower reaction time.

5. While movement time for any particular task can be quickened through

improved fitness and skill, reaction time cannot be appreciably improved by practice once the subject fully understands the stimuli and the appropriate response. However, there are several external as well as physiological conditions that can affect the speed of the reaction time.

6. When stimulated, certain sense organs lead to a faster reaction time than do others. For example, hearing and seeing are fastest while taste and smell are slowest.

7. Up to a point, a more intense stimulus leads to a quicker reaction time than does a softer, more subtle stimulus.

8. Subjects generally reach a peak of readiness for reacting from one to three seconds after being alerted. If the foreperiod is quicker than one second or slower than three seconds, reaction time is likely to be lengthened.

9. Reaction time improves during the childhood years, reaching a peak in the late teens or early twenties. The speed of reaction levels off and remains relatively unchanged until around the age of sixty, whereupon it gradually slows as one approaches feebleness.

10. Several studies have shown that males have slightly faster reaction times than females at all age levels. Some speculate that these findings have been culturally influenced.

11. Several studies report a relationship between reaction time and athletic performance. Specifically, it is reported that athletes have faster reaction times than do nonathletes.

SELECTED READINGS

CATTELL, J. McK. The influence of the intensity of the stimulus on the length of the reaction time. *Brain,* reprinted 1947, **9**, 512-15.

FULTON, C. D. and HUBBARD, A. W. Effect of puberty on reaction and movement times. *Res. Quart.,* 1975, **46**, 335-44.

GUILFORD, J. B. A system of psychomotor abilities. *Amer. J. Psychol.,* 1958, **71**, 164-74.

HENRY, F. M Factorial structure of speed and static strength in a lateral arm movement. *Res. Quart.,* 1960, **31**, 440-47.

HODGKINS, J. Reaction time and speed of movement in males and females of various ages. *Res. Quart.,* 1963, **34**, 335-43.

SLATER-HAMMEL, A. T. Reaction time and speed of movement. *Percept. Mot. Skills, Res. Exch.,* 1952, **4**, 109-13.

WELFORD, A. T., ed. *Reaction times.* New York: Academic Press, 1980.

WOODWORTH, R. S. and SCHLOSBERG, H. *Experimental psychology* (rev. ed.). New York: Holt, Rinehart and Winston, 1963.

References and Author Index

Numbers within parenthesis following each reference give the text page on which the work is cited. Citations in the text are by author and date of publication.

ADAMS, J. A. A closed-loop theory of motor learning. *J. Motor Behavior,* 1971, **3**, 111-50. (22, 91)

AMERICAN ALLIANCE FOR HEALTH, PHYSICAL EDUCATION, RECREATION AND DANCE, *Motor Development,* Basic Stuff Series I, K. Haywood scholar, 1981. (221)

AMERICAN ALLIANCE FOR HEALTH, PHYSICAL EDUCATION, RECREATION AND DANCE *Motor Learning,* Basic Stuff Series I, A. Rothstein, scholar, 1981. (33, 273, 305, 313)

AMERICAN ALLIANCE FOR HEALTH, PHYSICAL EDUCATION, RECREATION AND DANCE *Psycho-Social Aspects of Physical Education,* Basic Stuff Series I, C. A. Oglesby, scholar, 1981. (227, 261)

AMERICAN ASSOCIATION FOR HEALTH, PHYSICAL EDUCATION, AND RECREATION. *AAHPER Youth Fitness Test Manual.* Washington, D.C.: Author, 1965(a). (210)

AMMONS, H. and IRION, A. L. A. note on the Ballard reminiscence phenomenon. *J. Exp. Psychol.,* 1954, **48**, 184-86. (184)

AMMONS, R. B. Rotary pursuit performance with continuous practice before and after a single rest. *J. Exp. Psychol.,* 1947, **37**, 393-411. (50)

AMMONS, R. B. Le movement. In G. H. Seward & J. P. Seward, eds., *Current psychological issues.* New York: Holt, Rinehart and Winston, 1958. (139, 140)

AMMONS, R. B. and WILLIG, L. Acquisition of motor skill: effects of repeated periods of massed practice. *J. Exp. Psychol.,* 1956, **51**, 118-26. (186)

ANASTASI, A. *Psychological testing* (2nd ed.). New York: Macmillan, 1961. (332)

ANNETT, J. *Feedback and human behavior.* Baltimore, Md.: Penguin Books, 1969. (51, 52, 70)

ASMUSSEN, E. and HEEBELL NIELSEN, K. A dimensional analysis of physical performance and growth in boys. *J. Appl. Psychol.,* 1955, **7**, 593-603. (205)

ASTRAND, P. O. The child in sport and physical activity-physiology. In *Child in sport and physical activity.* Baltimore: University Park Press, 1976. (215)

AUSUBEL, D. P. Educational Psychology: A cognitive view. New York: Holt, Rinehart and Winston, 1968. (226)

AUSUBEL, D. P. *The psychology of meaningful verbal learning.* New York: Grune & Stratton, 1963. (190, 191)

AUSUBEL, D. P., SCHIFF, H. M., and GOLDMAN, M. Qualitative characteristics in the learning process associated with anxiety. *J. Abnorm. Soc. Psychol.,* 1953, **48**, 537. (226, 248)

BACHMAN, J. C. Specificity vs. generality in learning and performing two large muscle tasks. *Res. Quart.,* 1961, **32**, 3-11. (63, 320)

BAGLEY, W. C. *The education process.* London: Macmillan, 1905. (147)

BAKER, K. E., WYLIE, R. C., and GAGNE, R. M. The effects of an interfering task on the learning of a complex motor skill. *J. Exp. Psychol.,* 1951, **41**, 1-9. (139, 244)

BALLER, W. R. and CHARLES, D. C. *The psychology of human growth and development.* New York: Holt, Rinehart and Winston, 1961. (183)

BANNISTER, H. and BLACKBURN, J. H. An eye factor affecting proficiency at ball games. *Brit. J. Psychol.,* 1931, **21**, 382-84. (335)

BARCH, A. M. The effect of difficulty of task on provocation facilitation. *J. Exp. Psychol.,* 1953, **46**, 37-43. (218)

BARNET, M. Q. and STANICEK, J. A. Effects of goal setting on achievement in archery. *Res. Quart.,* 1979, **50**, 328-32. (258)

BAUER, W. W. and HEIN, F. V. *Exercise and health.* Chicago: A.M.A., 1958. (357)

BAYLEY, N. Some comparisons between growth in motor and in mental abilities in young children. *Psychol. Bull.,* 1934, **31**, 608. (194, 208)

BAYLEY, N. Some psychological correlates of somatic androgeny. *Child Develop.*, 1951, **22**, 47-60. (214)

BEHAVIORAL RESEARCH LABORATORIES. *American health and safety series.* Palo Alto, Calif.: Author, 1966. (302)

BELL, H. M. Retention of pursuit rotor skill after one year. *J. Exp. Psychol.*, 1950, **40**, 648-49. (171)

BELZER, E. G. and PETERS, B. Effect of a Gross Motor Activity on Recovery from Reactive Inhibition in a Rotary Pursuit Tast, *Res. Quart.*, 1972, **43**, 2, pp. 125-130. (274)

BERNARD, H. W. *Psychology of learning and teaching* (2nd ed.). New York: McGraw-Hill, 1965. (158)

BIGGE, M. L. and HUNT, M. P. *Psychological foundation of education.* New York: Harper & Row, 1962. (75)

BILODEAU, E. A., Ed., *Acquisition of skill.* New York: Academic Press, 1966. (102, 117, 118, 129)

BIRNEY, R. C. and TEEVAN, R. C., Eds. *Reinforcement: An enduring problem in psychology.* Princeton, N.J.: Van Nostrand, 1961. (129)

BLAKE, O. W. and VOLPE, A. M. *Lead-up games to team sports.* Englewood Cliffs, N.J.: Prentice-Hall, 1964. (312)

BLANK, G. Brauchbarkeit Optischer Reaktionsmessungen. *Indust. Pstechnik*, 1934, **11**, 140-50. (380)

BLAU, A. The master hand. *Amer. Orthopsychiatr. Assn. Res. Monogr.*, 1946, no. 5. (367, 372)

BLOOM, V. S. *Taxonomy of educational objectives.* New York: McKay, 1956. (13, 21)

BOOKWALTER, K. The relationship of body size and shape to physical performance. *Res. Quart.*, 1952, **23**, 271-79. (358)

BORING, E. G. *Sensation and perception in the history of experimental psychology.* New York: Appleton-Century-Crofts, 1942. (346, 354)

BORTNER, D. M. Pupil motivation and its relationship to the activity and social drives. In W. C. Morse & G. M. Wingo, Eds. *Readings in educational psychology.* Chicago: Scott, Foresman, 1962. (229)

BOURNE, L E. Jr. Information feecback in *Acquisition of skill*, E. A. Bilodeau, Ed. New York: Academic Press, 1966. (102)

BRACE, D. K. *Measuring motor ability, a scale of motor ability tests.* New York: Barnes, 1927. (332)

BRACE, D. K. Studies in motor learning of gross motor skill. *Res. Quart.*, 1946, **17**, 242-254. (328)

BRAY, C. C. Transfer of learning. *J. Exp. Psychol.*, 1928, **11**, 443-67. (139)

BREBNER, J. M. T. and WELFORD, A. T., Introduction: An historical background sketch: In *Reaction Times*, A. T. Welford, Ed. New York: Academic Press, 1980. (378, 379)

BREEDING, B. A. A study of the relative effectiveness of two methods of spacing archery practice. Unpublished master's thesis. University of Colorado, 1958. (268)

BREEN, J. L. Anxiety factors related to some physical fitness variables. Unpublished doctoral dissertation. University of Illinois, 1959. (244)

BROWN, R. C. The black gladiator—the major force in modern American sport. *Proceedings of the NCPEAM*, 1973, 43-50. (359, 372)

BRUNER, J. S. *The process of education.* Cambridge, Mass.: Harvard, 1963. (192)

BRYANT, W. L. On the development of voluntary motor ability. *Amer. J. Psychol.*, 1892, **5**, 123-204. (139)

BUGELSKI, B. R. *The psychology of learning applied to teaching* (2nd ed.). New York: The Bobbs-Merrill Co., Inc., 1971. (39, 74)

BURACK, B. and MOSS, D. Effect of knowing the principle basic to solution of a problem. *J. Educ. Res.*, 1956, **50**, 203-208. (143)

BUROS, O. K., Ed. *The sixth mental measurements yearbook.* Highland Park, N.J.: Gryphon Press, 1965. (332)

BURT, C. and MOORE, R. C. Mental differences between the sexes. *J. Exp. Psychol.*, 1922, **6**, 355-61. (328)

BURTT, H. E. An experimental study of early childhood memory: Final report. *J. Genet. Psychol.*, 1941, **58**, 435-39. (169)

CALFEE, M. College freshmen and four general intelligence tests. *J. Educ. Pedag.*, 1913, **24**, 227. (328)

CANNON, W. B. *Bodily changes in pain, hunger, fear and rage* (2nd ed.). New York: Appleton-Century-Crofts, 1929. (232, 233, 240, 241, 260)

CARROLL, H. A. *Genius in the making.* New York: McGraw-Hill, 1940. (229)

CARRON, A. V. *Laboratory experiments in motor learning.* Englewood Cliffs, N.J.: Prentice-Hall, Inc., 1971. (71, 242)

CASPER, B. Picture shot before address, 1969 National News Syndicate (reprinted in the *Philadelphia Bulletin*), January 7, 1970. (295)

CATTELL, J. McK. The influence of the intensity of the stimulus on the length of the reaction time. *Brain,* reprinted 1947, **9**, 512-15. (378, 379, 382, 384)

CHEFFERS, J. and EVAVL, T. *Introduction to Physical Education: Concepts of Human Movement,* Englewood Cliffs, N.J.: Prentice-Hall, Inc., 1978. (214)

CHRISTIAN, R. W. and MERRIMAN, J., Learning the direction and extent of a movement: A test of Adam's closed-loop theory. *Journal of Motor Behavior,* 1977, **9**, 49-60. (68)

CLAPPER, D. J. Measurement of selected kinesthetic responses at the junior and senior high school levels. Unpublished doctoral dissertation, State University of Iowa, 1957. (350)

CLARK, L. V. The effect of mental practice on the development of a certain motor skill. *Res. Quart.,* 1960, **31**, 560-69. (288, 290, 291, 299)

CLARKE, H. H. *Application of measurement to health and physical education* (4th ed.). Englewood Cliffs, N.J.: Prentice-Hall, 1967. (318, 332)

CLARKE, H. H. and GREENE, W. H. Relationships between personal-social measures applied to 10-year-old boys. *Res. Quart.,* 1963, **34**, 288-98. (256)

CLINTON, R. J. Nature of mirror drawing ability: norms on mirror drawing for white children by age and sex. *J. Educa. Psychol.,* 1930, **21**, 221-28. (329)

COLE, L. E. and BRUCE, W. F. *Educational psychology.* New York: Harcourt, Brace & World, 1959. (227, 228, 229, 230, 260)

COLVILLE, F. M. The learning of motor skills as influenced by knowledge of mechanical principles. *J. Educ. Psychol.,* 1957, **48**, 321-27. (143)

COOK, B. S. and HILGARD, E. R. Distributed practice in motor learning: progressively increasing and decreasing rests. *J. Exp. Psychol.,* 1949, **39**, 169-72. (176, 265)

COOK, T. W. Massed and distributed practice in the learning of rats. *Psychol. Rev.,* 1934, **41**, 330-55. (139)

COOPER, J. and GLASSOW, R. *Kinesiology.* St. Louis: Mosby, 1963. (347)

CORBIN, C. The effects of mental practice on the development of a unique motor skill. NCPEAM Proc., 1966. (63, 286, 287, 290)

CORBIN, C. *A Textbook of Motor Development.* Dubuque: Wm. Brown, 1973. (208, 213, 221)

COZENS, F. W. The measurement of general athletic ability in college men. *University of Oregon Phys. Educ. Ser.,* 1929, **1**, no. 3. (358)

CRATTY, B. J. *Movement behavior and motor learning* (3rd ed.). Philadelphia: Lea & Febiger, 1973. (33, 35, 55, 57, 71, 158, 195, 313, 321, 340)

CRONBACH, L. J. *Educational Psychology* (2nd ed.). New York: Harcourt, Brace & Wold, 1963. (190, 191)

CROSS, T. A comparison of the whole method, the minor game method, and the whole-part method of teaching basketball to 9th grade boys. *Res. Quart.,* 1937, **84**, 49-54. (306)

CROWDER, R. G. Improved recall for digits with delayed recall cues. *Journal of Experimental Psychology,* 1969, **82**, 258-62. (163)

CUNNINGHAM, B. V. An experiment in measuring gross motor development of infants and young children. *J. Educ. Psychol.,* 1927, **18**, 458-64. (357)

CURETON, T. K. *Physical fitness of champion athletes.* Urbana, Ill.: University of Illinois Press, 1951. (372, 383)

CURETON, T. K. Improving the physical fitness of youth. *Monogr. Soc. Res. in Child Develpm.,* 1964, **29**, no. 4 (Serial no. 95). (215)

DAHLERN, G. G. Gestalt approach to tumbling. *J. Hlth, Phys. Educ., Recreat.,* 1960, **31**, (no. 1), 38. (309)

DAMOS, D. L. and WICKENS, C. D. Dual-task performance and the Hick-Hyman Law of choice reaction time, *Journal of Motor Behavior,* 1977, **9**, 209-15. (68)

DANIEL, R. S. The distribution of muscular action potentials during maze learning. *J. Exp. Psychol.,* 1939, **24**, 621-29. (248)

DARWIN, C. J., TURUEY, M. T., and CROWDER, R. G. An auditory analysis of the Sperling partial report procedure: Evidence for brief auditory storage. *Cognitive Psychology,* 1972, **3**, 255-67. (163)

DASHIELL, J. F. A survey and synthesis of learning theories. *Psychol. Bull.,* 1935, **32**, 261-75. (88)

DAVIS, E. C. and LAWTHER, J. D. *Successful teaching in physical education* (2nd ed.). Englewood Cliffs, N.J.: Prentice-Hall, 1948. (154)

DAVIS, R. A. *Psychology of learning.* New York: McGraw-Hill, 1935. (326)

DAVIS, R. C. Set and muscular tension. *Indiana Univer. Sci. Ser.,* 1940, no. 10. (380)

DEESE, J., HULSE, S. H., and EGETH, H. *The psychology of learning* (5th ed.). New York: McGraw-Hill, 1980. (34, 74, 75, 96)

DEGARAY, A. L., LEWINE, L., and CARTER, J. E. L. *Genetic and anthropological studies of Olympic athletes.* New York: Academic Press, 1974. (357)

DELACATO, C. H. *The treatment and prevention of reading problems.* Springfield, Ill.: Charles C Thomas, 1959. (199, 372)

DELACATO, C. H. *The diagnosis and treatment of speech and reading problems.* Springfield, Ill.: Charles C Thomas, 1963. (199, 367)

DEMBO, T. Der Arger als dynamishers. *Psychol. Forsch.,* 1931, **15**, 1-144. (256)

DENNIS, W. and DENNIS, M. G. The effect of cradling practices upon the onset of walking in Hopi children. *J. Genet. Psychol.,* 1940, **56**, 77-86. (198)

DETERLINE, W. A. *An introduction to programmed instruction.* Englewood Cliffs, N.J : Prentice-Hall, 1962. (314)

DICKINSON, J. *Proprioceptive control of human movement.* Princeton, N.J.: Princeton Book Co., 1976. (346, 349, 354)

DICKSON, J. F. The relationship of depth perception to goal shooting in basketball. Unpublished doctoral dissertation, State Univer. of Iowa, 1953. (336)

DICTIONARY OF OCCUPATIONAL TITLES (4th Ed.). U. S. Department of Labor, 1977. (4, 5)

DIGIOVANNA, V. G., A comparison of the intelligence and athletic ability of college men. *Res. Quart.,* 1937, **8**, 96-106. (330)

DINUCCI, J. M. and SHOWS, D. A. Comparison of the motor performance of black and caucasian girls ages 6-8, *Res. Quart.,* 1977, **48**, 680-84. (360, 372)

DOLGENER, F. H., SPASOFF, T. C., and ST. JOHN, W. E. Body build and body composition of high ability female dancers. *Research Quarterly for Exercise and Sport,* 1980, **51**, (4), 599-609. (358)

DOMĄN, G., et al. Children with severe brain injuries. *J.A.M.A.,* 1960, **174**, 257-62. (199, 367)

DORÉ, L. R. and HILGARD, E. R. Spaced practices and the maturation hypothesis. *J. Psychol.,* 1937, **4**, 245-59.

DOUGLASS, H. R. and KITTLESON, K. L. An experimental evaluation of a modified Morrison procedure in teaching American history. *J. Exp. Educ.,* 1935, **4**, 20-25. (134)

DROWATSKY, J. N. *Motor learning principles and practices* (2nd ed.). Minneapolis, Mn.: Burgess Publishing Co., 1981. (34, 154)

DUFFY, E. The psychological significance of the concept of arousal or "activation." *Psychol. Rev.,* 1957, **64**, 265-75 (234)

DUKELOW, J. D. *A comparison of the effects of three short delays of augmenting videotape feedback on the learning and retention of a novel motor skill.* Unpublished doctoral thesis, Temple University, 1979. (52, 102, 103, 111, 112, 118)

DUROST, W. N. The development of a battery of objective group tests of manual laterality with the results of their application to 1300 children. *Genet. Psychol. Monogr.,* 1934, **16** (4), 229-35. (366)

EASON, R. G. Relation between effort, tension level, skill and performance efficiency in a perceptual-motor task. *Percep. Mot. Skills,* 1963, **16**, 297-318.

EASON, R. G. and WHITE, C. T. Relationship between muscular tension and performance during rotary pursuit. *Percept. Mot. Skills,* 1960, **10**, 199-210. (234)

EATON, M. L. The conditioned reflex technique applied to a less specialized type of learning. *J. Exp. Educ.,* 1937, **6**, 68-83. (265)

EBBINGHAUS, H. *Uber das Gedachtnis: Untersuchungen Zur Experimentellen Psycholgie.* Leipzig: Dunker and Humblet, 1885. (38, 161, 264)

EBBINGHAUS, H. *Grundzüge der Psychologie* (3rd ed.). Vol. I. Leipzig:Veit, 1911. (173)

EDWARDS, A. L. The retention of affective experiences—a criticism and restatement of the problem. *Psychol. Rev.,* 1942, **49**, 43-53. (177)

EGSTROM, G. H. Effects of an emphasis on conceptualizing techniques during early learning of a gross motor skill. *Res. Quart.,* 1964, **35**, 472-81. (64, 65, 286, 299)

EICHORN, D. H. and JONES, H. E. Maturation and behavior. In G. H. Seward & J. P. Seward (Eds.), *Current psychological issues.* New York: Holt, Rinehart and Winston, 1958, 211-48. (194)

ELLIS, W. D. *A source book of gestalt psychology.* New York: Harcourt, Brace & World, 1938. (328)

ENGLISH, H. B., WELBORN, E. L., and KILLIAN, D. C. Studies in substance learning and retention. *J. Genet. Psychol.,* 1934, **16**, 233-60. (265)

EPSTEIN, B. Immediate and retentive effects of interpolated rest periods in learning performance. *Teacher's College Continuing Education,* no. 989, 1949. (269)

ESPENSCHADE, A. Motor development. *Rev. Educ. Res.,* 1947, **17**, 354-61. (210)

EYSENCK, H. J. The measurement of motivation. *Sci. Amer.,* 1963, **208** (May), 130-40. (238, 243)

FARBER, L. E. and SPENCE, K. W. Complex learning and conditioning as a function of anxiety. *J. Exp. Psychol.,* 1953, **45**, 120-25. (248)

FISCHMAN, M. G., CHRISTINA, R. W., and VERCRUYSSEN, M. J. Retention and Transfer of Motor Skills: A Review for the Practitioner. *Quest,* 1982, **33**(2), 181-94. (158, 170, 188)

FITTS, P. M. Perceptual-motor skills learning. In A. W. Melton (Ed.), *Categories of human learning.* New York: Academic Press, 1964. (22, 64, 91, 93)

FITZHUGH, K. B. and FITZHUGH, L. C. Effects of early and later onset of cerebral dysfunction upon psychological test performance. *Percept. Mot. Skills,* 1965, **20,** 1099-1100. (328)

FLEISHMAN, E. A. A relationship between incentive motivation and ability level in psychomotor performance. *J. Exp. Psychol.,* 1958, **56,** 78-81. (248)

FLEISHMAN, E. A. *The structure and measurement of physical fitness.* Englewood Cliffs, N.J.: Prentice-Hall, 1964. (27, 50, 71, 318, 319, 321, 332)

FLEISHMAN' E. A. The perception of body position in the absence of visual cues. *J. Exp. Psychol.,* 1953, **46,** 261-70. (332)

FLEISHMAN, E. A. and PARKER, J. Factors in the retention and relearning of perceptual-motor skill. *J. Exp. Psychol.,* 1962, **64,** 215-26. (16, 186)

FLEISHMAN, E. A. Performance assessment on an empirically derived task taxonomy. *Human Factors,* 1967, **9,** 349-66. (51)

FLEISHMAN, E. A., THOMAS, P., and MUNROE, P. The dimensions of physical fitness a factor analysis of speed, flexibility, balance and coordination tests, Technical Report No. 3, The Office of Naval Research, 1961. (320)

FORT, M. A study of the emotions of high school football players. Unpublished doctoral dissertation, Boston University, 1959. (233)

FOX, M. G. The relation of dominance to motor ability. Paper read at AAHPER nat. convent., Minneapolis, Minn., April, 1963. (364, 368, 369)

FRANK, J. D. Individual differences in certain aspects of the level of aspiration. *Amer. J. Psychol.,* 1935, **47,** 119. (256)

FRANKLIN, J. C. and BROZEK, J. M. Relation between the distribution of practice and learning efficiency in psychomotor performance. *J. Exp. Psychol.,* 1947, **37,** 16-24. (265)

FREEMAN, G. L. The optimal muscular tension for various performances. *Amer. J. Psychol.,* 1938, **51,** 146-50. (247)

FROSTIG, M. and HORNE, D. *The Frostig program for the development of visual perception.* Chicago: Follett, 1964. (218, 221)

FULTON, C. D. and HUBBARD, A. W. Effect of puberty on reaction and movement times. *Res. Quart.,* 1975, **46,** 335-44. (381, 384)

GAGNE, R. M. *The condition of learning* (3rd ed.). New York: Holt, Rinehart and Winston, 1977. (13, 34, 96, 99)

GAGNE, R. M. and FLEISHMAN, E. A. *Psychology and human performance.* New York: Holt, Rinehart and Winston, 1959. (171)

GALLAHUE, D. The relationship between perceptual and motor abilities. *Res. Quart.,* 1968, **39,** 948-52. (341)

GARDNER, E. *Fundamentals of neurology.* Philadelphia: Saunders, 1963. (347)

GARFIEL, E. The measurement of motor ability. *Arch. Psychol.,* 1923, **9,** 1-47. (328)

GARRITY, H. M. Relationship of somatotype of college women to physical fitness performance. *Res. Quart.,* 1966, **37,** 340-52. (372)

GARRY, R. *Psychology of learning.* Washington: Cen. Appl. Res. Educ., 1963. (179, 208, 317, 332)

GENTILE, A. M. A working model of skill acquisition with application to teaching. *Quest,* 1972, **17,** 3-23. (17, 51)

GERDES, G. R. The effects of various motivational techniques upon performance in selected physical tests. Unpublished doctoral dissertation, Indiana University, 1958. (240, 241, 249)

GESELL, A. and AMES, L. B. The development of handedness. *J. Genet. Psychol.,* 1947, **70,** 155-75. (372)

GESELL, A. and THOMPSON, H. Learning and growth in identical infant twins. *Genet. Psychol. Monogr.,* 1929, **6,** 1-124. (197, 198)

GETMAN, G. N. and KANE, E. R. *The physiology of readiness.* Minneapolis: P.A.S.S., Inc., 1964. (218, 221)

GHISSELLI, E. Changes in neuro-muscular tension accompanying the performance of a learning problem involving constant choice time. *J. Exp. Psychol.,* 1936, **19,** 91-98. (248)

GIBSON, E. J. and BERGMAN, R. The effect of training on absolute estimation of distances over the ground. *J. Exp. Psychol.,* 1954, **48,** 137-49. (336)

GLENCROSS, D. J. and GOULD, J. H. The planning of precision movements. *Journal of Motor Behavior,* 1979, **11.** (68)

GODWIN, M. A. and SCHMIDT, R. A. Muscular fatigue and discrete motor learning. *Res. Quart.,* 1971, **42,** 374-83. (269, 270)

GOGGIN, N. L. and CHRISTINA, R. W. Reaction time analysis of programmed control of short, rapid aiming movements. *Res. Quart.,* 1979, **50,** 360-68. (382)

GRAYBIEL, A., JOKL, E., and TRAPP, C. Russian studies of vision in relation to physical activity and sports. *Res. Quart.,* 1955, **26,** 212-23. (336, 338), 354)

GREENLEE, G. A. The relationship of selected measures of strength balance and kinesthesis to bowling performance. Unpublished doctoral dissertation, State University of Iowa, 1958. (350)

GRIMALDI, J. V. Sensori-motor performance under varying noise conditions. *Ergonomics,* 1958, 2, 34-43. (243)

GROSE, R. F. and BIRNEY, R. C. *Transfer of learning,* Princeton, N.J.: Van Nostrand, 1963. (159)

GROSS, E. A. and THOMPSON, H. I. Relationship of dynamic balance to speed and to ability in swimming. *Res. Quart.,* 1957, 28, 342-46. (350)

GUILFORD, J. B. A system of psychomotor abilities. *Amer. J. Psychol.,* 1958, 71, 164-74. (175, 332, 375, 384)

GUTHRIE, E. R. *The psychology of learning* (Rev. ed.). New York: Harper & Row, 1952. (78, 79, 80, 99)

GUTTERIDGE, M. V. A study of motor achievements of young children. *Arch. Psychol.,* 1939, 34, no. 244, 1-178. (205)

GUYTON, A. C. *Function of the Human Body* (4th Ed.). Philadelphia, PA.: W. B. Saunders, 1974. (346)

HAHN, H. H. and THORNDIKE, E. L. Some results of practice in addition under school conditions. *J. Educ. Psychol.,* 1914, 5, 65-84. (264)

HAMBLEN, A. A. An investigation to determine the extent to which the effect of the study of Latin upon a knowledge of English derivatives can be measured by conscious adaptation of content and methods to the attainment of this objective. Unpublished doctoral dissertation, University of Pennsylvania, 1925. (134)

HAMMERTON, M. Retention of learning in a difficult tracking task. *J. Exp. Psychol.,* 1963, 66, 108-110. (179)

HARBY, S. F. *Comparison of mental practice-physical practice in the learning of physical skills.* Human Engineering Report. S.D.C. 269-77 to Spec. Device Cen. Office of Naval Res. Prepared at Pennsylvania State Coll., 1952. (292)

HARLOW, H. F. The formation of learning sets. *Psychol. Rev.,* 1949, 56, 51-56. (146)

HARMON, J. M. and JOHNSON, W. R. The emotional reactions of college athletes. *Res. Quart.,* 1952, 23, 391-97. (233, 245)

HARMON, J. M. and OXENDINE, J. B. Effect of different lengths of practice periods on the learning of a motor skill. *Res. Quart.,* 1961, 32, 34-41. (25, 266, 327)

HARRIS, T. L. and SCHWAHN, W. E. (Eds.) *Selected readings on the learning process.* New York: Oxford, 1961. (13, 21)

HAVIGHURST, R. J. Educational imperatives in a changing culture. Speech at Schoolmen's Week, University of Pennsylvania, March, 1966. (193)

HAWTHORNE, J. J. Somatotype and its relationship to selected motor performance of college men. Unpublished doctoral dissertation, University of Texas, 1952. (359)

HEBB, D. O. *The organization of behavior: a neuropsychological theory.* New York: Wiley, 1949. (91)

HEBB, D. O. *A textbook of psychology.* Philadelphia, PA.: W. B. Saunders, 1958. (199, 324)

HELLEBRANT, F. A. *Education.* December 1961. (140)

HELLEBRANT, F. A. and WATERLAND, J. C. Indirect learning. The influence of unimanual exercise on related groups of the same and opposite side. *Amer. J. Phys. Med.,* 1962, 41, 44-55. (140)

HENDRICKSON, G. and SCHROEDER, W. H. Transfer of training in learning to hit a submerged target. *J. Educ. Psychol.,* 1941, 32, 205-13. (137)

HENNIS, G. M. and ULRICH, C. Study of psychic stress in freshmen college women. *Res. Quart.,* 1958, 29, 172-79. (242)

HENRY, F. M. Independence of reaction and movement times and equivalents of sensory motivators of faster response. *Res. Quart.,* 1952, 23, 45-53. (375)

HENRY, F. M. Specificity vs. generality in learning motor skills. *Annu. Proc. Coll. Phys. Educ. Assn.,* 1958, 61, 126-28. (332)

HENRY, F. M. Factorial structure of speed and static strength in a lateral arm movement. *Res. Quart.,* 1960, 31, 440-47(a). (375, 384)

HENRY, F. M. Increased response latency for complicated movements and a "memory drum" theory of neuromotor reaction. *Res. Quart.,* 1960, 31, 448-57(b). (375)

HENRY, F. M. Influence of motor and sensory sets on reaction latency and speed of discrete movements. *Res. Quart.,* 1960, 31, 459-68(c). (375)

HENRY, F. M. Stimulus complexity, movement complexity, age, and sex in relation to reaction latency and speed in limb movements. *Res. Quart.,* 1961, 32, 353-66(a). (375)

HENRY, F. M. Reaction time-movement time correlations. *Percept. Mot. Skills,* 1961, 12, 63-67(b). (241, 375)

HERKOWITZ, J. Sex role expectations and motor behavior of the young child. In M. V. Ridenour (Ed.) *Motor Development Issues and Applications.* Princeton, N.J., Princeton Book Co., 1978. (215, 341)

HERTZBERG, O. E. Relationship of motor ability to the intelligence of kindergarten children. *J. Exp. Psychol.,* 1929, **20,** 507-19. (330)

HERZSTEIN, J. N. A comparison of the jumping of American Negro male college students with American white male college students as measured by the Sargent vertical jump test. Unpublished master's thesis, University of Maryland, College Part, 1961. (361)

HICKS, J. A. The acquisition of motor skill in young children an experimental study of the effects of practice in throwing at a moving target. *Univer. Iowa Stud. in Child Welf. J.,* 1931, **4,** no. 5. (201)

HILDRETH, G. The development and training of hand dominance: II. developmental tendencies in handedness. *J. Genet. Psychol.,* 1949, **75,** 221-54(b). (363)

HILDRETH, G. The development and training of hand dominance: IV. developmental problems associated with handedness. *J. Genet. Psychol.,* 1950, **76,** 39-100. (361)

HILGARD, E. R. *Theories of learning* (2nd ed.). New York: Appleton-Century-Crofts, 1956. (74, 88, 89, 99, 192)

HILGARD, E. R. Learning theory and its application. In W. Schramm Ed., *New teaching aids for the American classrooms.* Stanford, Calif.: Stanford Univer. Inst. Communicat. Res. 1960. (83)

HILGARD, E. R., SAIT, E. M., and MARGARET, G. A. Level of aspiration as affected by relative standing in an experimental social group. *J. Exp. Psychol.,* 1940, **27,** 411-21. (257)

HILGARD, J. R. Learning and maturation in preschool children. *J. Genet. Psychol.,* 1932, **41,** 31-56. (197)

HILGARD, J. R. The effect of early and delayed practice on memory and motor performance studied by the method of co-twin control. *Genet. Psychol. Monogr.,* 1933, **14,** 493-566. (197)

HILL, W. F. *Learning: a survey of psychological interpretations.* San Francisco: Chandler Publishing Co., 1963. (74)

HIPPLE, J. E. Racial differences in the influence of motivation on muscular tension, reaction time, and speed of movement. *Res. Quart.,* 1954, **25,** 297-306. (375)

HITCHCOCK, E. *An anthropometric manual.* Amherst, Mass.: Press of Carpenter and Morehouse, 1893. (356)

HOCHBERG, J. *Perception.* Englewood Cliffs, N.J.: Prentice-Hall, 1964. (354)

HODGKINS, J. Influence of age on the speed of reaction and movement in females. *J. Geront.,* 1962, **17,** 385-89. (375, 380, 381)

HODGKINS, J. Reaction time and speed of movement in males and females of various ages. *Res. Quart.,* 1963, **34,** 335-343. (384)

HOUSTON, J. P. *Fundamentals of learning.* New York: Academic Press, 1976. (34)

HUBBARD, A. W. and SENG, C. N. Visual movements of batters. *Res. Quart.,* 1954, **25,** 42-51. (340)

HUDSPETH, W. J. Delacato in Review. *28th Yearbook,* M. P. Douglas, Ed. Claremont Graduate School Curriculum Laboratory, 1964, p. 119-31. (199)

HULL, C. L. *Princples of behavior.* New York: Appleton-Century-Crofts, 1943. (80, 81, 83, 99, 129, 149, 180, 239)

HULSE, S. H., EGETH, H. and DEESE, J. *The psychology of learning* (5th ed.). New York: McGraw-Hill Book Co., 1980. (12, 34, 107, 129, 135)

JACOBSON, E. Electrical measurement of neuromuscular states during mental activities. II. imagination and recollection of various muscular acts. *Amer. J. Physiol.,* 1934, **94** (July-Sept.), 22-34. (285, 299)

JACOBSON, E. Electrophysiology of mental activities. *Amer. J. Psychol.,* 1932, **44,** 677-94. (285)

JAMES, W. *Principles of psychology.* New York: Henry Holt, 1890. (133, 163, 183, 235)

JAYACINSKI, R. J., HARTZELL, E. J., WARD, S., and BISHOP, K. Fitts law as a function of system dynamics and target uncertainty. *Journal of Motor Behavior,* 1978, **10,** 123-31. (68)

JENKINS, J. G. and DALLENBACH, K. M. Oblivescence during sleep and waking. *Amer. J. Psychol.,* 1924, **35,** 605-12. (180)

JENKINS, J. J. and PATERSON, D. G. *Studies in individual differences: the search for intelligence.* New York: Appleton-Century-Crofts, 1961. (332)

JENKINS, L. M. Comparative study of motor achievements of children five, six, and seven years of age. *Teach. Coll. Contr. Educ.,* 1930, no. 414. (364)

JOHNSON, G. B. A study of the relationship that exists between skill as measured and general intelligence of college students. *Res. Quart.,* 1942, **13,** 57-59. (140)

JOHNSON, G. B., Jr. Motor learning. In W. R. Johnson, Ed., *Science and medicine of exercise and sports.* New York: Harper & Row, 1960, 600-19. (330)

JOHNSON, W. R. A study of emotion revealed in two types of athletic contests. *Res. Quart.,* 1949, **20,** 72-80. (210, 253)

JOHNSON, W. R. (Ed.) *Science and medicine of exercise and sports.* New York: Harper & Row, 1960. (253)

JOKL, E. R. *Medical, sociological and cultural anthropology of sport and physical education.* Springfield, Ill.: Charles C Thomas, 1964. (202)

JONES, H. E. *Motor performance and growth.* Berkeley, Calif.: Univer. of California Press, 1949. (290)

JONES, J. G. Motor learning without demonstration of physical rehearsal, under two conditions of mental practice. Unpublished master's thesis, Univer. of Oregon, 1963.

JOST, A. Assoziationsfestigkeit in ihrer Ablangigkeit von Verteilong der Wiederholungen, *Z. Psychol.,* 1897, **14**, 436-472. (264)

JUDD, C. H. The relation of special training to special intelligence. *Educ. Rev.* 1908, **36**, 28-42. (136, 137)

KAPPERS, C. V. A. Further contributions on neurobiotaxis. IX. *J. Comp. Neurol.,* 1917, **27**, 261-298. (10)

KELLER, F. S. *Learning: reinforcement theory.* New York: Random House, 1954. (129)

KELLER, L. P. The relation of quickness of bodily movement to success in athletics. Unpublished doctoral dissertation, New York University, 1940. (383)

KEPHART, N. C. Perceptual-motor aspects of learning disability. *Except. Child.,* 1964, **31**, 201-207. (218)

KERR, B. A. Relationship between speed of reaction and movement in a knee extension movement. *Res. Quart.,* 1966, **37**, 55-60. (375)

KERR, R. *Psychomotor Learning.* Philadelphia: Saunders College Publishing, 1983. (34)

KIFER, E. Relationship between Academic Achievement and Personality Characteristics: A Quasi-Longitudinal study. *American Educational Research Journal,* 1975, **12**, 191-220. (226)

KIMBLE, G. A. Performance and reminiscence in motor learning as a function of the degree of distribution of practice. *J. Exp. Psychol.,* 1949, **39**, 500-10. (267, 271)

KIMBLE, G. A. Evidence for the role of motivation in determining the amount of reminiscence in pursuit rotor learning. *J. Exp. Psychol.,* 1950, **40**, 248. (270)

KIMBLE, G. A. *Principles of general psychology.* New York: Ronald, 1956. (318)

KIMBLE, G. A. and SHATEL, R. B. The relationship between two kinds of inhibition and the amount of practice. *J. Exp. Psychol.,* 1952, **44**, 355-59. (270, 271, 279)

KINGSLEY, H. L. and GARRY, R. *The nature and conditions of learning* (2nd ed.). Englewood Cliffs, N.J.: Prentice-Hall, 1957. (13, 74, 110, 151, 153, 159, 188)

KLAPP, S. et al. Simple and choice reaction time methods in the study of motor behavior. 1979, **11**, 91-101. (68)

KNAPP, B. *Skill in Sport, The Attainment Proficiency.* London: Routledge & Kegan Paul Ltd., 1963. (17, 18, 279)

KNAPP, C. and DIXON, R. Learning to juggle: I. a study to determine the effect of two different distributions of practice in learning efficiency. *Res. Quart.,* 1950, **21**, 331-36. (269, 279, 306)

KOERTH, W. A pursuit apparatus: eye-hand coordination. *Psychol. Monogr.,* 1922, **31**, 288-92. (49)

KOFFKA, K. Review of Tolman's "Purposive behavior in animals and men." *Psychol. Bull.,* 1933, **30**, 440-51. (84, 85)

KÖHLER, W. *The mentality of apes.* Trans. E. Winter. New York: Harcourt, Brace & World, 1925. (84)

KÖHLER, W. *Gestalt psychology.* New York: Liveright, 1947. (99)

KRAUSE, J. V. and BARHAM, J. N. *The mechanical foundations of human motion: A programmed text.* St. Louis: The C. V. Mosby Co., 1975. (302, 314)

KRETSCHMER, E. *Physique and character.* New York: Harcourt, Brace & World, 1925. Cited by P. V. Karpovich, *Physiology of muscular activity.* Philadelphia: Saunders, 1961, 292. (357)

KRIEGER, J. C. The influence of figure ground perception on spatial adjustment in tennis. Unpublished master's thesis, University of California, Los Angeles, 1962. (341)

KRUEGER, W. C. F. The effect of overlearning on retention. *J. Exp. Psychol.,* 1929, **12**, 71-78. (178, 179, 188)

KULCINSKI, L. E. The relation of intelligence to the learning of fundamental muscular skills. *Res. Quart.,* 1945, **16**, 226-76. (327)

KUSINITZ, I. and KEENEY, C. E. Effects of progressive weight training on health and physical fitness of adolescent boys. *Res. Quart.,* 1958, **29**, 294-301. (202)

LAMBERT, P. Practice effect of non-dominant vs. dominant musculature in acquiring two-handed skill. *Res. Quart.,* 1951, **22**, 50-57. (307, 351)

LANDERS, D. M. Arousal, attention, and skilled performance: further considerations. *Quest,* 1982, **33**(2), 271-83. (261)

LANDERS, D. M. The Arousal-Performance Relationship Revisited. *Research Quarterly for Exercise and Sport.* 1980, **51**(1), 77-90. (239, 261)

LARSON, R. L. Physical Activity and the Growth and Development of Bone and Joint Structures. In *Physical Activity: Human Growth and Development.* New York, Academic Press, Inc. 1973. (205)

LASHLEY, K. S. The requisition of skill in archery. *Papers Dep. Marine Biol. Carnegie Instn. of Washington,* 1915, **7**, 105-28. (268)

LAWRENCE, D. P. A reliability check of two interpolated time patterns in motor learning. Unpublished master's thesis, Boston University, 1949. (268)

LAWTHER, J. D. Learning motor skills and knowledge. In C. E. Skinner, Ed., *Educational psychology* (4th ed.). Englewood Cliffs, N.J.: Prentice-Hall, 1959, 499-525. (176)

LAWTHER, J. D. *The learning and performance of physical skills* (2nd ed.). Englewood Cliffs, N.J.: Prentice-Hall, Inc., 1977. (34, 201, 330)

LEAVITT, H. J. and SCHLOSBERG, H. The retention of verbal and of motor skills. *J. Exp. Psychol.,* 1944, **34**, 404-17. (171, 188)

LEE, A. M., Child-rearing practices and motor performance of black and white children. *Res. Quart. for Exercise and Sport,* 1980, **51**, 494-500. (360, 372)

LEITH, G. O., BIRAN, L. A., and OPOLLAT, J. A. The place of review in meaningful verbal learning. *Canadian Journal of the Behavioral Sciences,* 1969, **1**, 113-18. (265)

LERSTEN, K. C. Retention of Skill on the Rho Apparatus-After One Year. *Res. Quart.,* 1969, **40**, 418-19. (174)

LEUBA, C. J. *Man: a general psychology.* New York: Holt, Rinehart and Winston, 1961. (229)

LEWIN, K. *Principles of topological psychology.* Trans. F. Heider & G. M. Heider. New York: McGraw-Hill, 1936. (83, 86, 87, 99)

LEWIN, K., DEMBO, T., FESTINGER, L., and SEARS, P. S. Level of aspiration. In J. McV. Hunt, Ed., *Handbook of personal and behavioral disorders.* New York: Ronald, 1944, 333-78. (256)

LINDEBURG, F. A. and HEWITT, J. E. Effect of an oversized basketball on shooting ability and ball handling. *Res. Quart.,* 1965, **36**, 164-67. (139)

LITWHILER, D. *Baseball Coach's Guide to Drills and Skills.* Englewood Cliffs, N.J.: Prentice-Hall, Inc., 1963. (122, 123)

LOCKHART, A. S. and JOHNSON, J. M. *Laboratory experiments in motor learning.* Dubuque, IA.: Wm. C. Brown, 1970. (71)

LORGE, I. Influence of regularly interpolated time intervals upon subsequent learning. *Teach. Coll. Contr. Educ.,* 1930, no. 438. (266)

LYON, D. O. The relation of length of material to time taken for learning and the optimum distribution of time, part III. *J. Educ. Psychol.,* 1931, **14**, 400-13. (264)

MAGILL, R. A. *Motor learning: concepts and applications.* Dubuque, IA.: Wm C. Brown Co., 1980. (34, 102, 269)

MAGRUDER, M. A. An analytical study of the testing for kinesthesis. Unpublished doctoral dissertation, University of Oregon, 1963. (346)

MARGULIES, S. and EIGEN, L. D., Eds. *Applied programmed instruction.* New York: Wiley, 1962. (314)

MARTENIUK, R. G. *Information processing in motor skills.* New York: Holt Rinehart and Winston, 1976. (99)

MARTIN, H. A. Long-term retention of a discrete motor task. M. A. dissertation, University of Maryland, 1970 (Cited by Schmidt: 1975). (174, 250)

MARTIN, K. L. Handedness: a review of the literature on the history, development and research of laterality preference. *J. Educ. Res.,* 1952, **45**, 527-33. (366)

MARTIN, M. M. A study to determine the effects of motivational techniques on performance of the jump and reach test of college women. Unpublished master's thesis, University of Wisconsin, 1961. (174, 250)

MARTIRE, J. G. Relationship between the self concept and differences in the strength and generality of achievement motivation. *J. Pers.,* 1956, **24**, 364-75. (256)

MARX, M. H. and BUNCH, M. E., Eds., *Fundamentals and Applications of Learning.* New York: Macmillan Publishing Co., Inc., 1977. (172)

MASLOW, A. H. A preface to motivation theory. *Psychosom. Med. Monogr.,* 1943, **5**, 370-96. (228, 229, 230)

MASSARO, D. W. *Experimental Psychology and Information Processing.* Chicago: Rand McNally College Publishing Co., 1975. (376)

MASSEY, M.D. A study of the significance of interpolated time intervals on motor learning. Unpublished doctoral dissertation, Boston University, 1957. (266, 279)

MATARAZZO, R. G. and MATARAZZO, J. D. Anxiety level and pursuit meter performance. *J. Consult. Psychol.,* 1956, **20**, 70. (242, 248)

MCARTHUR, W. D. Speed of various neuro-muscular responses in children ages seven to thirteen. Unpublished doctoral dissertation, Oregon State Coll., 1957. (376, 380, 381)

MCCAIN, S. R. A comparison of the motion perception fields of athletes and nonathletes. Unpublished master's thesis, University of Alabama, 1950. (338)

MCCONNELL, T. R. The psychology of learning. *Yearb. Nat. Soc. Stud. Educ.*, 1942, **41**, Part II. (88)

MCCRAW, L. W. A factor analysis of motor learning. *Res. Quart.*, 1949, **20**, 316-35. (197, 198)

MCCRAW, L. W. Comparison of physical growth and development of athletes and nonathletes at the junior high school level. Report to Res. Sect., AAHPER Convention, Chicago, April 1956. (197, 202)

MCGEOCH, G. O. The intelligence quotient as a factor in the whole-part problem. *J. Exp. Psychol.*, 1931, **14**, 335-58. (307)

MCGEOCH, J. A. and IRION, A. L. *The psychology of human learning* (2nd ed.). New York: McKay, 1952. (131, 159, 188)

MCGEOCH, J. A. and WHITELY, P. L. The recall of observed material. *J. Educ. Psychol.*, 1926, **17**, 419-25. (173)

MCGRAW, M. B. *Neuromuscular maturation of the human infant.* New York: Columbia, 1943. (196, 197, 198, 221)

MCGUIGAN, F. J. and MACCASLIN, E. F. Whole and part methods in learning a perceptual motor skill. *Amer. J. Psychol.*, 1935, **68**, 658-61. (306)

MEDNICK, S. A. *Learning.* Englewood Cliffs, N.J.: Prentice-Hall, 1964. (200)

METHENY, E. Some differences in bodily proportions between American Negro and white male college students as related to athletic performance. *Res. Quart.*, 1939, **10**, 41-53. (359, 360, 372)

MILES, W. L. Ocular dominance demonstrated by unconscious sighting. *J. Exp. Psychol.*, 1929, **12**, 113-26. (381)

MILLER, D. M. The relationships between some visual-perceptual factors and the degree of success realized by sports performers. Unpublished doctoral dissertation. University of Southern California, 1960. (163, 338)

MILLER, L. A. The effects of emotional stress on high school track and field performance. Unpublished master's thesis, University of California, Los Angeles, 1960. (242, 244, 245)

MILLER, R. B. Task taxonomy: science or technology? *Ergonomics,* 1967, **10**, 167-76. (51)

MINAMI, H. and DALLENBACH, K. M. The effect of activity upon learning and retention in the cockroach. *Amer. J. Psychol.*, 1946, **59**. 1-58. (181)

MIRENVA, A. N. Psychomotor education and the general development of preschool children: experiments with turn controls. *J. Genet. Psychol.*, 1935, **46**, 433-54. (199)

MONTEBELLO, R. A. The role of stereoscopic vision in some aspects of basketball playing ability. Unpublished master's thesis. Ohio State Univer., 1960. (336)

MORRIS, P. C. A. comparative study of physical measures of women athletes and unselected college women. Unpublished doctoral dissertation. Temple Univer., 1960. (339, 358)

MOTT, J. A. Eye movements during initial learning of motor skills. Unpublished doctoral dissertation. University of Southern California, 1954. (340)

MOWBRAY, G. H. and RHODES, M. V. On the reduction of choice reaction time with practice. *Quart. J. Exp. Psychol.,* 1959, **11**, 16-23. (378)

MUELLER, C. G. *Sensory psychology.* Englewood Cliffs, N.J.: Prentice-Hall, 1965. (354)

MÜLLER, G. E. and PILZECKER, A. Experimentelle Beiträge Zur Lehre vom Gedachtnis. *Z. Psychol.,* 1900, **1**, 312, 322, 447. (182)

MUNN, N. L. Bilateral transfer of learning. *J. Exp. Psychol.,* 1932, **15**, 343-53. (140)

MURPHY, H. H. Distribution of practice periods in learning. *J. Exp. Psychol.,* 1916, **7**, 150-62. (269)

MURRAY, H. A. *Explorations in personality.* New York: Oxford, 1938. (226, 227)

MURRAY, M. J., Matching preferred cognition mode with teaching methodology in learning a novel motor skill. *Res. Quart.,* 1979, **50**, 80-87. (305, 314)

MUSSEN, P., CONGER, J., and KAGAN, J. *Child development and personality* (2nd ed.). New York: Harper & Row, 1963. (196, 221)

NASON, L. J. Physical coordination helps improve grades. Nason on education, 1965. (327)

NAYLOR, J. C. and BRIGGS, G. E. *Long-term retention of learned skills, and review of the literature.* Lab. of Aviation Psychol., Ohio State Univer. & Ohio State Univer. Res. Found., 1961. (16, 175, 307)

NEISSER, U. *Cognitive Psychology.* New York: Appleton-Century-Crofts, 1967. (163)

NELSON, D. O. Effect of swimming on the learning of selected gross motor skills. *Res. Quart.,* 1957, **28**, 374-78(a). (138, 139, 154)

NELSON, D. O. Studies of transfer of learning in gross motor skills. *Res. Quart.,* 1957, **28**, 364-73(b). (138)

NELSON, J. Analysis of the effects of applying various motivational situations to college men subjected to a stressful physical performance. Unpublished doctoral dissertation, Univer. of Oregon, 1962. (250, 258)

NEWMAN, E. B. Forgetting of meaningful material during sleep and waking. *Amer. J. Psychol.*, 1939, **52**, 65-71. (88, 175)

NIDEFER, R. M. The ethics and practice of applied sport psychology, Ann Arbor, MI.: Mouvement Publications, 1981. (299)

NIEMEYER, R. K. Part versus whole methods and massed versus distributed practice in learning of selected large muscle activities. Unpublished doctoral dissertation, University of Southern California, 1958. (307)

NISSEN, H. W. Analysis of a complex conditional reaction in chimpanzees. *J. Comp. Physiolog. Psychol.*, 1951, **44**, 9-16. (199)

NORRIE, M. L. The relationship between measures of kinesthesia and motor performance. Unpublished master's thesis, University of California, Berkeley, 1952. (351)

O'DONNELL, D. J. The relative effectiveness of three methods of teaching beginning tennis to college women. Unpublished doctoral dissertation, Indiana University, 1956. (306)

OETTINGER, L. Delacato in Review. *28th Yearbook,* M. P. Douglas, Ed. Claremont Graduate School Curriculum Laboratory, 1964, p. 119-31. (199)

OLSEN, E. A. Relationship between psychological capacities and success in college athletics. *Res. Quart.,* 1956, **27**, 79-89. (336, 337, 354, 383)

OSGOOD, C. E. The similarity paradox in human learning: a resolution. *Pyschol. Rev.* 1949, **56**, 132-43. (151)

OXENDINE, J. B. Effect of progressively changing practice schedules on learning of a motor skill. *Res. Quart.,* 1965, **36**, 307-15. (186, 266)

OXENDINE, J. B. Generality and specificity in the learning of fine and gross motor skills. *Res. Quart.,* 1967, **38**, 86-94. (27)

OXENDINE, J. B. Effect of mental and physical practice on the learning of three motor skills. *Res. Quart.,* 1969, **40**, 755-63. (284, 287, 290, 292, 293, 299)

OXENDINE, J. B. Emotional arousal and motor performance. *Quest,* 1970, **XIII**, 23-32. (239, 246)

PARSONS O. A., PHILLIPS, L., and LANE, J. E. Performance on the same psychomotor task under different stressful conditions. *J. Psychol.,* 1954, **38**, 457-66. (244)

PAVLOV, I. P. *Conditional reflexes.* Trans. E. V. Anrep. New York: Oxford, 1927. (12, 75, 104, 105, 129)

PECKSTEIN, L. A. Whole vs. part methods in motor learning: a comparative study. *Psychol. Monogr.,* 1917, **23**, 2. (307)

PENMAN, K. A. *Physical education for college students.* St. Louis: Mosby, 1964. (302, 314)

PERBIX, J. Relationship between somatotype and motor fitness in women. *Res. Quart.,* 1954, **25**, 84-90. (358)

PERKINS, F. T. Delacato in Review. *28th Yearbook,* M. P. Douglas, Ed. Claremont Graduate School Curriculum Laboratory, 1964, 119-31. (199)

PERKINS, W. L. Distributed practice with nonsense syllables. *Brit. J. Psychol.,* 1914, **7**, 253-61. (265)

PERRY, H. M. The relative efficiency of actual and imaginary practice in five selected tasks. *Arch. Psychol.,* 1939, **34**, 5-75. (285)

PHILLIPS, M. and SUMMERS, D. Relation of kinesthetic perception of motor learning. *Res. Quart.,* 1954, **25**, 456-69. (346, 349, 350, 354)

PHIPPS, S. J. and MOREHOUSE, C. A. Effects of mental practice on the acquisition of motor skills of varied difficulty. *Res. Quart.,* 1969, **40**, 773-78. (289)

PIAGET, J. *The origins of intelligence in children.* New York: International Universities Press, Inc., 1952. (193, 195, 221)

PIERSON, W. R. The relationship of movement time to reaction time from childhood to senility. *Res. Quart.,* 1959, **30**, 227-31. (375, 383)

PIERSON, W.R. and RASCH, P. J. Determination of representative score for simple reaction and movement time. *Percep. Mot. Skills,* 1959, **9**, 107-10. (375)

POND, F. L. Influence of the study of Latin on word knowledge. *Sch. Rev.,* 1938, **46**, 611-18. (134)

POULTON, E. C. On Prediction of Skilled Movements. *Psychological Bulletin,* 1957, **54**, 467-78. (17)

PRICE, N. The relationship between the level of aspiration and performance in selected motor tasks. Unpublished master's thesis, Women's Coll., Univer. of North Carolina, 1960. (257)

PROVINS, K. A. Handedness and skill. *Quart. J. Exp. Psychol.,* 1956, **8**, 79-95. (365)

PRUDDEN, B. How to keep your child fit from birth to six. New York: Harper & Row, 1964. (217)

PURDY, B. J. and LOCKHART, A. Retention and relearning of gross motor skills after long periods of no practice. *Res. Quart.,* 1962, **33**, 65-72. (184, 185, 188)

PYLE, W. H. Concentrated versus distributed practices. *J. Educ. Psychol.*, 1915, **5**, 247-58. (265, 269)

RADLER, D. and KEPHART, N. C. *Success through play*. New York: Harper & Row, 1960. (218, 219, 221)

RADOSAVIJEVICH, P. R. Das Behalten and Vergessen bei Kindern und Erwachsenesn Nach experimentellen Untersuchungen. *Päd. Monogr.*, no. 1. Cited by R. S. Woodworth & H. Schlosberg, *Expeimental psychology* (Rev. ed.) New York: Holt, Rinehart and Winston, 1963, p. 892. (173)

RAGSDALE, C. E. How children learn motor types of activity. *Yearb. Nat. Soc. Stud. Educ.*, 1950, **49**, 69-91. (308)

RANGAZAS, E. P. A comparative analysis of selected college athletes and nonathletes on several hand-foot reaction-time measures. Unpublished doctoral dissertation, Indiana University, 1957. (376, 378, 381)

RARICK, L. Growth and development theory and practice: implications for physical education. *Mich. osteopath. J.*, 1965, **30**, (Oct.), 21-24. (199, 205, 330)

RARICK, L. Cognitive-motor relationships in the growing years. *Research Quarterly Exercise and Sport*, 1980, **51**, 174-92. (330, 331, 332)

RARICK, L. and MCKEE, R. A study of twenty third-grade children exhibiting extreme levels of achievement on tests of motor proficiency. *Res. Quart.*, 1949, **20**, 142-52. (199, 202, 205, 332)

RARICK, L. and THOMPSON, J. J. Roentgenographic measures of leg muscle size and ankle extensor strength of seven-year-old children. *Res. Quart.*, 1956, **27**, 321-32. (214)

RASCH, P. J. and BURKE, R. K. *Kinesiology and applied anatomy*. Philadelphia: Lea & Febiger, 1963. (243, 244)

RAWLINGS, E., RAWLINGS, J. L., CHEN, S. S., and YILK, M. D. The facilitating effects of mental rehearsal in the acquisition of rotary pursuit tracking. *Psychonomic Science*, 1972, **26**, 71-73. (287, 288)

RAY, H. C. Interrelationships of physical and mental abilities and achievements of high school boys. *Res. Quart.*, 1940, **11**, 129-41. (328)

REED, H. B. Part and whole methods of learning. *J. Exp. Psychol.*, 1924, **15**, 107-15. (265, 307)

REJALL, A. E. Studies on long term retention. Cited by J. A. McGeoch, *The psychology of human learning*. New York: McKay, 1946, p. 328. (172)

RICHARDSON, A. Mental practice: a review and a discussion, part I. *Res. Quart.*, 1967, **38**, 95-107. (299)

RICHTER, C. P. Total self regulatory functions in animals and human beings. *Harvey Lecture Ser.*, 1942, **38**, 63-103. (225)

RIDENOUR, M. V. *Motor development: Issues and applications*. Princeton, N.J.: Princeton Book Co., 1978. (216, 221, 341)

ROBB, M. D. *The dynamics of motor-skill acquisiton*. Englewood Cliffs, N.J.: Prentice-Hall, Inc., 1972. (22, 34, 166, 176)

ROBINSON, E. S. The "similarity" factor in retroaction. *Amer. J. Psychol.*, 1927, **39**, 297-312. (151)

ROLOFF, L. Z. Kinesthesis in relation to the learning of selected motor skills. *Res. Quart.*, 1953, **24**, 210-17. (350)

ROSE, J. E. and MOUNTCASTLE, V. B. Touch and kinesthesis. In J. Field, ed., *Handbook of Physiology*. Vol. 1. Baltimore: Williams & Wilkins, 1959. (347)

ROYAL CANADIAN AIR FORCE. *VBX Plan for physical fitness*. Ottawa: Roger Duhamel, F.R.S.C., Queen's Printer and Controller of Stationery, 1962. (314)

RUBIN, E. Figure and Ground. In Beardsley, D. and Wertheimer, M., Eds. *Readings in Perception*. Princeton, N.J.: D. Van Nostrand Co. Inc., 1958. (340)

RUBIN-RABSON, G. Studies in the psychology of memorizing piano music: II. A comparison of massed and distributed practice. *J. Educ. Psychol.*, 1940, **31**, 270-84. (265)

RUBIN-RABSON, G. Studies in the psychology of memorizing piano music: VI. a comparison of two forms of mental rehearsal and keyboard overlearning. *J. Educ. Psychol.*, 1941, **32**, 593-602. (285)

RYAN, E. D. Effects of stress on motor performance and learning. *Res. Quart.*, 1962, **33**, 111-19(a). (185, 330)

SACKETT, R. S. The relationship between amount of symbolic rehearsal and retention of a maze habit. *J. Genet. Psychol.*, 1935, **13**, 113-30. (285)

SAGE, G. H. *Introduction of motor behavior: A neuropsychological approach*, Reading, MA.: Addison-Wesley, 1971. (11, 337)

SCHMIDT, R. A. *Motor control and learning: A behavioral analysis*. Champaign, IL.: Human Kinetics Publishers, 1982. (34, 71, 73, 102, 117, 118, 120, 149, 269, 279, 374)

SCHOTT, E. L. The development of learning capacity. Unpublished master's thesis, University of Missouri, 1923. (328)

SCOTT, G. M. Measurement of kinesthesis. *Res. Quart.*, 1955, **26**, 324-41. (346, 348, 354)

SCRIPTURE, E. W. Recent investigations at the Yale laboratory. *Psychol. Rev.*, 1899, **6**, 165. (139)

SCULL, J. W. The Amsel Frustration Effect Interpretation and Research. *Psychological Bulletin*, 1973, **79**, 352-61. (231)

SEARS, P. S. Levels of aspiration in academically successful and unsuccessful children. *J. Abnorm. Soc. Psychol.*, 1940, **35**, 498-536. (257)

SEASHORE, S. H. and SEASHORE, R. H. Individual differences in simple auditory reaction times of hands, feet and jaws. *J. Exp. Psychol.*, 1941, **29**, 342-45. (376)

SEEFELDT, V. Guidelines for Pre-School Children. *Proceedings* of the National Conference on Physical Fitness and Sports for All. 1980, 5-19. (204)

SEILS, L. G. The relationship between meausres of physical growth and gross motor performance of primary grade school children. *Res. Quart.*, 1951, **22**, 244-60. (205)

SELVE, H. *The stress of life.* New York: McGraw-Hill, 1956. (261)

SHAFER, L. F. Fear and courage in aerial combat. *J. Consult. Psychol.*, 1947, **11**, 137-43. (236, 237)

SHAW, W. A. The distribution of muscular action potentials during imaging. *Psychol. Rec.*, 1938, **2**, 195. (285)

SHAY, C. The progressive-part vs. the whole method of motor skills. *Res. Quart.*, 1934, **5**, 62-67. (307)

SHELDON, W. H. *Atlas of men.* New York: Harper & Row, 1954. (215, 357, 372)

SHICK, J. Relationship between depth perception and hand-eye dominance and free-throw shooting in college women. *Perceptual and Motor Skills*, 1971, **33**, 539-42. (337)

SHILLING, M. An experimental investigation of the effects of a decrease in the delay of reinforcement upon instrumental response performance. Unpublished master's thesis, University of Iowa, 1951. (117)

SHIRLEY, M. M. *The first two years.* Minneapolis: University of Minnesota Press, 1933. (194)

SILLS, F. D. A factor analysis of somatotypes and of their relationships to achievement in motor skills. *Res. Quart.*, 1950, **21**, 246. (359)

SILLS, F. D. and EVERETT, P. The relationship of extreme somatotypes to performance in motor and strength tests. *Res. Quart.*, 1953, **24**, 223-28. (359)

SINGER, R. N. Massed and distributed practice effects on the acquisition and retention of a novel basketball skill. *Res. Quart.*, 1965, **36**, 68-77. (268)

SINGER, R. N. *Motor learning and human performance* (3rd ed.). New York: Macmillan Publishing Co., Inc., 1980. (34, 99, 269, 299)

SINGER, R. N. *The learning of motor skills.* New York: Macmillan Publishing Co., Inc., 1982. (66)

SINGER, R. N. and GERSON, R. F. Task classification and strategy utilization in motor skills. *Research Quarterly for Exercise and Sport*, 1981, Vol. 52, No. 1, 100-16. (51, 71)

SINGLETON, W. T. *The analysis of practical skills.* Baltimore: University Park Press, 1978. (3, 12, 20, 26, 34)

SINNING, W. E., CUNNINGHAM, L. N., RACANIELLE, A. P. and SHOLES J L. Body composition and somatotype of male and female nordic skiers, *Res. Quart.*, 1977, **48**(4), 741-49. (357)

SKINNER, B. F. *The behavior of organisms: an experimental analysis.* New York: Appleton-Century-Crofts, 1938. (99)

SKINNER, B. F. Reinforcement today. *Amer. Psychologist*, 1958, **13**, 94-99. (129)

SKINNER, C. E. *Educational psychology* (4th ed.). Englewood Cliffs, N.J.: Prentice-Hall, 1959. (81, 82, 106)

SLATER-HAMMEL, A. T. Reaction time and speed of movement. *Percept. Mot. Skills, Res. Exch.*, 1952, **4**, 109-13. (375, 384)

SMITH, K. R. Intermittent loud noise and mental performance. *Science*, 1951, **114**, 132-33. (290)

SMITH, K. U. Cybernetic foundations of physical behavioral science. *Quest*, 1967 (May), no. 8, 26-82. (91)

SMITH, L. A. The effects of visual imagery ability upon the learning and retention of a gross motor skill acquired through mental and physical practice. Dissertation, Temple University, 1974. (290)

SMITH, L. E. Reaction time and movement time in four large muscle movements. *Res. Quart.*, 1961, **32**, 88-92. (375)

SMYTH, M. M. Attention and visual feedback in motor learning. *Journal of Motor Behavior*, 1978, **10**, 185-90. (68)

SNODDY, G. S. Learning and stability. *J. Appl. Psychol.*, 1926, **10**, 1-36. (43, 49, 328)

SNODDY, G. S. *Evidence for two opposed processes in mental growth.* Lancaster, Penn.: Science Press, 1935. (263, 266, 279)

SPEARMAN, C. E. *The nature of "intelligence" and the principles of cognition.* New York: Macmillan, 1923. (324, 325)

SPEILBERGER, C. D. State-trait anxiety and interactional psychology. In D. Magnusson and N. S. Endler, Eds. *Personality at the crossroads: current issues in interactional psychology.* Hillsdale, N.J.: Erlbaum, 1977. (223)

SPENCE, J. T. and SPENCE, K. W. The motivational component of manifest anxiety: Drive and drive stimuli. In C. D. Spielberger, Ed. *Anxiety and behavior.* New York: Academic Press, 1966. (239)

SPENCE, K. W. A theory of emotionally based drive and its relation to performance in simple learning situations. *American Psychologists,* 1958, **13,** 131-41. (117, 239)

SPERLING, G. The information available in brief presentations. *Psychological Monographs,* 1960, **74** (Whole No. 498). (163)

SPERLING, G. A model for visual memory tasks. *Human Factors,* 1963, **5,** 19-31. (163)

STALLINGS, L. M. *Motor learning: from theory to practice.* St. Louis: The C. V. Mosby Co., 1982. (94, 95)

START, K. B. The relationship between intelligence and the effect of mental practice on the performance of a motor skill. *Res. Quart.,* 1960, **31,** 644-49. (282, 289, 291)

START, K. B. The influence of subjectively assessed games ability on gain in motor performance after mental practice. *J. Genet. Psychol.,* 1962, **67,** 169-73. (329)

START, K. B. Kinesthesis and mental practice. *Res. Quart.,* 1964, **35,** 316-20. (299)

STAUFFACHER, J. C. The effects of induced muscular tension upon various phases of the learning process. *J. Exp. Psychol.,* 1937, **21,** 26-46. (248)

STEGGERDA, M. and PETTY, C. An anthropometric study of Negro and white college women. *Res. Quart.,* 1940, **11,** 110-18. (359, 360)

STELMACH, G. E., ed. *Motor control: issues and trends.* New York: Academic Press, 1976. (269, 270, 279)

STEPHENS, J. M. Transfer of learning. In *Encyclopedia of educational research* (Rev. ed.). New York: Macmillan, 1960. (159)

STERN, W. *The psychological methods of testing intelligence.* Trans. G. M. Whipple. Baltimore: Warwick and York, Inc., 1914. (325)

STRAUB, W. Psychische Alkoholwirkung and Blutalkoholgehalt, Z. *Arbeitsps,* 1938, **11,** 127-130. Cited by R. S. Woodworth and H. Schlosberg, *Experimental psychology* (Rev. ed.). New York: Holt, Rinehart and Winston, 1963, p. 38. (382)

STRONG, C. H. Motivation related to performance of physical fitness test. *Res. Quart.,* 1963, **34,** 497-507. (242, 249, 253, 257, 263)

STROUD, J. B. Apparatus for measuring muscular tension. *J. Exp. Psychol.,* 1931, **14,** 184-85. (247)

STROUP, F. Relationship between measurement of the field of motion perception and basketball ability in college men. *Res. Quart.,* 1957, **28,** 72-76. (338)

SUINN, R. M., ed. *Psychology in sports: methods and applications.* Minneapolis, Minn.: Burgess Publishing Co., 1980. (261)

SWIFT, E. J. Studies in the psychology and physiology of learning. *Amer. J. Psychol.,* 1903, **14,** 201-51. (139, 171)

SYMMONDS, P. M. Human drives. *J. Educ. Psychol.,* 1934, **25,** 694. (229)

TANNER, J. M. *Growth and development.* Springfield, Ill.: Charles C Thomas, 1955. (206, 207, 359, 360, 372)

TAYLOR, J. A. and SPENCE, K. W. The relationship of anxiety level to performance in serial learning. *J. Exp. Psychol.,* 1952, **44,** 61-64. (242, 352)

TEEPLE, J. Physical growth and maturation. *In motor development: issues and implications,* M. Ridenour, Ed. Princeton, N.J.: Princeton Book Company, 1978. (200)

THEUNISSEN, W. V. Part teaching and whole teaching of beginning group-golf classes for male college students. Unpublished doctoral dissertation, Indiana University, 1955. (306)

THOMAS, W. I. *The unadjusted girl.* Boston: Little Brown, 1923. (229, 306)

THOMPSON, M. E. A study of reliabilities of selected gross muscular coordination test items. *Human Resources Res. Cen. Res. Bull.,* 1952, 52-59. (328)

THORNDIKE, E. L. *Animal intelligence, experimental studies.* New York: Macmillan, 1911. (38, 52, 77, 78)

THORNDIKE, E. L. *Educational psychology.* Vol. 2. *The psychology of learning.* New York: Teachers College, 1913. (105)

THORNDIKE, E. L. Mental discipline in high school studies. *J. Educ. Psychol.,* 1924, **15,** 1-22, 83-98. (134)

THORNDIKE, E. L. *Human learning.* New York: Appleton-Century-Crofts, 1931. (52, 91, 99, 109, 110)

THORNDIKE, E. L. and HAGEN, E. *The measurement of intelligence.* New York: Teacher's College, 1927. (27, 325)

THORNDIKE, E. L. and WOODWORTH, R. S. The influence of improvement in one mental function upon the efficiency of other functions. *Psychol. Rev.,* 1901, **8,** 247-61, 384-95, 553-64. (134)

THURSTONE, L. L. Primary mental abilities. *Univer. of Chicago: Psychometer. Mongr.*, 1938, no. 1. (325, 332)

TITCHENER, E. B. Relearning after forty-six years. *Amer. J. Psychol.*, 1923, **34**, 468-69. (173)

TOLMAN, E. C. Theories of learning. In F. A. Moss, Ed., *Comparative Psychology*. Englewood Cliffs, N.J.: Prentice-Hall, 1934. (21, 83, 85, 86, 99)

TOLMAN, E. C. The determiners of behavior at a choice point. *Psychol. Rev.*, 1938, **45**, 1-41. (77)

TOLMAN, E. C. There is more than one kind of learning. *Psychol. Rev.*, 1949, **56**, 144-55. (13)

TORRES, J. The relationship between figure-ground perceptual ability and ball catching ability in ten- and thirteen-year-old boys and girls. Unpublished Master's thesis, Purdue University, 1966. (341)

TOWNE, B. M. An individual curve of learning: a study in typewriting. *J. Exp. Psychol.*, 1922, **5**, 79-92. (172)

TRAVERS, R. M. W. *Essentials of learning* (4th ed.). New York: Macmillan Publishing Co., 1977. (34, 101, 108, 129, 159, 184, 188, 230, 231, 265, 279)

TROW, W. C. *Educational psychology*. Boston: Houghton Mifflin, 1950. (172)

TRUSSEL, E. M. Mental practice as a factor in learning a complex motor skill. Unpublished doctoral dissertation. University of California, Berkeley, 1958. (287)

TSAI, C. A comparative study of retention curves for motor habits. *Comp. Psychol. Monogr.*, 1924, **2**, no. 2. (171)

TWEIT, A. H., GALLNICK, P. D., and HEARN, G. R. Effect of training program on total body reaction time of individuals of low fitness. *Res. Quart.*, 1963, **34**, 508-13. (380)

TWINNING, P. W. The relative importance of intervening activity and lapse of time in the production of forgetting. *J. Exp. Psychol.*, 1940, **26**, 483-501. (285, 292)

UHRBROCK, R. S. Laterality of champion athletes, *Journal of Motor Behavior*, 1970, **2**, 285-90. (369, 372)

ULRICH, C. Stress and sport. In W. R. Johnson, Ed., *Science and medicine of exercise and sports*. New York: Harper and Row, 1960. (242)

VANDELL, R. A., DAVIS, R. A., and CLUGSTON, H. A. The function of mental practice and the acquisition of motor skills. *J. Gen. Psychol.*, 1943, **29**, 243-50. (287, 299)

VAN DUSEN, F. and SCHLOSBERG, H. Further study of the retention of verbal and motor skills. *J. Exp. Psychol.*, 1948, **38**, 526-34. (171)

VAN ORMER, E. B. Retention after intervals of sleep and waking. *Arch. Psychol. N. Y.*, 1932, **21**, no. 137. (181)

VINCE, M. A. The part played by intellectual processes in a sensori-motor performance. *Quart. J. Exp. Psychol.*, 1953, **5**, 75-86. (326)

VINCENT, W. J. Transfer effects between motor skills judged similar in perceptual components. *Res. Quart.*, May, 1968, **39**(2), 380-88. (143, 144)

WAGNER, C. G. The effect of different lengths of practice on the learning of certain basketball skills among junior high school boys. Unpublished master's thesis, Temple University, 1962. (268)

WALKER, R. N. Body build and behavior in young children, body build and nursery school teacher's ratings. *Monogr. Soc. Res. Child Develop.*, 1952, **3**, 27, 84. (357)

WALTER, L. M. The relation of sex, age, and school achievement to levels of aspiration. *J. Educ. Psychol.*, 1951, **42**, 285-92. (257)

WATSON, G. What psychology can we feel sure about? In W. C. Morse & G. M. Wingo, eds., *Readings in educatonal psychology*. Glenview, IL.: Scott, Foresman. 1962. (97, 190, 231)

WAY, E. E. Relationship of lateral dominance to scores of motor ability and selected skill tests. *Res. Quart.*, 1958, **29**, 360-69. (369)

WEBSTER, R. W. Psychological and pedagogical factors involved in motor skill performance as exemplified in bowling. *Res. Quart.*, 1940, **11**, 42-52. (269)

WECHSLER, D. Measurement *of adult intelligence* (3rd ed.) Baltimore: Williams & Wilkins, 1944. (324)

WECHSLER, D. and HARTOGS, R. The clinical measurement of anxiety. *Psychiatr. Quart.*, 1945, **19**, 618-35. (242, 247)

WEIG, E. L. Bilateral transfer in the motor learning of young children and adults. *Child Develpm.*, 1932, **3**, 247-368. (139)

WEISS, R. F. Aspiration and expectations: a dimensional analysis. *J. Soc. Psychol.*, 1961, **53**, 249. (256)

WELFORD, A. T. *Skill performance: perceptual and motor skills*, Glenview, IL.: Scott Foresman and Co., 1976. (91, 95, 99, 264, 274, 384)

WERTHEIMER, M., Ed., *Readings in perception*, Princeton, N.J.: D. Van Nostrand Co., Inc., 1958. (84, 340)

WESTERDARP, D. Mental capacity and its relation to physical efficiency. *Amer. Phys. Educ. Rev.*, 1923, **28**, 216-19. (330)

WESTERLUND, J. H. and TUTTLE, W. W. Relationship between running events in track and reaction time. *REs. Quart.,* 1931, **2,** 95-100. (383)

WICKSTROM, R. *Fundamental Motor Patterns.* Philadelphia: Lea and Febiger, 1977. (202, 221, 269)

WIDDOP, J. Unpublished manuscript, Dept. of Phys. Educ., McDonald College, McGill University, 1963. (351)

WIEBE, V. R. A study of tests of kinesthesis. *Res. Quart.,* 1954, **25,** 222-230. (350)

WIENER, N. *Cybernetics* (2nd ed.). New York: Wiley, 1961. (91)

WILKINSON, J. J. A study of reaction-time measures to a kinesthetic and a visual stimulus for selected groups of athletes and nonathletes. Unpublished doctoral dissertation, Indiana University, 1958. (383)

WILLGOOSE, C. E. and ROGERS, M. L. Relationship of somatotype to physical fitness. *J. Educ. Res.,* 1949, **42,** 704. (359)

WILLIAMS, J. R. and SCOTT, R. B. Growth and development of Negro infants: IV. motor development and its relation to child-rearing practices in two groups of Negro infants. *Child Develpm.,* 1953, **24,** 103-21. (201, 337, 354)

WILLINGHAM, W. W. Performance decrement following failure. *Percept. Mot. Skills,* 1958, **8,** 197-202. (245)

WILLS, K. C. The effect of mental practice and physical practice on learning and motor skill, Unpublished Master's thesis, Arkansas State College, 1965. (289)

WILMORE, J. They told you you couldn't compete with men and you, like a fool, believed them. *Women Sports,* 1974, **1,** 40. (215)

WILSON, M. E. The relative effect of mental practice and physical practice in learning the tennis forehand and backhand drives. Unpublished doctoral dissertation, State University of Iowa, 1961. (284, 289, 292)

WITTE, F. Relation of kinesthetic perception to a selected motor skill for elementary school children. *Res. Quart.,* 1962, **33,** 476-84. (351)

WOODROW, H. The effect of type of training upon transference. *J. Educ. Psychol.,* 1927, **18,** 159-72. (146)

WOODRUFF, A. D. *The psychology of teaching.* New York: McKay, 1948. (28, 29, 30)

WOODWORTH, R. S. The accuracy of voluntary movement. *Psychol. Monogr.,* 1899, no. 13. (139)

WOODWORTH, R. S. and SCHLOSBERG, H. *Experimental psychology* (Rev. ed.). New York: Holt, Rinehart and Winston, 1963. (105, 163, 234, 261, 272, 279, 314, 354, 373, 374, 379, 380)

WORCESTER, D. A. Retention after long periods. *J. Educ. Psychol.,* 1923, **14,** 113-14. (173)

WORELL, L. Levels of aspiration and academic success. *J. Educ. Psychol.,* 1959, **50,** 47-50. (257)

WRIGHTSMAN, L. S. and SANFORD, F. H. Psychology: a scientific study of human behavior (4th ed.). Monterey, Calif.: Brooks/Cole Publishing Co., 1975. (324)

WYLIE, R. C. *The self concept.* Lincoln, Nebr.: University of Nebraska Press, 1961. (256)

WYNDHAM, C. H., STRYDOM, N. B., MORRISON, J. F., PETER J. WILLIAMS, C. G., BREDELL, G. A. R., and JOFFE, A. Differences between ethnic groups in physical working capacity. *J. Appl. Physiol.,* 1963, **18,** 361-66. (361)

YOUNG, D. New York Daily News Service Article carried in the *Philadelphia Inquirer,* October 13, 1980. (114)

YOUNG, O. C. A study of kinesthesis in relation to selected movements. *Res. Quart.,* 1945, **16,** 277-87. (261)

YOUNG, O. G. The rate of learning in relation to spacing of practice periods in archery and badminton. *Res. Quart.,* 1954, **25,** 231-43. (268, 350)

YOUNG, P. T. *Motivation and emotion.* New York: Wiley, 1961. (261)

ZAICHKOWSKY, L. D., ZAICHKOWSKY, L. B., and MARTINEK, T. J. *Growth and Development: the child and physical activity,* St. Louis: The C. V. Mosby Co., 1980. (190, 203, 213)

ZAICHKOWSKY, L. D. Tampering with performance—biofeedback and self-regulation, *Proceedings of NAPEHE,* Annual Conference, Milwaukee, Wisconsin, 1979, 75-82. (256)

ZARTMAN, E. N. and CASON, H. The influence of an increase in muscular tension on mental efficiency. *J. Exp. Psychol.,* 1934, **17,** 671-79. (247)

Subject Index

Abilities:
    general motor, 318-20
    intellectual, 324-26
Achievement motivation, 227-28
Acuity, Visual, 343
All-around athlete, 27, 28, 320-23
Ambidexterity, 362
Anthropometry:
    historic interest, 356
    relation to motor performance, 357
Anxiety:
    state, 223
    trait, 223
Applied research, 36-38
Arousal:
    conscious awareness, 235
    effect on intelligence, 243
    effect on motor performance and
        learning, 237-48
    physiological responses, 232-35
    reducing intensity, 255-56
    states of, 222-24
Aspiration, level of, 256-59
Autonomic nervous system, 233

Balance, 319, 321, 322
Basic research, 36-38
Behaviorism, 75-76
Bilateral transfer, 139-41
Biofeedback, 255, 256
Black Box model, 92
Body types, 357

Classical conditioning, 12
Closed loop theory, 92, 93
Closed skills, 17, 18
Cognitive learning theories, 78, 79, 82-87
Color vision, 344
Competition theory of forgetting, 182
Computers in research, 65-68
Connectionism, 77, 78
Contiguity theory, 78-80
Contralateral transfer, 139-41
Criteria for task selection, 50, 51
Cultural influences in motor skills, 213-15
Cybernetic theory, 90, 91

Depth perception, 334-37
Development, motor:
    activities, 216-19
    skills, 4
    stages, 195, 196

Dexterity, 362, 363
Distributed practice, 263-78
Dominance, 362
Drive reduction, 105, 106
Drive theory, 238, 239
Drives, 228, 230

Echoic memory, 163
Empericism, 35-37
Endurance activities for children, 215, 216
Experimental controls in research, 42, 43
Exteroception, 346
Extinction:
    of movement behavior, 126, 127
    of social behavior, 125, 126
Extrinsic feedback, 112
Eye dominance, 344

Feedback, Information:
    augmented, 121-24
    concurrent, 112
    definition, 101, 102
    extrinsic, 112
    intrinsic, 111, 112
    specificity of, 113-17
    temporal placement, 117-21
    terminal, 112
    timing of, 119-21
    types of, 111-13
Field theory, 86, 87
Figure-ground perception, 84, 340-43
Fine motor skills, 319, 320
Forgetting theories, 165-66, 181-83
Formal discipline, 132-34
Form in skill learning, 124
Fractionated reaction time, 374
Functionalism, 98

Galvanic skin response, 233
General motor development, 193, 194, 201
    during childhood, 203-5
Generality and specificity in motor skills,
    27, 28
Gestalt psychology, 83-85, 283
Goal setting, 256-59

Handedness, 362
Hawthorne effect, 48
Human differences, 315-18
Human subjects research, 45-47
Hypnotism, 250